MANAGING BEHAVIOR IN ORGANIZATIONS

TEXT, CASES, READINGS

McGraw-Hill Series in Management

Keith Davis and Fred Luthans, *Consulting Editors*

MANAGING BEHAVIOR IN ORGANIZATIONS

TEXT, CASES, READINGS

Leonard A. Schlesinger
Robert G. Eccles
John J. Gabarro

Graduate School of Business Administration
Harvard University

with the assistance of
Thomas B. Lifson
James P. Ware

McGRAW-HILL BOOK COMPANY

New York   St. Louis   San Francisco   Auckland   Bogotá
Hamburg   London   Madrid   Mexico   Montreal   New Delhi
Panama   Paris   São Paulo   Singapore   Sydney   Tokyo   Toronto

MANAGING BEHAVIOR IN ORGANIZATIONS
Text, Cases, Readings

7 8 9 0 DOCDOC 8 9 8 7

ISBN 0-07-055332-7

See Acknowledgments on page xviii.
Copyrights included on this page by reference.

This book was set in Times Roman by Rocappi, Inc.
The editors were Kathi A. Benson, James B. Armstrong, and Scott Amerman;
the production supervisor was Diane Renda.
The drawings were done by ECL Art Associates, Inc.
The cover was designed by Jane Moorman.
R. R. Donnelley & Sons Company was printer and binder.

Library of Congress Cataloging in Publication Data
Main entry under title:

Managing behavior in organizations.

    (McGraw-Hill series in management)
    Includes bibliographical references.
    1. Management—Case studies. 2. Organizational
behavior—Case studies. I. Schlesinger, Leonard A.
II. Eccles, Robert G. III. Gabarro, John J.
IV. Series.
HD31.M29398 1983   658   82-17308
ISBN 0-07-055332-7

CONTENTS

**PART 4   GETTING THE JOB DONE: ACTION PLANNING
AND IMPLEMENTATION 339**

FINAL

PREFACE

This book provides an in-depth exploration of the human aspects of management. As such, its purpose is (1) to provide a basic grounding in the issues to be confronted as you assume responsibility for managing people and organizations and (2) to provide a foundation of knowledge about organizations and organizational behavior, which is required for other courses in your academic program.

The major focus of this book is on developing an understanding of the basic dynamics of human behavior in organizations and their implications for managerial decisions and actions. At a more concrete level, the book is designed to familiarize you with some recurrent problems that managers face in working with and managing people; to develop your ability to diagnose the causes of organizational problems and your judgment to deal with them; to provide an understanding of the factors that influence human and organizational outcomes; and to provide a working knowledge of the tools a manager can use to affect these outcomes.

The book is organized into six major parts, each of which builds on knowledge gained in the previous parts. The remainder of this introduction broadly describes the focus, goals, and organization of the book.

PART 1: MANAGING GROUPS

In Part 1 we cover primary work groups, temporary work groups, and group process and decision making.

Managing Primary Work Groups

The major purpose of this section of the book is to develop the ability to systematically understand the forces that influence the behavior of primary, stable work groups. In particular, we are concerned with:

1 How a group's emergent culture becomes an important determinant of its productivity, satisfaction, and growth

2 How a group's emergent culture is influenced by contextual factors, organization and job design, leadership patterns, and the attributes and attitudes of its members

3 How these factors have implications for the way managers respond to problems and make changes

Managing Task Forces, Committees, and Other Temporary Work Groups

The purpose of this section is to familiarize you with some prototypical problems of temporary groups, the factors that influence their behavior, and ways to manage them effectively. Here we are concerned with:

1 How to organize a task force in terms of selecting members, setting ground rules, building effective norms, and setting goals

2 How to anticipate and manage problems of interdepartmental conflict, rivalry, dominant coalitions, and conflicting loyalties of members

3 How to manage a temporary work group in terms of coordinating effort, resolving conflict, and making decisions

Managing Group Process and Decisionmaking

The purpose of this section is to develop your awareness of ways to plan, participate in, and run effective group meetings. This section obviously draws heavily on the two preceding sections. In it, we deal with:

1 How to plan for a meeting in terms of anticipating "hidden agendas," doing "prework," and setting an agenda

2 How to lead a meeting in terms of member participation, dealing with conflict and digressions

3 How a group's process dynamics (that is, patterns of participation, dominance, avoidance, competition for leadership) affect the quality of its deliberations

4 How to observe these process dynamics and intervene to change them

PART 2 MANAGING INTERPERSONAL RELATIONSHIPS

Part 2 aims to develop familiarity with common problems that occur in working relationships, and ways to prevent or manage them. In particular, this section is concerned with:

1 How a person's frame of reference and self-concept affect the way he or she sees situations and behaves

2 How individual predispositions help explain behavior patterns that limit one's effectiveness and are often self-defeating

3 How a person's assumptions and predispositions act as filters that not only affect what he or she can or cannot see but also make it difficult to gain perspective, especially in stressful situations

4 How differences in predispositions and assumptions create failures of communication

5 How personal and task-related factors can cause or inflame conflict, and the implications of this for managing conflict

6 How to determine whether a conflict should be resolved, controlled, or left as is

7 How to intervene effectively in an interpersonal conflict

Managing and Working in Different Types of Relationships

Although the preceding issues are inherent in all kinds of relationships, they manifest themselves differently in various types of working relationships. For example, the problems involved in working with one's boss are apt to be somewhat different than those encountered in working with a subordinate, even though the underlying dynamics may be the same. For this reason, this section of the book is organized so that we can focus on the problems of managing subordinates, bosses, peers, and the external environment. In this context, we also explore the following issues:

1 How well-intentioned feedback or coaching can sometimes result in demotivation of a subordinate, anger, or feelings of hopelessness

2 How to give useful, specific, and nonthreatening feedback

3 How to receive feedback so that you learn the most from it

4 How to work with a boss to make the relationship as effective as possible, given the personal styles, predispositions, and traits that each of you bring to the relationships

PART 3: MOTIVATION, LEADERSHIP, AND INFLUENCE

Part 3 deals explicitly with influence processes that transcend situational settings. Its purpose is to familiarize students with the various means through which managers can influence behavior. It covers several commonly held theories of motivation, power, and leadership and their applicability and limitations to various managerial situations. The sections in this part provide a firm ground for developing an understanding of the underlying contingencies of personal, situational, and role-related variables and their implications for managerial action. Specifically, these sections deal with the following issues:

1 Motivation and its relationship to self-concept, expectations, and needs

2 Leadership style and its contingency on situational factors, personal style, sources of power available to the leader, and member motivation

3 The effect of job-person "fit" on satisfaction, motivation, and effectiveness

PART 4: GETTING THE JOB DONE: ACTION PLANNING AND IMPLEMENTATION

This part deals with the problems of detailed planning and implementation of management decisions. Similar to Part 3, this part aims to develop an awareness of the contingencies to be considered in taking action. Detailed attention is focused on developing action plans and implementation strategies which:

1 Relate to a diagnosis of the current situation and existing or potential problems

2 Consider the importance and urgency of the problems

3 Outline the time frame in which the problems must be addressed

4 Evaluate alternative types of changes appropriate for problem resolution

5 Address the risks and opportunities associated with individual and/or group involvement in the plan

6 Evaluate potential resistance to the implementation of the plan, the reason for and extent of resistance, and ways to reduce resistance

7 Assess the people whose cooperation is essential to the success of the plan, and determine the way to enlist their support

8 Consider your position vis-à-vis the persons impacted by the plan in terms of power, trust, authority, competence, etc.

9 Recognize the probability of having to develop different strategies for dealing with each affected individual and the group

10 Include contingency plans in case of an inability of secure desired results at significant points in the change process

PART 5: MANAGING ORGANIZATIONAL EFFECTIVENESS

In this part, we provide a framework for managing organizational effectiveness. Detailed attention is focused on organizational structures and systems, their relationship to managerial styles, and the activities necessary for successful short- and long-term organizational change.

Managing Organization Structure and Systems

In this section, we consider the effects of organizational structure on behavior and the extent to which structure can facilitate or impede the performance of key tasks. The major purpose of the section is to develop the ability to analyze tasks, environmental and human resource factors, and their implications for appropriate structures. In particular, we are concerned with:

1 How to identify key success factors and their implications for activities and desired outcomes

2 How to analyze key interdependencies among activities or subunits and their implications for the required organizational integration

3 How to assess the degree of differentiation that exists among different subunits and to judge its appropriateness for the organization and the environment

4 How to choose appropriate integrating devices given key interdependencies and levels of differentiation

5 How to assess the relative advantages and disadvantages of different forms of organizational structure

In dealing with these questions, we compare several different types of organizational structures, including functional organizations, product organizations, and matrix organizations. We also compare their relative advantages, disadvantages, and costs. In considering organizational structure, this section also focuses on the problems of managing geographically dispersed organizations, including multidivisional and multinational firms, and the role of organizational culture as an integrating force in these situations. Finally, this section also deals with the ways management systems can be used to supplement or complement organization structure to compensate for certain inherent disadvantages of a given structural design.

Managing Style, Structure, and Systems

This section goes beyond the work on management style in Part 3 and integrates it with information on structure and operating systems. We view the role of the key manager (or leader) as one of developing and sustaining a "fit" among the design elements. Recognizing that this role provides a large number of action options for the manager, we examine the ways in which a number of key managers have designed their organizations to support their operating style. In addition, we consider the implications of such design choices for organization members and the organization itself.

Managing Organizational Change and Development

This section deals with two related sets of organizational issues: planning and implementing major organizational change, and managing longer-term organizational development and effectiveness. Initially, we are concerned with understanding both the strategic choices involved in planning a major change and the tactical questions involved in implementing this change. In particular, we focus on:

1 Identification of the underlying situational factors that affect the choice of whether a change strategy should be implemented rapidly or slowly

2 Evaluation of whether the change should be planned fully in advance or in an evolutionary fashion

3 Evaluation of whether the change should attempt to overcome resistance or minimize it

4 Evaluation of whether the change should be implemented in a power-wielding or power-sharing approach

PART 6 PUTTING IT ALL TOGETHER: MANAGING INDIVIDUAL AND ORGANIZATIONAL CHANGE AND DEVELOPMENT

The case in Part 6 provides a major opportunity to study the growth and evolution of an organization in great depth and to propose a change strategy and implementation plan to address the human and organization issues faced by the company. As an integrative case, it provides a unique opportunity to review the issues and concepts covered throughout the book.

ACKNOWLEDGMENTS

Writing, reviewing, editing, and producing a book is an extraordinarily complex process. The fact that only three names appear as authors of this book belies the fact that a number of our faculty colleagues, present and past, made invaluable contributions to the development of many of the basic ideas underlying our organizational behavior course at the Harvard Business School and, therefore, to this book. We are especially grateful to Tony Athos, By Barnes, John Kotter, Jay Lorsch, Paul Lawrence, Jim Ware, and Tom Lifson. We also owe special thanks to Lisa Mooney, who helped us to manage the development of this book and who suffered through a never-ending barrage of administrative tasks to make it a reality.

With only a few exceptions the materials in this book have been individually copyrighted by the President and Fellows of Harvard College. They are reprinted here by special permission and may not be reproduced in whole or part without written permission. We also wish to thank the publishers and authors who have granted us permission to quote non-Harvard copyright material, as outlined below:

"*Bob Knowlton*" © 1955, Alex Bavelas
"Giving and Receiving Feedback" © John Anderson
"Understanding Individual Behavior in Organizations," adapted from Chapter 2 of *Managing Organization Behavior* (Boston: Little Brown) © 1979, David A. Nadler, J. Richard Hackman, and Edward E. Lawler III
"Hausser Food Products Co." © Steve Palesy and David A. Nadler
"Bancil Corporation" © Northwestern University
"Rondell Data Corporation" © 1981, John A. Seeger
"An Integrative Model of Organizational Dynamics," adapted from *Organizational Assessment* (New York: Wiley-Interscience) by Edward E. Lawler III, David A. Nadler, and Cortlandt Camman, © 1980, John Wiley & Sons
"Putting Excellence into Management," *Business Week,* July 21, 1980, © 1980, McGraw-Hill, Inc.
"Management Systems: The Language of Organizational Character and Competence," *Organizational Dynamics,* Summer 1980, © 1980, AMACOM, a division of American Management Associations

Even though we gladly acknowledge the many contributions of others to this book, we are fully responsible for this book and accept any and all of its faults.

Leonard A. Schlesinger
Robert G. Eccles
John J. Gabarro

WHAT IS A CASE?

A *case study* is a description of a management situation. The analysis of a case study in administration can be thought of as the business equivalent of medical "second opinion."

In medicine, an individual may seek a physician because of some perceived concern about how the body or mind is operating. The physician ordinarily compiles a preliminary problem statement called a *case history*. The case history is a combination of a patient's response to certain queries about his or her symptoms over time ("When did you first get the headaches?"), general history ("Was anyone in your family a diabetic?"), and life circumstances ("About how many hours do you work a week?"). Additionally, other data, both general and problem-related, are collected about the patient's state during the examination. One set, for example, that is routinely taken is called vital signs, and consists of pulse rate, blood pressure, and respiration rate.

From the sense of this case history, the physician attempts to reach a diagnosis, or statement of the patient's problem in terms suggestive of what might have caused it. Further, a treatment is specified, which is some course of action felt likely to remove or at least ameliorate the problem as diagnosed.

Where the patient's concerns and the physician's diagnosis are in conflict, or when the indicated treatment involves risk, a second opinion may be sought. Here, a new, consulting physician reviews the case history, diagnosis, and treatment plan generated by the first practitioner. The consultant often requires additional data generated by tests in an attempt to rethink the problem and its proposed solution. A course of action (for example, surgery) or, sometimes, no course of action is recommended.

[1] This material is adapted from material prepared by Thomas V. Bonoma.

When used in the study of an administrative situation, the *case study* offers the student and practitioner a legitimate learning vehicle and the scholar a useful research tool. The "patient" in administration is often the fictional actor called a corporation by the legal system, although a single division, department, or manager in the organization may be the case focus.

The perceived concerns of the individual(s) involved are as varied as those that send a patient to a physician. However, unlike the medical analogy, these concerns also include studies of especially excellent administrative health in addition to its more problematical aspects. And, also unlike the medical analogy, the practitioner more often seeks out the company than the company does the casewriter.

HOW IS A CASE WRITTEN?

The construction of the administrative case study is remarkably similar to that of the medical case history. Ordinarily, extensive interviews with management about their behavior and circumstances will be conducted. Also, measures of importance to the issue under investigation often are collected as in the case history. In the administrative world, these often include the "vital signs" of financial, marketing, or productive efficiency measures, depending on the nature of the problem under consideration. General measures of the firm's historical health and status, as well as an examination of its competitive environment, are also constructed or reviewed.

The business counterpart to the physician is the case preparer. He or she often spends 100 or more hours collecting information on the corporation and its situation, reducing it to a statement of the essential facts, and presenting it in a manner designed to (1) illustrate selected aspects of the situation, and (2) encourage "second opinions" about the issues facing the firm.

Unlike the general practitioner, who ideally should have no preformed biases or objectives which he or she hopes a patient will satisfy (but like the research physician), the casewriter will have a clear set of *objectives* in mind before approaching the company. Is the object of gathering case data to get students to consider the complexities of how a company buys back its distribution after involving numerous others during its growth period? Then a company that has had that experience recently is sought out.

The case study incorporates the writer's developing sense of what the issues of substance are in the situation facing management. In many respects, case preparation in medicine and business is a detective story, where the writer attempts to see and then reconstruct the underlying issues behind the current state of affairs. Thus, neither the case study (administrative) nor the case history (medical) is an inclusive, objective knowledge-seeking device. It is a subjective, targeted one, often much more valuable for that fact.

WHY DO COMPANIES COOPERATE?

Companies generally perceive several advantages in cooperating with an investigator in the development of a case study. The first is the insight possible from close scrutiny of a current issue with a professional casewriter who has seen other companies and other managers in somewhat similar circumstances. The second is that most managers feel a debt to the management education process, which equipped them to deal successfully with their own jobs. They often feel a corresponding desire to give back new materials to improve the educational process. Most importantly, management's opportunity to observe a number of bright and well-prepared students engage in a spirited discussion of their industry, company, or some current issue often provides a rich well of new ideas and perspectives to managers.

WHO GIVES THE "SECOND OPINION"?

The student does, and herein lies the power of the case for experiential learning. *Like* a consulting physician, students see a case "worked up" by someone else. They must review the relevant facts, analyze them, reach some conclusion about the problem and its cause (often different from both management's and the casewriter's own implicit diagnoses from the identical facts), and recommend some treatment. Also as in medicine, the most powerful and interesting cases are those that permit a multiple analysis of the same evidence to lead to several equally plausible and powerful problem statements, each with different action implications. *Unlike* the medical exercise, however, are these important differences:

1 An administrative case is examined not in isolation by one man or woman checking another's work, but in a community of many other students. Each student has individually invested 2–4 hours (or more) making sense of the evidence, diagnosing the problem, and thinking of treatments. Each has probably uncovered some aspect of evidence others have overlooked, and each probably has read identical pieces of information slightly differently. Further, each student has constructed his or her personal action plan, believes in its rightness, and therefore comes prepared to defend it.

2 Because administrative cases are dissected in a community of learners, not only "goodness" of analysis but also persuasiveness of presentation enter the discussion arena as factors with which to be reckoned. Cleverness and even brilliance unpresented, or presented poorly, will not necessarily dominate mediocrity presented with persuasive genius. Why? Because that is the way the world is, a group interaction in which volume can sometimes dominate veracity. Here is an important lesson in working with, in and, sometimes, around groups.

3 The individual student placed in such a community of learners is not some static receiver of truth from the mouth of a sage. Rather, he or she is an intimately invested participant (because of preparation and social exposure in a group of prepared peers), who, speak out or not, must dynamically rethink the validity of his or her individual analysis continually as the group discussion unfolds. Thus, different from many learning settings, the student spends much time *thinking* during the case discussion because of investment in his or her own point of view, which is implicitly but constantly challenged by different group construals of the identical facts reviewed during individual preparation. Understanding often becomes a matter of either having to defend one's view publicly, or to abandon it, as the group moves in some direction not supported by the individual's own analysis.

4 A discussion leader, present in this setting, has a delicate but powerful role. As part of his or her role, the leader must weave individual contributions toward a group discussion product better than, and sometimes different from, the sum of the individual analyses. The gestalt psychologists understood this phenomenon well when they wrote that the "whole is different from the sum of its parts" in their study of visual illusions.

WHAT DOES THE DISCUSSION LEADER DO?

The discussion leader serves as a recorder and organizer of the group's analysis as it emerges in the fragmented, back-and-forth form so characteristic of verbal interactions. Essentially, he or she can make the product of discussion look as good as the process by organizing and directing its flow. A very important part of this organization comes from the instructor's use of blackboards to leave a meaningful record of the group's progress and insight in front of all.

The discussion leader also may take a more interventionist role in the classroom, serving to point up critical conflicts in case issues and even playing the devil's advocate when no other participant seems inclined to do so. The purposes of challenging individual contributions, whether these challenges come from peers or the discussion leader, are to make the contributor push his or her thinking to its limits, to breed the toughness that comes from successfully coping with challenges, and to force students to grapple with the more subtle issues in the case.

A good discussion leader, more often than not, drives students not only toward diagnosis but also toward action. A leader reminds them that analytic brilliance expressed with persuasive efficacy is totally useless unless somebody does something as a result. However, he or she also encourages and wonders with students about what further thought, analysis, and tests might be necessary to inform right action, and is unaccepting of action recommendations unsupported by powerful analysis. Finally, when an action plan is decided upon, what will be looked at to see if the plan succeeded? At what time? No case analysis is complete without measures to monitor the acts being recommended.

WHAT HAPPENS WHEN IT WORKS?

More intense effort, both from students and instructors, is required for case learning than for any other form of instruction. Although an instructor may feel uncomfortable about his or her inability to control what contributions may be made in the classroom, the power of case learning is awesome. When students begin, they attack problems with raw, groping, undirected energy that more often than not leads them nowhere. In a short period of constant exposure to cases, they deal with the same ambiguous problem sets in a focused, assured manner that leads to firm and informed action regardless of the problem's fuzziness or the incompleteness of the facts. The reasons for such sweeping, changes from the case method of learning seem to include these:

1 The student is forced, by exposure to basically insoluble problems with no right answer, to formulate a personally workable approach to problem definition and formulation. Other learning methods teach some set of approved answers, and send students in search of problems to which to apply them. The case method teaches students to learn for themselves what the problems are and how to define the questions.

2 Repetitive exposure to these ambiguous problems has a remarkable confidence-building effect on those who eventually must deal with similar problems in management. What the psychologists call "tolerance for ambiguity" is cultured directly by case learning. The instructor constantly encourages students to drive toward specific actions in spite of incomplete information, uncertain circumstances, and unclear problems. Although this can sometimes provoke premature action, such a model is much more consistent with the way the "real world" works than is an insistence on complete information or unattainable certainty.

3 The experience of the problem in the case method precedes the structure created to solve it. This is in contradistinction to traditional learning methods, where someone (for example, a Linnaeus who names all the plants and animals) does the work of providing a useful taxonomy into which students are asked to partition their experiences. That model assumes experience is present, and only wants the addition of clever categorization to produce insight. The case method advocates, at least partially, the notion of throwing students into one end of the forest with a pencil and paper, to see what they come out with on the other side. Were there a business Linnaeus, case method instructors probably would vote not to let students know too much about his ideas before they learned more about administrative problems. *Then,* there would be some "pegs of experience" on which to hang the concepts—not before.

HOW DO I PREPARE A CASE?

For the student, case preparation is a personal matter of developing a totally individualistic and intimate problem-solving style. Cases are semistructured problems, and problem definition skills the main "product" of repeated exposure to these learning devices. However, even though there can be *no* formula for case preparation, most students seem to travel a general path that includes:

1 Reading the case quickly; almost skimming it for the major issues and the sense of its layout. One of the most important objectives of this quick reading is to get a sense of who the case protagonist is, and what his or her situation is like.

2 Rereading the case carefully, annotating, highlighting, and distinguishing important information, omissions, and questions raised by the reading.

3 Deciding what the action issues really are. Is this case really about a conflict? Or is the conflict, while an important issue, symptomatic of some deeper management issue needing examination and resolution?

4 Deciding on what analysis questions will inform the issue on what actions need to be taken.

5 Answering these analysis questions as formulated, using the data available from the case and making clear and well-informed assumptions about necessary but missing information.

6 Deciding on a course of action from the analysis, and explicitly considering and rejecting plausible alternative courses because of the analysis.

7 Developing a plan by which the desired action may be achieved or implemented within the company, people, and other constraints encountered in this situation.

8 Testing the plan and the analysis before class against the analysis of others, informally, in a small group. In this way, goodness of analysis and soundness of proposed action can be checked informally, without the social risks a presentation before many others implies. More importantly, in this way students can learn from each other's thought patterns and problem definition templates to improve their own thinking.

The good case learner analyzes each problem as if he or she *were* the case actor. He or she struggles to find a suitable construal of the problem, and then invests enormous effort in analyzing the quantitative and qualitative data to reach a useful set of action recommendations. But, in spite of this investment, he or she is continually reminded that problems are ambiguous, and other students' ideas may be as or more worthy than his or her own. In the best sense of the word, he or she remains ready to be an "idea chef," constantly melding the best of his or her own with the best of others' thoughts to reach a better understanding of the problem and its analytic requirements.

WHAT MAKES CASE LEARNING SO EFFECTIVE?

For both the instructor and the student, case learning requires sailing a very narrow channel between the rocks of overcontrol and the shallows of ambiguity. The promise of the case method, for those who successfully thread their course in this careful manner, is *not* that *it* will produce an excellent administrator. Rather, the student, with the discussion leader's aid, will over time produce this transformation and embody the differences rather than being "taught" them. In the case method, birds learn to fly; with other techniques, they are often given an airline pass.

MANAGING BEHAVIOR IN ORGANIZATIONS

TEXT, CASES, READINGS

PART ONE

MANAGING GROUPS

Part 1 concerns management of primary work groups, management of temporary work groups such as task forces and committees, and management of group process and decisionmaking. The basic model for understanding groups is presented in "A Framework for Analyzing Work Groups." The accompanying readings elaborate this basic model in the context of specific settings. The text, cases, and readings emphasize the development of both diagnostic understanding and action-taking skills.

"A Framework for Analyzing Work Groups" examines group behavior from a managerial perspective and focuses on how, both as a member and as a leader, to make groups effective. It presents what the manager needs to know in order to adequately understand a group. It details how the broad categories of a group's context and its design factors in terms of people, task requirements, and the formal organization are related to its culture, and how this contributes to group outcomes. While the model emphasizes that the design factors are the action levers of the manager, it forces one to recognize that group outcomes are a result of group culture, itself a product of the design factors, and context of the group. Group culture is discussed in terms of emergent activities and interactions; norms; roles and social ranking; sentiments; rituals, stories, and sagas; language conventions; and maps. These aspects of group culture determine the outcomes assessed in terms of productivity, satisfaction, and growth. The text shows how these broad categories are dynamically related through the use of a specific case that illustrates the elements of the model.

The first case, Slade Company, is rich in data that show the relationship between design factors and outcomes. Ralph Porter, the new production manager, needs to understand how the group in the plating department is achieving its outcomes, since he is faced with a difficult question. An illegal punchout system exists and he must decide what to do about it. This case raises the issue of how a manager takes action that affects group processes. It also raises some ethical issues.

The second case, Nuclear Tube Assembly Room, provides a somewhat more dynamic view of a group than Slade Company, which provides more of a snapshot. This second case presents data from Ralph Langley, the manager, and his subordinates on the actions Langley took to improve the performance of a group that was experiencing low outcomes. The case describes the changes made in the design factors of the group and the ways Langley demonstrates leadership and motivates workers. These first two cases provide the opportunity to develop a thorough understanding of the "Framework for Analyzing Work Groups."

Acton-Burnett, Inc., the third case, describes the sequence of events in task force management by David Baker, a young MBA. Although Baker's actions seem reasonable, a major crisis develops. Understanding the reasons for the emergence of this crisis requires an understanding of the complexity of group processes. Baker is faced with the problem of developing an action plan in an urgent situation.

West Point: The Cheating Incident (A), the last case in Part 1, provides the opportunity to apply the group concepts to a total organization. In spite of strong formal prohibitions against cheating contained in the cadet Honor Code, a major cheating scandal occurred at West Point in 1976. An understanding of some complex relationships among various aspects of group culture is required to explain the reasons for the cheating incident. This case also has a major action question for Lt. General Sidney Berry, the superintendent of the U.S. Military Academy. Berry must decide how to handle this incident in a situation of high stakes and substantial publicity with considerable pressure from many constituencies.

The three readings in Part 1 supplement the text and codify some of the lessons drawn from the cases. The readings emphasize the use of our understanding of groups to take effective action. Reading 1, on process observation, describes seven aspects of group behavior that apply across groups of all types. These aspects, which can be used to furnish clues as to the effectiveness of group function, include participation, influence, group climate, membership, feelings, task functions, and maintenance functions. Knowing how to assess the impact of these aspects on group effectiveness enables the manager to intervene to improve group effectiveness.

Reading 2, which considers aspects of problem solving and conflict resolution in management groups, focuses on two particularly important issues: how to best use groups in problem-solving situations and how to effectively resolve intragroup and intergroup conflict. Both issues are central to the quality of group decisions. This reading reviews the reasons for using groups for problem solving as well as the major weaknesses in using groups. It shows that the use of groups is most effective in particular situations, such as one of high complexity or uncertainty or when task interdependence is great. Effective group problem solving requires effective conflict resolution tactics. Various approaches, such as bargaining and forcing, smoothing and avoiding, and confronting, are reviewed to show that the last approach is generally the best.

Reading 3, on task force management, is a practical discussion of the steps involved in effectively managing a task force. It covers all phases of managing a task force, including its startup, the first meeting, and its operation and conclusion. In the startup phase, the importance of clarifying the purpose, defining the general operating procedures, determining the membership, contacting the prospective members, and preparing for the first meeting are emphasized. At this first meeting, the key objectives are reaching a common understanding of the group's task and defining working procedures and relationships. Ongoing responsibilities of the task force leader include holding frequent group meetings to review progress, dividing the group into manageable subgroups for specific tasks, setting interim project deadlines and ensuring adherence to them, and communicating important information to members of the task force and critical individuals in the organization not represented on the task force.

A FRAMEWORK FOR ANALYZING WORK GROUPS

Michael B. McCaskey

Groups are an inevitable feature of a manager's life. Much of what must be accomplished in organizations happens in, through, or in spite of the permanent and temporary groups that make up an organization. But being a familiar part of the landscape does not mean that groups are well-used. Groups can be a more or less effective means for attaining organizational goals. They can also be a forum for enhancing self-identity, a protection against excessive stress and uncertainty, and a home base in an otherwise impersonal corporation. More often, though, managers complain about the time wasted in committee meetings, the indecisiveness of the other person's work group, and the red tape of one's own group.

This note looks at groups from a managerial point of view. It focuses upon the features of group behavior important to the manager who wants to understand how to manage a group for increased effectiveness. The note considers the factors that influence the patterns of behavior that emerge over time in a group, and the way these patterns affect group performance. Throughout the note, the question addressed is: *What do managers need to know about groups?* We are concerned with what managers must know to effectively participate in, as well as lead, work groups.

In this note, *work groups* refers to the groups to which a manager might be assigned, either as a leader or as a member. Work groups then include such diverse gatherings of people as a company's sales force, workers on an assembly line, a board of directors, an ROI task force, and a division operating committee. Membership can range from three to dozens of people, maybe more. But, as will become clear later, not every named collection of people is a group.

The factors that can influence a group's behavior and performance include the people who comprise the group, the assigned task(s), the organizational constraints placed upon the group, and so on. Perhaps the best way to begin is to look at an actual situation and see how it might be analyzed. The case is presented in several installments, and provides a continuing example with which to ground the concepts of how work groups operate. In reading the note, work back and forth between the case and the concepts, letting each side enrich your understanding of the other. Now for part 1 of the case.

Merit Corporation: Part 1

The Merit Corporation was a medium-sized firm that manufactured and sold children's furniture nationally. From its inception, the company had been owned and operated by the Kirschner family. John Kirschner was the president of Merit. His grandfather and uncle had started the company, and control eventually passed to his father then to him. At the age of 54, Kirschner was considering early retirement, but he was still actively involved with every aspect of the company's operations. He felt that it was time for a close look at his organization.

Merit's headquarters and the largest of its three manufacturing plants were located in an industrial park 10 miles outside of Boston. Merit shared the building with a number of other firms, and had offices on the second and third floors of the six-story building. All employees worked a 40-hour, 5-day week. Work began promptly at 8:30 a.m. and ended at 4:30 p.m. Coming in early or leaving late was generally considered to be a sign of ineffectiveness by Kirschner. In fact, he set the pattern himself, just as his father and grandfather had before him. His car was always next to the front entrance of the building at precisely 8:30 a.m. and, with rare exception, he left at 4:30 p.m.

In a departure from the company's conservative philosophy and practice, Kirschner had brought in new managers from outside, some with MBA's, and most with backgrounds in plastics or consumer marketing. He emphasized continuing technical and managerial education and sent a number of his top people to Harvard's advanced management program. Kirschner also advocated managing by committee, and he shared the chief executive officer function with two other executives. Merit had generous fringe benefits and a pension plan that was a model in its area. Labor disputes had never been a significant problem. Turnover was generally low, and employee morale was high. Merit enjoyed a dominant position in the juvenile furniture market. In fact, Kirschner felt that the company's only troubling problem was the development of new products.

New products had traditionally been developed by a series of temporary task forces. On a rotating basis, managers would spend 6 months on a task force to develop a new product. This system had been used for years, since Kirschner's father and grandfather had both felt that line managers should have experience in the new products area.

Over the past 10 years, however, several changes warranted a new look at an area so fundamental to Merit's success. The birthrate was declining, and people seemed less inclined to spend a great deal of money on juvenile furniture. The consumers' movement was vocal about product imperfections and poor design features, such as sharp corners and toxic paints. Responding to these concerns increased production costs. The field had also become increasingly competitive as manufacturers of household furniture began to use their excess capacity to produce children's furniture. As a result of these and other factors, obtaining adequate financing had become increasingly difficult. The higher cost of debt had led to a price increase that did not help to attract customers to a highly competitive market where product differentiation was difficult. The company's sales had leveled off at approximately $120 million.

Kirschner had always been especially interested in new products because it was the first place he worked at Merit. Kirschner decided that before retiring, he wanted to significantly improve the new products area because strength here would help ensure the firm's continued success.

After giving the matter considerable thought and after brief discussions with his top managers, Kirschner decided that a radical change was necessary. He decided to form a group of six to eight people with diverse and possibly even unorthodox backgrounds to work full-time on developing new products. Kirschner felt that if he could find the right people and give them a good deal of encouragement, the company would considerably strengthen its new products development. Consequently, he set about finding and hiring the kind of people who could give real impetus to new-product development at Merit. Kirschner also began looking for office space to house the proposed new group. While no office space was presently available on the second or third floors, some space was available on the fourth floor.

CONTEXT

Whatever actions John Kirschner takes to improve new-product development at Merit will occur within the context of the existing organization and its wider environment. Even though he is president of the company, he does not have complete freedom. Any proposed changes must take into account the existing structure and people, the company's history and traditions, the economic and competitive climate, and many other features. If Kirschner wants to initiate a new group, background factors such as these will likely influence the size, independence, and behavior of the group.

For purposes of studying the way a work group operates, context or background can be conceptualized as follows:

1 The purposes for which the group was created
2 The physical setting in which the group works
3 The company: its size, the nature of its business, its location, its past history and proposed future
4 Competitors, suppliers, and regulators
5 Political, social, economic, and legal systems

These background factors will likely influence any efforts by John Kirschner to begin a new group. For example, one can imagine that some older executives might highly value their experience on temporary task forces and therefore resist any changes in existing procedures. This does not seem to be the case so far at Merit; but if such feelings and outlooks arose, Kirschner would have to deal with them. Failing to do so would endanger the ability of the group to carry out its mission or to survive after John Kirschner retires.

Contextual factors, then, are the background factors out of which a group arises and in which a group operates. Context affects the way a group behaves, at least indirectly, and must be part of any analysis of the way a work group operates. Turning to the case, what do you notice about Merit? What features are likely to be important for how the new work group, or any other group, performs at Merit?

Clearly one of the primary considerations affecting the proposed group are the purposes for which it is being called into existence. John Kirschner seems to like to introduce changes. His assessment of company strengths and weaknesses leads him to feel that the new products area is where the company needs the most improvement. He would like to retire soon and may want to leave a vital new-products group as a legacy. Since the proposed group would have the support of the president, it may enjoy unusual advantages in securing information and getting resources; but, of course, its success is not guaranteed. If there is a contest among aspirants to succeed Kirschner as president, some strange dynamics may endanger or support the fledgling group.

The physical location of the group on a different floor from the rest of corporate headquarters may also turn out to be important. Their mission will be to create new products, and they may want to set up procedures distinctly different from those geared to produce and sell existing lines. The physical separation of the group may help allow this to occur.

The company's history of family ownership and management through three presidents may incline other executives to go along with Kirschner's wishes. Kirschner has successfully introduced other changes and this may also provide "social capital," the credibility to introduce further changes. At the same time, the leveling off of company growth and the expectations created by bringing MBA's into the firm may fuel a desire to do a better job of creating new products. Pride in being the industry leader and the threat of new competition from general-purpose furniture manufacturers may also fuel a willingness to break with existing ways of developing new products. These contextual factors will influence the degree and kind of support group members are likely to receive from the rest of the organization.

One could go on, but the aim in outlining contextual factors is not to be exhaustive. Gathering information on these features could be carried to extremes. Remember that we are focusing on a work group and how to conceptualize the key features that affect its operation. Whatever conceptual framework we develop should serve to focus attention on what is most important for work group behavior. Now let us return to the Merit Corporation and see how John Kirschner proceeded.

Merit Corporation: Part 2

Within 6 months John Kirschner hired eight new people whom he felt had diversity of background, intelligence, enthusiasm, and imagination. They were all between the ages of 27 and 29, and had been educated at some of the best technical and liberal arts schools in the country. The eight members of the group and their backgrounds were:

Name	Age	Degree and major	School	Background
Christopher Kane	28	BA in mathematics, MBA	Tufts, Stanford	Worked for McKinsey & Company in a variety of areas, including marketing diversification and systems analysis.

Name	Age	Degree and major	School	Background
Andrew Jacobson	29	BS in mathematics	MIT	Systems analyst for Mitre Corporation for 1 year. Founder of a public interest research group under the auspices of Ralph Nader. Heavily involved with environmental and consumer issues.
John O'Hara	28	BA	Oberlin	Sculptor and painter. Had a one-artist show at the Cleveland Art Museum. Taught art and metal sculpting in U.S. and abroad.
Robert Vidreaux	28	BA in social relations	Harvard	Led two archeological digs to Iran, and spent 2 years working at the Museum of Natural History in New York City. Has three patents and a variety of inventions in the area of water filtration and purification.
Susanne Tashman	27	BA in English, J.D.	Hollins, Yale	Worked for Davis, Marshall and Polk, a law firm, for 2 years, specializing in S.E.C. work.
Joan Waters	27	BA in chemistry, MBA	Wellesley, Harvard	Worked for Sloan-Kettering Laboratories in New York City for 2 years in the area of chromosomal aberrations and viruses. After receiving an MBA, she worked in the financial office of Lilly Laboratories on long-range planning for 1 year.
Matthew Kiris	29	BS in chemistry	Cal Tech	Spent 3 years investigating the effect of high concentrations of pesticides in tidal regions in both the United States and the Far East. Was a consultant to the public health department in both the United States and Japan.
Raynor Carney	29	BA in political science, MBA	Northwestern, Columbia	Has had extensive political experience; organizing a major gubernatorial campaign, fund raising for the state Democratic Party. Served as the primary developer and contractor for modular low-cost housing project in Maryland.

John Kirschner wanted one person reporting directly to him, but decided against impos-ing any further structure on the group. He appointed Christopher Kane as group head, partly because he was the first to be hired and partly because Kane had made such a positive impression.

When the eight people began work at Merit, they did not know each other, and really did not know what they would be doing on a day-to-day basis. Additionally, their training and skills were very different. For example, Jacobson had worked as a systems analyst, and was also interested in consumer and environmental issues. He tended to be comfortable about the implications of the data in light of his other interests. His previous experience in a large company had led him to expect a "way of doing things" that he guessed was probably quite different from what others in the group expected. O'Hara, for his part, had never worked in a business environment. Although he was used to working long hours and to being committed to a project for an extended length of time, he brought fewer expecta-tions than Jacobson about his job at Merit. Vidreaux, on the other hand, because of his interest in inventing new ways of doing things, tended to approach a procedure by first looking for *other* ways in which it might be done.

Not only were their backgrounds and interests very different, but their personal charac-teristics were also quite varied. Kane, who had always worn a coat and tie to work, con-trasted sharply with O'Hara, who was more comfortable in jeans. Tashman had worked in a law firm before coming to Merit, and thus had become quite comfortable dressing for-mally every day. At the law firm, professional women differentiated themselves from women on the support staff partly by the way they dressed. In contrast, Waters preferred to dress informally. In fact, she saw the opportunity to dress even more informally as a major advantage of her new job.

The work styles of the eight were also quite different. O'Hara was extremely untidy and could only work comfortably with stacks of paper cluttering his desk and immediate area. On the other hand, Jacobson, as he put it, was "compulsively neat." Kiris felt that he worked better with low music in the room, while Waters and Tashman both had strong preferences for quiet when working.

John Kirschner felt that the new group would be creative if given lots of freedom and encouragement. He made it clear that the only things he required of them were a biweekly progress report so that the executive committee could keep abreast of new developments, and a monthly financial report. Other than this, Kirschner emphasized that they were free to work as they wished, as long as they focused their energies on developing new products that met the need for durable, but inexpensive, multipurpose children's furniture.

DESIGN FACTORS

In part 2 of this case, one can see a number of factors important to the patterns of behavior that will develop in the new-product-development (NPD) group. Those factors include the people who comprise the group, the tasks they are required to perform, and the formal structure and operating mechanisms of the organization in which they work. Part of a manager's job in managing a group is to arrange these factors in such a way as to enhance an organization's effectiveness.

In the new-product-development group, the task can be stated more simply than in many groups. The eight members are to develop "new products that meet the need for durable, but inexpensive, multipurpose children's furniture". The president has hired people he thinks are suited to this task. He has also set the group apart from the rest of the organization, both physically and in their reporting relationship to him. Thus, Kirschner is making decisions about what we have called the three design factors. He is trying to "fit" the design factors together in the strongest possible combination to increase their chances of success. Let us look at each design factor in turn.

People

First, there are the people who have been named to the NPD group. They are a diverse collection, primarily without much business experience. Since human beings are composed of a myriad of subtle and shifting characteristics, the possibilities for categorizing them are endless. For purposes of studying work groups, however, research on group behavior and organizational design has found some characteristics more useful to focus on than others. The short list of characteristics includes:

- The skills and interests individual members of the group have.
- Individual members' styles of learning. Some people learn best by actually doing things, while others learn best by reflecting and analyzing.
- The values and assumptions individual members hold. Particularly important in a group setting are members' expectations about leadership.
- Individual members' preferences for variety, for definition and structure, and for individual challenge. Some people feel more comfortable with loosely structured situations, where they have a great deal of autonomy. Other people strongly prefer clarity and definition in tasks and roles.

To manage the NPD group, one should consider the rich mix of people and the best way for them to work together. The company president has deliberately chosen a diverse range of skills and interests, including people who have sculpted, invented, and organized campaigns. They are all young and well-educated and so may expect to work together in a more or less democratic style. Leadership may emerge slowly and is unlikely ever to be dictatorial.

It may also make a difference to the operation of the group that O'Hara and Jacobson have quite different working styles. One is exploratory and messy, and the other is systematic and neat. Jacobson and Tashman are used to a corporate way of doing things; O'Hara, the sculptor, is not. Vidreaux, who has spent time on archeological digs and inventing, may well be a maverick with regard to procedures. These dispositions and skills must be taken into account in trying to manage the group effectively.

Task Requirements

The second major design factor that influences a group's behavior is the tasks that individuals or the group are required to perform. Once again the research on designing social systems is helpful for collapsing the wealth of possible dimensions down to a more manageable list. Task requirements can be classified according to:

- Interactions required between people
- Variety of activities involved
- Novelty or routineness of the tasks
- Breadth of skills involved to perform the task
- Degree to which the work pace is under an individual's control

Kirschner has deliberately kept the list of task requirements short and open-ended for the NPD group. The group is to develop new products for children's furniture within certain constraints. The fact that the group is called upon to innovate means that the task is more novel than routine and calls for a breadth of skills. The new product must appeal to parents, not offend consumer watchdogs, be low-cost and durable, and be capable of being manufactured by Merit. Kirschner has not specified or required any pattern of interaction among the eight group members, but the nature of the task suggests probable interaction between those who know marketing and those who understand engineering and manufacturing. O'Hara, Kane, Waters, and others will have to find ways to divide the work and to bring it together. Group members have high individual control over their work pace and work activities because the task is relatively unspecified, as compared, for example, to an assembly line work group.

Formal Organization

The third design factor is the organizational structure and operating systems, or the formal organization within which the group operates. This includes:

- Hierarchy of authority
- Pattern of reporting relationships
- Formal measurement, evaluation, and control systems
- Reward systems
- Selection and recruitment procedures

Because he wants to foster innovation, Kirschner has taken special pains to shield the NPD group from most structure and procedures that apply to the rest of the organization. He has appointed Kane to head the group for reporting purposes, and the only required reviews are a progress report every other week and a monthly financial report. The group reports directly to him and not, as might be true in many other organizations, to a vice president of research and development or marketing. We already know that he personally recruited and selected the eight members of the group into the organization. By so doing he has made it clear to the rest of the organization that this is a special project, high on his list of priorities. At this point, we know little about other organizational systems that might impact the NPD group. The major point is that there are few organizational procedures and very little structure to constrain or guide the group's behavior.

These then are the three basic design factors that a manager has to work with in managing a group. One must be careful not to presume that a manager can always readily change each factor. Because Kirschner is the president of the company and is starting up a new group, he has more freedom than most managers would ever have.

But even he must operate within the context of company history and traditions, the economic outlook, competitors' behavior, and so on.

In a given situation, a manager will have varying degrees of control over the three design factors. It may help to identify three levels of control:

- Those things over which a manager has complete control
- Those things requiring help from others to change
- Those things over which a manager has little or no control

In the case of the NPD group, Kane is unlikely to have direct control over how group members are rewarded or where it reports into the organizational hierarchy. But he can go to Kirschner and presumably could argue for changes in these factors with the president. For a wide range of other matters, Kane and the group have considerable control. This is due to the newness of the group, Kirschner's shielding efforts, and the relatively unspecified task in terms of required activities and interactions. In older, well-established groups, long-embedded in a particular organizational structure, the degrees of freedom about division of activities, required interactions, and pace of the work are often substantially less. In analyzing what a manager "should do" versus what a manager "can do" to improve work group performance, one should keep these three levels of control firmly in mind.

By virtue of being named to the NPD group, these eight people are not yet a group. Currently, they are a collection of people who will have to build a group. They are required to perform certain activities and interactions, such as developing a new product and reporting on their progress every other week. But beyond a few minimal requirements, the eight are free to evolve whatever patterns of thinking and behaving seem best to meet their needs. The emergence of these patterns of thinking and behaving is one of the most interesting and, for a manager, important aspects of group life. In reading the next part of the Merit case, keep close track of behaviors that *emerge*—those activities, interactions, and rules that are *not* required but which group members devise over time. Also keep track of how these emergent activities and interactions might affect group performance.

Merit Corporation: Part 3

On January 2, the eight members of the NPD group arrived at the Merit Corporation, and reported to Kirschner's office. Kirschner had planned an informal orientation day. He presented each person with a packet of information about the company, data about the products that Merit currently manufactured, and information about compensation and fringe benefits. Then they toured the offices and the plant with "Mr. K," as they quickly came to call him.

After lunch, which was held in a restaurant a few miles away, the group was introduced to the executives with whom they would come into contact. Then Kirschner took them to the fourth floor of the building where he had rented three offices next to one another. He explained that they would have one secretary who would be working directly with them and that they could use additional support staff, if necessary. He apologized for the condition of the offices, which were sparsely furnished and not air conditioned. He encouraged them to get to know one another, and to organize the space in any way they wished.

After Kirschner left, the group spent the rest of the afternoon organizing their work space. The three offices were adjacent to one another and interconnected. Each office had enough room for two or three desks. The middle office, the largest, contained three desks and a large table. Kane, whom Kirschner had introduced as being the group head, at least for reporting and administrative purposes, moved into the first office. Carney took the desk next to him because he wanted to be near a window. Tashman and Waters had already discovered the middle office. Kiris took the remaining desk in this room because he thought he sometimes might want to work at the large table. The three others shared the last office where the group decided to put the coffee machine that Jacobson had found in a storage closet. (See Exhibit 1 for the office layout.)

The group as a whole spent the next few weeks familiarizing themselves with the company. Kirschner usually came upstairs once or twice a week, and often brought new information that he thought they might be able to use. The group informally divided themselves into functional areas, on the basis of interest, training, and expertise. For example, while the group as a whole usually developed cash-flow projections, Tashman usually took responsibility for coordinating this activity. O'Hara used his artistic ability to translate ideas into three-dimensional drawings. Jacobson proved to be particularly adept at synthesizing complex data because of his background in systems analysis. Vidreaux was first seen as antagonistic, because of the disorderly way in which he worked. Then others began to see him as very helpful because his background and interest in social relations enabled him to

EXHIBIT 1   Office layout—fourth floor of the Merit Corporation headquarters building.

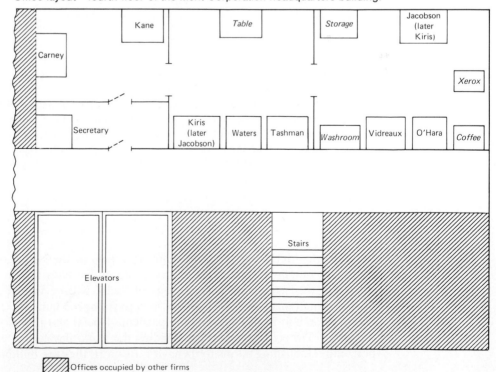

surface potentially disruptive issues about the group's process of working together. Kane was the nominal group head, but Waters soon became a coleader, partly because she had the technical expertise to communicate with engineers in the production department and because of the organizational ability she had acquired in her MBA training.

The group quickly developed some routines. Group members got into the habit of bringing their lunch and eating around the large table in the middle room. Almost daily over lunch they would brainstorm to elicit new ideas. Anyone could initiate such a session; but because they shared the middle office, Waters, Tashman, or Kiris tended to initiate. Since the physical layout brought the eight in contact with each other so easily, they interacted with each other a great deal.

Although working an 8-hour day was not specifically required of the group, individuals initially tended to come in at 8:30 a.m. and leave at 4:30 p.m. However, as ideas were gradually turned into viable products, they worked after hours and on weekends. After a while, some began to come in late in the mornings and work until 6 or 7 p.m., while others preferred to come in before work hours and leave early. However, it became the norm to work late or on weekends if a task was left unfinished. People were almost always in the office between 10 a.m. and 3 p.m., since it was during these hours that the brainstorming sessions and lunch tended to occur. As subgroups formed, and people tended to work together in twos or threes, tension and sometimes friction occurred.

One source of tension was Carney, who preferred to work a good deal on his own. He was often in the middle of something when the other members of the group wanted to begin a brainstorming session. Carney felt that it was more important to finish what he was doing than to work with the group. He eventually missed so many sessions that the other group members kidded him about his antisocial behavior. When this seemed to have no effect, they began to exclude him from informal conversations. At lunch one day when Carney was absent, Vidreaux suggested that the group discuss the purpose and frequency of the sessions, and the importance of everyone being present. As a result of this discussion, group members realized that exceptions to regular attendance could be made without affecting productivity. Subsequently, Carney was included in more informal conversations. But he still remained at the edge of the group.

A similar incident occurred around the issue of work space. O'Hara was extremely untidy and could only work comfortably in the midst of clutter. Jacobson, one of his office mates, was very orderly and found this very disturbing. Considerable antagonism developed between the two until Vidreaux kiddingly brought up the issue at a group session. As a result of the discussion, Jacobson agreed to change places with Kiris, who was indifferent to the "mess."

GROUP CULTURE

Part 3 of the Merit case shows the eight members of the NPD group busy with the process of building a group. As in any group, individuals are finding out who they can be in the group, and what aspects of "self" will be valued and confirmed by others. Simultaneously, each person is confirming certain aspects of others' self-presentation and is also learning the particular social and task skills others bring to the group. The eight members are dividing the work, developing patterns of interaction, and establishing norms for behavior. In short, they are building a group culture.

Emergent from Required

Group culture is the patterns of behavior and values that members *create for them-selves.* These are the ways of thinking and behaving that a group evolves over time. Even in the first weeks of being together, the members of the NPD group have developed a number of characteristic patterns that were *not required of them,* by either the way in which the task was specified or by formal organizational proce-dures. These emergent patterns of behavior are the members' interpretation of what they have been asked to do. And even more importantly, the emergent patterns of behavior are the members' inventions to fit their individual needs to the task and the social context. For example, they have developed a patten of working as many hours as needed to complete their work, even if it means coming in on weekends or working late. They have also developed patterns of mutual helping on the job. These activities and interactions are not required, but nonetheless they do affect group performance, for better or worse.

Since the group members are young and close in age, it is not surprising that an informal, loosely structured mode of interaction has emerged. They interact fre-quently and easily, and do not seem to greatly emphasize status differences, although some are emerging. They have found lunchtime brainstorming sessions useful in bringing the ideas of the group together, and these sessions are becoming a pattern.

Norms

The patterns outlined above are emerging, and some are being enforced as group norms. *Norms* are the expectations and guidelines shared by group members for how members should behave. Over time, group members define what is fair, and what is appropriate behavior. Almost all groups develop their own norms given enough time. Failure to follow group norms threatens the group cohesiveness and, typically, peo-ple who deviate from group norms suffer some form of social censure. For example, in the NPD group, Carney prefers working alone to attending the group's brain-storming sessions. At first he is kidded. When this fails to change his behavior, he is excluded more frequently from ordinary social contact. This could become a serious clash, but Vidreaux initiates explicit discussion. The end result is that Carney re-mains on the periphery of the group, a deviant from the group's norms. The episode illustrates a group's attempt to bring a member's behavior into line. In some groups, kidding may be followed by physical intimidation and eventually one may be totally cut off from the social life of the group. This ultimate sanction is to treat someone as a social isolate.

Even though norms are enforced by group members, they are not applied mono-lithically. They are far more subtle. Norms do not cover all behaviors and do not always apply equally to everyone. Some members may be given special allowance because of their personal needs or unique contribution. At Merit, Carney is allowed some deviation from group norms, although at the cost of remaining on the social periphery. One might expect group leaders to be allowed the most exceptions from group norms. However, research on groups shows that the leader tends to embody the central values and norms of the group even more so than other group members. Leaders may be allowed some exceptions from group norms because of their high status, but in so doing they use up a certain amount of the "social capital" they have accumulated.

If, as happens in most groups, members largely conform to the group norms, the norms help regularize interactions between members. It is much easier, for example, for everyone in the NPD group to attend impromptu brainstorming sessions if everyone follows the norm of being in the office between 10 a.m. and 3 p.m. This does not mean that a manager entering a group for the first time has to conform absolutely to its norms. It does mean that he or she must approach the task of possibly changing group norms with care and understanding of how they work.

Norms serve an important function for group members in stabilizing their interactions along predictable paths. Thus when a manager decides that some norms block group effectiveness, he or she must examine the purpose the norms serve before attempting to change them. Similarly, other features of group culture, such as roles, help give stability and predictability to the interactions of group members, and help the group attain a level of effectiveness.

Roles

Roles are the characteristic and expected social behavior of an individual. Roles may develop so that in addition to the formally appointed leader of a group, one or more *informal leaders* may arise as well. For example, Waters has emerged as a coleader of the group. And Carney has become a *social deviant,* because of his unwillingness to follow an important group norm. Carried further, a member who fails to follow several group norms in a strict group may become a *social isolate.* Roles such as these are often helpful in defining what the norms are in a group. At one end of the continuum, informal leaders are likely to closely adhere to group norms; at the other extreme, social isolates violate some and perhaps many of the group norms.

In the NPD group, several roles have developed based on the special skills and interests of different members. For example, Tashman coordinates the development of cash-flow projections, and O'Hara does the artwork. We know less about roles connected to the process of how the group works, except that Kane and Waters are coleaders. Kane is a formal leader and Waters is an informal leader. Vidreaux has become another informal leader because he explicitly raises process issues for discussion and can bring the discussion to a successful conclusion.

People in a group develop patterns of behavior that contribute or detract from the group's ability to achieve its social and task functions. You have probably been in a group where one person consistently tells a joke to break tensions and reharmonize relationships. In the same group, another person often supplies technical information, while a third person typically keeps an eye on the clock and returns the group to its agenda if discussion strays too far. Behaviors like these, often bundled into specialized roles, are quite important to the level of effectiveness that a group achieves.

Rituals, Stories, and Language

As part of its cultural ways, a work group may also develop rituals, stories about past deeds, and language shorthands. In the NPD group, members already have one ritual in the lunchtime discussions (along with a norm of consistent attendance). They are a young group and do not yet have "sagas" or "myths" to relate about previous heroic efforts, but when these develop they will also serve to reinforce the social ties among members. As is typical of work groups, members of the NPD group have several language shorthands to talk about different parts of their world. They attach special meaning to Mr. K, brainstorming, and antisocial behavior. The language shorthands can be clues to what is emotionally significant in a group's way of working together, what shared sentiments help hold the group together. For example, Mr. K conveys a mixture of deference and special relationship to the company president, especially if no one else in the company addresses him this way. It may signal their feeling that, if they are refused a hearing lower down in the organization, they can take their case to the top. Quite likely, members of the NPD group have other phrases and code words that make sense to themselves but are puzzling to outsiders. Like rituals and stories, special language conventions serve to draw boundaries around the group, differentiating members in the group from others.

Maps

One feature of group culture is the most invisible and often the most difficult for group members to articulate. It is the *map* that group members create of what is important to notice in the world around them. The eight members of the NPD group do not face a predefined, objective reality composed of hard facts. In their work world, there is so much that they can notice that it is overwhelming. Like individuals who must selectively perceive the world, a group also must selectively perceive from the world around it. Furthermore, out of what they notice they must build a coherent picture that makes sense to themselves and provides a common basis of understanding within the group. Rather quickly group members tacitly and naturally evolve agreements for what is most important and what the cause and effect linkages are. The process of formulating a shared map is not always smooth, and some groups can map only part of their world in common. To the extent that it can be formed, this version of reality is treated as real; *it is real* for group members, and is slow to change.

A map guides a group member's daily decisions about what to do and how to interact with others; it also facilitates predicting the likely outcomes of one action versus another. With the information provided so far about the NPD group, we know little about their map. But the map of a sales group, for example, may stress the importance of frequently "pressing the flesh" with customers. This represents a shared view of what is important in a customer's continuing to buy your product. *Mapping* is the mental process by which group members interactively comprehend and deal with the world around them. For a new group member, this means that a group has the power to influence the way she or he sees the world.

Thus far several features of group culture have been distinguished. Its components—emergent activities, norms, roles, rituals, stories, language, and mapping—are an ongoing, social construction of reality. Group culture is not something immediately obvious, but is the inferred change in its major outlines; over time, a group makes small modifications and adjustments. And, most important for managing groups, the group culture is outside the direct control of a manager. It can only be influenced by the manager's actions, example, and arrangement of the design factors discussed earlier. However, appreciation of the constructed nature of group culture opens new possibilities for leading and participating in groups. It separates what is easily changed from what is not, and focuses attention upon what can be directly influenced by a manager and what is more in the province of group members.

Understanding the process of forming a group culture and developing the ability to analyze it deserves a manager's attention, since group culture is closely connected to group performance. Let us return to the Merit case and see if the NPD group was successful in achieving its goals.

Merit Corporation: Part 4

After the NPD group had been in operation for 6 months, Kirschner and the executive committee saw that the group had developed a variety of innovative and unique product ideas. They could also see that group members were enthusiastic about their work.

At the end of the first year, the group came out with a new product. Within 6 months, the product had won a 20 percent share of an extremely competitive market and had been widely acclaimed for its low manufacturing cost, durability, and consumer appeal. To celebrate, the group had lunch away from the office one Friday, and the celebration lasted all afternoon.

OUTCOMES AND FEEDBACK

Although managers sometimes mistakenly consider group productivity solely in terms of work production, the outcomes of a group are actually multidimensional. We can consider the various outcomes a group produces under three headings:

- Productivity
- Satisfaction
- Individual growth

The productivity of the NPD group was quite high. They produced a variety of new product ideas and successfully introduced a new product into a competitive marketplace. They met the major purpose for initially establishing the group.

Beyond work productivity, an important outcome for the group was the sense of satisfaction with how they operated and what they achieved. The term *satisfaction* is shorthand for the rich mixture of feelings that a member can experience as a result of being a part of a group. These feelings can include strongly negative, as well as positive, ambivalent, and sometimes even contradictory emotions. They are part of what fuels each member's participation or lack of it in the group. Think, for a moment, of the groups you have especially enjoyed working in. What was characteristic of those groups? How did you feel during group meetings? How did that add to the amount and the quality of the work you did? As some scholars have phrased it, groups run on emotion.

Emotions—feelings of satisfaction or dissatisfaction—can be powerful stimuli for behavior in groups. The feelings that result from a period of work have feedback effects upon existing aspects of group life. As members see the group producing certain outcomes, this reinforces or weakens features in the group culture. For example, those in the NPD group who championed the product idea that later proved a market success probably saw their standing increased. The success of the group and the attendant positive feelings quite likely reinforced the map and the norms of the group about what was to be valued and what was not. In addition, feedback from outcomes can reinforce or weaken the patterns of interaction among people, task, and formal organization. Since the feedback in this case was positive, current patterns were strengthened. If the outcomes had been negative, this would have led to questioning the pattern of working together that the group had so far evolved.

Crucial for managing the long-term health of the group is the extent to which individuals feel they are learning and growing. In the NPD group, we have no direct information, but it seems a fair inference that many of the eight members see themselves as learning and growing. O'Hara and Kiris, who had nonbusiness backgrounds, are learning to operate successfully in a business setting. In exercising leadership skills, Waters is probably growing and developing as a manager. Such individual growth keeps a member involved and committed to group activities and provides the basis for even better future performance. If such individual commitment were lacking, the manager of a group would have to resort to increasingly heavy external pressures that would eventually be self-defeating.

A MODEL OF WORK GROUP BEHAVIOR

The concepts introduced so far can be brought together in a model of work group behavior. The model is devised for *managers* and focuses on the dominant features of how a group operates and the "action" levers available to a manager. The model does not aim for conceptual elegance, nor is it totally inclusive. Instead, it tries to shrink the number of categories to the smallest number possible that still accurately portray the main features of group life. The major elements of the model are presented in Exhibit 2.

The model indicates that group production, its outcomes, is influenced by a set of factors called *group culture*. Group culture refers to the patterns of behaving and thinking that develop in the group. Group culture arises from the interaction of the three design factors: the people in the group, the required tasks, and the structure and systems of the organization in which the group operates. The design factors and their interaction are in turn shaped by a set of factors called *context*. The company, its history and traditions, its size and economic clout, the physical setting in which the group works, the state of the economy, government action, consumer attitudes, and the actions of competitors are all contextual factors that could ultimately impact a given work group. Theoretically, arrows could be drawn between all parts of the

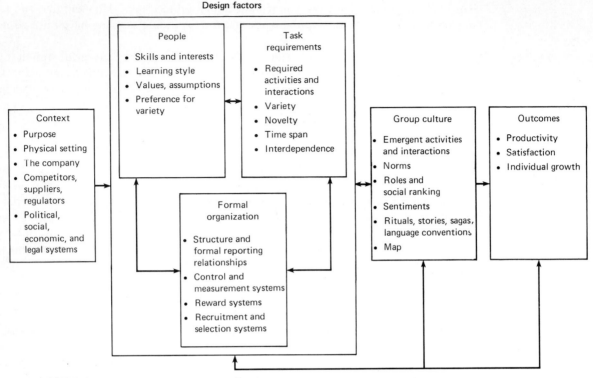

EXHIBIT 2   Model for analyzing a work group.

model. Group behavior is a complex and subtle phenomenon in which everything, to some degree, is interconnected. But since it is more useful to concentrate upon the typical patterns of interaction, arrows are used to describe only the most important relationships.

It is important to note that the whole system is alive and moving. Changes in any part of the model can eventually lead to changes throughout the model. For example, when the economy hits a severe downturn (a change in a contextual factor), top management may decide to lay off people. Some of these will be members of a work group. Remaining members may respond by increased emphasis on task requirements related to increasing production and lowering costs. (Or they may go out on strike or look for other jobs.) In response to a downturn, organizational systems, particularly budgeting and auditing systems, are likely to be tightened. This will interact with the group's norms about how much they should try to produce and how efficiently. It may well alter patterns of interaction and give new prominence to those members of the group who have special skills for dealing with the crisis. All the changes and adjustments percolate through the system, resulting in altered outcomes—perhaps higher productivity, higher or lower satisfaction, or a mixture of other feelings. The outcomes are multidimensional and have feedback effects upon the group culture and upon design factors.

Stop for a few minutes and study the model. You should be able to fill out a chart for the New Products Development group using these categories:

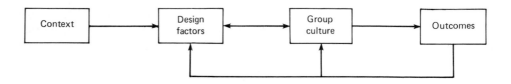

More importantly, you should also understand some of the interrelationships between the concepts.

Few social systems stand still, and events continued at Merit. Let us see what happened to the NPD group over the next several months. Part way through the case history, there will be a chance to test your understanding of the model.

Merit Corporation: Part 5

Three months later, Kirschner retired. The executive committee brought in Joe Donaldson as vice president of marketing. Donaldson had 15 years of experience in a large consumer product organization, and the NPD group was now to report to him. Donaldson was extremely interested in the group's work, but was concerned that no additional new products appeared to be imminent. Two months after his arrival at Merit, he asked Kane to come down to his office to discuss this problem. Kane explained that it had taken some time for the group to adjust to Merit but that things seemed to be going quite well; in fact, he was enthusiastic about the future of the group. Donaldson continued to express concern about the viability of such a group at Merit. Kane, somewhat flustered, finally told him that he could attribute some of the problems to the poor secretarial help and the lack of support staff on the fourth floor. Kane also stressed the fact that creativity in work groups tends to occur in cycles. He was confident that the group was in a "trough" right now, and would soon be out of it.

Two weeks after Donaldson's meeting with Kane, the group heard of his decision. The NPD group would move downstairs with the rest of the staff. Donaldson hoped that with better administrative assistance, closer contact with line executives, and with his personal involvement, the group could repeat their first success.

Within 30 days of Donaldson's decision, the NPD group moved downstairs to the second floor, and reported directly to Donaldson. Although the offices could not be located next to one another, they were redecorated, and each person was given ample secretarial and administrative help. In addition, the group was encouraged to increase expenses, if necessary, to quickly bring out another new product. Group members were also encouraged to work from 8:30 a.m. to 4:30 p.m., since the occupants of the adjoining offices might resent their unpredictable schedules.

Before reading further, use the model to predict what will happen.

At first, the new offices and novel atmosphere made up for the distance between offices. However, those group members who preferred to dress informally began to feel quite uncomfortable and changed to a more traditional business attire. Within a few weeks, the patterns of interaction that had proven successful as well as personally satisfying to individual members had fallen into disuse. Since group members could no longer easily enter and leave each other's offices and since they had no place to hold brainstorming sessions, their sense of what they "ought" to do on a given day became vague. Certain individuals, especially Carney, were more discomforted than others. Carney began to issue "working papers" on what the competition was likely to do and on social issues, neither of which was seen as particularly relevant to the work of the group. Soon he was ostracized from the group. Since there was no comfortable and accessible place to have lunch together, people began to go out to restaurants in subgroups. It soon became the exception rather than the rule for the group to meet informally. Individuals began to feel increasingly dissatisfied with their job and felt surrounded by people with different personal values. At the same time, the old roles seemed quite inappropriate in the new environment. During an infrequent group lunch at a nearby restaurant, numerous complaints were voiced, ranging from feelings of inadequacy to a sense of boredom, to dissatisfaction with the rigid work hours.

Within 2 months, O'Hara left Merit to be married and to live on the West Coast. Tashman and Carney also left. Kane suggested recruiting new people but Donaldson decided that it would be best to disband the group, assigning the remaining individuals to regular departments, and reinstituting the task force system that had earlier been used for new-product development. Three months later, every member of the group had resigned except for Kane.

On one of his rare visits to the office, Kirschner asked Kane what had gone wrong. Kane was reluctant to describe what he thought Donaldson's effect had been. So he told Kirschner that it was difficult to maintain a creative group over a long time and that most members had personal reasons for leaving. Kirschner seemed to accept the explanation, and did not pursue the matter further.

Donaldson looked at the NPD group and saw reduced outcomes. In his eyes, the absence of a new product in 2 months was cause for trying to change the group. He reached for action levers, changing the physical location and work schedule of the group without careful consideration of group culture and its operation. Unknowingly, he disrupted the culture that group members had devised to fit their diverse personalities to the task Kirschner had given them. The map, norms, and roles the group had established broke down. Carney and others became uncertain about what to do. Their previous excitement, satisfaction, and sense of purpose turned to confusion and hostility. The group as a social system floundered and became a collection of individuals once again. Several people quit and eventually the group was disbanded.

Donaldson used a deficient model of how groups operate. His actions seriously weakened and then broke the links between design and culture, and between culture and outcomes. He implicitly linked those things he could directly control, such as work schedule, reporting relationships, and physical setting, to group performance. He seemed unaware of the intervening role played by group culture and of how outcomes were multiple in nature. Use of a model that overlooked important features of how a group operates led him to make a number of ill-conceived changes.

One of the aims of presenting a *managerial* model of group behavior is to focus attention on the intelligent selection of action levers. The process can be summarized as follows:

1 Look at the outcomes of a group. Why does it perform the way it does? Part of answering this question means you should do the following.

2 Look at the culture of the group. What are its norms and values? What does it do that is *not required* but nonetheless affects its performance for better or worse? Why is the culture the way it is? Part of answering these questions is to do the following.

3 Look at the design factors. Which of these are under your direct control and which can you only indirectly influence? How can the design factors be changed in a desired direction to produce the intended outcomes?

4 Look at the context within which the group operates. Are the proposed changes consistent with contextual factors? Where should you anticipate difficulties?

Had Joe Donaldson thought through such an analysis for the NPD group, he would not have been guaranteed a success. Skills are needed to actually carry out any plan suggested by analysis. However, he would have increased his chances of successfully intervening and eventually achieving the intended results.

CONCLUSION

The model of group behavior presented in this note captures much of what happens in a work group and provides a platform for building further knowledge. Looking at groups in this way allows you to identify the multiple causes of group behavior and performance. Furthermore, the model suggests how one might think about participating in and leading a work group in its attention to action levers and what is and is not under a manager's control.

By showing how leadership functions can be distributed in a group and how a map is interactively constructed, the model refreshes one's thinking about leadership in work groups. One does not have to be appointed the formal leader of a group to help build a culture that fits together members, tasks, and organization. In fact, in high-performing groups, the behaviors that maintain a group socially and those that move it toward task accomplishment are usually shared by several members. Likewise, informal leaders can play a major role in formulating or reformulating the map that guides group efforts, even though the first attempt usually falls to the formal leader.

The culture constructed by group members represents a stance taken vis-à-vis the rest of the world and directly affects group effectiveness. The group tries it out and subsequent outcomes provide feedback. Feedback from the rest of the world leads to reinforcing, modifying or, in unusual cases, abandoning the map, norms, and roles that comprise the group culture. The revised patterns of thinking and interacting go through additional cycles over the life of the group. The possibilities lie within a group for either continued growth and development, or for settling into established routines.

In summary, group culture is closely connected to outcomes the group produces; and yet culture is beyond the direct control of a manager. A manager works through three design factors—people, tasks, and formal organization—to influence culture. These are the most readily available action levers for influencing group behavior. But managerial action should be taken only after a careful analysis of how the culture of the group will be affected and what the consequences will be for the group. As Donaldson discovered, it is a mistake to be concerned solely with productivity outcomes while ignoring emotional and individual growth outcomes. To improve work group performance, one must understand the multiple causes of group behavior. This model provides a practical starting point for acquiring such an understanding.

SLADE COMPANY

Paul R. Lawrence

Ralph Porter, production manager of the Slade Company, was concerned by reports of dishonesty among some employees in the plating department. From reliable sources, he had learned that a few men were punching the timecards of a number of their workmates who had left early. Porter had only recently joined Slade. He judged from the conversations with the previous production manager and other fellow managers that they were generally pleased with the overall performance of the plating department.

The Slade Company was a prosperous manufacturer of metal products designed for industrial application. Its manufacturing plant, located in central Michigan, employed nearly 500 workers, who were engaged in producing a large variety of clamps, inserts, knobs, and similar items. Orders for these products were usually large and on a recurrent basis. The volume of orders fluctuated in response to business conditions in the primary industries that the company served. At the time of this case, sales volume had been high for over a year. The bases upon which the Slade Company secured orders, in rank of importance, were quality, delivery, and reasonable price.

The organization of manufacturing operations at the Slade plant is shown in Exhibit 1. The departments listed there are, from left to right, approximately in the order in which material flowed through the plant. The diemaking and setup operations required the greatest degree of skill, supplied by highly paid, long-service craftsmen. The finishing departments, divided operationally and geographically between plating and painting, attracted less highly trained but relatively skilled workers, some of whom had been employed by the company for many years. The remaining operations were largely unskilled in nature and were characterized by relatively low pay and high turnover of personnel.

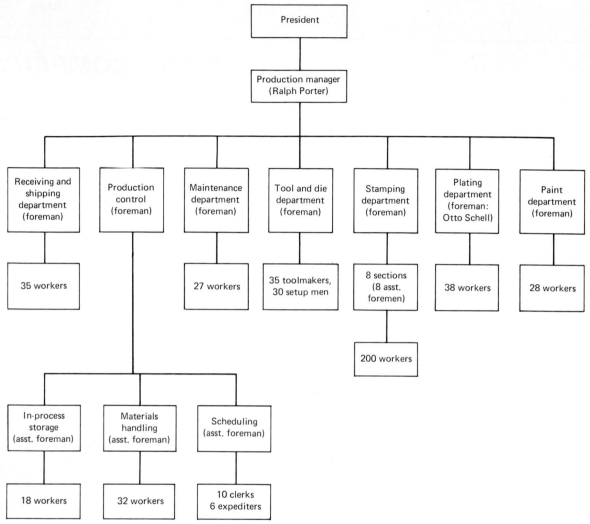

EXHIBIT 1   The Slade Company—manufacturing organization.

The plating room was the sole occupant of the top floor of the plant. Exhibit 2 shows the floor plan, the disposition of workers, and the flow of work throughout the department. Thirty-eight men and women worked in the department, plating or oxidizing the metal parts or preparing parts for the application of paint at another location in the plant. The department's work occurred in response to orders communicated by production schedules, which were revised daily. Schedule revisions, caused by last-minute order increases or rush requests from customers, resulted in short-term volume fluctuations, particularly in the plating, painting, and shipping departments. Exhibit 3 outlines the activities of the various jobs, their interrelationships, and the type of work in which each specialized. Exhibit 4 rates the various

EXHIBIT 2   The Slade Company—plating room layout.

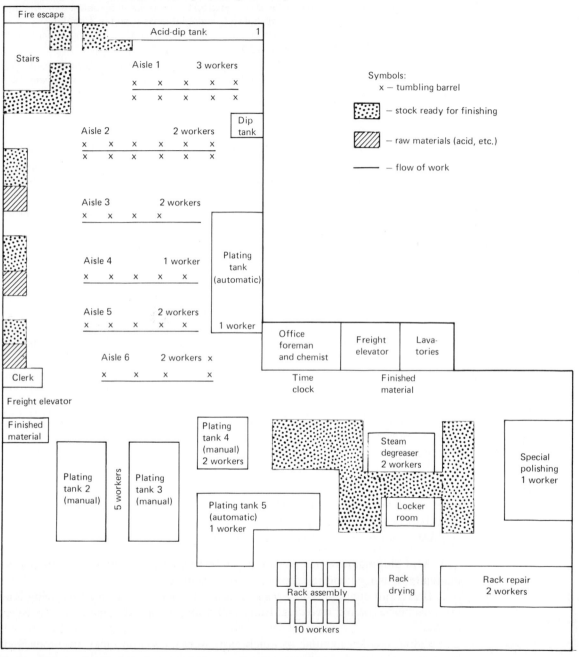

EXHIBIT 3 OUTLINE OF WORK FLOW, PLATING ROOM

Aisle 1	Worked closely with aisle 3 in preparation of parts by barrel tumbling and acid dipping for high-quality* plating in tanks 4 and 5. Also did a considerable amount of highly specialized, high-quality acid-etching work not requiring further processing.
Aisle 2	Tumbled items of regular quality and design in preparation for painting. Less frequently, did oxidation dipping work of regular quality, but sometimes of special design, not requiring further processing.
Aisle 3	Worked closely with aisle 1 on high-quality tumbling work for tanks 4 and 5.
Aisles 4 and 5	Produced regular tumbling work for tank 1.
Aisle 6	Did high-quality tumbling work for special products plated in tanks 2 and 3.
Tank 1	Worked on standard, automated plating of regular quality not requiring further processing in plating room, and on regular work requiring further processing in tank 5.
Tanks 2 and 3	Produced special, high-quality plating work not requiring further processing.
Tank 4	Did special, high-quality plating work further plated in tank 5.
Tank 5	Automated production of high- and regular-quality, special- and regular-design plated parts sent directly to shipping.
Rack assembly	Placed parts to be plated in tank 5 on racks.
Rack repair	Performed routine replacement and repair of racks used in tank 5.
Polishing	Processed by manual or semimanual methods, odd-lot special orders that were sent directly to shipping. Also, sorted and reclaimed parts rejected by inspectors in the shipping department.
Degreasing	Took incoming raw stock, processed it through caustic solution, and placed clean stock in storage ready for processing elsewhere in the plating room.

* In *high-* or *regular-quality* work, the quality of finishes could broadly be distinguished by the thickness of plate and/or care in preparation. In *regular* or *special work,* the complexity of the work depended on the routine or special character of design and finish specifications.

types of jobs in terms of the technical skill, physical effort, discomfort and training time associated with their performance.

Three main types of activities took place in the plating room:

1 Acid dipping, in which parts were etched by being placed in baskets that were manually immersed and agitated in an acid solution.

2 Barrel tumbling, in which parts were roughened or smoothed by being loaded into machine-powered revolving drums containing abrasive, caustic, or corrosive solutions.

3 Plating—either manual, in which parts were loaded on racks and immersed by hand through the plating sequence; or automatic, in which racks or baskets were manually loaded with parts that were then carried by a conveyor system through the plating sequence.

EXHIBIT 4   SKILL INDICES BY JOB GROUP*

Jobs	Technical skill required	Physical effort required	Degree of discomfort involved	Degree of training required†
Aisle 1	1	1	1	1
Tanks 2–4	3	2	1	2
Aisles 2–6	5	1	1	5
Tank 5	1	5	7	2
Tank 1	8	5	5	7
Degreasing	9	3	7	10
Polishing	6	9	9	7
Rack assembly and repair	10	10	10	10

* Rated on scales of 1 (the greatest) to 10 (the least) in each category.
† The amount of experience required to assume complete responsibility for the job.

Within these main divisions, there were a number of variables, such as cycle times, chemical formulas, abrasive mixtures, and so forth, which distinguished the particular jobs categorized in Exhibit 3.

The work of the plating room was received in batch lots whose size averaged 1000 pieces. The clerk moved each batch, which was accompanied by a routing slip, to its first operation. This routine slip indicated the operations to be performed and the scheduled completion time for each major operation so that the finished product could be shipped on time. From the accumulation of orders, each worker was to organize a personal work schedule to make optimum use of equipment, materials, and time. Upon completion of an order, each worker moved the lot to its next work position or to the finished material location near the freight elevator.

The plating room was under the direct supervision of foreman Otto Schell, who worked from 8 a.m. to 5 p.m. 5 days a week. Schell spent a good deal of his working time attending to maintenance and repair of equipment, procuring supplies, handling late schedule changes, and seeing that the workers were at their proper locations.

Working conditions in the plating room varied considerably. That part of the department containing the tumbling barrels and the plating machines was constantly awash, alternately with cold water, steaming acid, or caustic soda. Workers in this part of the room wore knee boots, long rubber aprons, and high-gauntlet rubber gloves. This uniform, consistent with the general atmosphere of the "wet" part of the room, was hot in the summer, cold in winter. In contrast, the remainder of the room was dry and relatively odorless, and provided reasonably stable temperature and humidity.

Exhibit 5 lists the workers employed in the plating room. It also provides certain personal data on each department member, including a productivity-skill rating (based on subjective and objective appraisals of potential performance), as reported by the members of the department.

EXHIBIT 5 PLATING ROOM PERSONNEL

Location	Name	Age	Marital status	Company seniority, years	Department seniority, years	Hourly pay	Education*	Familial relationships	Productivity-skill rating†
Aisle 1	Tony Sarto	30	M	13	13	$1.50	H.S.	Louis Patrici, uncle; Pete Facelli, cousin	1
	Pete Facelli	26	M	8	8	1.30	H.S.	Louis Patrici, uncle; Tony Sarto, cousin	2
	Joe Iambi	31	M	5	5	1.20	2 yr H.S.		2
Aisle 2	Herman Schell	48	S	26	26	1.45	G.S.	Otto Schell, brother	8
	Philip Kirk	23	M	1	1	0.90	College		‡
Aisle 3	Dom Pantaleoni	31	M	10	10	1.30	1 yr H.S.		2
	Sal Maletta	32	M	12	12	1.30	3 yr H.S.		3
Aisle 4	Bob Pearson	22	S	4	4	1.15	H.S.	Father in tool and die department	1
Aisle 5	Charlie Malone	44	M	22	8	1.25	G.S.		7
	John Lacey	41	S	9	5	1.20	1 yr H.S.	Brother in paint department	7
Aisle 6	Jim Martin	30	S	7	7	1.25	H.S.		4
	Bill Mensch	41	M	6	2	1.10	G.S.		4
Tank 1	Henry LaForte	38	M	14	6	1.25	H.S.		6
Tanks 2 and 3	Ralph Parker	25	S	7	7	1.20	H.S.		4
	Ed Harding	27	S	8	8	1.20	H.S.		4
	George Flood	22	S	5	5	1.15	H.S.		5
	Harry Clark	29	M	8	8	1.20	H.S.		3
	Tom Bond	25	S	6	6	1.20	H.S.		4
Tank 4	Frank Bonzani	27	M	9	9	1.25	H.S.		2
	Al Bartolo	24	M	6	6	1.25	H.S.		3
Tank 5	Louis Patrici	47	S	14	14	1.45	2 yr college	Tony Sarto, nephew; Pete Facelli, nephew	1

EXHIBIT 5 *(CONTINUED)*

Location	Name	Age	Marital status	Company seniority, years	Department seniority, years	Hourly pay	Educa-tion*	Familial relation-ships	Produc-tivity-skill rating†
Rack assembly	10 women	30–40	9M, 1S	10 (avg)	10 (avg)	1.05	G.S. (avg)	Six with husbands in company	4 (avg)
Rack maintenance	Will Partridge	57	M	14	2	1.20	G.S.		7
	Lloyd Swan	62	M	3	3	1.10	G.S.		7
Degreasing	Dave Susi	45	S	1	1	1.05	H.S.		5
	Mike Maher	41	M	4	4	1.05	G.S.		6
Polishing	Russ Perkins	49	M	12	2	1.20	H.S.		4
Foreman	Otto Schell	56	M	35	35	n.a.	H.S.	Herman Schell, brother	3
Clerk	Bill Pierce	32	M	10	4	1.15	H.S.		4
Chemist	Frank Rutlage	24	S	2	2	n.a.	2 yr college		6

* H.S. = high school; G.S. = grade school
† On a scale of 1 (top) to 10 (bottom), as evaluated by the members of the department.
‡ Kirk was the source of data for this case and, as such, was in a biased position to report accurately perceptions about himself.

The pay scale shown in Exhibit 5 was low for the central Michigan area. The average hourly starting wage for factory work in the community was about $1.25. However, working hours for the plating room were long—from 60 hours to a possible and frequently available 76 hours per week. The first 60 hours—the normal 5-day week—were paid for on straight-time rates. Saturday work was paid for at time and one half; Sunday work at double-time.

As Exhibit 5 indicates, Philip Kirk, a worker in aisle 2, provided the data for this case. After being in the department for several months, Kirk noted that certain members of the department tended to seek each other out during free time both on and off the job. He then observed that these informal associations were enduring, and were built upon common activities and shared ideas about what was and what was not legitimate behavior in the department. Kirk's estimate of the pattern of these associations is shown in Exhibit 6.

The Sarto group, so named because Tony Sarto was its most respected member and the one who acted as arbiter between the other members, was the largest in the department. The group, except for Louis Patrici, Al Bartolo, and Frank Bonzani (who spelled each other during break periods), invariably ate lunch together on the fire escape near aisle 1. On those Saturdays and Sundays when overtime work was required, the Sarto group operated as a team, regardless of weekday work assignments, to complete overtime work as quickly as possible. (Few department members not affiliated with either the Sarto or the Clark groups worked on weekends.) Off the

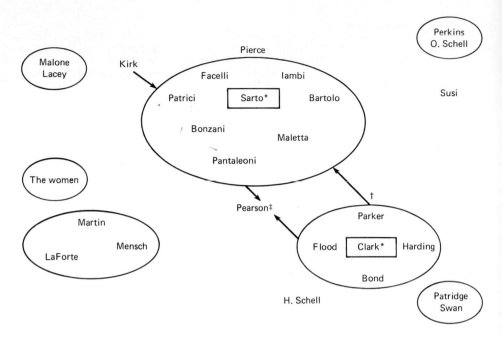

* The boxes indicate those workers who clearly demonstrate leadership behavior (most closely personified the values shared by their groups, were most often sought for help and arbitration, and so forth).

† While the two- and three-worker groupings had little informal contact outside their own boundaries, the five-worker group did seek to join the largest group in extraplant social affairs. These were relatively infrequent.

‡ Though not an active member of any group, Bob Pearson was regarded with affection by the two large groups.

EXHIBIT 6   The Slade Company—informal groupings in the plating room.

job, Sarto group members often joined in parties or weekend trips. Sarto's summer camp was a frequent rendezvous.

Sarto's group was also the most cohesive one in the department in terms of its organized punch-in and punchout system. Although workers were regularly scheduled to start at 7 a.m. and finish at 7 p.m. on weekdays, all supervision was removed at 5 p.m.; hence, it was possible almost every day to finish a "day's work" by 5:30 p.m. and leave the plant. What is more, if one worker were to stay until 7 p.m., he could punch the time cards of a number of men and help them gain free time without pay loss. (This system operated on weekends also, at which times members of supervision were present for short periods, if at all). In Sarto's group the duty of staying late rotated, so that no member did so more than once a week. In addition, a group member would also punch in another member in the morning if he were unavoidably delayed. However, such a practice never occurred without prior notice from the member who expected to be late and never if the tardiness was expected to last beyond 8 a.m., the start of the foreman's day.

Sarto explained the logic behind the system to Kirk:

You know that our hourly pay rate is quite low, compared to other companies. What makes this the best place to work is the feeling of security you get. No one ever gets laid off in this department. With all the hours in the week, all the company ever has to do is shorten the work week when orders fall off. We have to tighten our belts, but we can all get along. When things are going well, as they are now, the company is only interested in getting out the work. It doesn't help to get it out faster than it's really needed—so we go home a little early whenever we can. Of course, some guys abuse this sort of thing—like Herman—but others work even harder, and it averages out.

Whenever an extra order has to be pushed through, naturally I work until 7 p.m. So do a lot of the others. I believe that if I stay until my work is caught up and my equipment is in good shape, that's all the company wants of me. They leave us alone and expect us to produce—and we do.

When Kirk asked Sarto if he would rather not work shorter hours at higher pay in a union shop (Slade employees were not organized), Sarto laughed and said, "It wouldn't come close to an even trade."

The members of Sarto's group were explicit about what constituted a fair day's work. Customarily, they cited Herman Schell, Kirk's work partner and the foreman's brother, as a man who consistently produced below that level. Kirk received an informal orientation from Herman during his first days on the job. As Herman put it,

I've worked at this job for a good many years, and I expect to stay here a good many more. You're just starting out, and you don't know which end is up yet. We spend a lot of time in here; and no matter how hard we work, the pile of work never goes down. There's always more to take its place. And I think you've found out by now that this isn't light work. You can wear yourself out fast if you're not smart. Look at Pearson in aisle 4. There's a kid who's just going to burn himself out. He won't last long. If he thinks he's going to get somewhere working like that, he's nuts. They'll give him all the work he can take. He makes it tough on everybody else and on himself, too.

Kirk reported further on his observations of the department:

As nearly as I could tell, two things seemed to determine whether or not Sarto's group or any others worked on Saturday or Sunday. It seemed usually to be caused by rush orders that were received late in the week, although I suspect it was sometimes caused by the workers having spent insufficient time on the job during the previous week.

Tony and his group couldn't understand Herman. While Herman arrived late, Tony was always half an hour early. If there was a push to get out an extra amount of work, almost everyone but Herman would work that much harder. Herman never worked overtime on weekends, while Tony's group and the workers on the manual tanks almost always did. When the first exploratory time study of the department was made, no one in the aisles slowed down, except Herman, with the possible exception, to a lesser degree, of Charlie Malone. I did hear the workers in the dry end of the room slowed down so much you could hardly see them move; but we had little to do with them, anyway. While the workers I knew best seemed to find a rather full life in their work, Herman never really got involved. No wonder they couldn't understand each other.

There was quite a different feeling about Bob Pearson. Without the slightest doubt, Bob worked harder than anyone else in the room. Because of the tremendous variety of work produced, it was hard to make output comparisons, but I'm sure I wouldn't be far wrong in saying that Bob put out twice as much as Herman and 50 percent more than almost anyone else in the aisles. No one but Herman and a few oldtimers at the dry end criticized Bobby for his efforts. Tony and his group seemed to feel a distant affection for Bob, but the only contact they or anyone else had with him consisted of brief greetings.

To the members of Tony's group, the most severe penalty that could be inflicted was exclusion. This they did to both Pearson and Herman. Pearson, however, was tolerated; Herman was not. Evidently, Herman felt his exclusion keenly, though he answered it with derision and aggression. Herman kept up a steady stream of stories concerning his attempts to gain acceptance outside the company. He wrote popular music, which was always rejected by publishers. He attempted to join several social and athletic clubs, mostly without success. His favorite pastime was fishing. He told me that fishermen were friendly, and he enjoyed meeting new people whenever he went fishing. But he was particularly quick to explain that he preferred to keep his distance from the men in the department.

Tony's group emphasized more than just quantity in judging a member's work. Among them had grown a confidence that they could master and even improve upon any known finishing technique. Tony himself symbolized this skill. Before him, Tony's father had operated aisle 1 and had trained Tony to take his place. Tony, in turn, was training his cousin Pete. When a new finishing problem arose from a change in customer specifications the foreman, the department chemist, or any of the men directly involved would come to Tony for help, and Tony would give it willingly. For example, when a part with a special plastic embossing was designed, Tony was the only one who could discover how to treat the metal without damaging the plastic. To a lesser degree, the other members of the group were also inventive about the problems that arose in their own sections.

Herman for his part, talked incessantly about his feats in design and finish creations. As far as I could tell during the year I worked in the department, the objects of these stories were obsolete or of minor importance. What's more, I never saw any department member seek Herman's help.

Willingness to help was a trait Sarto's group prized. The most valued help to all was of a personal kind, although work help was also important. The members of Sarto's group were constantly lending and borrowing money, cars, clothing, and tools among themselves and, less frequently, with other members of the department. Their daily lunch bag procedure typified the "common property" feeling among them. Everyone's lunch was opened and added to a common pile, from which each member of the group chose his meal.

On the other hand, Herman refused to help others in any way. He never left his aisle to aid those near him who were in the midst of a rush of work or a machine failure, although this was customary throughout most of the department. I can distinctly recall the picture of Herman leaning on the hot and cold water faucets that were located directly above each tumbling barrel. He would stand gazing into the tumbling pieces for hours. To the passing, casual visitor, he looked busy; and, as he told me, that's just what he wanted. He, of course, expected me to act this same way, and it was this enforced boredom that I found virtually intolerable.

More than this, Herman took no responsibility for breaking in his assigned helpers as they first entered the department, or thereafter. He had had four helpers in the space of little more than a year. Each had asked for a transfer to another department, publicly citing the work as cause, privately blaming Herman. Tony was the one who taught me the ropes when I first entered the department.

The workers who congregated around Harry Clark tended to talk and behave like the Sarto group, although they never approached the degree of inventive skill or job helping that Tony's group did. They sought outside social contact with the Sarto group; several times a year, the two groups went "on the town" together. Clark's group did maintain a high level of performance in the volume of work they turned out.

The remainder of the people in the department stayed pretty much to themselves or associated in pairs or triplets. These people were not as inventive, helpful, or productive as Sarto's or Clark's groups, but most gave verbal support to the values those groups held.

The distinction between the two organized groups and the rest of the department was clearest in the punchout routine. The women could not work past 3 p.m., so they were not involved.

Malone and Lacey, Partridge and Swan, and Martin, La Forte, and Mensch arranged within their small groups for punchouts, or they remained beyond 5 p.m. and slept or read when they finished their work. Perkins and Pierce went home when the foreman did. Herman Schell, Susi, and Maher had no punchout organization to rely upon. Susi and Maher invariably stayed in the department until 7 p.m. Herman was reported to have established an arrangement with Partridge whereby the latter punched Herman out for a fee. Such a practice was unthinkable from the Sarto group's viewpoint. It evidently did not occur often because Herman usually went to sleep behind piles of work when his brother left or, particularly during the fishing season, punched himself out early. He constantly railed against the dishonesty of other men in the department, yet urged me to punch him out on several "emergency occasions."

Just before I left the Slade Company to return to school after 14 months on the job, I had a casual conversation with Mr. Porter, the production manager, in which he asked me how I had enjoyed my experience with the organization. During the conversation, I learned that he knew of the punchout system in the plating department. What's more, he told me, he was wondering if he should "blow the lid off the whole mess."

NUCLEAR TUBE ASSEMBLY ROOM

Cyrus Gibson
Paul R. Lawrence

The nuclear tube assembly room was a production unit of the American Radiatronics Corporation, one of the leading producers and an early pioneer in the nuclear electronics industry. The company manufactured a line of nuclear instruments and other electronic devices for nuclear applications. Its regular line of electronic tubes were assembled, tested, and prepared for shipment in the nuclear tube assembly room. Ralph Langley, general foreman of the process department, described the tube room group as the most successful and, from certain standpoints, the most interesting of the several units in his department. Exhibit 1 is an organization chart.

Before Langley assumed leadership of the department, some 24 months earlier, the workers in the room had acquired the reputation of being agitators, hotheads, and persistent troublemakers. Production was down, costs had risen markedly, and deliveries had become very unpredictable. Some thought had been given to eliminating the entire operation. A report prepared by the director of industrial relations, describing the existing problem, is presented in Exhibit 2.

Labor efficiency data during the subsequent 24 months are presented in Exhibit 3. During the most recent 3-month period the tube room's direct and allocated[1] monthly costs had averaged $12,350 while the actual sales value of the room's monthly production for the same 3 months averaged $35,800. A recent special management report presented some additional figures of interest. Between January of the previous year and March of the current year, the group had shown a 53 percent improvement in the dollar output of product per hour of work; direct labor efficiency had increased approximately 24 percent, and there had been an 11–12 percent im-

---

[1] Indirect costs were allocated to the department at the rate of 425 percent of direct labor dollars.

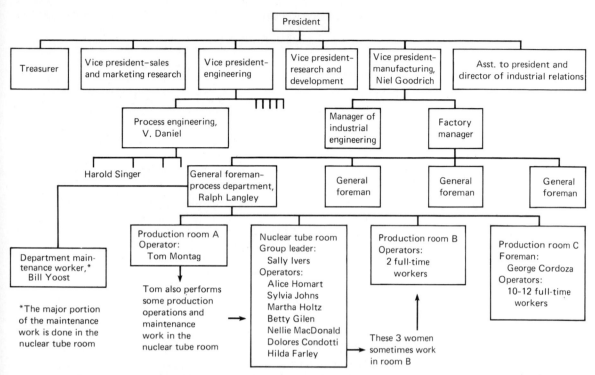

EXHIBIT 1 Partial organization chart of American Radiatronics Corporation.

provement in the use of raw materials on the tubes produced. During the same period, the department operated at 81 percent of its expense budget. In other words, it had used about $4000 less on miscellaneous expenses than had been budgeted for such items. During this period, the hourly wages of the women working in the room had risen from an average of $1.45 to $1.75 per hour. In summary, the profit position for tube manufacturing operations as a whole was now one of the best in the company, where previously the activity had been operating at a loss. In the most recent fiscal year, the tube manufacturing operations generated profits of $93,000 while the American Radiatronics Corporation's total profits were approximately $200,000.

In commenting about the group, Langley said, "The unique aspect of this performance was that it has been accomplished by the group itself—not so much by any tangible thing that I or management has done. These people, previously considered a problem group, are now performing in an efficient and profitable way. They have a very active interest in seeing not only their group, but also the company as a whole, progress and make profits. It seems to me that this is quite an impressive thing for them to have accomplished by their own efforts."

Before conducting the observations and interviews reported on in this case, the casewriter talked to Frank Halbert, president of American Radiatronics. In approving the study, Halbert said, in part, "I hope you find what you are looking for. It would be tremendously important for the whole economy to bust through this 'least

EXHIBIT 2   INDUSTRIAL RELATIONS DIRECTOR'S REPORT*

MEMORANDUM

RE: Process Department, Nuclear Tube Operation   July 10

TO: T. Bishop,† R. Langley

FROM: S. K. Lowe‡

Summary

A brief summary of history, data from supervisors (various levels), employees and exit interviews would indicate the following:

A This section has always had a reputation for being a "problem department." It is not as well organized as other sections (work flow, safety, basic processes, equipment, housekeeping, etc.) Group behavior gives evidence of intense frustration, personal differences, rumor-mongering, and concern over operations. Misunderstandings regarding wages have been reflected by new employees; discouragement about "getting ahead" is reflected by them after a few short weeks of work, after talking with the older workers in the department.

B Productionwise, the section has had a history of not meeting delivery dates or production quotas—with a high rate of product rejects.

Analysis

From examination it would seem that problems may result from the following:

A *Operations—basic product difficulty*   The products (fairly diverse and delicate) have not been "beaten down." Quality is dependent upon process, thus requiring a different *kind* of standardizing. Certain tube reactions are still technically unexplained. Is it a problem of basic design?

B *Instability of product*   Product results, therefore, have been unstable and/or unpredictable.

C *Work flow*   Organization of the work flow, methods used, and work steps do not appear as well defined as other operations, largely due, it would seem, to basic unresolved technical problems.

D *Work standards and conditions*   Standards of cleanliness and observation of eating and smoking restrictions (directly affecting operations) have not been rigidly observed.

E *Equipment*   Equipment failure and repair have, until recently, been a subject of complaint.

F *Coordination*   There is evidence of need for better liaison with sales—scheduling, planning, and meeting promise dates.

Attitudes

A *Top management*   With a myriad of pressures (merger, new plant, move, etc.,) perhaps this small department did not have adequate recognition of its fundamental technical dilemmas; or it did not know how to deal with the basic technical problems—thus unraveling the other tangled department threads. Perhaps in the pressure of bigger problems, it received stepchild treatment.

B *Supervisors*   To most management personnel concerned with its operation, the nuclear tube section was not only a headache, but a bewilderment. Had they been able to solve its basic technical difficulties, it would not have operated on a crisis basis, nor would a high degree of frustration characterize worker attitudes.

---

* Langley took over the Nuclear Tube Room Department on June 15.

† Factory manager.

‡ Director of industrial relations.

EXHIBIT 2   *(CONTINUED)*

For the supervision level nearest the employees, the same pattern has existed over a period of time—inability to organize due to basic technical product difficulties, poor equipment, and little attention or inadequate understanding *and solution* of basic technical problems.

C *Employees*   Employees reflect a high degree of frustration and worry for several reasons. They tend naturally to reflect the attitudes of their supervision. As a work group, they are older than average, tending to seek satisfaction from a well-ordered operation. This by reason of product process has not existed.

Employees are hourly and accustomed, from past employment, to more routine, less variable operations. They do not understand the *still experimental* technical debugging factors that must be resolved before operations run smoothly. It is not yet a traditional *production* department although we tab it thus; it is still in certain developmental stages.

Employees are distinctly upset by variations in tube results—not knowing the "reasons why," feeling they should be getting more consistent results. The high number of rejects on items produced is hardly a source of job satisfaction *unless recognized* and *understood* as part of the stage of product development.

Employees may be confused by the variety and types of things on which they work—upset by poor scheduling and crisis upon crisis, coupled with hazy work steps or unanalyzed processes.

---

work for the most pay' idea workers in this country have." Later he said, "Do you really think there is any substitute for fear as a motivator? I doubt it. All of these fringe benefits and things won't do it; we've certainly learned that."

About Langley and operations in the tube room, Halbert commented, "I don't want to downgrade Ralph Langley or anything like that—I think he has been extremely successful in what he is doing—but it should be kept in mind that the tube room is not such a tough place to handle. We have some real trouble spots in other parts of the company. The tube room, after all, because of the kind of work done there, lends itself to the women seeing the connection between what they do and the final product. The work has challenge; it's interesting. There are opportunities there for satisfaction in the work itself that you couldn't begin to find in these other places."

BACKGROUND FACTS ABOUT THE COMPANY AND ITS PRODUCTS

The history of American Radiatronics epitomized the pattern of development followed by many young companies in the nuclear electronics boom after World War II. Starting in a small garage workshop on a back street in Baltimore, the company had been founded approximately 10 years earlier by two young scientists convinced of the coming industrial applications for nuclear processes and instrumentation. Following an early period of rapid growth and a later series of mergers, the company had prospered and finally stabilized at an annual sales level of roughly $14 million. It had remained at this level for several years. In most recent years, the company had been experiencing increasing competition from other young companies that had also grown to formidable strength of size and resources, and from older electronics firms

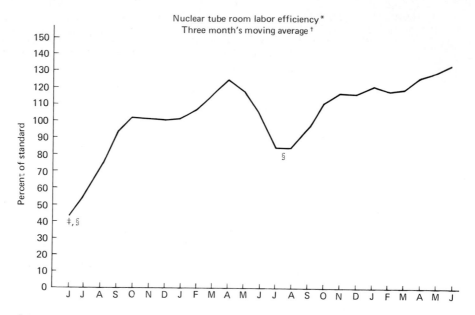

* Standard hours produced 4 hours on rated jobs (approximately 90% of time is spent on rated jobs).

† All percentages are calculated on new standards.

‡ Prior to this period labor efficiency figures are not available; however, the best estimates attainable indicate that efficiencies were averaging between 40% and 50% of standard.

§ Somewhat lower labor efficiencies are expected during the hot summer months than during the remainder of the year.

EXHIBIT 3   Nuclear tube assembly room 3 month's moving average.

that had more recently decided to enter the nuclear field. The later history of the company was marked also by a number of shifts in the top management structure; the present management team had been installed about 2 years earlier.

The Baltimore plant contained the main factory and home office headquarters for the company. Located in an industrial park area on Baltimore's outskirts, the plant employed approximately 600 people, most of whom commuted to work from Baltimore and its suburbs. The plant had been moved to its present site 2 years earlier from a downtown location. A new building had been erected at that time. The structure had been designed to incorporate into its features the latest conceptions in industrial architecture and general public appearance. Well over half the company's sales volume was derived from the Baltimore plant's operations.

NUCLEAR TUBE ASSEMBLY ROOM

The nuclear tube assembly room was one of several production units in the plant's process department. Under Langley's direction, the department produced a variety of equipment parts, some of which went into larger equipment units manufactured by the company, while others were sold directly to customers. Besides the nuclear tube assembly room, there were three other production units in the department, each housed in an adjacent separate room. The products and manufacturing processes for each of the production units was such that the work of one group was not linked to that of the others.

The nuclear tube assembly room produced all of the company's regular line of electronic tubes. These products varied considerably in size, shape, design, and materials. In appearance they ranged from delicate glass vials 3 or 4 inches in length to massive steel chambers with bolted covers. Some were all-glass construction; still others consisted of all-metal assemblies, with numerous variations in the thickness and kind of metals employed. In all, approximately 25 different types of tubes were manufactured on a regular production basis, although not all styles were in production at the same time. A normal production month would call for 8–10 separate tube styles to be produced in quantities of 300–500 per style. A number of miscellaneous small jobs consisting of repair, modifications, or experimental mockup of regular and/or experimental tubes were also assigned to the room each month. Out of the total number of tube types produced, four major tube styles accounted for approximately 80 to 84 percent of the dollar value of the room's output.

PRODUCTION PROCESS

The production process varied with each style of tube, depending upon the materials employed, the mechanical design of the tube, and the particular electronic properties called for by its function. The precise relationship between a given tube's design and its performance was not always clearly known. Certain tube designs were developed over the years by trial-and-error methods, while others were developed from known formulations and in accordance with standard design procedures. For this reason there was always an element of change in the air concerning details of the manufacturing process. For each tube, a set of written standard operating procedures had been developed by company engineers to describe each required assembly operation. From the viewpoint of production personnel, however, the history of modification and innovation that surrounded the evolution of many tube designs and production methods implied that the process of developing ultimate designs was not yet at an end.

Most operations performed in the assembly process were of a handwork nature, in which a variety of jigs, small implements, heating torches, and special-purpose machines were employed. Customarily, the work was performed on a batch of parts at a time until a sufficient inventory of parts had been accumulated to allow a number of tubes to be assembled in one operation.

The work of the tube room was roughly divided into (1) glass work, which consisted of making tube shells and internal glass parts; (2) metal work, wherein internal metal springs, wires, grids, leads, etc., were made and prepared for use; (3) tube assembly, at which time the entire tube was put together; (4) vacuum testing and exhausting, where tubes were lead-tested, exhausted, and filled with special gases; and (5) electronic testing, where tubes were tested as functioning units. After final testing, tubes were labeled, recorded according to individual serial numbers, and packaged for shipment or inventory storage. At all stages of assembly, tubes were given visual and electrical tests to minimize defective parts or subassemblies finding their way to final assembly. All testing and quality control measures were performed by the production workers themselves, including the final test before packaging.

PRODUCTION WORKERS

The major part of the production work in the tube room was performed by eight women, one of whom, Sally Ivers, served as group leader. Each worker performed several kinds of operations, although each had, at the same time, one or more operations that she regarded as her particular specialty. These special jobs, which were part of the regular production process, had emerged over time as the most suitable work for someone to do in view of skills and preferences, and the needs of the department. They were the most frequently recurring operations performed, accounting for roughly 50 percent or more of each worker's time, and were the chief identifying characteristic of the worker's job. In all, an almost infinite variety of combinations of worker and job were practiced in the room. It was not uncommon for several workers to perform the same operations at different times, and occasionally at the same time. Not even the special jobs were necessarily exclusive, since usually at least two workers had the special skills required to do a given job, and in the case of absence or emergency, one worker would take over for another.

The tube room production staff was augmented by Bill Yoost, a maintenance worker for the department, and Tom Montag, a part-time tube room worker who assisted with various production operations. Montag worked in the tube room when his normal assignment in room A, a single-person operation, did not keep him fully busy. Some additional personal and job information about these workers and Ralph Langley are given in Exhibit 4.

PAY RATES AND EMPLOYEE EVALUATION

As shown in Exhibit 4, tube room workers were paid on an hourly basis. Pay grades were established for each job classification by the industrial relations department according to an evaluation of the amount of skill and knowledge required of a worker in the job. Within each pay grade there was an established range through which the hourly wage rate could progress. An employee's progression within the range was determined by periodic merit reviews. At 4-month intervals, each employee was rated by the department general foreman on evaluation forms designed to reveal strengths and weaknesses. These evaluation forms were forwarded to the industrial relations department, where eligibility for pay increases was determined. The industrial relations department processed the wage increase, if warranted, and returned the completed evaluation form to the general foreman, who discussed the rating and salary increase with the employee.

The tube room workers were not unionized, although certain other manufacturing groups in the company had been organized some years before by a large international trade union.

EXHIBIT 4   JOB AND PERSONAL INFORMATION FOR TUBE ROOM PERSONNEL

Name	Job classification	Hourly wage	Age	Seniority with company, years	Seniority in tube room, years	Education	Marital status
Ralph Langley	Department general foreman	n.a.	41	3	2	MS in physics	M
Bill Yoost	Maintenance mechanic	$2.20	39	3	2	H.S. and trade school	M
Sally Ivers	Group leader, production worker AA	2.17	43	12	12	H.S.	S
Alice Homart	Production worker AA	2.05	53	3	3	H.S.	Widow
Nellie MacDonald	Production worker A	1.85	46	5	5	1 yr of college	M
Hilda Farley	Production worker A	1.81	46	11	1	G.S.	S
Martha Holtz	Production worker A	1.76	56	6	4	9 yr in Germany	M
Betty Gilen	Production worker A	1.74	42	4	4	H.S. and 3 yr of art school	Widow
Sylvia Johns	Production worker A	1.71	42	1	1	J.H.S.	Widow
Tom Montag	Production worker B	1.63	26	1/2	1/2	H.S.	M
Dolores Condotti	Production worker B	1.61	31	3	3	J.H.S.	M

WORK STANDARDS AND OUTPUT RECORDS

Approximately 95 percent of the tube assembly operations performed by the workers had been figured into standard hours by the company's industrial engineers. These standard hours were used in costing out direct labor costs for tube manufacturing operations by the accounting department, and they served as a standard of efficiency against which the room's actual performance was measured. Tube production for the total group was determined weekly when a physical inventory was taken of all finished and in-process tubes. Thus, labor invested in defective or destroyed tube parts or assemblies was "lost" to the group in figuring its net labor efficiencies. Monthly summaries of weekly efficiency figures were submitted to higher management for examination and review. Exhibit 3 presents these monthly efficiency figures for the previous 24 months.

The labor efficiency figures in Exhibit 3 were based on revised standards instituted 3 months before the writing of the case. The former standards, which had been set against the group's historical performance some years previously, has become inadequate in relation to the level of output then being achieved by the group. Consequently, Langley had initiated a review of all standards, "tube by tube, operation by operation," revising the allowed hours downward between 23 and 59 percent on individual tubes to an average 34 percent decrease on major tube types.

When Langley became supervisor of the tube room group, the work force had consisted of 14 production workers. In the ensuing 6 months, improvements in the group's performance created a surplus of labor which, because of a relatively stable volume of operations, required a series of layoffs to be made. It was during this period that the original force was reduced to its present size of eight. The layoffs were made in two steps, primarily on the basis of seniority with some secondary attention to the variety of work performed, and on the quantity and quality of work. Langley commented, "Those that stayed seemed to take it all right, even though none of them knew for sure whether she would be staying or not. They understood. One worker in the group I fired outright because of attitude. This worker just couldn't and wouldn't fit in with the others. We had had a long history of trouble with this one."

During the 24 months since Langley's arrival, there had been no major changes in the production facilities, manufacturing methods, or basic tube types in production. Much of the equipment in use was considered antiquated and inefficiently designed. The improvements in group performance were attributed primarily to improvements in labor efficiency, and informal production method innovations. Some minor alterations in tube design had been made by the company's scientific personnel, and a number of such changes had been initiated by members of the work group themselves. However, as these changes were made, their labor-saving effects had been largely incorporated into revised work standards.

OPERATION OF THE TUBE ROOM GROUP

The most immediate, apparent feature of the tube room was its physical layout and the location of various work positions within it. The room itself was a grey enclosure approximately 60 feet long and 50 feet wide, with a concrete floor. Closely assembled rows of tables, workbenches, production machines, and test stands filled its central area, while an ordered assortment of miscellaneous cabinets, shelves, benches, and additional production equipment banked its wall areas. A row of windows looked into production room C, immediately adjacent. A single door opened into the room.

Movement throughout the room was frequent and widespread; seldom were at least one or two people not in motion. The changing of settled work positions was likely to occur at any time during a day. Bantering, horseplay, and visiting frequently occurred; at times, periods of total inactivity, such as when a worker appeared to be daydreaming or silently contemplating her work, were observed. The pattern of activity did not appear to vary with the comings and goings of Sally Ivers, Langley, or other supervisory personnel.

The casewriter observed that most workers also participated in various nonwork activities. These activities were well-established and occurred regularly. For example, during coffee breaks, the total group invariably broke up into two smaller groups—one group gathering around Sally Ivers at her workbench desk, and the other group gathered at the rear of the room at Alice Homart's work station. The casewriter also observed that most workers ate lunch together at the same table in the company cafeteria. After finishing lunch, some people met back in the tube assembly room for a 10-or 15-minute card game before returning to work. The game was always played at Alice Homart's work station. In contrast, several other workers typically took a walk after lunch around the perimeter of the plant site and occasionally into the woods nearby.

The "pool" and the "poor box" were two activities in which most workers participated. The former was a weekly drawing for high and low stakes of a pool made up of 50-cent contributions from active members. The poor box referred to a weekly 10-cent collection (sometimes raised to 25 cents when the kitty was low) used to finance special events, such as going-away presents, wedding gifts, and sickness and death remembrances. For the most part, these activities had existed for 2 years or more, dating back to the day of the old downtown Baltimore location.

WORK ASSIGNMENTS AND SUPERVISORY PRACTICES

In performing their jobs, the workers customarily obtained instructions from Sally Ivers first thing in the morning. Ivers would move from worker to worker checking preparations, answering questions, and discussing the day's work schedule. At times, Ivers would give instructions during the work day as a worker finished the batch of work. Often the exchange would be phrased as an "Okay if I go to so and so now?" and "Sure." Or, if more detailed instructions were required, Ivers and the worker would go to the appropriate work station and discuss the details together. On many occasions, changes in work position or type of work took place without any apparent prior consultation with Ivers.

One of the most concrete features of work-scheduling practices in the tube room was a monthly production schedule delivered to the group by the company's production planning department just before the first of each month. Langley commented about the production sheet and how he and Ivers used it in scheduling work:

Ralph Langley: When the production sheet comes to us, Sally and I look it over. The production planning people can make a mistake like anyone else. Sometimes the company has so many tubes of one kind in stock that I just know they couldn't have wanted as many as the schedule calls for, so I will second-guess them. I keep an eye on the main company inventory, you know; it's in the room down the hall. All I have to do is walk in and look around and I can see the number of each kind of tube in stock. I often know how sales are running on particular tubes. People from the sales department come down and ask questions about things—about tubes, their cost, and any particular difficulty with them. In fact, I have often spoken directly with customers. Of course, I am not supposed to do that, but they will often refer a customer to me to talk about a particular tube, and in this way I have a feeling of how the sales of different kinds of tubes are going.

With this information about sales, inventory, stock situation, and the general work load, I am able to make some pretty fair guesses about the figures that production planning has set up—that is, whether we should follow their figures or adjust them slightly. Sometimes we miss, but usually our estimates of what the best schedule should be are good. In fact, it has happened more than once that the people from production planning have come to me and asked for my opinion on how many tubes I think they should put on the production planning sheet.

One production worker, Betty Gilen, spoke about the production schedule in the following manner.

Betty Gilen: You'll see satisfaction written over everyone's face the last working day of the production month when we've met schedule. You'll see them the last days before the end of the month walking to the production record over there, checking that, then checking the production schedule again on Sally's desk. It's amazing the change that begins to come over people when they move into the last part of the month and see we're going to have to step it up in order to make our quota. Everyone works a little harder, everyone tries to get her part of the work out of the way a little faster and on to the next worker. This is what makes this department work together so well. Everyone, and I would say there's not a single exception to this, is willing to cooperate, and we all feel the same way about meeting schedule. Now this is provided that no one is pushing us. We meet our own schedules and no one breathes down our backs. We do it ourselves.

WORK ATTITUDES

The casewriter also held conversations with other workers about their work and their attitude toward it.

Martha Holtz: I like my job. It's a good job as far as jobs go. Right now I'm doing mostly coating. I have done ceramic lining for Alice Homart over there, and fire polishing. And, toward the end of the month, I even do testing. I can do a lot of jobs.

I make the anodes for these tubes. We used to make them out of stainless steel, but now we always make them out of platinum. You know, that was funny. About 6 months ago, while we were still making them out of stainless steel, I made a mistake and made a whole batch out of platinum. When I finished, I told Sally Ivers about it. She said, "That's all right, Martha, let's test them out this way and see how they are." They tested out perfectly, so she told Ralph Langley about it, and the next time I made anodes for that tube, Sally told me to use platinum again because they had tested so well. Always before, we had trouble testing a whole batch of them without having some bad ones and, you know, since we've been making them out of platinum, we have had hardly any bad ones at all. And to think, just because I'd made a mistake.

Alice Homart (referring to some tube stem assemblies she was reworking from a batch made a few days earlier): We've been having a lot of trouble with leaking stems lately, and we're trying to figure out where the trouble is by studying these stems from rejected tubes. I'm spending quite a bit of time right now trying to find the trouble, so that we can get the production rate back up again.

Casewriter: Does anyone ever say anything to you when you get behind on production?

Alice Homart: You bet they do. We hear about it all right, and believe me, we hear about these leaky tubes, too. Nellie MacDonald shoots them right back at us when they don't make her leak test. That's what we're here for. No one stands over our shoulder counting what we do, but we know how many finished tubes we make and how many the production schedule calls for. Besides it's always nicer when things are going along without any trouble. You know we're not supposed to do this (indicating the defective stem she was examining), this is not our job. We're just production workers. We're not supposed to know the technical parts of this kind of work. The only thing is, there's no one else at the plant who knows much more about this kind of work than we do. There's just us here in the room, so I guess it's up to Sylvia Johns and myself to figure out what goes wrong when we have trouble. Ralph Langley can help us sometimes, but he can't do everything. Besides, we're closer to the work.

Sylvia Johns: I'm a glassblower. I learned the business from my husband in Philadelphia, where we operated a neon sign glass company for 25 years before he died. I had to go back to work after he died, and that's why I'm here. I like my work here. It's a good job, but it wasn't easy for me to find the kind of work I like to do after my husband died. Actually, glassblowing is all I do here, and it's what I prefer doing, too. I never work much on tube asembly, although I guess I would if I had to. Glass work is really my line. After 25 years, I know it. My husband taught me well before he died.

Casewriter (standing beside Betty Gilen at her customary workbench): Could you tell me the name of this place here where you seem to be working most often?

Betty Gilen: You could call this the heavy metal tube station. You see, I make all the heavy tubes here, and I guess I'm a sort of a specialist at it. But we're not making very many at the rate we're going now. Somebody goofed. These covers are made here in the machine shop, and the containers are made by a vendor, and you can see that the cover doesn't position right on the container, and that won't pass inspection.

Casewriter: Does this delay affect you personally?

Betty Gilen: Personally is right. It's driving me crazy. This is a big order, and we're way behind on it. We won't get them done—can't work on them at all. This means I haven't got anything to do, and I've got to hunt jobs. The day is 16 hours long for me these days. I like to keep busy.

Casewriter: Where else do you sometimes work?

Betty Gilen: Oh, you'll find me over at the glass machine; you'll find me at the wash basin; and you've probably seen me quite a bit over at the pump stand there. You see, I do all the glass welding, connecting tubes to the vacuum outlets. It's not that it takes any kind of particular genius to do it but I'm kind of familiar with that type of work. As I say, I do all kinds of things. If you want to see where I'm working, you'd better look fast because I won't be there long.

EMPLOYEE ATTITUDES TOWARD EACH OTHER

Here is how several workers talked and behaved with respect to their relations with one another:

Alice Homart (responding to a question about why there were two separate coffee groups): Why, I never thought about that until you mentioned it now. We've always had the two groups, but it doesn't mean anything. We're all friendly with one another. Why, we were the same way before when we were in Baltimore, except for Sylvia, who's only worked here 1 year. I can't imagine it being different.

Casewriter: How do you decide when to start and stop?

Alice Homart: Ralph Langley says it's up to us how long we take just so we get our work out. So we don't go by the company rule. Sometimes we take 20 minutes or so, and sometimes quite a bit less. At the end of the month, if we're rushed, we'll cut it pretty short, but no one ever says anything to us. We just gauge it by how busy we are.

Casewriter (addressing Betty Gilen one day at her workbench): Are there any topics of conversation or things to talk about that you tend to avoid with one another as you visit, say, during coffee breaks, at lunch, or even during work?

Betty Gilen: No, I don't think so. We'll talk about our work schedule, things that happened at home, weekends, just about anything. Politics can get pretty hot, and we have had a few scrapes in the past, so we leave that one alone entirely now. I guess there is another thing too, in a general sort of way. If anyone is particularly bothered about anything, we will avoid that subject, whatever it is that they're bothered about. We don't want to hurt anyone or make them feel bad by rubbing salt in wounds. This is especially so if it's something connected with our work here. If there is something going on that someone is particularly upset about, we'll avoid talking about it as long as it's happening. Later we will talk about it and laugh over it, but not at the time. We can't afford to hurt anyone. We get along by cooperating and being friendly with one another.

A WORK INCIDENT

One day, as the casewriter was working at an observation desk, a loud pop and the sound of breaking glass was heard. Looking up, the casewriter saw Betty Gilen standing at the finished-tube inventory cabinet, with the door open and a tray of finished tubes in her hand. At her feet were the remains of a broken tube (retail value, about $45). Ivers was standing about 8 feet away, working at a bench with her back to Betty. Nellie MacDonald was at her pump stand about the same distance away. Ivers did not look up, but continued steadily with her work. The noise was very audible and its point of origin was also quite clear.

Nellie, from her pump stand, looked over to Betty, shook her head slowly from side to side and said, "Tsk, tsk, tsk," then made a comment having something to do with what had caused the tube to fall out of the cabinet. Betty's elbow and tray were resting close to the shelf from which the broken tube had obviously fallen. Betty corrected her position, and at the same time looked forlornly at the smashed tube. Nellie walked over to the other side of the room, obtained a broom and dustpan, and swept up the mess. Betty proceeded to the electronic test stand with the tray of tubes. It would have been very easy for Betty to put the tray down and clean up the broken glass herself. Throughout the incident, neither Betty nor Nellie glanced in Sally's direction, nor did Sally change the pace of her work or look up.

BEHAVIOR OF RALPH LANGLEY

Langley had developed relationships with the group in a way that allowed him to retain a high degree of involvement in the affairs of the room without extensive personal presence. He would tour the room each morning near the beginning of the work day, speaking briefly with nearly everyone (although usually in a different order from day to day) and taking part in various technical discussions. From then on, he would reappear at fairly regular intervals, two or three times during the day or when some kind of unusual work event occurred.

During his periods of absence from the room, Langley visited the other rooms of his department, attended conferences and other scheduled meetings, paid informal visits to members of other departments in the company, or, as was more customary for extended periods of time, returned to his desk in one corner of room B, next door to the tube room. It was to this desk that members of the tube room group would come when they had a question or problem. Any worker was equally likely to visit Langley at his desk, and unless the situation prompting the visit was unusually complicated or pressing, Langley would respond with a few words of explanation, approval, or a promise to "do something about it." During a 2-day period in which Langley once happened to spend nearly all his time at his desk, these visits averaged about six or seven per day. His characteristic demeanor during interactions with subordinates was grave and intently serious, although his face would often break into fleeting smiles. Seldom effusive, he nevertheless usually managed to convey by his bearing and conversation an impression of friendliness and personal interest and of confidence in addressing problems.

COMMENTS OF THE WORKERS ABOUT LANGLEY

Sally Ivers: If anything does go wrong around here, we first of all try to find out what the trouble is ourselves and, if that doesn't work, we go to get Ralph. Ralph always helps us out. Ralph always knows the answers.

Betty Gilen: Ralph is fair, and he knows what he is doing.

Martha Holtz (in connection with a rumor that Ralph Langley was being considered for promotion to a bigger job): Ralph, he's the best. I don't know what we would do without him. He is always so fair, treats us all alike. We're very proud of Ralph. We would miss him terribly if he left.

Nellie MacDonald: If Ralph were promoted, we all would be very pleased for him. He deserves it, and it's time he went on to bigger things. But as for me, it would mean I'd lost my purpose for working. That guy made our work something it had never been before. I would never be able to feel the same way about George. (George Cortoza, foreman in production room C, was rumored to be Ralph's replacement.) George is all right. He's pleasant and he's a nice guy, but I have a respect for Ralph I'd never be able to develop for George. And it's not only respect I feel for Ralph. Ralph is my friend. I look forward to work every morning. We're a zany bunch—real screwballs. You couldn't find a bunch of people anywhere with more different personalities than we have. You've seen the way we horse around, the stunts we pull, and we don't feel the least bit embarrassed about it. We can get away with anything, but when it comes to our work, there's no one better than we are either. Now this is just a small department here, and I'm not over anyone, but I feel important. I feel there's a purpose in my life. I'm responsible for the pump stand and it's a critical part of the operation in there. It's a part of me and I'm part of it. I worry about how it's going. I'm checking it over all the time, and I'm turning out a lot of work on it.

But you see, it's not only the pump stand. It's how Ralph and people like him can make you feel about it. I know I'm not very bright and it doesn't take much for anyone to make me feel really stupid, but Ralph has never done that. He's always made me feel that I've got ideas that are useful. Now, I know my knowledge about the pump stand is very limited, and I lean a great deal on Ralph to help me out of scrapes, but you know, everytime I talk over a problem with him I feel as though I'm learning something. And I am learning!

Right now we've run into a problem with the pump stand. There's something wrong in the exhaust manifold system. We're not getting the tubes clean enough. Sally and I have gone over and over the system and we don't know what it is. We will wait for Ralph until he has time, and we know eventually he will help us out. Sure, we've got an engineer assigned to the department who is supposed to take care of these problems for us. We're not supposed to; we're just production workers, not supposed to know anything. And, brother, is the engineer convinced of that! I'd walk out of the plant before I'd turn to him for help on my pump. He doesn't really know much about them, and with what little he does know, he makes you feel so darn stupid in such a short time, you could scream. We don't need him in here and don't want him. Ralph, on the other hand, has a way of using his knowledge to help a person build up her own knowledge. He gives it to you—he doesn't use it on you. That's how I feel about Ralph as a friend and as the best boss I've ever had.

RALPH LANGLEY

The casewriter talked to Ralph Langley on a number of occasions about Langley's perceptions of his job and his concepts of himself as an administrator. Following are excerpts from some of these conversations.

Excerpt 1: Langley on His Relations with Tube Room Production Workers

Ralph Langley (speaking about what had been responsible for the marked improvement in group performance over the past 2 years): I would say it was mostly a matter of treating the workers the way they wanted to be treated and needed to be treated to feel as though they were part of American Radiatronics.

When I took over the department, one of the first things I told the workers was to forget about standards, to figuratively throw them out, pretend they didn't even exist—to just do the best job they knew how. I told them I felt they were working for American Radiatronics and not for me, that my job was to help them and not tell them what to do, and that they were strictly on their own as far as getting out production, scheduling their work, pacing themselves, watching their own waste, and so on. If they got into trouble they could ask me for help, and I would give it to them. Above all, I told them, we were going to be interested in making a better tube and learning how to do our job better at all times. They didn't believe me at first. Some of them gave me a really rough time, but gradually they learned I meant what I said and things began to improve.

I have no supervisor in the room. Sally is the group leader for the others, but each person in the room is responsible for her own operation. I'm always careful and insistent that they're given credit for everything they do. If she gets into trouble or has a question, she's free to come to me directly. I then work out the problem with her personally. When I'm presented with a problem, such as an order for extra work from another department, I'm able to just turn it over to one of the workers and it gets done.

I go in to them every now and then, just now and then, to keep an eye on things and to stay in touch. I check the production record to see how things are going, and I always speak to the workers. I try to be careful, whenever I come into the room to see that I always talk to a different person first each time. This way each one feels she is getting her fair share of attention. I talk with them about whatever is of interest to them. If it's about their families, fine; if it's about work, fine. Sometimes when I see that things are not going so well, and they don't always go just right, I'm careful to avoid any distressing or threatening discussion. The workers are not all the same. Some of them are pretty tough customers. Nellie MacDonald, in particular, has given me quite a lot of trouble in the past. So I'm extra careful in working with her.

I keep no secrets from them. They know as much about this operation and about what is going on in the top offices as I do. I'm honest with them and I ask that they be honest with me. This has paid off, too, because all of my workers aren't afraid to admit mistakes and are always anxious to learn to do something better. Of course, I may be exaggerating this a little bit. I have noticed here lately that there is almost a neurotic tinge in the way several members of the group have become so concerned about production and quality. It causes a little stir now and then.

Excerpt 2: Langley on Motivation

Ralph Langley: A person spends the majority of the waking hours on the job. It seems to me that the job should be important, that the job should represent the source of greatest satisfactions that a person experiences. To feel that satisfactions should be obtained only off the job is not realistic. People get drunk, or go to shows, but that doesn't always lead to the kinds of satisfaction that they really need. People need to feel important, to feel as though life is worthwhile, and to feel as though they're accomplishing something. These needs can be satisfied on the job, but it doesn't just happen by accident. You have to work at it.

One of my firmest beliefs is that the trouble with most managers is the way they think about their people. They see the company as the center of everything—and they're really thinking about themselves when they think about the company. They then see workers as something clustering around this central company or management; that is, they're only there to serve management's interests, to work for management. But these people, these workers, are the same as you and I, and they are the same as management.

The boss that uses workers to build his or her own ego, to satisfy a sense of power and prestige, is not doing right by the workers. They'll act just the way the boss treats them. As long as the worker is seen as something to be used by the company, the worker will resent it and give no more than necessary. But if the worker can be motivated, I'm convinced that any worker has a potential of productivity that's greatly in excess of anything that's usually given.

Excerpt 3: Langley on Controlling Subordinates' Task Choice

Ralph Langley: There is the kind of work you get out of people when they are doing what is prescribed for them to do, and then there is the bonus you get when they are doing what they want to do. I want Bill and Tom to figure out for themselves what they want to do, what they're happiest at, and let them do it as much as I can. That is my way of thinking.

Take Tom for instance. Before Tom went to room A, which was about a year to a year and a half ago, 65–70 units a month of work in there was considered to be a good production record. The person in there before Tom did manage to get it up to about 100 units a month. When Tom took over he managed to get up to 110 units per month quite quickly without trying too hard. So I just let him alone, raised the standards up to that, and he kept pushing it ahead. Now we are doing more work than ever in there—he has hit as much as 160–180 units a month and yet frequently is able to come in here and put in the equivalent of a full day's work in the tube room. That's what I mean by the bonus you get for letting people do the kind of work they want to do.

Tom is doing more than what was a full day's work in room A previously, and at the same time he is doing a lot in here besides. He wanted to do this so he just figured out how he could get things done in there quicker in order to spend more time in here. I want him to find out what he likes to do best. Right now I am kind of pushing him to take on the pump stand work, which he is doing besides picking up a lot of various maintenance work. No one knows at this time what he will end up liking best, but he is free to go in either direction without my telling him which one to take on. If it develops that he prefers maintenance equipment work, I'll ease off on the pump stand encouragement, and let Nellie MacDonald take on more of that. It's up to Tom.

One thing, and this is important. I'm not trying to handle Tom. Tom isn't trying to work harder, and I don't think I could make him work harder. The reason he is doing as well as he is is because he hasn't been thinking in terms of getting more work done; he has been thinking about learning and about getting ahead. I know he would think I was taking advantage of him if all he heard from me was getting more work out. For instance, if instead of feeling the way I do, I felt that Tom wasn't doing enough work in room A, I wouldn't push him. I would leave him alone to find his way. As it is now, he moves in, he learns more, he takes on more and more responsibility. This is the way you grow. I changed his grade when I opened the door for him to go into the tube room. I advanced him two grades. When I see he can take on still more work, I'll advance him again.

Excerpt 4: Langley on Use of Work Standards and Budgets

Ralph Langley: I believe in work standards as a yardstick of measurement that has no inherent validity of its own but does have a practical value. To me, standards serve as guideposts on the side of the road to tell us where we are today in relation to where we were yesterday and where we think we can go tomorrow. They provide management with a means of determining in advance what they can sell their product for while being competitive and profitable.

It isn't the standard that should determine how people work or pace themselves; instead the energy, drive, and interest they put in their work should be determined by how they *feel* about their work. I've indoctrinated my people to use standards just as a guide.

I tell my people, "You should be taking your incentive from yourselves." But I also emphasize that it is of vital interest to the company and therefore to themselves that they make the operation as profitable as possible because they, the workers, are just as meaningfully the company as management or the stockholders are, and in many ways even more so. I drive into them that one of the important satisfactions available to them is being engaged in a successful profitable activity. "After all," I tell them, "work is a way of life," and we've got to be getting something out of it as people. One of these things that can be important is the knowledge that we are connected with a successful operation that we helped make that way.

I have a budget, but I don't use my budget to control my people. Rather, I use it as something that they themselves can get satisfaction out of. For instance, we have cut our operating expenses way down since I took over, but I didn't do it, my people did it.

Our department's maintenance worker, Bill Yoost, administers the expense budget for supplies himself. He does all his own ordering and he does it in accordance with the amount of money that is available in his budget. These are supplies that are not used only by himself but by the workers in the department as well. Since they all know that it's up to them to control their expenses, they do it. If someone from another department comes and tries to borrow something that they know has been charged against their budget, they simply won't allow it. They'll say, "No, you'll run our expense budget over. You'll have to get it somewhere else."

I go over the budget with Bill once a month, whenever it comes out. We talk about it. From then on, it's up to him. I keep an eye on it every now and then just to see that he isn't running too far out on a limb, and if I see something wrong, I'll ask him about it. But if he tells me that he's making out all right, I let him go.

Excerpt 5: Langley on Required Features of His Department's Organization

Ralph Langley: There are three things I'm very firm on in the department. One of them is the production schedule. That's sacred! That is a must. Under all circumstances we must produce the schedule.

Casewriter: Is this because your superiors have imposed the schedule on you that same way too?

Ralph Langley: No, it's because I want it that way. This is what we're in business for. We want to get goods out the door. The way we go about doing that will, of course, make a difference in how successfully we accomplish the things not directly connected with production that are also real and important. But we want to keep the record straight. There is no wavering or compromise of the schedule. That will not be tolerated and everyone knows it.

Second are the employee evaluation sheets. These sheets are absolutely required by management and I can't get around them. I don't like them; I think they can do more harm than good at times, but they are there and I have to go along with them.

The third thing is that I expect my people to get along with one another. I say to them, "You must adjust to and with the group—become a part of it. At the least, you must have a willingness to try to do this." I think they all know this, I've told them so directly, and I've talked about and around it repeatedly on every occasion I could. This doesn't mean I forbid people to have personal differences. That would be stupid. But I do require that they overcome whatever personal differences they might have to the extent of being able to function cooperatively with one another. Two years ago, I had to get rid of a worker who just had to fight with everyone. I tried my best to help this worker, but it did no good. So I fired the worker, and everyone knew why, too.

Excerpt 6: Langley on Relations between Groups at American Radiatronics

Ralph Langley: Ryerson from the research department wants to use Sally on some special work in the electronics lab. He likes to have her do it because it's very delicate work and no one can do it as well as she can. I told him I'd speak to Sally and that he should check back later to talk to her himself. You know, we do this sort of thing back and forth all the time. We help them out and they help us out and there's a good relationship all around, but good relations have to be built. They don't just happen.

I started out in just small ways doing things for them and, as we began to build mutual trust and confidence, they started doing little things for us. Gradually, these exchanges got bigger. I once spent close to 4 weeks almost full time helping them out on some equipment setup they were working on. There were four of us, three of them and myself. We formed a team, made our own designs, then put it together. It worked out very well.

Their glassblower comes up here and does all our glass-system repair work for us. If we ever need any stopcocks or other parts in a hurry, we just ask for them and get them without any questions. Now, if any other department should try to do this, they would be out of them. There has never been a piece of paper passed between us. They've never asked us to sign for anything or keep records. We don't distinguish between ourselves as far as things we can do together or for one another are concerned. It's a good feeling.

This is an important problem at American Radiatronics—how to build relationships between different groups. Right now relations are generally pretty poor—foremen fighting with one another, saying this person is holding us up because he isn't getting the right parts to me or that person is holding us up for any one of a dozen reasons. They say they're overloaded. They just can't get the work out with the work force and equipment they've got. The schedule is too tight, parts are too slow. I just don't think this is true. I think there are plenty of workers here and the productive capacity of each department is at least twice what it is now. I think these problems are with the foremen themselves and in their relations with one another. They don't trust each another. They're fighting instead of cooperating; protecting themselves rather than working freely and confidently. It's around this problem, in little ways, that I'd like to do more. I'd like to begin to turn the tide if I could some way.

ANOTHER VIEW OF THE NUCLEAR TUBE ROOM

The casewriter interviewed Harold Singer, an engineer from the company's process engineering department who was familiar with the nuclear tube room. Singer and his colleagues served as central staff specialists for various operating departments and also worked on product development, production process planning, and technical aspects of long-range business planning. Excerpts from the interview are given below:

Harold Singer: I really can't understand how this operation makes money. The products are primitive in design, no changes have been made in years, and there's no engineering control of any kind. Everything is run on a casual hit-or-miss basis. It shouldn't make money, but somehow it does. . . .

Dollarwise, they're doing a pretty good job in here, as far as it goes, but they've got one overriding weakness in the way they are presently set up. Do you realize the workers do all their own testing in here? The same workers that make the tubes test them. It just isn't logical. It's against human nature. You can't trust the same people who make something to also test it. It's not healthy. They'll always try to protect themselves. This group of test equipment over here should be operated by a distinctly separate group of people completely removed from production and under different supervision.

We've got plans in the works for taking on this place and really making it over. And when we do, we'll see to it that the testing operations are carried on in a separate department. We'll really whip this operation into shape. . . .

There's a tremendous potential in this kind of activity, but it's never been exploited. We've got designs on the board right now that would revolutionize the way of doing things around here if we could get them going. I'd like to make this a model showplace for the company. Right now it's the worst in the company. Look at all this dirt, and the disorganization. . . .

This place has never been under engineering control. That's the trouble with it. The products and processes here now are what they've traditionally been from almost the start. Most product design changes have been developed and put into practice by the production people themselves. That's not good. Too much can creep into an organization that way that isn't good for it. They design their own products, they alter and maintain their own production equipment and processes and they are free to go off in all different directions at once. The first thing we would do if we could get hold of this room would be to put every operation under close engineering surveillance. The whole setup needs to be revamped and overhauled from one end to the other. We'll do it too. You won't recognize it 2 years from now.

Some of the new products we have in mind will call for a level of sophistication in production methods, equipment design, and cleanliness that'll make this look sick. You've seen pictures of how production departments look in other companies—

cleanliness precautions that make them look like operating rooms, temperature and humidity controls, white-painted walls and equipment. That's what we'll have here. Personnel is right now looking into available sources of production workers for us, and when we start getting them in here, training them properly, and installing modern production methods with the true mass production setup, then you'll see what this department can do. . . .

I'd like to think time zero for this department's operations in this company's history will start 3 months from now. We've got all the preliminary design work and process system concepts worked out already, and in about 3 months we'll begin to pick up some real speed. Two years from now you won't know the place. In contrast, everything that will have gone on before will be nothing. Take a good look around at what you see in here right now, you'll never see it again. Before long it will be like looking back at the covered wagon era.

ACTON-BURNETT, INC.

John J. Gabarro

At the conclusion of Acton-Burnett's executive committee meeting on June 12, Hale Acton III, chief executive officer and chairman of the board, asked Casey Ryan, vice president of marketing, and John Keene, vice president of corporate planning, to seriously reexamine the company's procedures for forecasting sales. Acton hoped that improved product demand projections would lead to better inventory control, financial planning, and factory scheduling. Acton-Burnett had suffered significant losses in the first quarter of 1975 and expected even greater losses in the second quarter (the first losses the company had experienced since 1936). Acton felt that poor forecasting was one of several underlying factors contributing to the firm's current, poor performance.

Ryan and Keene met subsequently with Robert Herd, president and chief operating officer, to briefly discuss his ideas on the subject. The two men then decided to form a task force to investigate the forecasting problem. Ryan and Keene agreed to put David Baker, a recent graduate of the Stanford Graduate School of Business, in charge of the task force. Baker had been with Acton-Burnett for 2 years and was currently a special assistant to John Keene. Before his present assignment, Baker had worked as a financial analyst in Keene's financial planning group, and was now assigned to Keene's market planning group. The assignment to market planning was an intentional move on Keene's part to broaden Baker's exposure to different aspects of Acton-Burnett's business. Baker was regarded by both Keene and Ryan as an especially promising and capable individual.

BACKGROUND ON ACTON-BURNETT, INC.

Acton-Burnett was the third-largest U.S. producer of precious metal alloys and other specialized alloys for commercial and industrial use; its 1974 sales exceeded $400 million. The company was headquartered in Chicago and had four major sales offices and five plants dispersed througout the United States. Its products included alloys of silver, gold, platinum, and other precious or rare metals. The company sold its alloys in the form of ingots, bars, coil, strip, and wire. Most of its raw material was purchased from abroad. Acton-Burnett sold its products to a wide range of customers, including dealers in precious metals, jewelry manufacturers, scientific firms, and industrial companies that used precious metals or special alloys in the manufacture of instruments and other devices.

The company's present difficulties were precipitated by two sets of related events. The first was the 1974–1975 recession, which had affected the company's sales to both industrial customers and jewelry manufacturers. The second factor was the rapid rise in the price of gold during the last 6 months of 1974. During 1974, the U.S. Congress had enacted legislation making it legal for private individuals and institutions to own and sell gold after January 1, 1975. Many industry sources felt that international gold speculators had intentionally driven up the price of gold during late 1974 in anticipation of a rush on gold by private U.S. investors. However, when the public market for gold opened in January, the expected demand did not materialize and the price of gold fell rapidly. The combination of the declining price of gold in early 1975 and Acton-Burnett's overly optimistic sales forecasts for the first two quarters of 1975 had resulted in excessive inventories of overvalued gold and sizable losses.

Acton-Burnett's current problems stood in dramatic contrast with the company's recent record of outstanding growth and profitability. The company had been founded by Acton's great-grandfather in 1881, and had always enjoyed a reputation for being a quality supplier of precious metals. However, during Hale Acton III's 10-year stewardship as chief executive officer, the firm had quadrupled in size and had become the most profitable firm in the industry. Acton attributed this recent success to the company's aggressive marketing efforts and to an infusion of "professionally" trained managers into the company's organization. Under Acton and Herd's direction, the company was the first firm in the precious metals industry to develop a marketing organization in which market managers and product managers were responsible for focusing on specific market segments and applications. (Herd had been vice president of marketing before his promotion to president in 1973.)

Despite his family's obvious influence in the company, Acton had "come up through the ranks" and had a solid grounding in the business. Before becoming president of the company in 1965, Acton had attended the advanced management program of the Harvard Business School. This experience had convinced him that several ideas he had developed over the years about marketing alloys were feasible, and he returned to Acton-Burnett determined to create a marketing organization and to hire business-school–trained managers. In the 10 years that followed, Hale Acton had hired a number of MBA's from Harvard, Stanford, Wharton, Columbia, and Dartmouth. It was generally acknowledged that many of these MBA's were received with some resistance from the oldtimers, although several of them had gained considerable influence and success within the company, including Ryan (Harvard MBA) and Keene (Dartmouth MBA), both of whom were now vice presidents.

FORMATION OF THE TASK FORCE

After some discussion, Keene and Ryan concluded that the major area for the task force to study should be the marketing division, because it was the four market managers who made the final forecasts for product demand. The market managers based their forecasts on information they received from their product managers, the vice president of sales, the vice president of manufacturing, and the macroeconomic forecasts made by the vice president of economic analysis and forecasting. (See Exhibit 1 for an organization chart of Acton-Burnett.)

Having decided on the task force's mandate, Ryan and Keene met with Baker and described the problem as they saw it. Ryan said that he would appoint three product managers to the task force to represent the marketing division and suggested that it would not be necessary to involve the market managers (to whom the product managers reported) because they were currently very busy and had been resistant to similar changes in procedures in the past. Keene, in turn, said that he would ask Vincent Ernst, vice president of sales, to appoint a representative from sales to the task force. He also suggested that two others, in addition to Baker, be assigned from corporate planning. The first was Cynthia Schrafft, a young Harvard MBA, who Keene felt would add analytic strength to the group; the second was Jason Cassis, a man in his mid-fifties, whom Keene thought would add "balance" because he was an oldtimer and would be able to relate well to the product managers. Keene added that he would ask Dr. Walter Hunneuus, vice president of economic analysis, to appoint a representative from his group.

The three men then agreed that the task force would report back to Keene, Ryan, and the market managers on August 4. After the presentation on August 4, Keene would arrange for a subsequent presentation to the president and chairman of the board later in the month.

INITIAL MEETING OF THE TASK FORCE

A week after his discussion with Keene and Ryan, Baker had his first meeting with the newly appointed task force. Its members included (in addition to himself, Schrafft, and Cassis) the three product managers from the marketing division; Steve Eldredge, an economic analyst from Hunneuus's group; and Ezra Bowe, a special assistant to the vice president of sales. (See Exhibit 2 for the names and positions of the task force members.)

The three product managers, men in their middle to late forties, were obviously uneasy at the beginning of the meeting. Baker had had few prior contacts with them and did not know them well. In contrast, he knew Cynthia Schrafft and Jason Cassis fairly well because they also worked for Keene in corporate planning. Baker had previously worked with Schrafft and had come to admire her analytic ability, quickness, and perceptiveness. Although he had never worked directly with Cassis, he knew that Cassis was widely respected within the company for his competence, knowledge, and thoughtfulness.

Steve Eldredge, the representative from the economic analysis and forecasting group, was a Wharton MBA and a contemporary of Baker and Schrafft. Baker had once worked with Eldredge on a project before Eldredge had been transferred from

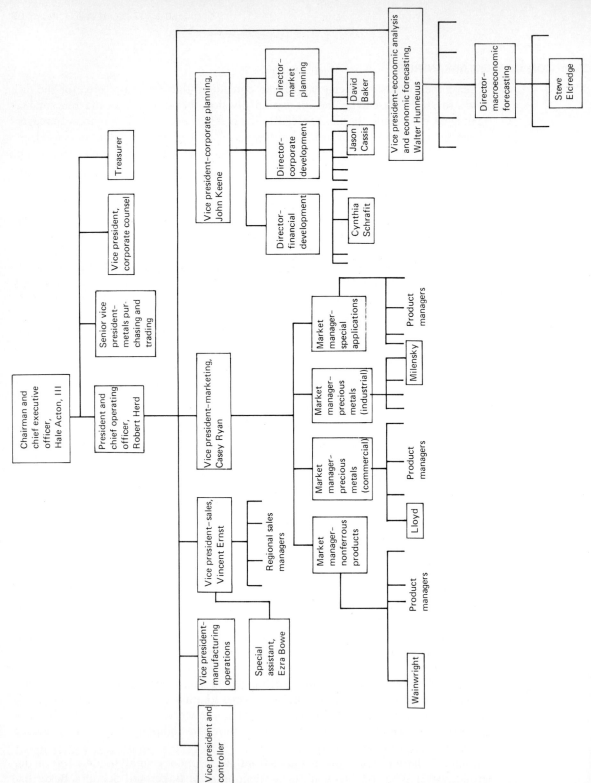

EXHIBIT 1   Acton-Burnett, Inc.—simplified organization chart.

EXHIBIT 2   MEMBERS OF THE FORECASTING TASK FORCE

Member	Age	Education	Position	Represents
David Baker (chairman)	28	MBA, Stanford	Market planning and analyst and assistant to the vice president of corporate planning	Corporate planning
Cynthia Schrafft	27	MBA, Harvard	Financial planning analyst	Corporate planning
Ezra Bowe	58	BMS, Massachusetts Maritime Academy	Special assistant to the vice president of sales	Sales division
Jason Cassis	54	BS, Missouri School of Mines	Corporate development specialist	Corporate planning
Stephen Eldredge	29	MBA, Wharton	Economic analyst	Economic analysis and forecasting group
Peter Wainwright	47	BS, Wayne State	Product manager, nonferrous products market group	Marketing division
Charles Lloyd	43	BS, Illinois Institute of Technology	Product manager, precious metals, commercial applications market group	Marketing division
Charles Milensky	48	Bronx High School of Science	Product manager, precious metals, industrial applications market group	Marketing division

corporate planning to Hunneuus's group. Baker had found this experience to be less than satisfying, with he and Eldredge disagreeing over several issues during their work together.

Ezra Bowe, the representative from the sales division, was in his late fifties and had spent almost all of his career in sales. His last 5 years had been as a trouble-shooter and special assistant to the vice president of sales. Bowe, like Cassis, was well-liked and widely respected within the company.

The meeting had a slow and awkward beginning, with Bowe, Schrafft, and the three product managers saying almost nothing. In contrast, Steve Eldredge was quite vocal and emphatic about the need to develop a model for the internal forecasting process. Eldredge argued that it was essential for the task force to identify the basic underlying assumptions upon which the present product demand forecasts were based, and then to make a model of the entire process. Schrafft finally interrupted Eldredge to say that although she agreed a forecasting model might be useful in the future, she thought that the creation of such a model should not be the task force's purpose. Rather, it should be one of the recommendations that the task force might make based on what they found. She also added that it was much more difficult to develop a single-firm forecasting model than it was to develop the macroeconomic models that the Hunneuus group worked with.

After a long pause, Jason Cassis suggested that the task force divide its work so that he and the three product managers could concentrate on the marketing division and Eldredge could concentrate on gathering whatever "hard data" he felt were necessary for a model. Baker thought that this was a good idea. He then asked Schrafft and Bowe if they would be willing to concentrate on the sales division's inputs into the forecast. Schrafft and Bowe exchanged ideas briefly and then agreed to take responsibility for this part of the project. Shortly thereafter the meeting adjourned, the consensus being that individual subgroups would stay in contact with Baker.

PREPARATION OF THE TASK FORCE REPORT

In the 5 following weeks, Baker spent much of his time working with Cassis and the three product managers on the marketing division's part of the study, and with Schrafft and Bowe working on the sales division's part. Cassis and the product managers worked well together and Baker found the meetings with them to be enjoyable and, at times, exciting. He also found that he, Schrafft, and Bowe enjoyed working together and that the three of them were making considerable progress in identifying how the regional sales managers prepared the sales estimates for the vice president of sales; (these estimates, in turn, constituted the sales division's inputs to the market managers). Eldredge, on the other hand, spent most of his time traveling to the various sales offices gathering data on historic sales trends as well as interviewing all product managers in company headquarters. Baker's exchanges with Eldredge were brief, infrequent, and occasionally strained. Baker suspected that Eldredge resented Baker's more rapid progress within the company. He had also heard through the grapevine that Hunneuus, Eldredge's boss, was disturbed that he had not been asked by Acton to look at the forecasting problem, or by Keene and Ryan to head the task force. Several of Eldredge's comments reinforced Baker's suspicions, since Eldredge made it clear that the internal product demand forecasting should be done by the Hunneuus group instead of by the market managers.

By July 23, Baker felt that the group had made enough progress to report back to Keene, Ryan, and the market managers. The next day, he called the task force together to exchange their findings and to discuss a strategy for presenting their recommendations to Ryan and Keene on August 4. All task force members attended except for Eldredge, who was in New York City gathering sales data and could not make the meeting. Cassis and the three product managers were quite enthusiastic about several recommendations that they were sure would improve the quality of the product demand forecasts. Bowe and Schrafft also reported that they had found "some systematic biases" in the sales division's inputs into the forecast. However, they felt that they needed more time before they could make specific recommendations. They did think that they could make some "recommendations of a general nature" at the August 4 presentation.

After the meeting had ended, Bowe took Baker aside and explained that the information on regional managers and their sales estimates was quite sensitive, and that he needed to discuss it with Vincent Ernst, the vice president of sales, before proceeding further. Bowe said that he would first prepare a report of his findings for only Baker and Schrafft to study; then, after the three had discussed it, he would take the report to Ernst. He said that he did not yet have all the information necessary and that the report would probably not be ready before the August 4 presentation. He also added that it would take several discussions with Ernst before his findings could be presented to the rest of the task force, because he thought his report would place the sales division in an embarrassing situation. He expected, however, that once Ernst understood the report and its implications, that some significant changes could be made to improve the sales division's inputs into the market manager's forecasts. He also felt that Ernst would support these recommendations. Schrafft joined Bowe and Baker part way through their conversation, and she concurred that all of this work could not possibly be completed by August 4. She suggested that their "general recommendations" be followed up at a later date with more specific recommendations after Bowe had discussed his report with Ernst.

During the following week, Cassis and the product managers spent most of their time preparing for the presentation, while Bowe worked as rapidly as he could on his report. In addition to consulting with Bowe on the report, Schrafft concentrated on preparing some general recommendations about the sales division's input into the forecast.

Baker had spoken with Eldredge as soon as he returned from New York, and had briefed him on the results of the earlier meeting. Eldredge agreed to outline a proposal for the development of an internal planning model as his part of the August 4 presentation. Eldredge added that the gathering of data had been frustrating and that he suspected that the regional sales managers were hiding information from him.

AUGUST 4 REPORT OF THE TASK FORCE

Before the task force's oral presentation on August 4, Baker, Cassis, and the three product managers agreed that Cassis should be the one to report his subgroup's findings and recommendations. The three product managers felt that if they made the presentation, it would put them in an awkward position with their bosses, the market managers, because several of their conclusions were critical in nature. Baker agreed with this strategy. He also decided (with the approval of the other task force members) on a tentative agenda. The plan was for Baker to begin the oral report with a 15-minute summary of the group's purpose, the group's perception of the general problems, and its major recommendations. Eldredge would then recommend that an internal forecasting model be developed to assist the market managers in making their individual product demand forecasts. Eldredge would also report on the historic sales data and on what he thought were the critical underlying assumptions that would have to be clarified in developing an internal forecasting model. Then, Cassis would report his subgroup's findings on how the marketing division should restructure its procedures for making future product demand forecasts. After Cassis's report was completed, Schrafft would present her general recommendations concerning the sales division's inputs into the product demand forecasts.

The presentation was scheduled to last from 10 a.m. until 1 p.m. in Casey Ryan's office. Baker had arrived at his own office at 8 a.m. to review his notes and flip charts. Shortly after 9 a.m., Bowe came into Baker's office with a copy of the report he had been working on all week. Bowe had stayed up most of the night typing it himself so that Baker could see it before going into the meeting. Baker skimmed the six summary statements on the first page and was indeed surprised by what they said. It was clear that the regional sales managers were consistently overstating their sales estimates to ensure adequate inventory and rapid delivery. He called Schrafft on the telephone and the three decided to discuss Bowe's report the next day, but not to report any of its findings at the presentation.

The presentation began promptly at 10 a.m. Everyone seemed very much at ease except for the three product managers. The meeting went smoothly until Eldredge finished his portion of the presentation. Eldredge solicited questions, and one of the market managers said he hoped that what the others had to say would be more relevant than Eldredge's recommendations. He added, "You guys in Hunneuus's group can't even forecast what the economy is going to do; how the hell are you going to tell me what our customers are going to do with your models?" The other market managers laughed at this remark and, to save Eldredge further embarrassment, Baker said that Eldredge's recommendations would make more sense after the market managers heard the other reports.

Cassis then presented the report on the marketing division's procedures for forecasting product demand and the task force's recommendations on how they should be changed. During Cassis's presentation, the product managers asked him several questions of a clarifying nature, and Baker felt these were useful in getting certain points across to the market managers. At the conclusion of Cassis's presentation, Lloyd, one of the product managers, said that all three of them felt that the conclusions and recommendations were sound and that they were prepared as individuals to stand solidly behind them and to take personal responsibility for their consequences.

Following this remark, Ryan, the vice president of marketing, asked his market managers what they thought of Cassis's report. One of them said he thought the recommendations might improve the forecasts, while the other three said that the recommendations could not possibly work. Their comments included such arguments as the recommendations would not allow enough room for necessary "subjective" factors, and that the new procedures would involve too much "red tape." The discussion became quite heated with most of the questions being addressed to Cassis. Several times, the product managers were cut off by their bosses in their attempts to answer questions or clarify certain points. Finally, one of the market managers said to Cassis, "Jason, frankly, I'm amazed that this kind of nonsense could come from you. I would expect it from a tenderfoot like Baker or Schrafft or Eldredge, but from you? You've been around here long enough to know our business better than to come up with this nonsense." A second market manager added, "Look, I'm just getting things under control again so we won't lose money next quarter. The last thing I need is this garbage." He then turned to Ryan and said, "In no way am I going to swallow this stuff." Ryan began to respond, but Keene interrupted to say that he thought tempers were hot and that the recommendations were not as controversial as they might first appear to be. He suggested that the meeting be adjourned until 3 p.m. to give everyone a chance to "cool off and think things over." Ryan agreed with the suggestion, and the meeting ended at 11:30 a.m.

Keene asked Baker to remain as the others began to leave. After everyone had left, Keene closed the door and said to Baker, "We've got one hell of a mess here, and you better figure out what you're going to do at 3 p.m. In the meantime Ryan and I will put our heads together and see what we can come up with." Baker picked up his notes and left.

When Baker returned to his own office, he found Eldredge sitting at his desk thumbing through the report that Bowe had left earlier in the morning. Baker explained that the report had been loaned confidentially to him for study only, and that Bowe had told him that he had to discuss the report with his boss before presenting it to the full task force. Baker added that none of the report's data would be presented in the afternoon meeting, except in the most general terms. Baker continued by saying that it was important to respect Bowe's wishes and that the report would be shared with the task force when the time was right. Eldredge responded by saying that Bowe's data would certainly have made his own task much easier. He said that he had suspected all along that the regional sales managers had been withholding information from him. Eldredge added that he had come by to say that he was angry that he had not received more support from Baker and Schrafft when the market managers had attacked him during the morning meeting. Baker explained his rationale for wanting to direct the discussion to another topic, and that one of his reasons for doing this was to get Eldredge out of the tough spot that he was in. He said he was sorry that Eldredge had interpreted it as a lack of support. Eldredge accepted his apology and left.

A few moments later, Schrafft came in to ask Baker to join her for lunch. The two spent most of their lunch discussing what Baker should do when the meeting reconvened at 3 p.m. After lunch, Schrafft accompanied Baker to his office; once there, they found Hunneuus waiting at the door. Hunneuus said that he wanted some information on two points that Bowe had made on the first page of his report. Baker noticed that Hunneuus was holding a piece of yellow-lined paper with Bowe's six major points written on it. Hunneuus stated that he needed this information for a 4 p.m. meeting with Vincent Ernst, the vice president of sales (and Bowe's boss), to get "some real progress going on the forecasting problem." Baker replied that it was impossible to give him that data, and that the report was considered confidential. Hunneuus smiled and asked how company information could be thought of as confidential when a corporate vice president asked for it. Hunneuus left by saying that he would get the information from Ernst himself when they met at 4 p.m.

Schrafft, who had overheard Baker's exchange with Hunneuus, seemed incredulous at what had transpired. Baker explained that Eldredge had seen the report before lunch and that he had explained its confidentiality to him. Eldredge had presumably understood the situation, but had not actually said that he would keep it confidential. By now Schrafft was quite angry, and said that if Bowe was in any way hurt or compromised by this turn of events, that it would be Baker's responsibility. She said that Bowe had taken a personal risk in sharing the information with them and that if Bowe ended up in trouble because of it, Baker's word would not "be worth a plugged nickel" in the future. Baker attempted to again explain what had happened but Schrafft cut him off by saying, "You've got a problem, man, which you'd better fix in a hurry."

WEST POINT: THE CHEATING INCIDENT (A)

Leonard A. Schlesinger
Lou Zambello

It was May 19, 1976, and Lt. General Sidney Berry, superintendent of the U.S. Military Academy at West Point, was faced with a difficult series of decisions. Roughly a month earlier, it had been brought to his attention that as many as 100 second-classmen (juniors) might have cheated on an electrical engineering exam. At West Point, cheating was a violation of the Cadet Honor Code, and violators were expelled from the Academy.

During the preceding month, Berry had set in motion an attempt to determine the guilt or innocence of the accused cadets through an investigation by a Cadet Honor Board.[1] The board's task was to assess the validity of the charges and to vote for expulsion if it determined that the cheating had in fact occurred.[2] The Cadet Honor Board investigation was a standard procedure for Honor Code violations, since at West Point cadets were responsible for the administration of the Honor Code and the Honor System.

Berry had found these standard procedures inadequate and overly time-consuming.[3] A further analysis by the professors who administered the electrical engineering exam in question revealed that an additional 135 cadets might have cheated. A complete independent investigation was demanded by *The New York Times* and other major newspapers and magazines; Senator Nunn, chairman of the Subcommittee on Manpower and Personnel of the Senate Armed Services Committee; and other government officials.[4] Superintendent Berry believed that unless the implicated ca-

[1] See for example, *Times-Herald Record,* Apr. 7, 1976.
[2] Ibid.
[3] See Sidney B. Berry's letter to West Point graduates, June 19, 1976.
[4] See, for example, Events Summary, Civil Action in U.S. District Court for District of Columbia, *D'Arcangelo et al. vs. Hoffmann et al.,* pp. 4–10.

dets were judged by their West Point peers and expelled if found guilty, the Cadet Honor Code and the overall Academy value system might be undermined.[5] Still, the Honor Board procedures threatened to drag on all year, bringing with them a continuing stream of adverse publicity for the Academy.

It was clear to Berry that he had two related decisions confronting him. First, he had to decide whether an investigation of each accused cadet, with automatic separation of the guilty, was necessary, fair, or even viable given the unprecedented number of accused cadets. Second, he had to decide whether to continue the standard Cadet Honor Board investigations or substitute a quicker and more systematic method of investigation that would use noncadets as judges and investigators. Whatever the decisions he reached on these issues, Berry realized that he also had to develop an implementation plan that would be acceptable to all interested parties: the cadets who favored continuing the honor board and automatic expulsion of the guilty; the press and the public, which were concerned with fair and equitable treatment of the accused cadets; and those associated with national defense who were determined that this incident would not undermine the long-term viability of West Point and the training of U.S. military officers.

The superintendent would have to arrive at a reasonable course of action immediately. On May 15, the Secretary of the Army, Martin R. Hoffmann, had been served with a request by three lawyers representing all the implicated cadets (as a group) to dissolve the Cadet Honor Board and personally oversee an alternative form of outside investigation. If Berry did not act quickly, it appeared that the decision might be taken out of his hands.

U.S. MILITARY ACADEMY

The U.S. Military Academy at West Point is America's oldest military academy. For almost two centuries, it has provided an impressive share of our greatest military leaders; Scott, Lee, Jackson, Sherman, Pershing, Eisenhower, MacArthur, Patton, Bradley, Grant, Haig, and Ridgeway. The Academy, a four-year institution supported entirely by government funds, is located in upstate New York on picturesque grounds near the Hudson River. In 1976 each graduate represented an investment of more than $100,000.[6] To be accepted into West Point, high school seniors must pass certain minimum academic and physical requirements and be recommended by their Senator, Congressman, or the Vice President or the President of the United States. Cadets entering West Point make a definite commitment to serve a mandatory 5-year term after graduation. If they leave the Academy after the first day of classes of their junior year, they are required to serve several years as enlisted personnel to fulfill their military obligation.

Cadets normally enter the Academy between the ages of 17 and 23. In 1976 the typical cadet had a B+ average in high school, received a letter in some sport (33

---

[5] See, for example, Sidney B. Berry, "Duty, Honor, Country," *The New York Times,* July 22, 1976.
[6] See the comptroller general's report to Congress, *Student Attrition at Five Federal Academies,* enclosure B 83, 1976.

percent were captains), and averaged 600 on the Scholastic Aptitude Test.[7] Many cadets had wanted to attend West Point since the beginning of their high school days or even earlier.[8] Slightly more than 13 percent of the cadets had fathers who were career military officers. For most new cadets, the Academy provides their first away-from-home experience. They enter with idealistic attitudes and are totally committed to West Point and its philosophy.[9] Plebes (first-year cadets) enter "Beast Barracks" (the Academy's summer training program) before their first school year and are introduced to the Academy's lifestyle and philosophy. Conditioned automatic deference to officers and cadet superiors is ingrained into each cadet from the first day of his Academy experience.[10] West Point graduates repeatedly told the casewriter that it was difficult to appreciate the intense conditioning experience that occurred during a Cadet's first year at the Academy. A glimpse is suggested by the following testimony from a second-year cadet:

> It really affects him just about every minute of the day. Whenever he is out of his room, he must be on guard and be performing properly. When he goes in passageways and the halls, he must double-time, stop, he must go in the center of the passageway. . . . During all this time his eyes are straight ahead. . . . If a plebe makes a mistake in front of an upperclassman while he is in the passageway, the upperclassman will tell him to do 10 pushups as punishment . . . counting "One, Sir" through "Ten, Sir." Freshman cadets are required to respond immediately to questions addressed to them with either, "Yes Sir"; "No Sir"; "No excuse, Sir"; "Sir, may I make a statement?"; or "Sir, may I ask a question?"[11]

A former cadet sums up the effect of such conditioning on first-year cadets:

> From the first day of Beast Barracks onward the cadets' primary motivation is survival. Cadets and their roommates, friends, and companymates band together as a group and help each other "survive."[12]

Academically, West Point is similar to many four-year private colleges, although its curriculum is heavily weighted in the areas of mathematics and applied sciences. The first-year core curriculum consists of two mathematics courses, English, a foreign language, environmental studies, and engineering fundamentals. This is followed in the second year by chemistry, physics, psychology, history, additional course work in mathematics, and further study of a foreign language. Juniors take a heavy load of electrical engineering and mechanics courses. The curriculum has little room for elective coursework. Cadets must take a minimum of six required courses each academic semester. In addition to the core curriculum, all cadets must take coursework in military science. All cadets graduate with a BS degree.

Unlike the atmosphere at the typical four-year college, the environment at the

---

[7] *Time,* June 7, 1976, p. 24.

[8] Ibid.

[9] Ibid.

[10] Michael T. Rose, *A Prayer for Relief: The Constitutional Infirmities of the Military Academies' Conduct, Honor, and Ethics Systems.* (South Hackensack, New Jersey: Fred B. Rothman & Co., 1973).

[11] See, for example, *U.S. Air Force Cadet Wing Manual,* 50–1, chap. II (5) (c) (4), 1968; Johnson, "The Tainted Image of West Point," *The Progressive* 13, 15, Feb. 1971.

[12] Letter from first-class cadet to dean of academic board, U.S.M.A., Sept. 28, 1971, cited from Rose, p. 62.

Military Academy is strictly business with little free time available. An Academy instructor commented:

> The academy abhors a temporal vacuum: free time. Too many cadets have lives of madcap, frenzied, disjointed activity: rushing from one class to another. . . . It is implicit that the cadets' four years at West Point somehow approximate the stress of combat.[13]

A typical day at West Point begins with reveille at 6:10 a.m., duties until 6:40 a.m., and classes from 7:50 to 11:50 a.m. Additional classes, military maneuvers, athletic requirements, and study continue until taps at 11 p.m. For many exhausted cadets, the major recreation is sleeping.

Cadets' lives are highly regimented. They cannot leave the campus without permission and leave occurs only during major Academy vacations. Each individual is required to comply with a large number of regulations, discipline codes, and traditional laws,[14] many of which are contained in a manual known as the Blue Book. Cadets may even be informed by their company commander of the type of shaving cream to be used and the color of toilet articles to be retained.[15] For many cadets, life at West Point consists in large part of finding ways around the regulations. It is nearly impossible for an individual to comply with all regulations all the time. A former cadet noted:

> Many cadets go through West Point virtually alone, almost in silence. My personal experience was just the opposite . . . but the lasting profound friendships I formed at West Point were born of rebellion against the system, not brotherhood within it.[16]

The rationale provided to cadets by West Point officers on the requirements for absolute honesty and strict compliance to even the most trivial regulation was that in combat, absolute obedience and integrity were critical.[17] Every cadet has frequently heard the classic story of the platoon leader who was ordered to move his troops from one position to another. His troops were too tired, and he thought the move unnecessary, so he did not move the platoon. When called on the radio 1 hour later and asked if the platoon was moved, he lied, and said it was. Subsequently, friendly artillery fire was called in on his position, which the company commander believed to have been vacated, and the platoon was wiped out. In this and many other ways every cadet is given the message that absolute honesty and strict obedience are necessary for survival in combat.

MISSION OF WEST POINT

The mission of West Point, which was established in 1802 by an act of Congress, has been to educate and train officers for the U.S. Army.[18] Its stated purpose is to

---

[13] Josiah Bunting III, "West Point Counterpoint," *Esquire,* vol. 86, Nov. 1976, p. 70.

[14] Lucian K. Truscott, "West Point and Honor: What We Haven't Told You," *Alicia Patterson Foundation Newsletter,* LKT IV-2, p. 14.

[15] Ibid.

[16] Ibid.

[17] Ibid., p. 8; Bunting, loc. cit., p. 122.

[18] *Report to the Secretary of the Army by the Special Commission on the United States Military Academy* (Borman Report), Dec. 15, 1976, p. 71.

instruct and train the corps of cadets such that each graduate shall have the qualities and attributes essential to progressive and continuous development throughout service in the regular Army.[19] West Point Superintendent Berry described the Academy's mission as follows:

> West Point seeks to build upon what the cadet brings into the military academy and to incubate and direct values, standards, attitudes, and expectations toward the demanding constraints of the battlefield. The values and standards may change out in society. The values and standards required of the soldier leader in the battlefield are constant.[20]

In pursuit of its mission, West Point developed a number of rigidly defined goals and procedures. Four of these goals are especially germane to an understanding of the cheating incident:[21]

1 West Point seeks to develop an intense sense of camaraderie and cooperation within the corps of cadets, especially among members of the same year group and among members of the same cadet company. Consequently, cadets are required to cooperate in a wide range of daily activities that reinforce a pervasive sense of interdependence.

2 The Military Academy attempts to teach cadets to operate under various forms of physical and mental pressures by arbitrarily creating situations of stress inside and outside academic classrooms.

3 West Point seeks to develop a strong cadet integrity. This goal is pursued through an absolute and unbending Honor Code.

4 West Point seeks to realize the cultivation of a sense of personal and group accountability. A primary force in implementing this goal is the large number of cadet regulations that define the boundaries of acceptable behavior.

HONOR CODE

The Honor Code simply and in its entirety states: "A cadet will not lie, cheat, or steal nor tolerate those who do." (Of all the military academies, only the U.S. Military Academy and U.S. Air Force Academy include toleration as an honor violation.) The code was a focal point for honorable and ethical practice at the Academy.[22] Adherence was not an end in itself. Rather, the Honor Code and the Honor System (West Point's mechanism for implementing the code) were designed to build integrity in the cadet.[23]

Dwight D. Eisenhower, speaking as a 1915 graduate of the Academy, reflected on West Point's Honor System:

[19] Ibid.
[20] Superintendent Berry as quoted in Bunting, *op. cit.,* p. 68.
[21] From U.S.M.A. Handbook as quoted in *Congressional Record,* vol. 122, no. 129, E 4941, Aug. 9, 1976.
[22] *The Cadet Honor Code and System 2,* 1970.
[23] Ibid. Also see Martin Hoffmann, opening statement of Senate Hearings on Academy Honor Codes, vol. I, June 21, 1976, p. 8.

The Honor System as a feature of West Point seems to grow in importance with a graduate as the years recede until finally it becomes something which he is almost reluctant to talk about. It occupies a position in his mind akin to the virtue of his mother or his sister.[24]

The evolution of the Honor Code coupled with an Honor System has been a gradual one. The Honor Code existed, in one form or another, since the beginning of the Academy in the early 1800s. The history of the formal Honor System did not begin until 1922 when Douglas MacArthur, then the superintendent of West Point, officially recognized a Cadet Vigilance Committee that had informally been rendering judgments and punishments to perceived Honor Code violators. Thus, throughout the first 120 years of its history, the Military Academy relied on peer pressure rather than a formalized enforcement mechanism.[25]

HONOR SYSTEM

The Honor System is the only facet of Academy life that has traditionally been completely under cadet control.[26] Plebes were informed by Honor System representatives that the code belonged to them alone and that they would be expected to attend meetings on the code and understand its intricacies.[27] Traditionally, cadets viewed with disfavor any actions that could potentially undermine their responsibility for teaching and administering the Honor Code and Honor System.[28]

There has been a tendency for Military Academy officials to adopt a defensive, outsiders-really-don't-understand-our-problem, tone. . . .[29]

As cadets were told in a paper evaluated by West Point's Honor Committee,

We should all recognize that it is unreasonable to expect information leaked outside of the Corps to be fairly or accurately reported. This is true simply because it is impossible for anyone but us to understand the Honor Code and System completely.[30]

The Honor Code, especially the toleration clause, posed a dilemma for cadets. On the one hand, the average cadet fervently believed in the importance and validity of the honor concept as a standard to live by. On the other hand, the cadet had developed an intense loyalty toward companymates and to avoid assisting them, or worse, to turn one in was unthinkable.[31] One cadet recognizing the conflicting forces involved stated:

At the Point, you're like a robot. They make every decision for you, even when to eat. You're in an atmosphere where everybody is trying to survive together. You're working on a quiz in the same room with guys you've crawled through the mud with. You are supposed to be comrades. But you can't ask "Am I on the right track? Is this almost right?" If you

---

[24] Unpublished paper by a member of 1976 West Point cadet honor committee, Company E-3, p. 1.
[25] Ibid.
[26] *The Cadet Honor Code and System 2,* 1970.
[27] Truscott, op. cit., p. 5.
[28] See, for example, Rose, op. cit., p. 84.
[29] Ibid., pp. 183–184, footnote 1102.
[30] Ibid., footnote 1103.
[31] "Ex-Point Doctor: Some Cheating Tolerated There," *Times-Herald Record,* Apr. 13, 1976.

even say that much and they don't turn you in, then they can be expelled, too. . . but . . . West Point's basic ideals are what I believe in.[32]

The administration of the Honor Code was carried out by cadet honor representatives who were elected by their fellow cadets each year. Honor representatives instruct and advise cadets on Honor Code matters and sit on Honor Boards during investigations. An honor investigation was initiated when a suspected violation was reported by a cadet (including the violator himself) or an officer. A cadet's allegation was initially reported to the elected company cadet honor representative. An allegation by an officer was reported to the deputy commandant of cadets, who informed the chairman of the Cadet Honor Committee. When there was evidence that an honor violation had occurred, the allegations were referred to a three-member subcommittee of the Cadet Honor Committee. After investigation the allegations would be dropped or recommended for referral to a 12-member Cadet Honor Board. The Board would conduct a hearing at which witnesses and the suspected cadet might testify. Officer and cadet spectators could attend unless the hearing was closed at the request of the cadet or the Honor Board. The cadet was present during the entire proceeding, except for Honor Board deliberations. The cadet was not entitled to question witnesses. He or she was allowed to confer with legal counsel but was not entitled to legal representation at this stage. However, the cadet was provided a nonvoting advisor from the Cadet Honor Committee. Verdicts were by secret ballot. Traditionally, a finding of an honor violation required the unanimous vote of all 12 Honor Board members. The cadet was immediately notified of the Board's findings and the superintendent received a written report. There is a right of appeal to the superintendent. The superintendent could overrule the Honor Board if he disagreed with its findings. The sole punishment available for a conviction of an honor violation was dismissal from the Academy. (A cadet found guilty of an Honor Code violation was asked to resign from the Academy.)[33] Although guilty cadets also had the opportunity to appeal to a board of Academy officers selected by the superintendent, few chose to do so. Between 1967 and 1972, all but 9 of 150 cadets found guilty of Honor Code violations resigned without requesting a board of officers hearing.[34] (See Exhibit 1 for a review of the Honor System decision-making process.)

Upon the rendering of a guilty verdict, a cadet offender was normally segregated from the rest of the Corps pending further action on his or her case. The cadet was assigned to a special dormitory designed to quarter those cadets undergoing separation actions, and was prohibited from attending class. Thus, even in the event of reversal, an initial finding of guilt is made known to the corps, and a cadet's reputation is damaged. In addition, West Point informs a convicted cadet's parents of his or her violation.[35]

A cadet whose honor conviction was reversed on appeal faced the prospect of individual ostracism (called silencing) by the entire cadet corps.[36] Cadets who im-

[32] "Bobby Jones: A Tragic Step out of the Long Grey Line," *Washington Post,* Sept. 29, 1976.
[33] Rose, op. cit., p. 37.
[34] *Borman Report,* op. cit., p. 52.
[35] Rose, op. cit., p. 61, footnote 318.
[36] Ibid., pp. 137–140, 41.

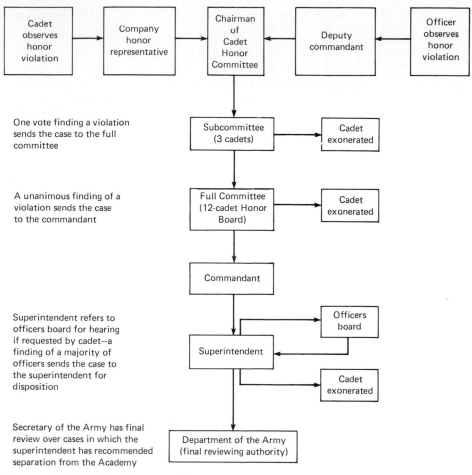

EXHIBIT 1   A diagram of the traditional honor system.

posed this unofficial punishment rationalized their actions on the grounds that the exonerated cadet was really guilty but could not be discharged due to legal techni- calities.[37] According to cadet lore, the Honor Board's verdict is the only one that matters because only cadets should administer the Honor Code. In 1960 the Cadet Honor Committee circulated a memo to the corps outlining the complete silencing procedure.[38] (See Exhibit 2.) The most widely publicized silencing occurred between 1972 and 1973 when Cadet Pelosi, whose honor board conviction during his junior year was reversed on appeal, was silenced during the remaining 19 months of his stay at the Academy.[39] A board of officers had determined that Pelosi could not be ex-

[37] Ibid., p. 42.
[38] Ibid., pp. 41–42, footnote 215.
[39] Ibid., pp. 139–143.

EXHIBIT 2   1960 CADET HONOR COMMITTEE OUTLINE OF SILENCING PROCEDURE*

---

1 The silence lasts his entire career in the Armed Forces.

2 He is not permitted to wear his class ring.

3 He is addressed only on official business, and then as Mister.

4 He will not be allowed to have roommates.

5 Seats next to him in mess hall will be left vacant.

6 If the man goes to the theatre or to athletic events, all seats adjacent to him (one seat on each side) will be vacated.

7 If he sits down at a table in the "Boodlers,"† that table will be vacated.

8 He will not be given the privilege of "cutting-in" or exchanging dances at the hop.

9 He will not participate in the fourth class system.

---

* Cited from *A Prayer for Relief*, p. 42.

† The Boodlers is a West Point recreation and entertainment room.

pelled because of command influence. Shortly after this successful appeal was announced, the Cadet Honor Committee held a vote asking the cadets whether Pelosi should be silenced. (Until the late 1960s, the decision to silence a cadet was made solely by the Honor Committee. The corps of cadets automatically upheld the Committee's decision.[40]) Thereafter, Pelosi was silenced. He had no roommate, few cadets talked to him, and three times a day he ate at a table by himself. He was required to forfeit his official position as an elected company honor representative, despite the protests of his companymates (who so wanted to retain him that they failed to elect a new representative to replace him). His rating on the Military Order of Merit fell from the top cadet in the company to the bottom and, later, to the bottom in the entire corps. He was prohibited from attending class for 42 days and was required to individually perform classroom academic exercises normally designed for groups. His slide rule was broken into small pieces and returned to his briefcase. He lost weight, he received threats; the corps's first captain, for example, said he would cut off the silenced cadet's finger before he would see him wear the West Point ring. Miscellaneous tactics employed to force Pelosi to resign included dousing his bed with water; theft of personal property; putting jelly between his sheets; and soaking his clothes in a shower. Until stopped by the warning of an attorney, cadets were arranging for Pelosi's yearbook picture to appear on a perforated page, for easy removal.[41]

Another case of silencing occurred in this time period when an officer appeal board found another cadet not guilty. The Honor Committee held a vote, similar to that for Pelosi, asking the corps whether or not to impose the silence on the cadet. Sixty percent voted that silence should not be imposed. The Honor Committee then held a revote, explaining that not everyone had voted and that it was important to obtain a decisive expression of opinion and thus ensure fairness. Immediately before the revote, the cadet circulated among the corps a letter explaining his case and offering evidence of his innocence. In response, the Cadet Honor Committe, post-

[40] Ibid., footnote 870.

[41] Ibid., pp. 143–144.

poning the vote for a few days, distributed to each company an *Honor Committee Fact Sheet* and held a meeting of each of the four classes to emphasize that the vote amounted to a test of the corps's confidence in its Honor Committee and that it did not matter whether or not the cadet in question was guilty or innocent but only that the committee's judgment be upheld. Subsequently, the corps voted 1419–1083, with approximately 300 abstentions, to silence the cadet. Many ballots were counted as votes for the silence merely because they wished to support the Honor Committee, even though they specifically expressed disapproval of the silence.[42]

Thereafter, the cadet was silenced. He was prohibited from attending class meetings, utilizing laboratory partners, studying with classmates, and visiting friends. Although he had received less than 50 demerits in his previous 2 years at the Academy, he received 83 demerits during the first semester of his second-class year. Someone substituted a rusty trigger assembly for the clean one in his rifle before he reported for inspection.[43] Following the publicity generated by the Pelosi incident, silencing was officially banned at West Point. Evidence exists that silencing continues on an unofficial basis.[44]

WEST POINT ORGANIZATION

As superintendent, Berry was charged by law with responsibility for the "immediate government of the Academy" (10 U.S.C. Sec. 4434b).[45] Selected from the ranks of Army general officers,[46] the superintendent had traditionally been an outstanding combat leader. The selection of a superintendent was not normally based upon ability and interest in providing educational leadership. Rather, the superintendent was expected to be a combat role model for the cadets.[47] Assignment as superintendent was considered to be a step toward higher responsibility, such as a chief-of-staff position. The typical superintendent spent slightly less than 3 years as head of the Academy.[48]

In carrying out his responsibilities, the superintendent was assisted by an academic board composed, by Army regulation, of the superintendent, the dean of the academic board, the commandant of cadets, the professor of military hygiene, and the heads of the various academic departments. The academic board was charged with the responsibility for "the course of study and methods of instruction."[49] Its dean advised the superintendent on academic matters and questions of general policy.[50] The dean served as the superintendent's deputy for the activities of the academic board and the academic departments.[51] The dean had no set term of office and

[42] Ibid., pp. 141–142.
[43] Ibid., p. 143.
[44] Professor Robert Moore, before Senator Nunn's Armed Services Subcommittee on Manpower and Personnel on Aug. 9, 1976 as quoted by Thomas J. Downey. *Congressional Record,* vol. 122, no. 129. E 4941.
[45] *Borman Report,* p. 77.
[46] Ibid.
[47] Ibid.
[48] Ibid.
[49] Ibid., p. 79.
[50] Ibid., p. 78.
[51] Ibid.

frequently remained in that position until retirement. Thus, a superintendent did not normally have the opportunity to select the dean that served under him.[52]

The commandant of cadets was in charge of the tactical department, which included all company tactical officers, the physical training program, the leadership evaluation system, and the Office of Military Leadership. (A tactical officer (TAC), was assigned to each of the 36 cadet companies as the company's officer commander. The TACs were responsible for the performance of their companies as a unit.) The responsibility for supervision of the Honor System also rested with the commandant.[53] The professor of military hygiene was responsible for academic instruction in the leadership and behavioral sciences.

The academic board was created out of a perceived need for a system of checks and balances. It was described in a 1975 Academy information paper as:

> . . . a unique crucible for a melding of viewpoints. The Superintendent and the Commandant, newly assigned approximately every three years, represent the guidance of the Secretary of the Army, the Army Chief of Staff, and a current senior officer view of the Army. The strong influence they have on the board is directly proportional to their experience, prestige, rank, and merited respect. The Department Heads, for their part, are able to maintain a current view of the young Army through their junior officer faculty members and also are influenced by their own and the younger officers' contacts with civilian academic institutions. . . . The resulting consensus reached by the Board, reflecting the operation of a classic check and balance system, is therefore based on a variety of experiences and backgrounds, and changes have traditionally been moderate, gradual, and evolutionary, governed by commitment to the mission of the Military Academy.[54]

Contrary to this view, the academic board was frequently criticized in the 1970s as unduly resistant to change and unrepresentative of the "young army." Academic board members acknowledged a lack of communication between the board and members of the junior faculty.

GENERAL SIDNEY BERRY

Berry, 50 years old, was a tough veteran of two wars and a 1948 West Point graduate. Shortly after finishing his tour of duty in Vietnam as a decorated division commander, he was appointed superintendent of West Point. Berry replaced Major General William Knowlton, who had completed a 3-year term. Knowlton, in turn, had replaced Major General Samuel Koster, who resigned and was demoted after being accused of taking part in the My Lai massacre cover-up while commander of the 9th American Division in Vietnam. On his departure, Knowlton provided Berry with a report concerning honor at West Point. The report, prepared at Knowlton's request by a group of faculty members in 1971, revealed widespread disaffection with the Honor System.[55] The report presented the following faculty observations:

> I believe, based on close contact with many cadets during my assignment to the faculty, conversations with others similarly assigned at that time and since, and comparison with

[52] Ibid.
[53] Ibid., p. 82.
[54] Ibid., p. 79.
[55] Ibid., pp. 32–33.

my own cadet experience only a decade before, that the Honor Code is in trouble at West Point. . . .

Reclaiming the Honor Code is a formidable task. There no doubt are in the Corps of Cadets (extrapolating from my faculty experience) a number of cadets who have violated the Honor Code and who have gotten away with it and know that they have. Some members of the Honor Committee share this knowledge. Cadets in general are aware of falling short of the cherished ideal in this area. The starting point for any improvement would have to be a mutual recognition on the part of cadets and faculty that a problem exists.[56]

Although Knowlton did little with the report, in response to its strong warning, Berry established in October 1974 a joint officer-cadet task force (Special Group on Honor at West Point) with a defined mission of "examining and challenging all tenets and facets of the Honor Code and System considering nothing sacrosanct or above question."[57] This group prepared and administered a survey to all cadets and officers concerning attitudes toward the Honor Code and the Honor System. On May 23, 1975, the group issued a two-volume study that concluded that attitudes toward the Honor Code and the Honor System were deteriorating.[58] Exhibit 3 contains a brief sample of the report's findings. Berry forwarded the task force's report to the academic board and the Cadet Honor Committee.[59] He believed that it was important that he do little more. He commented:

The cadets want full responsibility for the Honor System. That is a healthy attitude. No Superintendent can run the Honor System. No Commandant of Cadets can. No Dean of Academics, no Association of Academics, no Association of Graduates, no outside group can run the Honor System—only the Corps of Cadets themselves can do so.[60]

In late March of 1976, the Cadet Honor Committee, acting on the study group report, offered a number of recommendations for change, which were voted upon and accepted by the cadets:

1 Initial investigations and appeal hearings would occur at the cadet Honor Board level; the officer board would be eliminated.

2 A less than unanimous vote (11 to 2) would be required for a finding of guilt.

3 Cadets other than honor representatives would participate in the investigation and adjudication of honor violations.

These items, although passed by the corps, were not yet implemented on May 19, 1976. In addition, the end of mandatory expulsion for Honor Code violators was recommended by the committee but not passed by the corps. In January 1976, without informing the corps as a whole, the Honor Committee passed a resolution requiring that a two-thirds majority had to favor the end of mandatory expulsion before it could be abolished. Shortly before the cheating incident, a majority of the corps (51 percent) but less than the required two-thirds, voted to end the single sanction.

---

[56] Ibid., p. 33.
[57] Ibid.
[58] Ibid., pp. 33–35.
[59] Ibid., p. 35.
[60] Berry's letter to graduates, June 10, 1976, p. 5.

EXHIBIT 3   SAMPLE OF FINDINGS BY THE 1975 SPECIAL STUDY GROUP ON HONOR AT WEST POINT*

The "Honor Code is a clear and simple statement of an unattainable level of human behavior." It "is a goal suitable for the entire professional life of a military man and is a goal to which he should aspire in the challenging environments outside the Academy as well as in the training period of his cadetship."

The nontoleration clause makes the Honor Code "philosophically hard to digest by American society, in general and, to a degree, by the Army Officer Corps."

[O]perational interpretations of the Honor Code vary widely and are modified frequently without the benefit of any regularized process. . . .

The Honor System has "relied on mystique to cloak the very many issues and difficult judgments involved in prescribing and enforcing a system of ethics."

The "inflexible application" of the single sanction of separation "in conjunction with an idealistic code is certain to place considerable strain on a human system."

"The drift . . . toward an increasing list of specifics . . . tends to obscure the spirit of the code and exacerbate the conflict that cadets conjure up between honor and regulations."

Dubious 11–1 acquittals, the lack of convictions for toleration, the absence of fundamental fairness in the proceedings, and the rare conviction of first classmen result in the perception of many that the Honor System has been hypocritical, corrupt, and unfair.

70 percent of the cadets deny that the Honor Code is uniformly adhered to throughout the corps.

60 percent of the cadets and 61 percent of the officers agree that adherence to the spirit of the Honor Code is deteriorating.

39 percent of the cadets and 24 percent of the officers do not believe the Honor System is fair and just.

26 percent of the cadets do not believe that the Honor System is effective in accomplishing its mission of imparting to cadets a sense of personal honor; an additional 16 percent were "neutral" on whether the Honor System has this effect.

45 percent of the cadets and 45 percent of the officers do not believe that the Honor Code is realistically interpreted by the corps.

76 percent of the cadets believe that the Honor Code is used to enforce regulations.

73 percent of the cadets would not report a good friend for a possible honor violation and 34 percent of the cadets would not report a good friend for a clear-cut violation.

45 percent of the cadets want toleration removed as an honor violation.

* From the *Borman Report,* footnote 22.

Shortly after the cheating incident, another vote was taken and 65 percent of the cadets voted against expulsion, still less than the required two-thirds.[61]

In early March of 1976, Berry reversed a Cadet Honor Committee and an officer board's finding of guilt and ordered a cadet returned to the corps. The case extended back to 1975. At that time 19-year-old Stephen Verr, a slight (5-feet 9-inches, 140 pounds) plebe, still in Beast Barracks, was seen crying by an upperclassman.[62] Verr had been subjected to a traditional form of harassment: upperclassmen ordered him

[61] Ibid.
[62] *Newsweek,* May 24, 1976.

not to put certain foods on his tray and made him stand at attention while others ate. After going hungry for 2 days, Verr had tears in his eyes as he left the dining hall. When an upperclassman demanded, "Mister, what are you crying about?", the plebe told him that his parents had been injured in an automobile accident. Verr later admitted that this was a lie and blamed his outburst on suffering from an insufficient diet while training as a long-distance runner. He was charged with an honor violation and brought before a Cadet Honor Committee, which recommended expulsion from the Academy. An officer board concurred but Berry overturned the decision, saying that the cadet had had "no intent to deceive" and that he had not been in control of his faculties. Berry's decision proved to be very unpopular with the corps; a number of members of the Cadet Honor Committee submitted resignations. During the period of the hearings, and after Berry's decision, Verr was silenced.[63] He was placed in transient barracks, harassed, and isolated. He was given a room by himself and was forced to eat alone. Verr claimed that his mail was intercepted and his room ransacked. He allegedly received telephone threats on his life until the Academy assigned him a bodyguard.[64] Only 1 month after Berry reversed the Verr decision, the cheating incident occurred.

CHEATING INCIDENT

The most unpopular course at West Point was electrical engineering.[65] All juniors were required to take two electrical engineering courses, one each semester. The courses were known as "juice," and consisted of EE 301 (electrical circuits) and EE 304 (electronics). The former was theoretical overview, the latter a more involved applied electronics course featuring such topics as frequency selectivity in communication circuits, characteristics and modeling electronic devices, diode circuits, amplifiers, oscillators, etc.

Cadets' negative attitudes toward these electrical engineering courses stemmed from the extreme difficulty of the work and the absence of a relationship between the coursework and the cadets' ultimate career orientations.[66] Cadets viewed the courses as a burdensome requirement. Furthermore, cadets who failed the course were required to repeat it their senior year. A large number of less quantitatively oriented cadets struggled with electrical engineering each year.

EE 304 featured assigned study problems for each class that allowed collaboration. Since the course was particularly difficult for many cadets, cooperation among cadets was well-ingrained and encouraged, as was the case with other particularly difficult Academy courses.[67]

On March 3 and 4 a take-home problem was distributed to 823 juniors. This time-consuming problem, to be turned in by each cadet on either March 17 or 18, was to count for less than 5 percent of the cadet's semester grade. The instructions on the

---

[63] Ibid.
[64] "Cadet under Guard after Threats," *The New York Times News Service,* May 26, 1976.
[65] Bunting, op. cit., p. 70.
[66] Ibid.
[67] Bunting, op. cit., p. 122.

cover page of part 1 of the examination were explicit. *"Upon issuance of this problem there will be no discussion of the problem with anyone except Department of Electrical Engineering Instructors."* [68] Part 2 of the exam was a team project for which collaboration was mandatory.

The discovery of the cheating occurred as follows:

Before handing his exam in Cadet Paul Nardi of Section 12F wrote on the cover page of his examination: "To whom it may concern: I have received help in completing this special problem from my roommate." The grading instructor, Lieutenant Colonel Leonard L. Friesz, made a mental note to call in Nardi and continued grading. Soon he noticed a discomforting similarity in certain answers, both absurdly wrong, on Nardi's and Cadet Garret Keane's exams. Friesz called in Keane, showed him the two papers, and asked him his roommate's name.

Mr. Keane, who, we must imagine, was a terrified young man, went to Nardi and asked him if he had copied from his (Keane's) paper. Nardi said, "I might have, thinking it was my roommate's." Nardi's roommate was Cadet Gerald M. Ousley. Now Keane returned to Colonel Friesz and repeated Nardi's surmise. Friesz checked Ousley's paper and found what he had already begun to suspect: more identical answers.

On March 24, three days before the corps of cadets left the Academy for spring vacation, Colonel Elliot C. Cutler, permanent head of the department of electrical engineering at West Point, had learned not only of this collusion but of "disturbing similarities" in other groups of examinations as well. He called in the director of the EE 304 course, Captain Billy W. Frazier, and called for a comprehensive examination and comparison of the 823 papers. The survey yielded dramatic evidence of widespread collusion involving many groups of cadets (pairs, threes, and fours). The groups usually involved roommates or members of the same cadet company. Of the thirty-six companies at the Academy, all but ten had juniors who were implicated. Superintendent Berry was advised of the Survey findings.[69]

The investigation continued, and on April 4, the day the corps of cadets returned from vacation, 117 exams were submitted by the deputy commandant of cadets to the Cadet Honor Committee charged with investigating the allegations. By April 7, news of the scandal, already guardedly referred to as the worst since the famous cribbing incident of 1951, was in *The New York Times*.[70] (The cribbing incident involved some 40 West Point football players, among others, who were expelled when it was discovered that they cheated on exams to maintain their eligibility.) Berry received a great number of inquiries from reporters, the parents of the cadets, and alumni concerned about the breakdown of discipline. On April 10, the superintendent issued a letter (see Exhibit 4) to both parents and alumni. The letter restated the Academy's commitment to the Honor System and Berry's belief that, despite the number of implicated cadets, the Honor System was working.

Of the original 117 cadets, 102 appeared before full, 12-member Cadet Honor Boards. Fifty-two were found guilty, but only 4 resigned, leaving 48 who requested appeal hearings before officer boards. It was considered unusual for so many cadets

[68] Ibid.
[69] Ibid.
[70] Ibid.

EXHIBIT 4   GENERAL BERRY'S LETTER TO ACADEMY GRADUATES

Office of the Superintendent
UNITED STATES MILITARY ACADEMY
West Point, New York 10990

MASG   10 April 1976

Dear West Point Graduate:

I am writing to all graduates to give direct information about the recently publicized honor incident.

In early March the Department of Electrical Engineering issued a homestudy computer problem for grade to approximately 800 cadets of the Class of 1977. The instructions required each cadet to do his own individual work without collaboration with any other cadet. In mid-March as the papers were being graded, it appeared that some unauthorized collaboration might have taken place.

The Chairmen of the 1976 and 1977 Honor Committees asked that the questionable papers be referred to the Cadet Honor Committee for review for possible honor violations. Three-member sub-committees of the Cadet Honor Committee reviewed the papers and interviewed cadets involved. As a result of these interviews, 101 cadets of the Class of 1977 will appear before twelve-member boards of the Cadet Honor Committee.

If a twelve-cadet Honor Board determines by unanimous vote that a cadet has violated the Honor Code, the allegation will be submitted to the Commandant of Cadets for further official action. At this point, the cadet will appear before a *de novo* hearing by a Board of Officers unless he elects to resign from the Corps of Cadets. The proceedings of the Cadet Honor Committee and Board of Officers will be accomplished as thoughtfully, thoroughly and expeditiously as possible with full regard for the rights of the individual and interests of the institution. I personally review and evaluate all applications for resignation and all findings of Boards of Officers and forward them with my recommendations to the Secretary of the Army, who is the final authority in such cases.

It is important to note that as of this writing no cadet has been found by a Cadet Honor Board to have violated the Honor Code in this incident. The Cadet Honor Committee has accomplished its work thus far in a calm, professional manner which I know would gain your respect and confidence.

Although this incident appears to be serious, I do not believe it reflects a widespread lack of concern for the Honor Code in the Corps of Cadets. On the contrary, cadets remain strongly supportive of the principles of the Honor Code and this action of their Honor Committee.

Please understand that because of my role in the review process, I must avoid personal involvement in the individual cases until I receive the official record of board proceedings for my evaluation and appropriate recommendation to the Secretary of the Army. Further, I must be absolutely correct in statements or actions that might prejudice any proceedings underway. As soon as I can properly do so, I will report to you the outcome of this situation. That time may be several months hence.

A similar letter is going to the parent of each cadet.

Sincerely,

Sidney B. Berry
Lieutenant General,
U.S. Army Superintendent

to appeal.[71] Historically, cadets had accepted the judgment of the Cadet Honor Board and had immediately resigned to spare themselves and the Academy further embarrassment.[72] On April 16, Berry issued instructions to assign those cadets found guilty to different quarters and companies, presumably so that the remainder of the corps could settle down to some semblance of normal operations.[73] On April 22, counsel for all the convicted cadets requested that reassignment be stopped until the cadets appealed the conviction.[74] Their request was denied by Berry.[75] On April 24, Berry, realizing that the cheating incident was occupying more and more of his time and becoming more complex, assigned Colonel Hal B. Rhyne, deputy commandant, to a new, full-time job of handling Honor Code questions and issues.[76] Berry simply needed an aide to help him keep current on press releases and to answer the deluge of requests for interviews and information on the cheating incident.

As rumors of widespread cheating spread, attention focused on a statement by accused cadet Tim Ringgold to the undersecretary of the Army, Norman Augustine, that "roughly one-third of my class cheated and the other two-thirds tolerated it." A recheck by the electrical engineering department of the original 823 papers produced evidence that an additional 135 cadets might be involved. The recheck was stimulated by press accusations of an Academy cover-up and by the charges of many of the accused cadets that many of the cheaters had not been caught.[77]

On May 3, defense counsel formally petitioned the Secretary of the Army to dissolve the Honor Boards composed of cadets, and convene instead a closed board of inquiry at the Secretary of the Army level or higher. The counsel also requested that immunity be granted to all cadets testifying to this outside board. Counsel argued that the Cadet Honor Boards were not the appropriate vehicle for investigation because they were corrupt and biased. Counsel felt strongly that its clients would be made scapegoats for a massive cheating wave that would never be fully investigated by Cadet Honor Boards.[78] Attached to their request, counsel enclosed a series of sworn statements by cadets giving examples of Honor Board corrupt practices and undisclosed Honor Code violations (see Exhibit 5).

Upon receiving the request, the Secretary of the Army, Martin Hoffmann, was forced to involve himself in the incident. Hoffmann was a civilian, but had the legal authority to intervene in West Point matters and overrule Berry's decisions. In fact, it was his duty to do so if he perceived that the viability of the Army was threatened. Subject to the direction and control of the President (as commander in chief) and the Secretary of Defense, he had responsibility and authority for the conduct of all affairs of the Department of the Army. (For a brief biography of Hoffmann, see Exhibit 6.) Usually, Hoffmann was reluctant to interfere in Army matters that could

---

[71] David W. Moore, "Revolution at West Point," *Boston Globe.*
[72] Rose, op. cit., p. 103.
[73] U.S.M.A., April 16 memo from Berry.
[74] U.S.M.A., April 22 memo from counsel to Berry.
[75] U.S.M.A. memo from Berry to counsel.
[76] *Times-Herald Record,* May 25, 1976.
[77] "Point Official Gets Cover-up Charge," *Times-Herald Record,* May 29, 1976.
[78] From the formal petition to the Secretary of the Army by attorneys of the accused cadets.

EXHIBIT 5   CADET AFFIDAVITS GIVING EXAMPLES OF CORRUPT PRACTICES AND HONOR VIOLATIONS*

Examples of honor board corrupt practices

I, *(name), (company),* class of 1977, wish to make the following sworn statement. I have personal knowledge of the following events:

About one week prior to the boards, cadets were seeing the president of the board, *(name),* class of 1976, who was president of about 18 boards to ask him if the board could be weighed toward an innocent vote.

Through my personal observation, the following individuals requested from the president, *(name),* that he do all he could for them to be found innocent:

> *(name),* class of 1977
> *(name),* class of 1977

I had an Honor Board and I found out that *(name)* was going to be my president, so I asked him if he would help me out. I was subsequently found innocent.

I have personal knowledge of three individuals who had the power in their hands to give an innocent vote. They are:

> *(name)*
> *(name)*
> *(name)*

All of the above are honor reps.

Through indirect channels I heard that the honor reps were contacted by friends of those who were going up for boards that they be found innocent.

I don't know if all those other cadets actually made contact, but assumed they did.

I have personal knowledge of collaboration. The following names are:

> *(name)*
> *(name)*
> *(name)*

Examples of undisclosed cadet honor violations

I, *(name)* have personal knowledge of the following violations of the Cadet Honor Code:

(name), '77, used his cadet credit card while on leave in June 1974, to force people to take his personal check. He told these people that he was acting as an official agent of the United States Government and that they were required to take his personal check when supported by the credit card. *(name),* '77, was witness to the actual event. *(name)* related the incident to me. One night while on confinement, *(name)* went to Grant Hall with his card marked. His roommate, *(name)* '77, confronted him with the violation. *(name)* told him that if he reported him he would break him in half. *(name)* tolerated *(name's)* violation.

(name), '77, and I made numerous honor violations together while roommates, in cheating outright, lying, and violation of the absence card.

(name) and I left post *(date)* with our cards marked "on limits." As roommates we committed numerous violations, including coming back after taps on Homecoming Weekend, '75 and when stopped by a guard, we told him we were on weekend status. We related our story to *(name),* '77, who tolerated our violation and admitted to committing numerous violations with *(name),* particularly limits violations.

EXHIBIT 5   *(CONTINUED)*

(name), '77, tolerated my honor violation while on summer leave, June 1974. I had stolen parachute gear from the airborne detachment and sold it while on leave. *(name)* was aware of the source of the equipment I was selling.

(name), '77, and *(name),* '77, both lied as the *(offense)* disciplinary board in . . .

(name) tolerated my honor violation when I admitted to him of knowing of many cadets cheating in the EE 304 computer project. He later lied as to our conversation having ever taken place.

(name), '77, and I committed frequent limits violations together. *(name)* has relayed to me many incidents of known violations of the honor code within his company. For example, on the EE 304 computer project, he told me that of the 29 second classmen in his company only six did not collaborate. *(name)* has told me of many accounts of widespread cheating on . . .

---

* Cited from the cadets' defense counsel's official request to the Secretary of the Army for an impartial board of inquiry, May 3, 1976.

be handled by career officers, since he felt that they had a lifetime of relevant experience, which he did not have, to draw on.[79]

Concurrent with counsel's request to Hoffmann, Representative Melvin Price, chairman of the House Armed Services Committee, stated that his committee intended to thoroughly review the Honor Code and System at the Academy if those responsible did not do so.[80]

On May 19, Hoffmann informed Berry that he would respond to the request for independent hearings in whatever manner the superintendent felt was best.[81] Berry favored continuing the present proceedings, continuing to seek out evidence of additional violations and using the Cadet Honor Boards. That same day Hoffman denied the request for independent hearings.[82] The controversy increased. Congress, Hoffman, current cadets, Academy graduates, cadet counsel, the public press, and day-to-day routine operations in the face of deteriorating cadet and officer morale, all required Berry's immediate attention. (See Exhibit 7 for a brief chronology of the cheating investigation.)

CONGRESSIONAL ACTIONS

For Berry a major problem was having to react to repeated congressional requests for an independent investigation. Initially, a number of members of Congress, including Senator Adlai Stevenson, Senator Charles Percy, and Representative Edward Dirwinski, at the request of cadets and their relatives, asked that the cheating incident be

[79] From an interview with Michael T. Rose.
[80] Melvin Price's letter to Donald Rumsfeld on June 16.
[81] Berry's letter to graduates, June 10, 1976, p. 4.
[82] Ibid.

EXHIBIT 6 BIOGRAPHY OF MARTIN R. HOFFMANN*

Mr. Hoffmann was sworn in as the Secretary of the Army on August 5, 1975. Born April 20, 1932, Mr. Hoffmann was graduated from Princeton University in 1954 with an AB degree, and from the University of Virginia Law School, Charlottesville, in 1961 with an LLB degree. He was admitted to the District of Columbia bar in August 1961. An honor graduate of the field artillery officer candidate school in 1955, Mr. Hoffmann served 2½ years with the 101st Airborne Division, as aide-de-camp to General William Westmoreland.

Prior to becoming Secretary of the Army, Mr. Hoffmann's government service included tenures as general counsel of the Department of Defense, special assistant to the Secretary of Defense and Deputy Secretary of Defense, and general counsel to the Atomic Energy Commission.

* From published proceedings of Subcommittee on Manpower and Personnel, Armed Services Committee, U.S. Senate, August 23, 1976.

thoroughly investigated by a congressional committee.[83] Senator Barry Goldwater asked for a full investigation as an outgrowth of his concern that the Academy was pressuring cadets into resigning without appeal. Independent congressional requests for a complete investigation (and an Honor System change, if necessary) were channeled to the U.S. Armed Services military personnel subcommittee, which began initial investigations. As evidence of improprieties mounted, requests for action moved from the House of Senator Nunn, chairman of the Subcommittee on Manpower and Personnel of the Armed Services Committee, to Representative Melvin Price, chairman of the Armed Services Committee. Price, in turn, recommended to both the Secretary of Defense, Donald H. Rumsfeld, and Hoffmann that they appoint a "high-level, blue-ribbon panel of inquiry to look into various facets of the operation of the Military Academy, including the Honor Code System."[84] This panel would consist of civilians with no stake in West Point matters and could therefore be the most objective.[85] (The head of the panel ultimately established was Frank Borman, a West Point graduate with two sons who attended the Academy. His appointment raised the questions of whether the panel could be entirely objective.)

PRESS PROBLEMS

Another problem area that Berry faced was the press. Every day major newspapers and magazines ran stories, summarized new findings, and supplied editorial comment. Many of the books written about West Point in the last 50 years were being recirculated and reread. Berry wondered if and how he should respond to the articles and public comment. Exhibit 8 contains a sample of typical commentary illustrating the different viewpoints being circulated at the time of the incident.

[83] "West Point Cadet Faces New Charges: His Congressman Demand an Inquiry," *The New York Times,* Apr. 28, 1976.

[84] Melvin Price's June 16, 1976, letter to Donald Rumsfeld.

[85] See, for example, Senator Bartlett's (Oklahoma) address to the Senate, 94th Congress, 2d session, Sept. 21, 1976.

EXHIBIT 7   CHRONOLOGY OF THE 1976 CHEATING INVESTIGATION

March 3–4	Department of Electrical Engineering issued the first of two parts of a home-study problem to approximately 823 cadets of the class of 1977 in the required course EE 304.
March 17–18	Mandatory turn-in dates for part 1 of home-study problem. 823 cadets turned in problem for grades.
March 19	Generally, each EE 304 instructor commenced grading of students' home-study problems. However, an instructor in EE 304, while grading papers, suspected possible unauthorized collaboration between two cadets. The head of the Department of Electrical Engineering was notified.
March 24–25	The head of the Department of Electrical Engineering directed the assembly and review of all EE 304 home-study problems on a company basis to determine the extent of unauthorized collaboration.
April 5	Commandant of cadets decided to refer EE 304 cases to Cadet Honor Committee for investigation.
April 6	Subcommittee hearings of 117 cases commenced and completed. As a result of these hearings, 101 cases were referred to the Cadet Honor Committee for full hearings. Fifteen cases were not referred and one cadet resigned.
April 21	Cadet Honor Committee hearings substantially completed. Fifty cadets found to have violated the Honor Code by unauthorized collaboration. Fifty cadets wre exonerated, and one cadet resigned.
May 3	Request for convening of an impartial board of inquiry by counsel for the respondents to the Secretary of the Army. Counsel informed the superintendent that 300–600 cadets were implicated in the cheating scandal.
May 19	Reply from the Secretary of the Army denying counsel for respondents' request for convening an impartial board of inquiry. Attorneys encouraged to offer matters raised for consideration by regularly appointed boards of officers.
May 20	EE 304 review team began to review all 823 papers, first on a company-by-company basis, and later on various associational and organizational lines, such as varsity teams, clubs, etc.
May 21	Government counsel (prosecution) informs the superintendent that 300–400 cadets could be referred to boards of officers and, if properly investigated, that as many as 600 cadets may be involved.
May 23	Superintendent selected a permanent professor to head up a five-man internal review panel to investigate and determine whether there is sufficient cause to refer additional cases to a board of officers.

* Compiled from District Court Civil Proceedings (see footnote 4), Defense Council.

WEST POINT OFFICER REACTIONS

Berry faced a concerned but divided West Point officer corps. West Point officers could be split into two camps. The senior officers, the commandant, and the rest of the tactical officers were generally adamant that the Honor Code and System be maintained in its present form and that the alleged cheaters be tried by Cadet Honor Boards and expelled if guilty.[86] Conversely, the 300 junior officer instructors in the

[86] "Point Code Revision at Least a Year Away," *Times-Herald Record*, May 22, 1976.

EXHIBIT 8   SAMPLES OF PUBLISHED COMMENTARY

Articles suggested the idea that cheating on the electrical engineering examination was a common occurence.

> For the record, there have been three publicized scandals at West Point in the last 25 years. In 1951, 90 cadets were dismissed, 37 of them were members of the football team. In 1966, 42 cadets were dismissed; and in 1973, 21 cadets were separated. Simple deduction suggests that the EE 304 exam could not have been the first time these cadets cheated. Since the exam was only 5% of their grade and had no bearing, it is reasonable to assume that the offenders had cheated before and were quite sure they wouldn't get caught. The scandal was brought to light not because the cheating itself was an isolated event but because the rigorous search for duplicate answers and cheating by the professors was an uncommon occurrence.

> Former West Point Instructor
> *Esquire,* Nov. 1976

Articles looked at the Honor System as the cause of the problems.

> That the administration at West Point can condone a system of discipline that actually promotes the potential for man's inhumanity to man is unbelievable. The entire system seems not only repressive, undemocratic, and physically dangerous but shamefully adolescent as well. The fine image of the Academy is being destroyed by the ones who are commissioned to protect it. If the image is to be restored, this system which is not only archaic and unrealistic but apparently corrupt as well, must be cut out immediately.

> *The New York Times,* May 19, 1976

> [one must] understand the dangers of a military establishment that clings to two mistaken traditions: the notion that the soldier can only emerge after the destruction of the man; and the belief that the pure image of the corps' honor justifies any strategy that prevents public exposure of military wrongdoing.
>
>   The authorities at West Point and in the Pentagon apparently need to be reminded that a democracy cannot condone totalitarian brutality in the name of military conditioning. The greatest threat to honor at West Point is a cover-up of dishonorable policies.

> *The New York Times,* May 12, 1976

> Increases in size and heterogeneity of the student body have distorted the ability of the cadets to assimilate the ethical guidelines to the degree of respect required to follow the honor code unhesitatingly. With the establishment of the system, the framework of the code began to disappear beneath the weight of the machinery erected to administer the enforcement of the code.

> A Second Classman
> *Cadet Study Report of Honor System*

> [Rejection of the Honor System] is caused by the rigid, idealistic character of the conduct, honor, and ethics systems which require cadets to adhere to inflexible ethical standards and notions of honor which far exceed those generally accepted by the remainder of society. . . .
>
>   Newly entering cadets are far more "abstract" than their predecessors. They are more open-minded and flexible; have increased tolerance of ambiguity, increased creativity under stress, greater ability to think and act in terms of hypothetical situations; and are less prone to form and generalize impressions of others from incomplete information. . . .
>
>   Such cadets are more likely to be resistant to arbitrarily imposed rules, procedures, and standards of honor and justice. At least some degree of cynicism and lack of acceptance

EXHIBIT 8   *(CONTINUED)*

must be attributable to the cadets' perceptions of injustice and unnecessary inflexibility in the academy's Honor System.

Air Force Academy Graduate
A Prayer for Relief (see footnote 10)

Many commentators noted that the public behavior of notable West Pointers in the early 1970s may have had an affect on Academy graduates.

What lessons are impressionable cadets to draw from the remarkable career of Alexander Haig? Haig retired from the military to become Richard Nixon's principal aide and ardent defender in the later cover-up years. In Nixon's final days Haig adroitly moved to save himself and help unseat an obviously doomed Commander-in-Chief. . . . Some, such as Major General Samuel Koster, who resigned as West Point Superintendent because of involvement in the cover-up of the My Lai massacre, brought particular discredit to the Academy.

Authors of a Book about West Point
New Republic, June 1976

Other commentators placed the blame on Vietnam veterans serving as officers at West Point.

. . . the way of the Army in Vietnam—falsifying body counts, illegally barraging hamlets and villages, covering-up atrocities, covering-up what would eventually be revealed as a massive drug problem among American troops over there—that way of life was carried back to West Point on the shoulders of graduates and translated this way: If you could lie, cover-up, and generally do bad in combat in Vietnam, then why not at West Point? . . .
These officers abused the Honor Code or used it against the cadets to maintain discipline. Cadets became disillusioned. They felt the Honor Code was applied to the cadets but not to the officers who administered the Academy. Cadets cheat because it feels good.

Former Cadet
Patterson Foundation Newsletter (see footnote 14)

Finally, other writers concentrated on explaining the apparent cover-up:

. . . cadets develop a sense of moral superiority after being told repeatedly by academy officials that they are the cream of the crop of American youth and that their experience with the honor and ethics systems furnishes them with moral training far superior to that afforded their peers at similar colleges. As a result cadets come to view themselves as moral standard bearers for the rest of the nation. This superiority attitude is coupled with a super-loyalty attitude which begins with the academy's efforts at creating an intense cohesiveness among members of their respective cadet corps. This emphasis on the development of a strong sense of brotherhood and community leads to the cadets' internalization of an intense loyalty to their academy and to the military in general. Thereafter. . .the cadets come to perceive loyalty to the country they serve as loyalty to each other and to the military—the defender of the country.

Air Force Academy Graduate
A Prayer for Relief (see footnote 10)

. . .the United States Army's obsession with image borders on institutional paranoia.

Chaplain (Colonel) Kermit D. Johnson
CDRS Call (Army Newsletter)

academic departments believed that the Honor System, and indeed the strong emphasis on military instead of academic training, was often counterproductive in producing capable military officers.[87]

In a May 1976 press conference, a spokesman for the pro–Honor System officers, Commandant Walter F. Ulmann, forcefully asserted:

- The West Point Honor Code is alive and well, although there are some flaws and some points of illness.
- If it ever died, the Academy would die with it.
- I do not believe cheating at the Academy is widespread. What we have here is a very selective violation of the Code.
- The System is essential to a military career.[88]

Junior faculty members, at the same time, asserted that "the class of '77 was not unique. We are seeing only the tip of the cheating iceberg."[89] Junior faculty believed that the Honor Board investigations would be insufficient and that it was the "failure of the Academy constituencies to agree on the relative importance of the educational components of the mission that had hindered the development of an academic atmosphere which discourages dishonesty."[90] The junior faculty believed that academics should have priority over military training, at least from September to May, and viewed the cheating scandal as an opportunity to push the Academy toward adopting a more academic emphasis.[91]

Berry, however, had the task of appeasing both junior faculty officers and senior tactical officers. His failure to do so would promote a further deterioration of officer morale and support, both of which Berry needed in order to return West Point to its normal operations.

LEGAL PROCEEDINGS

Berry was also concerned with pending legal action against the Academy. Cadets fighting the Academy in court were a unique experience for the superintendent and the Academy. A West Point graduate writing about the uniqueness of the situation stated:

> The current scandal is significant . . . [because] rather than submit, the guilty are challenging the Academy in court. This cavalier disregard for the honor system and unprecedented challenge of the Academy's authority by so many third-year cadets, who next year were to be leaders of the corps, suggests an atmosphere of rebellion that is indeed profound.
>
> The widespread and deliberate rejection of a tradition as important as the honor code is no minor aberration. It is mass revolution.[92]

[87] For example, Borman Report, pp. 71–75.
[88] *Times-Herald Record,* May 25, 1976.
[89] Borman Report, p. 3.
[90] Ibid., p. 11.
[91] "Military Honor Code at a Crossroads," *Sunday Record,* Middletown, N.Y., May 23, 1976; and Borman Report, pp. 73–74.
[92] Moore, op. cit.

Berry was aware that the defense counsel was continuing to fight for hearings from an independent body. One of the 10 defense lawyers, who refused to be identified, exclaimed:

> The suggestion that the lawyers submit their allegations of widespread cheating and bad-faith practices by the cadet honor committees to the honor committee themselves . . . is ludicrous. It's a perfect Catch-22. Obviously, we are not going to take our charges to these agencies because they are who we are accusing of initiating or condoning the wrongdoing.[93]

The defense counsel was to provide evidence of the fact that virtually every cadet in the junior class was guilty of some violation of the Honor Code. Their plan was to force the Academy either to prosecute hundreds of alleged honor violations, thus potentially decimating the corps' rising senior class, or to acquit everyone on the grounds that the Honor Code was unenforceable.[94] Berry also faced the prospect of a court determining that the Honor Code proceedings were unconstitutional. As far back as 1961, the judge advocate general of the Navy had publicly stated that when it was achieved, fairness in such Honor Committee proceedings came "in spite of the procedures employed which can only be described, at best, as poorly designed to assist . . . in discovering the truth of the allegation.[95] The president of the New York State Criminal Courts Association stated that the association would initiate formal hearings into the legal protection of cadets.[96]

OTHER PROBLEMS

Berry also faced pressure from the graduates of West Point. Most graduates still believed that the Honor Code and the Honor System were critical to a successful military. General William Westmoreland (class of 1936) summarized the majority of the graduates' views when he said:

> . . . the school's honor code is immutable. I am disappointed with the country's deteriorating morality which is affecting us now.[97]

Presidential candidate Jimmy Carter received thunderous applause when he began his speech to the 1976 American Legion National Convention by stating:

> We will not lie, cheat or steal, nor tolerate among us those who do.
>   These words comprise the ancient code of honor which was adopted and still is used by the military academies and which recently has been questioned as being too strict and rigid for the future leaders of our armed forces.
>   Is this too strict a code for cadets? I think not. Is this too strict a code for senior military officers who defend our country? I think not. Is this too strict a code for any public officer who serves our nation? I think not.[98]

[93] "Study Sought by West Point Legal Staff Is Ruled Out by Secretary," *The New York Times,* May 20, 1976.
[94] "Accused Cadets to Involve Hundreds of Classmates," *The New York Times,* May 26, 1976.
[95] Rose, op. cit., p. 41.
[96] "Bar Moves into West Point Scandal," *Times-Herald Record,* May 26, 1976.
[97] *Times-Herald Record,* May 29, 1976.
[98] Opening lines of presidential candidate Jimmy Carter to the 1976 American Legion Convention.

Berry sent a letter to every living West Point graduate in the early stages of the scandal assuring them that the situation was limited in scope and under control (see Exhibit 4). All that they read in the popular press implied that that was not the case. Berry knew that any action he took limiting or changing the Honor Code or System would be viewed negatively by most graduates. Moreover, a large number of graduates were expected at West Point during the week of May 26 for graduation ceremonies and reunions. They would arrive expecting answers and assurances.

As more and more cadets were implicated in the scandal, Berry realized he faced a further problem. The students on cadet honor boards at a time of the year close to final exams, were being forced to spend a major part of their time trying other cadets. It appeared as if every cadet in the junior class was either a judge or defendant. Berry commented on this problem:

> The emergence of increasing new numbers made it painfully obvious that due process, speed, and thoroughness were about to be overwhelmed by the administrative magnitude of the case.[99]

Berry realized that, at its present rate, the entire investigation could take a year, providing a continuing flow of bad press and preventing the Academy from returning to a state of normalcy.[100] Furthermore, it was becoming clear that the verdicts of the Honor Board would probably be challenged by the courts and the general public due to questions of the board's legal legitimacy and impartiality.[101] Finally, the superintendent realized that there was a good chance that, unless he took decisive action, Secretary of the Army Hoffmann would become directly involved in resolving the problems and would remove Berry from the decision-making process. Hoffmann was already spending more and more time at West Point, personally interviewing key witnesses.[102] Although Hoffmann publicly supported Berry's decision to continue normal Honor Board proceedings, he had privately urged Berry to call in an outside agency to investigate the cadet Honor System—someone who understood the Academy, but who still could remain independent in the public eye to stifle any suggestion of a cover-up.[103]

Berry realized that the lives of many cadets, the future of the Honor Code and Honor System, his career, and the future of the Academy itself could well depend on his decisions. He stated to a *Time* magazine reporter:

> I do not think the code is anachronistic. Integrity is essential to the development of leader officers. The honor code fosters integrity.
>
>   I have never been in more of a combat situation than I am now. There are things that make me heartsick in the whole situation—so many young men may have violated the honor code. But, by God, I've been heartsick in battle and done what I had to do.[104]

---

[99] Berry's letter of June 10, 1976.
[100] Berry's letter of August 26, 1976 to faculty and administration.
[101] Borman Report, p. 25.
[102] Martin Hoffmann, Senate Hearings on Academy Honor Codes, vol. I, June 21, 1976, p. 8.
[103] "Get Outsider to Probe Honor System," *Times-Herald Record*, May 20, 1976.
[104] *Time*, June 7, 1976, p. 24.

PROCESS OBSERVATION

John J. Gabarro
Anne Harlan

"A camel is a horse put together by a committee" is a cliché that is frequently applied to group decisionmaking. What is it that makes so many groups inefficient, slow, and frustrating, instead of effectively combining the insights and expertise of its members? To some extent, the answer may be found in the formal group design. Perhaps the people chosen were not the ones who should have been included in such a group, or perhaps the group goal was simply unattainable. More often, however, the difficulties encountered have less to do with the content of task issues than with the *group process,* or how the group is going about achieving its formal task.

Because each group member is an individual, he or she bears certain expectations, assumptions, and feelings —about not only his or her own role but also the roles of other group members. As a result of these expectations, certain patterns of relating to others in the group develop. These patterns may become beneficial or detrimental to the group's purpose. Spotting the detrimental patterns is the first key to understanding and improving the functioning of any group; but often these patterns are hard to identify because you cannot see inside each person's mind. For instance, how do you know that everyone understands what the agenda is, or that person X understands it but is likely to deviate from it if he can, or whether person X has the leverage to change the agenda if he wants to? While you cannot see inside another person's mind, you can develop a greater awareness of what is and what is not likely to happen in a group, and of what the group is or is not capable of doing at a given meeting by being attentive to what is happening among group members while the group is working.

Being able to observe and understand a group's process is important for two reasons. First, it enables you to understand what is taking place covertly as well as overtly in the group's behavior. Secondly, it can provide you with insight into what you and others can do to make group interaction more productive.

Below are listed seven aspects of group behavior that can furnish valuable clues as to how effectively a group is functioning. It is unlikely that all aspects are relevant to your concerns at a given time or that you can attend to them all simultaneously. However, the more you are to observe and assess them, the more likely it is that you will spot potential difficulties early and act on them to improve group effectiveness.

PARTICIPATION

Participation (who participates, how often, when, and to what effect) is the easiest aspect of the group process to observe. Typically, people who are higher in status, more knowledgeable, or simply more talkative by nature tend to participate more actively; those who are less experienced, lower in status, uninformed, or who are not inclined to express their feelings and ideas verbally generally speak less frequently. Even in groups composed of people of equal status and competence, some people speak more than others; this variation is to be expected, and is not necessarily a sign of an ineffective group. However, when *large* disparities exist between the contributions of individual members, it is usually a clue that the process is not effective— particularly when individuals or coalitions dominate group discussion.

There are many reasons why unequal participation can reduce group effectiveness. Low participators often have good ideas to offer but are reluctant to do so, or they cannot contribute their ideas because they are squeezed out by high participators who dominate the meeting. This imbalance can be a potential problem when we consider that those ideas that receive the most "air time" inevitably become the ones that are most seriously considered when it is time to make a decision. Considerable research has shown that the most frequently stated ideas tend to be adopted by the group, *regardless of their quality*. Maier calls this the "valence" effect; it is one of the reasons why groups often make poor decisions. Thus, large imbalances in participation can result in potentially good ideas being underrepresented in the discussion, lost by the wayside, or perhaps not even expressed.

Another negative consequence of uneven participation, which is borne out by common sense as well as by research, is that low participators are likely to tune out, lose commitment to the task or become frustrated and angry (especially if they have tried to enter the discussion but have been ignored or cut off by high participators). These negative attitudes result not only in poorer quality decisions, but also in less commitment to implementing the group's decision.

Several factors contribute to uneven participation. One factor is that people who have the most at stake in a given issue (and may thus be the least objective) are more motivated to participate than those who may simply have better ideas to offer. Another factor is that different people have different internal standards on which they judge whether or not an idea they have is worth offering to the group. Thus, people with higher internal standards may be less apt to contribute than those with lower internal standards, with negative consequences for the quality of group discussion.

A marked change in a person's participation during a meeting is also a clue that something important may be going on. If a person suddenly becomes silent or withdraws during part of a meeting, it could suggest a number of possibilities, depending on the person's nonverbal behavior. For example, it might simply mean that the person has temporarily withdrawn to mull over the comments of a previous speaker. It may also be that the person has "tuned out" and has lost interest. Or, it may be a sign of hostility or frustration. Whatever the case, it is a sign that something is "off."

Some questions to consider in observing participation include the following:

1 Who are the high participators? Why? To what effect?

2 Who are the low participators? Why? To what effect?

3 Are there any shifts in participators: for example, an active participator suddenly becoming silent? Do you see any reason for this in the group's interaction, such as a criticism from a higher-status person or a shift in topic? Is it a sign of withdrawal?

4 How are silent people treated? Is their silence taken by others to mean consent? Disagreement? Disinterest? Why do you think they are silent?

5 Who talks to whom? Who responds to whom? Do participation patterns reflect coalitions that are impeding or controlling the discussion? Are the interaction patterns consistently excluding certain people who need to be supported or brought into the discussion?

6 Who keeps the discussion going? How is this accomplished? Why does that person want the discussion to continue in that vein?

Interventions

A number of simple and unobtrusive process interventions can be made by the group leader or a group member to bring about a better balance in participation. These interventions are particularly important if you observe that potentially valuable minority views are not getting their share of time, that certain people have not had a chance to develop their ideas fully, or that some group members seem removed from the discussion. One intervention is to try to *clarify* a point made earlier that seemed to "fall through the cracks"; for example, you could return to someone's point by saying something like "Tom, let me see if I understood what you said a moment ago." A related technique is simply to reinforce a previous point by asking the person to elaborate on it, for example, "Sue, I was interested in what you were saying earlier. Can you elaborate on it a bit more?" Similarly, a very direct technique for drawing out silent people is to simply *query* them, for example, "Mary, you haven't said a word during this discussion. What are your ideas on it?" Or a direct comment can be made, such as "We've heard a lot from the marketing people, but very little from production scheduling. What do you guys think about the problem?"

INFLUENCE

Influence and participation are not the same thing. Some people may speak very little, yet capture the attention of the whole group. Others may talk frequently but their words go unheard. Influence, like participation, is often a function of status, experience, competence and, to some degree, personality. It is normal for some people to have greater influence on a group's process than others, and this fact is not necessarily a sign that a group is ineffective. However, when one individual or subgroup has so much influence on a discussion that others' ideas are rejected out of hand, it is usually a clue that the group's effectiveness will suffer and that the discussion will fail to probe alternatives in depth. This imbalance is particularly dangerous when minority views are systematically squelched without adequate exploration.

An asymmetrical influence can have a number of negative consequences on group effectiveness. As we have already noted, it can result in the suppression of potentially valuable minority views, it can contribute to imbalanced participation, and it inevitably results in hostility and lack of commitment by group members who feel that they have been "muscled out." As with participation, considerable research on group behavior and alienation shows that the more influence people feel they have had on a group's discussion, the more committed they are likely to be to its decisions, regardless of whether their own point of view has been adopted by the group.

One way of checking relative influence is to watch the reactions of other group members. Someone who has influence is not only likely to have others listening attentively, but is also less likely to be interrupted or challenged by others. He or she may also be seated at or near the head of the table or near the center of a subgroup.

Struggles for influence and leadership often characterize the early stages of a group's life, especially in temporary groups such as task forces, project teams, or committees. To some extent, these struggles occur in most groups, although usually in a mild, covert fashion. Vying for leadership can become a problem, however, when it disrupts the group's ability to deal with the task at hand. The disruption occurs when being dominant is an important need for those who are vying for leadership. Under these circumstances, the competition takes place in a *sub rosa* fashion with one person disagreeing with the other because of his or her need to establish dominance, regardless of the relative merits of the other's arguments. The hidden agenda then becomes "scoring points" rather than working on the problem. Frequently, two people engaged in such a power struggle are not even aware of their hidden motives and genuinely think that they are arguing about the problem at hand.

In assessing influence patterns within a group, you may find the following questions useful:

1 Which members are listened to when they speak? What ideas are they expressing?

2 Which members are ignored when they speak? Why? What are their ideas? Is the group losing valuable inputs simply because these members are not being heard?

3 Are there any shifts in influence? Who shifts? Why?

4 Is there any rivalry within the group? Are there struggles between individuals or subgroups for leadership?

5 Who interrupts whom? Does this reflect relative power within the group?

6 Are minority views consistently ignored regardless of possible merit?

Interventions

If you observe that the opinions of an individual or subgroup of people appear to be unduly influencing group progress, several brief interventions can open up the discussion. One strategy is simply to *support* or *reinforce* the views of minority members, for example, "I think there is some merit to what Jane was saying earlier and I'd like to elaborate on it," or "I think that we're not giving enough thought to Jane and Sam's position and I think we should explore it further before dropping it." Another intervention is to actually *point out* that the opinions of certain people are dominating the discussion, for example, "Mary, you've made your point quite forcefully and clearly, but I'd also like to hear the other side of the question before we go further." Similarly, another technique is to ask the group *to open up* the discussion, for example, "So far we've spent a lot of time talking about Jane and Bill's proposal, but I'd like to hear some differing opinions," or "The managers seem to agree strongly on what needs to be done, but I'd like to hear more about what the customer representatives think are the problems."

GROUP CLIMATE

Group members bring with them many assumptions of how groups in general should function and how their particular group should function. Frequently, these expectations or assumptions are quite different from one member to another. One person may feel that the way for a group to work effectively is to be "strictly business"—an absence of socializing and tight leader control over the group. Another may feel the only way a group can work creatively is to give each person equal time for suggestions, to meet informally, and to have relatively loose leadership. Still others may have different preferences. After group members have tested each others' assumptions early in this history of the group, a *climate* or *atmosphere* becomes established that may or may not facilitate effective group functioning. Different group climates are effective in different situations; and what is good for one situation isn't necessarily good for another.

For example, if a problem demands a creative, new solution and the collaboration of a number of different experts (such as on a task force problem), then a climate of openness in which everyone has an equal opportunity to participate will be most effective. In other situations, however, a more competitive or structured group climate might encourage a higher-quality solution, especially if expertise is not distributed equally among all group members. To gauge a group's climate, you should observe:

1 Do people prefer to maintain a friendly, congenial discussion? Or do they prefer conflict and disagreement?

2 Do people seem involved and interested? Is the atmosphere one of work? Play? Competition? Avoidance?

3 Is there any attempt to suppress conflict or unpleasant feelings by avoiding tough issues?

For most task groups, an unstructured, *laissez faire* or conflict-smoothing climate is ineffective. It results in important issues and conflicts not being explored sufficiently, and the quality of group work is sacrificed for the maintenance of friendly, smooth relations. Conversely, a highly structured climate can impede effective problem solving because members do not allow each other enough freedom to explore alternatives or consider creative solutions. A highly competitive climate can also be dysfunctional; competition can preclude thoughtful deliberation and exchange, resulting in failure to build on other people's ideas.

Interventions

Intervening to alter a group's climate is more difficult than the previous interventions described. It can be done, however, by reinforcing and supporting desirable behavior, as well as by raising the issue directly. For example, if a group is smoothing conflicts and avoiding important problems, a useful intervention would be, "We seem to have a lot of agreement, but I wonder if we have really tackled some of the tougher underlying issues, such as . . ." When a group seems to be bound by its own structure, a comment as simple as the following frequently suffices: "I think that maybe we're looking at the problem too narrowly and it might be useful to consider whether we should also consider X, which isn't in the agenda but seems to have relevance to what we're talking about."

MEMBERSHIP

A major concern for group members is their degree of acceptance or inclusion in the group. Different patterns of interaction may develop in the group, providing clues to the degree and kind of membership:

1 Is there any subgrouping? Sometimes two or three members may consistently agree and support each other or may consistently disagree and oppose one another.
2 Do some people seem to be "outside" the group? Do some members seem to be "inside" the group? How are those "outside" treated?
3 Do some members move physically in and out of the group, for example, lean forward or backward in their chairs, or move their chairs in and out? Under what conditions do they come in or move out?

The problem of "in-groups" and "out-groups" is closely related to the earlier discussion of influence within a group. The interventions described earlier—supporting, querying, and opening up the discussion—are also useful for bringing in marginal members.

FEELINGS

During any group discussion, feelings are frequently generated by the interactions between members. These feelings, however, are seldom talked about. Observers may have to make guesses based on tone of voice, facial expressions, gestures, and other nonverbal cues.

1 What signs of feelings (anger, irritation, frustration, warmth, affection, excitement, boredom, defensiveness, competitiveness, etc.) do you observe in group members?

2 Are group members overly nice or polite to each other? Are only positive feelings expressed? Do members agree with each other too readily? What happens when members disagree?

3 Do you see norms operating about participation or the kinds of questions that are allowed, for example, "If I talk, you must talk"? Do members feel free to probe each other about their feelings? Do questions tend to be restricted to intellectual topics or events outside the group?

Most groups in business develop norms that allow only the expression of positive feelings or feelings of disagreement as compared to anger. The problem with suppression of strong negative feelings is that these feelings usually resurface later. For example, a person who is angered by someone in a meeting may seek revenge later in the discussion by disagreeing with that person or by criticizing his or her idea regardless of its merit. The hidden motive becomes revenge and the person pursues it by resisting ideas, showing stubbornness, or derailing the discussion. This retaliation is usually disguised in terms of substantive issues and often has an element of irrationality to it. Often it is more effective to bring out the person's anger in the first place and deal with it when it first occurs.

TASK FUNCTIONS

For any group to function adequately and make maximum progress on a task, certain task functions must be carried out. First of all, there must be *initiation;* that is, the problem or goals must be stated, time limits ordained, and some agenda agreed upon. This function most frequently falls to the leader, but may be taken on by other group members. Next, there must be *opinion seeking and giving,* and *information seeking and giving,* on various issues related to the task. One major problem affecting group decision quality and commitment is that groups tend to spend insufficient time in these phases. *Clarification and elaboration* are vital not only for effective communication but also for creative solutions. *Summarization* includes a review of ideas to be followed by *consensus testing,* that is, ensuring that all the ideas are on the table and that the group is ready to enter into an evaluation of the various ideas produced. The most effective groups follow this order rather than the more common procedure of evaluating each idea or alternative as it is discussed. Different group members may take on these task functions, but each must be covered:

1 Are suggestions made as to the best way to proceed or tackle the problem?

2 Is there a summary of what has been covered? How effectively is this done? Who does it?

3 Is there any giving or asking for information, opinions, feelings, feedback, or searching for alternatives?

4 How is the group kept on target? Is topic-jumping or going off on tangents prevented or discouraged?

5 Are all ideas presented before evaluation begins? What happens if someone begins to evaluate an idea as soon as it is produced?

MAINTENANCE FUNCTIONS

Groups cannot function effectively if cohesion is low or if relationships among group members become strained. In the life of any group, there will be periods of conflict, dissension, and misunderstanding. It is the purpose of maintenance functions to rebuild damaged relations and bring back harmony to the group. Without these processes, group members can become alienated, resulting in the loss of valuable resources.

Two maintenance activities that can serve to prevent these kinds of problems are *gate-keeping*, which ensures that members wanting to make a contribution are given the opportunity to do so, and *encouragement*, which helps create a climate of acceptance. *Compromise* and *harmony* are activities that have limited usefulness to the actual task accomplishment, but are sometimes useful in repairing strained relations.

When the level of conflict in a group is so high that effective communication is impaired, it is often useful for the group to suspend the task discussion and examine its own processes to define and attempt to solve the conflicts. The following questions focus attention on a group's maintenance functions:

1 Are group members encouraged to enter into the discussion?

2 How well do members relate their ideas? Are some members preoccupied and inattentive? Are there any attempts by group members to help others clarify their ideas?

3 How are ideas rejected? How do members react when their ideas are rejected?

4 Are conflicts among group members ignored or dealt with in some way?

PROCESS OBSERVATION AND FEEDBACK

This note has covered several aspects of group process that can influence group effectiveness. The suggested interventions are relatively simple and can be made naturally and unobtrusively during the normal progress of a meeting. The more people in a group skilled at making process observations, the greater the likelihood that the group will not "bog down," waste valuable time, or make poor decisions. For this reason, an increasing number of U.S. and foreign firms have developed norms that encourage open discussion of group process. In many companies, meetings end with a brief feedback session on group process, during which a meeting's effectiveness is critiqued by group members.

It is not necessary, however, to be in such a firm or to use such terms as "process feedback" to contribute to group effectiveness. Most of the ideas presented in this note rest on common sense; their practice does not require use of jargon, or even the terms used here. It is the underlying ideas rather than the specific labels, such as "task" and "maintenance" functions that matter.

SOME ASPECTS OF PROBLEM SOLVING AND CONFLICT RESOLUTION IN MANAGEMENT GROUPS

James Ware

We have seen that management groups deal with organizational problems in a wide variety of ways. Clearly, some styles of problem solving are more effective than others, and some management groups are much more capable of handling and resolving internal conflict than others. Because group decisionmaking is so common in organizations, effective managers must be highly skilled at influencing group processes.

The purpose of this note is to review several characteristics of managerial groups that enhance and detract from their problem-solving effectiveness, and to describe the most common ways in which groups deal with conflict. The previous reading has suggested specific guidelines for managing meetings and task force projects productively, and for observing important aspects of group processes. Here we consider more systematically how styles of problem solving and conflict resolution affect the nature and quality of group decisions. We also look more explicitly at the dynamics of interdepartmental conflict, since most important organizational problems involve two or more departments with differing goals, priorities, and needs. Although many of the ideas covered here refer primarily to interactions in face-to-face meetings, the same processes generally apply to group behavior over extended periods of time.

STRENGTHS AND WEAKNESSES OF GROUPS AS PROBLEM SOLVERS[1]

Group problem solving has some distinct advantages over individual problem solving in organizations. However, it also has several disadvantages. First, let us consider

---

[1] This section draws heavily, although not exclusively, on "Assets and Liabilities and Group Problem Solving," by Norman R. E. Maier, *Psychological Review,* vol. 74, no. 4, July 1967, pp. 239–249.

the most compelling reasons for using a management group to deal with organizational problems:

1 *Diversity of problem-solving styles*   Different people have different ways of thinking about problems. Although almost any problem can be viewed from several different perspectives, most of us tend to develop relatively fixed patterns of thinking. Some people, such as engineers and accountants, tend to rely on highly quantitative techniques. Other people, such as architects and designers, think more graphically, using pictures and diagrams. Still others, such as entrepreneurs and commodity traders, tend to rely more on feelings and intuition about what will work in a given situation.

Individual problem solvers too often get into "ruts" that prevent them from seeing other productive ways of dealing with a particular problem. When people with different styles interact with each other in a group, however, they can stimulate each other to try new ways of approaching a problem.

2 *Greater knowledge and information*   Individuals also bring different specialized knowledge and current experiences to a problem-solving discussion. Even when some group members are much more highly skilled or formally educated than others, the diversity of knowledge, skills, and thinking styles in a group can lead to more innovative solutions than the "experts" could produce working alone. For example, a sales manager who has worked closely with customers may be able to suggest very creative product design modifications that simply would not have occurred to a product engineer.

Furthermore, if group members exchange their tentative ideas as they explore the problem and possible solutions, they can challenge and improve each other's thinking. During a group discussion, one person's comment often triggers a new idea for someone else. This process of sharing and building increases both the number and the quality of solution ideas.

3 *Greater understanding and commitment*   When people are involved in the deliberations that lead to a decision, they clearly understand the problem more thoroughly. Furthermore, even if they disagree with the ultimate decision, they are more likely to accept it if they have had an opportunity to express their disagreement during the decision process. Participation is one of the major reasons that task forces are so often successful in achieving major organizational changes.

These are powerful reasons for having groups work on organizational problems. Unfortunately, however, many management groups develop patterns of behavior that seriously detract from their problem-solving effectiveness. Among the most important weaknesses of group problem solving are the following:

1 *Use of organizational resources*   Group decisionmaking clearly consumes more time and other resources than does individual problem solving. After all, a 1-hour meeting of eight people requires as much managerial time as one person working all day on the problem. Furthermore, it usually takes a significant amount of time for all group members to achieve an equal and adequate understanding of the problem. Each individual approaches the problem with a personal understanding and perspective; achieving agreement on the nature of the problem, let alone its solution, can be a very difficult and time-consuming process.

2 *Pressure to conform* Groups often develop such strong norms of conformity that members spend more time and energy figuring out the "party line" than they do analyzing a problem on its merits. Agreement becomes more important than being right, and conforming to the majority point of view becomes a requirement for remaining part of the group. Conformity is a particular danger in management groups whose members differ in their levels of authority, status, and power. It is especially difficult for less powerful members to confront or disagree with their organizational superiors.

Extensive research on group decisionmaking has repeatedly shown that the solution or argument mentioned most frequently in a group is almost always the one finally chosen, regardless of its validity. This "valence" effect is particularly pervasive in overly conforming groups. Solutions are often selected simply because they are repeated frequently, and no one suggests any viable alternatives.

3 *Advocacy and individual domination* Perhaps the most common weakness of problem-solving groups is their susceptibility to control by individuals or small coalitions. Decisionmaking turns into a contest in which winning becomes more important than being right. Individuals advocate their own points of view, vying for leadership to satisfy personal needs or to achieve organizational influence that benefits one group or department rather than the total organization.

Although a group discussion may appear to focus on substantive issues and the pros and cons of each alternative, at a deeper level the debates can and often do involve issues of power, prestige, and influence. If a domination attempt is being made on the basis of information or ideas directly related to the focal problem, the group may actually benefit. Often, however, those who argue the loudest and strongest do so precisely because of the logical weakness of their position.

4 *Diffusion of responsibility* Group members often lose their individual identity and sense of responsibility during problem-solving deliberations. Discussion often moves so swiftly that members lose track of who initially mentioned specific ideas, and most finished ideas are combinations of several persons' recommendations. While this process can be highly creative, research suggests that it also leads to a group's reaching riskier decisions than any of its members would have agreed to individually. Under these circumstances, a group can make very poor decisions, yet individual members will actively deny personal responsibility for the decisions and their consequences.

5 *Groups are solution-oriented* Most people dislike being faced with a problem; it is unsettling not to know what is going to be done about it. Thus, many management groups tend to short-circuit problem analysis, jumping quickly to solution proposals. Experienced managers are often very sure they "know" what the problem is, and thus are opposed to spending very much time exploring its underlying causes. Often, of course, the "problem" as it is first defined is only a symptom of a much bigger and more complex situation. Yet when problem-solving groups are formed, they rarely spend enough time simply exploring the nature of the problem.

WHEN TO USE A GROUP

Given the kinds of strengths and limitations described above, what are the circumstances in which a group problem-solving process should be used? Groups certainly have the potential to produce highly effective, innovative solutions, yet they often develop behavior patterns that prevent fulfillment of their potential. Unfortunately, simple generalizations are not very helpful. The important task for a manager is to determine when a *specific* group should work on a *particular* problem.

There are, of course, many organizational situations in which a manager has little choice about whether to handle a problem alone, assign it to a single subordinate, or involve a group. Organizational traditions frequently restrict the manager's options; almost every company has standing committees, regular staff meetings, and other settings that bring together specialists from different functional or geographic areas to address both recurring and isolated problems. Similarly, there are other situations in which the pressures of time and individual responsibility, the need for specific expertise, or the requirements of confidentiality clearly point to an individually determined decision. Between these two extremes, however, it is often difficult for a manager to decide whether individual or group effort will be most productive.

The choice of when to refer a particular problem to a management group depends upon both the characteristics of the problem and the skills and interests of the group. The most important factors in each of these areas will be discussed below.

Characteristics of the Problem

The nature of the problem, and the organizational requirements for a solution, define the primary criteria for determining whether to use a group problem-solving process.

Complexity, Uncertainty, and Conflict   Organizational problems can usually be described as involving uncertainty, complexity, or conflict. *Uncertain* problems are those in which the problem solver lacks information about underlying causes, potential solutions, or even solution criteria. *Complex* problems are those in which more is known about related causes and possible choices, but so many factors affect the situation that their interactions and consequences are difficult to trace and understand. *Conflict* problems are, obviously, those in which different individuals or subgroups have differing priorities or goals that cannot be mutually satisfied. In conflict situations, both the choices and their consequences may be very clear; the difficulty lies in choosing among the alternatives, and in determining how to make that choice when there are competing goals and interests at stake.

Most real-world problems involve all three of these elements in varying degrees. Definition of the problem in terms of its uncertainty, complexity, and conflict potential is a useful exercise because it helps to clarify what additional information is needed, who possesses it, and who is affected by the problem (or will be affected by its solution). Generally, the more uncertain, the more complex, and the more conflict-laden the problem, the greater the likelihood that involving others in developing a solution will be appropriate and effective.

Business Stakes The more important the problem, the more appropriate it is to involve others in its solution. Problems with higher organizational stakes (whether such tangible outcomes as costs, profits and market share or such intangible ones as public reputation, status, and power) call for more thorough analysis, wider awareness of issues, and shared responsibility for solutions and their consequences. A group process is much more likely to be effective when the risks and potential payoffs are large, because group members will pay more attention, take more time, and devote more energy to finding a widely acceptable solution.

Task Interdependence When a work procedure or information system crosses departmental boundaries, procedural changes are almost impossible without bringing together people from all affected departments. To use a simple example, imagine a materials control manager attempting to modify an inventory control system without involving sales, accounting, purchasing, manufacturing, and production control. Each department is affected by the system changes and can influence the success of the implementation effort. The problem simply cannot be resolved by one manager in one functional area.

Need for Acceptance and Commitment Another reason for leaning toward group processes is that those who are involved in group deliberations will understand the problem and its solution much better, and will normally accept and support the group decision much more readily. This aspect of group problem solving is especially important when the solution includes a major implementation effort involving several people. When many of these people are not direct subordinates of the manager responsible for making the change, then their acceptance and commitment is doubly important.

Deadline Pressures Group processes consume more managerial time and related organizational resources than individual problem solving. If a decision deadline is too immediate, it may be impossible to involve others even though the substantive nature of the problem calls for their inclusion. On the other hand, a tight deadline may be a very compelling reason for bringing in more people. If there is an adequate understanding of the problem, a group can divide the work and attack several aspects of it simultaneously.

To summarize, a group problem-solving process is generally called for when:

- The problem is relatively uncertain or complex, and has potential for conflict.
- The problem requires interdepartmental or intergroup cooperation and coordination.
- The problem and its solution have important personal and organizational consequences.
- There are significant but not immediate deadline pressures.
- Widespread acceptance and commitment are critical to successful implementation.

Characteristics of the Group

Organizational problems do not develop in a vacuum, and management groups certainly differ in their ability to work on various kinds of problems. Several important characteristics of problem-solving groups also have a bearing on the decision to use a group process.

Relevant Knowledge and Skills   The most obvious criterion is whether the group possesses the knowledge and skills to solve the problem productively. This is not a simple issue, however, because individuals often have problem-solving capabilities well beyond what they have previously demonstrated. Furthermore, groups develop problem-solving skills primarily through practice; both individuals and groups grow when they are stretched slightly beyond their present capacity.

Unfortunately, the immediate need to solve a problem and get the organization back on track very often overshadows the longer-term developmental needs of a group. Managers frequently justify individual problem solving in terms of lack of time, group work overload, and the group's lack of knowledge and experience. However, when developing the group's problem-solving skills is an important objective, the manager should consciously submit to the group problems whose nature might otherwise suggest individual attention.

Current Workload   If a group is already working at or near its normal capacity, addition of another important problem to its agenda is generally ineffective. Not only would the problem receive less attention and effort than it should, but other group tasks will probably suffer as well. An overloaded group is generally characterized by high levels of stress; and high stress typically leads to brief and shallow diagnosis, a preference for solutions that are simple and certain (rather than creative and effective), and usually severe and inflexible conflict. Overloaded groups are not effective problem solvers.

Group Expectations   Company norms sometimes value group participation in certain kinds of decisions, regardless of whether that participation actually improves the quality of the solution. In fact, many of the tensions that develop between managers and subordinates derive from differing assumptions about the appropriateness of group participation in certain types of decisions. Thus, a manager must be concerned not only with the substance of a problem but also with its emotional components. If a group feels strongly about its right to be involved in a decision, then that is another factor that the manager must take into account, regardless of whether he or she agrees with the group's feeling.

Norms for Conflict Resolution   Perhaps the most critical aspect of a group's problem-solving capacity is its approach to handling conflict. Group decisionmaking is especially difficult when group members have different and/or conflicting goals and needs. If the problem has the potential to create serious and heated controversy and the group is not skilled at confronting its differences, then the group solution will probably not be an effective one. On the other hand, a group that has developed healthy confronting norms can be a highly appropriate forum for hashing out an issue with many alternative solutions.

Because conflict resolution skills are such a critical factor in group problem-solving effectiveness, the next section describes alternative modes for handling conflict in much greater detail.

Thus, a management group is more likely to develop an effective solution to an organizational problem if:

• Group members possess the required knowledge and analytic skills, or are capable of developing them.
• The group is not already overloaded with other work.
• The group's expectations about involvement are taken into account.
• The group is highly skilled at resolving conflict, and is characterized by open, confronting norms.

These factors highlight the extent to which the manager's task is indeed one of finding the most workable fit between the problem and the problem-solving group. Neither element can be addressed in isolation; and none of the specific characteristics described above can be treated independently of the others. Since an ideal fit almost never occurs on its own, much of the manager's work involves trying to modify one or more of these characteristics. Finding the leverage points is not simple, and there are no formulas that will substitute for careful diagnosis of the most important elements in each situation.

MODES OF CONFLICT RESOLUTION

Because styles of problem solving and conflict resolution are such important variables in determining group effectiveness, they are among the most frequently studied aspects of group behavior. The literature on management groups contains numerous models of problem solving, group and intergroup conflict, bargaining, and techniques for managing conflict. We focus here on three predominant styles of conflict resolution, describing each style and its related assumptions in some detail. We are less concerned with the underlying causes of conflict, or with generalized strategies of conflict management.

Research on styles of group problem solving suggests that there are three primary modes of conflict resolution: *bargaining and forcing, smoothing and avoidance,* and *confrontation and problem solving.* Research suggests that confrontation and problem solving is by far the most effective approach, even though it is by no means the most common one. This assertion draws upon a substantial body of research. For example, Lawrence and Lorsch,[2] in their extensive study of product innovation groups in several different industries, found that the management groups of the more profitable firms invariably employed confronting styles of decisionmaking more than other

---

[2] Paul R. Lawrence and Jay W. Lorsch, *Organization and Environment,* Homewood, Ill.: Irwin, 1969.

modes, and generally did so more often than their less profitable competitors. In fact, the predominant mode of conflict resolution that characterized a company's management groups was found to be the most consistent variable that discriminated between profitable and unprofitable companies in the different industries.

The remainder of this section describes each of these three modes in some detail, and suggests their relative strengths and weaknesses as styles of conflict resolution.

Smoothing and Avoidance

A group employing smoothing tactics is more interested in maintaining harmony and agreement than in confronting the problem or the individual members' differences. Group members assume that conflict is destructive; because they value membership in the group, they avoid confronting their differences out of fear that the resulting conflict will split the group irreparably. People who favor smoothing over their differences often have little confidence in their own ability to articulate their reasoning or to persuade others of their position; they assume that the group is generally incapable of dealing with problems that involve conflict.

Groups that develop a smoothing and avoidance style tend to favor the status quo; they try to maintain an even keel, and not to rock the boat. Such groups actively redefine their problems so that minimum disagreement occurs; they develop powerful norms of avoiding conflict, actively withdrawing from controversial issues, and withholding critical comments. Members of a smoothing group describe their beliefs by quoting proverbs, such as "Soft words win hard hearts," "Kill your enemies with kindness," or "Smooth words make smooth ways." (These and similar proverbs were actually used to identify smoothing and avoidance groups in the Lawrence and Lorsch research, and in earlier studies as well.)[3]

Group members may privately express sharp criticisms of each other and group operation, but these criticisms are kept private. Meetings are often perfunctory and always polite, although a sensitive observer can usually pick up nonverbal signals that contrast sharply with the surface verbal behavior. Even when the stakes are high for some members on some issues, the pattern of smoothing is very hard to break out of. Membership in a smoothing group can be extremely frustrating, especially for persons interested in making changes or improving organizational performance.

Bargaining and Forcing

In a group characterized by bargaining and forcing, the participants view each other as adversaries, and work actively to define the problems in terms of what each person, subgroup, or department stands to gain or lose. Decisionmaking is viewed as a win/lose proposition, in which it is clearly better to win than to lose. Groups operating in this mode develop norms that justify pushing for one's own point of view regardless of the merits of others' views; forcing when one has an advantage, and seeking compromise when one does not; concealing unfavorable information; and digging for data that the "opponent" is hiding.

[3] See, for example, Robert R. Blake and Jane S. Mouton, *The Managerial Grid,* Houston: Gulf Publishing Co., 1964.

The kinds of proverbs that typify a bargaining and forcing climate include "Tit for tat is fair play," "Might overcomes right," and "You scratch my back, I'll scratch yours." Conflict is viewed as inevitable, necessary, and even desirable, but it is treated almost like a poker game in which one bluffs, conceals data, and seeks to scare the other participants from the game. Most decisions are reached through a series of compromises and tradeoffs, or by powerful parties forcing the issue. Participants assume the worst about each other, and each party seeks to maximize its own share of the "pot."

The poker analogy is important and appropriate, because in this mode of conflict resolution there is rarely any attention paid to increasing the total size of the pot, or to finding a solution in which everyone wins. Attention tends to be concentrated on the division of limited resources, whether they be budgetary funds, sales territories, management bonuses, or such intangibles as prestige and status.

Confrontation and Problem Solving

Groups operating in a confrontation mode work from the assumption that disagreements are healthy if they are worked through in pursuit of a solution that is good for the total organization. The basic difference between this orientation and the preceding ones is that here the individual parties recognize that their goals are interdependent, and that everyone will be better off in the long run if the total organization benefits. A confrontation group believes that the solution will be better if each party is open about its needs and objectives and the differences that are causing the conflict. Sharpening these differences clarifies goals and interests, and leads to creative solutions. Confronting the differences helps individuals find areas of common interest as well; the parties explicitly search for ways to increase the total payoff so that everyone can "win" rather than merely argue over the relative shares of a fixed outcome.

In identifying the underlying norms that typify this mode, people cite such proverbs as "Come now and let us reason together," "Try and trust will move mountains," and "By digging and digging the truth is discovered."

A problem-solving group focuses on the needs and objectives of the total organization as well as on those of each member. It also focuses on the relationships between members, not on the individuals or their personalities. Group members recognize that the "problem" lies in their differences and interdependencies, rather than within any individuals or their positions. Furthermore, emphasis is placed on resolving the problem, not on simply accommodating different points of view.

A confrontation style is a risky one that requires participants to challenge each other's underlying values and assumptions, and to share openly personal concerns and criticisms. Trust and integrity are essential ingredients in an effective confrontation and problem-solving climate.

Comparison of the Three Modes

It is important to keep in mind that these three modes are being described as prototypes, or even stereotypes: actual management groups often act in ways that contain elements of two or even all three modes. Most groups develop a dominant style, but typically each group has its own mixture of styles, and may vary its style over time or depending on the type of problem considered.

Exhibit 1 provides a brief comparison of these three styles. Each style is characterized briefly in terms of the group members' assumptions about the nature of problem solving, the role of conflict, the attitudes of the participants and the nature of the outcomes. The final two rows describe characteristic norms and representative proverbs that capture the beliefs and values implicit in the norms.

As noted earlier, confrontation and problem-solving norms are generally the most effective mode for resolving group conflicts. There are also situations in which a smoothing or a bargaining orientation may be not only appropriate but also necessary. Consider a group faced with an unavoidable deadline and a decision with several mutually exclusive alternatives. Because of the significant time pressure, the group may be forced to reach a decision without fully confronting all members' positions and needs. Even if the members are highly skilled at productive confrontation, the group leader may choose to explicitly suppress conflict to reach a quick decision.

Clearly, however, there is a difference between a one-time, short-term strategy of

EXHIBIT 1   MODE OF CONFLICT RESOLUTION

Category	Smoothing and avoiding	Confrontation and problem solving	Bargaining and forcing
Problem	Define to minimize differences	Define relative to the total organization's needs	Define in terms of the stakes for each subgroup
Role of conflict	Destructive	Can be healthy	Good to win, bad to lose
Participants	Accommodators	Collaborators	Adversaries
Outcomes	Maintain status quo	Interdependent; all come out ahead if the total group benefits	Win/lose
Typical norms	Withdraw when attacked Avoid conflict Keep your tongue in cheek	Confront differences Be open and fair Decide questions by reason, not power	Push when you have the advantage Compromise when you do not Maximize your own share
Representative proverbs	Soft words win hard hearts Kill your enemies with kindness Smooth words make smooth ways	Come now, and let us reason together Try, and trust will move mountains By digging and digging, the truth is discovered	Tit for tat is fair play Might overcomes right You scratch my back, I'll scratch yours

avoiding differences to meet a deadline, and the longer-term development of norms that actively suppress conflict time and time again. There is also a danger of using successive short-term crises to justify a smoothing leadership style; unfortunately, it takes only a few short-term crises to build up a long-term pattern.

A bargaining style also has its place in group problem solving. In fact, bargaining is probably the most common (but not necessarily the most effective) form of conflict resolution when the problem involves scarce resources and two or more departments in an organization. Budgets and sales territories *are* limited; and organizational resources that go to one department clearly cannot go to another. Actually, in the absence of clear organizational priorities, bargaining is often the only means for resolving interdepartmental conflict. Bargaining can be a particularly useful mode of operating for groups that meet infrequently, when the individuals involved do not know each other well, or when the overall organization does not have a clear sense of direction.

The difficulty is that all too often the bargaining climate degenerates into the kinds of forcing tactics described earlier. The "game" and winning become more important than achieving the best solution. The interests of the total group, and even of the subgroups, get lost in the battle to acquire scarce resources or to achieve organizational prominence.

Thus, even under these special circumstances, an open, confronting climate remains a highly desirable goal. It is an elusive goal, however, because an active confrontation of differences requires highly skilled participants. Open discussion of important differences is not only inherently stressful, but is productive only when group members possess both analytic and interpersonal skills. An effective problem-solving group continually risks falling apart in disagreement; creative problem solving is almost impossible without creative tension.

INTERGROUP AND INTERDEPARTMENTAL DECISIONMAKING

Managing group problem solving effectively is difficult under any circumstances. As we have already seen, the process is especially complex when the group is a temporary one composed of people from several different primary groups. Most difficulties are only heightened versions of those that arise within a single group, but the differing orientations and goals of people from different departments complicate the process significantly.

There are two major factors that make interdepartmental problem solving a more complex and difficult process to manage. First, we will briefly discuss the primary sources of interdepartmental conflict, going beyond the obvious differences in goals and personal styles that were identified earlier. Secondly, we will look much more closely at the individual problems faced by people serving as departmental representatives. Being a departmental representative can create particularly intense internal conflict; and the differences in the ways that different representatives resolve these conflicts can lead to relationship problems among the representatives and with their home departments.

Each of these factors is discussed briefly below.

Interdepartmental Conflict

We have already identified the major sources of interdepartmental conflict: competition for scarce resources; different interests and priorities; and different personal values, orientations, and styles of thinking and problem solving. Problem-solving groups composed of people from different functional areas clearly begin with a wider range of goals and opinions about the problem. In addition, the stakes are usually higher, the problems are almost always more complicated, and individuals' positions on most issues are much less flexible.

Interdepartmental conflict stems from more than just different goals and priorities. Natural differences in departmental size and power also affect the problem-solving process. Larger, more powerful departments can generally exercise more control over joint operations and decisionmaking. If one department is highly dependent on another for a critical resource (raw materials, information, even people), it may be overly willing to give in to avoid losing its critical resources. This kind of power imbalance frequently leads to decisions being determined by political "clout" rather than on their merits, and the company often suffers as a result. Furthermore, one-sided control usually leads to resentment by the weaker department, and working relationships deteriorate as a result.

Differences in departmental workloads and stress can also contribute to conflict. An overworked department is generally less open to change, and its members are especially resentful of other departments' relative lack of pressure. Furthermore, overworked departments are more likely to resort to either bargaining and forcing or smoothing and avoidance strategies. They simply do not have the time to carefully work through differences.

Departmental Representatives

Given the many potential sources of conflict, it is easy to understand the difficulty behind interdepartmental problem solving and decisionmaking. In most situations, the "glue" that holds the group together is the recognition of a common overriding interest in the success of the total organization. Often, however, that success is taken for granted, and individual departmental interests and prestige become more important. In interdepartmental decisionmaking, each group member acts as a *representative* of his or her department. This role creates particular difficulties for the representatives; in turn, these difficulties affect their behaviors in the interdepartmental group.

Individual Problems of Departmental Representatives Each representative experiences internal conflict as he or she attempts to balance commitments to the home department with those to the interdepartmental group. Maintaining membership in both groups forces each representative to conform to two sets of norms and expectations. Departmental representatives usually learn rather quickly to vary their behavior and language depending on the group they are currently interacting with, but there are often times when conforming with one group's expectations places the representative directly at odds with the other group. For example, membership on a task force that is developing new sales forecasting methods may require a product manager to share marketing department data and procedures that reflect poorly on his or her own staff. More significantly, the marketing department may have a history of resolving internal conflict by hard-nosed bargaining, while the task force group is being managed in a more open, confronting style. The product manager is caught in the middle: if he or she shares data openly with the task force, he or she risks being ostracized by his or her own department; yet if the manager reflects his or her department's bargaining stance, he or she will antagonize other task force members and could weaken his or her influence (and thus the marketing department's influence) on the task force's recommendations.

This dual membership problem places considerable stress on the departmental representative. Not only must each representative live with dual (and often conflicting) sets of goals, norms, and values, but each must also answer to two constituent groups for the actions taken and the decisions made. Even when the representative disagrees with the position taken by one group, he or she must explain it to the other. Furthermore, each constituent group typically holds the representative responsible for *all* the actions and decisions of the other group. The representative is pressured by each group not only to explain its own position to the other group, but also to influence the other group as well. And since all representatives on the interdepartmental group feel the same kinds of pressure, each individual is a target for influence attempts from both directions, at the same time that he or she is attempting to exercise influence on both the home department and the problem-solving group.

Relationship Problems of Departmental Representatives   This internal conflict also contributes to several kinds of relationship problems for departmental representatives. The pressures they feel often lead them to interpret the challenges or criticisms of their home departments as personal attacks. In fact, many managers do express procedural criticisms in a personal fashion. Since the representatives view each other as symbols of their respective departments, substantive departmental conflicts often escalate quickly into emotional interpersonal disputes.

Another relationship problem arises from the fact that the representatives feel different levels of commitment to their two constituencies. While some representatives remain oriented primarily toward their home departments, others may develop more loyalty to the interdepartmental group (in effect, redefining their role as representatives of the group to the department, rather than vice versa). The group members may also differ in the degree of independence they have to make commitments on behalf of their departments and in the willingness of their departments to accept the decisions of the interdepartmental group. These differences in orientation and influence further complicate the way the representatives are able to work with each other.

Personal Skills of Departmental Representatives   Obviously, the group and interpersonal skills of the individual department representatives also have a major impact on group effectiveness. And the greater the role conflict, the more important personal skills become. Perhaps the most important characteristic for a representative to possess is a high tolerance for stress, ambiguity, and conflict. Unless an individual can live with competing goals, irreconcilable values, and unresolved organizational problems, then perhaps he or she should avoid interdepartmental assignments. Representatives also must be highly skilled at listening. Understanding the needs and motives of others is an essential prerequisite to effective problem solving. Similarly, representatives must be able to explain their own positions and needs articulately and persuasively, and they must be capable of making quick, on-the-spot judgments. Interdepartmental groups usually make decisions that have major implications for individual departments; group members must be able to trace the consequences of new ideas rapidly to influence group decisions as they occur.

MANAGERIAL IMPLICATIONS

This note has identified a rather extensive and diverse set of ideas for understanding group problem-solving behavior. Up to this point, there have been very few specific suggestions for how individual managers can develop and reinforce healthy problem-solving norms in the groups to which they belong or hold responsibility. The difficulty is that the appropriateness of any particular action depends greatly on the group's present skills and existing norms. We have stressed the importance of careful diagnosis precisely because generalized prescriptions are so obviously inadequate. Nevertheless, we can suggest several basic strategies for effectively influencing group behavior. Many of these ideas have already been discussed; reviewing them here should help to tie together the concepts underlying group problem-solving behavior.

1 *Understand the sources of current behavior.* We have repeatedly stressed the idea that both individuals and groups develop patterns of behavior that are *useful* to them. Thus, if you set out to change someone's behavior, it is essential that you understand the reasons why that behavior is functional for that person. A manager cannot always change underlying conditions and personal characteristics, but it is futile to try to influence current behavior without understanding its sources, and without considering its benefit to the individual.

2 *Demonstrate desired behavior yourself.* Serving as a role model is one of the most powerful ways a manager can affect his or her subordinates' behavior; an obviously capable and successful manager can have an equally significant impact on peers and even superiors in the organization.

With respect to problem-solving behavior, this principle suggests demonstrating your own commitment to making decisions on the basis of facts and objective criteria. Furthermore, if you stress your own interest in finding solutions that maximize the goals of the total organization, others will also become more aware of their common objectives. You can model problem-solving behavior in all kinds of ways: suggest several solution alternatives rather than just one; do your homework and present factual support for your suggestions; avoid becoming involved in coalitions and compromises; and define your underlying assumptions so that you and others can question their validity.

Underlying this suggestion is the assumption that a problem-solving orientation will in fact lead to effective decisionmaking. Your own success will encourage others to act similarly, and should lead gradually to a more open, confronting set of decision-making norms and procedures.

3 *Monitor the decision-making process.* Reading 1 suggested a number of processes that generally occur during group discussions. By increasing your sensitivity to the dynamics of group decisionmaking, you can improve your ability to influence how the group works together. The counterpart of modeling problem-solving behavior is to insist on it in others as well. Press group members for factual evidence to back up their assertions; do not let minority views get squeezed out; work on achieving a balance of participation; and so on.

Your leadership style should vary depending on the phase of group problem solving. During problem definition and solution finding, you should encourage open, nonevaluative exploration. Later, when a decision is required, you may need to press individuals to make personal commitments, and you will again want to ensure that minority concerns receive a full airing before the group decision is considered final.

Although these suggestions are easiest to implement if you are the formal leader of a group, most of them can also be acted upon by other group members. It may be more difficult to influence group norms from a member role, but it is by no means impossible. The principles of effective problem solving that have been discussed here and elsewhere have a high degree of legitimacy in our society; acting on these ideas will rarely be viewed as inappropriate behavior. In fact, just the opposite is true; by appealing to group members' personal values, you will generally gain a great deal of respect. Even when you have to confront strongly held opinions, you can be successful if you have done your homework and know you stand on solid ground.

MANAGING A TASK FORCE

James Ware

Companies establish task forces to work on problems and projects that cannot be easily handled by the regular functional organization. Typically, the problems extend across existing departmental boundaries or are simply so time-consuming that working on them would disrupt routine departmental tasks.

A task force can be a powerful management tool for resolving complex and challenging problems. Several factors contribute to this strength:

1 The group is usually very task-oriented because it was formed to solve a specific problem or achieve a well-defined outcome. When the problem is solved or the task is accomplished, the group disbands.

2 If the task force brings together managers from the affected functional areas, it will possess a diversity of skills and understanding that can potentially produce a high-quality solution.

3 If group members are selected on the basis of their individual competence relative to the problem, there is rarely any "deadwood."

These same characteristics, however, can present a task force leader with several difficult managerial problems.

1 The group represents an inherent criticism of the regular organization's failure to deal with the problem, and thus there may be significant tensions and even battles between members and nonmembers.

2 Individual task force members who come from different parts of the organization usually bring with them a wide diversity of viewpoints, goals, and loyalties. The task force can become a battleground for fighting longstanding departmental conflicts.

3 The temporary nature of the task force may limit members' willingness to commit personal time and energy to the project.

4 Personally ambitious managers often view a task force assignment as a major opportunity to "score points" with upper management. These private agendas can seriously interfere with the group's problem-solving effectiveness.

5 If the group members do not know each other well, or are competing with each other personally or as departmental representatives, the leader will find it very difficult to create the shared sense of purpose and mutual respect that is so necessary for issue-oriented problem solving.

Clearly, the success of a task force's efforts depends heavily on the management of its activities. This note suggests a number of simple operating guidelines for increasing the effectiveness of any temporary management group. These suggestions have been grouped into four categories, based on the sequence in which the leader will confront the problems:

1 Starting the task force
2 Conducting the first meeting
3 Running the task force
4 Completing the project

These guidelines apply primarily to a task force leader. However, the most effective groups are often those in which several members carry out the leadership activities. Thus, you may find many of these ideas personally useful even in groups in which you do not have formal leadership responsibilities.

STARTING THE TASK FORCE

Your work as task force leader begins the moment you accept the responsibility of chairing the group. The period before the first formal meeting presents several opportunities for making decisions that will affect many of the group's later activities. Careful attention to details at the very beginning will pay subsequent dividends as the group confronts tough issues during the course of its deliberations. In fact, these "front-end" activities probably represent your greatest opportunity for defining the group's working style.

These start-up activities should focus on the following basic tasks: clarification of the reason for task force formation, definition of general operating procedures, membership selection, contact with prospective members, and preparation for the initial task force meeting.

Clarification of the Reason for Task Force Formation

Although the specific circumstances surrounding each project are unique, most task forces are established to accomplish one or more of the following general objectives.

1 To investigate a poorly understood problem

2 To recommend and/or implement a high-quality solution to a recognized problem

3 To respond to a crisis that results from a sudden change in the organization's business conditions

4 To bring together the people with the knowledge and skills to work on the problem

5 To gain commitment to a decision by involving the people affected by its implementation

6 To develop managers by providing them with exposure to other functional areas and people

7 To force resolution of a long-standing problem, or to work around an obstacle, such as a particular individual or group

Usually, the commissioning executives (the upper-level management group who determined that a task force should be established) will have several purposes in mind. For example, a new-product-development project can also be an excellent training experience for junior marketing managers. Similarly, a study of excessive inventories could be part of a strategy to reduce the power of an ineffective but well-entrenched purchasing manager.

Often, however, multiple objectives are incompatible, in that one objective may be attainable only at the expense of another. Additionally, the various commissioning executives may have differing objectives, or differing priorities for conflicting objectives. In many cases, these differences will not be openly expressed or even recognized.

Thus, one of your first critical tasks will be to meet with the commissioning executives and with other managers who have an interest in the project's outcome. In those meetings, you will want to explore the relevance and relative importance of each possible objective. You may even find it necessary to define alternative objectives and possible conflicts yourself. You can be a very active participant in the process of clarifying the task force's mission.

It is also important to determine if the task force is expected to conduct a preliminary investigation, to engage in problem solving and decisionmaking, or to implement an already agreed-upon change. The choice of emphasis obviously depends upon the history and nature of the particular problem, but you should seek an explicit statement about the boundaries of the project.

The nature of the task influences decisions about the composition of the task force, and the appropriate kinds of operating and decision-making procedures. For example, an exploratory investigation of a customer service department's efficiency would require very different analytic skills and working procedures than the installation of a computerized invoicing and inventory control system. Consequently, you will want to select task force members whose skills match the project requirements.

A useful technique for confronting these issues is to write a proposed statement of purpose, and then to ask each commissioning executive to assess how well your statement reflects their expectations. As the executives help you revise the statement, they will develop personal commitment to it—and to the task force's success.

Definition of General Operating Procedures

1 Will members be assigned to the group on a full-time or a part-time basis?
2 When should the task be completed?
3 What will the group's budget be?
4 What organizational reports and other information will be available to the group?
5 How much decision-making power is being delegated to the group?
6 What information should be reported to functional managers, and how often?

There is no way to anticipate all the procedural issues that the group will face, and many of those that can be anticipated will have to be worked out by the whole task force group. Again, however, you should discuss these questions in advance with the executives who are establishing the task force. It is far better to be told explicitly that some topics and decisions are beyond the group's charter than to discover those boundaries only by crossing them.

One of the most important procedural issues to be resolved concerns the way in which the group will make task-related decisions. The more exploratory and open-ended the basic project is, the more open and participative the discussion and decision-making procedures should be. Considerable research evidence suggests that task-oriented groups prefer relatively directive leaders, and that decisionmaking is usually more efficient in a structured climate. However, if the problem requires an imaginative or wholly new perspective, then a more unstructured climate will generally produce more innovative ideas.

Although you should discuss leadership and decision-making styles with both the commissioning executives and the prospective task force members, this is not a decision to make once for the entire project. The effectiveness of each approach depends very much on the nature of the current problem, and you will probably want to vary your procedures as the project progresses.

Selection of Task Force Members

As much as possible, members of the task force:

1 Should possess knowledge and skills relevant to the task
2 Should have a personal interest in the problem
3 Have, or can get, the time to devote to the task force
4 Enjoy working in groups, and are effective in group settings
5 Will not dominate the meetings or decisions solely on the basis of personality or power

While individual competence is important, it is not an adequate basis for constructing the project group. It is equally important to consider the overall composition of the group. Does each member possess organizational credibility and influence relative to the problem? Is each functional area that will be affected by the group's work represented? The exclusion of important departments not only generates re-sentiment and resistance, but may also reduce both the quality of the task force's recommendations and the probability that the recommendations will eventually be implemented.

A major membership selection dilemma is whether to include persons who are likely to obstruct the group's investigations and to impede progress toward a solution. Although including such individuals may reduce problem-solving efficiency, it does increase substantially the probability of their later supporting (or at least not actively opposing) group recommendations. Lowered efficiency in early deliberations is usually more than compensated for by smoother implementation. In addition, when individual resistance is based on valid information or experience, a solution that ignores the sources of that resistance is likely to be suboptimal or even unworkable.

It is vitally important that you be involved in membership selection. You may have information about prospective members that will have a direct bearing on the appropriateness of their involvement. In addition, your participation in the selection process adds your personal commitment to the group's effectiveness. Finally, your involvement in selecting task force members provides you with an additional opportunity to learn more about upper management's expectations for task force operation.

Contact with Prospective Members

Your first contact with each prospective task force member gives you an opportunity to begin defining not only the problem the group will be addressing but also the procedures it will be using. Whenever possible, this contact should be made in person; and you may want to include the prospective member's functional supervisor in the same meeting. The presence of the supervisor ensures that all three parties agree on the basic purpose of the task force and on the prospective member's level of involvement.

These first contacts also provide an opportunity to explore each person's current knowledge and feelings about the problem, and then build a productive personal relationship if one does not already exist. This information and experience can prove invaluable as you prepare for the first full task force meeting.

Preparation for the First Meeting

Because the quality of the first meeting sets the tone for all later activities, you will want to prepare a careful agenda. There are two major objectives for this first meeting:

1 To reach a common understanding of the group's task
2 To define working procedures and relationships

Since the most important function of the first meeting is to define the problem and the organization's expectations for the group's output, the commissioning executives should be asked to attend the meeting, if possible. Be certain to review everything you have learned about the problem and the group members with your supervisor in advance of the meeting to ensure that the group begins with a positive, productive experience.

It is highly unlikely that you can carry out all these start-up activities as thoroughly as you would wish. Time pressures, physical separation of group members, and previous relationships may all prevent the kind of thorough, rational analysis these suggestions imply. In addition, the commissioning executives may find it difficult to provide a clear statement of the problem. After all, most task forces are established because the organization actually does not fully understand the nature of its problem.

You have to accept some responsibility for defining the problem. But you also have to know when to stop *discussion* and start *action*. This difficult managerial judgment can be made only within the context of a specific situation. These suggestions can help you start well, but you may not be able to follow all of them. Often you will have no choice; other decisions will limit your alternatives. But you *can* become aware of the risks you incur by omitting a preparatory step, and can thereby be more alert to potential future problems.

CONDUCTING THE FIRST MEETING

This meeting is important not only because it represents the first gathering of all task force members, but also because patterns of interactions begun here will influence all later group activities. The two major objectives for this first meeting are to reach a common understanding of the group's task and to define working procedures and relationships.

Common Understanding of the Group's Task

This goal is clearly the most important item on the agenda; yet, in most instances, it is the most difficult to accomplish. Few of the other members have devoted as much time or attention to the task as you have. Until these members become acquainted with the problem and see it in the same general terms as you, they will be a "group" in name only.

Each manager enters this meeting with a feeling of responsibility to represent his or her own department's interests. Each interprets the problem in terms of those interests, and each possesses a distinct combination of ideas and information about the problem. Furthermore, many group members feel highly defensive, since they assume that other managers blame their departments for the problem. These feelings are not only natural, but are also very likely based on past personal experiences. If you know or suspect that such feelings exist within the group, try to find a positive way to bring them to the surface. Encourage everyone to participate by expressing an opinion and offering suggestions, but ask everyone to withhold judgment until all relevant information is presented. You can serve as the role model for other group members by asking questions that focus on facts, by maintaining strict neutrality on the issues, and by eliciting ideas from all members.

At this point, the group probably does not possess enough information to achieve a deep understanding of the problem and its probable causes. Indeed, the lack of information and understanding is generally one of the major reasons for establishing a task force. Nevertheless, it is essential for the group to achieve at least a general agreement that the problem exists, and where its boundaries lie.

Your most difficult task at the first meeting may be to prevent a premature consensus on an appropriate solution. Most experienced managers are sure they "know" what the problems are and what actions are required. Thus, even though you are seeking some level of agreement on the nature of the *problem,* you do not want the group to settle on a *solution* just yet.

You *do* want group members to develop a sense of their joint responsibilities and of the appropriate next steps to be taken. An explicit recognition of the area in which group members differ is also highly desirable. Member participation in a task-focused discussion of this kind will serve to generate commitment to the group and its general goals, even if differences of opinion as to appropriate strategies are openly recognized.

Definition of Working Procedures and Relationships

A second essential topic for the first meeting is the question of how the group will work on its task. Among the issues that require explicit attention are the following:

1 The frequency and nature of full task force meetings
2 The need for subgroups and, if needed, their structure
3 Ground rules for communication and decisionmaking within the task force between meetings
4 Ground rules or norms for decisionmaking and conflict resolution
5 Schedules and deadlines for accomplishing subtasks and completing the final report
6 Ground rules for dealing with sensitive issues; agreement on which issues require the involvement of other managers
7 Procedures for monitoring and reporting progress, both within the task force and to functional area managers
8 Explicit processes for critiquing and modifying task force working procedures

Spending time on these procedural issues serves two primary purposes. First, the discussion helps group members form clear expectations about their projected activities and working relationships. These expectations reduce the tensions inherent in an otherwise very unstructured situation. Secondly, the process of reaching agreement on procedural matters can become a model of how the task force resolves other problems.

Resolution of these issues at the first meeting can provide all participants with a positive experience associated with the group. However, this is obviously a full agenda, and you will probably need to carry these topics over into subsequent meetings. Try to end the first meeting on a note of agreement, however. If you can achieve a solid consensus on some portion of these procedural matters at the first meeting, you will have taken a major step toward a successful project no matter how deeply divided the group is on substantive issues.

RUNNING THE TASK FORCE

Once the front-end work has been completed, your efforts focus on keeping the project moving and on monitoring and reporting the group's progress. Although specific circumstances vary, there are several general principles to keep in mind.

1 *Hold full task force meetings frequently enough to keep all members informed about group progress.* Although each meeting should have a specific purpose, periodic meetings should be scheduled well in advance, and all members should be required to attend. A meeting can always be canceled if there is nothing substantial to discuss. However, full meetings do have an important symbolic value. They are the only time the full group is physically together, and anything said there is heard simultaneously by everyone. Very often the most valuable and creative discussions are those that evolve spontaneously in response to someone's raising a nonagenda item. For example, the most successful fund-raising project in the history of public television (the cast party after the final episode of *Upstairs, Downstairs*) grew out of two spontaneous comments during an informal staff meeting at WGBH in Boston.

While that kind of creativity cannot be purposefully planned, you can most definitely create opportunities for unstructured, exploratory discussions.

2 *Unless the task force is very small (fewer than 5–7 members), subgroups are virtually mandatory.* You must manage this process very carefully, however. Dividing the project into separate tasks that can be worked on simultaneously can be a very efficient mechanism for achieving rapid progress. But remember that one of the virtues of the task force approach is the synergy that results from new combinations of individuals investigating problems in areas they are not overly familiar with. If you permit the task force members to work only in their own areas, or with persons they already know and work well with, you are throwing away one of your major advantages.

Of course, when managers enter areas of the company that are entirely unfamiliar, they may ask questions that insult or unintentionally threaten the functional managers they work with. Warn your group members of this danger, and be prepared to spend some time telling functional managers about your group's work and smoothing ruffled feathers as they occur.

You must also recognize that working in subgroups can cause individuals to lose their overall perspective. If the task force becomes too differentiated, the various subgroups may form their own identities and develop an advocacy style of pushing for "their" solutions. The more the total job is divided for subgroup work, the more you must encourage formal intergroup sharing of problems, findings, and ideas as the project moves along.

3 *Be careful not to align yourself too closely with one position or subgroup too early.* This principle is particularly important if there are clearly opposing and mutually exclusive sides to the issue. Although you will eventually have to make a commitment to a plan of action, you will serve the group most effectively by being as concerned with the problem-solving *process* as you are with the specific outcomes of that process.

4 *Set interim project deadlines and demand adherences to them.* When you are in charge of the schedule and know the arbitrariness with which some key checkpoints were set, it becomes far too easy to assume you can make up lost time later. Despite the arbitrariness of interim deadlines, a missed interim deadline leads to a missed final deadline.

Insistence on meeting deadlines is doubly important when the task force members are assigned to the project only on a part-time basis. If they continue to carry out functional responsibilities, they feel pressure to spend time on operating tasks with immediate outcomes. The pressure to accomplish immediate tasks always outweighs the needs of the longer-range task force projects. Part-time task force members face a real dilemma, and are under continual stress. As the project leader, you must be prepared to spend a major portion of your time prodding group members to complete their tasks on schedule. At the same time, however, you must remain sympathetic with the legitimate needs of the functional areas, and be careful not to antagonize group members or their functional bosses. Your task will be especially delicate in situations where you have no formal authority over these part-time members, or where the lines of authority have been drawn but vaguely.

5 *Be sensitive to the conflicting loyalties created by belonging to the task force.* As task force members work together in group activities, they normally begin to develop commitments to the project and to each other. These commitments often become another source of stress, as members feel loyalties to both the task force and to their home departments. On the one hand, they continue to feel responsible for representing the interests of their functional areas, and, on the other hand, they feel growing pressures to help the task force accomplish its goals.

Assisting the task force frequently requires group members to share confidential information with you or with other members. You must recognize the risk this sharing involves. Whenever feasible, the source of confidential information should remain anonymous. As the task force leader, you may be able to play a valuable intermediary role in this regard. But remember that once someone has entrusted you with confidential information, that person has become dependent on your integrity. If you are ever indiscreet, you are unlikely to be so trusted again, and your value to the organization will be seriously diminished.

6 *Your most important leadership role is to communicate information to task force members and between the task force and the rest of the organization.* This communications role is time-consuming but absolutely essential to the success of the project. You must take personal responsibility for monitoring group progress, for bringing appropriate subgroups together to share information and ideas, and for reporting both progress and problems to your supervisor and to the functional managers in whose areas the task force is working.

Very often your most important activities involve listening to individual managers, passing information from one task force member to another, and bringing together managers who must exchange or share information and ideas. While these activities often seem inordinately time-consuming, they bind the individual task force members together. As individuals and subgroups pursue their investigative tasks, you probably become the only manager who retains an overall understanding of the total project. Communicating that understanding to others, and reminding them of their interdependence, is a critical responsibility.

BRINGING THE PROJECT TO COMPLETION

The work of an investigative task force typically culminates with a written report and a summary presentation of findings and recommendations to upper management. An implementation task force normally has more concrete operating results to demonstrate its accomplishments, but even so there is often a formal meeting at which the task force officially relinquishes its responsibilities to an operating group.

The written report documents the work of the task force, but its importance lies in the decision-making process it generates. In fact, the preparation of the final report can provide a structure and focus for the task force's concluding activities. You should prepare a tentative outline of this report early in the project and circulate it widely among group members. This outline can actually serve as a guide to the development of specific recommendations; the need to write the report forces the group to reach specific decisions.

Drafts of the report can then become the basis for working out any differences remaining among the task force members. Except in highly charged situations with major organizational consequences, you should strive to reach a group consensus before presenting any recommendations to upper management. Unless group members agree on the actions needed, you can hardly expect management acceptance or approval of the report.

The summary presentation of findings and recommendations to management is just as important as the task force's first meeting. The presentation should be carefully organized, with explicit attention to who will say what, in what sequence, and with what visual aids. The importance of these preparations varies in direct proportion with the extent to which the recommendations will be surprising, controversial, and/or expensive.

You should brief your superior and other key executives before the formal presentation. This briefing does not necessarily require their approval or agreement, but their advance understanding can help to prevent defensive reactions or categorical rejections of your group's recommendations. This kind of briefing can be especially important if your recommendations involve major changes in organization structure, budget allocations, or strategic focus for any of the executives who will be present at the formal presentation.

As important as this formal presentation is, however, it rarely constitutes an adequate wrap-up of the task force project. Only if the recommendations are very straightforward and noncontroversial will the management group be able to understand and act on them at one sitting. A more effective strategy will be to plan *two* meetings. In the first, you summarize the findings and recommendations, as described above, and distribute the formal report. At the end of this presentation, you then schedule a second, decision-making meeting for the near future. The interval between the two meetings gives the executives an opportunity to read the report and consider its implications.

This period will be a busy time for the task force members, who can meet individually and in subgroups with key executives to clarify the report. Only when the report has been acted upon can the task force consider its work actually ended.

PART TWO

MANAGING INTERPERSONAL RELATIONSHIPS

Part 2 narrows our focus from groups to two-person relationships, but at the same time magnifies the examination. After all, groups are composed of a number of two-person relationships. Effective management at all levels requires the ability to establish interpersonal relationships that contribute to desired outcomes. In this part, we review the central issues and problems in managing all types of interpersonal relationships—with supervisors, peers, or subordinates. The basic framework for this part is built upon the concepts of an individual's frame of reference and self-concept. His or her assumptions, perceptions, and feelings influence the quality of communications, an integral component of any interpersonal relationship. Failures in communication often lead to conflict. This part also further develops the issue of managing conflict, which was discussed briefly in Part 1.

The text for this part considers communication in a one-to-one relationship. It discusses how to develop and maintain effective interpersonal relationships. Communication is the key to effective relationships, but many problems can inhibit good communication. The text discusses some common communication problems before developing a framework for understanding the role of communication in interpersonal relationships. This framework has as its basic concepts the assumptions, perceptions, and feelings of a person. These act as filters on what is heard from others. When these are different for both persons, problems can develop in the relationship. Other factors that inhibit good interpersonal relationships are the tendencies to evaluate and judge. This note uses a specific case to illustrate the principles of the framework of assumptions, perceptions, and feelings as a way of understanding interpersonal relationships.

The first case in Part 2 concerns a recently promoted manager who ends up quitting his job much to everyone's surprise, including Dr. Jerrold, his supervisor.

His action is an outgrowth of an interpersonal conflict and a lack of communication, both of which are not appreciated by Jerrold. Using the concepts developed in the text, we can understand the reason for Knowlton's resignation and the possible ways to have prevented it. The case is a classic example of the increasing cycles of misunderstanding that result from poor communication.

Case 2 involves another surprise resignation, but one of potentially much greater significance due to the sensitive and explosive issues involved. John Baker, an English expatriate manager in the Caribbean nation of Barracania, is leaving his position as chief engineer for another position in the company. He is being replaced by Matthew Rennals, a bright, young, promising Barracanian who Baker has had the responsibility of developing for the position of chief engineer. Baker's well-intentioned final feedback interview with Rennals results in the angry resignation of Rennals. Political and racial sensitivities exacerbate this situation. The concepts for understanding interpersonal relationships help to explain the reason for Rennals's resignation and must be considered in developing an action plan in a situation of high urgency and large stakes.

Case 3 presents another type of conflict situation, between Bill Eden and his subordinate Al Abrams, in which the manager responsible for managing this conflict, Harris Johnson, does not have direct authority over either of these individuals. As in the previous two cases, the conflict results in a resignation, this time of Al Abrams. In order to decide what to do, Johnson must understand the underlying causes of the conflict. He is then faced with the choice of resolving or controlling the conflict.

Case 4 describes a conflict situation between Frank Mason and his supervisor, Ed Nolan, and is the first case to focus explicitly on managing one's boss. Mason, the new vice president for marketing and sales, has seen his relationship with Nolan gradually deteriorate in the 6 months he has been on the job. Mason is left with little power, autonomy, or credibility and is unsure of the reason for this turn of events. Case 5 describes subsequent events leading to Mason's dismissal.

Case 6 is another conflict situation with one's supervisor. Young Roger Clarke has experienced rapid progress in his company, receiving a double promotion 6 weeks ago and a substantial pay increase. However, he finds himself in conflict with his boss, the former incumbent in Clarke's position and whom Clarke suspects of making overly optimistic or even fabricated sales forecasts. With little information, Clarke must develop an action plan to resolve his job and interpersonal problems.

The three readings deal with three of the most important issues every manager faces: giving and receiving feedback, managing interpersonal conflict, and managing one's boss. The readings codify many of the lessons derived from the case analyses and offer some very practical suggestions that can be applied by managers. Reading 1 reviews the regularly given reasons for not engaging in feedback sessions and describes how the lack of feedback can lead to interpersonal problems. This serves as the basis for describing how to effectively give feedback to an individual. Important considerations are the person's ability to understand, accept, and use the feedback. Eight criteria are provided for deciding if and how to give someone feedback. This reading also discusses some considerations for receiving feedback.

Reading 2 explores the nature and sources of interpersonal conflict to understand its determinants and dynamics. This understanding is directed toward deriving some specific approaches to managing conflict, whether as an adversary or as a third-party mediator. This reading discusses the positive and negative outcomes of conflict, the relationship between substantive and emotional issues, and the role of situational and personal/internal factors. The three basic approaches to managing conflict (bargaining, controlling, and confrontation), originally discussed in Reading 2 of Part 1 are here applied to interpersonal conflict situations.

Reading 3 is a "how to" article on an important skill found in many of the best managers—managing one's boss. The first step in doing this is to have a good understanding of the boss's world in terms of the goals and pressures on him or her, and his or her strengths, weaknesses, and work style. A similar understanding is required of oneself, including an understanding of one's dependence on authority figures. For developing and maintaining an effective working relationship with one's boss, the following are important: (1) finding a relationship that fits the needs and styles of both parties, (2) establishing mutual expectations, (3) keeping the boss informed, (4) demonstrating dependability and honesty, and (5) selectively using the boss's time and resources.

UNDERSTANDING COMMUNICATION IN ONE-TO-ONE RELATIONSHIPS[1]

John J. Gabarro

Most people working in organizations, and particularly managers, have relationships with a wide range of people. Typically, a manager works with subordinates and important peers whose input, support, and cooperation is vital to the manager's effort. The manager also has a relationship with his or her own boss and other important seniors who are in positions to allocate scarce resources, influence important decisions, and provide advice and support. Even a portfolio manager in a financial institution (who is likely to have few, if any, direct subordinates) must rely heavily on analysts, researchers, and outside contacts to perform effectively.

The value of interpersonal effectiveness and communication seems fairly apparent. Not so obvious, however, is what a person can do to develop and maintain effective interpersonal relationships.

PROBLEMS OF COMMUNICATION

Almost everyone has experienced interpersonal conflicts and misunderstandings in both their personal and professional lives. So pervasive is this phenomenon that it takes up a disproportionately large amount of space in the literature written for and by managers. Indeed, the expression "communication problem" is now used so commonly that it is often applied to just about any difficulty that exists between two people, whether or not a communication problem actually exists. Not all interpersonal problems or conflicts are communication problems. Two managers may have

---

[1] Several of the ideas presented in this note draw heavily from Renato Tagiuri, "A Note on Communication," Harvard University, 1972, and Arthur N. Turner and George F. F. Lombard, *Interpersonal Behavior and Administration,* New York: Free Press, 1969. Special acknowledgment is given to Eileen Morley, who assisted in preparing an earlier draft.

131

difficulty working with each other for many different reasons. They may understand each other extremely well (and therefore do not have a communication problem), but one of them may not act as the other wishes. Take for example the following possibilities:

Political in-fighting and power struggles   Two people do not really want to reach a resolution because each wants the other to "lose" for political or other reasons. Each might understand the other's intentions and needs quite well. The real agenda in such a situation is to increase one's power and resources at the expense of the other's.

Personality conflicts   For reasons of a psychodynamic and unconscious nature, two people may have a propensity to dislike each other's personal styles, personality predispositions, or personal techniques. Again one person may understand what another person wants, but still have difficulty working with him or her.

Conflicting goals   Two people may have sharply conflicting goals, making it difficult for them to collaborate. This may not result from an individual's failure to understand another's position, or to communicate his or her needs. Indeed, both individuals may understand and communicate very well; it is just that they don't like what the other does, says, or wants.

Many other examples could be given of interpersonal problems that are not, strictly speaking, problems of communication. The problems listed above involve influence, trust, intention, and competition over scarce resources. However, many, if not most, interpersonal difficulties faced by managers actually do involve problems in communication or in understanding another person's point of view. This note focuses explicitly on problems of communication.

EFFECTIVE COMMUNICATION VERSUS GOOD COMMUNICATION

Renato Tagiuri, a specialist in interpersonal perception and communication, has presented a useful distinction between effective and good communication.

The major common concern is with effective communication. And it is a suitable concern for people in management and administration who are constantly trying to use communication to obtain specific results. When a communication does obtain the intended outcomes, it can be properly called "effective." But effective communication requires in most instances "good" communication, which means that party B has understood a concept that party A wished to convey to B.

"Good communication" is a pre-requisite but does not insure "effective" communication. If A said to B "Jump out the fourth floor window," B would probably not do it unless there were a fire and no other escape alternatives. Yet if we can assume that B has understood A perfectly well, this communication was "good" but not "effective." It is important not to confuse "good" with "effective" communication, for the latter includes aspects of behavior such as persuasion, motivation, power, coercion and the like. . . .

In practice it is not easy to separate the communication process itself from other processes involved in effective communication. But the "communicator" should be alert to this distinction.

TOM, STEVE, AND AN "OPPORTUNITY"

If we assume that effective communication depends at least partly on good communication, it is worth considering what obstructs good communication and causes misunderstandings. As a way of doing this, let us look at an actual situation in which good communication did not occur and carefully examine what took place. The situation involved two people in a work situation, and although the setting and names have been changed, the important elements of the story remain the same. The relationship between these two people was not an intimate one, but nonetheless an important one in each of their lives. As you read about what took place in this situation, imagine that it is not "just a case," but a company in which you might be employed, that you are well acquainted with both individuals concerned, that you like them both, and that you care about the outcome.

Tom Ellery was vice president of sales and Steve Watson was a regional sales manager in charge of four district managers. Steve reported to one of three area managers who, in turn, reported to Tom. Tom had followed Steve's career with interest and considered him one of the best sales managers in the company. It was not surprising, then, that Steve's name came immediately to mind when Tom received a memo from the marketing vice president asking for recommendations for someone to take over the marketing services department.

Marketing services employed about 400 people and provided promotional support and special services to the sales division. In terms of salary grade, the position was one level higher than regional sales manager, so it would offer Steve a promotion. Tom felt Steve was the ideal candidate for the job for several reasons. First, people in both marketing and sales divisions felt marketing services had become unresponsive to the needs of the sales division. The department was now more of a bottleneck than a service, and Steve's extensive experience as a sales manager would give him a clear idea of what kind of support the department ought to be giving.

Second, the department had begun to suffer from an "image problem" that Steve's transfer could do much to correct. Marketing services had developed a reputation for being a place where people were assigned when they ceased being effective in product management or in field sales. Putting an acknowledged "comer" like Steve in charge of the department would go far in dispelling that image. The position would also provide Steve with an opportunity for wider corporate exposure and one in which he could influence total company marketing and sales efforts.

After consulting with the marketing vice president, Tom sent Steve a copy of the original memo with the added note, "Are you interested? I think you're the best person for the job. Come by and let's talk about it." Tom was pleased that his own division was finally strong enough to allow him the flexibility to offer one of his best managers to another division. It had taken 3 years of systematically identifying weak spots and moving strong new people like Steve into them to provide this luxury, and he planned to make the most of it.

Pause for a moment before you read on and consider the assumptions Steve *might* make on receiving the memo, and what his feelings might be. Note them briefly on a separate piece of paper.

A few days later, Steve came by to discuss the memo. Tom was surprised to find Steve both uninterested in the transfer, and a little curt and ill-at-ease as well. Steve began by saying he didn't think he had the background to do the job and that he still had a lot to do in the region before he felt he could move on to another job. Sensing that Steve might be a little anxious about moving into the marketing division, Tom went into more detail on the reasons why he thought Steve could hande the job and do it well. Steve remained unconvinced, however, and as a last resort Tom suggested that Steve talk with the marketing vice president before making a final decision. Tom couldn't help feeling a little annoyed at the end of the conversation, and found himself questioning his original judgments about Steve's flexibility and adaptability.

Pause for a moment more and consider what inferences and assumptions Tom is making about Steve's response, and why these lead to feelings of annoyance.

To Tom's continued disappointment, Steve's talk with the marketing vice president failed to change his mind, and Tom began to feel his relationship with Steve had become strained. Soon afterwards, Tom noticed Steve was avoiding him in the company cafeteria, and seemed especially silent in his presence. About a month later, Tom received a call from Steve's area manager saying that Steve had resigned to take a position with a competitor.

Consider what perceptions and assumptions could lie behind Steve's action. How do you sense Steve feels in taking such an action?

Tom later learned from a mutual friend that Steve had left because he had concluded that his career with the company was finished when Tom offered him the marketing services job.

Did you deduce this from what went before? How do you think Tom felt when he heard the news?

A CASE OF MISUNDERSTANDING

A misunderstanding had taken place, the roots of which we cannot begin to understand without getting a better sense of what Steve was experiencing before and during his dealings with Tom. To begin with, Steve had no serious intention of moving to another company until after the memo from Tom arrived. On the contrary, he was very satisfied with his career in the company. He had enjoyed his work and had received two promotions within 3 years. Why then did his interpretation of the transfer differ so much from Tom's intention?

While Tom saw the transfer as a recognition of Steve's performance, Steve saw it as a sign that his past performance was not good enough. Steve had reasons on which to base this supposition. As long as Tom Ellery had been in charge of sales, he had never transferred an *effective* sales manager out of the division—only ineffective managers. Similar to other sales managers, Steve was very much aware of Tom's practice of identifying weak areas and bringing new life to them in the form of new managers. Indeed, he had been a major benefactor of this policy, and was one of the people who had advanced rapidly as a result. But now he wondered if it was his turn to be replaced as a regional sales manager. He had accepted his promotions and Tom's praise as clear signs of approval but now wondered if Tom had been less satisfied than he had seemed. The thought that this might have been the case especially angered him because neither Tom nor his area manager had given Steve any indication they were unhappy with his results.

The more Steve thought about the situation, the more suspicious and angry he became. If they wanted to get him out of the way, he could not think of a better place to send him than marketing services. Hadn't he joked with other sales managers about it being the burial ground for old product managers?

Steve's talk with Tom failed to dispel these suspicions. All Steve heard were Tom's attempts to sell him on the marketing services job and Tom's obvious annoyance when he refused to transfer. The whole series of events left him so suspicious and uncertain of his status that he decided to leave the company.

UNDERSTANDING THE MISUNDERSTANDING

The sources of this and other misunderstandings can be made clearer if we can describe and understand what each person *experienced* before and during the events described above. One relatively simple but effective way of doing this is by thinking about what each person experienced in terms of important *assumptions* he brought to the interaction, what he *perceived* as taking place, and what his *feelings* were during this series of episodes. By *assumptions,* we mean the values, attitudes, and beliefs that a given person has about how things *should* be in a given situation. By *perceptions,* we mean what the person actually sees, hears, or otherwise perceives as taking place in a given situation, as compared to what he or she might think should be occurring. By *feelings,* we mean the emotive and affective responses of a person in reaction to what happens in a given situation. In simplest terms, feelings are the emotions a person feels, which are triggered by what he or she sees taking place.

Tom's initial assumption was that he should recommend an outstanding individual with sales experience for the job. He decided to recommend Steve based on his perceptions of Steve's past effectiveness. He further assumed Steve *should* see the transfer as an opportunity for further advancement and as recognition of his past achievements. Given these assumptions, it was not surprising that he further assumed that Steve *should* be pleased and interested in the transfer. When Tom perceived Steve's negative reaction to the offer, he felt surprised because Steve's behavior was inconsistent with his assumptions. When Steve failed to respond to his arguments for taking the transfer, Tom felt annoyed, and ended up questioning his original assumptions about Steve's flexibility and adaptability. Very possibly Steve's behavior also may have threatened some of Tom's assumptions about his own ability as a manager and judge of people. Tom's annoyance no doubt reflected itself in his nonverbal behavior with Steve.

Steve's assumptions, based on past perceptions, were that "effective" sales managers do not receive transfers from the sales division and that marketing services was an assignment for people the company wanted out of the way. Both of these assumptions/perceptions were based on observations of what had taken place in the past, and provided the basis for concluding that the transfer was a sign of Tom's dissatisfaction with Steve's past performance. But this conclusion was inconsistent with his own assumption about himself, "I am a good manager," and his perceptions of the feedback Tom and his boss had given him earlier. This conflict between his own assumptions and the subjective meaning of the transfer led him to feel surprised, anxious, and threatened.

From Steve's point of view, Tom's behavior in the meeting gave Steve little reason to change his new assumptions; rather it gave him a further basis to reinforce them. Tom tried to sell the transfer, and appeared annoyed when Steve was not interested—behavior that could reasonably be expected from someone who wanted him out of the division. This led Steve to conclude that he no longer had a future in sales, and he resigned in anger to take another job. (The assumptions, perceptions, and feelings of these two men have been diagrammed in Exhibits 1 and 2, and it may be useful to look at them before proceeding.)

You may wonder how such a misunderstanding could possibly have occurred between two reasonably bright and probably sensitive people. Why didn't Tom explain his intentions better or anticipate how Steve's assumptions may have differed from his own? How could Steve so seriously misinterpret the offer? Admittedly, these questions also came to my mind. But these questions are reactions from *our* point of view about what took place. They deny the actuality of what each person must have experienced for the situation to develop the way it did.

EXHIBIT 1   Tom's experience.

Assumptions	Perceptions	Feelings	Behavior

Before the job offer

1. We ought to clean up marketing services.
2. We need a good manager to do it.
3. The job should be a challenge and an opportunity to the right man.
4. Steve ought to be pleased/honored at being invited to do it.

1. Steve appears to be a good manager. → Enthusiasm → Send the memo.

At the interview

5. Steve will be pleased at what I have to tell him.
6. Steve is anxious about moving into marketing division. (I must reassure him.)
7. Steve is not as flexible and adaptive as I thought.
8. He wants to stay where he is.

2. Steve appears curt and ill at ease. → Surprise (My perception of Steve's behavior doesn't fit my assumption.)

3. Steve still seems unyielding. → Annoyance

Goes into detail about why he thinks Steve can do job well.

Later

4. Steve has resigned. → Total astonishment (My assumption about Steve does not match his action.)

Before thinking about ways the problem could have been avoided, try to develop an empathetic understanding of how each person experienced his feelings and perceptions in the relationship and how this influenced each person's behavior in relation to the other.

Try to imagine for a moment how each person might have experienced the situation. Imagine Tom's sense of surprise when Steve refused an offer that seemed to him a compliment and an opportunity; how it must have conflicted with his assumptions about himself as well as Steve. Consider how this surprise slowly turned to annoyance and possibly anger as he experienced what he saw as irrational behavior on Steve's part. Consider the strength of Steve's feelings in terms of the extent to which his self-concept of an effective sales manager was in jeopardy, his expectations about the future, his sense of identity in the organization, and his ability to master a complex situation effectively. Consider how all these feelings were being challenged by his perceptions and assumptions about Tom's view of him.

EXHIBIT 2   Steve's experience.

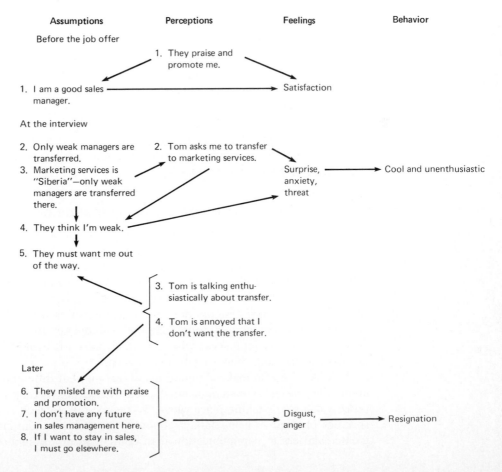

FACILITATING UNDERSTANDING IN ONE-TO-ONE RELATIONSHIPS

Having glimpsed at how these two people experienced the situation, it becomes easier to understand the misunderstanding. The actual situation as it was experienced by Tom and Steve was no doubt a great deal more subtle and complicated than this simple description implied. For example, our understanding of what happened would be sharper if we knew more about the personal histories of the two men and the expectations they had of their careers and broader lives.

However, even with the little information we have about the episode, we know a great deal more than either man knew at the time about some of the important *differences* in the way each was experiencing it. We have had the advantage of seeing some of the points of view and assumptions of *both* men, an advantage that unfortunately neither had until it was too late. The ability to recognize when important and disabling differences exist in assumptions is a skill that people seldom cultivate in their relationship with others. It is easy to do when the data are presented as in a case, a film, a story, or in some way, outside ourselves. But what do you do when you are one of the people in the relationship? Even more importantly, what do you do when you are part of the problem, as Tom and Steve were? What do you do when your own assumptions structure your perceptions and create feelings that prevent you from hearing or seeing how the other person's views and feelings differ from your own?

The simple, although not easy, answer to this question is to increase your awareness of what the other person is experiencing, of what their important assumptions, perceptions, and feelings are. This takes practice in trying to "imagine" the reality of the other person, and trying to keep separate your own point of view from how you think the other person might see it. Development of awareness is similar to any other skill; it requires practice in everyday interactions. There are also other actions you can take to minimize problems in communication that have to do with understanding the process of communication itself.

ASSUMPTIONS ABOUT COMMUNICATION THAT IMPEDE UNDERSTANDING

Much of the misunderstanding between Steve and Tom stemmed from their different sets of assumptions. Many of these assumptions were about the other's intentions and the specifics of what they were talking about, that is, the transfer, its symbolic effect, and its implications. In a sense, these were assumptions about the *content* of what Steve and Tom were communicating to each other. To a great extent, all of us constantly make such assumptions in our relationships with others. It could be argued that such content assumptions enable us to operate in a world in which we can never know in any total sense what the other person is experiencing, or how his or her specific meanings may vary from our own.

However, we also make assumptions of a somewhat different kind—assumptions about the *process* of communication itself. These are assumptions about the very process of what is taking place when two people talk to each other, rather than the specifics of what is being talked about. These process assumptions can be much greater barriers to communication than content assumptions because they keep us from discovering that our content assumptions may differ. For this reason, they can be especially dangerous. For example, consider the following process assumptions, which we often make in day-to-day communications with others.

- That the other person perceives the situation the same way we do
- That the other person is making the same inferences and assumptions we are
- That what is taking place should be logical from our point of view
- That the other person is experiencing or should experience the same feelings we do
- That the communication process in a given situation has little or no relation to other events in the situation or to past history
- That the other person's understanding of the situation should be based on your logic rather than their feelings

Most of these process assumptions were implicit in Tom's behavior. These process assumptions were much more critical in impeding his understanding of how Steve experienced the situation than were the set of content assumptions in Exhibit 1, because these process assumptions kept him from discovering how different his content assumptions were from Steve's.

TENDENCY TO EVALUATE AND JUDGE

One reason why both content and process assumptions impede understanding is that we tend to pass judgments on what we think others are saying based on these assumptions without ever getting to hear *the other person's* underlying assumptions.

Carl Rogers, a therapist who has spent much of his career studying the process of increasing understanding and communication, has postulated that "the major barrier to mutual interpersonal communication is our very natural tendency to judge, to evaluate, to approve (or disapprove)" of what the other person is saying. We approve when our perceptions of the other person's behavior fit our assumptions about how he or she "should" behave. We disapprove when they do not.

It is interesting to note that both Tom and Steve were most judgmental when they were experiencing strong emotions, and this is where the "rub" is. It is most difficult to listen nonevaluatively and refrain from passing judgment when feelings are strongest. And feelings are strongest when important assumptions are being violated. This is especially the case when what the other person is saying threatens us, because our defenses against anxiety are highest at those times. It is only by listening nonevaluatively that we can hear enough from the other person's frame of reference to begin to understand his or her assumptions, perceptions, and feelings. If, for example, Tom had been able to suspend his judgments and inferences about why Steve was reluctant and instead had inquired about Steve's lack of enthusiasm for the job, the misunderstanding might have ended there. If Steve had been able to suspend judgment on Tom's intentions long enough to hear him out, he may have discovered that Tom's intentions were quite different from what he assumed they were.

The difficulty, of course, is to be aware that our own *feelings* are signaling us that we are not really hearing the other person and to shift our emphasis from focusing on our own reactions to focusing on the other person's concerns as well. Trying to hear the other's concerns is the first step toward listening less evaluatively and improving communication. This nonevaluative stance is a precondition to understanding another person from his or her point of view and for imagining what that person's reality is like. This does not necessarily mean that your view must agree with the other person's view of the situation, but it does mean suspending judgments to understand the other's point of view. For example, try putting yourself into the shoes, first, of Tom and then of Steve.

Sit back for a moment, and feel your way through Tom's experience:

- His initial enthusiasm for Steve's transfer
- His hopes for the marketing services group
- His surprise and disappointment at Steve's lack of enthusiasm and curtness
- His need to reassure Steve about his ability
- His irritation when Steve remained unresponsive
- His disappointment when Steve's interview with the marketing vice president failed to influence Steve's decision
- His gradual estrangement from Steve around the company
- His astonishment at Steve's resignation

Now put yourself in Steve's shoes and follow the same process. Try to recreate within yourself a sense of the flow of Steve's feelings, beginning with his sense of pride and confidence in his performance as an effective manager. Try to imagine the sequence of his feelings so that you begin to share some sense of what his experience meant to him. Then, if you can, try to use this approach in a relationship that you are currently involved in which is important to you.

SOME FINAL POINTS

To anticipate and deal with communication problems, three things are necessary. First, a person must develop a sense of awareness of what the other is experiencing, as well as an awareness that difficulties in communication arise more often than we assume. (This is a matter of attitude.) Secondly, a person needs a conceptual understanding of how and why people are apt to see the same thing differently. (This requires finding a useful framework.) The simple concepts of assumptions, perceptions, and feelings, and how they might differ for two people, can be very useful in gaining this understanding. Thirdly, a person needs a way of examining and acting upon what is taking place in the communication process. This requires an understanding of some of the process assumptions that obstruct good communication and understanding. (This is a matter of both attitude and behavior.)

Tagiuri suggests the following strategies and attitudes as useful guides in preventing and anticipating communication problems:

- Suspend judgments of right and wrong—at least temporarily until you have understood the other person's point of view (attitude and behavior).
- Assume the legitimacy of another person's view (attitude).

- Try to see the situation from the other's point of view (behavior).
- Define terms (behavior).
- Deal with "facts" rather than with interpretations or inferences (behavior).
- Take the other person's and your own emotions and feelings into account as being important and, if appropriate, recognize them (behavior).
- Reopen communication—the balance between telling and listening (behavior).
- Restate issues as the other party sees them. This serves as feedback to the other person and a check on your own understanding (behavior).
- Attend to and stimulate feedback in terms of the consequences of the communication (behavior).

BOB KNOWLTON

Alex Bavelas

Bob Knowlton was sitting alone in the conference room of the laboratory. The rest of the group had gone. One of the secretaries had stopped and talked for a while about her husband's coming induction into the Army, and had finally left. Bob, alone in the laboratory, slid a little further down in his chair, looking with satisfaction at the results of the first test run of the new photon unit.

He liked to stay after the others had gone. His appointment as project head was still new enough to give him a deep sense of pleasure. His eyes were on the graphs before him, but in his mind he could hear Dr. Jerrold, the head of the laboratory, saying again, "There's one thing about this place that you can bank on. The sky is the limit for the person who can produce!" Knowlton felt again the tingle of happiness and embarrassment. Well, dammit, he said to himself, he had produced. He wasn't kidding anybody. He had come to the Simmons Laboratories 2 years ago. During a routine testing of some rejected Clanson components, he had stumbled onto the idea of the photon correlator, and the rest had just happened. Jerrold had been enthusiastic; a separate project had been set up for further research and development of the device, and he had gotten the job of running it. The whole sequence of events still seemed a little miraculous to Knowlton.

He shrugged out of the reverie and bent determinedly over the sheets when he heard someone come into the room behind him. He looked up expectantly; Jerrold often stayed late himself, and now and then dropped in for a chat. This always made the day's end especially pleasant for Bob. It wasn't Jerrold. The man who had come in was a stranger. He was tall, thin, and rather dark. He wore steel-rimmed glasses and had on a very wide leather belt with a large brass buckle. His wife remarked later that it was the kind of belt the pilgrims must have worn.

The stranger smiled and introduced himself. "I'm Simon Fester. Are you Bob Knowlton?" Bob said yes, and they shook hands. "Doctor Jerrold said I might find you in. We were talking about your work, and I'm very much interested in what you are doing." Bob waved to a chair.

Fester didn't seem to belong in any of the standard categories of visitors: customer, visiting fireman, stockholder. Bob pointed to the sheets on the table. "There are the preliminary results of a test we're running. We've got a new gadget by the tail and we're trying to understand it. It's not finished, but I can show you the section that we're testing."

He stood up, but Fester was deep in the graphs. After a moment, he looked up with an odd grin. "These look like plots of a Jennings surface. I've been playing around with some autocorrelation functions of surfaces—you know that stuff." Bob, who had no idea what he was referring to, grinned back and nodded, and immediately felt uncomfortable. "Let me show you the monster," he said, and led the way to the work room.

After Fester left, Knowlton slowly put the graphs away, feeling vaguely annoyed. Then, as if he had made a decision, he quickly locked up and took the long way out so that he would pass Jerrold's office. But the office was locked. Knowlton wondered whether Jerrold and Fester had left together.

The next morning, Knowlton dropped into Jerrold's office, mentioned that he had talked with Fester, and asked who he was. "Sit down for a minute," Jerrold said. "I want to talk to you about him. What do you think of him?" Knowlton replied truthfully that he thought Fester was very bright and probably very competent. Jerrold looked pleased.

"We're taking him on," he said. "He's had a very good background in a number of laboratories, and he seems to have ideas about the problems we're tackling here." Knowlton nodded in agreement, instantly wishing that Fester would not be placed with him.

"I don't know yet where he will finally land," Jerrold continued, "but he seems interested in what you are doing. I thought he might spend a little time with you by way of getting started." Knowlton nodded thoughtfully. "If his interest in your work continues, you can add him to your group."

"Well, he seemed to have some good ideas even without knowing exactly what we are doing," Knowlton answered. "I hope he stays; we'd be glad to have him."

Knowlton walked back to the laboratory with mixed feelings. He told himself that Fester would be good for the group. He was no dunce, he'd produce. Knowlton thought again of Jerrold's promise when he had promoted him—"the person who produces gets ahead in this outfit." The words seemed to carry the overtones of a threat now.

The next day, Fester didn't appear until mid-afternoon. He explained that he had had a long lunch with Jerrold, discussing his place in the laboratory. "Yes," said Knowlton, "I talked with Jerry this morning about it, and we both thought you might work with us for a while." Fester smiled in the same knowing way that he had smiled when he mentioned the Jennings surfaces. "I'd like to," he said.

Knowlton introduced Fester to the other members of the laboratory. Fester and Link, the mathematician of the group, hit it off well together, and spent the rest of the afternoon discussing a method of analysis of patterns that Link had been worrying over for the last month.

It was 6:30 when Knowlton left the laboratory that night. He had waited almost eagerly for the end of the day to come—when everyone would be gone and he could sit in the quiet rooms, relax, and think it over. "Think what over?" he asked himself. He didn't know. Shortly after 5 p.m. everyone had gone except Fester, and what followed was almost a duel. Knowlton was annoyed that he was being cheated out of his quiet period, and finally resentfully determined that Fester should leave first.

Fester was reading at the conference table, and Knowlton was sitting at his desk in the little glass-enclosed cubicle that he used during the day when he needed to be undisturbed. Fester was carefully studying the last year's progress reports. The time dragged. Knowlton doodled on a pad, the tension growing inside him. What the hell did Fester think he was going to find in the reports?

Knowlton finally gave up and they left the laboratory together. Fester took several reports with him to study in the evening. Knowlton asked him if he thought the reports gave a clear picture of the laboratory's activities.

"They're excellent," Fester answered with obvious sincerity. "They're not only good reports; what they report is damn good, too!" Knowlton was surprised at the relief he felt, and grew almost jovial as he said goodnight.

Driving home, Knowlton felt more optimistic about Fester's presence in the laboratory. He had never fully understood the analysis that Link was attempting. If there was anything wrong with Link's approach, Fester would probably spot it. "And if I'm any judge," he murmured, "he won't be especially diplomatic about it."

He described Fester to his wife, who was amused by the broad leather belt and the brass buckle. "It's the kind of belt that pilgrims must have worn," she laughed.

"I'm not worried about how he holds his pants up," Knowlton laughed with her. "I'm afraid that he's the kind that just has to make like a genius twice each day. And that can be pretty rough on the group."

Knowlton had been asleep for several hours when he was abruptly awoken by the telephone. He realized it had rung several times. He swung off the bed muttering about damn fools and telephones. It was Fester. Without any excuses, apparently oblivious of the time, he plunged into an excited recital of how Link's patterning problem could be solved.

Knowlton covered the mouthpiece to answer his wife's stage-whispered "Who is it?" "It's the genius," replied Knowlton.

Fester, completely ignoring that it was 2 a.m., proceeded excitedly to start in the middle of an explanation of a completely new approach to certain photon laboratory problems that he had stumbled onto while analyzing past experiments. Knowlton managed to put some enthusiasm in his own voice and stood there, half-dazed and very uncomfortable, listening to Fester talk endlessly about what he had discovered. It was probably not only a new approach but also an analysis that showed the inherent weakness of the previous experiment and how experimentation along that line would certainly have been inconclusive. The following day Knowlton spent the entire morning with Fester and Link, the mathematician, the morning meeting having been called off so that Fester's work of the previous night could be gone over intensively. Fester was very anxious that this be done and Knowlton was not too unhappy to suspend the meeting for reasons of his own.

For the next several days, Fester sat in the back office that had been turned over to him and did nothing but read the progress reports of the work that had been done in the last 6 months. Knowlton felt apprehensive about the reaction that Fester might have to some of his work. He was a little surprised at his own feelings. He had always been proud (although he had put on a convincingly modest face) of the way in which new ground in the study of photon-measuring devices had been broken in his group. Now he wasn't sure, and it seemed to him that Fester might easily show that the line of research they had been following was unsound or even unimaginative.

The next morning, as was the custom in Bob's group, the members of the laboratory, including the secretaries, sat around a conference table. Bob always prided himself on the fact that the work of the laboratory was guided and evaluated by the group as a whole, and he was fond of repeating that it was not a waste of time to include secretaries in such meetings. Often, what started out as a boring recital of fundamental assumptions to a naive listener, uncovered new ways of regarding these assumptions that would not have occurred to the researcher who had long ago accepted them as a necessary basis for his or her work.

These group meetings also served Bob in another sense. He admitted to himself that he would have felt far less secure if he had had to direct the work out of his own mind, so to speak. With the group meeting as the principle of leadership, it was always possible to justify the exploration of blind alleys because of the general educative effect on the team. Fester was there; Lucy Jones and Martha Smith, the laboratory secretaries, were there. Link was sitting next to Fester, their conversation concerning Link's mathematical study apparently continuing from yesterday. The other members, Bob Davenport, George Thurlow, and Arthur Oliver, were waiting quietly.

Knowlton, for reasons that he didn't quite understand, proposed for discussion this morning a problem that all of them had spent considerable time on previously, with the conclusion that a solution was impossible, that there was no feasible way to treat it in an experimental fashion. When Knowlton proposed the problem, Davenport remarked that there was hardly any use in reviewing it again, that he was satisfied that there was no way to approach the problem with the equipment and the physical capacities of the laboratory.

This statement had the effect of a shot of adrenalin on Fester. He said he would like to know about the problem in detail, and walking to the blackboard, began to write the "factors" as various members of the group began to discuss the problem and simultaneously list the reasons for its abandonment.

Very early in the description of the problem, it was evident that Fester would disagree about the impossibility of attacking it. The group realized this and finally the descriptive materials and their recounting of the reasoning that had led to its abandonment dwindled away. Fester began his statement which, as it proceeded, might well have been prepared the previous night although Knowlton knew this was impossible. He could not help being impressed with the organized, logical way that Fester was presenting ideas that must have occurred to him only a few minutes before.

Fester had some things to say, however, that left Knowlton with a mixture of annoyance, irritation and, at the same time, a rather smug feeling of superiority over Fester in at least one area. Fester thought that the way the problem had been analyzed was really typical of group thinking and, with an air of sophistication that made it difficult for a listener to dissent, he proceeded to comment on the American emphasis on team ideas, satirically describing the ways in which they led to a "high level of mediocrity."

During this time, Knowlton observed that Link stared studiously at the floor, and he was very conscious of Thurlow's and Davenport's glances toward him at several points during Fester's speech. Inwardly, Knowlton couldn't help feeling that this was one point at least in which Fester was off on the wrong foot. The whole laboratory, following Jerry's lead, talked if not practiced the theory of small research teams as the basic organization for effective research. Fester insisted that the problem could be approached and that he would like to study it for a while himself.

Knowlton ended the morning session by remarking that the meetings would continue and that the very fact that a supposedly insoluble experimental problem was now going to receive another chance was another indication of the value of such meetings. Fester immediately remarked that he was not at all averse to meetings for the purpose of informing the group of the progress of its members—that the point he wanted to make was that creative advances were seldom accomplished in such meetings, that they were made by the individual "living with" the problem closely and continuously, a sort of personal relationship to it.

Knowlton went on to say to Fester that he was very glad that Fester had raised these points and that he was sure the group would profit by reexamining the basis on which they had been operating. Knowlton agreed that individual effort was probably the basis for making the major advances, but that he considered the group meetings useful primarily because of the effect they had on keeping the group together and on helping the weaker members of the group keep up with the members who were able to advance more easily and quickly in the analysis of problems.

It was clear as days went by and meetings continued as they did, that Fester came to enjoy them because of the pattern that the meetings assumed. It became typical for Fester to hold forth and it was unquestionably clear that he was more brilliant, better prepared on the various subjects that were germane to the problems being studied, and more capable of progress than anyone there. Knowlton grew increasingly disturbed as he realized that his leadership of the group had been, in fact, taken over.

Whenever the subject of Fester was mentioned in occasional meetings with Jerrold, Knowlton would comment only on Fester's ability and obvious capacity for work. Somehow he never felt that he could mention his own discomforts, not only because they revealed a weakness on his part but also because it was quite clear that Jerrold himself was considerably impressed with Fester's work and with the contacts he had with him outside the photon laboratory.

Knowlton now began to feel that perhaps the intellectual advantages that Fester had brought to the group did not quite compensate for what he felt were evidences of a breakdown in the cooperative spirit that he had seen in the group before Fester's coming. More and more of the morning meetings were skipped. Fester's opinion of the abilities of other group members, with the exception of Link, was obviously low. At times, during the morning meetings or in smaller discussions, he had been on the point of rudeness, refusing to pursue an argument when he claimed it was based on the other person's ignorance of the facts involved. His impatience with others led him to make similar remarks to Jerrold. Knowlton inferred this from a conversation with Jerrold in which Jerrold asked whether Davenport and Oliver were going to be continued on; and his failure to mention Link led Knowlton to believe that this was the result of private conversations between Fester and Jerrold.

It was not difficult for Knowlton to make a quite convincing case on whether the brilliance of Fester was sufficient compensation for the beginning of the breakup of the group. He took the opportunity to speak privately with Davenport and Oliver, and it was quite clear that both were uncomfortable because of Fester. Knowlton didn't press the discussion beyond the point of hearing them in one way or another say that they did feel awkward and that it was sometimes difficult for them to understand the arguments Fester advanced, but often embarrassing to ask him to provide the background on which his arguments were based. Knowlton did not interview Link.

About 6 months after Fester came to the photon laboratory, a meeting was scheduled in which the sponsors of the research would visit the laboratory to get an idea of the work and its progress. It was customary at these meetings for project heads to present the research being conducted in their groups. The members of each group were invited to other meetings, which were held later in the day and open to all, but the special meetings were usually attended only by project heads, the head of the laboratory, and the sponsors.

As the time for the special meeting approached, it seemed to Knowlton that he must avoid the presentation at all cost. He felt that he could not trust himself to present the ideas and work that Fester had advanced, because of his apprehension as to whether he could present them in sufficient detail and answer questions correctly. On the other hand, he did not feel he coud ignore these newer lines of work and present only the material that he had done or had been started before Fester's arrival. He also felt that it would not be beyond Fester at all, in his blunt and undiplomatic way (if he were present at the meeting, that is), to comment on his own presentation and reveal the inadequacy that Knowlton felt he had. It also seemed quite clear that it would not be easy to keep Fester from attending the meeting, even though he was not on the administrative level that was invited.

Knowlton found an opportunity to speak to Jerrold and raised the question. He remarked to Jerrold that, with the meetings coming up and with the interest in the work and with the contributions that Fester had been making, Fester would probably like to attend these meetings, but that there was a question of the feelings of the others in the group if Fester alone were invited. Jerrold dismissed this very lightly by saying that he didn't think the group would fail to understand Fester's rather different position, and that he thought Fester by all means should be invited. Knowlton then immediately agreed, adding that Fester should present the work because much of it had been done by him and that, as Knowlton put it, this would be an opportune way to recognize Fester's contributions and to reward him since he was eager to be recognized as a productive member of the laboratory. Jerrold agreed and so the matter was decided.

Fester's presentation was very successful and in some ways dominated the meeting. He attracted the interest and attention of many in attendance, and a long discussion followed his presentation. Later in the evening, with the entire laboratory staff present, a small circle of people formed about Fester in the cocktail period before the dinner. One of them was Jerrold himself, and a lively discussion took place concerning the application of Fester's theory. All of this disturbed Knowlton and his reaction and behavior were characteristic. He joined the circle, praised Fester to Jerrold and to the others, and remarked on the brilliance of the work.

Without consulting anyone, Knowlton began to take an interest in the possibility of a job elsewhere. After a few weeks he found that a new laboratory of considerable size was being organized in a nearby city, and that his training would enable him to secure a project-head job equivalent to his present one, with slightly more money.

He immediately accepted it and notified Jerrold by a letter, which he mailed on a Friday night to Jerrold's home. The letter was quite brief and Jerrold was stunned. The letter merely said that he had found a better position; that there were personal reasons why he didn't want to appear at the laboratory anymore; and that he would be glad to return at a later time from where he would be, some 40 miles away, to assist if there was any mixup at all in the past work. It also mentioned that he felt sure that Fester could supply any leadership for the group, and that his decision to leave so suddenly was based on some personal problems; he hinted at problems of health in his family, his mother and father. All of this was fictitious, of course. Jerrold took it at face value but still felt that this was very strange behavior and quite unaccountable since he had always felt his relationship with Knowlton had been warm and that Knowlton was satisfied and, as a matter of fact, quite happy and productive.

Jerrold was considerably disturbed, because he had already decided to place Fester in charge of another project that was going to be set up very soon. He had been wondering how to explain this to Knowlton, in light of the obvious help and value Knowlton was getting from Fester and the high regard in which he held him. He had, as a matter of fact, considered the possibility that Knowlton could add to his staff another person with Fester's kind of background and training, which had proven so valuable.

Jerrold did not make any attempt to meet Knowlton. In a way, he felt aggrieved about the situation. Fester, too, was surprised at the suddenness of Knowlton's departure and when Jerrold asked him whether he had reasons to prefer to stay with the photon group instead of the impending Air Force project, he chose the Air Force project and went on to that job the following week. The photon laboratory was hard hit. The leadership of the laboratory was temporarily given to Link until someone could be hired to take charge.

THE ROAD TO HELL

Gareth Evans

John Baker, chief engineer of the Caribbean Bauxite Company of Barracania in the West Indies, was making his final preparations to leave the island. His promotion to production manager of Keso Mining Corporation near Winnipeg—one of Continental Ore's fast-expanding Canadian enterprises—had been announced a month before and now everything had been tidied up except the last vital interview with his successor, the able young Barracanian, Matthew Rennalls. It was crucial that this interview be successful and that Rennalls should leave his office uplifted and encouraged to face the challenge of a new job. A touch on the bell would have brought Rennalls walking into the room, but Baker delayed the moment and gazed thoughtfully through the window considering just exactly what he was going to say and, more particularly, how he was going to say it.

John Baker, an English expatriate, was 45 years old and had served 23 years with Continental Ore in the Far East, several African countries, Europe and, for the last 2 years, the West Indies. He hadn't cared much for his previous assignment in Hamburg and was delighted when the West Indian appointment came through. Climate was not the only attraction. Baker had always preferred working overseas (in what were termed the developing countries) because he felt he had an innate knack—better than most other expatriates working for Continental Ore—of knowing just how to get along with the regional staff. However, after 24 hours in Barracania, he realized that he would need all of this "innate knack" to deal effectively with the problems in this field that awaited him.

At his first interview with Hutchins, the production manager, the problem of Rennalls and his future was discussed. There and then it was made quite clear to Baker that one of his most important tasks would be "grooming" Rennalls as his successor. Hutchins had pointed out that not only was Rennalls one of the brightest

Barracanian prospects on the staff of Caribbean Bauxite—at London University he had taken first-class honours in the BSc engineering degree—but, being the son of the minister of finance and economic planning, he also had no small political pull.

The company had been particularly pleased when Rennalls decided to work for it rather than for the government in which his father had such a prominent post. The company ascribed his action to the effect of its vigorous and liberal regionalization program which, since World War II, had produced 18 Barracanians at mid-management level and given Caribbean Bauxite a good lead in this respect over all other international concerns operating in Barracania. The success of this timely regionalization policy has led to excellent relations with the government.

This relationship had been given an added importance when Barracania, 3 years later, became independent—an occasion that encouraged a critical and challenging attitude toward the role foreign interests would play in the new Barracania. Therefore, Hutchins had little difficulty in convincing Baker that the successful career development of Rennalls was of primary importance.

The interview with Hutchins was now 2 years old and Baker, leaning back in his office chair, reviewed his success in grooming Rennalls. What aspects of the latter's character had helped and what had hindered? What about his own personality? How had that helped or hindered? The first item to go on the credit side would, without question, be the ability of Rennalls to master the technical aspects of the job. From the start he had shown keenness and enthusiasm and had often impressed Baker with his ability in tackling new assignments and the constructive comments he invariably made in departmental discussions. He was popular with all ranks of Barracanian staff and had an ease of manner that placed him in good stead when dealing with his expatriate seniors. These were all assets, but what about the debit side?

First and foremost, there was his racial consciousness. His 4 years at London University had accentuated this feeling and made him sensitive to any sign of condescension on the part of expatriates. It may have been to give expression to this sentiment that, as soon as he returned from London, he threw himself into politics on behalf of the United Action Party, which later won the preindependence elections and provided the country with its first prime minister.

The ambitions of Rennalls—and he certainly was ambitious—did not lie in politics for, staunch nationalist that he was, he saw that he could serve himself and his country best—for bauxite was responsible for nearly half the value of Barracania's export trade—by putting his engineering talent to the best use possible. On this account, Hutchins found that he had an unexpectedly easy task in persuading Rennalls to give up his political work before entering the production department as an assistant engineer.

Baker knew that it was Rennalls's well-repressed sense of race consciousness that had prevented their relationship from being as close as it should have been. On the surface, nothing could have seemed more agreeable. Formality between the two men was at a minimum; Baker was delighted to find that his assistant shared his own peculiar "shaggy dog" sense of humor so that jokes were continually being exchanged; they entertained each other at their houses and often played tennis together—and yet the barrier remained invisible, indefinable, but everpresent. The existence of this "screen" between them was a constant source of frustration to Baker, since it indicated a weakness that he was loath to accept. If he was successful with all other nationalities, why not with Rennalls?

But at least he had managed to "break through" to Rennalls more successfully than any other expatriate. In fact, it was the young Barracanian's attitude—sometimes overbearing, sometimes cynical—toward other company expatriates that had been one of the subjects Baker had raised last year when he discussed Rennalls's staff report with him. He knew, too, that he would have to raise the same subject again in the forthcoming interview because Jackson, the senior draftsperson, had complained only yesterday about the rudeness of Rennalls. With this thought in mind, Baker leaned forward and spoke into the intercom, "Would you come in, Matt, please? I'd like a word with you." As Rennalls entered the room, Baker said, "Do sit down," and offered a cigarette. He paused while he held out his lighter and then went on.

"As you know, Matt, I'll be off to Canada in a few days' time, and before I go, I thought it would be useful if we could have a final chat together. It is indeed with some deference that I suggest I can be of help. You will shortly be sitting in this chair doing the job I am now doing, but I, on the other hand, am 10 years older, so perhaps you can accept the idea that I may be able to give you the benefit of my longer experience."

Baker saw Rennalls stiffen slightly in his chair as he made this point. Consequently, he added in explanation, "You and I have attended enough company courses to remember those repeated requests by the personnel manager to tell people how they are getting on as often as the convenient moment arises and not just the automatic 'once a year' when, by regulation, staff reports have to be discussed."

Rennalls nodded his agreement, and Baker went on, "I shall always remember the last job performance discussion I had with my previous boss back in Germany. He used what he called the 'plus and minus' technique. His firm belief was that when a senior, by discussion, seeks to improve the work performance of his staff, his prime objective should be to make sure that the latter leaves the interview encouraged and inspired to improve. Any criticism must, therefore, be constructive and helpful. He said that one very good way to encourage a person—and I fully agree with him—is to tell him about his good points—the plus factors—as well as his weak ones—the minus factors. I thought, Matt, it would be a good idea to run our discussion along these lines."

Rennalls offered no comment, so Baker continued, "Let me say, therefore, right away, that, as far as your own work performance is concerned, the plus far outweighs the minus. I have, for instance, been most impressed with the way you have adapted your considerable theoretical knowledge to master the practical techniques of your job—that ingenious method you used to get air down to the fifth-shaft level is a sufficient case in point—and at departmental meetings I have invariably found your comments well taken and helpful. In fact, you will be interested to know that only last week I reported to Mr. Hutchins that, from the technical point of view, he could not wish for a more able man to succeed to the position of chief engineer."

"That's very good indeed of you, John," cut in Rennalls with a smile of thanks, "My only worry now is how to live up to such a high recommendation."

"Of that I am quite sure," returned Baker, "especially if you can overcome the minus factor which I would like now to discuss with you. It is one that I have talked about before so I'll come straight to the point. I have noticed that you are more friendly and get on better with your fellow Barracanians than you do with Europeans. In point of fact, I had a complaint only yesterday from Mr. Jackson, who said you had been rude to him—and not for the first time either.

"There is, Matt, I am sure, no need for me to tell you how necessary it will be for you to get on well with expatriates because until the company has trained up sufficient people of your calibre, Europeans are bound to occupy senior positions here in Barracania. All this is vital to your future interests, so can I help you in any way?"

While Baker was speaking on this theme, Rennalls sat tensed in his chair and it was some seconds before he replied. "It is quite extraordinary, isn't it, how one can convey an impression to others so at variance with what one intends? I can only assure you once again that my disputes with Jackson—and you may remember also Godson—have had nothing at all to do with the color of their skins. I promise you that if a Barracanian had behaved in an equally peremptory manner I would have reacted in precisely the same way. And again, if I may say it within these four walls, I am sure I am not the only one who has found Jackson and Godson difficult. I could mention the names of several expatriates who have felt the same. However, I am really sorry to have created this impression of not being able to get along with Europeans—it is an entirely false one—and I quite realize that I must do all I can to correct it as quickly as possible. On your last point, regarding Europeans holding senior positions in the company for some time to come, I quite accept the situation. I know that Caribbean Bauxite—as they have been doing for many years now—will promote Barracanians as soon as their experience warrants it. And, finally, I would like to assure you, John—and my father thinks the same too—that I am very happy in my work here and hope to stay with the company for many years to come."

Rennalls had spoken earnestly; although not convinced by what he had heard, Baker did not think he could pursue the matter further except to say, "All right, Matt, my impression *may* be wrong, but I would like to remind you about the truth of that old saying, 'What is important is not what is true but what is believed.' Let it rest at that."

But suddenly Baker knew that he didn't want to "let it rest at that." He was disappointed once again at not being able to break through to Rennalls and having yet again to listen to his bland denial that there was any racial prejudice in his makeup. Baker, who had intended to end the interview at this point, decided to try another tactic.

"To return for a moment to the 'plus and minus technique' I was telling you about just now, there is another plus factor I forgot to mention. I would like to congratulate you not only on the calibre of your work but also on the ability you have shown in overcoming a challenge which I, as a European, have never had to meet. Continental Ore is, as you know, a typical commercial enterprise—admittedly a big one—which is a product of the economic and social environment of the United States and Western Europe. My ancestors have all been brought up in this environment for the past 200 or 300 years and I have, therefore, been able to live in a world in which commerce (as we know it today) has been part and parcel of my being. It has not been something revolutionary and new that has suddenly entered my life." Baker went on, "In your case, the situation is different because you and your forebears have only had some 50 or 60 years in this commercial environment. You have had to face the challenge of bridging the gap between 50 and 200 or 300 years. Again, Matt, let me congratulate you—and people like you—once again on having so successfully overcome this particular hurdle. It is for this very reason that I think the outlook for Barracania—and particularly Caribbean Bauxite—is so bright."

Rennalls had listened intently and when Baker finished, replied, "Well, once again, John, I have to thank you for what you have said, and, for my part, I can only say that it is gratifying to know that my own personal effort has been so much appreciated. I hope that more people will soon come to think as you do."

There was a pause and, for a moment, Baker thought hopefully that he was about to achieve his long-awaited breakthrough, but Rennalls merely smiled back. The barrier remained unbreached. There remained some 5 minutes of cheerful conversation about the contrast between the Caribbean and Canadian climate and whether the West Indies had any hope of beating England in the Fifth Test before Baker drew the interview to a close. Although he was as far as ever from knowing the real Rennalls, he was nevertheless glad that the interview had run along in this friendly manner and, particularly, that it had ended on such a cheerful note.

This feeling, however, lasted only until the following morning. Baker had some farewells to make, so he arrived at the office considerably later than usual. He had no sooner sat down at his desk than his secretary walked into the room with a worried frown on her face. Her words came fast. "When I arrived this morning I found Mr. Rennalls already waiting at my door. He seemed very angry and told me in quite a peremptory manner that he had a vital letter to dictate that must be sent off without any delay. He was so worked up that he couldn't keep still and kept pacing about the room, which is most unlike him. He wouldn't even wait to read what he had dictated. Just signed the page where he thought the letter would end. It has been distributed and your copy is in your tray.' "

Puzzled and feeling vaguely uneasy, Baker opened the confidential envelope and read the following letter:

From: Assistant Engineer

To: Chief Engineer, Caribbean Bauxite Limited

14 August 198–

Assessment of Interview between Baker and Rennalls

It has always been my practice to respect the advice given me by seniors, so after our interview, I decided to give careful thought once again to its main points and so make sure that I had understood all that had been said. As I promised you at the time, I had every intention of putting your advice to the best effect.

It was not, therefore, until I had sat down quietly in my home yesterday evening to consider the interview objectively that its main purport became clear. Only then did the full enormity of what you said dawn on me. The more I thought about it, the more convinced I was that I had hit upon the real truth—and the more furious I became. With a facility in the English language which I, a poor Barracanian, cannot hope to match, you had the audacity to insult me (and through me every Barracanian worth his salt) by claiming that our knowledge of modern living is only a paltry 50 years old whereas yours goes back 200 or 300 years. As if your materialistic commercial environment could possibly be compared with the spiritual values of our culture. I'll have you know that if much of what I saw in London is representative of your most boasted culture, I hope fervently that it will never come to Barracania. By what right do you have the effrontery to condescend to us? At heart, all you Europeans think us barbarians, or, as you say amongst yourselves we are "just down from the trees."

Far into the night I discussed this matter with my father, and he is as disgusted as I. He agrees with me that any company whose senior staff think as you do is no place for any Barracanian proud of his culture and race—so much for all the company "clap-trap" and specious propaganda about regionalization and Barracania for the Barracanians.

I feel ashamed and betrayed. Please accept this letter as my resignation, which I wish to become effective immediately.

cc: Production Manager
     Managing Director

STURDIVANT ELECTRIC
CORPORATION

Richard Nolan
F. Warren McFarlan

Personnel of the Sturdivant Electric Corporation were entering the stage of running final acceptance tests on a special-purpose computer they had subcontracted to supply to the Armed Services. One stipulation in the computer contract was a demonstration by the supplier that the machine would function correctly and reliably under test conditions. The special operating system of the computer was prepared by Sturdivant Electric's chief programmer, Al Abrams. Several days before beginning these tests, Abrams submitted his work to his immediate superior, Bill Eden, who was computer project engineer (see Exhibit 1). Eden was to review the design of the operating system and compare it to the specifications. It was not intended that Eden check the correctness of the operating system itself, since forthcoming operational tests would accomplish that check.

In the course of his check, Eden found that Abrams had taken some liberties in one of the terms of the specification, and had told Abrams to reverse the changes. Abrams had become enraged. He shouted that Eden was not capable of passing judgment on his work. Abrams had stormed out of the computer room, bellowing and cursing, and had bumped into Harris Johnson, the Sturdivant test facility supervisor, in the hallway. Johnson tried to calm Abrams down, but Abrams pushed past him, claiming he would leave his security pass at the gate as a sign of his permanent departure.

Johnson knew that Eden and Abrams had had difficulties before, and that the project, nearing completion, was in a particularly sensitive stage of development. Realizing that he did not have direct line authority over Abrams within Sturdivant, Johnson needed to decide quickly what his next step should be.

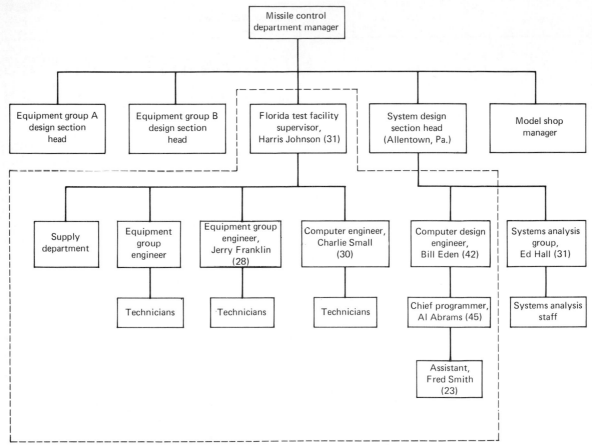

EXHIBIT 1   Sturdivant Electric Corporation—abbreviated organization chart of the missile control department.

COMPANY BACKGROUND AND ORGANIZATION OF FLORIDA TEST FACILITY

Sturdivant Electric was a large manufacturer of electrical equipment for industry, the Armed Services, and the consumer. Their industrial electronics division specialized in radar and all types of communication equipment. One subdivision of this operation was engaged in the development of missile guidance equipment. This group had a field test facility at the U.S. government's special weapons test center in Florida. The purpose of the facility, which had been under construction and partial operation for 14 months, was to conduct performance tests on missile guidance systems.

Although located on a military base, the test facility operated as an independent entity insofar as the direction of its activities was concerned. It relied on military personnel and supply for support only. For instance, the buildings were within a classified area guarded by military police, but the company retained responsibility for security of the project and could give or withhold permission to enter the test compound. When shipments had to be unloaded, it was done under the direction of the company, but with the help of military personnel and equipment. The military also supplied certain types of vehicles, which were driven by Sturdivant employees unless some specialized skill was required. In general, the arrangement was intended to allow the Armed Forces to provide services and facilities required by Sturdivant and the various other contractors with test facilities on the base, and thus to avoid unnecessary duplication.

Organizationally, the Sturdivant Electric test facility supervisor reported directly to the manager of the missile control department at corporate headquarters in Allentown, Pa. Harris Johnson had been placed in charge of the Florida center when it was first set up and took with him from Allentown several key people who would form the nucleus of the field organization (Exhibit 1).

In addition to the transplanted Pennsylvania personnel, Sturdivant employed several technicians and others from the local area. These people lived in their own homes or in nearby apartments. The workday for 15 members of the test facility staff began at 7 a.m. A coffee break took place at 8 a.m. when the post exchange coffee wagon made a stop at the building. The lunch period extended from 11:15 to 11:45 a.m. but, because of the nature of their work, the personnel took the half-hour when it was convenient rather than observing a strict schedule. The staff members were very congenial and enjoyed many outside activities together, such as beach parties, fishing trips, etc. The workday ended at 3:30 p.m., except when overtime was scheduled.

The bulk of the missile control equipment was built by the company in its Allentown plants and shipped to Florida. To assist with the start-up process, temporary assistants had been sent from Allentown. These people reported to Johnson for administrative purposes while in Florida, although any technical direction specifically relating to their equipment grouping came from their respective supervisors at headquarters.

Several members of Sturdivant's computer group had also been assigned temporarily to the Florida facility. Of this group, Bill Eden, the chief computer engineer, Al Abrams, the chief programmer, and Fred Smith, assistant, had stayed with the project on a full-time basis; other temporary personnel rarely stayed more than a week at a time. These three employees and their families occupied adjoining two-room motel apartments at a tourist court not far from the military base. Although their spouses saw each other daily and their children played together, the families did not share many common social activities. The apartments consisted of one bedroom, a large living room made into a bedroom, a combination kitchen and dining area that opened off the living room, and a bath. The motel was located on the ocean and, while reasonably comfortable, did not constitute luxurious accommodations by any means. Transportation to and from work was generally by company car, although because of the extended duration of the assignment, all three families had brought their own cars to Florida.

THE COMPUTER

A central component of the test facility was a digital computer. Although Sturdivant had prepared the performance specifications for the computer, it was the only major piece of equipment not designed and built by the company. When the subcontractor delivered the machine to the test facility, its installation and software development remained to be done. Consequently, a group of technicians from the subcontractor accompanied the computer to help the Sturdivant staff bring it up to operation. Eden, Abrams, and Smith had all spent considerable time in the design and production stages of the computer project back and forth between Sturdivant's headquarters and the subcontractor's headquarters in Concord, Mass., so they were familiar with the problems involved. Sturdivant's contract with the government stipulated that the supplier demonstrate that the computer would perform correctly and reliably. This demonstration was to be the acceptance tests, based on the performance specifications.

Sturdivant Electric's chief programmer, Al Abrams, had been working on the operating system of the computer under the supervision of Bill Eden, the computer project engineer. The many unresolved problems in the computer when it was delivered made the work day rather hectic. The computer contractor's personnel had first priority in working on the machine, since they were vitally interested in completing their fieldwork as rapidly as possible. Their headquarters' interest in completing the contract along with the ever-mounting costs associated with the installation and check-out operation provided a sense of pressure on the daily work.

Bill Eden's purpose in Florida was to represent Sturdivant on installation questions with the computer contractor, to make preparations for the acceptance tests of the machine, and generally to keep track of progress on the operating system. He did not have a great deal to keep him busy. His work day soon settled down and became rather routine. Much of the time he merely observed the work being done by the contractor's personnel in the computer room. He was always willing to take on special jobs suggested by Mr. Johnson from time to time and relished the opportunity to do something tangible. Fred Smith was kept busy running detailed computations for Abrams.

In addition to the tension created by the push to debug the computer quickly, further tension was produced by the necessity for Al Abrams to begin checking out the computer portions of the system that he was developing. It was necessary for Sturdivant to have a finished operating system before the computer could be put through exhaustive acceptance tests, yet the testing of the system required operational machine time. This made it mandatory to use any time when the contractor's employees were not performing development work that interfered with machine operation. Much of this available time was lost, however, because Abrams was unable to abruptly interrupt his efforts on one phase of the system to place other parts of it, which he may have mapped out several weeks earlier, in the machine, to run them, and to evaluate the results.

The stresses inherent in this working arrangement were manifest in an incident that took place earlier in the computer installation and development process. One day after lunch Al Abrams walked into Johnson's office with a look of disgust on his face.

Abrams: I'm sorry, Harris, I just can't take it any longer. I've talked it over with my wife and she agrees that my health is more important. I want to resign, effective immediately. I've never had to take the kind of guff that I'm getting around here.

At this point, Bill Eden, obviously disturbed, walked into the office.

Abrams: I don't know what this guy [pointing to Eden] expects of me. I've never taken the kind of treatment he's been giving off of anyone—even during the recession when jobs were tough to find. He hounds me all day long. I just can't be driven and I can't be paced by that machine.

Eden: Al, you know I do no such thing. I try to be as considerate of you as I possibly can. We've got a job to be done, and you've got to work on the machine when it's free.

Abrams: I don't work that way! When I get on a train of thought at my desk, I've got to follow it through. When you interrupt me I lose the train and it means I have to repeat the entire mental process that led up to it. I just can't stop in the middle of a sequence and run back to that damn computer just because it's free for a couple of minutes. I've been on a milk and crackers diet for the past 2 weeks because my ulcers are acting up again and it's all because of this work. You're driving me crazy.

Eden: That's not so. Al, you know damn well that I try not to aggravate you. You're so doggone touchy, it's pitiful.

Johnson: Hold on now! It's not going to do either of you any good to get hot under the collar. Let's try to get at the root of the trouble without all the fuss.

Abrams: Just take today for instance. You call me down to the machine this morning because it's going to be free for an hour. What happens? The damn thing isn't working and all my efforts were wasted. It took me 2 hours to retrace the steps up to the point at which you interrupted me.

Eden: It wasn't the machine, Al, your system had a mistake in it. The machine is okay.

Abrams: That's not so! You know damn well the computer was consistently failing to meet the maintenance routine density test limits for disk storage. How in the hell do you expect me to test part of my program with an unreliable disk?

Eden: The program checks you were making didn't involve the disk.

Abrams: How the hell do you know what I was checking?

Johnson: All right, come on back to earth!

Abrams: This business had me so upset this morning that I called my wife and asked her to meet me at the PX right away so we could discuss it in private. I left here on the 11 a.m. bus. We decided that it just wasn't worth it. My health is more important than this job. I know I'm not doing myself any good professionally by quitting, but it's the only answer. And that's not all; I got back here at noon and the first crack out of the box this guy says, "Where the hell have you been?" in a nasty tone of voice.

Eden: I did not use a nasty tone of voice! You'd been gone for an hour and a half and you didn't even have the courtesy to tell me when you left or where you were going!

Abrams: It was none of your damn business! I don't have to tell you every time I want to walk away from my desk. And for your information I told Mary [the office stenographer] when I left and when I'd be back.

Johnson: How about it, Bill, did you check with Mary? You know she keeps pretty good track of us.

Eden: No.

Abrams: Harris, I didn't have any trouble working in this group until Bill took over from McAlpin. Mac and I got along fine. And I don't want to put the company in an embarrassing spot by walking off before the system is complete. But I've got to think of myself.

The conversation continued along these lines for another half-hour. Eden walked out after a while, and Johnson and Abrams discussed in detail some factors behind the blowup. It became evident that Abrams had been stewing over the interruptions to his work at the desk for several weeks. A previous incident that had occurred in Allentown was also rehashed. At that time, Abrams had mistakenly interpreted Eden's request for the name of one of the computer contractor's programmers as an indication that the company was trying to hire a replacement for him and that he was going to be fired. Eden simply asked the question and gave no explanation. After Abrams had thought about it for an hour or so, he had become so incensed that he marched into the manager's office, broke up a meeting, and asked if they wanted him to quit.

When Abrams related this to Johnson in Florida, Johnson assured him that "the company did not operate in that fashion," and that if they were ever dissatisfied with his work, that fact would be discussed completely with him. The conversation drew to a close with an agreement that Abrams would continue to work on the program until its completion. Johnson promised to try to arrange a transfer to another department as soon as it was complete, and also to attempt to find a solution to his difficulties with Eden. Then Johnson called Eden back into the office.

Johnson: Bill, Al has agreed to finish up on the operating system. I hope you two will try to keep in mind the other fellow's feelings and try to be a little more tolerant and considerate. You know Al is doing the sort of work that involves uninterrupted concentration, so make sure that the free machine time is really worth breaking in for.

And, Al, you know that Bill's chief concern is the schedule and that he is afraid that we won't meet it. Understand that when he becomes apprehensive over your progress he is not being critical but just wants to know where we stand.

One thing more, I want it understood that neither of you has prejudiced his position by what has been said here today. You have honest differences and we'll try to resolve them, but we'll need the cooperation of each of you.

With this, Abrams left, but Eden stayed behind.

Eden: You know, Harris, I bend over backward with that guy. I'm just as nice as I can possibly be. I never go near him unless it's absolutely necessary. I leave him completely free for the program and screen out all small detailed matters. But he's so damn suspicious of everything you do. Why, one day in Allentown the boss asked me to check on the name of a programmer. The Concord crowd owed us some instruction time under the terms of the contract and since the fellow in question was familiar with our machine, the boss felt we might collect the time by sending some work up there. All I did was to ask Al for his name, nothing more, and darned if he didn't think we were going behind his back and trying to hire someone to take his place. After he blew up and learned the whole story, he changed his tune to the effect that he wasn't being consulted on such matters as he should be.

CHIEF COMPUTER ENGINEER

Bill Eden, age 42, had graduated from college after the Korean war, during which he had served as a first-class petty officer in the U.S. Navy. He was fortunate in not being required to take the laboratories associated with his major field, electrical engineering, at a large midwestern university, because his full-time job was in the university's research laboratory. In spite of the tremendous work load, Eden managed to complete the requirements for a bachelor's degree in 3 years. His wife, whom he met and married while they were in the Navy, also obtained her degree. Following graduation, Bill continued to work as an engineer in the research laboratory, occupied with basic development work for the defense effort. A year later he accepted a position with a large West Coast aircraft manufacturer, and was placed in charge of a group preparing technical manuals. He left this position in 1967 to accept a position with Sturdivant Electric Corporation as project engineer in the systems section. Eden had been dissatisfied with his previous job, partly because a golfing friendship had developed between one of his subordinates and his boss. The subordinate's professional loyalty appeared to be open to question, and Eden felt that he used the golf course to further his own cause.

With Sturdivant, Eden did an excellent job of coordinating the many system functions assigned to him. Before his coming, the entire design department had grown very rapidly. This—coupled with the new personnel's lack of familiarity with system concepts and requirements, the steady progress in the design of the many hardware components of the system, and the pressure of early design and dates—had created impetus for assigning the detailed coordinating responsibility to one person who could work with all design sections and gather, sort, analyze, and evaluate data and design considerations. With the help of two assistant engineers, Eden accomplished the desired results. He continued in this capacity until the promotion of the former computer project engineer created the vacancy into which he moved.

CHIEF PROGRAMMER

Al Abrams, age 45, had worked in three distinct fields: accounting, teaching, and engineering. His undergraduate training had prepared him primarily for teaching, but his interest in mathematics led him into graduate work preparatory for a master's degree in that field. His quest for further knowledge carried him into electronics, and he completed more than 150 semester hours of undergraduate and graduate study in radio engineering.

Abrams began his business career in the tax department of New York State, but left after 2 years to take a position as test planning engineer for Northern Electronics, Inc. While there he also began to teach electronics for the Army Air Force. Following this, he returned to accounting and served for a year as an Internal Revenue Service (IRS) agent in charge examining the tax returns of individuals, corporations, estates, and trusts. During this period, he also began to teach freshman and sophomore engineering physics at a New York college and continued there for 7 years. Concurrently, he operated his own business, preparing financial statements and tax returns, which he continued until mid-1966. During an 8-month period, he also tried various positions with four different companies in which he reviewed tax reports, gave advice on items that might invite IRS examination, audited books, and prepared financial statements. In late 1968, he accepted a position as a circuit and applications engineer with Erie Tube Corporation, and remained with them until he came to work for Sturdivant in April 1970.

Upon his arrival at Sturdivant, Abrams was assigned to the missile control project, where he assisted in the preparation of the purchasing specification for the computer. During the time lag while the contractor was beginning production of the machine, he assisted the analysis group at headquarters on the solution of mathematical problems. Following this he was sent to the computer contractor's plant in Concord, where he attended their school for programmers and filled a minor capacity in the coordination of the equipment manufacture. It was during this period that he also began work on programming the actual operating system to be used in Florida. It was also during this period that the original Sturdivant computer project engineer, McAlpin, was promoted and Eden was assigned the technical responsibility for the computer.

Abrams had spent 2 months at the computer contractor's school for technical programming. During this period he learned the logic of the computer he was to work with, that is, the characteristics of the various sections of the machine, their functional relationship to one another, the forms in which data were placed in and taken from the machine, the speeds with which computations could be handled, and many other factors that provided him with the basic tools needed to develop the operating system. From there on, development work was left to the ingenuity of the programmer. This task required a high degree of proficiency in mathematics and the type of mind that could, in an orderly, systematic fashion, juggle a vast number of factors, trying first one arrangement and then another, until the desired result was obtained. Generally, provision had to be made to store bits of information in the memory sections of the machine since the value was to be used later in a subsequent step. Particular attention had to be given to the amount of time taken to perform each operation, since the problem was being solved in "real time," that is, the time required for the performance became an integral part of the problem and affected the final answer. Because of the close interlocking relationship between computation time and sequence of operations, it was possible to have several days' work proved worthless because of a sudden incongruity. When a particular element of the operating system was completed, it was then pieced with a number of other elements to form a larger part of the entire sequence, in effect pyramiding the complications that could arise from incompatibility. Each element was a building block and it was not uncommon to find misfits, resulting in many painful and time-consuming repeats. In absolute magnitude, the job had hundreds of separate and distinct operations. Abrams was the only member of the Sturdivant computer staff who had been through the entire training program at the computer manufacturer's school, although Eden and Smith had been exposed to portions of it.

EARLIER ENCOUNTER

When Johnson had to leave the office for several days, he always designated one member of the permanent staff as being responsible for the operation of the test facility. On one such occasion Jerry Franklin, who generally filled this spot, was playing bridge with several other members of the staff, as was the lunchtime custom. As the group was completing the final hand, Eden walked over to the group, who was sitting around a desk that served as its card table, and observed for a minute or two. He cleared his throat a couple of times and finally said, "Don't you fellows think it is about time that you all got back to work?"

When the group broke up, Eden followed Abrams over to his desk and said, "Al, I'd like to get a progress report from you. Would you let me have the parts of the system you have completed?" Abrams' reply was to the effect that none of the work was in such a form that it would mean anything to Eden. He maintained that he had a series of notes in his file that contained the rough outline of the system and some finalized elements. He stressed that, in their present form, they would be valueless to Eden and were more likely subject to change in any event. Eden was nevertheless insistent. The level of their voices rose. After several heated exchanges in which charge and countercharge were hurled, Eden stalked off.

When Johnson returned the following day, Eden visited with him.

Eden: If you've got a minute, there's something I'd like to discuss with you.

Johnson: Sure thing, pull up a chair.

Eden: Well, I had another run-in with Al the other day and, frankly, I'm worried. He just will not give me anything concrete in the way of a progress report. He maintains that he is making satisfactory progress and will tell me if he feels he is getting behind.

You will recall that when he made his original estimate of how long it would take him to do the job, I made a point of letting everyone know that I didn't agree that he had allowed sufficient time. Now, with his reluctance to let me see what he has done, I'm more convinced than ever that we will not finish on time and that he is hiding the fact. Every time I try to find out where we stand he becomes temperamental. And if there's anything I can't stand it's a prima donna! When he finds that time has run out, he'll probably up and quit on us.

Johnson: Ouch! That's all we'd need! I hope you are misjudging Al.

Eden: I hope so, too, but the fact remains that I have no means of measuring his progress and have only his word for assurance that we are on schedule. You know the blood will be on my hands if we miss our dates. I'm plenty worried.

Johnson: Well, for peace of mind, if nothing more, we have to determine the status of the operating system. After all, our schedule for the entire test facility is based to a large extent on Al's end date. If you had his file on the system, could you do a sufficiently comprehensive analysis of the contents to establish our position?

Eden: Possibly, but I doubt it. Ed Hall up in Allentown would be in a much better position to do it since he has had a great deal of general operating system experience. But I know if you call in Hall for that purpose, it'll make Al mad.

Johnson: You're certainly right about that! However, if Hall would come down for a visit on a related matter, the progress report might be obtained as a byproduct. With his work on system simulations, there should be plenty of common ground on which the two of them can get together.

Eden: That's a thought.

Johnson: Suppose I discuss the matter with the boss and see what we can cook up.

A visit with Hall was arranged. As a result of some rescheduling at headquarters, it was convenient to shift some work associated with the Florida testing to Allentown. Abrams had originally planned to do this work after completing the main operating system. The stated purpose of Hall's visit was to coordinate the transfer of this small block of work. After making the arrangements, Johnson called Abrams into his office and informed him of the plan and the reasons. Abrams thought it was a good idea and promised to help in any way possible. After the visit, Hall assured everyone that Abrams appeared to be making satisfactory progress and that for the present, at least, he had every chance of meeting the schedule.

OVERTIME INCIDENT

On a Friday, several weeks after the work status controversy, Abrams stopped Johnson in the laboratory.

Abrams: Say, Harris, Bill wants Smith and me to work tomorrow, but I don't see the need for it. I'm keeping up with the schedule I've set for myself and until I get behind I see no reason for putting in overtime. Besides, I'd like to spend some time with my family.

Johnson: Can't say I blame you for that. Why does Bill feel that it is necessary?

Abrams: He just said that we should make use of every available minute now as a cushion against missing our schedule. I'm being very careful to be sure I maintain a progress rate consistent with our dates and I feel that overtime now is a needless imposition. If I find myself falling behind in any week, I'll certainly tell you and request overtime.

Johnson: From what you've told me, I've got to agree with you. Suppose I talk it over with Bill and see what he has in mind.

Abrams: Okay.

On his way back to the office, Johnson stopped by Eden's desk and asked him about the overtime situation.

Eden: Two fellows from Concord who are experts on the disk section are leaving for home on Sunday. So far this week we haven't gotten in more than 2 hours of actual operating time on the machine and I figured that if we worked Saturday we could get in a solid 8 hours with these boys standing by in case of trouble. In fact, they suggested that we do it so that they could be sure that the reliability of that section of the computer was up to par. Besides, it won't do any harm to get in all of the time we can now. I know Al is sore about it because he had planned to take off for Miami with his family tonight to spend the weekend with relatives.

Johnson agreed that they should work Saturday under the circumstances and walked back to the computer room to find Abrams. When Johnson related Eden's full story, Abrams quickly agreed to work. His closing remark was, "If Bill had only said something about the fellows leaving for Concord, there wouldn't have been any argument in the first place."

JOHNSON'S CURRENT PROBLEM

As Sturdivant moved into the stage of testing the computer, Eden reviewed Abrams's work. Abrams had finished the operating system a few days earlier and had submitted it to Eden.

In the course of his review, Eden found that Abrams's design of the operating system differed from the approved government specifications. When asked about it, Abrams replied that he was aware of the discrepancy but that it would make no difference in the end result. Eden discussed the matter with Charlie Small, another computer engineer for Sturdivant, and they agreed that the program was not acceptable as presented. When Abrams met with Eden and Small, Eden told him to correct the discrepancy. Abrams became enraged and made some caustic comments about their ability to pass judgment on his work. His closing comments were "I'm not going to have my work checked by everyone! I've been working on this system a long time and I'm the only one who can say whether or not it is okay! You guys have made my life miserable from the start! You sneak around behind my back and pull all sorts of stunts. I deserve to know what's going on around here. Eden, you've driven me like a common laborer since you were assigned to this job. You've never given me any help—I've been all alone on this job. I don't know what to expect next! As far as I'm concerned this is the finish. I quit!"

With that he stormed out of the computer room. Johnson, who had heard the last part of the conversation, caught up with him at the outer exit. Abrams tried to turn in his security pass.

Johnson: I won't take your pass now. Take a minute to relax and calm down.
Abrams: Damn it! Take it!
Johnson: No! Go on home and cool down. If you still want to quit in the morning, I'll accept your pass then.
Abrams: I don't want to be mollified! I don't want to cool down! If you won't take my pass, I'll leave it with the guard at the gate!

Once again, Johnson was faced with the problem of how to handle an administrative situation over which he had no direct line responsibility. Abrams and Eden worked for the systems section head, and although Johnson had kept him informed on all developments in Florida, the geographical separation seemed to Johnson to make him the one who had to cope with the problem on the spot. There was always a question about the lengths to which he could go in handling the matter because of his inability to make any commitments that would be binding for the section head.

FRANK MASON (A)

John J. Gabarro
N. J. Norman

"It was like stepping out of a steam bath into a cold shower," Frank Mason reflected as he recalled the day he left Great Pacific Paper Company. He now wondered if he would have left had he known what awaited him at the Abbot Business Supply Company. Frank sat in his office on Monday morning, September 14, and glanced out the door, noting that Ed Nolan, president of Abbot, had not yet arrived. In recent months, working for Nolan had been the most difficult experience of his otherwise successful career. When Frank had joined the company in March as vice president of marketing and sales, Nolan seemed to be a delightful, charming, almost charismatic gentleman. Nolan had given Frank a free hand in reorganizing the marketing area and practically guaranteed that Frank would be president of Abbot within 2 years. But then, things began to go wrong. He and Nolan no longer got along, his autonomy had been severely limited, company sales were again declining, and matters in general were rapidly deteriorating. To make things worse, Daryl Eismann, president of Houston Electronics, Abbot's parent company, would be flying in the following week to review the company's current situation.

The previous week, Frank had decided to take some action before Eismann arrived, and to him it seemed like it was time to have a candid talk with Nolan and try to resolve their differences. Frank had thought that Nolan would surely want to discuss these matters before Eismann's impending visit, but even after working for Nolan for 6 months, Frank still found him unpredictable. On Tuesday, Frank had asked Nolan to have a drink with him that afternoon, but Nolan declined. He also declined Frank's invitations for lunch on Wednesday and Thursday with no explanation. However, Frank noted that Nolan continued to have lunch with other managers in the firm. Frank still felt that a candid discussion about their relationship and the problems of Abbot could no longer be delayed, and he was determined to see Nolan as soon as he arrived. Nolan usually arrived at 9 a.m., which gave Frank almost half an hour to review the situation and gather his thoughts.

FRANK MASON

Frank was 35 years old, single, and a native of Peoria, Ill. He received his BA in economics from Antioch College, served 4 years in the Navy, and earned an MBA from the Harvard Business School. He then joined the Great Pacific Paper Company in Spokane, one of the country's largest and most profitable manufacturers and marketers of consumer paper products. The company sold nationally advertised facial tissue, bathroom tissue, paper towels, paper napkins, and other paper products. It was primarily Great Pacific's good reputation in the consumer products field that had appealed to Frank. His success in the marketing division had been spectacular— product manager in 2½ years (a company record), and senior product manager in only 6 more months. His salary had more than doubled by the end of his fifth year at Great Pacific.

But Frank also recalled the sense of personal stagnation that was growing during his last months there. Establishing new products had lost its charm. It was the same procedures again and again, and he felt that there was simply nothing new to learn there. Moreover, because of Great Pacific's strong hierarchical control, everpresent committee work, and endless rounds of required approval, he felt that he had not really tested himself. In fact, with such strong control and competent staff support, it seemed almost as difficult to fail as to succeed. He also recalled Great Pacific's disastrous acquisition of a regional chemical company, which forced them into austerity measures and restriction of expansion and advancement.

For these reasons, Frank left Great Pacific and went to Gleason Pro Shops, a retail sporting goods chain based in Seattle, as vice president for planning and marketing, receiving a 15 percent salary increase over his Great Pacific pay as well as a bonus. His autonomy there was indeed like an exhilarating cold shower. But corporate financial problems seemed to follow him from Great Pacific, for Gleason fell into a severe cash flow bind a few months after his arrival. Being unable to afford Frank's salary, the company sent him on his second search for employment in less than 18 months.

As he thought back on the experience, two things about his 15 months at Gleason Pro Shops still concerned Frank. Although he did not consider himself a "job hopper," he found himself beginning to fit this unattractive mold. Secondly, not one of his coworkers was a college graduate, and all used strong profanity, which seemed crude and unsophisticated to Frank. In retrospect, however, he suspected that he may have been too severe in his assessment of them which, in turn, may have caused some personal animosities.

After he left Gleason, Frank was contacted by an executive search agent, who told him of the position at Abbot Business Supply. The executive search firm had been engaged by Houston Electronics to find a vice president of marketing and sales for its Abbot subsidiary. Abbot had been a family-owned company with a very paternalistic style of management before its acquisition a year earlier by Houston Electronics, a producer of military avionics and space-tracking radar systems. Abbot was a regional manufacturer of stationery and other paper products, as well as a distributor of related business supply items. The company sold over 2000 products with annual sales of about $10 million. In addition to stationery and business forms, the product line included envelopes, typewriter paper, machine rolls, folders, loose leaf sheets, pens, pencils, duplicating supplies, staplers, blotters, and stenographic supplies. Stationery and business forms were Abbot's largest items, accounting for 45 percent of sales, and were produced and printed on Abbot presses. About 50 percent of their orders were received from stationery and business supply stores, 30 percent from businesses, and 20 percent from school systems and colleges. Abbot was located in San Francisco, with 70 percent of company sales in the Bay area, 20 percent in Los Angeles, and the remainder in Sacramento. School systems, colleges, and businesses were contacted by the company's sales force on a regular basis, while stationery and business supply stores sent their order directly to the sales department. The company had been urgently in need of a vice president of marketing and sales, and the agent offered Frank a salary 20 percent higher than his salary at Gleason Pro Shops, as well as a 25 percent bonus at the end of the year. Although not initially interested, Frank eventually agreed to a luncheon interview later that month with Ed Nolan, president of Abbot Business Supply.

INTERVIEWS WITH ED NOLAN

After a discouraging interview for an unattractive job in Burbank, Frank arrived in San Francisco on a beautiful, clear day in late February. It was at the Top of the Mark Restaurant in the Mark Hopkins Hotel that Frank first met Ed Nolan.

Nolan appeared to be in his mid-fifties, about medium height, slightly overweight with large, heavy jowls, and a full head of grey hair. Frank remembered how Nolan had initially reminded him of Laurence Olivier. Nolan was originally an engineer and had spent much of his career in high technology companies. He had impressed Frank with his excellent mind, which could accumulate, sort, and evaluate a large amount of information and reach a conclusion in a very short time. Frank was also impressed with Nolan's personal charm, good sense of humor, and attentive interest, which made him seem, at least to Frank, almost benevolent. But the one thing that Frank remembered most strongly about the meeting was that it seemed strangely unnecessary to "score points" with Nolan. It was as if Nolan was selling him on the job, rather than the other way around.

Frank also remembered his surprise when Nolan told him that he was also president of another division within Houston Electronics, with $300 million in sales. But Nolan had explained that he was only acting as steward of Abbot until he could find an aggressive, intelligent, young manager to take his place there. It soon became apparent to Frank that the next vice president for marketing and sales was very likely to become the next president of Abbot within 2 years. Frank expressed interest in the job and, without making firm commitments, they left the restaurant and Frank took a cab to the airport.

Ten days later, Nolan called Frank at his parents' home in San Diego and asked him if he was still interested. Since he was, they agreed on a date for Frank to fly to

San Francisco for a visit to the company plant and offices. Nolan told Frank he would pick him up at San Francisco International Airport on the morning of March 6. In thinking back to that morning, Frank was a little amused at the comedy of errors that had occurred. Nolan had not shown up as expected, so Frank called his apartment. Nolan's wife explained that Ed had already left for the office, and a second call to Nolan's secretary revealed that he was not yet in. but was expected shortly. Frank felt it would be a waste of time to wait at the airport, so he took a cab to the Abbot offices. Nolan greeted Frank warmly upon his arrival and seemed genuinely sorry for the mixup. Nolan then discussed company operations with him for the rest of the morning. Frank had researched the company thoroughly and was able to conduct an intelligent, knowledgeable discussion. In fact, it had seemed to Frank that he was more prepared to discuss specifics than Nolan.

However, Nolan seemed to have some strong general opinions on running a business. He was a strong believer in management-by-objectives and stressed the importance of good communication among top management. But he was equally convinced that each manager should run an area simply and without help from other functions. Nolan emphasized the importance of the controller as the guardian of the company's assets, and he stressed the need for efficiency and tight inventory control in production. He then added, "But in this business, control and marketing are the most important functions." Frank got the impression that Nolan saw people as either competent or incompetent, with great contempt and distrust for the latter. Nolan also talked for considerable time about his experience at Houston Electronics and the importance of accurate cost estimates in calculating required margins for their government contracts. According to Nolan, there were no serious pressures from the parent company, even though Abbot's sales had been declining. Until things were turned around, Houston Electronics could make up any Abbot losses. Frank talked with Nolan until mid-afternoon and then returned to San Diego.

Two matters bothered Frank about his prospects at Abbot. First, Nolan had failed to introduce him to any of the other people in the company (see Exhibit 1), explaining that they were busy with the quarterly report. Second, the job was in industrial marketing, which lacked the excitement of surveys, mass advertising, packaging, and so on. However, Nolan had promised the autonomy that Frank wanted, and there seemed to be a very good chance that he might be president with 2 years. To Frank, the autonomy and challenge of making major marketing decisions seemed to greatly outweigh the less exciting marketing problems of a small, nonconsumer company such as Abbot. Additionally, he could live in the San Francisco area, which he had always liked. When Nolan offered him the job the following week, Frank accepted with no hesitation.

A TALK WITH ST. CLAIR

On March 22, Frank began his job as vice president for marketing and sales of Abbot Business Supply Company. He soon met Bob St. Clair, a consultant to Abbot, who was also a graduate of Harvard Business School (class of 1957) and who had been a consultant to Great Pacific Paper Company. They quickly became good friends, and Frank asked St. Clair to talk with him about the company's background. One after-

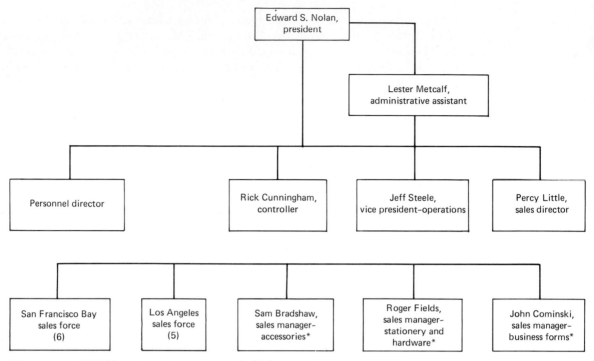

*The company is divided into three product groups, each with its own product manager:
  — The accessories group: bulletin boards, rubber bands, paper clips, maps,
    and art supplies (18% of sales)
  — The stationery and hardware group: stationery and envelopes, appointment books,
    scratch pads, calendars, card indexes, steno supplies, fasteners, and paper punchers
    (39% of sales)
  — The business forms group: business forms, business envelopes, machine rolls,
    typewriter paper, indexes, folders, and expanding envelopes   (43% of sales)

EXHIBIT 1   Partial organization chart, Abbot Business Supply Company (March 1).

noon they met for lunch, and St. Clair explained that Nolan was apparently the
protégé of Art Lincoln, executive vice president of Houston Electronics (see Exhibit
2). St. Clair was on good terms with Lincoln, since they had been roommates in
college. Nolan had been the only high-level manager in Houston Electronics that was
in favor of acquiring Abbot. His influence with Lincoln and his record as a high
performer had apparently outweighed any objections to acquiring a company in such
a different industry. Nolan was made president of Abbot and put under heavy pressure from Eismann to improve its performance. St. Clair confided to Frank that
Nolan had just told Lincoln that Abbot was in serious trouble. Lincoln had recommended that Nolan spend all his time in San Francisco and leave his division in
Houston in the hands of his capable deputies. However, Nolan was still spending
half his time in Houston.

St. Clair also told Frank that, while most people seemed to have difficulty in
getting along with Nolan, Rick Cunningham, the controller, and Lester Metcalf, the
administrative assistant, were on good terms with him. They usually had lunch with
Nolan 3 or 4 days a week. Both had worked for Nolan at Houston Electronics. A

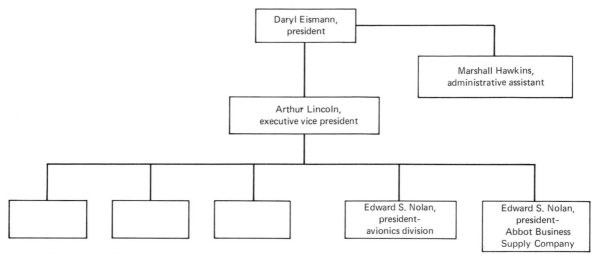

EXHIBIT 2   Partial organization chart, Houston Electronics Company (March 1).

rumor had it that several years earlier Metcalf had been near personal bankruptcy, and Nolan had saved his career. St. Clair told Frank that Metcalf was very loyal to Nolan. Cunningham was an accountant who strongly emphasized cost control but reportedly had no sympathy for salespeople's problems. He, too, was very loyal to Nolan, and they occasionally attended Warrior games during the basketball season. As far as St. Clair knew, basketball games with Cunningham were Nolan's only social life.

St. Clair knew that Nolan considered Frank a possible candidate for the president's job. However, he warned Frank that Jeff Steele, vice president for operations, also wanted to be president of the firm and that Frank could be in for a difficult time with him. As a final word of advice, St. Clair urged Frank to move into the vacant office next to Nolan's office, "before someone else tries to gain the favored position." Frank thanked St. Clair for the information and advice, and he returned to his office. The next day, he moved into the room next to Nolan's office, as St. Clair had suggested. At first Frank had been very apprehensive over St. Clair's warning about Jeff Steele. Later on, however, Steele became one of Frank's best friends, while his relationship with Nolan became worse over the summer.

FIRST 3 MONTHS AT ABBOT

Initially, Nolan seemed to have absolute confidence in Frank's ability. Frank's recommendations on marketing strategy met no resistance, and he seemed to be the commanding influence on Nolan for his first few months at Abbot. Nolan had given Frank full autonomy over pricing, even though St. Clair had recommended that Nolan retain pricing control over very large orders. Although St. Clair also recommended that Frank be allowed at least 2 months to gain a foothold in marketing before taking over sales as well, Nolan wanted Frank to take responsibility for sales in early April. Frank was reluctant to take on too much too soon, but he hesitated for other reasons also.

When Frank first joined the company, Percy Little was in charge of sales. Frank saw Little as a highly regimented person who paid careful attention to detail but often could not see the forest because of the trees. He thought that if Little had a personal motto, it would be "Everything to please the customer." Although Little had excellent relationships with the sales force, he seemed to have little administrative ability. Nolan would often ask detailed, probing questions of Little, which he could rarely answer without checking his books or asking a salesperson. Little's failure to have the answers at his fingertips invariably angered Nolan, who made it clear to Frank that he thought Little was incompetent and should be fired immediately. Frank also recalled the attitude of the sales force at that time. They were mostly oldtimers, with more than 25 years of service with the company. In his initial contacts with them, Frank found them to be shy, very responsive to his questions or requests, and seemingly frightened of him. For Frank, this did not appear to be a situation in which he wished to become involved at that time.

But Nolan was persistent, and Frank finally yielded and took charge of sales. He felt that he would have to manage the sales force as best he could, dealing with them primarily through Little. Little proved to be loyal to Frank, even though he, too, was one of the company oldtimers. Little seemed to be relieved when Frank took charge of sales. After this change the organizational chart for Abbot Business Supply was redrawn as shown in Exhibit 3.

In early May, the company received a visit from Art Lincoln, executive vice president of Houston Electronics. The main purpose of the visit was to hear Frank present Abbot's business plan. When Nolan introduced Frank to him, Lincoln remarked, "So this is the guy who walks on water." Frank was somewhat surprised, but replied, "It depends on how deep it is." The presentation for Lincoln was a one-person show, and Frank was the star performer. Much of his presentation concerned a reorganization of the marketing function and its communication needs. He recalled that after his presentation everyone had been happy except him, because he knew that he now had to deliver.

In his first 3 months at Abbot, Frank had been faced with several difficult decisions. In late May, he found it necessary to release the entire Los Angeles sales force, since the volume for that region was not large enough to justify the operating costs involved. He contacted four large stationery stores and three distributors in the Los Angeles area, which agreed to order exclusively from Abbot. Frank felt that this action would retain most of the volume in Los Angeles without the high operating costs of the sales force. He appointed James Au, the Los Angeles warehouse manager, to oversee these accounts and to call on them at regular intervals. Although the salespeople were released because of financial considerations and not age, Frank still had mixed feelings about firing them. One salesperson was 69 years old, even though the company had a policy of retirement at 65. He reportedly had a private agreement with Nolan to remain in his job past the normal retirement age. Frank felt a great sense of relief when he later learned that all of them had obtained jobs within 2 weeks of their severance from Abbot Business Supply. Another unpleasant but nec-

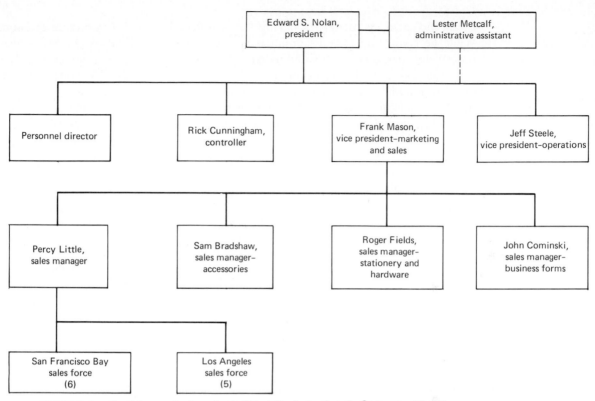

EXHIBIT 3 Partial organization chart, Abbot Business Supply Company (May 1).

essary action was to fire Sam Bradshaw, one of the sales managers. Sam was 57 years old, had 32 years of service with the company, and was afflicted with Parkinson's disease. Frank had discussed firing Bradshaw with Percy Little, and after a long and labored discussion, Little begrudgingly admitted that it probably was not necessary to keep Bradshaw. Although he did not find it easy, Frank eventually gave Bradshaw his notice.

As he began to get the feel of his new job, Frank also made friends with Roger Fields and John Cominski, his two sales managers, who seemed quite happy for Frank to be taking the lead role in the company. Both also seemed to have considerable difficulty in dealing with Nolan. But Frank had dismissed any concerns he might have had about Nolan, believing that they were simply too unsophisticated to effectively deal with him.

In mid-May, Frank added Steve Lewis to his staff as a product manager. When Frank first met him, Lewis was working for Cunningham in the controller's office. Frank and Lewis were both bachelors in their mid-thirties, and they soon discovered that they were very similar in lifestyle and sense of humor. One evening over drinks, Lewis expressed an interest in working for Frank. Frank had been impressed with Lewis's ability, and he remembered Cunningham commenting favorably on Lewis's competence. When Cunningham later returned from a meeting in Los Angeles,

Frank indicated his interest in having Lewis transferred to the marketing division. While he could understand Cunningham's reluctance to let Lewis go, Frank was nevertheless persistent, and Cunningham eventually agreed to the transfer.

Frank also hired Tony Buccini as a product manager in May. Although Buccini often appeared abrupt and stubborn, his enormous energy and strong ability with numbers made him a good product manager. Frank thought back to the day in mid-May when both Lewis and Buccini were officially assigned to marketing. He had remembered how Nolan had emphasized that each manager should be able to run his own area without help from other functions. Therefore, he told Lewis and Buccini that, although their official functions were in marketing, they should keep themselves informed of other aspects of the company as well. The following week, Buccini approached Frank with what he saw as an impending problem in the company's cash position. They discussed it with Cunningham, who assured them that there was no problem with the projected cash flow. Neither Frank nor Buccini was convinced, and later that afternoon they met with Nolan to explain the problem. Nolan failed to see a problem and, over their objections, dismissed the issue as unimportant. Frank remembered the staff meeting 2 days later in which Nolan had emphasized the soundness of the company's cash position and how it was not a subject of concern. In retrospect, Frank felt that this incident may have strained Buccini's relationship with Cunningham. Now that Lewis and Buccini were working for Frank, the company organizational chart was again redrawn, as shown in Exhibit 4.

EXHIBIT 4   Partial organization chart, Abbot Business Supply Company (May 25).

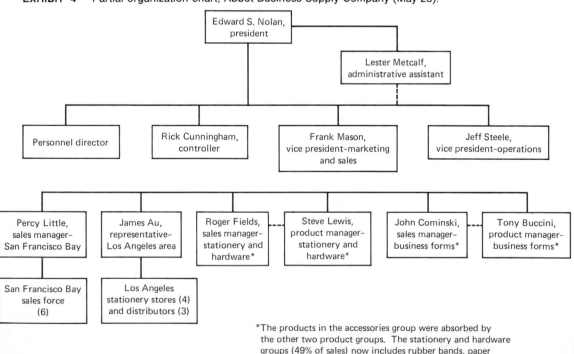

*The products in the accessories group were absorbed by the other two product groups. The stationery and hardware groups (49% of sales) now includes rubber bands, paper clips, and bulletin boards, and the business forms group (51% of sales) now includes maps and art supplies.

After a short time, Frank began to have mixed feelings about his job at Abbot. After searching for greater autonomy, he had suddenly found himself thinking that he almost had too much autonomy. While the Great Pacific Paper Company approach emphasized tight control supplemented by strong staff support, the approach within Houston Electronics could be summed up as "self-sufficiency," or as Frank often put it, "parochial functionalism." For Frank, this meant providing his own control, budgeting, planning, and so on. Also, it seemed to Frank that he, not Nolan, was supplying the leadership for the company. This seemed to him like such excessive autonomy that it was a little frightening.

PROBLEMS WITH NOLAN

During May and June, Frank began to see unexpected and unpleasant aspects of Nolan's personality. He recalled the volatile and unpredictable side of Nolan, particularly in the way he treated other people, such as Percy Little. Frank's tour in the Navy had taught him that when dealing with subordinates the rule was, "Praise in public, censure in private." Nolan seemed to take exactly the opposite view. It seemed to Frank that Nolan was a "Theory X manager—if something goes wrong, raise hell!" Also, during his frequent outbursts, Nolan would liberally use strong profanity, even during staff meetings, which Frank found personally distasteful and at times upsetting. At Great Pacific Paper, he had never heard an oath stronger than "SOB," and even that was seldom used. He was shocked that a man of Nolan's stature would use such language at any time, but especially when conducting company business. At first, Frank had attributed such behavior to the other managers' ineptness in dealing with Nolan, but even so, he felt that Nolan's methods and language were unnecessary.

One particular incident stood out in Frank's memory. At a staff meeting in May, Nolan had wanted Jeff Steele to set up the warehouse like a supermarket, to move away from the computer printouts currently being used in inventory control. "When I want to know what we have in inventory," he shouted, "I want to walk through the warehouse and see it with my own eyes!" Steele had argued that the computerized location system was efficient and reliable, and that there was no need to group and display their products in the warehouse like supermarket merchandise. Frank remembered Nolan's anger during the conversation. Nolan apparently disliked computer printouts and believed that a good manager should have the relevant information in his head. What seemed quite strange to Frank was that Nolan seemed to look to him for reassurance as he argued with Steele. Nolan even interrupted the meeting to ask Frank for advice on the matter. Frank responded that from his own perspective there would probably be no problems, but the real issue was whether or not the company would incur incremental costs by changing to the supermarket-type arrangement. The company changed over to Nolan's system within a month.

In June, Frank first noticed that his relationship with Nolan was growing more tense. Nolan had become very concerned about Abbot's recent financial performance, especially the firm's low margin. The low margin was primarily the result of Frank's price-cutting strategy aimed at reversing Abbot's declining sales. Also, the price of paper had sharply increased shortly after Frank took over pricing, which further hurt performance. Although the company's performance was not good in comparison to the business plan, Frank pointed out to Nolan that it was still an improvement over the February figures. But his reasoning had little impact on Nolan, who continued to complain about the poor margin.

Frank's relationship with Nolan grew more strained in July, and early in the month they had their first major argument. Frank had approved the sale of an order at below the break-even point. Since he believed that the customer would not pay a higher price, and since the firm was experiencing high inventory levels, he approved a price that at least covered variable costs and provided some contribution, rather than lose the order. Cunningham informed Nolan of Frank's decision, and Nolan became very upset with Frank, since his decision would further reduce the margin. After expressing his anger at Frank for several minutes, Nolan suddenly demanded to know the margin on a small order for desk pens. Since Frank regarded his role in the company as strategist, he left such details to his subordinates. When he told Nolan that he would have to check, Nolan became furious. During the next few minutes, Nolan also expressed his displeasure that the former owner of Abbot had somehow obtained some sensitive information about their operations in Los Angeles. He was sure that one of the marketing people had leaked this information, and he demanded to know what Frank was going to do about it. The entire discussion left Frank feeling very disturbed, confused, and angry, but he managed to tell Nolan that he would bring it up at his next staff meeting.

A few days later, Frank opened his staff meeting with a few words on the sensitivity of company information. He later informed Nolan of this action, but Nolan demanded to be present at the next meeting to see for himself. A week later, Frank presented the same information to his staff, as Nolan had instructed, while Nolan sat by the wall near the head of the table. When Frank finished his opening remarks, Nolan abruptly left the room, slammed the door, and did not return.

At Nolan's next staff meeting, he told Frank that he should send Percy Little to Los Angeles on Mondays to visit the major stationery stores there. Frank protested that there was no need to send Little to Los Angeles, and that he could be of more help in the home office. Nolan became visibly angry at Frank's response and instructed Frank that he wanted Little in Los Angeles on Mondays "even if all he does is sit there!" Then, without looking directly at Frank, he said, "When I tell someone to do something, I expect them to do it!"

Shortly after the incident over the break-even sale, Frank felt the need to talk with Nolan about how things were going. He spoke to Nolan one morning and expressed his frustration and confusion over what was expected of him. Nolan, however, responded that things were going fine and there was nothing to be overly concerned about. This discussion left Frank feeling very unsatisfied. It seemed to him that such a discussion should have had a more powerful impact on Nolan, but instead Nolan had been very calm and approving. He decided that it would be better to discuss the matter with Nolan during their trip to Los Angeles the following week.

Frank and Nolan arrived in Los Angeles on a hot, smoggy afternoon in late July. During the ride from the airport in their rented car, Frank began to tell Nolan about the problems he saw at Abbot Business Supply. He said that since Nolan spent much of his time in Houston, there were communication problems, a lack of central focus, and a power vacuum in the company. Also since Lester Metcalf, the administrative assistant, also went to Houston fairly often, no one was in charge of the company for fairly long periods of time. Frank felt that Nolan needed to be at Abbot all the time or not at all. Frank also felt that if Nolan could not be there at all, then he should make some sort of power arrangement. After expressing these thoughts to Nolan, Frank suggested that a conference phone hookup from Houston might be feasible. Nolan listened to Frank and seemed to be very understanding of the problems and frustrations Frank was experiencing. He agreed with Frank's analysis, seemed appreciative of his candor. Frank began to feel optimistic, since Nolan seemed ready to make the needed changes.

CONSTRUCTION PAPER INCIDENT

After their conversation, Nolan casually mentioned to Frank that the company ought to sell more school construction paper. Frank agreed and, upon his return to San Francisco, began to gear up for increased construction paper sales. One week later, Frank was surprised to discover that no more construction paper remained in inventory. For an explanation, Frank went to Jeff Steele, who told him that Nolan had ordered him to stop purchasing construction paper a few days earlier. Frank then went to Nolan and expressed his distress that he had not been informed of this decision. Nolan remarked, "This is a small company. When I tell one guy something, he should tell the others." He had little else to say, so Frank returned to Steele's office and they discussed the matter for over an hour.

The following Tuesday, a salesperson from a major paper producer offered to sell 40,000 reams of construction paper to Abbot at a very good price. Frank talked to Steele and then to Nolan, explaining that the supplier would guarantee the order to the company's specifications and would allow Abbot to inspect the shipment before delivery. Nolan, however, did not think it was a good idea. Although 40,000 reams is a small amount of construction paper, Nolan still disagreed with the purchase, stating that "I don't want to go into it. I've talked to paper experts and they say we're too small to be hedging in the paper market." The next day, Steele asked Frank about the order and Frank told him of Nolan's decision. Steele responded, "I want to talk to Nolan," and went straight to the president's office. Twenty minutes later, Steele returned to say that Nolan had changed his mind and had decided to buy the 40,000 reams of construction paper. When Frank confronted Nolan about this reversal, Nolan explained, "For that amount, we can sell it. Besides, Frank," he continued, "you didn't give me all the facts about this deal. You never told me that we could reject the order at no cost to us, if it wasn't prepared to our specifications." When Frank pressed him, Nolan simply dismissed the issue, saying that Frank need not be concerned about it. Frank left Nolan's office feeling very angry and frustrated.

NEW PRICING SCHEME

In early August, Nolan took control of all pricing. The margin for July was as poor as that of May and June, and Nolan decided to remedy this problem with his own pricing scheme for Abbot's products. His pricing scheme was based on a required overall company margin of 24 percent.[1] Since the cost of each item was known, Nolan could calculate a price for each of the company's products that would produce a margin within 2 or 3 percentage points of the required figure.

However, Frank felt that this scheme was far too simple. It treated every product the same, regardless of differences in demand, competitive situation, or the distinct qualities of each item. Also, it had the effect of lowering the price on high-margin, low-volume goods and raising the price on low-margin, high-volume goods. Since stationery stores often carried thousands of items, they could not absorb large orders and, therefore, would be unable to take immediate advantage of a lower price on the high-margin, low-volume items. Furthermore, if prices were raised on high-volume, low-margin items, which were typically price-competitive, the company might lose sales to lower-priced competitors. Although Frank voiced these objections, Nolan insisted on going ahead with his plan. When Frank saw the new price list, he protested that he could not possibly generate the volume at these prices. Nolan replied, "When did I expect you to worry about volume?"

As Frank had expected, Nolan's pricing scheme was a complete failure, and the company's performance for August was even poorer than it had been for May, June, and July. Nolan had received the August performance results on September 4, and since that time had spoken to no one, except Cunningham and Metcalf. Since Frank's autonomy was now very limited, and since Nolan was no longer speaking to most managers, it seemed to Frank that there was no longer any leadership in the company.

RICK CUNNINGHAM

It occurred to Frank that his deteriorating relationship with Nolan paralleled his deteriorating relationship with Cunningham. During April and May, he and Cunningham got to know each other fairly well, and they would occasionally have drinks and dinner. Although they related well after working hours, it seemed to Frank that Cunningham was a completely different person at the office. Frank felt that "apple polisher" would be too kind a word for Cunningham, who blamed everyone else for any problems and always answered Nolan with "Yes, sir," "No, sir," and "Right away, sir." Cunningham also saw Percy Little as a major problem in the company because he was "giving the products away" with low prices and easy credit terms.

It seemed to Frank that Cunningham and Nolan always stood on the same side of every issue. After Nolan's reprimand over the break-even sale, Frank discovered that Cunningham had informed Nolan of Frank's decision to approve the order. That afternoon, Frank had found Cunningham in the hall, and asked him why he had gone directly to Nolan and not seen him first. Frank made it clear that if Cunningham didn't have the decency to deal with him directly instead of running to Nolan, then he too could play that game. In response, Cunningham demanded that Buccini mind his own business and accused Frank of letting Percy Little operate in his usual

---

[1] Margin, in percent, was calculated by dividing the gross margin by sales revenue. Gross margin equals the sales revenue minus the cost of goods sold.

way, which was causing the company to lose money. After a short time, both men calmed down and returned to their offices.

After this incident, it seemed to Frank that his relationship with Cunningham became more openly hostile. A few days later, Buccini drove to Sacramento and returned via San Rafael on company business, but neglected to acquire receipts for bridge tolls. The controller's office had recently established a new policy that specifically prohibited reimbursement of expenses for company business without a receipt, and Buccini's request for $2.35 was refused. Buccini explained the situation to Frank, who was amazed at the pettiness of the refusal. Frank was so angered by it that he went directly to the company clerk and complained. However, the clerk argued that he could not make the payment under the company's policy, and Buccini never received payment for this expense. A few days after this incident, Frank received a memo from Cunningham which said, essentially, "If you have a complaint, don't talk to my people, talk to me." To Frank, the note seemed to be the last straw. By the time he reached Cunningham's office, Frank was so angry that he simply crumpled up the note, dropped it in Cunningham's waste basket, and told him, "I got your note."

CURRENT SITUATION

The most recent problem facing Frank involved Nolan's insistence that he dismiss James Au, the Los Angeles area representative. Frank had put Au in charge of the Los Angeles accounts after he had released the Los Angeles sales force. He had felt that the volume of business in Los Angeles was large enough to warrant a company representative to service these accounts. It seemed to him that, without a local representative, the company would probably lose these accounts to competitors. Nolan, however, felt that these accounts could be serviced equally well from San Francisco, and that Frank should dismiss Au to cut costs. Although Frank had recommended that no raises be given to himself, his product managers, or his sales managers in an effort to reduce costs, Nolan still insisted that Au be fired. Frank felt that this problem, as well as the pricing problem, had to be settled before Daryl Eismann arrived. The impending visit of the parent company's president created an added sense of urgency to resolve these and other problems that had developed over the last few months.

Over the weekend, Frank had even considered resigning from Abbot. At first the idea seemed appealing, under the circumstances, but the more he thought of it, the more distasteful it became. A resignation, to Frank, would be an admission of failure and, if he took another job, it would be his third in less than 2 years. Additionally, he had recently purchased a house overlooking the Bay, and the prospect of being without income again for an undetermined period of time would strain his resources. Frank had invested most of his savings in the property, and he did not have enough cash to sustain a prolonged job search. Also, he liked the Bay area and did not look forward to leaving it, if he could not find a job nearby.

Frank leaned back in his chair and tried to put the last 6 months into perspective. He had taken a job with substantial autonomy, a good chance for advancement, and a very good relationship with the company president. But the relationship had deteriorated, his autonomy had been severely curtailed, and his chances for advancement looked dim. Nevertheless, he felt that he could not continue much longer with things as they were, and believed that he had to take some immediate action to improve the situation with Nolan and Cunningham. Frank became lost in his thoughts for a few minutes until he heard the familiar sound of heavy, purposeful footsteps in the hall. Frank looked up and stared at the president's door, waiting expectantly.

FRANK MASON (B)

John J. Gabarro
N. J. Norman

Nolan walked into his office and closed the door behind him. Frank entered Nolan's office and began to tell him of his frustrations. As he became more excited, Frank heard himself saying, "What do you expect from me? I don't understand my role in the company. If Cunningham is your chief of staff, let me know." For each of these statements, Frank provided examples. Nolan was very quiet and nodded slowly as Frank reeled off point after point. Nolan finally broke his silence while Frank was discussing Cunningham. "I feel comfortable with Rick," he interrupted. "I know him from our days in Houston Electronics. I communicate with him very often, and I probably shouldn't." Frank continued to complain that, as vice president for marketing and sales, he should be involved in pricing. Nolan countered by stating that the new scheme was his own idea and he would run it himself. "Besides, Frank," he continued, "you let me down before. Try it my way now." Then Nolan became more active, complaining that Buccini was interfering with other areas. Frank defended him, stating that he believed Buccini was doing a fine job. Nolan suddenly demanded, "Why haven't you fired Little?" Frank explained that Little was his link to the salespeople, and firing him would be a mistake. They continued their discussion for about 20 minutes and, as Frank, was about to leave, Nolan said, "Frank, you shouldn't feel that we have to get away from the office for us to talk. My door is always open, you can come in anytime."

Frank left Nolan's office feeling somewhat relieved. What had begun as a difficult, emotional argument had ended surprisingly well. Nolan seemed to understand the problem Frank was facing and indicated that he would try to be more reasonable. On the whole, it had gone better than Frank had expected, and he was looking forward to a better relationship with Nolan and a gradual return of his autonomy.

The next morning, it was as if they had not talked at all. Nolan began his staff meeting by criticizing Cunningham, but looking at Frank as he did so. Then, Nolan began to complain loudly about the poor margin for the last 4 months. Although he was very active during the staff meeting, Nolan was aloof the rest of the week, except for lunch with Cunningham and Metcalf.

The following Monday, Daryl Eismann arrived and met with Nolan and his managers all day. Eismann asked many difficult and pointed questions, and Frank got the impression that Nolan and Cunningham were attempting to smooth over the problems at Abbot. After Eismann left, Frank drafted a letter to him on yellow paper, but did not mail it. (See Exhibit 1.) Later in the week, Nolan had another staff meeting, announcing that Marshall Hawkins, Eismann's administrative assistant, would arrive at Abbot on Monday for additional meetings. Nolan's opening words were, "Eismann is sending his sleuth for a visit."

Hawkins arrived on Monday and talked with each top manager in Abbot. Frank believed that this was the time to state his position. He talked with Hawkins privately, and candidly explained his own view of the situation at Abbot. Frank also showed Hawkins the letter to Eismann he had drafted a week earlier. When Hawkins read it, he remarked, "It's a good thing you didn't send it." It seemed to Frank that Hawkins was sympathetic to his problems. Hawkins thanked him for his time and candor and left his office. Frank noted that Nolan and Cunningham were again attempting to smooth over the company's problems. The next day, Hawkins issued a list of six actions that he designated as high priority, three of which involved marketing. Hawkins left on the afternoon plane for Houston, and Nolan left for Houston the following morning.

One priority on Hawkins's list was to increase the prices on Abbot's line of desk calendars and appointment books. However, when Frank showed Metcalf the new price list, Metcalf refused to approve it. Frank reminded him of Hawkins's instructions, but Metcalf replied, "Hawkins is staff, not line. As long as Ed Nolan is president of this company, we sell these items at the lower price." Frank asked for a memo of his decision, but Metcalf remarked, "I'm sending a letter straight to Hawkins!"

EXHIBIT 1   FRANK MASON'S UNSENT LETTER TO DARYL EISMANN

Dear Daryl,

I enjoyed meeting you and found your comments helpful in moving the business ahead.

While you were exposed to many of our problems during your visit, there are others of which you may not be aware. I would like to speak with you further about these problems at your convenience.

Sincerely,

Frank Mason

Two weeks later, Steele received a call from Hawkins, who asked for his observations on the company's progress since his visit, expressing a particular interest in Frank's area. Steele informed Frank of the call, explaining that he had said a few encouraging words in general but had declined to discuss Frank, stating that he felt it inappropriate to evaluate a peer.

A few weeks after Hawkins called Steele, Metcalf invited Frank to lunch and explained that "some things are going on" that he could not divulge. After making sure that Frank was doing his utmost to comply with Hawkins's instructions, Metcalf added, "If you have any problems, call me. I'll be in Palm Springs." A week later, Metcalf called Frank to see what progress he was making on Hawkins's instructions. Frank made a favorable report, adding that he had also completed James Au's severance papers as Nolan had wanted. During most of the following month, Frank worked to implement the priorities on Hawkins's list, as did most of the other managers at Abbot. Nolan was beginning to play a conspicuously small role in the management of the firm. Since Eismann's visit, Nolan had spent about 1 day a week at Abbot and the rest in Houston.

Two months after his initial visit, Eismann returned to Abbot and informed the top management group that Nolan had been relieved of his duties. He went on to add that in his opinion Abbot was in serious trouble and every member of top management was suspect. He also pointed out that an "internal person" would not be chosen to replace Nolan. Eismann concluded by promising them an answer about their future with the company as soon as circumstances permitted.

A week later, Hawkins arrived at Abbot and informed Frank that he was fired. Hawkins explained that the only reason for dismissal was Houston Electronics's policy of "cleaning house" whenever a division president was fired. "It's nothing against you," he added, "it's just company policy." In a strange way, Frank felt relieved and vindicated by his statement. Two weeks later, Frank called Buccini to inquire about the situation at Abbot. Buccini replied that Hawkins had become acting president, but that no one else had been fired so far.

ROGER CLARKE (A)

W. Earl Sasser

Six weeks after his promotion to advanced market development specialist, Roger Clarke realized that he was in trouble. The glowing reports and forecasts that had provided the momentum for his predecessor's promotion to marketing manager were either overly optimistic or outright fabrications. There was no chance of meeting the 6-month or 12-month goals unless Clarke continued the creative accounting and report writing so brilliantly engineered by Brad Carter, who was now his boss. In fact, as he reread a memorandum from Carter to Conrad Dawson, the group vice president, he was convinced that Carter was building a case to fire him.

PATH TO ADVANCED MARKET DEVELOPMENT SPECIALIST

Roger Clarke was born in 1948 in a small midwestern town. Of modest financial means, he worked his way through Indiana State University, receiving a bachelor's degree in engineering management at the age of 22. His first job after college was in a sales capacity with IBM. Clarke compiled an outstanding sales record and was recruited to Universal Computers in March 1973 to assume a sales representative's position for the securities industry group in the Chicago office. In Clarke's mind, the opportunities to advance rapidly at Universal appeared outstanding.

In July 1973, Clarke made a well-received presentation to Robert Simmons, the national sales manager, and Conrad Dawson, the group vice president, during a regional meeting. Shortly thereafter, during a 4-week training program at group headquarters in New York, Clarke asked Conrad Dawson to promote him to market development specialist, stating that "most of the market development specialists are not qualified to carry my briefcase." At the end of a 6-hour dinner, the group vice president gave Roger his blessing and promoted him to the position of advanced marketing development specialist assigned to group headquarters in New York City. The group's organizational structure is depicted in Exhibit 1. The promotion had been a double advancement because it normally took a marketing development specialist several years in the field to obtain the advanced status. All other market development specialists were in their early to mid-thirties. The advanced market development specialist in the other region was 40 years old; Clarke was only 25. His salary was $27,000, a 50 percent improvement over his previous salary.

Clarke had direct responsibility for the three market development specialists in his region. They, in turn, had "dotted-line" responsibility for the sales representatives in their districts. Clarke reported to Brad Carter, the marketing manager of securities industry group. Carter had recently been promoted from the position Clarke assumed.

FIRST MONTH

After the promotion had become effective on September 10, Clarke had spent a week with his boss in New York City, making a whirlwind tour of brokerage firm clients. The next week he had spent the majority of his time getting to know most of the New York sales representatives of the securities industry group and making introductory sales calls with a few salespeople. He had spent the next 2 weeks visiting brokerage firms in New York and visiting sales offices in Philadelphia, Baltimore, and Boston, where he met local sales representatives and clients. He also participated, along with the eight other marketing specialists and Brad Carter, in a marketing plan review for 1974. Clarke recalled the hectic nature of the first month in his new position, "Besides meeting all the sales representatives and clients during this period, I was in the

EXHIBIT 1   Roger Clarke (A)—organization chart, the securities industry group.

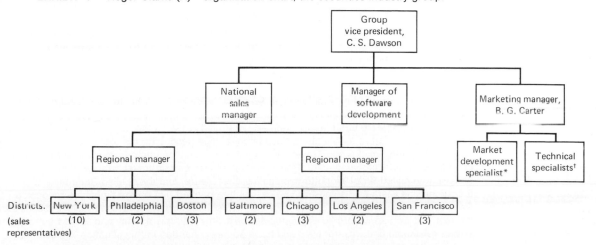

*There are two advanced market development specialists (one for each region) and seven market development specialists (one for each district). Roger Clarke was advanced market development specialist for the New York–Philadelphia–Boston region.

†There are seven technical specialists (one for each district).

process of buying a house on Long Island, getting married (on September 21), and arranging to move my possessions from Chicago to Long Island."

MEETING WITH THE MARKETING MANAGER

On October 15, 1973, Roger Clarke met with Brad Carter for 2 hours to discuss his performance to date. Quite to Clarke's surprise, Carter had prepared a list of problems he had had with Clarke's performance in the first month on the job. The day after the meeting, Carter had written a memorandum to Dawson, who had promoted Clarke, outlining the points covered in the meeting; he had also sent a copy to Clarke (Exhibit 2).

EXHIBIT 2   CARTER'S MEMORANDUM TO DAWSON

October 19, 1973   Personal and Confidential

TO: C. S. Dawson

SUBJECT: Roger Clarke's Performance

Since Clarke's commencement as a market development specialist on September 10, 1973, a number of incidents have reflected unfavorably upon his performance. We had discussed most of these incidents as they occurred, but I felt it necessary to meet with him on October 15, 1973 to review all my displeasures with his performance and chart a positive course for the future. The following is a summary of our approximately 2-hour discussion.

I told Roger I was not at all pleased with his performance to date and that we would be watching him closely over the next 30 days with the expectation of marked improvement. We reviewed a number of problems including the following:

1 Reports of Roger being pompous and a "smart ass." I indicated that I supported those descriptions. We discussed these impressions in some detail and how to change them.

2 Failure to let our office know where he is when he changes plans. Discussed the importance of his whereabouts and the fact that he is not free to drastically change his plans without my knowledge. For example, on October 12, the Philadelphia office and I were trying to locate him. His itinerary said Philadelphia office. At 3 p.m. he called from Boston and said he was there because "there was nothing to do in Philadelphia." He did not have two assignments ready for me that were due that day. He had left Philadelphia on the evening of October 11. In his behalf, he did leave a note at the Philadelphia office describing his plans.

3 Trouble with Small World Travel. The negative information came from my secretary, Rena, in an incident on October 4, 1973. Roger was upset with certain travel arrangements made for him. He had called Small World to express his displeasure, and they called Rena back to further determine Clarke's displeasure in that they had booked him on the flights we requested. Rena reports he grabbed the phone from her, complained further, and hung up. We discussed the fact that we had never had any particular problems with this agency and valued our cooperative relationship. It was not his place to be so heavy handed in this situation. He said he preferred to use his own air travel card in the future and not to deal with a travel agent. I agreed, but will reverse my decision and advise him that my signature on ticket advance forms is, in effect, my *required* approval of his travel plans. I know of no one else in marketing who does not work in this manner, so he is not being singled out.

EXHIBIT 2   (CONTINUED)

---

4 Does not follow up on requested information. Several incidents here, but the major ones are as follows. First, on September 27, I asked him to check why Dean Witter had not purchased our equipment. After approximately three reminders, I still have not received a good answer. A visit to Dean Witter is now planned.

Secondly, on or about September 20, I requested the status of Merrill Lynch. The only answer I ever received was he would check into it next week.

Next, on September 27, I requested organizational charts for the operations function at several major brokerage houses. His reply at that time was that he "doesn't see the reason to have these." I told him they were important, explained why, and still never received them.

5 Perhaps Clarke was playing the devil's advocate, but he appeared very negative in the marketing plan review meeting on September 28.

I would say that Roger accepted and discussed this criticism in a humble and constructive manner. Plans to alter or correct the previous five problems are as follows:

1 Plan constructive, positive calls when dealing with field market development specialists. Have the purpose and necessary sales aids to complete an objective. Avoid making calls simply to meet people.

2 Call the office at least once a day, preferably twice.

3 Travel plans to be arranged like everyone else. I will tell Roger not to use his air travel card, as I had previously agreed.

4 Roger now says he understands that my requests are not of a "jog-the-memory" type, but rather a request for information in my hands.

5 Says he will try to show a more positive attitude within the company while maintaining a positive attitude with outside contacts.

Roger plans to move his wife and household goods to Long Island on October 26. Perhaps a more settled home life will improve his work performance. Roger and I plan to discuss his overall performance again in mid-November.

Brad G. Carter
Securities Industry Marketing Manager

BCC:rps
cc: Roger Clarke

CLARKE'S DILEMMA

After his promotion and marriage, Clarke had been in a state of euphoria. The meeting with Carter and the subsequent memorandum came as quite a shock. However, in retrospect, Clarke believed that he should have seen it coming:

> I should have realized that trouble was brewing at the September 28 marketing plan review meeting. At the meeting, I was not as optimistic about the future as Carter thought I should be. However, everywhere I went, brokerage firm executives were complaining about excess computer capacity. At the meeting, Carter assigned 1974 performance commitments for all market development specialists. I expressed concern that my goals would be impossible to achieve. After the meeting, Carter called me aside and gave me a pitch on the huge growth opportunities of our market. I nodded my head but after 2 weeks visiting our customers, I had been more optimistic at the meeting than what I had seen made me want to be.

As he sat at his desk looking at the copy of Carter's memorandum, Clarke recalled Dawson's advice about his new position:

> Conrad Dawson warned me that I was entering a political situation. He told me that Carter was not exactly overjoyed with my promotion; he had wanted to promote a market development specialist to my position.
>
> If I have a sponsor in this organization, it has to be Conrad. He took a high risk promoting me despite Carter's objection. However, he told me that he expected my performance, and not our relationship, to be the key to my next advancement.

Clarke acknowledged that he had not been very concerned with politics when he assumed the new position; his only concern had been with understanding his new duties as quickly as possible. But what should he do now? Should he arrange a meeting with Dawson? Should he respond in writing? Should he avoid rocking the boat and do exactly what Carter tells him even when he is convinced it is a waste of time? Should he try to move laterally to another group in Universal Computers? Should he send out his resume to other firms? These were simply a few of the questions on his mind after rereading Carter's memorandum. Next week he, his wife, and their belongings would settle into a new house on Long Island. He thought the fall would prove rather interesting.

GIVING AND RECEIVING FEEDBACK

John Anderson

PURPOSE

This reading discusses a few considerations involved in telling other people how you feel about them—"how to do it" considerations that are apt to be important, if your objective is to help someone become a more effective person, and also to arrive at a more effective interpersonal working relationship.

BACKGROUND

A common central purpose of group interaction in a learning environment is to help each participant become more clearly aware of the impact he or she has on others. That is, during the learning experience, the participant has an opportunity to talk with others, to solve problems with others, and to generally interact with others in ways that are characteristic for the individual. The image an individual projects—the impression that others have of his or her behavior—is communicated back by other group members. This sort of exchange is usually a good deal more open than what is common in everyday life. The intent, at least as far as the objectives of the program are concerned, is that this feedback will be helpful to the recipient—that people may see, for example, some discrepancies between effects they desired to create (and, in fact, thought were created), and what actually took place, with the hope that individuals can use this information to make more intelligent choices of behavior with which to deal with similar situations in the future.

Unfortunately, such feedback (for reasons of content, timing, and presentation) does not always turn out to be useful to the recipient. And, although the very large majority of managers who participate in public sensitivity or feedback training environments return saying that the overall experience was very helpful personally, still

189

many have felt that "This is the kind of thing you sure couldn't do with people you work next to all the time!" The fear is that if the members of a work team did attempt to enter into an experience of this kind together, either (1) they would not dare to be open and candid with one another, and the result, therefore, would be a superficial and useless experience; or (2) they would dare to be open and candid with one another, and the result would be one of disruption in team working relationships, escalation of ill feelings carried over from old grievances, etc.

Several companies have experimented with some sort of small-group feedback experience. In my own experience, the design used has varied considerably depending on the needs of the particular group. But in no instance have the two fears mentioned above (organized slumber or total destruction) materialized. Each has turned out to be, in the judgment of the large majority of participants, a very useful and worthwhile experience from the standpoint of building more effective working relationships on the job. In general, people seem to be both concerned enough for one another, and trusting enough of one another that they are able to be *appropriately* open in exchanging feedback. It is my belief that instances in which people have only hurt or confused one another have resulted not primarily from motivational problems but from problems of skill in giving feedback—that is, knowing how to do it well and what kinds of pitfalls to watch out for.

Now, I will summarize some of the more important considerations drawn from fairly limited and scattered literature as well as from my own personal observations of some of the holes people seem to dig themselves into in experiences of this kind. I believe it is particularly important that these thoughts be given some attention in groups conducted without outside assistance—that is, without a skilled, experienced outside observer who can direct the group if they begin to wander in nonproductive directions. The following considerations have, no doubt, some application to the conduct of "performance appraisal" discussions as well as other informal exchanges that often take place between people in or out of the working environment.

FIRST GENERAL TEST

The first, most general, and most significant criterion that "helpful feedback" must meet is simply that it be *intended* to be helpful to the recipient. That is, the sender of the message should ask himself or herself beforehand, "Do I really feel that what I am about to say *is likely to be helpful to this person?* Do I unload a burden of hostility from my breast for my benefit, regardless of the expected effect on the receiver?" Otherwise, the sender of the message may imagine that the only obligation is to be open and honest—that the aim is candor—and that as long as he or she is truly and completely straightforward, the only obligation has been fulfilled.

If the objective is to *help* the recipient of the feedback, the following three things are necessary:

1 The other person must *understand* what has been said.
2 He or she must be willing and able to *accept* it.
3 Both parties must be *able to do* something about it if they choose to.

ACHIEVING UNDERSTANDING

The two most important considerations for achieving understanding of feedback are:

1 The feedback should be *specific* rather than general. If the person who is being given feedback can be provided with specific examples of instances in which he or she has behaved in the way described, it will be much easier to understand what has been said than if the message is given only in terms of generalizations. For example, if a person is told that he or she talks too much, or doesn't express thoughts very clearly, this is likely to be *less* helpful than if a particular instance can be cited, related to time and place, where this behavior was exhibited. If you can recall vividly to a person's mind a particular instance in which he or she rambled on long after having conveyed an idea to an individual or a group, then that person is more likely to be able to grasp your meaning. At the very least, an area will have been opened up that can be explored further. If people can understand what actually happened in particular situations, they are more likely to gain a clearer idea of what to do differently in the future. The key here is to avoid generalizing about the kind of person the individual is; give clear examples.

2 Provide *recent examples of behavior,* which are more effective than old ones. In order for an individual to understand what has happened in a particular situation, he or she must be able to recall the instance somewhat vividly. What took place 2 minutes ago can usually be more vividly recalled than what took place an hour ago— which, in turn, will be more easily remembered than what took place yesterday, last week, last year, etc.

GAINING ACCEPTANCE

Circumstances occur in which any person finds it quite difficult to accept critical, negative feedback—times at which it will be very difficult to maintain an open, objective frame of mind. It may be helpful to use the following guidelines to gain acceptance:

1 It is important to establish at least a minimum foundation of *trust* among members of a group before this sort of learning experience is undertaken. If person A is to accept critical feedback from person B, then A must be already somewhat convinced from other previous associations with B that B's motivations regarding A are not entirely self-serving—that is, that B *does care* for A and can be trusted to give helpful feedback that, in the end, will benefit A. In a situation where A has a deep distrust of B, there is probably very little that can be done to get A's voluntary acceptance of what he has been told.

2 The way person B addresses person A in this specific situation can be an important factor. If B's tone of voice, facial expression, choice of words, and general manner convey directly to A the impression that, "I value you, and I really would like to help you, and that is the only reason I am telling you this," then A is more likely to attend to the message with an open mind than if B merely rattles off a list of intellectual observations about A's behavior, perhaps without even looking directly at A while doing so.

3 In sending negative feedback to another person, the receiver is more likely to respond in an accepting way if the message is descriptive rather than evaluative—that is, if the sender describes what happened and communicates the personal effect it had, as opposed to evaluating its goodness or badness, rightness or wrongness, in more general terms. For example, if B were to tell A that "This may not be your problem—it may be mine. However, I want you to know that when you act toward me the way you do sometimes (describe a situation, in time and place), it is very difficult for me to think straight (or keep from getting angry, or keep my mind on what we're talking about—whatever fits the situation)," it is much more likely for the message to be accepted openly than if B were to tell A that "I think it is just awful when you act toward people that way, you really shouldn't do that, that's a senseless way to behave, why don't you grow up, etc. . . ."

4 Before giving a person any negative feedback, the sender should consider whether *the present* is a good time to do so—whether the other person *appears* to be in a condition of readiness to receive information of this kind. If he or she appears, for example, to be angry, confused, upset, highly distraught, defensive, etc., the answer is probably no. This is not the appropriate time to give negative feedback. Perhaps it is for this reason that feedback solicited by the recipient is more likely to be responded to openly than feedback that is simply sent to the person, whether asked for or not. And the more specific the area in which feedback is solicited, the more likely it is to be expected and received openly. For example, suppose the leader of a group says, "How about the decision I made last Friday—do you feel that I arrived at it in an appropriate way, or do you feel that I should have involved all of you more deeply before arriving at a conclusion?" As a member of a group, one would feel that this solicitation of feedback was more genuine and could be responded to more openly, and with more confidence that it would be received in an open frame of mind, than one would feel if the leader of the group, perhaps a bit too intensely or with a slightly loud laugh should say, "O.K., this is my turn in the barrel! Really level with me now! I want to hear everything you don't like about me!" That may be true and it may not—all I am suggesting is that if overt solicitation is indicative of probable acceptance, the former sort is apt to be more meaningful than the latter.

5 There is always the problem that feedback sent to one person by another will be accepted as valid when, in fact, it should *not* be. For example, if person A tells person B that there is a certain thing that B does in their relationship that A finds upsetting, it may be that the problem isn't B's at all, but rather that it is A's. One value of entering into this sort of exchange in a group, as opposed to doing so only in a one-on-one relationship, is that the feedback that each person gives another can be routed around the group to see if another person has an experience of this kind, which would support or clarify the meaning of what has been said. This should be done, whenever possible, to check the validity of the observation as well as to ensure that the recipient receives as many examples as possible to help him or her understand what has been said.

ASSESSING THE RECEIVER'S ABILITY TO USE FEEDBACK

The third criterion that useful feedback should meet is that the recipient must be able to do something with it. Consider the following:

1 Suppose you feel that a particular person does not present her ideas as forcefully and persuasively as needed to receive attention from the group; and you decide to tell her about this. This is still a pretty general feeling, and before saying anything, therefore, it should be considered what there is, specifically, about her delivery that prompts your feeling. You may think, for example, that she fails to organize her thoughts as well under some circumstances as you know she is capable of (from other shared experiences). This is an example of something you might assume she could do something about, and so you should probably tell her about this feeling, especially if she can be given specific examples of this type of behavior. Or suppose that she conveys her ideas effectively but that, at the first sign of static, she withdraws, either from indifference, lack of confidence in her ideas, or whatever. This, again, might be useful to mention to her because it is very likely that she can do something about it.

2 On the other hand, suppose you feel that the only thing that interferes with her ability to persuade, to convey her ideas forcefully to a group, is that she is physically a very small person, with a very squeaky voice, or possibly an even more pronounced speech impediment. If you are really trying to be helpful, there obviously is no point in calling attention to these characteristics.

3 So, by this criterion, you may or may not decide that it would be helpful to tell the other person that you felt she did not project her ideas in the group as forcefully or persuasively as possible. Whether you choose to do so or not would depend on your best estimate of her ability to remove the particular obstacles to her effectiveness in this particular area.

4 During a group session in which members are exchanging their views of and feelings about one another in this way, there may be a tendency to feel that you have not really done justice unless you have told people "everything that bothers you" about them. It is not necessarily desirable, however, to be "complete" in the negative feedback you might give a person. It may be quite a large enough task, for example, for anyone to understand, accept, and consider doing something about characteristic ways of behaving in two or three key areas. To give someone more than this to think about may be simply spreading attention beyond what one is capable of dealing with at present. Also, other things being equal, the more you unload, the more threatening the experience is liable to be, and the more difficulty the receiver is likely to have accepting any criticism in an open frame of mind.

SUMMARY OF FEEDBACK CRITERIA

In summary, to be fully useful to the recipient, feedback should meet the following criteria. It should be:

1 Intended to help the recipient
2 Given directly and with real feeling, and based on a foundation of trust between the giver and the receiver

3 Descriptive rather than evaluative

4 Specific rather than general, with good, clear, and preferably recent examples

5 Given at a time when the receiver appears to be in a condition of readiness to accept it

6 Checked with others in the group to be sure they support its validity

7 Inclusive only of those things that the receiver might be expected to be able to do something about

8 Not more than the receiver can handle at a particular time

A MAJOR RISK: EXCESSIVE CAUTIOUSNESS

Finally, the question might be asked, "Isn't there some risk that if all these cautions are followed, people might be induced to be overly cautious and decline to take any risks (and what may probably be desirable risks) in being open with one another?"

This is a reasonable question, and may well be answered affirmatively—this is a risk in itself. Many of us tend to feel that we could not possibly share with other people the negative feelings we have about them. They would be crushed if we did so. Or they would never forgive us. All of the criteria listed above are simply considerations that should be given some attention by the sender of feedback. But it will no doubt be impossible to meet all of them, all of the time, and still have something to say. And so, in such cases it is appropriate to take prudent risks—to be open more than closed, experimentally, and to see what happens. If you at least really *intend* to help—and there is no doubt that you intend to help by the manner in which you say what you say—then a good deal of clumsiness is almost certain to be overlooked by the receiver. Even if people fail to understand or agree with what you are saying they will, at least, not hold it against you. If their defenses stay down, together you may be able to clarify meanings, draw out essentials, and generally compensate for your initial clumsiness in trying to help.

RECEIVING FEEDBACK

A few key things for the recipient of feedback to keep in mind are:

1 First of all, you should make a sincere effort not to be defensive. This has as much to say about what you allow to go on inside yourself as about what you allow yourself to say overtly to those who are giving you feedback. You should try to look at what is being said with an open mind, try to understand it, and not all the while say to yourself "They simply don't understand, it isn't what I meant at all."

2 If you are having trouble understanding what has been said to you and the giver of the feedback is unable to provide examples that clarify things for you, you should begin to seek and speculate on possible examples of yourself with the group—to say, for example, "Remember the time we met last Friday, and I did such and so. Is that the kind of thing you are talking about?"

3 To be certain you understand, try to summarize briefly for the group what you understand them to be saying. This gives a final opportunity to check misunderstandings that might have occurred.

4 It can be very helpful to an individual and a group if the recipient of the feedback is allowed, and encouraged, to share his or her feelings with the group about the particular behavior(s) they have been discussing. The risk of defensiveness is one that all involved should be alert to. However, if people can openly explore their feelings about why they tend to behave in particular ways at particular times, two things can happen. First, people may arrive at a better understanding themselves of why they behave in the way they do, simply by talking it through, and thereby be in a better position to consider what they might do about it. Second, if they find it difficult or impossible to correct behaviors that have been negatively described to them by the group, even though they try, if they have genuinely shared with the group some of their concerns and internal struggles they have in these situations, the group may at least find it a little easier to understand and accept them as they are in the future.

5 Finally, some people react negatively to the very idea of doing this sort of thing—meeting as a work team, for example, and exchanging views openly of how people see each other, positively or negatively. The feeling may be that, "I am what I am, and I have a right to be that. And no group of people has a right to dictate to me what I should be like." My feeling is that this is exactly right. It remains, and should remain, the right of every individual to evaluate what he or she hears, decide what to believe, and decide in what respects, if any, it is personally worthwhile to make an effort to change. The purpose of a learning experience of the kind described here, and of the kind of information exchanged in it, is simply to give individuals better and clearer information than would ordinarily be received on which to judge their personal effectiveness in working with others, and to allow them to plan or decide to further develop that effectiveness.

MANAGING INTERPERSONAL CONFLICT

James P. Ware
Louis B. Barnes

History is largely the record of conflict.

Kenneth Boulding

Dealing with conflict that involves oneself or one's bosses, peers, or subordinates is a task that few managers enjoy. Whether the conflict is openly hostile or subtly covert, strong personal feelings may be involved. Furthermore, there are often valid points of view on both sides, and the process of finding an acceptable solution can be mentally exhausting and emotionally draining. Yet the ability to productively manage such conflict is clearly critical to managerial success. Interpersonal differences often become sharpest when we perceive the organizational stakes to be high, but almost all organizations also include their share of petty issues blown into major conflicts. The problem for a concerned manager is to build upon human differences of opinion while not letting them jeopardize overall performance, satisfaction, and growth.

The purpose of this reading is to explore the nature and sources of interpersonal conflict, to understand its determinants and dynamics, and to discuss several specific approaches to managing conflict—whether as an adversary or as a third-party mediator.

SOME ASSUMPTIONS AND DEFINITIONS

Several basic assumptions and definitions are key to the ideas that will be expressed here. To help the following discussion, these are noted below:

Interpersonal conflict typically involves a relationship that has a sequence of conditions and events tending toward aggressive behavior and disorder. However, conflict can also be viewed in terms of its background conditions, the perceptions of the involved parties, their feelings, their actual behavior, and the consequences or outcomes of their behavior.

Conflict is an organizational reality that is inherently neither good nor bad in and of itself. It can be destructive, but it can also play a productive role both within a person and between persons. The problems usually arise when potential conflict is either unrealistically suppressed or when it escalates beyond the control of the adversaries or third-party intermediaries. Whereas most managers seek to reduce conflict because of its negative repercussions, some seek to use it for its positive effects on creativity, motivation, and performance. The management of conflict usually entails maintaining a delicate balance between these positive and negative attributes.

There is no "one best way" for managing interpersonal conflict, either as an involved adversary or as a third party. Rather, there are a number of strategies and tactics involving the external conditions, differing perceptions, internal feelings, behavior, and outcomes. In addition, the relationships of the involved parties (for examples, superiors and subordinates, peers, etc.) and their past histories as adversaries, allies, or relatively neutral third parties pose another key variable. The relative power of the involved parties is another consideration in deciding whether to withdraw from the conflict, compromise, work toward controlling a conflict within certain boundaries, seek constructive confrontations, force conflict into a win/lose pattern, smooth it over with friendly acts, or try to enact a variety of other subtle or forceful approaches.

Conflict as an involved participant is emotionally very different from conflict as a relatively objective third party. Indeed, as we will see, one strength of involving third parties lies in their potential to add an objective perspective to the perceptions, feelings, and behavior of the involved adversaries. In this reading, we view the management of conflict from the vantage point of both the biased adversary and the outside third party who might be a boss, colleague, friend, or even subordinate. Each of these roles poses its own distinct strengths and weaknesses.

QUESTIONS ON CONFLICT MANAGEMENT

A manager often becomes concerned with conflict when it leads to negative outcomes in individual or organizational productivity, satisfaction, or growth. In analyzing conflict management, he or she might start with these consequences or outcomes, partly with the idea of looking at both the positive and negative sides of the coin. A second area of examination is the behavior patterns manifested by the involved parties. A third entails the different feelings and perceptions. And a fourth looks for the underlying and background conditions that help to initiate and perpetuate the conflict. It is important for a manager, either as a participant or a third party, to appreciate that any of these four areas may be an appropriate action point for dealing with conflict. With regard to these four areas, a manager might pose the following questions:

1 What are the important personal and organizational outcomes or consequences of the conflict as they currently exist? What of future outcomes?

2 What are the behavior patterns that seem to characterize the conflict? How do these patterns highlight the substantive issues, perceptions, and underlying causes of the conflict?

3 What are the substantive issues involved? To what extent are they colored by one-sided perceptions? To what extent are the perceptions further colored by feelings and involvement? Where in the organization is there potential for relative objectivity on the part of a third party?

4 What are the apparent underlying and background conditions leading to the conflict feelings, perceptions, behavior, and outcomes?

Question 1: Outcome Considerations

We have already suggested that conflicts generally have both positive and negative consequences. An increased awareness of both kinds of outcomes complicates the diagnosis, but can lead to significantly more effective intervention decisions. Examples of both positive and negative consequences are briefly discussed below.

Positive Outcomes   The competitive nature of conflict can increase the motivation and creativity of the participants. A manufacturing manager who gets angry at being pushed around by a sales vice president may respond by trying harder to produce a workable production schedule ("just to show him I can do it"). The same competitive dynamics—the urge to win—often leads to innovative breakthroughs, because of the effort and willingness to consider new approaches. Interpersonal conflicts frequently clarify persistent, underlying organizational problems. Furthermore, intense conflict can force attention to basic issues and, therefore, lead to productive resolution of long-standing difficulties, since the problems can no longer be smoothed over or easily avoided.

Conflict involvement can also sharpen an individual's approaches to bargaining, influence, and competitive problem solving. In addition, the paticipants often increase their own understanding of personal values and positions on important issues. Conflict often forces a manager to clarify an idea more effectively to explain it to someone who clearly disagrees with it.

Thus, conflicts are often functional, or at least can lead to functional outcomes, for the organization and for one or both of the individuals involved. In addition, however, there are often negative consequences, and conflict can escalate to a level where the negative outcomes clearly outweigh the positive ones.

Negative Outcomes   Interpersonal conflicts are often unpleasant emotional experiences—a subordinate who suppresses anger with a boss; a pair of managers who exchange angry words with each other; two colleagues who avoid each other because of previous tensions, and jeopardize a department's productivity as a result; two other associates who "play games" by not sharing relevant and important information. All of these patterns penalize the organization and have an emotional impact on the people involved. The organizational landscape is littered with managers who could not get along with their bosses, colleagues, or subordinates. Put one way, this might mean that they were not good "people managers," but put another way we could say that the firm had failed to develop effective procedures for dealing with the outcomes of conflict.

When a person is engaged in conflict, these negative outcomes spill out as emotions of anger, frustration, fear of failure, and a sense of personal inadequacy. Careers can be sidetracked or ruined. The stress of conflict relationships can make life miserable for the people involved, disrupt patterns of work, and consume an inordinate amount of time for those involved as well as for those affected or indirectly concerned. The direct loss of productivity is but one negative business outcome; the danger of continued poor decisionmaking because of withheld information is yet another. The irony is that those parties determined to "win" their own limited battles often cause major losses for themselves and the organization in the final analysis.

Short-term negative outcomes can also lead to patterns of worsening relationships unless some remedial action is taken, and both the involved and third-party managers have the problem of deciding when the time has come for action. While on rare occasions managers deliberately maintain tensions for their positive outcomes, most managers seek to change the situation before the schisms become too great. Before they can take appropriate steps, though, they usually need to understand the behavior taking place.

Question 2: Behavior Patterns

As we noted above, interpersonal conflicts tend to develop patterns. That is, the two parties engage in open conflict over a particular issue, then separate or gather forces before coming together and going at each other again. Often an organizational procedure like budgeting, scheduling, or work assignments precipitates the conflict and serves as part of the background. Sometimes an apparently trivial issue sets one party against another. There may even be periods of time when two people seem to work relatively well together or are effectively buffered from each other. Then, once again, some event or change in circumstances sets them off. While these triggering events are not always predictable, there is often a pattern to them that can be identified. Poor listening, one-upmanship, power plays for resources, perceived insults, and overcontrolling comments can all serve to kindle the fires of distorted perceptions and feelings. The initial triggering behaviors can set in motion reactions and reciprocal behaviors that then begin a conflict cycle. Careful attention to when and how a conflict arises is an important part of developing a conflict management strategy.

It is equally important to note the way the conflict principals express their differences. When the conflict is open and active, the behaviors are usually obvious: shouts, sulking, continued insults, heated debate, unwillingness to listen, hardening of positions, and so on. However, when conflict is latent, the signs are not so evident The behavior is usually more subtle: writing memos to avoid face-to-face contact; delaying decisions to block the other party; interacting only through subordinates or third parties; avoiding direct exchanges; and changing times of daily arrivals and departures to avoid meeting. The list could go on and on. Detecting such suppressed conflict requires great sensitivity, but is also highly important since many conflicts are expressed indirectly.

Developing an understanding of behavior patterns in a particular conflict situation is an important prelude to planning the way to manage the conflict. If particular events trigger open conflict, those events can sometimes be stopped or actively constrained. This kind of understanding can also lead participants or third parties to make more effective role choices as to when and where to enter the conflict. Finally, as noted earlier, the patterns of conflict can provide important clues to the underlying reasons for the conflict.

Question 3: Substantive Issues, Perceptions, and Feelings

Most conflicts include two distinctively different kinds of issues. *Substantive* issues involve disagreements over policies, procedures, decisions, use of resources, roles and responsibilities, or other organizational practices. *Emotional* issues, in contrast, involve the distorted perceptions and feelings that two people can feel about each other and about the substantive issues over which they are contending. Because our social customs and the norms of most organizations discourage the open expression of negative personal feelings, intense emotional conflicts are often expressed and rationalized as substantive issues. In fact, we often seek out substantive disagreements on trivial issues to provide justification for what has become basically an emotional conflict with another individual.

This tendency to distort and magnify differences means that conflicts often escalate rapidly in intensity and importance. Each person builds a grievance list of real and perceived problems. We seek support wherever we can find it, repeatedly citing our evidence to justify our feelings as a means of gaining sympathy. Worse yet, we attribute all kinds of negative motives and intentions to the other person while thinking of ourselves as the injured "good guy."

Conflicts also escalate because each time two people interact they try to "score points," and each interaction then becomes part of the history of the conflict. Any time one person perceives that he or she has lost a round, the effort to win the next one becomes that much more intense.

> A product manager and an inventory control manager had to meet regularly to review and update product-line sales forecasts. Their interests conflicted somewhat since the product manager wanted to minimize unit costs and avoid stockouts, while the inventory control manager wanted to minimize total purchasing costs and inventory levels. When their forecasts became inaccurate, the two managers had several substantive disagreements over the forecasting procedures and their divergent goals. Gradually, however, the two managers lost sight of each other's different basic assumptions and organizational needs. They began to personalize their differences. Each felt threatened and attacked by the other, and these feelings intensified each time they interacted. Their growing distrust and lack of respect spilled over into personal antagonism, with each manager perceiving ulterior motives and unpleasant personality traits in the other. It got even worse with personal threats, name calling, and accusations of stupidity, self-interest, and dishonesty. Thus, a legitimate set of substantive differences was transformed into the vicious cycle of a heated emotional battle. Most of us have seen or been in such situations.

Some managers involved in a conflict dispute are determined to work it out with the other party by themselves through bargaining, control procedures, confrontation, or other forms of negotiation. Still other managers perceive the conflict as something to avoid, withdraw from, or smooth over as though it were not there. Colleagues and bosses are probably less reluctant to take the first approach than subordinates, who may feel forced to fall back upon the second approach, and all parties may prefer a third-party mediator. One's choice has much to do with one's own tolerance for conflict and the uncertainties that surround it. With experience, a manager can get a sense of how much to "trust" his or her perceptions and feelings during such stressful times. Even though there is evidence that some degree of stress may indeed be a productive motivator, most people have difficulty remaining open-minded and flexible during periods of very high stress. In addition, performance shortcomings may challenge one's assumptions about personal abilities and self-concept. The most natural response is then to look outward for a scapegoat—for example, "If only they would give me more accurate sales forecasts, then I wouldn't be stuck with all this excess inventory." It is much easier to change my perception about someone else's ability ("She just doesn't know how to forecast") or motives ("He's deliberately feeding me false data to make me look bad") than it is to admit personal failure or the need for help. This scapegoating tendency is another personal characteristic that contributes to escalation in conflict situations.

The advantage of having a third party trusted by both adversaries is that those more objective perceptions and feelings can serve as a reality check for both adversaries. If the third party can help work out a procedure for coping with the conflict, that may be a major step toward further agreement or resolution. A boss acting as a third party has the added power of being able to arbitrate or tip the power imbalance one way or the other, but even this apparent advantage can have negative effects in the long run if the boss is perceived as "taking sides" too often. One of the hardest, yet most important, challenges for the third party is to stay in touch wth the perceptions and feelings of the two adversaries while at the same time keeping his or her own views separate, thereby dealing with the conflict *relationship* rather than being pulled into a single point of view.

Question 4: Underlying and Background Conditions

The underlying causes of interpersonal conflict are just as numerous and varied as the ways in which conflicts are expressed. Indeed, several of the more common reasons that conflicts develop have already been identified. The difficulty of assessing the factors that "really" cause or reinforce a particular conflict is that there are usually multiple factors involved. Separation of the primary causes is often almost impossible, since most serious conflicts have reached a point of being self-reinforcing. That is, they have such a powerful history and have become so personalized that their original sources are almost irrelevant to the current level of conflict. Nevertheless, any attempt to understand a conflict must consider the kinds of factors behind the two people's actions. Management of the conflict then means changing the situational factors surrounding it or the ways in which the two people respond to the situation and to each other.

For discussion purposes, we divide these causal factors into two categories: situational or external characteristics and personal/internal characteristics. Keep in mind, however, that these distinctions are somewhat arbitrary, and are treated here as more distinctive than they usually are in fact.

Situational External Characteristics This category includes all external conditions surrounding the two people—the pressures of time and deadlines; competition for budgetary funds, staff, organizational influence, and other scarce resources; performance pressures from bosses, peers, and other departments; promotion opportunities; and the organizational rules and procedures that affect their interaction.

We have previously seen the way interdepartmental conflict in complex organizations works. When two people from different departments (such as the market analyst and inventory control manager described above) must interact, they often represent and reflect their own reference group's differences in goals, values, and priorities. Thus, interdepartmental conflict frequently becomes interpersonal conflict unless the two representatives can rise above the special interests of the groups they represent.

But even two people from the same department can be put into competition for scarce resources, whether it be budgetary funds, subordinates, control over key procedures and decisions, office space, or the boss's time or job. The pressures to perform can make the personal stakes so high that individual managers become highly inflexible and defensive. These stakes are particularly important when middle managers are placed in competition for promotion opportunities that stress individual responsibilities and rewards. Since most organizations reward managers who are "winners" both formally (promotions and salary increases) and informally (influence, status, credibility), the *social* pressues to compete and win can be extremely intense.

Personal/Internal Factors The personal goals, styles, and abilities of two people in conflict can also have a powerful effect on their behavior and their relationship. Personal career goals and ambitions can develop in response to the organizational pressures just described. However, people often experience feelings of rivalry and interpersonal competition even when there is little *external* basis for such emotions. Sometimes, of course, there is actually a poor fit between a person and the job requirements, and his or her poor performance may indeed create serious problems for someone else. More frequently, however, conflict erupts and escalates because one manager perceives another to be actively blocking a personally important goal. Whether that perception is accurate or not is almost irrelevant. The resulting feelings of anger, frustration, and anxiety contribute to the emotional escalation of conflict in ways such as those we saw earlier. These kinds of feelings are particularly strong among ambitious, competitive, achievement-oriented individuals.

In addition, we often hear of bad "chemistry" between two people. If they have very different personal values, styles, or basic assumptions that affect their work habits, they are likely to disagree over the ways to accomplish important tasks. For example, consider the tensions between an aggressive, high-energy manager and a careful, methodical analyst; or between a talkative, easygoing plant manager and a quiet, reserved manufacturing manager. Sometimes personal styles are complementary, but sometimes they become basically incompatible. When the people involved feel strongly about their ways of doing things, conflict is almost inevitable.

One of the most critical personal characteristics that feeds a conflict is one's capacity for coping with stress. When personal and organizational stakes are high, we tend to develop "short fuses" and become intolerant of others' mistakes or even of their legitimate needs. When two people are under extreme pressure and must interact frequently, it is very difficult for them to avoid blaming each other for the problems they experience.

By the time the external conditions of a situation become fueled by each person's internal anxieties and stress levels, it is easy to see how conflict can surface into the areas of perceptions, feelings, and behavior. Faced with these realities, and with the outcomes of a conflict situation, either as an adversary or an onlooker, a manager is faced with a series of action choices. The first is whether to avoid or try to manage the conflict. Although the choice may seem clear-cut on paper (that is, managers should manage), it seems fair to say that most managers are better at conflict avoidance, or smoothing over than they are at conflict management. The skills and strength for managing a conflict, either as an involved participant or as a third party, do not come easily for most people. At the same time, it is important to note that there are times when avoidance or smoothing over negative outcomes and stress can make sense in the short term—and even in the long term if satisfaction is valued more highly than performance or growth. This is true in many family situations and in some family businesses. But in other situations where management is trying to optimize the balance of the three outcomes—performance, satisfaction, and growth—there is probably a greater need for managing the conflict.

MANAGING CONFLICT

If a manager chooses to try to manage and not to withdraw from or smooth over a conflict situation, he or she must first evaluate where he or she is in the situation. Am I an adversary or a third party? Boss or subordinate? Representative or free agent? With power and dependencies or, relatively speaking, without them? Any of these roles poses its own set of demands and choices. Some of these demands and choices also depend upon one's personal attributes, for example: How do I feel about using what power I have in this fashion? Am I willing to take on this conflict? In this section, we wish to briefly discuss three general approaches to conflict management and to raise several questions that a manager might ask before taking one of these or still another approach.[1]

The three approaches can be roughly categorized as (1) bargaining, (2) controlling, and (3) confrontation. Bargaining behavior is probably most prevalent under conditions of required interdependence and an approximate balance of power. Controlling behavior is more apt to be used when one party (including the third party)

---

[1] Ideas in this section are drawn from various sources, including Richard Walton, *Interpersonal Peacemaking,* Boston: Addison-Wesley, 1969; Louis R. Pondy, "Organizational Conflict: Concepts and Models," *Administrative Science Quarterly,* vol. 12, no. 2, Sept. 1967, pp. 296–320; and Robert R. Blake and Jane S. Mouton, *The New Managerial Grid,* Houston: Gulf Publishing, 1978.

has relatively high power but where the interdependence requirements are more flexible. Confrontation behavior may be used under either of the above conditions but seems to depend more upon the personal attributes of the involved parties and the assumptions they make about the setting and time pressures. During our discussion of each of these approaches below, we make the assumption that the acting manager "understands" the conflict situation in terms of the outcomes and consequences, the behavior, the perceptions and feelings as they relate to the substantive issues, and the underlying/background conditions. Each of these dimensions offers an entry point for either an adversary or a third-party mediator, but the choice of an approach heavily depends upon the individual's position, skills, and personal preferences.

Option 1: Bargaining

For a manager involved as adversary or mediator in a conflict situation, the only rational approach often appears to be negotiation or bargaining with the other party on the substantive issues. The assumption behind this is usually that the conflict has involved a win/lose game in which one party would gain or lose at the other's expense. However, if two parties come to the bargaining table in a union-management fashion, they would each then signal that they wished to consider and seek new ways to resolve or compromise the conflict. The alternative presumably means win/lose warfare or withdrawal into a stalemate.

The advantage of a bargaining approach is that the goal of compromise is a step beyond the goal of conflict. In approaching such negotiations, the two parties, with or without a third-party mediator, usually prepare to lose as well as to win some points. The goal is to obtain an acceptable solution in a rational way for public consumption. At the same time, many bargaining situations involve games such as bluffing, behind-the-scenes negotiations, an attempt to marshal outside power sources, a tendency to overstate one's initial demands, and the heavy use of legalistic procedures since these preserve the appearance of a rational process. Each bargaining tactic can involve risks as well as rewards. Another problem with a bargaining approach is that the parties often place a higher premium on acceptable compromises than on sound solutions. A manager who engages in a bargaining approach, either as a party in conflict or as a third party, can lose sight of the organization's well-being and become consumed in the limited goals of reaching an acceptable solution.

Option 2: Controlling

Four general ways can be used to control interpersonal conflict. These usually appear when there is a power imbalance, for example, when one party can exert pressures to make them happen. Conflict control can also be used temporarily until the crisis is concluded or conditions improve enough to permit bargaining or confrontation. Other times, two adversaries will tire of the controls or a third party appears who gains the trust of the two adversaries. The four controlling behaviors open to either adversaries or mediators are (1) prevention of interaction or reduction of its frequency; (2) structuring the forms and patterns of interaction; (3) reduction or alteration of the external situational pressures; and (4) personal counseling to help the two parties accept and deal with the process and realities of the conflict. This fourth approach involves a kind of third-party help different from mediation, and can also be used with bargaining and confrontation approaches. We now examine each of the controlling approaches more closely.

Prevention of Interaction or Reduction of Its Frequency   This strategy is often useful when emotions are high. It controls conflict by reducing the possibility of triggering events. If the two people are physically separated and no longer need to interact with each other, then there is little opportunity for them to express differences. While the differences continue to exist, the intense feelings are likely to dissipate without recurring conflict episodes, or at least to settle sufficiently to permit other approaches.

There are many ways to reduce or eliminate interaction, some of which have already been suggested. Sometimes operating procedures can be modified to eliminate the necessity for two people to work together. If that option is impossible, perhaps peers or subordinates can substitute for one or both parties; however, if the conflict stems from an underlying conflict of interest, it is just as likely to flare up in the new pair. One or both of the people could be transferred to a new job or even to a new physical location.

Several of these options are relatively expensive and time-consuming. However, they may be useful if there is no other way to work out the differences, or if the mutual hostility has reached such a level that a confrontation would be either impossible or inordinately long and drawn out. Keep in mind, however, that separation of the two parties may create more serious long-term problems or only delay an eventual necessary confrontation. When adversaries are separated, their hostilities sometimes merely go underground and may become more rather than less intense because of the absence of any opportunity to express them. When that happens the eventual confrontation may be even more serious, as the suppressed emotions finally are released. At times like this, the trusted third parties can help to judge whether reducing interaction makes sense.

Structuring Forms of Interaction   Often the separation options listed above simply are not feasible. When the two parties must continue to interact, the conflict can be controlled by imposing clear limitations on their behavior. These procedures can be as specific and narrow as the parties wish. For example, they might specify the time and place of meetings, the allowable discussion topics, the specific information to be provided by each individual, or even the types of questions or comments that are *not* allowed. Alternatively, the imposed procedures might specify or imply new channels of communication: meetings could be replaced by memos, messages, or telephone calls. These new forms of structured interaction are often limited only by the imaginations of the involved parties.

The way in which these ground rules are established depends greatly on the specific situation, and on the relationships between the involved people. A manager can generally impose these kinds of procedures on subordinates or other adversaries with less organizational authority. In the absence of a clear mandate from above, the ground rules are often arrived at by negotiation, mutual agreement, or the help of a third party.

This approach permits the continued exchange of vital information but seeks to prevent the exchange of hostile judgmental emotions that would interfere with necessary communication. Similar to physical separation, this strategy should be considered temporary. Here again the suppression of strong emotions can easily lead to move violent and destructive flareups subsequently. Once again, too, involved adversaries may find that their own perspectives need the objectivity of outsiders to reduce distortion in making judgments on when to use and when to abandon this approach.

Reduction or Alteration of External Pressures   Instead of focusing on the interactions that characterize the conflict, a strategy of changing the conditions that fuel it is often more effective. When the diagnosis of the conflict suggests that situational factors are largely responsible, dealing with those factors directly can control the conflict, or even eliminate it completely. Of course, the factors to be changed depend on the specific circumstances, each manager's power to affect the critical factors, and the organizational consequences of the changes (sometimes a change that might control the conflict would not be appropriate for other, more important reasons). Situational factors that could be changed include extension of deadlines, addition of new project personnel, modification of organizational policies or allowance of temporary exceptions, arrangement of periodic informational meetings, an increase in budget allocations, and protection of the principals from harassment by peers or even organizational superiors. Sometimes these mechanisms are in the hands of one of the adversaries and can be acted upon. Sometimes they need actions from outside or above the conflict.

Personal Counseling   In contrast to the other control strategies, this approach does not address the conflict itself, but focuses on the way the two people react to it. The underlying assumption here is that providing counseling, reassurance, and emotional support helps make the conflict more tolerable. In addition, the process of ventilating feelings about an "enemy" to a colleague or friend usually releases built-up tensions, and may become a first step toward personally discovering new ways to deal directly with the conflict. Alternatively, discussion of the problem with a third party can lead an individual to invent new procedures or personal goals that make him or her less dependent on the other party, thus reducing the inherent stress in the conflict.

As noted above, control of a conflict situation by oneself or a third party is a useful short-term strategy, because either the situation or the parties can often be changed. Where this is unlikely, though, or when interdependence needs are high, managers may do well to think about ways in which to constructively confront the conflict.

Option 3: Confrontation

As with the other approaches to managing conflict, a manager, either as adversary or mediator, has choices in confronting a conflict. One major choice lies in his or her intent. Is the intent to confront the differences in a constructive, getting-beyond-the-conflict manner or is it to confront differences in a way that is more destructive and attacking than integrative? The problem with adversarial confrontation is that even though one adversary wants to be constructive, the other adversary may perceive the initial attempt as an attack. Consequently, constructive confrontation must almost always begin with a serious and well-communicated attempt to *understand* and *explore* the other party's perceptions and feelings. Of course, this process can be aided by a third party who helps to build an exploratory climate while going beyond the initial temptations to support one of the two adversaries. But the important point to remember is that a constructive confrontation does not usually begin with a confrontation. It begins with an attempt to understand. Once a climate of exploration has been introduced, constructive confrontation has the advantage of conveying the possibility of a win/win solution. It seeks an information exchange of data—substance as well as perceptions and feelings—that provides new definitions of the problem and new motives for a common solution. These processes require skill and patience, but more than that they often require persistence and an active effort to help each party listen to the other while constantly looking for ways to move beyond the deadlock. This is true for adversaries *and* mediators. Each operates under considerable stress at times, but a crucial expression is often the simple question of "What if . . .?" as a way of searching for new action alternatives.

At the same time, confrontation behavior can walk a narrow tightrope initially while the two adversaries seek to release their emotions and feelings. Once again, a third party can help to legitimate these expressions while also channeling or policing the ways in which negative or hostile feelings are expressed. For example, the third party—or even one of the adversaries—may suggest that the parties agree to express and explore feelings that result from the actual behavior of each adversary rather than venting feelings based upon inference and speculation of the other's motives and perceptions. Without such ground rules for the expression of feelings, confrontation can easily become more destructive than constructive. With them, it is usually easier to move to new stages of information exchange and problem solving.

SOME RELEVANT ACTION QUESTIONS

In line with taking action to help manage a conflict instead of to avoid it, smooth it over, or use power to suppress it, an involved *or* third-party manager might well pause and raise the following questions. These questions are probably most important when considering a confrontation strategy, which is potentially both the most difficult and the most rewarding, but they also apply to the other approaches.

1 *To what extent is there a productive level of tension and motivation in the conflict relationship? Or has the conflict become highly destructive in nature?* If conflict resolution is to be successful, there typically must be enough stress in the situation for the participants to desire a resolution but not so much that they are unable to deal with the issues or each other. Insufficient tension may require someone to call attention to the personal or organizational outcomes that make the latent conflict dangerous or dysfunctional. Excessive tension may require cooling-off steps or temporary controlling measures.

By the same token, interpersonal conflict often persists because only one party is motivated to do something about it. When this happens, little can be done until the tension level is again high enough so that *both* adversaries at least *say* that they want to work toward a resolution. Such stated motivation can at least serve as a starting point.

2 *What are the balances of status and power positions between the two or three parties?* The balance-of-power configurations can play a major part in determining appropriate paths to conflict resolution or avoidance in a given situation. For example, there may be less chance for successful resolution when one party in a two-party relationship is much more powerful or influential than the other. It is often harder to secure third-party involvement in such situations as well, particularly when the power imbalance involves a superior and a subordinate. At the same time, those are also the times when third-party mediation can be most helpful, in that the third party can help to rebalance the power equation. Conflict resolution advantages are clearly on the side of the higher-status person, whether that person be an adversary or a third party.

3 *To what extent are there time and flexibility resources available?* Conflict resolution in almost any form can require considerable time, new procedures, offsite meetings, outside help, painful adjustments, restructuring of relationships, and tolerance for uncertainties. As conflict conditions develop and change, so might the participant needs for time and resources. It may indeed be easier to change situational or external variables, such as new procedures, than to change the internal perceptions of *all* parties in the conflict arena, particularly those who are reference group members or advocates standing behind the two adversaries. Under these conditions, active counseling by a number of managers may help provide new perspectives throughout the conflict arena. In other words, changing the feelings and perceptions of the two adversaries may not be enough if their reference groups do not allow them to let go of the conflict. To work on all involved parties will take more time.

CONCLUSION

Interpersonal conflict can be both a constructive and a destructive force within an organization. More importantly to recognize, though, is the fact that such conflict is almost inevitable in any human organization. A manager's first choice is whether to ignore or avoid such realities, or whether to find ways to manage the complexities of conflict. The first alternative is quite often easier in the short run but more costly in the long run. At the same time, the management of conflict requires some understanding of its outcomes, its destructive behavior and reciprocity patterns, the perceptions and feelings that drive the behavior, and the underlying and background conditions that help to perpetuate the conflict. Each of these approaches provides entry points for managing conflict in bargaining, controlling, or confronting fashions—separately or in combination with each other. While these action approaches are rough in concept, they help a manager to explore his or her options in dealing with the realities of a conflict situation. Almost every manager has ample opportunity to view such situations as both an outsider and as an involved adversary. While this reading may capture some issues in interpersonal conflict, it cannot capture the emotional qualities that pervade such situations. Fortunately, most readers can do that for themselves. If not, they may be in the most difficulty in the future.

MANAGING YOUR BOSS

John J. Gabarro
John P. Kotter

To many the phrase *managing your boss* may sound unusual or suspicious. Because of the traditional top-down emphasis in organizations, it is not obvious why you need to manage relationships upward—unless, of course, you would do so for personal or political reasons. But in using the expression *managing your boss,* we are not referring to political maneuvering or apple polishing. Rather, we are using the term to mean the process of consciously working with your superior to obtain the best possible results for you, your boss, and the company.

Recent studies suggest that effective managers take time and effort to manage not only relationships with their subordinates but also those with their bosses.[1] These studies show as well that this aspect of management, essential though it is to survival and advancement, is sometimes ignored by otherwise talented and aggressive managers. Indeed, some managers who actively and effectively supervise subordinates, products, markets, and technologies, nevertheless assume an almost passively reactive stance vis-à-vis their bosses. Such a stance practically always hurts these managers and their companies.

If you doubt the importance of managing your relationship with your boss or how difficult it is to do so effectively, consider for a moment the following sad but telling story:

Frank Gibbons was an acknowledged manufacturing genius in his industry and, by any profitability standard, a very effective executive. In 1973, his strengths propelled him into the position of vice president of manufacturing for the second largest and most profitable company in its industry. Gibbons was not, however, a good manager of people. He knew this, as did others in his company and his industry.

---

[1] See, for example, John J. Gabarro, "Socialization at the Top: How CEOs and Their Subordinates Develop Interpersonal Contracts," *Organizational Dynamics,* Winter 1979; and John P. Kotter, *Power in Management,* AMACOM, 1979.

Recognizing this weakness, the president made sure that those who reported to Gibbons were good at working with people and could compensate for his limitations. The arrangement worked well.

In 1975, Philip Bonnevie was promoted into a position reporting to Gibbons. In keeping with the previous pattern, the president selected Bonnevie because he had an excellent track record and a reputation for being good with people. In making that selection, however, the president neglected to notice that, in his rapid rise through the organization, Bonnevie himself had never reported to anyone who was poor at managing subordinates. Bonnevie had always had good-to-excellent bosses. He had never been forced to manage a relationship with a difficult boss. In retrospect, Bonnevie admits he had never thought that managing his boss was a part of his job.

Fourteen months after he started working for Gibbons, Bonnevie was fired. During that same quarter, the company reported a net loss for the first time in seven years. Many of those who were close to these events say that they don't really understand what happened. This much is known, however: while the company was bringing out a major new product—a process that required its sales, engineering, and manufacturing groups to coordinate their decisions very carefully—a whole series of misunderstandings and bad feelings developed between Gibbons and Bonnevie.

For example, Bonnevie claims Gibbons was aware of and had accepted Bonnevie's decision to use a new type of machinery to make the new product; Gibbons swears he did not. Furthermore, Gibbons claims he made it clear to Bonnevie that introduction of the product was too important to the company in the short run to take any major risks.

As a result of such misunderstandings, planning went awry: a new manufacturing plant was built that could not produce the new product designed by engineering, in the volume desired by sales, at a cost agreed on by the executive committee. Gibbons blamed Bonnevie for the mistake. Bonnevie blamed Gibbons.

Of course, one could argue that the problem here was caused by Gibbons's inability to manage his subordinates. But one can make just as strong a case that the problem was related to Bonnevie's inability to manage his boss. Remember, Gibbons was not having difficulty with any other subordinates. Moreover, given the personal price paid by Bonnevie (being fired and having his reputation within the industry severely tarnished), there was little consolation in saying the problem was that Gibbons was poor at managing subordinates. Everyone already knew that.

We believe that the situation could have turned out differently had Bonnevie been more adept at understanding Gibbons and at managing his relationship with him. In this case, an inability to manage upward was unusually costly. The company lost $2 to $5 million, and Bonnevie's career was, at least temporarily, disrupted. Many less costly cases like this probably occur regularly in all major corporations, and the cumulative effect can be very destructive.

MISREADING THE BOSS-SUBORDINATE RELATIONSHIP

People often dismiss stories like the one we just related as being merely cases of personality conflict. Because two people can on occasion be psychologically or temperamentally incapable of working together, this can be an apt description. But more often, we have found, a personality conflict is only a part of the problem—sometimes a very small part.

Bonnevie did not just have a different personality from Gibbons, he also made or had unrealistic assumptions and expectations about the very nature of boss-subordinate relationships. Specifically, he did not recognize that his relationship to Gibbons involved *mutual dependence* between two *fallible* human beings. Failing to recognize this, a manager typically either avoids trying to manage his or her relationship with a boss or manages it ineffectively.

Some people behave as if their bosses were not very dependent on them. They fail to see how much the boss needs their help and cooperation to do his or her job effectively. These people refuse to acknowledge that the boss can be severely hurt by their actions and needs cooperation, dependability, and honesty from them.

Some see themselves as not very dependent on their bosses. They gloss over how much help and information they need from the boss in order to perform their own jobs well. This superficial view is particularly damaging when a manager's job and decisions affect other parts of the organization, as was the case in Bonnevie's situation. A manager's immediate boss can play a critical role in linking the manager to the rest of the organization, in making sure the manager's priorities are consistent with organizational needs, and in securing the resources the manager needs to perform well. Yet some managers need to see themselves as practically self-sufficient, as not needing the critical information and resources a boss can supply.

Many managers, like Bonnevie, assume that the boss will magically know what information or help their subordinates need and provide it to them. Certainly, some bosses do an excellent job of caring for their subordinates in this way, but for a manager to expect that from all bosses is dangerously unrealistic. A more reasonable expectation for managers to have is that modest help will be forthcoming. After all, bosses are only human. Most really effective managers accept this fact and assume primary responsibility for their own careers and development. They make a point of seeking the information and help they need to do a job instead of waiting for their bosses to provide it.

In light of the foregoing, it seems to us that managing a situation of mutual dependence among fallible human beings requires the following:

• That you have a good understanding of the other person and yourself, especially regarding strengths, weaknesses, work styles, and needs.

• That you use this information to develop and manage a healthy working relationship—one which is compatible with both persons' work styles and assets, is characterized by mutual expectations, and meets the most critical needs of the other person. And that is essentially what we have found highly effective managers doing.

UNDERSTANDING THE BOSS & YOURSELF

Managing your boss requires that you gain an understanding of both the boss and his context as well as your own situation and needs. All managers do this to some degree, but many are not thorough enough.

The Boss's World

At a minimum, you need to appreciate your boss's goals and pressures, his or her strengths and weaknesses. What are your boss's organizational and personal objectives, and what are the pressures on him, especially those from his boss and others at his level? What are your boss's long suits and blind spots? What is his or her preferred style of working? Does he or she like to get information through memos, formal meetings, or phone calls? Does your boss thrive on conflict or try to minimize it?

Without this information, a manager is flying blind when dealing with his boss, and unnecessary conflicts, misunderstandings, and problems are inevitable.

Goals & Pressures

In one situation we studied, a top-notch marketing manager with a superior performance record was hired into a company as a vice president "to straighten out the marketing and sales problems." The company, which was having financial difficulties, had been recently acquired by a larger corporation. The president was eager to turn it around and gave the new marketing vice president free rein—at least initially. Based on his previous experience, the new vice president correctly diagnosed that greater market share was needed and that strong product management was required to bring that about. As a result, he made a number of pricing decisions aimed at increasing high-volume business.

When margins declined and the financial situation did not improve, however, the president increased pressure on the new vice president. Believing that the situation would eventually correct itself as the company gained back market share, the vice president resisted the pressure.

When by the second quarter margins and profits had still failed to improve, the president took direct control over all pricing decisions and put all items on a set level of margin, regardless of volume. The new vice president began to find himself shut out by the president, and their relationship deteriorated. In fact, the vice president found the president's behavior bizarre. Unfortunately, the president's new pricing scheme also failed to increase margins, and by the fourth quarter both the president and the vice president were fired.

What the new vice president had not known until it was too late was that improving marketing and sales had been only *one* of the president's goals. His most immediate goal had been to make the company more profitable—quickly.

Nor had the new vice president known that his boss was invested in this short-term priority for personal as well as business reasons. The president had been a strong advocate of the acquisition within the parent company, and his personal credibility was at stake.

The vice president made three basic errors. He took information supplied to him at face value, he made assumptions in areas where he had no information, and—most damaging—he never actively tried to clarify what his boss's objectives were. As a result, he ended up taking actions that were actually at odds with the president's priorities and objectives.

Managers who work effectively with their bosses do not behave this way. They seek out information about the boss's goals and problems and pressures. They are alert for opportunities to question the boss and others around him to test their assumptions. They pay attention to clues in the boss's behavior. Although it is imperative they do this when they begin working with a new boss, effective managers also do this on an ongoing basis because they recognize that priorities and concerns change.

Strengths, Weaknesses & Work Style

Being sensitive to a boss's work style can be crucial, especially when the boss is new. For example, a new president who was organized and formal in his approach replaced a man who was informal and intuitive. The new president worked best when he had written reports. He also preferred formal meetings with set agendas.

One of his division managers realized this need and worked with the new president to identify the kinds and frequency of information and reports the president wanted. This manager also made a point of sending background information and brief agendas for their discussions. He found that with this type of preparation their meetings were very useful. Moreover, he found that with adequate preparation his new boss was even more effective at brainstorming problems than his more informal and intuitive predecessor had been.

In contrast, another division manager never fully understood how the new boss's work style differed from that of his predecessor. To the degree that he did sense it, he experienced it as too much control. As a result, he seldom sent the new president the background information he needed, and the president never felt fully prepared for meetings with the manager. In fact, the president spent much of his time when they met trying to get information that he felt he should have had before his arrival. The boss experienced these meetings as frustrating and inefficient, and the subordinate often found himself thrown off guard by the questions that the president asked. Ultimately, this division manager resigned.

The difference between the two division managers just described was not so much one of ability or even adaptability. Rather, the difference was that one of the men was more sensitive to his boss's work style than the other and to the implications of his boss's needs.

YOU & YOUR NEEDS

The boss is only one-half of the relationship. You are the other half, as well as the part over which you have more direct control. Developing an effective working relationship requires, then, that you know your own needs, strengths and weaknesses, and personal style.

Your Own Style

You are not going to change either your basic personality structure or that of your boss. But you can become aware of what it is about you that impedes or facilitates working with your boss and, with that awareness, take actions that make the relationship more effective.

For example, in one case we observed, a manager and his superior ran into problems whenever they disagreed. The boss's typical response was to harden his position and overstate it. The manager's reaction was then to raise the ante and intensify the forcefulness of his argument. In doing this, he channeled his anger into sharpening his attacks on the logical fallacies in his boss's assumptions. His boss in turn would become even more adamant about holding his original position. Predictably, this escalating cycle resulted in the subordinate avoiding whenever possible any topic of potential conflict with his boss.

In discussing this problem with his peers, the manager discovered that his reaction to the boss was typical of how he generally reacted to counterarguments—but with a difference. His response would overwhelm his peers, but not his boss. Because his attempts to discuss this problem with his boss were unsuccessful, he concluded that the only way to change the situation was to deal with his own instinctive reactions. Whenever the two reached an impasse, he would check his own impatience and suggest that they break up and think about it before getting together again. Usually when they renewed their discussion, they had digested their differences and were more able to work them through.

Gaining this level of self-awareness and acting on it are difficult but not impossible. For example, by reflecting over his past experiences, a young manager learned that he was not very good at dealing with difficult and emotional issues where people were involved. Because he disliked those issues and realized that his instinctive responses to them were seldom very good, he developed a habit of touching base with his boss whenever such a problem arose. Their discussions always surfaced ideas and approaches the manager had not considered. In many cases, they also identified specific actions the boss could take to help.

Dependence on Authority Figures

Although a superior-subordinate relationship is one of mutual dependence, it is also one in which the subordinate is typically more dependent on the boss than the other way around. This dependence inevitably results in the subordinate feeling a certain degree of frustration, sometimes anger, when his actions or options are constrained by his boss's decisions. This is a normal part of life and occurs in the best of relationships. The way in which a manager handles these frustrations largely depends on his or her predisposition toward dependence on authority figures.

Some people's instinctive reaction under these circumstances is to resent the boss's authority and to rebel against the boss's decisions. Sometimes a person will escalate a conflict beyond what is appropriate. Seeing the boss almost as an institutional enemy, this type of manager will often, without being conscious of it, fight with the boss just for the sake of fighting. His reactions to being constrained are usually strong and sometimes impulsive. He sees the boss as someone who, by virtue of his role, is a hindrance to progress, an obstacle to be circumvented or at best tolerated.

Psychologists call this pattern of reactions counterdependent behavior. Although a counterdependent person is difficult for most superiors to manage and usually has a history of strained relationships with superiors, this sort of manager is apt to have even more trouble with a boss who tends to be directive or authoritarian. When the manager acts on his or her negative feelings, often in subtle and nonverbal ways, the boss sometimes *does* become the enemy. Sensing the subordinate's latent hostility, the boss will lose trust in the subordinate or his judgment and behave less openly.

Paradoxically, a manager with this type of predisposition is often a good manager of his own people. He will often go out of his way to get support for them and will not hesitate to go to bat for them. At the other extreme are managers who swallow their anger and behave in a very compliant fashion when the boss makes what they know to be a poor decision. These managers will agree with the boss even when a disagreement might be welcome or when the boss would easily alter his decision if given more information. Because they bear no relationship to the specific situation at hand, their responses are as much an overreaction as those of counterdependent managers. Instead of seeing the boss as an enemy, these people deny their anger—the other extreme—and tend to see the boss as if he or she were an all-wise parent who should know best, should take responsibility for their careers, train them in all they need to know, and protect them from overly ambitious peers.

Both counterdependence and overdependence lead managers to hold unrealistic views of what a boss is. Both views ignore that most bosses, like everyone else, are imperfect and fallible. They don't have unlimited time, encyclopedic knowledge, or extrasensory perception; nor are they evil enemies. They have their own pressures and concerns that are sometimes at odds with the wishes of the subordinate—and often for good reason.

Altering predispositions toward authority, especially at the extremes, is almost impossible without intensive psychotherapy (psychoanalytic theory and research suggest that such predispositions are deeply rooted in a person's personality and upbringing). However, an awareness of these extremes and the range between them can be very useful in understanding where your own predispositions fall and what the implications are for how you tend to behave in relation to your boss.

If you believe, on the one hand, that you have some tendencies toward counterdependence, you can understand and even predict what your reactions and overreactions are likely to be. If, on the other hand, you believe you have some tendencies toward overdependence, you might question the extent to which your overcompliance or inability to confront real differences may be making both you and your boss less effective.

DEVELOPING & MANAGING THE RELATIONSHIP

With a clear understanding of both your boss and yourself, you can—usually—establish a way of working together that fits both of you, that is characterized by unambiguous mutual expectations, and that helps both of you to be more productive and effective. We have already outlined a few things such a relationship consists of, which are itemized in Exhibit 1, and here are a few more.

EXHIBIT 1   MANAGING THE RELATIONSHIP WITH YOUR BOSS

Make sure you understand your boss and his context, including:
  His goals and objectives
  The pressures on him
  His strengths, weaknesses, blind spots
  His preferred work style
Assess yourself and your needs, including:
  Your own strengths and weaknesses
  Your personal style
  Your predisposition toward dependence on authority figures
Develop and maintain a relationship that:
  Fits both your needs and styles
  Is characterized by mutual expectations
  Keeps your boss informed
  Is based on dependability and honesty
  Selectively uses your boss's time and resources

Compatible Work Styles

Above all else, a good working relationship with a boss accommodates differences in work style. For example, in one situation we studied, a manager (who had a relatively good relationship with his superior) realized that during meetings his boss would often become inattentive and sometimes brusque. The subordinate's own style tended to be discursive and exploratory. He would often digress from the topic at hand to deal with background factors, alternative approaches, and so forth. His boss, instead, preferred to discuss problems with a minimum of background detail and became impatient and distracted whenever his subordinate digressed from the immediate issue.

Recognizing this difference in style, the manager became terser and more direct during meetings with his boss. To help himself do this, before meetings with the boss he would develop brief agendas that he used as a guide. Whenever he felt that a digression was needed, he explained why. This small shift in his own style made these meetings more effective and far less frustrating for them both.

Subordinates can adjust their styles in response to their bosses' preferred method for receiving information. Peter Drucker divides bosses into "listeners" and "readers." Some bosses like to get information in report form so that they can read and study it. Others work better with information and reports presented in person so that they can ask questions. As Drucker points out, the implications are obvious. If your boss is a listener, you brief him in person, *then* follow it up with a memo. If your boss is a reader, you cover important items or proposals in a memo or report, *then* discuss them with him.

Other adjustments can be made according to a boss's decision-making style. Some bosses prefer to be involved in decisions and problems as they arise. These are high-involvement managers who like to keep their hands on the pulse of the operation. Usually their needs (and your own) are best satisfied if you touch base with them on an ad hoc basis. A boss who has a need to be involved will become involved one way or another, so there are advantages to including him at your initiative. Other bosses prefer to delegate—they don't want to be involved. They expect you to come to them with major problems and inform them of important changes.

Creating a compatible relationship also involves drawing on each other's strengths and making up for each other's weaknesses. Because he knew that his boss—the vice president of engineering—was not very good at monitoring his employees' problems, one manager we studied made a point of doing it himself. The stakes were high: the engineers and technicians were all union members, the company worked on a customer-contract basis, and the company had recently experienced a serious strike.

The manager worked closely with his boss, the scheduling department, and the personnel office to ensure that potential problems were avoided. He also developed an informal arrangement through which his boss would review with him any proposed changes in personnel or assignment policies before taking action. The boss valued his advice and credited his subordinate for improving both the performance of the division and the labor-management climate.

Mutual Expectations

The subordinate who passively assumes that he or she knows what the boss expects is in for trouble. Of course, some superiors will spell out their expectations very explicitly and in great detail. But most do not. And although many corporations have systems that provide a basis for communicating expectations (such as formal planning processes, career planning reviews, and performance appraisal reviews), these systems never work perfectly. Also, between these formal reviews expectations invariably change.

Ultimately, the burden falls on the subordinate to find out what the boss's expectations are. These expectations can be both broad (regarding, for example, what kinds of problems the boss wishes to be informed about and when) as well as very specific (regarding such things as when a particular project should be completed and what kinds of information the boss needs in the interim).

Getting a boss who tends to be vague or nonexplicit to express his expectations can be difficult. But effective managers find ways to get that information. Some will draft a detailed memo covering key aspects of their work and then send it to their bosses for approval. They then follow this up with a face-to-face discussion in which they go over each item in the memo. This discussion often surfaces virtually all of the boss's relevant expectations.

Other effective managers will deal with an inexplicit boss by initiating an ongoing series of informal discussions about "good management" and "our objectives." Still others find useful information more indirectly through those who used to work for the boss and through the formal planning systems in which the boss makes commitments to his superior. Which approach you choose, of course, should depend on your understanding of your boss's style.

Developing a workable set of mutual expectations also requires that you communicate your own expectations to the boss, find out if they are realistic, and influence the boss to accept the ones that are important to you. Being able to influence the boss to value your expectations can be particularly important if the boss is an overachiever. Such a boss will often set unrealistically high standards that need to be brought into line with reality.

A Flow of Information

How much information a boss needs about what a subordinate is doing will vary significantly depending on the boss's style, the situation he is in, and the confidence he has in the subordinate. But it is not uncommon for a boss to need more information than the subordinate would naturally supply or for the subordinate to think the boss knows more than he really does. Effective managers recognize that they probably underestimate what the boss needs to know and make sure they find ways to keep him informed through a process that fits his style.

Managing the flow of information upward is particularly difficult if the boss does not like to hear about problems. Although many would deny it, bosses often give off signals that they want to hear only good news. They show great displeasure—usually nonverbally—when someone tells them about a problem. Ignoring individual achievement, they may even evaluate more favorably subordinates who do not bring problems to them.

Nevertheless—for the good of the organization, boss, and subordinate—a superior needs to hear about failures as well as successes. Some subordinates deal with a good-news-only boss by finding indirect ways to get the necessary information to him, such as a management information system in which there is no messenger to be killed. Others see to it that potential problems, whether in the form of good surprises or bad news, are communicated immediately.

Dependability & Honesty

Few things are more disabling to a boss than a subordinate on whom he cannot depend, whose work he cannot trust. Almost no one is intentionally undependable, but many managers are inadvertently so because of oversight or uncertainty about the boss's priorities. A commitment to an optimistic delivery date may please a superior in the short term but be a source of displeasure if not honored. It's difficult for a boss to rely on a subordinate who repeatedly slips deadlines. As one president put it (describing a subordinate): "When he's great, he's terrific, but I can't depend on him. I'd rather he be more consistent even if he delivered fewer peak successes—at least I could rely on him."

Nor are many managers intentionally dishonest with their bosses. But it is so easy to shade the truth a bit and play down concerns. Current concerns often become future surprise problems. It's almost impossible for bosses to work effectively if they cannot rely on a fairly accurate reading from their subordinates. Because it undermines credibility, dishonesty is perhaps the most troubling trait a subordinate can have. Without a basic level of trust in a subordinate's word, a boss feels he has to check all of a subordinate's decisions, which makes it difficult to delegate.

Good Use of Time & Resources

Your boss is probably as limited in his store of time, energy, and influence as you are. Every request you make of him uses up some of these resources. For this reason, common sense suggests drawing on these resources with some selectivity. This may sound obvious, but it is surprising how many managers use up their boss's time (and some of their own credibility) over relatively trivial issues.

In one instance, a vice president went to great lengths to get his boss to fire a meddlesome secretary in another department. His boss had to use considerable effort and influence to do it. Understandably, the head of the other department was not pleased. Later, when the vice president wanted to tackle other more important problems that required changes in the scheduling and control practices of the other department, he ran into trouble. He had used up many of his own as well as his boss's blue chips on the relatively trivial issue of getting the secretary fired, thereby making it difficult for him and his boss to meet more important goals.

WHOSE JOB IS IT?

No doubt, some subordinates will resent that on top of all their other duties, they also need to take time and energy to manage their relationships with their bosses. Such managers fail to realize the importance of this activity and how it can simplify their jobs by eliminating potentially severe problems. Effective managers recognize that this part of their work is legitimate. Seeing themselves as ultimately responsible for what they achieve in an organization, they know they need to establish and manage relationships with everyone on whom they are dependent, and that includes the boss.

THREE

MOTIVATION, LEADERSHIP, AND INFLUENCE

Part 3 focuses on the individual manager: the implications of individual motivation for exercising leadership and influencing behavior. The concepts developed have general application to all managerial situations, although a central concept is the importance of "fit" between the job or situation and the person. By understanding the way individual needs influence particular motivations, a manager can decide what he or she needs to do to obtain effective behaviors that provide positive outcomes for both the individual and the organization. Effective managerial action requires the development and use of power, a necessity of leadership. The concept of power is central to Part 3 in the same way that group culture was to Part 1 and conflict was to Part 2.

The text "Understanding Individual Behavior in Organizations," presents a model of individual behavior based on the expectancy theory of motivation. At the foundation of this theory is the principle that individual behavior is a result of the interactions of individual characteristics, such as abilities, needs, and beliefs, and organization characteristics, such as jobs, reward systems, and control systems. Individuals have a variety of needs, arranged hierarchically, that they seek to satisfy and that motivate them to act in certain ways. In considering what actions to take to satisfy these needs, individuals consider the probability of successful performance for a given level of effort as well as the probability of receiving certain outcomes if performance is successful. To these outcomes, individuals attach positive or negative values. They weigh these against their expectations of the effort-performance relationship and the performance-outcome relationship in deciding what to do. Although somewhat complex, this model of individual behavior is developed step by step in a way that makes it useful for analyzing the cases in Part 3.

Case 1 considers James Edwards, a young, black MBA who is currently dissatisfied with his job situation despite his high level of performance. An extensive transcript of his remarks on his current situation provides data on his needs, motivations, and expectations. The model presented in the text can be used to understand why Edwards is frustrated. One factor is the response of his company to an article he wrote about black managers. Thus, in addition to general issues of human motivation and behavior, this case requires an analysis of many specific issues attendant to being a minority. In Case 2, Edwards is offered a job in which he would report directly to the company president. The risks and opportunities are both considerable, and Edwards must decide whether to accept the job. The model can be used to anticipate whether or not he *will* accept this job and whether or not he *should* accept it.

Cases 3–5 describe the strategy taken by Elizabeth Best upon becoming undersecretary of environmental affairs in the Water Division of the state of Delaware. From the very beginning, she is treated with politeness but indifference by all her subordinates. Much to her amazement, she also finds absolutely no files left by her predecessor. In addition to operating in a highly political and constrained situation, Best finds some major operating problems in the division, including very slow water-revenue collections from cities and towns and the lack of adequate pipeline transportation for fresh water. Many of the employees in the division are poorly motivated, but, as civil servants, cannot be dismissed. An analysis of these cases shows how Best made use of her personal characteristics and the situation to develop the necessary power to influence people in the division to improve their performance. Similar to Cases 1 and 2, these cases involve general issues of human motivation and performance, as well as specific issues confronting minority group managers.

Case 6 describes the structure and role of the product manager at United Brands. A person in this job must influence a number of people, both inside and outside the company, in such areas as sales, production, market research, product research, finance, and advertising, over whom he or she has no direct responsibility. It is a high-status job and a common step on the way to positions of higher responsibility. This case includes data from product managers, assistant product managers, and others on what is required for someone to be successful in this job.

David Alpert is a very effective product manager. Case 7 provides data that, along with the preceding case and the note on expectancy theory, help explain the reasons for Alpert's success. These data include dialogues from Alpert's meetings with subordinates and bosses and his comments about his managerial approach. This case also builds heavily on concepts developed in Part 2.

Case 8 consists of reflections by Alpert about his family, childhood, and youth. It provides data that can be used to understand Alpert's needs and consequent motivations, and how his personal characteristics enabled him to develop effective influence skills. Comparisons can be made between Alpert, Best, and Edwards to gain further understanding of human motivation and behavior.

Case 9 requires the use of all concepts developed thus far to prepare an action plan for a manager caught in a difficult situation. Brenda Cooper, a young MBA, is the southeastern regional sales manager and is responsible for the Florida sales force. Cooper is under strong pressure to find ways to improve the slowly growing infant food business in her region. While the entire company is experiencing difficulties with this mature product line, the Florida sales force continually meets its objectives and obtains a performance bonus, although Cooper does not know how. In fact, the sales force has found that baby food can be sold to nursing homes through supermarkets, but is withholding this information from the company. The two basic questions are why is the sales force behaving in this fashion and what should Cooper do if she were to find out about it.

The three readings address the related issues of power and leadership. Reading 1 reviews five especially important and common sources of social power: reward power, coercive power, referent power, legitimate power, and expert power. Reading 2 addresses three issues: (1) the reason that the dynamics of power are an important part of managerial processes, (2) the ways that effective managers acquire power, and (3) the ways that effective managers use power and to what purposes. This reading emphasizes the central importance of the interdependence between managers and their subordinates in both directions. Four different types of power—sense of obligation, belief in a manager's expertise, identification with a manager, and perceived dependence on a manager—are identified and discussed. Various influence methods that involve the use of power are presented in terms of what they can influence and their advantages and disadvantages.

Reading 3 addresses the question of what type of leadership style is best—boss-centered or subordinate-centered. These types are regarded as anchoring a continuum of seven leadership styles. As one moves from boss-centered to subordinate-centered leadership, the use of authority by the boss declines and the area of freedom for subordinates increases. This reading argues that no one method is necessarily superior but that the most appropriate method to be used depends upon three major factors: forces in the manager, forces in the subordinate, and forces in the situation. Forces in the manager include his or her value system, his or her confidence in subordinates, his or her own leadership inclinations, and his or her feelings of security in an uncertain situation. Forces in the subordinate include the need for independence, readiness to assume responsibility for decisionmaking, a degree of tolerance for ambiguity, and degree of experience and knowledge. Finally, forces in the situation include characteristics of the organization, the level of group effectiveness, characteristics of the problem being addressed, and extent of time pressure. Effective managers are those who adapt their leadership style as necessary.

UNDERSTANDING INDIVIDUAL BEHAVIOR IN ORGANIZATIONS

David A. Nadler
J. Richard Hackman
Edward E. Lawler III

Mrs. Ellen Johnson has a routine, repetitive job. She works in a garment factory where she sits over a Singer sewing machine from 8 a.m. until 4 p.m., and by the end of a week she has guided 1500 linings into 1500 coats.

How does Mrs. Johnson feel about her job? She likes it. Mrs. Johnson has been with her present employer since the death of her husband 29 years ago. Her day begins at 6:40 a.m. when she leaves her home in Brooklyn. Two subway trains and 50 minutes later, she changes into a work smock in a makeshift dressing room.

She can do any job on the assembly line in the garment factory where she works. Most of the time, by her own preference, she sews linings into coats. She moves with astonishing speed and deftness and her productivity rate is far above the engineered standard for the job. After more than 25 years of practice, she can carry on a lively conversation with coworkers and still keep the coats flowing through her sewing machine with faultless precision.

Mrs. Johnson earns about $125 a week. She has more than made her peace with the job. "I wouldn't recommend it to someone with an education," she says, "but for someone like me, it's good. You learn to take it in stride. You make up your mind It's your livelihood and then you don't get bored."

Mrs. Johnson cannot imagine any other way of spending a day. To her, going to the garment factory is almost an involuntary function of the body and mind. It is, she says, "like everything else—you gotta eat, you gotta sleep, you gotta work." Indeed, to her, the rundown garment factory is almost like a home. "I'd come in here with a fever," she says. "Even if there's a blizzard, I come."

Mrs. Johnson is fiercely proud of her good record as a worker and is scornful of younger workers who are not willing to devote as much to the job as she does. "They want easy jobs, like office jobs. I like this place here, but I do sweat for a dollar. We know what a dollar is worth here."

One of the women Mrs. Johnson is scornful of is Mrs. Janet Henson. Mrs. Henson works in the same garment factory as Mrs. Johnson. Most of the time her job consists of cutting loose threads off finished coats and packing the coats in boxes. She is 20 years old and a high school graduate. Mrs. Henson failed to find an office job when she graduated from high school 2 years ago. As she says, "This was the cleanest factory job I could find at the time."

Although she used to try hard, Mrs. Henson has never mastered her job and her performance is constantly below standard. She seems to lack the finger dexterity and hand speed required to do her job.

How does she feel about her job? "I dread coming to work. The pay is too low and the boredom is driving me crazy. I am starting to have nightmares about it. If I could get a better job, I would take it in a minute. My biggest fear is that I am trapped in this job and that I will never be able to get an office job."

Mrs. Henson may not find an office job, but there is a good chance she will be leaving her present one before long. Her supervisor, Ms. Abelson, has just about given up on her. According to Ms. Abelson, "Janet is a nice girl, but she just doesn't fit here. She doesn't seem to be able to learn the job and she is more interested in her appearance than in the work. I just cannot tolerate this any longer. I am afraid I am going to have to let her go."

Clearly the reactions of Mrs. Johnson and Mrs. Henson to their jobs are quite different. They differ in how they feel about their jobs as well as in how effectively they are able to perform, despite the fact that their jobs are similar in many important respects.

Can the differences between these two women be explained, or should they simply be dismissed as due to unexplainable differences in people? Although it is not easy to explain differences like these, they usually can be dealt with by models that are available to analyze individual behavior. Basic to all these models and to understanding the work behavior of individuals is the principle that human behavior is jointly determined by characteristics of individuals and characteristics of the work environment.

EXHIBIT 1   A general model of behavior in organizations.

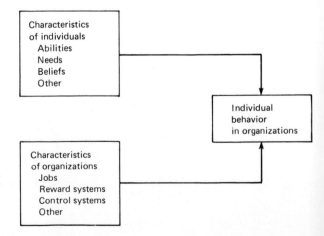

As shown in Exhibit 1, human behavior is a function of the characteristics of both the *person* and the *environment.* Individuals bring things to the organizational setting, including abilities, personal beliefs, expectations, and past experiences. The environment provided by the organization has a number of features: jobs, relationships between people, work that needs to be done, rewards that are available to individuals, and so on. Neither the nature of the individual nor the nature of the organization completely determines behavior. Rather, behavior results from the interaction of individual and organizational characteristics. As the field of organizational behavior has matured, researchers and theorists have developed more complex views of the key attributes of individuals, and similarly they have developed more complex views of the salient characteristics of organizations. At the same time, the concept of behavior as a joint function of the person and the environment has persisted as the underlying model of behavior.

The remainder of this note is organized around this model, and it considers some of the characteristics of individuals that can help us understand individual behavior in organizational settings.

UNDERSTANDING THE NATURE OF INDIVIDUALS

Psychology has developed many ways of viewing the nature of people. Although the concept of people accepted by most researchers in organizational behavior draws on some of these approaches, it is different and has its own character. It is performance-oriented, and views most job behavior as the result of conscious thought processes within the individual. The best way to understand this view is to review its basic principles.

People Differ in Their Behavior Capabilities

An important limiting factor on an individual's behavior is capability. People cannot respond in all ways that might seem desirable. People can only lift so much weight, think so fast, run so far. Furthermore, and of great significance, individuals differ widely in their response capabilities. Some people can lift many times what others can, think much faster, run much farther. Mrs. Johnson, for example, was able to master the complex manual skills that are involved in garment manufacturing, while Mrs. Henson was not.

Traditionally, psychologists have divided behaviors into those that are innate and therefore not subject to improvement by training, and those that can be altered and learned. This way of thinking about human characteristics is outmoded. Even such measures as intelligence (IQ), once thought to be innately determined and fixed, can be influenced by training and experience. It remains true, however, that IQ can only be influenced within a limited range because physiological limitations exist. The same is true of the kinds of manual dexterity skills that are important in performing the jobs of Mrs. Johnson and Mrs. Henson. Consequently, it now seems reasonable to describe human response capabilities by placing them on a continuum. At one end are those behaviors that are difficult to influence by training and experience (for example, reaction time), and at the other end are those behaviors that are relatively open to change and not significantly constrained by genetic or physiological factors (for example, reading speed).

A large number of psychological tests have been developed that are valid measures of behavior capability, and research has shown that some of them can predict job performance. Tests have been developed to measure those behavior capabilities that are relatively fixed and those that are more susceptible to change as a result of experience and training. The latter are often called *skill tests,* while the former are called *aptitude tests.* Both kinds can, and often do, play an important role in a variety of staffing decisions, including hiring, firing, promotion, and training. The significance of the fact that individuals have different behavior capabilities is not limited to decisions concerning staffing. It is also important to keep this point in mind when training decisions are being made and when jobs are designed. For an organization to be effective, individuals must hold jobs that they are capable of performing. As we will see, a number of strategies exist for creating good fits between the capabilities of an individual and the demands of a job.

People Have Different Needs That They Try to Satisfy

Psychologists generally talk about human behavior as being motivated by a set of needs. A *need* is some internal state in a person that causes clusters or groups of objects or outcomes to be sought. For example, various food objects are sought by individuals and are clustered together, so that when people desire one food object, they usually desire others as well; when they get enough of one food, they often lose interest in the others. Thus, we say people have a need for food rather than saying that people have a need for roast beef or potatoes. Similarly, performing well in certain kinds of competitive activities seems to be attractive to individuals and, as a result, we speak of a need for achievement even though we cannot tie this need to any physiological basis.

Human beings are motivated toward a great diversity of ends. For instance, Mrs. Johnson seems attracted to work because it satisfies her social needs as well as her need for security. Furthermore, needs are constantly changing. What motivates people today may or may not be potent in determining their behavior tomorrow. This, however, does not mean that the concept of need is not useful for dealing with human behavior in organizations. It is necessary if we are to explain and predict the goal-oriented behavior that occurs in organizations. It can also help us to understand why outcomes are important to individuals, and it can help us predict which outcomes will be important to specific individuals.

What needs do individuals have? The following list, or one similar to it, enjoys broad acceptance:

1 A number of existence needs, including sex, hunger, thirst, and oxygen
2 Security
3 Social relations
4 Esteem and reputation

5 Autonomy, self-control, and independence
6 Competence, achievement, and self-realization

One distinction between the first four needs and the fifth and the sixth is that these can only be satisfied by outcomes that are external (extrinsic) to the person and have a concrete reality (food, money, praise from another). The need for self-realization and competence and, to some extent, the need for autonomy and self-control seem to be satisfied only by outcomes that are given intrinsically by persons to themselves (for instance, the feeling of accomplishment). It is true that certain environmental conditions must be present before internal outcomes can be obtained, but the outcomes themselves are not observable to others or controlled by others. Behavior in organizations is motivated by individuals seeking *both* intrinsic and extrinsic rewards.

Maslow's well-known need theory specifies that needs are arranged in a hierarchy. According to this theory, people move successively up a need hierarchy (like the list above). As their lower-order needs are satisfied, their higher-order needs, such as self-realization, become more important. In essence, Maslow talks as if needs are arranged like a ladder that must be climbed one rung at a time. Thus, people are only concerned with self-realization if their existence needs, their security needs, and so on are satisfied. Further, if the satisfaction of a lower-order need is threatened, that need immediately becomes predominant, and all higher-order needs will be forgotten.

Maslow also points out that a satisfied need is not motivating. Once a person has obtained a satisfying amount of food, the opportunity to obtain more food is not motivating. The one exception to this conclusion is the need for self-actualization or growth. This need seems to be insatiable: the more individuals obtain outcomes that satisfy it, the more important it becomes and the more of it they desire. Because of this, self-realization, unlike other needs, continues to be important, and people are continually motivated by the desire to experience more of it. One important implication is that no matter how much satisfaction someone has, he or she will always want more.

Research supports the view that unless existence and security needs are satisfied, people are not concerned with the needs above them. However, very little evidence exists to support the view that a hierarchy exists once one moves above the security level. For example, studies do not indicate that social needs must be satisfied before people are concerned with the need for self-realization. Thus, based on the research evidence, it seems best to assume a two-level hierarchy, with existence and security needs at the lower level and the remaining needs at the upper level. This means that unless the lower-order needs are satisfied, the others do not come into play. It also means that when the satisfaction of lower-order needs is threatened, these needs predominate. Thus, attempts to influence behaviors that threaten lower-order needs always have an impact because these dominate all others.

The existence of a two-level hierarchy also means that if the basic needs are satisfied, no one need is likely to be the "best" or "only" motivator. In fact, the evidence suggests that more than one need may simultaneously be important. For example, a person can be motivated by both social and autonomy needs. It also suggests that people differ widely in which need or needs come into play once existence and security needs are satisfied. As a result, it is to be expected that at any point in time most organizations employ individuals who are motivated by different needs, as exemplified by the differences between Mrs. Johnson and Mrs. Henson.

People Think about the Future and Make Choices about How to Behave

People's needs can only be satisfied by their engaging in behaviors. In many situations, individuals are faced with a number of potentially need-satisfying behaviors from which to choose. The most widely accepted current approach to explaining how individuals make choices among a large set of alternative behaviors is called *expectancy theory*. Expectancy theory is based on the relatively simple proposition that individuals choose to attempt those behaviors that they see as leading to outcomes (rewards such as pay, recognition from the boss) that are attractive to them (that meet their particular needs). Based on this proposition, the theory shows how to analyze and predict what courses of action individuals will follow when they can choose their behavior.

Exhibit 2 presents expectancy theory graphically. It shows that as individuals contemplate the performance of an act, they consider several factors. First, the probability that if they put forth effort, they will be able to attain the required level of performance (the effort to performance, or EP, expectancy); second, if the level of performance is obtained, the probability that it will lead to acquiring outcomes (the performance to outcome, or PO, expectancy); third, the attractiveness of the outcomes, seen as accruing from performance; and fourth, the degree to which some outcomes may have additional attractiveness because their acquisition in turn leads

EXHIBIT 2   Major expectancy theory terms.

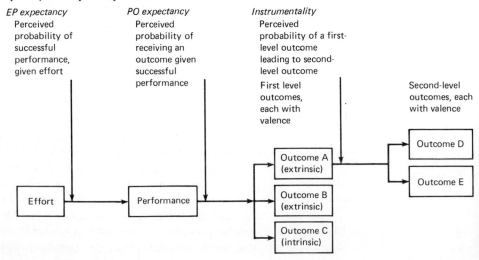

to the obtaining of other desired outcomes (such as money, which is attractive because of what it can buy). Given this model, the motivational force to behave in a certain way is greatest when:

1 The individual believes that performance at the desired level is possible (high EP expectancy)
2 The individual believes that the behavior will lead to outcomes (has a high PO expectancy)
3 Those outcomes have positive value (have high attractiveness)

Given a number of alternative behaviors (for example, 10, 15, or 20 units of production per hour, or vacation versus work), the model predicts that individuals choose the behavior that has the greatest motivational force associated with it. In other words, when faced with choices of behavior, the individual goes through a process of asking questions, such as: Can I perform at that level if I try? If I perform at that level, what will happen? How do I feel about those things that will happen? The individual then decides to behave in the way that appears to have the best chance of producing positive outcomes.

Applying this model to the performances of Mrs. Johnson and Mrs. Henson, we can see why Mrs. Henson has a low motivation to perform her job effectively. To begin with, she does not believe that she can perform at a high level because she lacks the necessary capabilities. Furthermore, she does not believe that good performance on the job will lead to the rewards she values. The situation for Mrs. Johnson is just the reverse. She knows she can do well if she puts forth the effort, and good performance on the job leads to feelings of self-esteem and competence.

It is important to note that the expectancy model does not predict that people always behave in the best way to obtain what they desire. It assumes that individuals make rational decisions based on their perception of the situation, but it does not assume that people have accurate or complete information when they make those decisions. People often stop considering alternative behaviors when they find one that is at least moderately satisfying, even though more rewarding behaviors remain to be examined. Searching is time-consuming and takes effort; thus, it is not surprising that people limit their explorations. People are also limited in the amount of information they can handle at one time, and the outcomes associated with many behaviors are multitudinous; therefore, people often do not consider all the outcomes that might result from a certain behavior. Finally, as we discuss below, people see the world in terms of their past experience. This leads them to misperceive the world on many occasions.

People Perceive the Environment in Terms of Past Experiences and Needs

Similar to most approaches to understanding behavior, the expectancy model assumes that people behave according to their perceptions of the world. It indicates that perceptions lead to beliefs about what performance is possible and what outcomes will follow performance.

Perceiving the environment is an *active* process in which people try to make sense out of their environment. This active process involves individuals selectively noticing different aspects of the environment, appraising what they see in terms of their past experience, and evaluating what they are experiencing in light of their needs and values. Since people's needs and experiences often differ markedly, their perceptions of the environment do likewise. For example, people in the same organization often develop very different expectations of what kinds of behavior lead to rewards, such as pay increases and promotions.

Environments provide their members with many more objects and events than an individual is cognitively able to handle. Therefore, in perceiving an organization at any given time, individuals do not notice many of its aspects. What aspects are noticed and processed depends partly on the nature of the objects and events themselves and partly on the individual's previous experience. Highly distinctive objects within the usual organizational context are more likely to be noticed than those that do not stand out in some unusual way. The written memo on the bulletin board may not serve as a very distinctive input to organization members, but a meeting in the cafeteria with the company president, an extremely rare occurrence, may have high distinctiveness and will be attended by most employees. In addition to distinctiveness, the previous learning of organization members plays an important part in determining what is noticed. Organization members learn to discriminate between those things that they need to pay attention to in order to satisfy their needs and those that they may safely overlook.

Even when an event or object is noticed or attended to, there is no guarantee that it will be perceived accurately. The meaning that any given object or event has for an individual organization member is influenced by the needs of the member. Events and objects are often distorted so that they are more congruent with needs and values. The specific nature of the distortion of a particular event or object is difficult to predict; simply too many idiosyncratic factors are involved, both in the nature of the event or object and in the psychological and emotional makeup of the individual. However, the degree of distortion is predictable; it is a function of the degree to which the situation involves important needs. Thus, organizational events around such matters as pay and promotion are particularly likely to be misperceived.

It is precisely because people misperceive the world that their behavior sometimes appears irrational. In fact, they often have erroneous performance outcome beliefs and behave in what they think is a rational manner. Because of this phenomenon, many things that organizations do to motivate and control behavior fail, and indeed often lead to counterproductive behavior.

Individuals Have Affective Reactions

People are rarely neutral about things they perceive or experience. Instead, they tend to evaluate most things by whether they like or dislike them. Moreover, this evaluative response is one of the most crucial factors in influencing future behavior because it establishes the importance and attractiveness of actions and outcomes. For instance, Mrs. Johnson's relatively positive experiences at work have led her to stay at the same job for 29 years, while Mrs. Henson's unpleasant experiences appear to be leading to her dismissal. Literally thousands of studies have been done on job satisfaction. Studies have focused on overall job satisfaction as well as on people's satisfaction with such specific aspects of the work environment as pay, promotion opportunities, the task to be performed, fringe benefits, personal relationships, security, and the leadership style of the supervisor.

Part of the reason for the original interest in job satisfaction was the widely held belief that job satisfaction was a major determinant of job performance. Research has not supported the view that job satisfaction causes job performance. Quite the contrary, recent research shows that when a relationship exists between satisfaction and performance, it is usually because performance influences the level of satisfaction. This has by no means signaled an end to interest in studying job satisfaction for two quite different reasons. First, satisfaction has become an important topic of study in its own right because it is an indication of the quality of work life. Secondly, satisfaction has turned out to be a reasonably strong determinant of absenteeism, tardiness, and turnover. The more satisfied an employee, the less likely he or she is to be absent, to be late to work, and to resign from the organization. This seems to come about because satisfaction influences people's expectations about the consequences of coming to work. Satisfied employees see more positive outcomes associated with going to work and, hence, are more likely to show up for work and remain members of their organization (as in the case of Mrs. Johnson).

In general, it appears that satisfaction is determined by the difference between what a person receives and the amount that he or she feels *should* be received. The larger the discrepancy, the greater the dissatisfaction. Moreover, the amount a person feels *should* be received has been found to be strongly influenced by what others are perceived to be receiving. People seem to compare what they are putting into a work situation and what they feel they are getting out of it with what others receive in return for what they put into their work situation. If this comparison reveals that their outcomes are unfair when compared to those of others, dissatisfaction results. As would be expected, since this is an important area, individuals often misperceive the inputs and outcomes of other people as well as those of themselves, and end up being dissatisfied when perhaps they would not be if they perceived the situation accurately. In some instances, however, they misperceive in ways that make them satisfied when, in fact, they might not be if they correctly perceived the situation. Precisely because misperception is so common in important areas, it is difficult for organizations to distribute rewards, such as pay increases and promotion, in a way that satisfies the majority of people.

Behavior and Attitudes Are Caused by Multiple Factors

At the beginning of this note, we pointed out that behavior is a function of both the person and the environment. Now we can elaborate on what characteristics need to be considered in order to understand and manage organizational behavior.

We have identified a number of factors that influence the degree of individual motivation, and we have stressed that the capability to perform is an important influence on performance. Organizations can influence individual behavior by changing one or more of the crucial determinants of individual behavior. None of them is easy to change, but all are open to influence. Needs and certain capabilities are particularly hard to influence because they are often limited by the physiological characteristics of individuals as well as by background and nonwork experiences that are beyond the capability of the organization to influence. Expectancies and certain learned capabilities, on the other hand, are often open to influence, since these emanate from the work environment. In fact, it is through its influence on these factors that the work environment can have a direct impact on individual behavior. Based on expectancy theory, we know that those parts of the environment that involve desirable outcomes are especially important, since they can directly affect motivation. Thus, it seems only logical that every manager should determine what these desirable outcomes are and then develop a plan that relates them to performance.

The environment can also influence behavior by placing constraints on the behavioral options available to an individual. For example, a broken machine could prevent Mrs. Johnson from achieving her production quota no matter how motivated she is. Similarly, walls may prevent employees from talking and forming groups, even though employees might enjoy the social companionship. One implication of this is that organizations need to give considerable attention to the work environment to prevent obstruction of desirable employee behavior.

Because behavior is determined by many factors, it is often difficult for organizations to establish the conditions that lead to effective individual performance. The manager concerned with creating the right conditions for effective performance is in a similar position to the football coach who is designing an offensive play. For the play to work, a great deal has to go right, and some luck is also required. Nevertheless, it is usually best to have a game plan that recognizes the key factors and tries to deal with them. The same can be said for the manager who wants effective performance.

SUMMARY: NATURE OF INDIVIDUALS

In this note, we have presented a view of individual behavior that can be described by the following statements.

1 People have only limited behavior capabilities; individuals differ greatly in their capabilities.

2 Individuals differ in what outcomes are attractive to them; the internal conditions that make outcomes important are called *needs;* it is possible to list them in a two-step hierarchy of higher- and lower-order needs.

3 People make conscious choices of how to behave based on their needs and their perceptions of the environment, particularly their perceptions of what kinds of behavior will lead to what kinds of outcomes. One way of predicting those choices is through the use of models like expectancy theory.

4 Given the perceptual basis of behavior, it is important to note that perceptions are susceptible to distortion by individuals.

5 Once people enact a piece of behavior and experience consequences of behavior, they have affective reactions to the event, the most common being satisfaction/dissatisfaction. These affective reactions have implications for subsequent sequences of behavior, since they affect both perceptions and needs.

6 Capabilities, expectancies, needs, past experience, and environmental constraints are all important influences on behavior.

Exhibit 3 presents a general model of behavior in organizational settings that follows the concepts presented thus far. Working from left to right in the model, motivation can be seen as the force on the individual that encourages performance in a certain manner. Thus, motivation leads to a level of effort by the individual. Effort alone, however, is not enough. Performance results from a combination of the individual's effort, level of capability (skills and training), and constraints in the situation (broken machinery, behavior of others, and so on). As a result of performance, the individual attains certain outcomes that lead to satisfaction. As this process of performance-reward occurs, time after time, the actual events serve to provide information that influence the individual's perceptions and thus influences motivation in the future. This is particularly true in the case of the individual's expectations; these are strongly influenced by the past relationships individuals have encountered between their performance and outcomes (see the dashed line in Exhibit 3).

EXHIBIT 3   The basic motivation-behavior sequence.

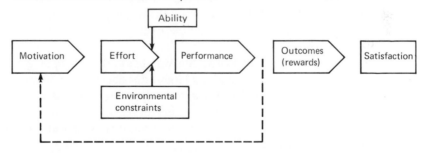

JAMES EDWARDS (A)

John J. Gabarro

James Edwards was 33 years old, black, and a graduate of the Harvard Business School. He had received his MBA with high distinction and was one of the first blacks to be named a Baker scholar in the school's history. After leaving Harvard, Jim returned to his former employer, a large consumer products company that had sent him to Harvard. Jim had joined the company upon graduation from college and had worked his way up to a middle management position before being sent to the business school.

After completing an MBA, Jim was made district manager of the metropolitan Chicago sales district, one of the largest districts in the company (see Exhibit 1.) Jim had held this position for over a year when this case was written, and had begun to experience increasing doubts about his future with the company. He had been particularly disturbed by top management's response to an article he had written for a national business magazine on the difficulties of being a black manager. He had based the article on his own personal experiences as a black man working his way up the management ladder. Jim suspected that the company's management had reacted negatively to the article (which they had seen prior to publication) and had misunderstood and resented what he was trying to say.

Knowing of these concerns, the casewriter asked Jim if he would be willing to discuss them and have his comments taped for possible use as a case. Jim agreed, and the following is a transcript of his remarks.

> What it comes down to is I will soon have to make a decision about which way to go. I've been running the district for well over a year now with no sign from anyone about what the next step is . . . what the future holds. They told me when I came back that it would be a short assignment—a year at the most. That period has come and gone and I've met or exceeded every objective during the past year and I'm beginning to wonder if performance

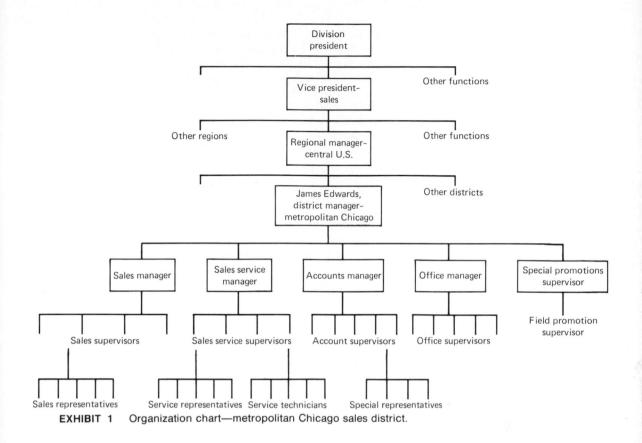

EXHIBIT 1   Organization chart—metropolitan Chicago sales district.

is what counts. That's part of the frustration. The rest of . . . the other part of it is the reaction to the article . . . they didn't understand it. . . . They didn't understand what I was trying to say. I think they took it as a slap in the face. In fact, several people that I confide in have told me it was not a politically wise thing to do, to write that article. And this is what grates at me, because if I cannot speak the truth on something that is basic to me, then maybe I'm in the wrong company. Should I suppress what I have lived through and I know is important? Suppress what I know can help make it less of a hell for other black guys? Not tell what the experience is like, the built-in obstacles a black manager faces? Suppress that? I don't know that it's worth the price.

I guess I'm really wrestling with a more basic question, which is what can I do to make a maximum contribution. I can stay here and show them that I can withstand whatever they give me, and become a proven performer so that there can be no doubt. That's the obvious option. I could go back to school and get a PhD or something that would allow me to focus on the whole problem of black managers and write about it. Or I could switch. I could go to another company, which is not a solution but is at least a change. . . .

Which is why, I guess, I am coming to realize that there are some things that are bigger than me as a person. It's been a trauma for the last 2 months, since I first sent the rough draft of the article around the company. I didn't get any response for weeks—and, when it finally came, it was noncommittal as hell. I guess I am learning that with some things you can't go right through the middle. I am having to develop the graciousness to accept that Jim Edwards cannot necessarily go out and change the world. I have to suppress the temptation to stand up and scream, "Can't you see what you're doing?" and "Don't you understand?" I'm fighting to get myself geared up after this vacation—to reinstill my pride that says, damn it, if there's an objective, I'll meet or exceed it. I won't fall prey to disappointment or disillusionment.

But I have had great disappointment in terms of my ideals as a black thinking of all blacks. There's also disappointment as a person thinking of his own career. On the other hand, I'm caught with the fact that if I can't do it here, then, God damn it, I look behind me and I don't see anyone else who I judge is able to really do it. And there's a danger in thinking of yourself as omnipotent—which I'm not . . . which I damn well . . . I found that out these last few months when I found that I couldn't sleep at night. But, I think I came damn close to the breaking point. In fact, one of my sales service supervisors told me yesterday, "You seem much more relaxed now. Some of us were starting to notice that you were getting tense beyond compare." And they were recognizing it, and that's one of the things that started me to fight it because one thing I am not willing to sacrifice is my personal effectiveness.

I've been feeling so tense these last couple of months, it's unreal, and that's due to the article basically, and the inability of some people to look upon the article in terms of its purpose and message as opposed to Jim Edwards, the guy who wrote the article. I think that I will have to accept a slightly longer horizon about influencing the company. I have other options. I could go out and get another job, and probably make more money if I wanted to sell my blackness. But the fact of the matter is that I don't want to sell my blackness for more money to get in a showcase position where I'm as useless as a tit on a bull. In which I have no authority, no responsibility, no decision-making power, and where I cannot influence the direction of an organization. As a person, it grates against me because I would not be a performer—if I am not a performer and I don't—I want the chance to prove myself.

 The last 2 months I have been trying to decide my course of action because I find it very difficult to be a passive entity in life—to just sit here and wait. And I've considered all the options. I could leave the company, and find some way of devoting full time to raising people's awareness of the problems facing black managers and what companies can do to give them a fair chance. I could go back to school and do that, get a PhD and make that my research specialty. That would be a way which could allow me to do that directly—use leverage on business as a whole. But, the other alternative is to stay here and prove that I can go to the top and become the first black vice president in the company. And this is also direct, but in a different way—by showing it can be done.

And this company matters to me; it's an important part of me. I want to shape my own direction and I guess the part I have been wrestling with is whether to mount an offensive or dig in for a moral issue, on which I know I'm right. I'm very frustrated because I can't get other people to see that it's not Jim Edwards, the person, looking for selfish ambitions—at least not necessarily ambitions by themselves. But what I'm trying to say is something that's far more general and far broader, and I have received some satisfaction from the letters I have gotten from outside the company. But those who know me as an individual in the company refuse to look beyond their nose for what I'm trying to say—and they don't evaluate the statement; they evaluate the person making the statement, and then it comes down to missing the whole point.

They say that I am ungrateful for what the company has done for me. The fact of the matter is, I am doing as well or better than any guy who came into the company when I did.

And that's frustrating, it's frustrating and when I say it's frustrating I mean frustrating to have to back off, to accept the fact that maybe it's not wise to consume one's self in trying to idealistically plow straight through, no matter what the odds are. The reason is, you see, I'm playing in someone else's ballgame and they are allowing me to play, and I'd better damn sure recognize that. It's funny I've become especially aware of that limitation now that I've got a daughter. This has changed perhaps my motivations—which were almost all self-centered to now include someone else.

Having a baby has suddenly made a big difference because, you know, a marriage is a type of thing where, if two people get married in their late thirties or forties, instead of in their twenties, they are looking for different things out of marriage because they have spent a long time alone, they have had a chance to do things. But when people get married in their early twenties, they haven't really fulfilled themselves. And, in that case there's a tendency and a desire, after being together for, let's say, 7, 8, 9 years, as in my case, to say, "Damn it, if I don't achieve self-realization now, I never will," and that sort of makes you a little selfish. There is a tendency to say, "Well, I know what my wife wants, but on the other hand, I want this, and hell, my needs are just as good as her needs. I have as much of a right as she has," so you become a little selfish. But the inclusion of a child where both of your goals and desires and ambitions are totally coincident changes that. So, my daughter's arrival has started to shift my thinking and all of a sudden I have to start to suppress myself in many ways.

So the baby certainly has made me more cautious and, it's funny, because I was talking to a friend of mine no more than 2 weeks ago, and he's followed this whole thing about the article. He's one of the few guys who really appreciates what I am saying. Being a white guy, it's rather difficult for him and he has found that many of his peers have turned him off when he tries to explain that I'm trying to make a general statement about what it's like to be a black manager—not just about me. And in sharing these things, we have become pretty friendly. A couple of weeks ago I made the statement to him that I was quite capable of going after a *pure* victory if that's the only victory I could score, and I'd be damned if I'd admit defeat in making my point because I don't want other black guys to go through the grief I went through. And I want them, the company, to get the message one way or another. And, he said, "Well, Jim, you know, what about your family?" And, I said, "Well, some things are more important than family" and it's funny looking back; I have to smile because a couple of weeks later after the baby was born I can see exactly what he meant. And it's only been 3 weeks since she was born. He's on vacation now, and I've been waiting to see him because I'm dying to tell him that very thing. Because I can really understand what he meant now. Other things are more important to me now than just *my own goals.*

I think that the thing that frustrates me most is my inability to get an acceptance within the company about the article, and I was really trying to say something to the company, not just to business in general. There's no doubt in my mind that it's more important for me to communicate this to the company than to business as a whole. I'm glad that the article got a favorable acceptance, nationally, but, on the other hand, my pride in working for my company and wanting the company to be ahead of the others and for the company to be right in what it does, to be successful, frustrates me in not getting the message across to them or, at least, in their not acknowledging it. And I guess that frustration has increased even more with the receipt of each positive letter from outside companies.

In fact, I received a letter from Honeywell that said Jim Edwards is probably a pen name—he could have been one of *our* black managers and we have noticed the same things he describes. And, General Electric is going to use that article as a training vehicle for increasing the awareness of its white managers. On the other hand, in my company the reaction, from at least one of the people who has been most important to me in my career and whose opinion matters to me, was, "That God damned ingrate." And I put that together by tapping my various, well, my grapevine. The other source of frustration is that I, as a person, as an MBA, and as a business person, I guess I've always met or exceeded all objectives before going to Harvard Business School. I also met or exceeded all objectives while at the Harvard Business School, and I broke everyone's expectations at the B School. I have never acknowledged the fact that certain limitations were on me because I was black. But the fact of the matter also is that at one time I didn't think it would be possible for me to go farther than what my present level is. But, when the company sent me to the B School, that changed. I became totally dedicated to the books and made what some people considered ridiculous sacrifices, and at this point I'm not sure they weren't right. I was determined to be a Baker scholar, and somehow, by God, it came about through determination because—while I think I'm of above average intelligence—I don't think I'm of exceptional intelligence. Most of the guys up there are above average, you know, and I think I'm comparative with them, but certainly not the genius that outshined everyone else. I have to get mine from sweat and determination. But I made it there—in that field of competition—and I was determined to become a Baker scholar and I made it.

But having been there, and then coming back with broader horizons—with raised horizons—I became very frustrated when I got here. It was like, when all of a sudden, say, I'm out there playing basketball and they start playing football, and I'm out dribbling on the court and they've changed the backboard to a goalpost and they didn't tell me the new name of the game. What happened was very similar to Mr. Moynihan's benign neglect. I came back, and I was told by the vice president of sales, "You don't have to do anything, Jim, you've proven how smart you are. All you have to do now is show you can get along with people, and I wouldn't be surprised if in 3 or 4 months. . . ." Well, hell, I heard him, and, of course, this didn't depress my horizons, this confirmed that my evaluation was correct. I had a reputation for being a hard charger before I went to Harvard and for getting results—but not necessarily for being a Mr. Nice Guy. But then my pride said, "I'll be damned. I've never been a cake eater and I don't intend to start now." So, I figure there's got to be a way to prevent blowing this place to hell as far as getting along with people is concerned. On the other hand, I've gotta meet or exceed my objectives, and there's no way that I'm gonna let someone say, if I do get a promotion, that I got it because I was black. So, that old determination went into play again, and after getting back from exams and graduation I shifted into high gear. And, we had an awful lot of problems and a long way to go, and there were questions of sales and service and receivables, and with the economy going bad in the particular area that I'm responsible for, and we geared up—in fact, my boss told me that I could not achieve a top rating at that time.

And it's not because the district was in such bad shape. They don't assign guys that they don't think highly of to a district like Chicago metro. It's probably one of the most difficult in the division or in the whole company for that matter. But my boss didn't think that I could get a top rating for the simple reason that I was relatively new and untried. Well, I pointed out a few other cases where fellows had gotten top ratings who, in effect, had had less field experience than me because I had, in effect, run a district without the title before going to the B School. In fact, before I went to B School, when I was a level lower, I was assigned to a district sales manager south of Chicago, and was told to turn his district around without upsetting the apple cart. Which I did in 5 months. I brought him from number 12 out of 13 in the region to number 2. And, of course, I didn't have the title. And, I did his job. I retrained his entire district. I got things understood and I got them clicking. . . . Well, ah, well, but my current boss didn't think I had the experience, and I gave him a few examples of other guys who didn't have much field experience but whom I guessed were top-rated, and I challenged him to tell me what he wanted and to evaluate me based on performance—not seniority.

So, he came up with objectives—and it wasn't the mutual goal setting that we're taught at the B School. He told me what he wanted, and I said, "Well, gee, that's pretty rough—in this area and that area, etc." And he said, "That's what it's got to be." And, the objectives were set down even though I wasn't able to change his mind in lots of areas. But, when the year was finished, all the objectives had been met or exceeded in every category. And, he had no choice but to give me the rating that I told him I was determined to get.

So, I had come back to the company and after a year the district hadn't blown apart, but that's another frustration in that I don't think the company realizes the internal chaos and additional problems I faced in preventing the district from blowing apart. First of all, I am the only black guy in a field job. There are a couple of guys in public relations and other BS jobs but that isn't the same. I walked into that district, and I anticipated many problems and, unfortunately, my anticipation was correct. When I went into that district, I made myself promise that I was going to act like any other manager who would go into a district. But I had been there all of 3 days before the tension and the tightness that I saw all around me made me back up. And, quite frankly, I saw that I had a problem which, if I didn't deal with, was going to result in an explosion and in failure. And, my honest evaluation was that if there was an explosion for whatever reason—whether I was right or wrong—I would have, in fact, lost the game. So, while I wanted to approach it as any other manager, I had no choice but to deal with what I saw was creating the tension—which, of course, was me and the response that people had to me—because their response would preclude me from being effective. What I felt was tension everywhere—among the nonmanagement employees, among the first-level supervisors, and among my managers—everywhere. And I had four white managers working for me, and all were college graduates. Two of whom had come into the business the same time I did, all of whom had heard that I was coming from the Harvard Business School. And, my grapevine had confirmed that there had been rumors flying all about the place when it was announced that I was being assigned to that district.

The significance of the assignment to that district was evident—it's one of those districts designated as *the* most difficult and as being a stepping stone to a promotion. It's historical that certain assignments such as that one are the steps prior to moving up. When I went in I met everyone, and I smiled and I shook hands and I was polite and courteous. In fact, I tried to observe and keep my mouth shut and just see what was going on. But, after 3 days the tension was . . . and I don't think I'll ever know whether it was something that only I felt or that was really present. But I think that some of the things that I found out since then verify that it was real, and still is, to some degree, present. I felt at that time that all they saw was a black district manager; they never saw Jim Edwards, the man.

And, it's funny. This wasn't a problem of just the whites who worked for me, but it was a universal problem within the district. From both sides, both ends. For example, blacks would say, "Any guy who can get to this level is an Uncle Tom." Or, I remember when I was a kid, you know, you used to get mad at someone, and the worst thing you could say to them was, "You black so-and-so," and then you'd stop and you'd think about that. In effect, you were dealing in self-deprecation just as the white guy who saw you and didn't like you would give a remark such as that and you would make a remark such as that, too, to your own friends, buddies, or sisters when *you* got mad—which says a lot about the psychological damage that's been done to all of our minds, both black and white. The tendency is for whites to think that maybe blacks don't feel that way, but I don't think that's true. Black pride and years and years of processed minds being exposed to newspaper headlines that say, "Black Man Kills So-and-So," "Black Man Rapes Someone," or "Black Man Robs Bank," and everything that a black man did wrong, it was mentioned that it was a *black* man and, on the other hand, when it was a white man it just said "Man." Or the exposure to blacks on TV, which is a recent phenomenon. But, when you saw them in the past they were maids, janitors, Step 'n' Fetchits, or Amos 'n' Andys. Or they lacked an ability to get a job, or were totally associated with everything low, or lower status, or lesser importance. Ah, this has to have an effect on people's minds. Around 1968–1969 black pride got to be fashionable—people began saying black is beautiful. Well, that's really great, but that's just a phrase and blacks and whites don't realize what's been done to their minds in this shaping that's been taking place from birth to the place where they can say black is beautiful. And just saying black is beautiful doesn't erase 10, 15, 20 years of, say, having a processed mind. We develop natural hairdos now because black is beautiful, yet, and still—remember when Sugar Ray Robinson was fighting he used to have a process? He used to go out and get a comb and grease to get his hair to look long and straight. That's called a process and, in effect, black's minds were also being processed when they got their hair straightened. But psychologically, internally, they weren't aware that they had been processed, that they had been programmed by everything they had been exposed to since they were children that black was inferior. Did you ever see the cowboy and Indian shows? You know that if the good guy's on a white horse, the guys on the black horses are bad? It's black and white—very seldom do you see a pinto in those movies. And you think about that, it's frightening. Everything good is white. Everything bad is black—and it has affected people.

And that's why, getting back to the district and what I was saying before, I have thought about these things, and my experience has taught me that blacks were not yet where it was all "Right on, brother" and total pride. They themselves have their prejudices against blacks which, in many cases, is built-in just like white prejudice. For example, I have observed that it is very difficult for one black to be second best to another black. But when blacks are in a competitive situation with whites, it is not as damaging to their ego to come out second. It's almost as if blacks have said to themselves, "O.K., I gotta be second best when it comes to whites, but I'll be damned if I'm not the best when it comes to blacks." And, I've read about some studies that I think verify those observations. Some tests taken at Lincoln University show that blacks, when they are in mixed groups, tend to be nonaggressive, more political, and more tactful; when they're pitted against blacks, they are more competitive. It's as if they have learned to back off, and it's more of a blow to be second best, to another black. It's as if they can no longer rationalize—that they can't do something because of the color of their skin—which is a damaging thing to you as a person—to have to say, "I didn't reach a certain level because I just didn't do it." When, maybe for 30 years, you have said to yourself, "I never got that promotion because they're prejudiced and they don't like blacks." But, if another black gets it, I anticipated some of these reactions.

The blacks were saying, "He's gotta be an Uncle Tom. If he's an Uncle Tom, he's gonna play favorites with them. At least we had a chance with his white predecessor." Well, on the other hand, I saw whites who were uptight and I perceived them to be thinking, "Well, we're gonna swing the other way, now. Black is in charge, black is beautiful, and all of a sudden, you know, we have gotta change our whole stance." It seemed to me necessary to call it for what it was because if I ever started to let subjective factors change my evaluations, then I would become inconsistent. So, I have tried to develop a knack for removing all feelings, all emotions from making decisions, because if ever I veer from the line—if I veer toward the blacks then I have become a militant to my white staff—I'll have part of my force that doesn't want to work with me or cooperate with me. If I veer toward the whites, then I'm an Uncle Tom to the blacks, and that's a cause for double dissension because there are always going to be some whites who are going to side with the blacks simply because they think it's a moral thing to do (laughs). These are some of our liberal friends who feel guilty or something (laughs).

That's the situation I saw. So after—well—it was as if everyone was sitting there like turtles with their heads pulled back in their shells, expecting me to come in like the grim reaper, changing things, doing things different, or, "Oh, my God, what's about to fall on us," like there was a great scythe about to come down and decapitate them, and this tightness was something that I had to deal with one way or another. First of all, I recognized that no matter what I did, it was going to be a losing proposition because someone would be able to find fault with it. What I finally decided was to take a low-key approach, but be very candid about my recognition of the problem. I decided to work through my managers, so after that day I called my managers in. And I told them that if I were in their position and I had heard there was a black district manager who had just left Harvard Business School, I would have some serious problems. These problems would be enhanced in my mind if I had come into the company about the same time as him, because, after all, why does this guy go to Harvard and I not go to Harvard? So, I said, "I want to assure you of several things. Number one, I do not leap tall buildings with a single bound. Number two, I expect from you total honesty, and I expect you to be totally candid." And, I said, "I recognize that some of you don't know me well enough to just take my word and give me that trust." I said, "However, I am going to *demand that trust* until you have reason to tell me to my face that this should not exist. And my reason for saying this is simple—that none of us are going to achieve our objectives unless we understand the extent of the problems."

And I told them that while I knew that I was very strong-minded and opinionated, and had a tendency to be forceful at times, that I did not expect anybody to back off. If they disagreed with me, I expected them to say so because I did not want a yes man. Well, that was the tenet that I approached them on. And, so, what I then did was sit back for 3 months and, thank goodness, things generally went OK. I did not go out and talk to the folks or become buddy-buddy with the supervisors, the sales people, or the office people. I tried to run that operation through the managers and, at the end of about 3 months, I thought I detected some people's heads coming out and saying, "Hey, the sky hasn't fallen down on us. This isn't so different than what it was before." Now doing this was very difficult for me though, from a personal point of view, because my style is basically one of putting my nose in every corner and talking to everyone so that I understand exactly what the problem is.

You see my style is to be with the people—eyeball to eyeball, and in close to the problems. And one of the things I learned about myself during that period was that I don't like being out of the action. But, you see, it was important in those first few months to keep a low profile—to avoid that explosion.

Then the audit came and that's when I found I couldn't hold back any longer. The district was audited by the overall company. Not the division headquarters, but the company headquarters, and there's only one audit in each division a year. There are roughly 50 districts in my division and, unfortunately, mine was the one that was chosen, which, I must admit, I wonder about. Because I thought that was one hell of a chance—a district run by a black man, the only district of 50 to be run by a black man, and it gets audited. But be that neither here nor there, I had only been there about 3½ months. It was early enough so that my predecessor, who had a good reputation, could not totally disclaim any responsibility, and I hoped they couldn't hit me all the way. But what I did after that audit was rather embarrassing in many ways. I reaudited the audit. I took almost a solid month of my personal time out of my nights and weekends and I turned into a doer in addition to an administrator, because I was determined to find out the truth, whether the audit reflected the operations properly. I tore into the audit. I audited every part of it, and I found out where it had been distorted. And, in a 25- or 35-page epistle, which was probably the best written analysis I have ever done, I put egg all over the auditor's face, and dared them to come back and reaudit and disprove my claims and my statements. And we came out smelling like a rose.

And, at this point, my basic nature said this is the time to stop letting the managers run the show totally. My nature, which had been grated by my acting in a way that was basically uncomfortable for me, took over. All of that time being passive—of working through others—where instead of driving the car, I was in the shotgun seat saying, "OK, fellers, . . . now driver, make a right turn here at the corner," or worse yet, "What do you think about making a right turn at the corner?" Ah, that's a little uncomfortable when things get hot and heavy! I don't like to miss objectives, and now I was faced with the need to take charge. There hadn't been the trauma or explosion that I had to avoid earlier and, if I was ever going to take charge, I had to do it then. So, I did. I told the managers that I wanted to talk to all of the supervisors in the district—all 25 supervisory people. I put together a 1-hour course that I gave to all the supervisors. And it was amazing. I had given out copies of the audit and my report to all the management, and they were absolutely befuddled to see that I walked, talked, thought and wrote, and that I was vicious with a pen! And, they grinned from ear to ear and said, "Wow!" And some of them thought the words I used were a little big, but they were impressed (chuckle). So I guess they were pleasantly surprised. So I guessed that now they knew what it was all about to be a District Manager.

All of a sudden, without any trauma, the black district manager had become *the* district manager! And there was no doubt in anyone's mind that I was in charge when I stood in front of the management people and I took on their questions one by one, telling them what direction we were going to take, and why we were gonna go that way, what the alternatives were and the rest of it—all off the cuff. There was no doubt in anyone's mind who was running that district. And I think I was rather proud of myself that there was such a smooth transition from "that black district manager" to seeing Jim Edwards *as* the district manager! No one could say, "He took charge this day," or "He took charge that day." They just didn't know; all of a sudden this thing happened. They looked in the driver's seat, and I was winking in the rear view mirror, saying "leave the driving to me now. Everything's gonna be OK."

So, I began to be on top of things—on all fronts. For instance, several incidents sort of confirm this. We have a black union steward and I started talking to him as a person because I was fighting this Uncle Tom thing, and I wanted somehow to spread the word without my going out and hanging around every black's neck telling him that I wasn't an Uncle Tom. On the other hand, I wasn't going to play favorites either, but I wanted to let them know I was a regular guy, so a couple of little things, like, for example, one night they were having a little going-away party for someone who was leaving the district and people were playing cards in the lounge. Now there's a black game that's called Bid Whist—almost all blacks know how to play Bid Whist. Well, I went by and, you know, I'm a nut about Bid Whist. I happen to think I'm *the* best that ever played Bid Whist, as all blacks do (laugh). It's an ethnic game—it's part of the rap that if you can't play Bid Whist then you just can't make it among the ethnic—you just can't, but you gotta be good at it. So, they were looking for a fourth as I went by, so I said, "I'll play a couple of hands." And I sat down, and sure enough, we played Bid Whist—you have to talk bad and loud and deliver. I played bad and loud and delivered, and got up and left a winner (laughs)! And I think that helped set the stage. And, then I went over to the whites and I talked with them. So, I wasn't just saying, "Brother, right on," and rest of it, but, on the other hand, I wanted them all to see that I was a normal black guy and that I wasn't an Uncle Tom—that I could write, and I could talk, and I could walk, and I could think. And I could play Bid Whist—and damn well, too (laughs).

But then the black guy, the union steward, confirmed that I wasn't being paranoid when I first took over the district. That all kinds of rumors had been going around, that people had heard I was a hard nose or an Uncle Tom. Everyone, both black and white, had diverse opinions about me, but I think the consensus was generally negative. They had me indicted, tried, and judged before I could prove who I was. I had to prove that I wasn't any of those things—that's a form of prejudice, you know, that's what prejudice means, prejudgment.

I guess that it was a very tough period, it's still tough. I'm still in the process of mentally and emotionally trying to adjust to the fact that it's not necessarily pure performance that counts. I guess I can be a well-oiled performance machine, but I now have to recognize realistically that it's not my actual performance that counts so much—that's not really what will move me ahead. And that's disappointing to me at this point because I'd like to think that's what the system is all about—that performance is what counts.

But it seems as if the guys who really get ahead are those who have rabbis. A rabbi is like a patron, a godfather; he looks after you from up higher in the organization. Those guys who have rabbis don't have to have good performance behind them. They seem to move out of tight spots just before they explode, and move into good spots and then leave them before they explode. And, I've seen several guys who are top-rated but have never met an objective, and they are still top-rated and they keep on moving. It's as if someone up above has deemed that they had the ability from the day they came into the company, and they are going to make it. So they've been moving them along. On the other hand, it's sort of OK to say that if a man proves himself, then he can determine his own destiny. When that's the case it's entirely up to you, but it may be a real fact of life that it may not be what you do but who you know that's important. And I'm caught between these two things because my personal pride says that I *should* perform, *be number one*, no matter how difficult it is. And, I've got to achieve no matter how difficult because that gives me the feedback that says, *you are able, you are capable, you can do it.* If I ever fail to get that type of feedback from my own performance, then I'm in trouble. I need to be in a situation where I can prove myself, because if I'm not I would not be a performer—and if I am not a performer and I don't perform—there's nothing for me to test, then how the hell am I going to have the assurance that I am still capable as a person? Because I have had to accept the reality that I may never be able to rely on accurate feedback from my boss or my peers because of their own prejudices. So if I lose my ability to perform, or if I ever fail to meet or exceed my objectives and begin to have self-doubts, or am in an environment in which I cannot totally trust the quality of the feedback, then I've got problems. I've got serious problems.

Serious problems, and that's part of what bothers me now, because I am starting to realize that—I don't know—accept that I am no more than a pawn on a board, that I am being moved around and my success is being determined by the judgments of others more than my own individual performance. In fact, my boss perhaps accepted that same idea when he said to me when I came in, "You don't have to prove how smart you are. All you have to do is get along with people." That's a hell of a contradiction. Well, he is in effect saying we've got one thing in theory and another thing in actuality. And, I guess it worries me from the point of view that if we are ever going to have real equal opportunity in this country, it's going to have to be based upon performance. And, if we don't now have real equal opportunity among whites based on performance, damned if we haven't got one hell of a problem when we mix blacks in there! And, if you don't have the chance to prove that you can do it before you move ahead, then how the hell do you ever get the reassurance that you can do it? Now, I know that's not true in 100 percent of the cases, but it's true in far too many cases, more than I'd like to accept.

And this bothers me; it worries me at times. I feel that if there are blacks who are going to do well in my company, and on a larger scale in the system in this country, then they have be guys who *can* perform, and these guys have got to take the additional burden of the crap that comes along because they're black and be able to handle that *as well as* be a performer. And, if necessary then, they have got to be . . . they've got to be the meanest son-of-a-bitch in the valley. And, I—maybe—I don't know whether I ever told you my motto. I have to admit that I have to smile when I say my motto is that "Ye, though I walk through the valley of the shadow of death I will fear no evil for I shall be the meanest son-of-a-bitch in the valley." I have to smile for the simple reason that this motto is an admission that I have survived when there was little possibility of survival. The cards were not stacked for my survival. There was certainly no one planning for my survival. And I don't want it to sound as if I had a plan for survival because there wasn't any. There was more or less benign neglect and there were no steps taken to ensure my survival; therefore, I was subjected to everyone's prejudices—which they weren't even aware of, but which I had to deal with. Like my going into that office, that district. I'll be willing to bet you that nobody above my level, none of my supervisors other than my boss Frank recognizes what I went through. (Pause.) The crossroads I'm at now, I'm fighting to get myself geared up after this vacation to reinstill that pride that says, damn it, if there is an objective I'll meet it or exceed it. (Long pause.)

It's important to me to prove myself as a performer. . . . I guess part of it has to do with the way I grew up, because I moved so many times, and you know you have to reestablish yourself every time you move. Kids being kids, they always want to try the new guy, and if you couldn't fight—man, I got sucker-punched so many times, it was unreal. And so I had to learn how to fight. I had to prove myself everytime we moved.

I think also that a lot of it probably comes from my old man. My father comes from a large family in the South. He was the oldest boy, and after his real father died, he was about 12, well I guess his stepfather kicked him out because he wouldn't work in the cotton fields to help support the family. Dad wanted to stay in school and become a pullman porter. That was hot stuff for a black guy in those days. And, two old maids who were school teachers in North Carolina had seen how bright dad was and they took him in, and they said, "No, son, you deserve to be more than a pullman car porter." Well, they gave him a place to live and guidance, and he shined shoes, and he told me how he ate peanut butter sandwiches to save money, but somehow he got to school. He got a scholarship, and he also worked as a waiter, and he boxed, and he did just about everything under the sun to get through. He came out salutatorian or valedictorian—I forget which—in his class. He then went on to a theological seminary and got to be an ordained Presbyterian minister, and I think that's one of the things that carried him through. He has a very deep faith and a religious outlook on life. But he was still not satisfied. He wanted to achieve more and he went on to the University of Pittsburgh, and worked on his PhD in physics, which was his undergraduate major. And he completed everything except he was failed on his orals. The reason for this was that he had made it known that he wanted to go into business rather than teach in some black school when he finished his PhD and that was against their values. So, he had his master's and he'd completed his requirements for the PhD, with an A average in classwork, but I remember that even with all that, my dad still had to work as a dishwasher to keep his family fed and sheltered. Even with his master's in physics, and that was about 1947.

But we moved some 20 times. He was determined, however, that we would make it, and that he would make it for us, and boy, some of the things he's done. I would never have had the guts. He moved from company to company, which was par in the defense industry, 20 some times before I got out of high school, back and forth. His calling was to the ministry, but his obligation was to succeed, and his calling was torn, really. He had a personal inquisitiveness that could not be satiated but combined with a very strong idealism. He is very intelligent. He'll whip a word on me today and I'll have to go look it up. Although I'll never admit it to his face now, he'll use a term I've never heard of before, and I'll have to look it up (laughs). He's very articulate. And he's got to be *the* most forceful person I've ever met, although I gotta say that he has been too forceful at times.

That's also a trait of mine, which I am sure I take after him—that forcefulness. I also look at his other weakness, which is political naivete. And, I try not to make the same mistake. Dad went on and worked in engineering and physics. He helped design guidance systems for missiles, and has written a lot of articles on guidance and space. But my father could never really get into the big stuff. As bright as he was, he never made it big, he never played the game quite right. He finally got hung up from his own doing. There were little shenanigans going on in his company—missiles were blowing up after lunch and the company knew they had a mistake but wouldn't correct it, and millions of tax dollars were going down the drain. They asked him to analyze the problem and he said, "OK, here's your problem—nose cone stress. You underdeveloped your nose cone." And, then he was told, "OK, thanks a lot but we're going to shoot off the rest of them anyway." And he said, "But that's dishonest." And he threatened to write the President. And, of course, that was not too smart a thing to say, because that meant he was being disloyal to the company. At any rate, he wound up in a jam. He was also getting older, so he went over to the government civil service to work, and then was let go when Nixon had his big layoff. Dad is really giving himself away in the sense that he's got a hell of a lot more ability, potential, and capability. He has been forced to teach high school to make it these days. And that's a long drop for a guy who was once an assistant dean and head of a physics department and who helped design guidance for missiles.

But even to this day, I see my old man sit there and dig into his books, and he's determined. He never, never, never says die, and I have to admire that in him. I guess I get that from Dad that I'll never say die—I don't want to back off, just like Dad does. But I want to use more prudence and judgment than he did; I don't want to make the same mistakes Dad made.

You know, we were very, very close and he is such a dominant guy that there has to be a certain, well, if you're going to grow up, you run into conflict. When I look back and analyze it, that's exactly what happened. We got into a physical conflict that was unreal. I got my head banged a few times, and I always had the utmost respect. I said my Dad boxed in college, and I had always respected my Dad because I've seen him lift a block of an engine out of a car—a sight that was overwhelming to me. Well, I'll never forget when I was 16, I was sassing Mom about something—kid stuff. I didn't want to wash the floor. It was my sister's turn to wash the floor, and Dad got mad, and he ran into the living room and backed me into the corner. And, all of a sudden he did something he'd never done before—

he always hit me with a belt. All of a sudden Dad swung and when Dad swung on me—as I said you learn the hard way, when you get sucker-punched—my reflexes took over and I knocked him across the chair. Well, that was the beginning of 3 or 4 years of knockdown, drag out fights. He was kicking me in and out of the house all the time. Of course, at that time I was determined that I was going to be my own man and it was about the time I went to college. Looking back on it, it's so funny. It teaches me certain things that I don't want to repeat as far as my own kids go. But I've always respected him.

And a lot of my competitiveness also comes from him. In fact, all of us—my sister and my younger brother—are very competitive. My older sister is one of the most determined women you ever want to meet. She won't back off for anybody. She is a competitor all the way. I'm a competitor, and my youngest brother is a competitor. It's funny. My middle brother was always the baby. Dad always thought he was small and puny. So, he always sort of sheltered the middle one, and he never developed the aggressiveness that the rest of us did. But my sister, I look at her, and she has three kids and went back to get a master's degree after her second. She won't be counted out. And my brother was a leader in the demonstrations at Cornell—when the takeover occurred. There were certain things he would not accept. He doesn't know how to back off either. He and I are the closest, even though we've taken very different paths. His has been confrontation while mine has been working through the system. But we can talk to each other about anything. There isn't anything we can't say to each other. It's funny, I could respect what he was doing and the reasons he was doing it, and he could respect what I was doing and the reasons I was doing it. And one thing that we both respect about each other is we are damned good at what we do. For example, he was called on to testify before Senator Kennedy's committee on health care while he was teaching at Cornell.

It's interesting what I used to talk to my brother about—about the system. About how you develop power and get into a position to change the system. He has accepted it, and he's playing the game beautifully. He has come 180 degrees, and he's basically going in the same field, the consulting field, as I am. He's just changed jobs and the president of his company didn't want him to leave and promised him a vice president's job to stay. My brother, at the age of 23, was making $24,000 as a consultant—and he had already taught at Cornell.

And here again, it's that thing about being competitive. Because he and I *are* competitive. I root for him all the way, but I want him to be just a half step behind me. It's more a matter of family pride, you know. Just for that. Neither one of us knows which one is really the best. I think I am and he thinks he is. As far as my other brother, my Dad still worries about him, and I tell him, "You've got to let him stand up and be his own man—that's the only way, or he'll never develop responsibility." That's a rough spot for him, being the middle guy of three knockdown competitors, the only one without a college degree. In fact, the only one without at least a master's. And, it's a rough situation, one in which I happen to be sensitive, at least as far as his feelings are concerned. So, that's basically my family except for my mother. Mom was dominated by Dad, although I'm very fortunate in having a very good mother. A very good homemaker, a very good mother, very dedicated and very loyal. Mom used to teach school and, after we grew older, she went back. She just stopped teaching school about 2 years ago.

We lived in so many places that the family was very important because it was constant. We lived all over, lived in so many places. If I had to select two cities where we spent the most time, they were Philadelphia and Pittsburgh. But we have lived in Minneapolis, North Carolina, upstate New York, New Jersey, Queens—hardly anywhere over a year. So, it's a situation that, I guess, helps explain why in some ways I might appear to be cold to some people, because I think it is difficult for me to develop close relationships. I can think back about certain relationships that I have developed, but as you get older it's more and more difficult. Then, you put your nose to the grindstone and you don't worry about that any more. And, as I say, there's no in between with me. So, if something worries me, I give my energies to it, and it's full speed ahead, come hell or high water. In fact, have I ever told you what Frank told one of the vice presidents who visited me while I was at Harvard? You know who Frank is, don't you? He is the one I refer to in the article who really squared with me—the one who helped me get moving. Well, he's a good friend of one of our vice presidents, who came to visit me in Boston to see the Harvard-Yale game. This vice president was asking me how it was going, and I explained how it was rather difficult, and that it was one of the most difficult things I had ever done. And he went back after his visit, and he told this to Frank, my old boss, and Frank's remark was, "Well, if it can be done, he'll do it. In fact, if they make it too rough, that bastard will find a way to steal their exams if he has to, but he'll get it." (Laughs.) So, there was no doubt—he said that facetiously—in his mind that one way or another I would find a way to prevail. Frank's an excellent manager who did a lot for my development. He really helped me come into my own. His is one of the relationships that I really value in the company and, as you can imagine, leaving the company would not be an easy choice.

JAMES EDWARDS (B)

John J. Gabarro

Several weeks after his conversation with the casewriter, Jim Edwards was surprised to receive a telephone call from Robert McIntosh, one of the company's three executive vice presidents.[1] McIntosh began the conversation by saying that he had read Jim's article and thought it was very interesting, but that it left him with several questions that he wanted to discuss personally. McIntosh continued to say that he would be in Chicago the following week and wondered whether Jim could meet him for lunch. Jim immediately agreed, and a date was set for the following Wednesday.

Jim's grapevine had told him that several of the company's top management had been "put off" by his article, and he wondered if this was why McIntosh wanted to talk with him. McIntosh was widely respected within the company and, from what Jim knew of the man, he found it hard to imagine that McIntosh would have reacted negatively. On the other hand, Jim really could not be sure. The only area that Jim felt certain about was his district's performance: he had met or exceeded every sales, service, and collection objective and the record stood for itself. Nonetheless, Jim's curiosity began to grow. In many ways, the lunch meeting would provide an ideal opportunity to explain to a key member of top management what he was trying to say in the article.

Jim arrived for the appointment several minutes early and was surprised to see McIntosh enter with Wayne DeVoto, another executive vice president of the com-

---

[1] The company Edwards worked for had sales of about $2.5 billion and employed nearly 80,000 people. The company's corporate offices were located in Los Angeles, while its divisional headquarters were scattered throughout the country. Edwards reported to a regional sales manager who, in turn, reported to the sales vice president of one of the company's several consumer product divisions. The division's president reported to a group vice president who, in turn, reported to McIntosh. See Exhibit 1 for a simplified organization chart of the company.

EXHIBIT 1   Company organization (simplified)

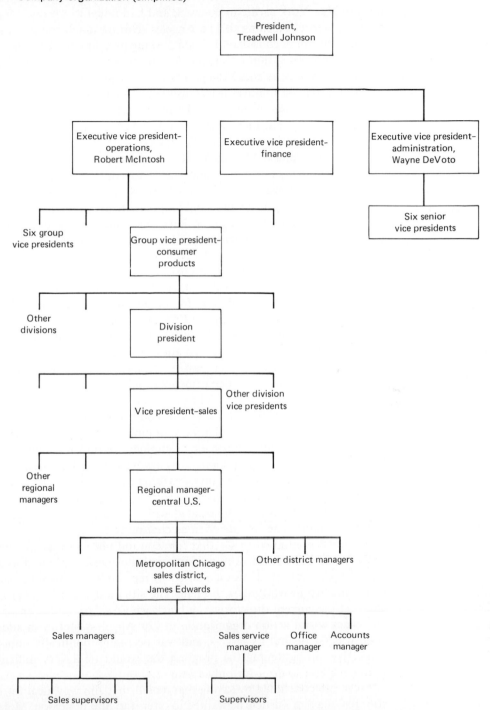

pany. After the preliminary introductions were made, DeVoto explained that he had been in New York earlier in the week and had flown to Chicago to join them for the meeting before returning to Los Angeles. During lunch the two men discussed the article with Jim in considerable detail, asking him why he felt as he did about certain issues and probing him on others. Jim attempted to answer their questions and to explain as well as he could the points he had tried to make.

After about 45 minutes, McIntosh concluded the discussion by saying that the points that Jim was trying to make in the article were valid and made sense. He added, however, that there were several officers of the company who did not agree with Jim's perceptions, but that did not necessarily mean they were right.

After a brief pause, McIntosh told Jim that there was a second reason why the two men had come to talk with him. They had come to offer him the job of special assistant to the president of the company. If Jim accepted the job, he would be in charge of a special project and would report directly to the president. The assignment would require that he move to the corporate headquarters in Los Angeles. McIntosh explained that the assignment would be to serve as director of the Job Action Coalition of Los Angeles (JACLA), of which the company's president, Treadwell Johnson, was chairperson. JACLA was a coalition of business organizations, social action groups, labor unions and local, state, and federal agencies. The organization had as its purpose the creation of jobs for members of disadvantaged groups, Vietnam veterans, ex-convicts, and youth. If Edwards accepted the job, he would have to work directly with many different organizations, and especially with representatives of local black and Chicano groups. In addition, he would have to work with Southern California businesspeople, the mayors of major cities in the area, boards of education, and state and federal departments of labor.

McIntosh pointed out that Johnson, the company's president, had been chairperson of the coalition for over a year and had become very dissatisfied with its lack of progress. Johnson was particularly disappointed with JACLA's unsuccessful attempt to create jobs for youth the preceding summer. McIntosh added that JACLA's initial lack of success had been a source of growing personal embarrassment to Johnson, and that Johnson intended to do everything he possibly could to make the program work. Johnson had made a special trip to Washington to tell the secretary of labor that he did not wish to be associated with a failure and, unless he could "turn the program around," he would resign as chairperson.

McIntosh continued to say that Johnson did not feel that the present director of JACLA had been effective in working with businesspeople and as a result had not gained their support. Johnson wanted to replace him with someone who would be more effective in working with them. The situation was further complicated by the fact that the current director was a black whose salary had been paid by an important black social action organization in Los Angeles. McIntosh added that the program was far behind its targets, and was becoming politically unpopular as well as ineffective. Straightening the program out would be a very difficult job, but they would ask him to do it for only a year.

McIntosh concluded by saying that he felt that Jim was ideal for the job, but that after reading Jim's article he wanted to offer it to him in person. McIntosh was afraid that Jim might think it was a "show-case" job, and for that reason he wanted to explain the context of the offer. McIntosh finished by saying that he hoped that Jim would accept the job, but that it definitely would not be held against him if he chose not to take it. At this point, Jim asked McIntosh if he thought the position really had the potential for effecting change, to which McIntosh replied that he thought it did but that it would be "damn tough," and that was the reason they were asking Jim to do it. DeVoto added that unless JACLA began to deliver on some of its promises, both Johnson and the company would be publicly embarrassed. McIntosh concurred with DeVoto's observation and then asked Jim if he would accept the offer.

ELIZABETH BEST (A)

Ardis Burst
C. Wickham Skinner

On July 1, 1969, Elizabeth Best assumed the position of undersecretary of the Department of Environmental Affairs, Water Division, for the state of Delaware. The water division was responsible for the engineering and construction of dams, the pipeline transportation of fresh water, and the collection of all water revenues from the various cities and towns throughout the state. In addition to these responsibilities, the Water Division was charged with overseeing sewerage disposal and marine transportation.

Elizabeth Best had received notification of her appointment from the governor's office only 2 weeks earlier. The position involved jurisdiction over the directors of the five sections of the Water Division and the 330 employees of the Water Division. (See Exhibit 1.) Although she did not know exactly what working for the state government would be like, she felt that she was entering territory both familiar, because of her extensive volunteer experience in the area of environmental affairs, and presumably friendly, because of her previous professional association with the secretary of environmental affairs and one of the deputy secretaries.

She arrived at the state office building at 9 a.m. and went to the Water Division on the tenth floor. There she introduced herself to the receptionist, was shown to her large but spartanly furnished office and met the department secretary, who told her that the secretary of environmental affairs had arranged for her to meet the other undersecretary (in charge of the environmental standards division) and the directors of the various environmental agencies at 9:15 a.m.

At 9:15 a.m., Best went to conference room A, where 22 men were assembled around a huge table They all stood up when she entered, and the secretary introduced her. Everyone sat down and one by one the agency directors introduced themselves to her and told her what agency they headed. Elizabeth then said a few words

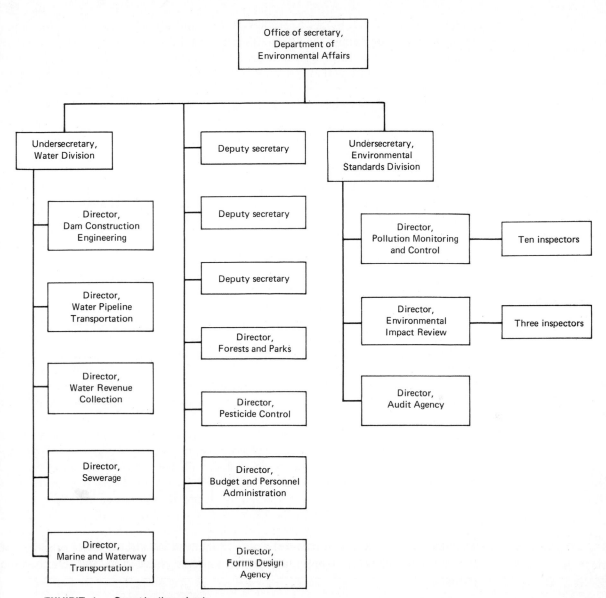

EXHIBIT 1   Organization chart.

about her expectations for felicitous working relationships. At 9:30 a.m., the secretary adjourned the meeting, nodding politely and agreeably to Best as he left the conference room.

Elizabeth returned to her office. She began to look for the files of her predecessor. There were none. This surprised her for she knew that the Water Division collected millions of dollars annually in water revenues and reviewed engineering specifications for pipeline construction and sewerage treatment. She noticed the other undersecretary as he walked by her open door, but he did not speak to her or show any recognition. At lunchtime, she went out alone and did some errands. Afterward she returned to her office and began to order and organize supplies. The afternoon mail arrived but there was nothing of apparent significance nor were there items that required action. She then asked her five directors to come in, one by one, and each uniformly and respectfully reported that everything was fine and politely excused themselves.

At 3:30 p.m., the undersecretary walked by her office again. When she heard his footsteps as he returned down the hall, she went to the door of her office. "Hello, George," she said. "Won't you come in and talk?"

George stepped into her office and welcomed her to the division, but then he excused himself almost immediately to return to a meeting. Elizabeth returned to her desk. She decided she needed to plan a strategy to become a working member of the Water Division.

BEST'S BACKGROUND

Elizabeth Best was born in Indianapolis, Indiana, in 1927. The only child of middle-class parents, she always assumed she would go to college and pursue a career. After graduating from Radcliffe, she worked in New York for *Newsweek* as a researcher, a job that was considered highly desirable by her and her classmates. After a year with *Newsweek,* she resigned and married J. B. Best, whom she had met while in college. The Bests traveled for a year, first in Europe on an extended honeymoon, then around the United States, assessing possible places to live. They finally settled in Seattle, Washington, in 1950.

There Elizabeth worked for a large corporation on a market research study of the effect of TV advertising on consumer behavior. As an economics major in college, she had anticipated a career in market research and while her job was interesting because television was a new field at the time, she became disenchanted with market research and lost confidence in the techniques used in the project. While she held this job, she also began volunteer work with the League of Women Voters. After 18 months at this paid job, she had her first child and left the position. She continued to do volunteer work, however, and over the next 18 months was elected a vice president of the Seattle league and a representative to the national convention. She described the period:

> I found the league extremely rewarding. Within the first year there, I worked on TV programs on league subjects. As was the case in my market research job, TV was so new that anybody knew as much as the next person and they needed someone in that field.
>
> This work was important not because I ever went into TV or market research, but because it gave me quick feedback on the fact that I could do something, I could achieve. It was a reinforcement of identity so I didn't have to feel a sense of helplessness about my environment or my situation as a woman. My success was a combination of being assertive and awfully lucky.

In 1953 the Bests returned to the East Coast so that J. B. could attend the Wharton School. For the next 2 years, Elizabeth spent most of her time caring for her daughter and her son, who was born in December 1953. After J. B.'s graduation, the Bests moved to a suburb of Wilmington, Delaware. The 2 years at Wharton and the first year in Delaware were difficult for Elizabeth; first she felt overwhelmed by the two children. Then J. B. could not decide what job to take after he finished school. The Best family's financial situation during the year after J. B.'s graduation was less than ideal. Finally, J. B. bought a small manufacturing company with a classmate and began working. Elizabeth again found time to become active in the league.

> The first year I went back to being active in the league I was asked by the state board to act as program chairperson for the school of foreign affairs. The woman who had chaired the school the year before knew me and my experience in Seattle and recommended me to the board. We had a budget that seemed enormous to me then—$3000 or $4000—to be used in obtaining any speakers we wanted on any foreign affairs topic.
>
> The board wanted the program to focus on Latin America but this was during the peak of interest in China's 5-year plans and I wanted to do China. I was in awe of the board, but something inside me said, "China." I don't know how I managed to get away from home but somehow I got sitters and spent days in the library, researching both topics: who the speakers would be, what the specific topics would be.
>
> This was in 1957, when there was a lot of concern about the whole communism question. So I went to the board with my proposal. The president said we would do China if I could get the most secure, respectable person around to speak—John Foster Dulles. I spent 3 months that summer calling the state department. We didn't get Dulles but we did have the program on China. Every seat was sold out; the auditorium was overflowing. It was the most enormously successful program they had ever had.

Shortly after the foreign affairs school ended, elections for Elizabeth's local league chapter were held.

> The local league didn't have anyone to be president. They asked me and I think I surprised them by accepting. Both the presidency and the chairperson's position, I feel, were the result of having good luck plus a willingness to move forward, leap in when the opening arrived, and not hold back. There I was with two small children, a husband barely on his feet. . . .
>
> A few feathers were ruffled when I became president. Some of the oldtimers were horrified at the idea of a young new person whom they didn't know, and whom they suspected of having radical ideas, because of the China program. Although I wasn't a radical, I made it very clear that I was open to change and open to reevaluating every single thing the league did. There was a real problem there at first, which was very threatening to me at the time, because I was afraid I'd end up as a social outcast in town and the league.

Around the time she became president of the local chapter, Best also realized that there were no women involved in the government of the suburban town in which the Bests lived. Furthermore, the women in the league were reluctant to monitor and evaluate the work of the men in town government. As league president, Best set up observer squads to oversee key boards (such as finance) in the town. Meanwhile, she set her sights on being appointed to one of the boards herself.

> One day the town moderator, who had the power to make board appointments, called me. I remember the conversation very well. He started with a lot of flattering remarks and then he asked me if I would serve on the Fourth of July committee. I said no very definitely. You

have to be willing to have a view of where you're going, hold to that view, and not take the first thing that comes along. I wanted to be on a planning board and I was willing to wait.

Now, I coud have run for office. Let's face it: I could have run and not sat around and waited to be appointed. But I don't recall that it ever occurred to me to run for office. I take that as a reflection against me as much as against the times. Finally, I was appointed to the conservation board, in which I was keenly interested, and also to the finance committee, one of the most important positions in town.

During this period (1958–1963) of league presidency and town government activity, Best began and completed a master's program in philosophy and had a third child. By the time she was asked by the town "fathers" to run as a selectperson, she had decided that she was more interested in state politics than in town politics. She declined to run and instead became more involved in the league at the state level.

ENVIRONMENTAL STUDY AND ENVIRONMENTAL PLANNING COMMISSION

In 1964 Best was asked to become chairperson of the state league's Environmental Policy Committee and a member of the Delaware Planning Commission. These two jobs meshed very well, and consumed as many hours as a full-time job for the next 4 years.

The Environmental Planning Commission had been established by the state legislature to work with the Delaware business community and various citizen groups in planning for the state's industrial expansion in an environmentally sound way. Best asked the league to recommend her appointment to the commission to the governor. The league did so and she was appointed.

> This turned out to be really a stellar committee because it had some of the outstanding members of the senate, legislature, and business communities. This, of course, was back in the days before federal legislation established the Environmental Protection Agency, and environmental standards. We were really concerned with balancing economic and environmental needs in a program of sensible growth and expansion. I asked to be assigned to a subcommittee chaired by a former environmental affairs secretary, a person who took the whole thing very seriously. It was like having a superior tutor.
>
> One of the major assets for me was that it was a real entrance into the legislative and business communities. I didn't appreciate at the time how great it was, but later I got some perspective on what a break it was.

The Environmental Planning Commission's project centered on policy recommendations for the future. According to Best:

> The basis of the League of Women Voters is study, consensus on a program of action, and then action. We studied the entire environmental policy issue, including budgetary procedures, and methods as well as environmental planning at both the local and state levels, a tremendous undertaking for a volunteer group. We set up discussion groups, briefed discussion leaders, prepared all our own materials, and organized panels and programs throughout the state.
>
> In spring 1968, after the study period, we were waiting for local league recommendations to come in. We were basically looking for a model that we could use in pinpointing the economic tradeoff of various environmental controls. One of the other women on the commission came up with the model. We thought it was good but we didn't want to do

anything until we had a chance to test it on the computer, its impact on individual cities and businesses. We'd seen too many models adopted that turned out to be awful.

The husband of a committee member ran the local university computer center. He volunteered to help and provided computer time and a student who wrote the program. League volunteers keypunched the data from local league study groups, and a rather complete profile was developed for each city and manufacturing firm in the state.

Using all this we tried our model. It worked. It was a beautiful model. It highlighted the cost of various pollution control devices and equalized the cost impact so that small businesses did not bear an inordinately high percentage of the total cost. At the same time, we found that the governor's initial environmental proposals had been voted down by the legislature. We said "Ha, let's use our model to evaluate the governor's new legislative proposals."

Now, the league is nonpartisan. We knew what we had was a great gift. We didn't want to give it to the Republicans and not to the Democrats or to the executive branch and not to the legislature. So we drew up a plan to introduce the proposal. We'd had some lobbying experience and because of the committee I knew who the inside people were, the people to whom we should leak it before we gave it to the leadership.

So we timed it very closely, first distributing it to a few key people. Then we stood in the middle of the state house and distributed it simultaneously to the leadership, and the executive offices. Next we asked for, and received, interviews to explain it.

The model gained the total support of the speaker of the house and some support from the secretary of internal affairs, who met with us but who "couldn't quite take the fact that the women would come up with the model." A few weeks went by before the governor's amended proposals were distributed.

We rushed for a copy, read it, and our hearts fell. The model they used wasn't ours. But, in fact, the proposals looked good. If they were good, we'd have to submerge our own interests in true League of Women Voters fashion. But we rushed to the library and we had enough data on our printouts to do a quick extrapolation to see what the impact would be on communities and business we had identified as bellwethers. And the governor's model didn't work. In fact, it was a terrible model. It did all the wrong things, such as pushing some smaller companies into bankruptcy with the cost of new pollution-control devices, and imposing no costs on other companies. It was marvelously awful.

So we handwrote some of the odd outcomes, pairing some small companies with larger ones for maximum effect, and took it to the internal affairs offices and said, "Look, ha, ha, at what you've just proposed." Of course, they'd never analyzed it that way. We really shamed them.

By the time the next hearings came up, we had lobbied heavily with other organizations and businesses and had lined up support. It may sound odd but at that time computers were still not used much in this kind of research. And women lugging around printouts of economic tradeoffs made people sit up a bit. First, we were the only ones doing it. Secondly, we were women. And lastly, we were volunteers.

At the public hearing, we packed the auditorium and it was a triumph when the mayor of Wilmington stood up and endorsed the result of our model. The governor's budget was then amended to include it. The amazing thing was that all this took place within 2 months of the end of the league study.

The original environmental proposal was adopted by the house, but lost in the senate by two votes. However, the results of the model were adopted for use by cities and towns for local environmental planning, so it was on the books. Best felt that the campaign had been a real educational experience about action in the state house and what was involved in changing state law.

BECOMING UNDERSECRETARY

"In February 1969, I saw in the paper that the job of undersecretary of the Water Division in the Department of Environmental Affairs had been vacant for 18 months, and I remember at breakfast saying to J. B., 'Well, you know, I think I'll apply for that' and he said, 'Why not. You're working hard enough as a volunteer and you might as well get paid for it'."

She talked to a friend who was a member of the Delaware congress. The friend checked around and found that the job was still open. The friend then recommended that she run her job application like a campaign and develop a strategy that involved touching base with people from a number of different communities within the state— business, academic, and political. Best began to do so.

> I guess it doesn't sound unusual to someone else, but to me, at the time and even in retrospect, it seemed like an extraordinary amount of *chutzpah* for me to have gone forward that aggressively. I called business people, very prominent people, made appointments and went to see them. I would talk with them for half an hour about why I wanted the job and why I wanted them to write a letter on my behalf. I was really surprised myself that I did it.

After 4 months of gathering support, Best was appointed undersecretary in June 1969. She felt that she got the job because of three factors: (1) she was a woman; (2) she had the league, nonpartisan, good government image; and (3) no one in the department wanted the job. The position was nontenured, non–Civil Service, and paid a lower salary than that of the directors.

Best was interested in understanding how the government administered a large statewide service such as water. She was also concerned with how local communities and interest groups participated in decisions, such as dam construction or rate setting. She also hoped that, eventually, as a participant in state government, she would have some influence in seeing the league's environmental proposals adopted on a statewide basis.

After Best was notified of her appointment, she met the secretary of environmental affairs for the first time on a person-to-person basis. He was, it seemed to her, "cool, neutral, and yet perfectly pleasant." She then spent some time trying to make a realistic appraisal of where she was to fit into the division.

All but three of the employees in the entire division were Civil Service appointees with guaranteed jobs. All directors (see Exhibit 1) were over 50 years of age. She also knew that her immediate predecessor had been moved to a much lower position in the division because he had fallen out of favor. This could imply that the secretary hoped to replace him with someone more dynamic, or it could mean that he didn't really want anybody who would create any waves. In this case, her job would consist of doing little. She was, after all, a political appointee, a newcomer to state government. She decided that she would simply have to feel her way and see what the first days brought before making any decisions as to how to approach the situation.

ELIZABETH BEST (B)

Ardis Burst
C. Wickham Skinner

In 1971, 2 years after she first assumed the position of undersecretary of the Water Division for the state of Delaware, Elizabeth Best discussed her strategy for establishing herself in the department with an interviewer.

Elizabeth Best: First, I mapped out a strategy. In fact, I even worked it out in terms of a time sequence—how I was going to go about doing things and what I was going to do in what order.

Interviewer: This was the second day?

Elizabeth Best: Yes, the second day. It had to be because there was nothing to do but sit there in that office. For the first 3 weeks, I would visit each of the agencies and take notes on what I observed in terms of things that I thought ought to be done and things that I thought that I could perhaps make a contribution toward. I stretched this out over the full 3 weeks. It was really sort of fun because it was a little bit like playing Queen Wilhelmina touring the provinces. I was very careful to wear a different dress each day. I would go around and talk with the assistant director and the director, and personally meet all of the clerks and the secretaries and chat about their violets and the pictures on the desks of their children. I then sat down and had a fairly lengthy talk with the director about the agency. Then, after I visited all the agencies, I drew up a list of things I could do.

Never during this time did I see the secretary of environmental affairs. So, toward the end of the 3 weeks, I called and formally made an appointment. My office is just three doors away from his, but I made a formal appointment to talk with him. At that conference, I brought out my list of things that I felt needed to be done and that I could handle. And the last thing on the list was the one that I really wanted to work on and that I really felt was the most important. So I started with the first item, the need for a centralized information service. He said right away, "No, no, no. That wouldn't be appropriate for you to do." Then I suggested that I establish some kind of security system to use throughout the agencies, both to ensure confidentiality of the files and to prevent loss and destruction of papers. I had noticed files lying around that could be stolen or even simply mixed up, causing considerable confusion. He disagreed with that, too. We went right down the list and every one of them he knocked out. Then we came to the last one: the budget. My presentation was essentially that the incredibly limited budget that the department was working on was seriously restricting the activities of all bureaus. Because of the league study on Delaware budget procedures, I knew how the state's budget was prepared and I knew the people in the budget bureau and in internal affairs personally. I wanted an opportunity to really develop the budget needs of the department for the appropriation requests for the following year. The important point was that although the secretary hesitated and I felt he really didn't want me to do it, I said, "I don't want you to strike this down today, because I really feel very strongly about it. And I want you at least to think about it. Let me talk with you tomorrow."

At the time there were three top men in the department: one undersecretary and two deputy secretaries. After leaving the secretary's office, I went to the office of the one who acts as his top advisor, the one with whom he works very closely. I presented the whole thing to him and he snapped it up. Then I went back into my office, and I could see him marching down to see the secretary and sometime later I could see him coming back. The next day I went in and the green light was on.

I think the secretary's initial reluctance to give me the go-ahead came from two things. First, many of the areas I suggested working in were areas for which he had responsibility. He wasn't eager to give up those areas and the power and control that goes with them. Second, he is by nature a very cautious individual who takes his work very seriously. He didn't know what my capabilities were or what I should be entrusted with. He reasonably likes to have the final say about things, and I've found he can almost always make a positive contribution when I take something to him.

But although he was reluctant to say "yes," he couldn't just tell me to go back to my office. He knew I had to have some role in the division. Before I even started my job, but after my appointment, I had been contacted by some of his political enemies who invited me to have lunch with them and talk about the division. I had put them off—told them I didn't want to talk about the job until I started it. But I had also called the secretary at home to tell him what had happened. He had been pleased by that. I also think he felt there wasn't much to lose since the budget problems were so severe, so I think that's why he told me to go ahead.

With regards to water revenue, there were two major problems facing the agency at the time. The first involved the collection of revenues from the various cities and towns. Although our meters kept accurate track of the volume of water being piped to each municipality, we were very slow in collecting fees. At $248 per million gallons, we were, in effect, a short-term source of funds for most cities and a longer-term source for some. Because the water revenue collection unit was so understaffed, there was little pressure on the cities and towns to reduce the float, which amounted to as much as 18 months.

The second problem involved the pipeline transportation of fresh water. Although Delaware had adequate reservoirs to serve the needs of the entire state, the lack of adequate pipeline facilities meant that many cities and towns in northern Delaware bought water from neighboring Pennsylvania. This area was an untapped source of revenue. Investing in additional pipeline to northern Delaware would substantially increase the state's water revenue.

I drafted two memos to be sent to all the agency directors. One of the memos requested workload data: all the data they had to demonstrate how much and what kind of work had been accomplished by their bureau in the previous year—the number of audits performed, the number of bills processed, the number of pipeline inspections, anything they could put out numerically in terms of workload handled. The second memo was addressed to the budget itself. I essentially reminded them of the needs they had expressed to me in those initial interviews and asked them to come up with requests for implementing a change in their operation that would result in more revenue being raised. It could be a reorganization of their agency, it could be new personnel, it could be new equipment. But I wanted them to present a plan and accompany it with an estimate of the amount of revenue that would be raised as a result of the plan. This idea was met with hesitation by the secretary but finally he approved it and the memos went out.

During the time when I started this project, I was willing to put myself into a staff type of situation. I think that willingness is because I'm a woman. Later I was doing clerical work at times as part of pulling the budget together. I was willing to pitch in and do whatever was needed if the time pressure demanded it. Men, it seems to me, are more likely to feel that their position calls for setting policy only. I think that is really a mistake because a lot of good policy can be generated from actual involvement.

But to return to those early months. The memo went out and the agency directors were given about 3 weeks to come up with their proposals and data. While they were doing that, I, in good League of Women Voters' fashion, really delved into doing research on what other states appropriated for their water divisions. It's tough to do this because, of course, you're dealing with apples and oranges when you compare states, and it's very hard to find any common denominator to make a comparison. But suddenly, out of this morass of data, I found that from some states I could get a figure on the relationship between money invested in audits and computerized billing systems, and the revenues raised. I was able to produce comparable figures for Minnesota, Wisconsin, New York, and California.

Then I received data on the amount of money that came in from water revenues and the number of field personnel in Delaware so that I could make comparisons. This put me in contact with our personnel records. My office was heaped with papers at the time. It became virtually a branch office of the budget and personnel offices. I didn't realize until later how unique this was. I considered myself to be just doing a research project. I didn't think of it in terms of the potential power. The power part, in many people's eyes, means getting to know where the jobs are, where the openings are, and where the money is. I think my attitudes helped my relationships with my peers and the secretary. I didn't have the power-play approach to what I was doing; I was simply doing what was useful for the research project on the budget. In other words, I wasn't being competitive. I was trying to be a staff aide for the good of the division. It was the kind of a staff role that they didn't have anybody else doing, because the division was so limited in its personnel that they'd never had a person to do that kind of research on the budget.

So I came up with these tables in which I projected that if we invested x amount into, say, improving pipeline transportation of water, we'd receive y amount of revenue. I worked out a whole format, a presentation, really. It was a presentation with tables, graphs, summary sheets, and things of that sort for our budget requests. The secretary is quite a conservative person and he was obviously uneasy but his friend, Scott Walters, the deputy secretary who was acting as advisor, thought it was "great, just great." Even though when I'd leave the secretary's office, and he'd be appearing to sort of shake his head and be on the verge of backing down from the whole thing, the other man would go in and buttress it back up. So that worked out well. In the meantime, as luck would have it, an old buddy from the days when I was an activist for the league, Ralph Winston, had gotten himself the job of undersecretary of internal affairs in charge of budgets. So who should come down to the revenue division as the liaison from internal affairs but my old friend. Not only was he my old friend, but he's also very ambitious. He's really reaching, very bright, and carries things out. And he took one look at these tables and figures and he said, "You mean that if we gave your division an additional $2 million, that you'd be able to bring in $6 million?" I said "Yes," and fortunately at this point Scott Walters was in and he said, "Why, absolutely." And then Ralph said, "Well, I wonder if we gave you $4 million, how much would you raise?" At this point Scott said, "$12 million." Ralph said "OK. Prepare your budget for an additional $4 million," which was a 30 percent increase.

In the meantime, our budget had already been drawn up. Preparing a budget in state government is a very tedious proposition. We had to figure the precise personnel and equipment accounts on which to spend the $4 million. The budget deadline was during the Christmas season. I really felt at that point like, "What have I done?" Scott Walters was the key architect of the plans, but the entire budget had to be taken apart and integrated with the new. We had to develop the justification statements and additional tables and charts. I was making up personnel titles when the ones we wanted weren't in the Civil Service book. It was really a very unusual kind of situation in state government, where everything's so tight. But we did it. Again, it was an unusual kind of role I played. Here I was an undersecretary sitting and compiling and taking things to the duplicating room. In state government, where jobs are so defined, they aren't used to that. I don't know for sure if this was a good or bad way to be in the division, but on the whole I have the impression it was good, and my commitment and willingness to work was respected. So we prepared the new budget and we received everything we asked for. It was a tremendous victory in a year of very tight budgets for all other divisions.

ELIZABETH BEST (C)

Ardis Burst
C. Wickham Skinner

By January 1970, Elizabeth Best had been undersecretary of environmental affairs in charge of the Water Division for 7 months. During this period she had influenced several major changes within her division and the department as a whole. She appraised her work as being quite successful. In February 1970, the department's only other undersecretary, who was in charge of the Environmental Standards Division, resigned. Best asked the secretary for a lateral transfer to that position.

The Environmental Standards Division included three agencies: (1) the Pollution Monitoring and Control Agency, which was responsible for conducting pollution inspections throughout the state; (2) the Environmental Impact Review, which was responsible for reviewing proposals for new construction; and (3) the Audit Agency, which worked with local environmental planning agencies. The secretary approved her request, and in February 1970 she took over her new position.

Of the three agencies, Best believed that the problems and functions of the Pollution Monitoring and Control Agency were the most critical and urgent. The agency was charged with the responsibility of gathering data on air and water quality throughout Delaware and monitoring this data against standards. The primary use of this data was to ensure that all communities (both residential and industrial) enjoyed reasonably clean air and water. If, for example, a particular industry was found in violation of a pollution standard, the Pollution Monitoring and Control Agency would turn over this information to the Audit Agency. The Audit Agency would then contact local business and community leaders and work with them to correct the problems.

Best felt that the monitoring and control function was especially important. Air and water pollution had received considerable attention at both the state and national level and was becoming an increasingly important political issue. Any of Delaware's efforts to equalize and implement air- and water-quality standards depended on the Pollution Monitoring and Control Agency's ability to gather relevant data and initiate action. Moreover, a new state law had been passed the previous year, requiring that the agency compile air- and water-quality data on more than 250 cities and towns in Delaware. As of February, less than a year remained before the January 1971 deadline for compiling and reporting this information.

The Pollution Monitoring and Control Agency had a director, 2 assistant directors, and 10 field representatives, all of whom were civil service employees. The field representatives were assigned on a geographic basis and were responsible for gathering data on air and water quality within their districts. This gathering and monitoring function was to be performed through periodic inspections. The 10 inspectors reported to the 2 assistant directors, each of whom was responsible for part of the state. In addition, all of Delaware's cities and towns had been asked to forward citizen complaints on air or water quality.

Best commented on this work:

> This is a politically sensitive task. The Environmental Standards Division is in the process of drawing up new air- and water-quality standards. Many local businesses and labor unions are fearful that if new standards are too strict that compliance with the law will cause loss of jobs and other economic hardships throughout the state. On the other hand, many citizen groups have been lobbying for the state to take more aggressive action in curbing flagrant polluters. In order to draw up a reasonable set of standards, we have to rely on data submitted by the field inspectors on what current emissions levels are.

Because of the January 1971 deadline date mandated by the new state law, Best began to work on the project as soon as she took charge of her new division. As a first step, she asked to review all the pollution data the agency had thus far collected. To her surprise, she discovered that many of the folders she had asked for were not in the files, and those that were typically contained only a single page of handwritten notes. After questioning the agency director and the assistant directors, it became clear that the process was incomplete and had been conducted in a haphazard manner. Less than half the cities and towns in the state had been inspected. Worse, over a third of the collected data had been taken from industry records rather than from actual inspection.

Best became painfully concerned that the whole inspection system had become a sham. Although this awareness and concern were in no way shared by the agency director, his staff, or the inspectors, it was shared by the secretary for environmental affairs. Best felt that although the secretary's background was in another area, he was a person of integrity and intelligence and was politically attuned to how pollution monitoring inspections were viewed by those outside the division. Since little formal information existed on agency techniques for conducting inspections, Best sought some time and advice from the secretary, but was mainly left to rely on her own methods for getting results.

> I started the project by trying to use the League of Women Voters' group discussion approach with the agency directors and the senior field representatives. I really wanted to involve the people themselves in the project, and I wanted them to understand what it was

about, and why it was so important. I was also trying, of course, to develop a sense of urgency about the task, and to get them to take more responsibility for it.

I also tried to develop through group discussion what our goals were, how inspections should be done, and a calendar and a schedule for accomplishing them. By participatory goal setting, I hoped to get their commitment to the goals. I explained in detail how the figures were used.

But it really seemed like nothing registered. There was very little that could be called discussion. In part, I think it was such a novelty for them to be in an organized meeting. The agency and even the whole section had always been run without any organizational meetings. The field representatives weren't used to discussing problems or setting work objectives. Also, don't forget, there was the novelty of their undersecretary being a woman. I don't think they had ever known a woman in a position of authority before.

Best gave the director and his assistants the responsibility for supervising the inspections and ensuring that they took place effectively. She had noticed that, at first, they had tried to stay out of the meetings and she wanted to make sure that they understood their responsibility. After the meetings, she began to question the director and his assistants about the progress of the inspections. By July, 4 months had passed and Best's hopes had sunk.

By then, I was beginning to get suspicious. I had put trust in these people. I had assumed that the system of using the agency directors would work, after they understood better what the urgency or circumstances were. By July, it appeared that possibly no one had produced any work at all. Although the men had been in the field for weeks, there was no tangible evidence to show for it. At one meeting, I asked a young field representative to show me his work. First, he said it was in the other office and I could see it there. I told him firmly to bring it to me. Then he said it was in his briefcase among his papers. I said, "Then let me see your papers." It turned out that his briefcase was heavily loaded with blank forms.

Best felt that she could not, and should not, take complete responsibility for managing the project herself, but it seemed clear that the three directors could not handle the responsibility. She did not want to go against the traditional table of organization that existed in the agency by ignoring the directors and assigning a senior field representative to serve as a supervisor. The final option, to replace them, was not really an option because everyone in the division either held a Civil Service position or, if high enough in rank, had received his position due to a strong reservoir of political support. In order to dismiss anyone, a solid case of deliberate misconduct would have to be made.

The data on which new environmental standards would be based had to be publicly reported. Best wondered if there would be enough time to train and develop the inspectors. Would they even care if it got done, she wondered? And if not, what option did she really have?

PRODUCT MANAGEMENT AT UNITED BRANDS[1]

Richard Harmer
Jay W. Lorsch
Cyrus Gibson

"They are the chosen few . . . the MBA club. They're on the fastest track in the company."

"They're a bunch of young, bright, and terribly egotistical guys."

"It's the Momma's-chicken-soup syndrome. These guys *assume* they know how to do it best."

"What they call creative thinking would be called BS in any other place."

"That department brings people in from the outside all the time, because they don't know their own business. They can't develop their own people; they promote them instead."

"They have charisma. They are always great personalities . . . a bunch of actors . . . a superior race. They're the prestigious group, the comers."

All these statements are about product managers. They were made by people in the various departments of the Butternut Division of United Brands, Inc. Only the last statement was made by a product manager.

DEVELOPMENT OF PRODUCT MANAGEMENT AT UNITED BRANDS

Established in the late 1920s through the merger and acquisition of a number of independent packaged food producers, United Brands was one of the first U.S. multiproduct packaged food marketers. United Brands was also a pioneer in the use of the product management form of organization.

Originally, at United Brands, as in most companies, each function—production, research, marketing, and financial services—played a specialized role in the total

---

[1] Disguised name, which has no relationship to the real company of the same name.

operation of the company. The general manager of a division coordinated the work of the functions in implementing the corporate strategy. However, as the number of products each division produced and sold increased, the job of coordination became increasingly complex. The product-management type of organization was United Brands' response to this complexity in coordinating the functional departments in the development, production, and marketing of a large number of products.

The product management organization was superimposed over the traditional functional organization, cutting across functional lines, as shown in the matrix below:

	Functions				
	Market research	Sales	Production	Accounting and control	Product research
Product group A					
Product group B					
Product group C					
Product group D					
Product group E					

Each product manager played a role similar to that of the division general manager, coordinating the work of people in the functional departments in implementing the strategy for the product (or products) for which he or she was responsible. An important difference, however, was that the product manager had no structural authority over the people whose work he coordinated, as did the general manager. In fact, a product manager sometimes had to compete with other product managers for the services of the functional departments. For example, in the Butternut Division of United Brands, the same sales force handled all the products of all five product groups. In other departments, such as financial services and, to some extent, marketing research, employees were assigned to work with particular product groups, while at the same time working for their superiors within the function.

In 1970, United Brands marketed a wide range of packaged food products in the United States through four operating divisions, each of which was treated as a relatively autonomous unit.

BUTTERNUT DIVISION

The Butternut Division of United Brands maintained its own production facilities, sales organization, product management section, marketing research group, research and development organization, raw foodstuffs purchasing group, and personnel and controllership functions. (See Exhibits 1 and 2 for the organization chart and division headquarters floor plan.) Its products included peanut butter, jams, jellies, honey, and maple syrup.

According to Lee Edwards, Butternut's marketing manager, the Butternut Division had traditionally been United Brands' largest division and had accounted for 37 percent of domestic sales.

However, although Butternut sales had continued to increase steadily over the past 5 years, its share of United Brands' total and domestic sales had decreased over the same period. This was due to a leveling off of the market for its group of products, United Brands' renewed acquisition program, and United Brands' increased activity in the institutional and international markets.

According to United Brands' 1970 annual report, the business of the Butternut Division would "remain a dependable and profitable business, but will account for a relatively smaller share of overall sales and earnings as other areas of the company grow more rapidly."

Product Management in the Butternut Division

According to Edwards, the product manager's role was a key one in the operations of the division. Characterizing this position as a "little general manager," he described how the product manager was central to the planning and execution of marketing strategies:

> The product groups, with the advice of the various functional departments, formulate the marketing strategies and then pass them up the line of management for modification and/ or concurrence. When agreement on the strategy is finally achieved, responsibility for the execution of the strategy rests with the product manager. This approach keeps senior management in control of policy and strategy, but it puts the burden of "managing" on the product manager. It also serves as a built-in personnel development program, as the product manager must constantly think up solutions to business problems and accomplish their successful execution.

The product manager's work in executing product strategy could be divided into two broad categories: (1) the administration of trade discounts on current products, and (2) management of advertising and product changes.

Butternut management considered most of its products to be commodities in the packaged food business. Therefore, in terms of marketing expenditures, the division's marketing emphasis was on price competition. Three-fourths of the division's marketing expenditures were spent on trade deals.[2] Trade deals were administered on a

---

[2] Trade deals were promotional expenditures aimed at distributors and retailers, rather than directly at customers. These included discounts from regular trade prices and allowances to retailers for running special newspaper advertising and retail coupon offers. These expenditures were often made with the intent that price reductions be passed on to the customer. Sometimes trade discounts or dealer promotions required action by the retailer before the money was turned over; sometimes they did not. Trade deals did not include consumer promotions, such as sweepstakes contests, merchandise send-ins, etc.

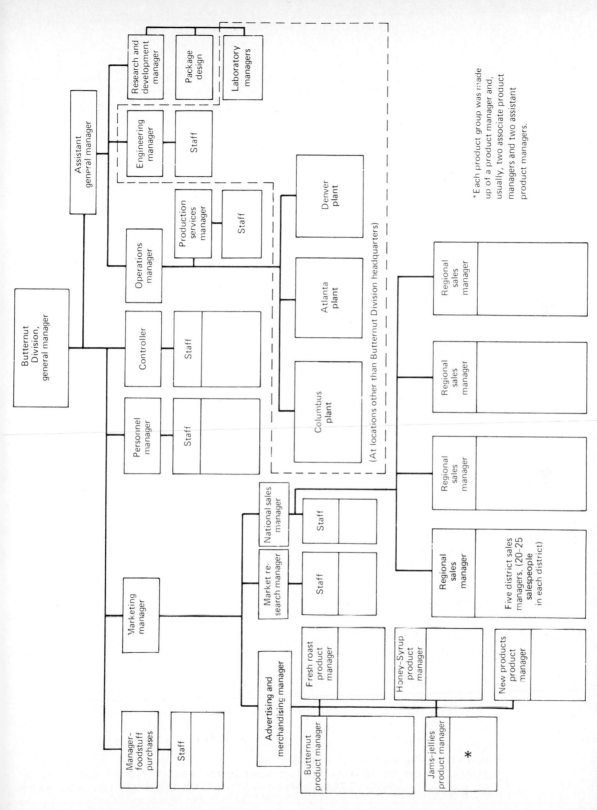

EXHIBIT 1 Product management at United Brands—Butternut Division organization chart.

*Each product group was made up of a product manager and, usually, two associate product managers and two assistant product managers.

(At locations other than Butternut Division headquarters)

Five district sales managers. (20–25 salespeople in each district)

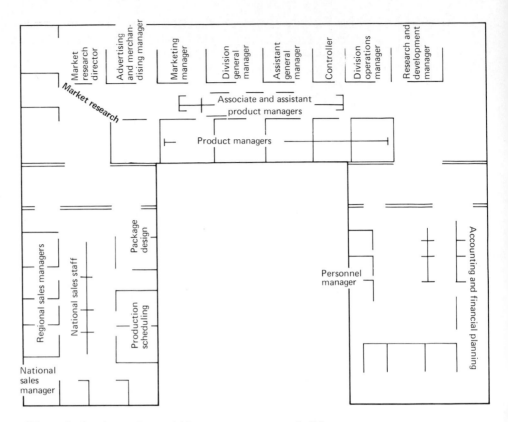

*The production plants and research laboratory were at separate facilities

EXHIBIT 2   Product management at United Brands—floor plan of Butternut Division headquarters.

district-by-district basis over the 20 sales districts. (The four regional sales managers each had five district sales managers working for them, who in turn each had 20–25 salespeople.) Managing trade deals required negotiating the types and amounts of the trade deals for each district with the regional sales managers and coordinating the volume requirements with production. In the negotiations with the regional sales manager, the product manager had the final say as to how and where the marketing money would be spent; he controlled the purse strings.

The management of advertising and product changes could entail introducing a new product, changing a current product, or changing its advertising. These activities required working together with the product research group, the market researchers, the product group's advertising agency, sales, and production. An extremely simplified example of the process follows: product management and market research determined what could sell. This had to be reconciled with what product research could create and what production could produce within cost limits. Production was then established on a limited basis. Product management, market research, and the advertising agency then developed selling concepts and introduced them through the sales force to test-market the product. Test-market data were evaluated and decisions were made on a final strategy. The controller was involved in financial analysis throughout the complete process.

While this example is sequential, in actuality all the different functional departments were involved in the process at all points to some degree. A large number of unforeseen problems would occur while coordinating the work of the functional departments. Much of the product manager's job involved getting these cross-functional conflicts resolved and getting decisions made, so that schedules and objectives could be met. The product group served as the focal point of most coordination and decisionmaking.

When the casewriter asked Edwards for the basis on which product managers were evaluated, he answered, "On how well they did their job." He was reluctant to be more specific, explaining that even though a product manager had met all the financial and market objectives of a product strategy, he or she could still be judged as performing poorly because of other circumstances, such as momentum in the product before his or her arrival, or an ineffectiveness in dealing with other people.

A successful product manager, he pointed out, must be able not only to coordinate the work of others but also to get good ideas from them and to motivate them to carry out his or her decisions following the timetable.

The casewriter discovered that product management in the Butternut Division had traditionally been the route to top management positions in the company. The chairperson, president, and 12 of the corporation's 16 top nonproduction operating officers[3] were once product managers in the Butternut Division.

On the whole, people in the product management group were younger and more highly paid than their counterparts in the other departments of the division. Most of them had MBAs.

PRODUCT MANAGEMENT AS SEEN BY THE OTHER DEPARTMENTS

The casewriter arranged to talk with people in each of the functional departments and with representatives of the advertising agency with whom the product managers came in contact. The intention was to find out what constituted "effective dealings" with each of the groups. The casewriter asked these people two questions: (1) What are the basic conflicts between your department and product management? (2) In terms of helping you do you own job more effectively, what constitutes a good product manager and what constitutes a poor product manager?

Representative answers to question 1 appear below.

Advertising Agency

The thing that's always bothered me about Butternut is, where its businesses are so huge and the funds are there, it doesn't try new approaches to advertising enough. It spends too

---

[3] Division managers, marketing managers, national sales managers, advertising and merchandising managers.

much time on the day-to-day operations, making sure the deals are effective, making sure it meets its monthly share objectives. Product management simply does not experiment enough.

Production

Plants are basically big thick machines. Product management is constantly thinking of ways to market the products that don't fit those big machines, that require a significant amount of change. These big machines don't like to get changed. So this basic plant wish—in an ideal world, to produce everything in a one-pound jar—is basically at odds with product management, which is trying to make up exotic things to sell, exotic ways to make products, and exotic ways to package it.

The product management people seem to continually come up with new ideas that the plant cannot do.

One conflict is the speed with which product management would like to react. Once they have an idea, our cycling time to get that idea from the drawing board into the package is usually far too long for product management; and they try their damnedest to get us somehow to commit to a date that's unrealistic.

Market Research

What keeps competent people in this department is the opportunity to be personally creative, to develop new market research techniques. Too often product management gets in the way of that. They're constantly sending us out to put out brush fires—little projects, the same kinds of things all the time. What's worse is when they ignore your research results, because they don't fit the product manager's preconceived conclusions.

Controllership

Our main job is helping product managers project the results of their programs and then tracking what they've done and determining how successful it's been. They've got so many programs going at the same time—and these programs overlap—that it makes our job very difficult. And there's always something new and different that doesn't fit our ways of doing it. It's really a can of worms. But, then, that's what we're paid for. I shouldn't really complain about that.

Product management has traditionally not paid close enough attention to profits and has emphasized market share. They have rationalized that they were buying future profits; but until recently they haven't tried to cash in on their past investment. That's beginning to change now. Mr. Parkes, the new division general manager, is putting increasing emphasis on the profitability of brand strategy; and the product managers are catching on. But it is still something of a problem.

Sales

Some of the product managers are inexperienced. They don't know what the hell they're talking about. For the most part, they're trained to think profits and how to increase profits and spend the least amount of money. Or maybe it's the reverse—spend the least amount of money and, therefore, get more profits. Unfortunately, it doesn't work out that way.

Product management's job is to make sure the consumer wants our product. Sales' job is to make sure the products are there. That means sales has to know what is the best way to present it to the trade, which is the key execution in getting the product to the shelf.

Every market is different. But our salespeople are in each and every market. So we know our customers' needs; we have accumulated knowledge of those markets. Given our intimate knowledge of each of these markets, we can recommend to the product management people how they should spend their promotion money. Sometimes they follow our recommendation; sometimes they don't. When they don't, then there's conflict.

The major complaint in sales is that we don't handle the money. Product management has complete control of the purse strings. We try to get x amount of dollars from the product group for a program we feel will be beneficial to the division. They may not give it to us. And they have the final say.

Product Research

The overriding basic conflict is we can't make what they want as cheaply as they want it. And they don't want what we can make. Of course, that's an overexaggeration. But the conflict is there.

There's a tendency on the part of the product management people to theorize and postulate, etc. They see themselves as being very creative. They'd much rather argue than go out and try to get the information, to run the experiment. They shouldn't be creative to the point that they neglect facts. There's too great a tendency, I think, to fly by the seat of their pants, and not to get the facts.

Representative answers to question 2 appear below.

Advertising Agency

A good product manager doesn't use me just for working up copy. He includes me in the full range of marketing strategy formulation. That makes it very satisfying for me personally. It also ensures that what we're thinking at the agency is in step with what's brewing in the division. And, occasionally, I'm able to contribute something valuable that may have been overlooked by the product management people.

Production

A good product manager understands the production function. So when we are unable to meet some of his or her timetables, he or she better understands the situation. The product manager should be open-minded, quite willing to listen, and perhaps give some part of the day, or some importance, to production.

Some product management people are honest and aboveboard. They tell you what they want, their reasons, and the impact on the company if they get it and if they don't get it. Others, you feel they're not really being honest with you. Their objective is to make short-term heroes out of themselves at the expense of long-term gains. They are in such competition with each other. There's a lot of backbiting.

Production persons will bust their rear ends to get something for a product manager if they know it's in the interests of the division or the corporation. But if they think it's just to make the manager look like a hero, they're not going to.

A good product manager is willing to make a decision and stand by it.

Marketing Research

Good product managers ask the staff to make recommendations on how best to solve a problem. They will *not* tell the staff what test to use, what kind of sample, etc. Instead, they will allow the market researcher to do his or her job and make recommendations. Of course, product managers have the right to question the program. You know, "Is this question really answered?" But they won't tell you what to do; they will define the problem and then await your recommendations.

Good product managers give us the opportunity to be directly involved in the formulation of marketing strategy, the chance to make and defend our own recommendations.

What I don't like in product managers is indecisiveness. If I work out programs with product managers, and they like and buy it, I think they should support me in their recommendations to senior management. If there are points of conflict, they should be willing to let the market researcher into the discussion, where senior management is present, and let him or her defend it, too.

Controllership

The man who fails as a product manager is not able to meet schedules and timetables. The good product manager is not only good at dictating, but also at listening.

Sales

Good product managers have to have good personalities—almost a sales-type personality. They have to be able to come down like they've just stepped out of the shower, and give an amusing, enlightened presentation to the sales force. They've got to be extroverted, to be able to project a good image.

I have never seen a negative, introverted, or ill-dispositioned product manager make it.

A good product manager will come right out and tell it like it is. "Here's how much I have. I'm sorry I can't give you more," rather than say "We feel this strategy would be better for you."

My approach to them is, "Tell me what your story is and, if you don't have the funds, I can sit down with my people and explain that to them." But I can't tell my people we didn't get x promotion dollars because product management didn't think we were right. Because we know we were right!

You've got to have people to deal with who will act, who will make decisions, not the ones who think, "If I don't do anything, it will go away."

A good product manager can develop a strong point of view, articulate it correctly, and stand up to his or her superior with it.

Product Research

The ineffective product managers tend to look down on people in the other departments—like "you're my lackey."

A product manager must be able to speak the languages of the people he or she deals with, which is quite different from technical research, operations, or financial people.

He or she must have a basic desire to communicate with the different functions and be sympathetic to their needs as they relate to the total business. Not to cater to their gripes, but to really try to understand and appreciate the problems a person is trying to explain. He or she must be willing to give up valuable time to communicate to these people what he or she is trying to do and the reasons why.

PRODUCT MANAGEMENT AS SEEN BY SUBORDINATES OF THE PRODUCT MANAGERS

Another group each product manager dealt with was his or her own subordinates. The casewriter asked several junior members of the product management group what kind of product manager they preferred to work for. Some of their answers appear below:

A good product manager will give his or her subordinates new chances to develop their skills and new types of things to work on. I don't want to stay on one thing for too long after I've learned it. Then I'm just wasting time. I want to move on and up in the business. To do that, I've got to learn all aspects of the business. A good product manager won't hold me back. . . .

A good boss will always be ready to help you out with a problem, but won't hover so closely over you that you can't grow through overcoming the difficulties of the problem yourself. A good boss will be there when you're in need. . . .

A good product manager will include me in on what's happening in the product group, beyond the particular project I'm working on, so I know where my work fits in.

PRODUCT MANAGEMENT AS SEEN BY PRODUCT MANAGERS

The casewriter also asked two product managers to describe what they thought differentiated the successful product manager from the less successful one.

Product Manager 1

The most difficult part of the job is to get the uninvolved, uninterested people to be involved and interested in the business, like the production and packaging people, the nine-to-five's, the people who have no future in their jobs. A good product manager can do that.

You have to understand what the fellow needs—a kick in the ass or a pat on the back. Some fellows like to be loved. So you ask, "How's your dog today? Did you sleep well last night?" The fellow will think, "Hey, there's a nice guy. I'm going to take care of him next time." If you're sending pen and pencil sets to retailers as a promotion gimmick, you send the fellow one. So he feels part of the brand. Others you have to lean on, get tough with, threaten. It depends on the person.

Let me give you an example—the purchaser in the production department. If you don't get her attention and miss your target date, you may have the best program, but without glass to pack the product in, you don't have *any* program. And she is the one who orders glass. She is the one who can make the supply area work extra hard for you. But she works for 5 product groups, 7 brands, and 30 different sizes. If she doesn't like you, you're in trouble.

So it's a function of how you show your respect for a person, and how you communicate, and how you build this rapport.

If you need to get something done in 3 weeks, and the book says it takes 4 to 6 weeks to get it done, but you know if she wants to help you she can do it in 3 weeks, then it's that critical area of whether she's going to help you that makes or breaks you, or makes you look good.

That's why it's important to know how to deal with each person. There are other things too, of course. If a person can't handle the complexity of many things going at the same time, he or she will never make it.

Also, there are some people who have great ideas, but can't sell them. They're just poor salespeople. They will yield right away when the boss gives them the pressure treatment, even if it's just to test them. They don't last.

There's another type that is extremely competent, but won't succeed because they can't live within the system; they won't observe all the protocols, they won't follow the procedures. If you want to succeed, you can step out of bounds only once in a while to show you're a tiger. You can be sort of a bastard—but not much, just sort of. You step on people's toes only once in a while.

The organization demands that its people be good Christian soldiers. That also means that you may stay in a position longer than you should, or take a job that you don't want; but you don't say no, you say "Yes, but." You have to strike the right balance between independence and compliance.

Product Manager 2

To become a product manager, you have to be smart, aggressive, and creative. The smarter you are, the better. By aggressive, I'm referring to a people-oriented aggressiveness. To get ahead and succeed as a product manager, that aggressiveness must be attached to a commitment to get things done. Creativity is very important, but it's not necessary that the person be creative with new and appropriate ideas. It's more important that the product manager can recognize appropriate creativity in others. The product manager should continually be running across things others do with the reaction, "Gee, I wish I'd thought of that." The important thing is that he or she isn't bothered by not coming up with an idea, but is delighted to accept an idea someone else has had.

To get ahead as a product manager, you have to have a commitment to the results rather than to a particular technique, personality, or source of the ideas. A product manager has to show aggressiveness and a toughness, a tenacity that doesn't stop when somebody says, "No, you can't do it." A product manager will try to figure out another way to do it.

Another thing you need to get ahead in product management is the broadest view of the job possible—that means the product manager goes beyond the requirements of his or her job. There are three kinds of people who start off in product management: (1) those who look upon the job as a crappy job, who go through the motions, and who don't want to do it—and the job suffers; (2) those who manage to do the job adequately, who are committed to it, and who want to do it well so they can move on to something that's more fun and exciting; (3) those who do the job adequately and have the time—no, make the time—to do other things as well that they think are important. They are the ones who go beyond their jobs. They are the ones who will succeed in product management.

Another important factor is what I call public relations. (The cynic would probably call it politics.) The fact that someone is using a great new idea in his or her work doesn't do any good unless the right people know about it. That is the job of the product manager. I am continually sending things up just to keep them posted as to what people in my product group are doing that is good.

Finally, a little humility goes a long way. That's trying to know as much as you possibly can without flaunting it. The person who says, "I've been in this business 20 years, so I ought to know more about it than you do," is categorically wrong. That person knows more about his or her job, but I know more about how his or her job relates to what I'm trying to do—which is what that person and I are sitting down to talk about.

So his or her attitude is wrong. But making that person see that doesn't move the ball ahead. Playing "gotcha" is sometimes satisfying, but it doesn't help much.

DAVID ALPERT (A)

Richard Harmer
Jay W. Lorsch
Cyrus Gibson

In 1971 David Alpert was the product manager for Butternut Peanut Butter in the Butternut Division of United Brands, Inc.[1] (See the organization chart in Exhibit 1.) The previous year, 5 years out of Harvard Business School, he had assumed responsibility for Butternut Peanut Butter, one of United Brands' top selling products. (Over the previous 5 years, Butternut sales and profits had been 9.1 percent and 15.4 percent of corporate sales and profits, respectively.)

EVALUATION OF ALPERT AS A PRODUCT MANAGER

As far as the casewriter could tell, Alpert was doing well as product manager. Lee Edwards, Butternut Division marketing manager, had referred Alpert to the casewriter as a good example of a strong, effective product manager. Other people from the various functional areas in the division described Alpert as follows. Sales considered him "flexible, prompt, decisive, a decision maker." The controllership found him "receptive to different ways of looking at the business." Product research considered him "sympathetic to problems we might have in accomplishing our task, . . . tries to understand, . . . a good communicator." Market research found him a "very fair-minded person, . . . generally given to listening to all sides of a thing, given to letting people express their opinions, . . . parochial in terms of pushing for his brand's priorities, but easy to work with." Production found him "excellent, . . . a good listener; . . . he keeps us informed as to how we fit into the overall picture."

---

[1] Disguised name, which has no relationship to the real company of the same name.

ALPERT'S EVALUATION OF THE JOB

Alpert told the casewriter he liked his job for a number of reasons:

First, I like the responsibility the job entails and I like the fact that I can measure my accomplishments. There are measures like market share targets and return on investment. There is also a certain measurement in the sense that we deal with programs that can be completed. We've just completed a successful program that involved spending an awful lot of money. It had a lot of little pieces to it. It was a real executional nightmare. It was satisfying to fit all these pieces together.

Secondly, I find a lot of personal satisfaction in being responsible for the expenditure of a lot of money and spending it well. I guess beneath that is the fact that I like to be looked upon as a guy who has things under control. It means something to me to have that reputation in the company.

Another thing about project work that is fairly appealing to me is the fact that on no given Tuesday do I have the same thing to do from week to week. There are no routines in the work.

Then I guess that I would have to say that there are people who I like to work with. First, there are those outside the product group. I find a great deal of satisfaction in cranking these people up to get a job done. Secondly, within the product group I have four people working for me, and I think I'm relatively good at getting them to progress—getting them to feel they are progressing.

There are two aspects to this. The first one is the training aspect. I enjoy working with my people and helping them to develop along the lines that I think are important for product manager types to have.

David then paused for a moment before he went on.

The second aspect you might call the public relations job. I like to ensure that my people will have their day in court and be exposed in the way that will help them to get promoted. I think I'm pretty good at that.

Finally, the material rewards—the money—are, of course, very important. It's strange how you are consistently able to live just beyond your income, so that you're looking forward to each raise as it comes. I guess that's very much the American way of life. In any case, my salary progression has been fairly dramatic. My salary has increased fourfold since coming to United Brands. I am making in the high thirties now, and that's pretty damned important. Especially when it comes by doing something I like—that I'm making progress by doing things I enjoy doing.

Of course, it's not all a bed of roses.

It's aggravating to any product manager who wants to get the job done to sit and listen to somebody else tell you about their problems. If they didn't have problems, they wouldn't have a job; and because they've got problems, they become one of your problems. On the other hand, if reciting their problems to you helps to solve their problems through some ego satisfaction or whatever, and your job is to solve their problems, then you are doing your job by listening to them talk about it.

But that's really not the most important part of our job—listening to somebody create a problem before your very eyes, which he will then proceed to solve and be a great big hero. When they do that it's a fairly obvious ploy.

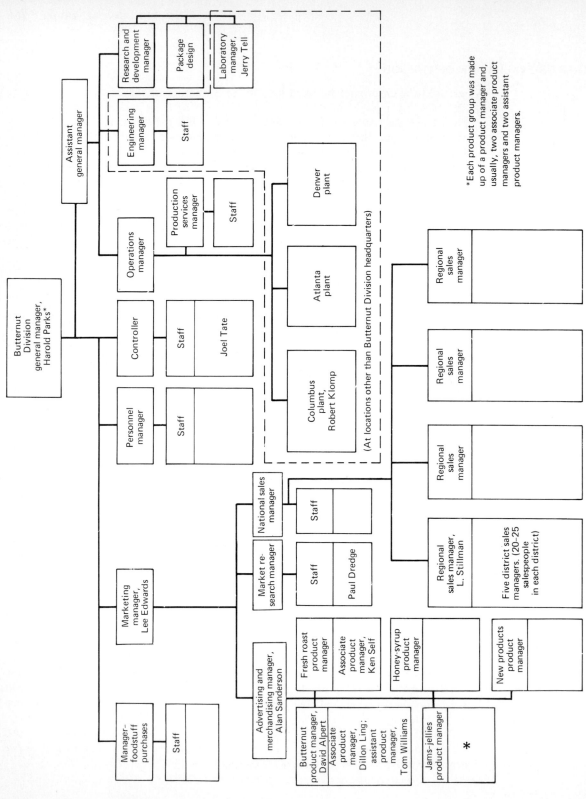

EXHIBIT 1 Butternut Division organization chart. (Only names mentioned in the case are given.)

*Each product group was made up of a product manager and, usually, two associate product managers and two assistant product managers.

(At locations other than Butternut Division headquarters)

282

ALPERT'S DEALINGS WITH OTHERS IN THE BUTTERNUT DIVISION

The casewriter spent 3 days with Alpert, recording his dealings with others in the Butternut Division. Later he asked David to comment on these exchanges.

Monday's Task Force Meeting

Among his other current duties, Alpert headed a special temporary task force that had been formed to make up the 5-year plan for the two peanut butter brands sold by the Butternut Division. Alpert represented Butternut Peanut Butter, United Brands' popularly priced line. Representing Fresh Roast Peanut Butter, United's premium brand, was Ken Self, an associate product manager in the Fresh Roast Product Group. Other task force members representing other groups in the division were:

Production	Robert Klomp
Control	Joel Tate
Sales	Larry Stillman
Market research	Paul Dredge
Product research	Jerry Tell
Advertising agency representative	Ned Ashby

Below are excerpts from one of the task force meetings (the control and sales representatives were absent).

The meeting began at 9 a.m. Jerry Tell summarized the results of a meeting with higher management on task force objectives. He had attended the meeting representing Alpert, who had been on vacation. Fifteen minutes into the presentation, Ned Ashby, the advertising agency representative, walked into the meeting late. He gave a short apology and excuse, and took a seat.

Alpert answered his apology:

Alpert: I told the secretaries there were two things we were missing—Ned Ashby and the coffee. And I wasn't sure which we were missing most.
Ashby: You're being polite. (Everybody laughs.)

The meeting then continued. Tell finished the summary with a comment on the use of market research in the division.

Tell: The next issue was that, in a business that is as consumer-oriented as ours is, we are not spending really enough time, money, or effort on basic marketing research, so that we can improve our ability to communicate with and to the consumer. The comment was generally made that there should be a great deal more effort in this area.
Alpert: Did you make the comment or did higher management?
Tell: I did. That's a personal thing I've been carrying around for quite a while.
Alpert (jokingly): You got that off your chest?
Tell: Yes, I felt a lot better. I slept very well that night.

Later, the discussion turned to looking into areas of peanut products other than peanut butter, such as peanut candy bars and peanut cake frosting mixes. The group engaged in animated discussion of several possibilities for about 10 minutes. During that time, Alpert remained silent. He then cut off the discussion, saying that what they were discussing were areas for the division to look into, but that they were probably more appropriate for the new products group, and that the peanut butter group would not have to worry about them.

Alpert then went through the 5-year plan point by point with the group. All task force members participated freely in the discussion.

Robert Klomp raised the question of whether changes in taste preferences were going to come about in the next 10 years, or whether it had been assumed that tastes would stay the same. Klomp suggested that it should be possible to project future changes in taste preferences on the basis of changes over the past 10 years. Alpert answered him in a roundabout way:

Alpert: Well, you've gotta have some givens. You've got to establish some base objectives. And the easiest ones to establish are markets and margins. You just can't cope with all the variables.

You have no control or relatively no control over what the market's going to be. We hope we can expand it, but we made the best guess we can.

Tell: With our share of market, we have more control than I think we tend to exercise.

Alpert: Well, we don't know how to exercise it.

Tell: But with margins . . .

Alpert: Yes, we've gotten some control over margins. But if the cost of peanuts is 70 percent of the cost of goods sold, and if Fred (the raw foodstuffs buyer) doesn't know what the cost of peanuts is one day to the next, let alone one week or month to the next, then all you can do is assume you will take an active pricing action and adjust it as you go along.

The casewriter noticed that during the meeting, Ken Self, the associate product manager from the Fresh Roast Group, challenged Alpert a number of times on such points as use of merchandising methods, perceptions of the consumer, and advertising possibility of the brands. Each time, when Alpert answered his challenge with a milder response, Self backed off.

The meeting concluded at 12:15 p.m. After it was over, the casewriter asked Alpert about aspects of the meeting that intrigued him.

Rivalry and Competition among Product Managers

Casewriter: I thought what I saw going on between you and Ken Self was friendly rivalry. Was it?

Alpert: No, it wasn't. I haven't been in a position to develop a lot of respect for his talent. The guys he works with think he's pretty good. I just haven't seen it. He hasn't really been any help on the task force. I thought it was nitpicking.

Casewriter: How did you try to handle it?

Alpert: Just as briefly as possible without being rude. Because, obviously, any obvious dissension between product manager and associate product manager in a group like that would be picked up by the other functions—probably with some relish, even though they are pretty mature people. There was nothing there to call for his being put down. In meetings like that, when somebody like Ken brings up something, I just tend to lose interest in the conversation. I let it wander around for a while, then pick it up again after a few minutes.

Casewriter: But, still, it looked like rivalry. Is there much competition among the product management people?

Alpert: Not really. I can't think of any. There is no reason to be. United Brands needs all the good product managers it can get.

Use of Humor

Casewriter: Let's turn to something else in the meeting. I noticed you used humor a number of times.

Alpert: Humor goes a long way.

Casewriter: Like when you asked Jerry Tell if it felt good to have it off his chest, after his analysis of the marketing situation. It seemed to me he wanted to get involved in marketing decisions.

Dealings with Product Research

Alpert: Nearly everyone does. That's where they think the action is. It's where the status is.

Jerry Tell is very easy to work with. He is far and away the most competent man at the laboratory from my standpoint. He thinks more like a manager than a technician. He evaluates a proposal on rational return-on-investment criteria rather than on whether it would be technically fun. He is a delight to talk to, a real breath of fresh air in the organization. But there are others who don't act that way. Really, he is the exception.

Casewriter: How do you deal with others in product research?

Alpert: Those are the kind of guys you coddle. They have just as much education as you do. But they need experience on the job before they become effective. We spring full blown from business school as "marketing experts." They don't, so our counterparts there are generally older than we are. Therefore, we tend to exclaim loudly and make a terribly big fuss over their accomplishments.

For example, I'll call a guy down in the bowels of the laboratory someplace and congratulate him, and make it very clear that a product improvement was his accomplishment. Which it was.

Dealings with Production

Casewriter: How about the production man, Robert Klomp? His major contribution was some speculations on the probability of taste preferences changing. it seemed he wanted to play marketer too, perhaps.

Alpert: Could be. He was really here primarily so the production people would feel included. Although some things could come up where I could use his knowledge.

I've simply learned that bridges built to the plant will pay innumerable dividends. Primarily the junior product managers deal with them, but I try to keep in touch because they can screw us up badly.

And those are the kinds of people that, if they want to, will ruin an entire plan just to prove they're right and you're wrong. And they can do it.

I have no idea what goes on down there in the plants. And most of it, I suspect, would horrify me if I did. But that's not really important, as long as I can get them to do what needs doing for us. And change is, by definition, bad at the plants. So it's very important that I win them over to my side. It is important that they feel that they can come into my office and tell me that they are not able to do what I want them to do. If they don't come, but shove the problem under the rug, we can't work things out before it's too late. So the key there is communication—direct and easy communication and access. When they come to me with a problem, we sit down and try to figure out what we can do to overcome it.

Dealings with Market Research

Casewriter: What about Paul Dredge, the market researcher?

Alpert: He is a bit parochial, but that's what he's paid to be. When he says he'll go away and think about ways we can incorporate research into our task force presentation and make it a little more research-oriented, he'll probably be back in here first thing Tuesday morning with a bunch of ideas about how to do it. He's a good man. I've got few worries in that department. I was the market research director for 4 months before I got this position. Now they're convinced, true or false, that I know enough of what's going on down there that they can't fool me. The key there is to keep them informed about the business so that they can keep their research program up to date. They don't need a lot of guidance.

Casewriter: Your sales and control people were not at the meeting.

Alpert: They are both out of town. I'll be meeting with Joel Tate, the accounting guy, tomorrow morning to discuss ROI calculations. I have to find out how United Brands does it before the next task force meeting. Our sales representative is a very good man for this job. He worked in product management for a while and has a broader view of things than most of those guys.

Dealings with Sales

Casewriter: Tell me about your dealings with sales.

Alpert: The day-to-day dealings are handled almost exclusively by our junior people in product management. I usually get involved when they can't get a problem worked out.

The people in sales resent us. And yet maybe they are the most crucial people we have to work with. That whole relationship is a difficult one from their point of view. The regional sales manager sees you as younger and less experienced than him (which we are). And yet, as his volume and sales promotion planners, his success depends on our ability to get him his share of the total dollars for promotion and spending. So I can certainly understand the resentment—particularly against the people who don't do well at it.

We treat them with a combination of deference—because they are a little older, and particularly when we are junior—and candor. Candor is the key to the thing.

They like to deal with decisionmakers. It's good for their own self-image, plus it saves time—which is an important commodity for any guy.

When they make a request for a program that they think is necessary, they would far prefer they be told that we don't have enough money to do it. Whether it's a good idea or a bad idea, it's wasting time to debate it when you don't have the funds.

But if *you* don't think it is a good idea and can convince the sales manager yourself, that can take you miles. If you can disagree and give him your reasons and really communicate, so that you end up working out something that you agree to, or that at least he can understand your position, then that's very good. There's a lot of respect built in that kind of relationship. Say, "I can't afford it," when you can't afford it; say, "I don't agree," when you don't agree.

Tuesday's Meeting with Control

The next morning, Alpert had a short meeting with Joel Tate, the control representative to the task force, to discuss ROI calculations for the 5-year plan. Alpert needed the material for a meeting with his superiors, Alan Sanderson, the advertising and merchandising manager, and Lee Edwards, the marketing manager.

Alpert: Where are your ROI calculations for the 5-year plan? I've got to get some by Thursday. I need at least one, and perhaps several exhibits on that subject. Because those are probably the most important numbers—at least the second most important after share—that we'll talk about. And I can't just go say to Edwards it ought to be approximately 35 percent.

Tate: I'll have to do some work on it. I'm not too sure I can have all the data and all the . . . a . . . things together by Thursday.

Alpert: I mean we've got something, haven't we, we've got . . .

Tate (cuts in): Oh, I have the actual of how we came up with fiscal 1970—the 35 percent.

Alpert (impatiently): Well.

Tate: And, and I just got pieces for the other years.

Alpert (firmly): I'd like to see what those pieces are.

Tate: OK . . . as far as projections. We can maintain, I'm sure we can. . . . We should say that minimum is 35 percent.

Alpert (growing even more impatient): I mean over the last 3 years. Can I see the calculations?

Tate (leaving): Sure, . . . I'll bring them in.

Alpert (turning to the casewriter after Tate left): You needn't worry about stifling creative ideas that the elves down in accounting may have—because they don't have any. I think the secret with those guys is that you not deal with them at the middle management level, that is, Tate's level. Because I think that the truth of that department is that they occasionally get lucky and hire somebody that's good. But they can't keep them long enough to promote him through the ranks to get them to Tate's position. It's only the relative dullards, like Joel, that stay. I suppose he is a capable guy in his own right. He is not really stupid. He's not awfully smart; he can add a column of figures. But he is not going to become treasurer of the corporation, controller of the division, or anything else.

The best way to get real performance there is to latch on to a young guy who's aggressive and good and very junior in the organization, and just have him work his ass off for you.

We've got a financial analyst under Joel who's assigned directly to Butternut. He is very good. He's the guy through whom we get things done. He is practically a member of the product group. A very, very junior member, because he doesn't create anything, he just does what he is told. But he is a tremendous help.

Tuesday's Meeting with Subordinates

Later that same day, Alpert met with Dillon Ling and Tom Williams, associate and assistant product managers on Butternut, about a test market they were proposing in Atlanta. Ling was Chinese; Williams was black. Alpert listened quietly to the presentation, now and then probing their assumptions, asking additional questions to see how well they had thought things out. After Williams finished his last points, Alpert began the following exchange.

Alpert: That's a very thorough way to go about analyzing what it ought to be. . . . The only question I have is that we've traditionally gone from a northeastern test market, such as Albany, south and west without any compunction. If it tested well in Albany, Syracuse or Indianapolis, we'd take it south. We don't have any experience testing it in the South and taking it to the North.

Ling: We don't?

Alpert: I don't see any radical differences. But we don't want to get ourselves into situations where we've selected test markets that rationally people would think OK, but when it comes right down to it, they won't accept it emotionally.

They discussed the issue. Ling pushed for Atlanta, citing advantages with media and outlet control.

Alpert: OK, let's assume it will be Atlanta. In the meantime, I'll do a little spade work across the hall with the advertising and merchandising manager and the marketing manager and see if that makes people uncomfortable. Because I think it clearly is the best market. But I think we ought to be pragmatic about it. We want it, not because it's Atlanta, but because it's the best way we can think of to test our product.

Williams: We had a couple minor positives and negatives to going into Atlanta.

Alpert: OK, I'm convinced.

Williams: I think you want to hear these, though. One thing, a positive, is I'd go to the Hyatt House. I've never seen it.

Another, a negative one, it's not a great area for minority groups to take their field trips. [Williams laughs cautiously.]

Alpert: Well, Atlanta's all right, but I'm not so sure about eastern Tennessee. [Everyone laughs.]

Ling: Johnny Cash is the spokesman for Nashville.

Alpert: Yes. For eastern Tennessee, you want to send your white Anglo-Saxon Protestants; and we don't have any of those kind of people.

Williams: Buy somebody some cut-off Levi's and get him a rope to tie 'em up and a T-shirt, and send him to eastern Tennessee. [Everyone laughs.]

Ling: The introductory promotion in March could be a shotgun; then, for 50 cents, you can get the shot and shoot the revenuer. [Laughter.]

Alpert: Make the ammunition the continuity. [Laughter.]

After the meeting the casewriter asked Alpert about his dealings with the subordinates in his product group.

Casewriter: How do you train your people?

Alpert: A lot of the training is in your expectations. Junior product managers are, in their individual ways, terribly anxious to please. You don't have to give them orders, you just have to make known simply what you want and be clear about what it is you want done, and then stay out of their way, because they will go to great lengths and work terribly hard to get it done just the way they think you would want it done. That's awfully important. That's a characteristic of the good junior product manager. The thing that separates the good ones from the excellent ones is that the good ones get it done just the way they think you want it done, and the excellent ones will get it done that way, unless they think there might be a better way—and they'll stop and think about it. They will come back to you and say, "I heard you, but this is a better idea." That's sort of a step beyond. I think my people know about the distinction, because we've discussed it and will continue to discuss it. The key is initiative.

The most important thing is getting the job done, achieving the objectives. I don't have a lot of pride of authorship. I'm not really creative in bringing up new ideas of my own. I'm better at being able to take other people's ideas and adapting things that have been done before to problems that we have now.

Wednesday's Meeting with Superiors

On the morning of the third day, Alpert met with his two immediate superiors, Alan Sanderson and Lee Edwards, to discuss the final stages of the 5-year plan. Alpert was concise in his remarks and candid in his presentation. Several times Edwards disagreed with market assumptions he had made. Alpert defended his ideas, saying that he thought the issues were more complicated than the marketing manager perceived them. He suggested that they look into them further.

After the meeting, the casewriter commented on Alpert's skill in making a persuasive, concise presentation.

Alpert: I've learned most of that from Alan (the advertising and merchandising manager). He's a very good businessman and he's hard nosed. And he doesn't like to beat around the bush. If you start to give him something in a roundabout sort of fashion, he's very good at cutting right through to the meat of it. And, he will do it disapprovingly, because he doesn't like you to be wasting his time telling him something in five sentences when you should be able to tell him in one. He doesn't like you to take 5 minutes on justification when 1 minute will do. He's a terribly busy guy. He has an incredibly time-consuming job. He can't afford the luxury of people who can't afford to talk straight, and his style is blunt enough; he'll tell you if you're wasting his time.

Casewriter: You were pretty candid in the meeting yourself.

Alpert: Ed and Alan encourage that. They encourage opposition. They're open enough so that if they don't agree with you, and you tell them you think they're wrong, they'll very quickly admit it if they agree with you. Alan, in particular. He'll sometimes test you to see whether you've thought things out. He'll ask for five reasons you feel the way you do, and very often, he will cut you off after the second reason and say, "OK."

That starts, of course, with the general manager—to tell people what you think. That's Harold Parks's style.

DAVID ALPERT (B)

Richard Harmer
Jay W. Lorsch
Cyrus Gibson

David Alpert and the casewriter went to a small French restaurant on the outskirts of Dayton, Ohio, to cap off the casewriter's 3-day visit with Alpert at United Brands. (See Case 7.) As the evening wore on, the conversation turned to Alpert's personal life. The casewriter was interested in learning more of his background, his lifestyle, and his aspirations.

Casewriter: Let me ask you two questions together, David. First, what is it about yourself—your personal skills, your likes and dislikes—that keeps you in product management? And second, what kinds of things in your upbringing, family life, and education helped develop these skills and made these likes and dislikes important?

Alpert: Well, I guess the basic ingredient is a good sense for dealing with people, and a liking for it. That's what really sends someone into this area of business. At least that is the most valid reason for me. Sociability, having friends, being with them, enjoying them, making sure they enjoy me—this is something that is important to me and always has been, and manifests itself in different ways at different stages of life.

I was the oldest of two children. (I have a sister who is 7 years younger. I always thought 7 years was a natural interval between children, until I started having them.) When I was very young, there were very few children in my neighborhood. I didn't have very many close friends, in terms of neighbors that I could play with all the time, the way my kids do. I find that just absolutely delightful that we're falling over children at our house all the time. (Usually, I find that delightful; sometimes, I get sick of it.) But I can remember that as being rather significant. I could go three or four blocks before finding friends to play with. I don't know. . . . I have no idea if this made me more outgoing when I was with people or what.

That was probably a pretty good summary through grade school. I had friends, not a great many. I don't remember a great many. I remember a couple of them. We didn't live too close; we weren't together constantly. I don't remember myself as being much of a leader when I was younger, in grade school.

I'm not sure what denotes a "leader" in grade school anyway. But I became one in high school. It was a small school for boys. And my parents thought it would be a good thing for me to go to a private school; this turned out to be very wise of them. I didn't think it was a very good idea at the time, but I think so now. I got very close to one of my English instructors, who was also the dramatic coach; and I played the lead in my high school play as a sophomore. It just happened that the role fit me. The play was "The Man Who Came to Dinner." I played Sheridan Whiteside's part, which was a great deal of fun, and I guess tended to single me out in a very favorable way, because it was a very successful play and a lot of fun to do. A lot of people enjoyed watching it. It made me known as someone with a good sense of humor—which I think is pretty true anyway. It just magnified the thing and called it to everybody's attention all at once.

I worked on the school newspaper and the student council, and ended up editor of the paper and president of the student council. There were 36 in the class, and there were two or three of us who were running the organization at the school. I think we were well-liked, without any question; but we were *not* the social leaders to the same degree as we were the organizational leaders. We weren't outcasts in any sense. An interesting part of that was that 2 of the 3 of us were the only Jewish students in the class. (No, there were 3 Jewish boys in the class.) One of them, a fellow who is still my best friend, was president of the senior class and I was president of the student body.

I guess that's an issue, religion, which is something that will crop up occasionally, because it's important. Here and there, more important in some places than in others. I don't really think it was the drawback. I'm sure it was not a drawback, because the offices that I held were elective, the friends that I made in high school are still among my closest friends. But it was something that was there, and it tended to set the three of us apart a little bit. More so in the minds of some parents than in the minds of their children.

Casewriter: After high school, you went to Harvard College, didn't you?

Alpert: Yes.

Casewriter: What are the most important things you remember from your college days, in terms of friendships made and things that had an impact on your future?

Alpert: For some reason, my closest friends in college were Jewish. In high school they hadn't been; but in high school there hadn't been as many Jewish boys to choose from. In college I didn't seek out Jewish friends. I really don't understand why that occurred; although my roommate was Jewish, and I met some of them through him (his father was chairperson of the board of the Continental Publishing Company). The guys that I knew were rich and Jewish and generally from New York and the East.

Casewriter: Were you rich?

Alpert: No.

Casewriter: Were you a Harvard son?

Alpert: Yes.

Casewriter: What about important activities during your college days?

Alpert: I was involved in a couple of them. The best of them (which was a great thing I did because, at the business school, I needed it to put on that application) was that I ran the combined charity drive at Harvard College, the United Fund drive, with another guy in our junior year. It was a big undertaking. We had a couple of hundred guys working for us through this organization that we set up. Compared to the previous year, we were quite successful. And I made some very close friends in the process.

Casewriter: Do you miss the fellowship of your college days?

Alpert: Yes, I do, to a degree. At the same time, the product management system gives ample outlet to a guy who wants to be with people and wants to get things done on a basis of forming friendly relationships with people. That, I guess, as I work myself around to your original question, is probably as good a reason as any for why this job fills some important needs for me. I enjoy those kinds of relationships with people, even though they are a smaller portion of my total life now than they were in college—even if it is with a regional sales manager, for example, that I don't really spend a lot of time with, that I see occasionally at the office. They are *not* my kind of people, really. I mean, I wouldn't seek them out socially . . . some of them. But there's a couple that I would.

Casewriter: After you graduated from college, you went to Harvard Business School, didn't you?

Alpert: Yes.

Casewriter: Why did you pick business as a profession?

Alpert: Partly because I eliminated the other professions for one reason or another, but also because I had some fairly positive attitudes towards business. I had spent summers working for various family businesses. I worked for my Dad first when I was about 15. At the time, he was a wholesale distributor for a large company. He was for about 8 or 9 years.

He has had, that I remember, I guess, about four different jobs since he's gotten out of business school. He worked for a stationery and envelope company in St. Louis. It's a national company, but with its headquarters in St. Louis. He started out when he graduated from business school. He started out hauling paper from the dock to the envelope machines in 1933, and thought he was very lucky to get the job. But he was eventually to become a vice president or something or other—one of their three or four top employees. But the two or three above him happened to have the same name as the president. So he decided that was as far as he was going to go. He was with them about 15 years.

Casewriter: He had gone to Harvard College and Harvard Business School?

Alpert: Yes, I guess he must have been a little better at that system than I was, because he graduated from Harvard College when he was 16 and graduated from the business school when he was 18.

After he left the stationery and envelope company, he acquired and ran a charcoal briquette business for another part of his family. He did pretty well with that business for a while, but the intrafamily relationship, as often happens, proved to be a difficult one. He was running a piece of the business that they weren't really close to;

they were buying and selling grain on the floor of the Board of Trade, in St. Louis. And that led to frictions. And I think basic to the whole thing was that my father enjoyed being his own boss and he wasn't in that kind of situation. And when they did call that fact to his attention, it was over things that they were generally wrong about and he was generally right, and he knew that. So he got out in plenty of time to keep the family together, because he thought that was more important than the business relationship. And they continued the business on a good deal smaller scale than it was when he was there.

When he left there, he bought a stationery office supply company in downtown St. Louis. He sells office supplies to offices in the area and has a retail store. He's done that for the last 6 or 7 years, and has been very happy about it. It's been hard work.

Casewriter: How old is he now, David?

Alpert: 59.

Casewriter: Are you in pretty close communication with him on business decisions and other kinds of things?

Alpert: Yes. We talk every Sunday. They call. Primarily now to talk to the children. They call nonetheless, and they ask us what's new before they ask if the children are there.

Whenever we're in St. Louis . . . I was in St. Louis last week for the sales meeting there. I figured as long as I was running the sales meeting—we were having it for the whole midwestern area—we should jolly well have it in a place like St. Louis. It was fun. I invited Dad to come to the sales meeting. He sat in the back and enjoyed himself thoroughly. We had about 125 salespeople. Put on a hell of a fancy show.

We generally take some time to sit down and talk about things. I think we stay pretty close.

Casewriter: Tell me what it was like to work for your father.

Alpert: It was a pretty successful circumstance for me, because what I set out to do was to get people to say, "He's pretty good in spite of the family relationship." And I really had the same thing going for me for the next four or five summers when I worked for the same family milling and grain company that my father eventually worked for. The most important thing to me was to be thought of by peers and superiors as one who would carry his own weight even if he had a different name and belonged to a different family.

But I guess it was also important in making a longer-term decision not to be involved in a company your family owns—that you make it on your own without worrying about that. I wouldn't really be interested, I think, in a family business.

Casewriter: What kind of relationship did you have with your parents?

Alpert: I think the relationship with my parents was always pretty candid. We sought to make it that way. Our rules with the family would always err toward the side of communicating with each other. "We don't care if you smoke, but if you smoke, smoke at home. We don't care if you drink, but if you drink, drink at home. Make up your own mind but don't try and do something when we are not here that's different than when we're here." I think that was a good description of our relationship.

Casewriter: What about their hopes and expectations of what you'll be professionally?

Alpert: They're convinced, my mother in particular, that I will be president of United Brands. And I don't do much to dissuade her. I don't suppose I could.

Casewriter: What about your own personal goals? Do you plan to stay in this business, or is there perhaps something else you'd like to get involved in?

Alpert: At times I've thought I'd like to get involved in politics. I did do some work in St. Louis for the John Kennedy campaign the summer he was running for president. I had gone to Washington right after school let out to try to get in on the campaign at the national level, but it was before the convention and they weren't hiring anybody.

Getting involved in politics wouldn't be as much of a change as you may think because, in many respects, politics is what product management is. A good product manager, I think, would be a good politician, in the way politics ought to be. Staying with United Brands, I should progress to positions where the emphasis is less on marketing and more on management. The fact that you could be moving up to a point where you are spending most of your time worrying about and concerned with showing your interest in people seems like something really worth working for to me.

The problems we are dealing with are fascinating. But I get a little sick of the peanut butter business once in a while. I think it can only take you just so far. Peanut butter will come and go, but people will be around for a while.

Casewriter: How was it that you decided originally to work for United Brands?

Alpert: Several factors counted in making the decision. On the one hand, it was the big leagues. If I hadn't tried it in the big leagues, I would always wonder if I could have made it. On the other hand, although it looked like a high-risk place, it was actually pretty safe, in terms of going to a known quantity and going to a company that knew how to use the talent I had developed. The third factor was location; Dayton seemed like a nice place to live.

Casewriter: We have talked about your father, but we haven't talked about your mother. Do you have a Jewish mother?

Alpert: Oh yes.

Casewriter: Is she like the one in the television commercials?

Alpert: Yes, oh yes. She's close. I thoroughly enjoy those commercials. I identify with that guy. But my mother can be put down, and goes down with a great deal of grace and style when necessary. I have a Jewish mother, but I don't have a Jewish wife. And that sometimes befuddles my mother.

Casewriter: How do you mean?

Alpert: Well, my mother is terribly careful about stepping on my wife's toes. She doesn't mix in. Sometimes I know she's biting her tongue. As a matter of fact, the last time we were in St. Louis we all sat down and talked about it, because I thought she was frustrating herself unnecessarily, holding back. Because, as long as she realized that we were perfectly free to ignore her advice, I thought she should know we valued her advice as long as it was given in the spirit of, "Here's some free advice, which is worth what you paid for it."

Casewriter: To me there seems to be a similarity between that kind of conversation and the kind of conversations you have every day at United Brands. Does it strike you the same way?

Alpert: Never had before. Well, I guess to the extent that I feel a lot more comfortable in being candid with people, because people respond so well when they know you are. It's really a very selfish thing. I like to be candid with people because I know people like it. Because people like it, our bonds are closer, and I enjoy that. I do it only partly because it is good for the other side, too. With that aspect of it, it's very true.

Casewriter: Sitting in your office, I noticed the poem "If" framed and on your wall (Exhibit 1). The last line caught my eye, and it said something like . . .

Alpert (breaking in): "Be a Man, my son!"

It's really the first verse of that poem that has always seemed the most appropriate to me, which . . . I don't remember the words . . . but it's something about keeping your cool when things are going adversely. If you can accept blame when it really isn't yours, or if you can keep your head when all those about you are losing theirs, that's really what the poem is about. Product management, when it's working right, should always be the eye of the storm. And that fits very well with my disposition. I don't tend to get excited; I roll with the punches.

On the other hand, there is a lack of great emotional involvement on either the high side or the low side that accompanies that. It is a fairly steady, even disposition. I am pleased when things are going well, but I don't reach the heights that some people do. I don't reach the depths either. And I'd just as soon have it that way.

That obviously extends to more than business—it's a personal thing, too. It bothers my wife sometimes. She says I don't get enthusiastic enough about the things that happen with the children or us, or whatever; but by the same token, I don't get as dejected.

I really don't think that's a qualification that you need for the job. It could be helpful.

Casewriter: Would you like to be different? Or is that a moot question?

Alpert: Well, it's pretty much a moot question the way I go about things, because one of the outgrowths of that disposition or attitudes is pragmatism. I try to recognize things as they are and make the best of them, instead of wasting a lot of time wishing things weren't that way. I guess it would be nice to get more enthusiastic about successful things and get more involved and excited, but then you're opening yourself up to a lot of crap that's got to come on the other side of the coin. On balance, I'm satisfied with it the way it is.

EXHIBIT 1

If

Rudyard Kipling

If you can keep your head when all about you
Are losing theirs and blaming it on you,
If you can trust yourself when all men doubt you,
But make allowance for their doubting too;
If you can wait and not be tired by waiting,

Or being lied about, don't deal in lies,
Or being hated, don't give way to hating,
And yet don't look too good, nor talk too wise:

If you can dream—and not make dreams your master;
If you can think—and not make thoughts your aim,
If you can meet with Triumph and Disaster
And treat those two imposters just the same;
If you can bear to have the truth you've spoken
Twisted by knaves to make a trap for fools,
Or watch the things you gave your life to, broken,
And stoop and build 'em up with worn-out tools:

If you can make one heap of all your winnings;
And risk it on one turn of pitch-and-toss,
And lose, and start again at your beginnings
And never breathe a word about your loss;
If you can force your heart and nerve and sinew
To serve your turn long after they are gone
And so hold on when there is nothing in you
Except the Will which says to them: "Hold on!"

If you can talk with crowds and keep your virtue,
Or walk with Kings—nor lose the common touch,
If neither foes nor loving friends can hurt you
If all men count with you, but none too much;
If you can fill the unforgiving minute
With sixty seconds' worth of distance run,
Yours is the Earth and everything that's in it,
And—which is more—you'll be a Man, my son!

HAUSSER FOOD PRODUCTS COMPANY

Steven Palesy
David A. Nadler

Brenda Cooper, the southeastern regional sales manager for the Hausser Food Products (HFP) Company, expressed her concern to a researcher from a well-known eastern business school:

> I think during the past year I've begun to make some progress here, but the situation is a lot more difficult than I thought when I first arrived. Our current methods of selling products just are not adequate, and the people in the field don't seem interested in coming up with new ideas or approaches to selling.

BACKGROUND

Hausser Food Products Company is a leading producer and marketer of infant foods in the United States. The company manufactures and markets a whole line of foods for the infant market, including strained meats, vegetables, fruits, and combination dishes. The product line includes foods that are completely strained, for infants, as well as foods that are partially strained or chopped, for children 6 months of age and older. HFP has traditionally been the leader in this field. The company has no other major product lines. Its products are known for their high quality and its name is well-known to most consumers.

HFP owns its production and warehousing facilities. Its well-developed distribution network provides direct delivery of products to the warehouses and stores of most major food chains. The smallest segment of its market is composed of a limited number of institutions for children that purchase HFP products in bulk.

HFP has had a long history in the infant food business. Traditionally the market leader, it has over the years maintained a market share of approximately 60 percent. During the 1960s, the firm experienced rapid expansion and growth. The number of different types of infant food products increased tremendously to keep up with increasing demand for a greater number of foods and a greater variety of products. From the mid-1960s to the mid-1970s, growth in sales approached 15 percent compounded yearly.

During the past few years, HFP has faced a greatly changing market for infant foods. The sudden decrease in the birth rate brought about major changes in the whole infant food business, and projections of sales had to be altered drastically. In addition, the new concern about food additives, including flavorings, dyes, and preservatives, also had its impact on the baby food market. Many consumer advocates argued that mothers would be much safer in making their own baby foods, rather than purchasing the commercially prepared products, such as those manufactured by HFP. Finally, competition in the baby food market also increased with private brands competing on the basis of price against the nationally advertised brand names.

These changing conditions had been viewed with great alarm by the top management of HFP. The drop in growth of sales (to 3 percent in the most recent year) was accompanied by an even greater drop in earnings, as management felt itself faced with unused plant and warehouse capacity. Management is currently concerned with looking for new ways to stimulate demand for HFP products as well as with the longer-range problem of finding other complementary products to develop and market.

MARKETING ORGANIZATION

In 1975 a researcher from a major business school became involved in studying the marketing organization of HFP as part of a larger-scale research project. His inquiries led him to look closely at the sales department and to investigate some of the problems that were being experienced there.

The marketing function at HFP is directed by a vice president for marketing, who reports directly to the president of HFP. (See Exhibit 1 for a partial organization chart.) The vice president for marketing has five functional directors reporting to him. Each director is responsible for one of the major areas of marketing activity, including market research, market planning, sales promotion, advertising, and sales. The sales department, which has been the focus of much recent concern, is headed by the director of sales. This person directs selling activities in the entire United States. The country is divided into seven major regions, each of which has a regional sales manager. Regions are further divided into districts—each district may include a range of geographic areas, from several states to part of a city, depending upon the particular location. The district manager heads the HFP sales team for each district. The sales team has the ultimate job of selling HFP products to customers, offering promotions, maintaining contact with the customers, ensuring adequate shelf space, etc.

A key element in the marketing organization is the regional sales manager position. This position has been an entry position for many bright, aggressive, and well-trained young people who subsequently have risen to high-level positions within the

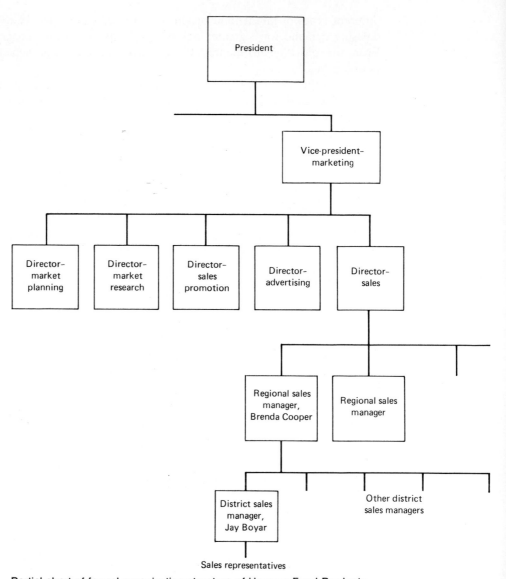

EXHIBIT 1   Partial chart of formal organization structure of Hausser Food Products.

company. The current president of the company, the vice-president for marketing, and three of the five marketing directors began their careers at HFP as regional sales managers.

Brenda Cooper, the southeastern regional sales manager, is fairly typical of the kind of person placed in that position. Brenda entered an MBA program immediately after graduation from one of the best women's colleges in the country. Majoring in marketing, she did extremely well in business school and graduated near the top of her class. Upon graduation she received many job offers and took a position as an assistant product manager in a large nonfood consumer products company. During 4 years at that firm, she performed extremely well both in the management of existing products and in the launching of new products. By the end of her fourth year, however, she was becoming restless and, seeing no opportunities for quick advancement, decided to accept an offer to become a regional sales manager at HFP. The salary was attractive, and she would receive a potentially large bonus based on the profit performance of the entire company. What also attracted Brenda was the possibility of advancement within the company; she had heard that many of the senior staff had started in the regional manager position. At the end of her first year, Brenda is still very much concerned about doing well in her job; in particular, she is adjusting to her role as a manager, with six district managers reporting to her.

SALES PLAN

Much of the activity of the regional managers centers around the yearly sales plan. The sales plan is essentially a budget that includes projections of sales, expenses, and profit. It serves as the basic yardstick against which the performance of regional managers is measured.

Each year the sales plan is developed through a multistage process, as follows.

1 The director of market planning projects sales for the coming year. At the same time, the director of sales asks the regional managers for their projections of sales for the next year. These projections are usually extrapolations of previous-year figures with adjustments for major changes in the market year, if any.

2 The directors of market planning and sales, along with their staffs, negotiate to resolve the differences that usually exist between their two projections (market planning always tends to be higher). Out of these negotiations emerges the sales plan for the coming year. This plan includes budgeted expenditures for promotions, advertising, expenses, and so forth, as well as projected sales volume and profit.

3 The sales director allocates portions of the sales plan to each of the regional managers, who are responsible for meeting the plan within their own region. Regional managers, in turn, allocate parts of the plan to each of their district sales managers and teams.

4 The district managers receive the plan in the form of sales targets and expense budgets for the coming year. The district manager typically receives a relatively low base salary combined with a relatively large yearly bonus, which is based entirely on the performance of the sales team, measured against the sales plan. At the end of the year, the district manager is also given a pool of bonus dollars, also based on team performance against plan, to be distributed to the individual salespeople. Salespeople also receive relatively low base salaries and look to their yearly bonuses as a major source of income.

PROBLEMS OF REGIONAL SALES MANAGERS

As part of the investigation, the researcher visited Brenda Cooper in her Atlanta office. After describing the operations of her region, Brenda began to talk about some of her problems.

> We in HFP are currently wrestling with the problem of a very mature product line. Top management has begun to see the critical need to diversify, in other words to hedge our bets with some other lines of products which are not dependent upon a steadily increasing birth rate. They have been talking about some interesting and exciting things, but any new product is still a few years away from being introduced. . . . In the meantime, it is the job of us out here in the field to come up with new ideas to help keep up sales of our existing product line. I think there must be better ways of selling our product and I am sure that there are new things that we can do to get much more performance out of the line than we are seeing now. The problem is that the best ideas usually come in from the field, from the salespeople themselves, and we really have had very little from our sales teams. They seem content to continue to let the products sell themselves and just keep the shelves stocked, as they have for years. I just don't get any new ideas or approaches from my sales teams.

Brenda and the researcher then reviewed the sales figures for her region, in particular the sales performance of the different areas. Brenda noted:

> Look here at Jay Boyar and his group in Forida. This is a prime example of the kind of problem I am facing. While we have been facing decreasing growth in sales, and actual drop off of sales some places, Jay's group consistently comes in at 10 percent above the sales plan. I've been down there and met with them and I've talked with Jay numerous times, but I can't figure out how they do it. They must be doing something that could be used in other places, but everytime I ask how they do it I get very vague answers, such as, "Well, we work very hard down here" or "We work together as a group; that's how we are able to do well." I'm sure it must be more than that, but I can't seem to get them to open up.

VISIT TO THE FLORIDA SALES TEAM

Intrigued with the Florida figures, the researcher arranged an extensive visit (during January and February) with the Florida sales team. The researcher was given a letter of introduction from the vice president for marketing. This letter explained that the researcher was collecting background information for a major research project that would be of help to the company, that any information collected would be confidential, and that the sales team should provide any needed assistance.

At first Jay Boyar and his group made no attempt to hide their suspicion of the researcher. Slowly, however, as the researcher spent numerous days in the field, riding the Florida roads with each salesperson, they began to trust him and reveal how they felt about their jobs and the company. (See Exhibit 2 for a listing of the staff of the Florida Sales team).

David Berz, the unofficial assistant team manager, talked at length about why he liked his job.

EXHIBIT 2   STAFF OF THE FLORIDA SALES TEAM

Name	Position	Age	Years with HFP	Education
Jay Boyar	District sales manager	52	30	High school
David Berz	Salesperson (assistant manager)	50	30	High school
Neil Portnow	Salesperson	56	36	High school
Alby Siegel	Salesperson	49	18	½ yr college
Mike Wolly	Salesperson	35	12	2 yr college
John Cassis	Salesperson	28	4	BA
Fred Hopengarten	Salesperson	30	3	BA

> What I really like is the freedom. I'm really my own boss most of the time. I don't have to be sitting in an office for the whole day, with some supervisor hanging over my shoulder and looking at all of my work. I get to be outside, here in the car, doing what I like to be doing—being out in the world, talking to people, and making the sale.

Neil Portnow, who had been with the company longer than the other team members, commented on the group:

> This is really a great bunch of guys to work with. I've been with a couple of different groups, but this is the best. I've been together with Dave and Jay for about 15 years now and I wouldn't trade it for anything. Jay is really one of us; he knows that we know how to do our jobs and he doesn't try to put a lot of controls on us. We go about doing the job the way we know is best and that is OK with Jay.
>
> The guys are also good because they help you out. When I was sick last year, they all pitched in to cover my territory so that we could make our plan plus 10 percent without reporting my illness to the company. They can also be hard on someone who doesn't realize how things work here. A few years back, when one of the young guys, Fred, came on with us, he was all fired up. He was going to sell baby food to half the mothers in Florida, personally! He didn't realize that you have to take your time and not waste your effort for the company. The other guys gave him a little bit of a hard time at first—he found his orders getting lost and shipments being changed—but when he finally came to his senses, they treated him great and showed him the ropes.

Picking up on the references to "the company," the researcher asked Neil to talk more about HFP as a place to work:

> It's all pretty simple: the company is out to screw the salespeople. Up in Atlanta and New York, all they are concerned about is the numbers, meeting the plan no matter what. The worst thing is if you work hard, meet the plan, and then keep going so you can earn some decent money. Then they go and change the plan next year. They increase the sales quota so that you have to work harder just to earn the same money! It just doesn't pay to bust your ass. . . .
>
> The people in Atlanta also want all kinds of paperwork: sales reports, call reports, all kinds of reports. If you filled out all of the things that they want you to fill out, you'd spend

all your time doing paperwork and no time selling, looking for new accounts, making cold calls, or any of the things that a salesperson really is supposed to do if he's going to keep on top of his area.

As the researcher talked with the other salespeople, he found general agreement with Neil's views on the company. Alby Siegel added:

> The biggest joke they got going is the suggestion plan. They want us to come up with new ideas about how the company should make more money. The joke of it is, if you come up with an idea that, for instance, makes the company a couple of hundred thousand in profit across the country, they are generous enough to give you $500. That's the top figure, $500 for your idea. That amount of money is an insult. . . .
>
> One thing you have to remember is that in one way or another, we're all in this for the money. Despite what they say, it's not the greatest thing to be out on the road all of the time, staying in motels, fighting the competition. But it's worth it because I can earn more money doing this job than anything else I could do. I can live better than most "professionals" with all their college degrees. . . . Jay is pretty good about the money thing too. He makes sure that we get our bonus, year in and year out, and he keeps the people in Atlanta from taking our bonus checks away from us. He's not management—he's one of us. You can really tell it during the team meetings. Once every 2 months we all meet in Tampa and spend a day going over the accounts and talking about ideas for selling. We spend the whole day in this hotel room, working, and then we go out and spend the whole night on the town, usually drinking. Jay is one of us. . . . Many is the night that I've helped carry him back to the hotel.

After about 4 weeks with the team, the researcher participated in one of the bimonthly team meetings. During lunch, Jay came over to him and began to talk:

> Listen, I need to talk over something with you before we start the afternoon meeting. We trust you so we're going to let you in on our little discovery. You may have noticed that we aren't doing so badly, and you're right. The reason is a little finding made by Alby about 3 years ago. He was out in one of the stores and he noticed that a lot of people buying our products were not mothers of young children, but old people! We started looking around and we began to notice that a lot of older people were buying HFP jars. We talked with some of them and it turns out that they like our stuff, particularly those people who have all kinds of teeth problems.
>
> Since then we've developed a very lucrative trade with a number of the old folks's homes, and we've been able to sell to them through some of the supermarkets who are located in areas where there is a large older population. It's a great new piece of the market: it takes the pressure off us to make plan, and we don't even have to push it very hard to keep making plan and about 10 percent.
>
> We've also been pretty successful in keeping Atlanta from finding out. If they knew, they'd up our plan, leaving us no time to sell, no time to develop new customers, no time to make cold calls, or anything. This way we use this new area as a little cushion, and it helps us to stay on top of our territory. I had to tell you because we'll be talking about the old people this afternoon. The boys seem to think you are OK, so I'm trusting you with it. I hope I'm not making a mistake telling you this.

BACK IN ATLANTA

Soon after the Tampa meeting, the researcher left the Florida sales team and returned to New York. On the way back, he made a final brief visit with Brenda Cooper. He found her even more concerned about her problems.

> I'm getting all kinds of pressure from New York to jack up my sales in the region. They are pushing me to increase the plan for the next year. I really am beginning to feel that my job is on the line on this one. If I can't come up with something that is good in the coming year, the future for me at HFP looks bleak.
>
> At the same time, I'm getting flack from my district managers. They all say that they're running flat out as is and they can't squeeze any more sales out of the district than they already are. Even Jay Boyer is complaining that he may not make plan if we have another increase next year. At the same time, he always seems to pull out his 10 percent extra by the end of the year; I wonder what they're really doing down there.

SOURCES OF SOCIAL POWER

Robert W. LeDuc

The subject of power is one of the most difficult areas of management to understand and to put into perspective. In part, this complexity is due to the fact that the topic of power—its acquisition, its use, and its misuse—often evokes strong negative feelings among people who discuss the issue. McClelland, a researcher who has written extensively on human needs and motivation, has observed that

> In American society in general, individuals are proud of having a high need to Achieve, but dislike being told they have a high need for Power. It is a fine thing to be concerned about doing things well (n Achievement) or making friends (n Affiliation), but it is reprehensible to be concerned about having influence over others (n Power).[1]

On the other hand, it seems apparent that individuals do influence other people all the time and that organizations require their members to exercise power to function effectively. McClelland explains this paradox by suggesting that there are "two faces of power." The *negative* face of power is characterized by dominance and submission and the feeling that if one person wins then the other loses. In this case, the primary motivation for gaining power is to have an impact on others for one's own benefit or simply to experience the sensation of personal power. In contrast, McClelland argues that the *positive* face of power is characterized by "a concern for group goals, for finding those goals that will move men, for helping the group to formulate them, for taking initiative in providing means of achieving them, and for giving group members the feeling of competence they need to work hard for them."[2] In this case, the primary motivation for gaining power is to exercise power for the benefit of others.

[1] David C. McClelland, *Power: The Inner Experience* (New York: Wily, 1975), p. 255.
[2] Ibid., p. 263.

It is not the purpose of this note to exhaustively discuss the definitions of power. However, McClelland's observations raise many important issues that effective managers must resolve as they try to understand the faces of power. These issues cannot all be discussed here. Rather, this note is intended to provide a descriptive framework for subsequent discussions on managerial power and the responsibilities that accompany the exercise of that power.

BASES OF SOCIAL POWER

The subject of this note is a set of ideas that was originally presented by French and Raven in 1959.[3] Since that time their conceptual scheme has been widely used by both managers and researchers. The major thrust of their work was to develop a way of thinking about power that focused on the *sources* of one individual's power to influence another. From the many potential sources of social power, they have identified five especially common and important ones: reward power, coercive power, referent power, legitimate power and expert power.

Reward Power

Reward power is based on the ability of certain persons or groups to control the rewards that will be received by other individuals. Typically, managers derive reward power from their ability to obtain pay increases for subordinates, to recommend them for promotion, and to offer meaningful recognition for good work. French and Raven also suggest that the ability to terminate punishments (for example, to transfer an individual from an undesirable assignment) is also an example of reward power. In general, the amount of available reward power depends on (1) the magnitude of the rewards involved and (2) the probability that a reward will actually be provided for behaving in the desired manner (this probability must be higher than the probability of obtaining a reward without conforming).

Coercive Power

Coercive power is based on the ability of an individual or group to punish another person. It is similar to reward power in that the amount of coercive power depends on the magnitude of the punishments and the probability of punishment for nonconformity. Managers generally derive some potential for coercive power from their ability to demote or fire subordinates. Similarly, managerial groups may use the threat of rejection to exert coercive power over one of their members. In this context, the ability to terminate previous rewards (for example, cutting executive bonuses or transfering a salesperson from a choice sales territory) is also considered by French and Raven to be a source of coercive power.

[3] John R. P. French, Jr., and Bertram H. Raven, "The Bases of Social Power," in D. Cartwright (ed.), *Studies in Social Power* (Ann Arbor: University of Michigan Institute for Social Research, 1959).

French and Raven are careful to point out that the exercise of reward or coercive power does not typically result in a genuine change in attitude on the part of the person being influenced. They suggest that compliance with the influence attempt is a more likely result, that is, a change in observable behavior with no change in underlying attitude. One implication of this argument is that the person exercising reward or coercive power must be able to closely monitor the behavior of those being influenced in order for that power to be effective over time. This is particularly true of coercive power.

The repeated use of coercive power by a manager is likely to create resentment, mistrust, and hostility among those affected. These feelings, in turn, may generate resistance against future attempts at coercion and the possibility of covert retaliation when the opportunity presents itself. Reliance on coercive power, therefore, requires diligent observation of those persons being influenced and some means of ensuring that they will not simply escape coercion by leaving the organization.

On the other hand, French and Raven argue that the successful use of reward power may serve to reinforce the manager's overall position of influence. For example, the manager's reward power for subsequent influence attempts is enhanced because others are likely to attach a new, higher probability to the prospect that they will actually be rewarded for behaving in the desired manner. Anticipation of future rewards also provides an incentive to stay with the organization. In addition, it is possible that the mutually beneficial arrangement implicit in the successful use of reward power may create additional bases of managerial power, such as those outlined below.

Referent Power

The basis of *referent power* is the desire of one person P to "be like" or to "identify with" another person or group O. In this context, the process of identification implies consciously or unconsciously taking on another person's behavior and expectations as one's own. French and Raven describe the origins of referent power as follows:

> If O is a person toward whom P is highly attracted, P will have a desire to become closely associated with O. If O is an attractive group, P will have a feeling of membership or a desire to join. . . . P's identification with O can be established or maintained if P behaves, believes, and perceives as O does. Accordingly O has the ability to influence P, even though P may be unaware of this referent power. . . . The stronger the identification of P with O the greater the referent power of O over P.[4]

Managers may have referent power because they are part of a group (management) that others aspire to join or because of other more personal qualities with which others identify. Note that the person being influenced may be aware or unaware of this referent power. French and Raven suggest that referent power is likely to be especially pervasive when an individual is not conscious of his or her identification with a person or group.

---

[4] Ibid., pp. 161–162.

The following examples may help clarify the distinction between referent power and reward or coercive power. If a person is influenced by a group because he or she fears ridicule or rejection, that would be an example of coercive power. On the other hand, if a person accepts the group's influence to win praise from other members, that would be labeled reward power. If a person is influenced by the group because he or she finds the group's expectations for behavior to be attractive, that would be an example of referent power.

Legitimate Power

Legitimate power exists when people comply with the directions or wishes of an influencing person because they believe he or she has a legitimate right to influence them and that they have an obligation to accept that influence.

French and Raven outline three common bases of legitimate power. The first occurs when cultural values ascribe the right to people who possess certain characteristics (such as age, intelligence, or caste) to prescribe behavior for other people. Another basis of legitimate power is the acceptance of a given social structure by the members of a group or organization. In formal organizations (such as companies and government agencies), much of the influence of "officeholders" resides in their offices rather than in themselves as individuals. French and Raven give the following brief examples of roles that are vested with legitimate power: "A judge has a right to levy fines, a foreman to assign work, a priest is justified in prescribing religious beliefs, and it is management's perogative to make certain decisions."[5] An organization's hierarchy of authority usually implies that people who hold certain offices or titles have the right to prescribe (within limits) the behavior of others lower in the structure.

French and Raven cite "designation by a legitimizing agent" as a third source of legitimate power. In such cases, the designated (or delegated) person's power is seen as legitimate by those being influenced because the person has been granted that power by a legitimizing agent whose authority they accept. An example of this would be a vice president delegating authority in a particular area to a department head.

Note that legitimate power requires that the person being influenced willingly accept the legitimacy of the influence attempt; that is, it must be consistent with his or her values. When individuals go along with the boss even though they don't believe the boss has the right to prescribe behavior in a particular area, it is probably because of the boss's power to reward and/or punish and not a case of legitimate power. Such a case highlights French and Raven's point that the exercise of legitimate power is often explicitly limited.

The areas in which legitimate power may be exercised are generally specified along with the designation of that power. A job description, for example, usually specifies supervisory activities and also designates the person to whom the job-holder is responsible for the duties described. Some bases for legitimate authority carry with them a very broad range. Culturally derived bases for legitimate power are often especially broad. It is not uncom-

[5] Ibid., p. 160.

mon to find cultures in which a member of a given caste can legitimately prescribe behavior for all members of lower castes in practically all regions. More common however, are instances of legitimate power where the range is specifically and narrowly prescribed. A sergeant in the army is given a specific set of regions within which he can legitimately prescribe behavior for his men.[6]

Expert Power

Expert power derives from recognition of an individual's knowledge, skill, or experience in a particular area. Evaluations of expertise may be made relative to one's own knowledge as well as to an absolute standard. Managers often develop expert power in a number of areas. For example, they are often more knowledgeable than others in subject areas directly related to their task, for example, engineering design, inventory control, and finance. In addition, they may be more familiar with company policies and procedures than their subordinates or have a better understanding of "company politics."

French and Raven point out that expert power may also be limited to specific areas. The expert is often seen as having superior knowledge or ability in very specific areas and his or her power will generally be limited to these areas, although some "halo effect" may occur. In addition, whenever expert influence develops, it is probably necessary for the person being influenced to believe that the other person is knowledgeable and that he or she can trust the other person to be truthful.

SUMMARY

In this brief note, five common sources of managerial power have been identified and discussed: reward power, coercive power, referent power, legitimate power, and expert power. In actual practice, a manager's influence within his or her organization is almost never based on just one of these sources of power. A manager often makes use of all sources of power simultaneously. In other cases, a manager may temporarily rely on those sources of power that seem particularly relevant to a given situation.

In the final analysis, a manager's influence is based on a complex network of relationships with other people that changes substantially over time. Patterns of power and influence are an integral part of these relationships. Just as important, however, is the recognition that managers are also strongly *dependent* on the activities of others to accomplish their goals. Typically, the most important relationships to a manager involve mutual influence and mutual dependence. Consequently, it is the acceptance and quality of a manager's decisions concerning the exercise of power that most often determine whether he or she will gain or lose influence over important others.

[6] Ibid., pp. 160–161.

POWER, DEPENDENCE, AND EFFECTIVE MANAGEMENT

John P. Kotter

Americans, as a rule, are not very comfortable with power or with its dynamics. We often distrust and question the motives of people whom we think actively seek power. We have a certain fear of being manipulated. Even those people who think the dynamics of power are inevitable and needed often feel somewhat guilty when they themselves mobilize and use power. Simply put, the overall attitude and feeling toward power, which can easily be traced to the nation's very birth, is negative. In his enormously popular *The Greening of America*, Charles Reich reflects the views of many when he writes, "It is not the misuse of power that is evil; the very existence of power is evil."[1]

One of the many consequences of this attitude is that power as a topic for rational study and dialogue has not received much attention, even in managerial circles. If the reader doubts this, all he or she need do is flip through some textbooks, journals, or advanced management course descriptions. The word *power* rarely appears.

This lack of attention to the subject of power merely adds to the already enormous confusion and misunderstanding surrounding the topic of power and management. And this misunderstanding is becoming increasingly burdensome because in today's large and complex organizations the effective performance of most managerial jobs requires one to be skilled at the acquisition and use of power.

From my own observations, I suspect that a large number of managers—especially the young, well-educated ones—perform significantly below their potential because they do not understand the dynamics of power and because they have not nurtured and developed the instincts needed to effectively acquire and use power.

---

[1] Charles A. Reich, *The Greening of America: How the Youth Revolution Is Trying to Make America Liveable* (New York: Random House, 1970).

In this article I hope to clear up some of the confusion regarding power and managerial work by providing tentative answers to three questions:

1 Why are the dynamics of power necessarily an important part of managerial processes?
2 How do effective managers acquire power?
3 How and for what purposes do effective managers use power?

I will not address questions related to the misuse of power, but not because I think they are unimportant. The fact that some managers, some of the time, acquire and use power mostly for their own aggrandizement is obviously a very important issue that deserves attention and careful study. But that is a complex topic unto itself and one that has already received more attention than the subject of this article.

RECOGNIZING DEPENDENCE IN THE MANAGER'S JOB

One of the distinguishing characteristics of a typical manager is how dependent he is on the activities of a variety of other people to perform his job effectively.[2] Unlike doctors and mathematicians, whose performance is more directly dependent on their own talents and efforts, a manager can be dependent in varying degrees on superiors, subordinates, peers in other parts of the organization, the subordinates of peers, outside suppliers, customers, competitors, unions, regulating agencies, and many others.

These dependency relationships are an inherent part of managerial jobs because of two organizational facts of life: division of labor and limited resources. Because the work in organizations is divided into specialized divisions, departments, and jobs, managers are made directly or indirectly dependent on many others for information, staff services, and cooperation in general. Because of their organization's limited resources, managers are also dependent on their external environments for support. Without some minimal cooperation from suppliers, competitors, unions, regulatory agencies, and customers, managers cannot help their organizations survive and achieve their objectives.

Dealing with these dependencies and the manager's subsequent vulnerability is an important and difficult part of a manager's job because, while it is theoretically possible that all of these people and organizations would automatically act in just the manner that a manager wants and needs, such is almost never the case in reality. All the people on whom a manager is dependent have limited time, energy, and talent, for which there are competing demands.

Some people may be uncooperative because they are too busy elsewhere, and some because they are not really capable of helping. Others may well have goals, values, and beliefs that are quite different and in conflict with the manager's and may therefore have no desire whatsoever to help or cooperate. This is obviously true of a competing company and sometimes of a union, but it can also apply to a boss who is

---

[2] See Leonard R. Sayles, *Managerial Behavior: Administration in Complex Organizations* (New York: McGraw-Hill, 1964) as well as Rosemary Stewart, *Managers and Their Jobs* (London: Macmillan, 1967) and *Contrasts in Management* (London: McGraw-Hill, 1976).

feeling threatened by a manager's career progress or to a peer whose objectives clash with the manager's.

Indeed, managers often find themselves dependent on many people (and things) whom they do not directly control and who are not "cooperating." This is the key to one of the biggest frustrations managers feel in their jobs, even in the top ones, which the following example illustrates:

> After nearly a year of rumors, it was finally announced in May 1974 that the president of ABC Corporation had been elected chairman of the board and that Jim Franklin, the vice president of finance, would replace him as president. While everyone at ABC was aware that a shift would take place soon, it was not at all clear before the announcement who would be the next president. Most people had guessed it would be Phil Cook, the marketing vice president.
>
> Nine months into his job as chief executive officer, Franklin found that Phil Cook (still the marketing vice president) seemed to be fighting him in small and subtle ways. There was never anything blatant, but Cook just did not cooperate with Franklin as the other vice presidents did. Shortly after being elected, Franklin had tried to bypass what he saw as a potential conflict with Cook by telling him that he would understand if Cook would prefer to move somewhere else where he could be a CEO also. Franklin said that it would be a big loss to the company but that he would be willing to help Cook in a number of ways if he wanted to look for a presidential opportunity elsewhere. Cook had thanked him but had said that family and community commitments would prevent him from relocating and all CEO opportunities were bound to be in a different city.
>
> Since the situation did not improve after the tenth and eleventh months, Franklin seriously considered forcing Cook out. When he thought about the consequences of such a move, Franklin became more and more aware of just how dependent he was on Cook. Marketing and sales were generally the keys to success in their industry, and the company's sales force was one of the best, if not the best, in the industry. Cook had been with the company for 25 years. He had built a strong personal relationship with many of the people in the sales force and was universally popular. A mass exodus just might occur if Cook were fired. The loss of a large number of salesmen, or even a lot of turmoil in the department, could have a serious effect on the company's performance.
>
> After one year as chief executive officer, Franklin found that the situation between Cook and himself had not improved and had become a constant source of frustration.

As a person gains more formal authority in an organization, the areas in which he or she is vulnerable increase and become more complex rather than the reverse. As the previous example suggests, it is not at all unusual for the president of an organization to be in a highly dependent position, a fact often not apparent to either the outsider or to the lower level manager who covets the president's job.

A considerable amount of the behavior of highly successful managers that seems inexplicable in light of what management texts usually tell us managers do becomes understandable when one considers a manager's need for, and efforts at, managing his or her relationships with others.[3] To be able to plan, organize, budget, staff, control, and evaluate, managers need some control over the many people on whom they are dependent. Trying to control others solely by directing them and on the basis of the power associated with one's position simply will not work—first, because managers are always dependent on some people over whom they have no formal authority, and second, because virtually no one in modern organizations will passively accept and completely obey a constant stream of orders from someone just because he or she is the "boss."

Trying to influence others by means of persuasion alone will not work either. Although it is very powerful and possibly the single most important method of influence, persuasion has some serious drawbacks too. To make it work requires time (often lots of it), skill, and information on the part of the persuader. And persuasion can fail simply because the other person chooses not to listen or does not listen carefully.

This is not to say that directing people on the basis of the formal power of one's position and persuasion are not important means by which successful managers cope. They obviously are. But, even taken together, they are not usually enough.

Successful managers cope with their dependence on others by being sensitive to it, by eliminating or avoiding unnecessary dependence, and by establishing power over those others. Good managers then use that power to help them plan, organize, staff, budget, evaluate, and so on. *In other words, it is primarily because of the dependence inherent in managerial jobs that the dynamics of power necessarily form an important part of a manager's processes.*

An argument that took place during a middle management training seminar I participated in a few years ago helps illustrate further this important relationship between a manager's need for power and the degree of his or her dependence on others:

> Two participants, both managers in their thirties, got into a heated disagreement regarding the acquisition and use of power by managers. One took the position that power was absolutely central to managerial work, while the other argued that it was virtually irrelevant. In support of their positions, each described a very "successful" manager with whom he worked. In one of these examples, the manager seemed to be constantly developing and using power, while in the other, such behavior was rare. Subsequently, both seminar participants were asked to describe their successful managers' jobs in terms of the dependence *inherent* in those jobs.
>
> The young manager who felt power was unimportant described a staff vice president in a small company who was dependent only on his immediate subordinates, his peers, and his boss. This person, Joe Phillips, had to depend on his subordinates to do their jobs appropriately, but, if necessary, he could fill in for any of them or secure replacement for them rather easily. He also had considerable formal authority over them; that is, he could give them raises and new assignments, recommend promotions, and fire them. He was moderately dependent on the other four vice presidents in the company for information and cooperation.

---

[3] I am talking about the type of inexplicable differences that Henry Mintzberg has found; see his article "The Manager's Job: Folklore and Fact," *Harvard Business Review*, July-August 1975, p. 49.

They were likewise dependent on him. The president had considerable formal authority over Phillips but was also moderately dependent on him for help, expert advice, the service his staff performed, other information, and general cooperation.

The second young manager—the one who felt power was very important—described a service department manager, Sam Weller, in a large, complex, and growing company who was in quite a different position. Weller was dependent not only on his boss for rewards and information, but also on 30 other individuals who made up the divisional and corporate top management. And while his boss, like Phillips's, was moderately dependent on him too, most of the top managers were not. Because Weller's subordinates, unlike Phillips's, had people reporting to them, Weller was dependent not only on his subordinates but also on his subordinates' subordinates. Because he could not himself easily replace or do most of their technical jobs, unlike Phillips, he was very dependent on all these people.

In addition, for critical supplies, Weller was dependent on two other department managers in the division. Without their timely help, it was impossible for his department to do its job. These departments, however, did not have similar needs for Weller's help and cooperation. Weller was also dependent on local labor union officials and on a federal agency that regulated the division's industry. Both could shut his division down if they wanted.

Finally, Weller was dependent on two outside suppliers of key materials. Because of the volume of his department's purchase relative to the size of these two companies, he had little power over them.

Under these circumstances, it is hardly surprising that Sam Weller had to spend considerable time and effort acquiring and using power to manage his many dependencies, while Joe Phillips did not.

As this example also illustrates, not all management jobs require an incumbent to be able to provide the same amount of successful power-oriented behavior. But most management jobs today are more like Weller's than Phillips's. And, perhaps more important, the trend over the past two or three decades is away from jobs like Phillips's and toward jobs like Weller's. So long as our technologies continue to become more complex, the average organization continues to grow larger, and the average industry continues to become more competitive and regulated, that trend will continue; as it does so, the effective acquisition and use of power by managers will become even more important.

ESTABLISHING POWER IN RELATIONSHIPS

To help cope with the dependency relationships inherent in their jobs, effective managers create, increase, or maintain four different types of power over others.[4] Having

---

[4] These categories closely resemble the five developed by John R. P. French and Bertram Raven; see "The Base of Social Power" in *Group Dynamics: Research and Theory,* Dorwin Cartwright and Alvin Zandler, eds. (New York: Harper & Row, 1968), Chapter 20. Three of the categories are similar to the types of "authority"-based power described by Max Weber in *The Theory of Social and Economic Organization* (New York: Free Press, 1947).

power based in these areas puts the manager in a position both to influence those people on whom he or she is dependent when necessary and to avoid being hurt by any of them.

Sense of Obligation

One of the ways that successful managers generate power in their relationships with others is to create a sense of obligation in those others. When the manager is successful, the others feel that they should—rightly—allow the manager to influence them within certain limits.

Successful managers often go out of their way to do favors for people whom they expect will feel an obligation to return those favors. As can be seen in the following description of a manager by one of his subordinates, some people are very skilled at identifying opportunities for doing favors that cost them very little but that others appreciate very much:

> Most of the people here would walk over hot coals in their bare feet if my boss asked them to. He has an incredible capacity to do little things that mean a lot to people. Today, for example, in his junk mail he came across an advertisement for something that one of my subordinates had in passing once mentioned that he was shopping for. So my boss routed it to him. That probably took 15 seconds of his time, and yet my subordinate really appreciated it. To give you another example, two weeks ago he somehow learned that the purchasing manager's mother had died. On his way home that night, he stopped off at the funeral parlor. Our purchasing manager was, of course, there at the time. I bet he'll remember that brief visit for quite a while.

Recognizing that most people believe that friendship carries with it certain obligations ("A friend in need. . ."), successful managers often try to develop true friendships with those on whom they are dependent. They will also make formal and informal deals in which they give something up in exchange for certain future obligations.

Belief in a Manager's Expertise

A second way successful managers gain power is by building reputations as "experts" in certain matters. Believing in the manager's expertise, others will often defer to the manager on those matters. Managers usually establish this type of power through visible achievement. The larger the achievement and the more visible it is, the more power the manager tends to develop.

One of the reasons that managers display concern about their "professional reputations" and their "track records" is that they have an impact on others' beliefs about their expertise. These factors become particularly important in large settings, where most people have only secondhand information about most other people's professional competence, as the following shows:

> Herb Randley and Bert Kline were both 35-year-old vice presidents in a large research and development organization. According to their closest associates, they

were equally bright and competent in their technical fields and as managers. Yet Randley had a much stronger professional reputation in most parts of the company, and his ideas generally carried much more weight. Close friends and associates claim the reason that Randley is so much more powerful is related to a number of tactics that he has used more than Kline has.

Randley has published more scientific papers and managerial articles than Kline. Randley has been more selective in the assignments he has worked on, choosing those that are visible and that require his strong suits. He has given more speeches and presentations on projects that are his own achievements. And in meetings in general, he is allegedly forceful in areas where he has expertise and silent in those where he does not.

Identification with a Manager

A third method by which managers gain power is by fostering others' unconscious identification with them or with ideas they "stand for." Sigmund Freud was the first to describe this phenomenon, which is most clearly seen in the way people look up to "charismatic" leaders. Generally, the more a person finds a manager both consciously and (more important) unconsciously an ideal person, the more he or she will defer to that manager.

Managers develop power based on others' idealized views of them in a number of ways. They try to look and behave in ways that others respect. They go out of their way to be visible to their employees and to give speeches about their organizational goals, values, and ideals. They even consider, while making hiring and promotion decisions, whether they will be able to develop this type of power over the candidates:

> One vice president of sales in a moderate-size manufacturing company was reputed to be so much in control of his sales force that he could get them to respond to new and different marketing programs in a third of the time taken by the company's best competitors. His power over his employees was based primarily on their strong identification with him and what he stood for. Emigrating to the United States at age 17, this person worked his way up "from nothing." When made a sales manager in 1965, he began recruiting other young immigrants and sons of immigrants from his former country. When made vice president of sales in 1970, he continued to do so. In 1975, 85 percent of his sales force was made up of people whom he hired directly or who were hired by others he brought in.

Perceived Dependence on a Manager

The final way that an effective manager often gains power is by feeding others' beliefs that they are dependent on the manager either for help or for not being hurt. The more they perceive they are dependent, the more most people will be inclined to cooperate with such a manager.

There are two methods that successful managers often use to create perceived dependence.

Finding & Acquiring Resources   In the first, the manager identifies and secures (if necessary) resources that another person requires to perform his job, that he does not possess, and that are not readily available elsewhere. These resources include such things as authority to make certain decisions; control of money, equipment, and office space; access to important people; information and control of information channels; and subordinates. Then the manager takes action so that the other person correctly perceives that the manager has such resources and is willing and ready to use them to help (or hinder) the other person. Consider the following extreme—but true—example.

When young Tim Babcock was put in charge of a division of a large manufacturing company and told to "turn it around," he spent the first few weeks studying it from afar. He decided that the division was in disastrous shape and that he would need to take many large steps quickly to save it. To be able to do that, he realized he needed to develop considerable power fast over most of the division's management and staff. He did the following:

He gave the division's management two hours' notice of his arrival.
He arrived in a limousine with six assistants.
He immediately called a meeting of the 40 top managers.
He outlined briefly his assessment of the situation, his commitment to turn things around, and the basic direction he wanted things to move in.
He then fired the four top managers in the room and told them that they had to be out of the building in two hours.
He then said he would personally dedicate himself to sabotaging the career of anyone who tried to block his efforts to save the division.
He ended the 60-minute meeting by announcing that his assistants would set up appointments for him with each of them starting at 7:00 A.M. the next morning.

Throughout the critical six-month period that followed, those who remained at the division generally cooperated energetically with Mr. Babcock.

Affecting Perceptions of Resources   A second way effective managers gain these types of power is by influencing other persons' perceptions of the manager's resources.[5] In settings where many people are involved and where the manager does not interact continuously with those he or she is dependent on, those people will seldom possess "hard facts" regarding what relevant resources the manager commands directly or indirectly (through others), what resources he will command in the future, or how prepared he is to use those resources to help or hinder them. They will be forced to make their own judgments.

[5] For an excellent discussion of this method, see Richard E. Neustadt, *Presidential Power* (New York: Wiley, 1960).

Insofar as a manager can influence people's judgments, he can generate much more power than one would generally ascribe to him in light of the reality of his resources.

In trying to influence people's judgments, managers pay considerable attention to the "trappings" of power and to their own reputations and images. Among other actions, they sometimes carefully select, decorate, and arrange their offices in ways that give signs of power. They associate with people or organizations that are known to be powerful or that others perceive as powerful. Managers selectively foster rumors concerning their own power. Indeed, those who are particularly skilled at creating power in this way tend to be very sensitive to the impressions that all their actions might have on others.

Formal Authority

Before discussing how managers use their power to influence others, it is useful to see how formal authority relates to power. By *formal authority,* I mean those elements that automatically come with a managerial job—perhaps a title, an office, a budget, the right to make certain decisions, a set of subordinates, a reporting relationship, and so on.

Effective managers use the elements of formal authority as resources to help them develop any or all of the four types of power previously discussed, just as they use other resources (such as their education). Two managers with the same formal authority can have very different amounts of power entirely because of the way they have used that authority. For example:

By sitting down with employees who are new or with people who are starting new projects and clearly specifying who has the formal authority to do what, one manager creates a strong sense of obligation in others to defer to his authority later.

By selectively withholding or giving the high-quality service his department can provide other departments, one manager makes other managers clearly perceive that they are dependent on him.

On its own, then, formal authority does not guarantee a certain amount of power; it is only a resource that managers can use to generate power in their relationships.

EXERCISING POWER TO INFLUENCE OTHERS

Successful managers use the power they develop in their relationships, along with persuasion, to influence people on whom they are dependent to behave in ways that make it possible for the managers to get their jobs done effectively. They use their power to influence others directly, face to face, and in more indirect ways.

Face-to-Face Influence

The chief advantage of influencing others directly by exercising any of the types of power is speed. If the power exists and the manager correctly understands the nature

EXHIBIT 1 METHODS OF INFLUENCE

Face-to-face methods	What they can influence	Advantages	Drawbacks
Exercise obligation-based power.	Behavior within zone that the other perceives as legitimate in light of the obligation.	Quick. Requires no outlay of tangible resources	If the request is outside the acceptable zone, it will fail; if it is too far outside, others might see it as illegitimate.
Exercise power based on perceived expertise.	Attitudes and behavior within the zone of perceived expertise.	Quick. Requires no outlay of tangible resources.	If the request is outside the acceptable zone, it will fail; if it is too far outside, others might see it as illegitimate.
Exercise power based on identification with a manager.	Attitudes and behavior that are not in conflict with the ideals that underlie the identification.	Quick. Requires no expenditure of limited resources.	Restricted to influence attempts that are not in conflict with the ideals that underlie the identification.
Exercise power based on perceived dependence.	Wide range of behavior that can be monitored.	Quick. Can often succeed when other methods fail.	Repeated influence attempts encourage the other to gain power over the influencer.
Coercively exercise power based on perceived dependence.	Wide range of behavior that can be easily monitored.	Quick. Can often succeed when other methods fail.	Invites retaliation. Very risky.
Use persuasion.	Very wide range of attitudes and behavior.	Can produce internalized motivation that does not require monitoring. Requires no power or outlay of scarce material resources.	Can be very time-consuming. Requires other person to listen.
Combine these methods.	Depends on the exact combination.	Can be more potent and less risky than using a single method.	More costly than using a single method.
Indirect methods	**What they can influence**	**Advantages**	**Drawbacks**
Manipulate the other's environment by using any or all of the face-to-face methods.	Wide range of behavior and attitudes.	Can succeed when face-to-face methods fail.	Can be time-consuming. Is complex to implement. Is very risky, especially if used frequently.
Change the forces that continuously act on the individual: Formal organizational arrangements. Informal social arrangements. Technology. Resources available. Statement of organizational goals.	Wide range of behavior and attitudes on a continuous basis.	Has continuous influence, not just a one-shot effect. Can have a very powerful impact.	Often requires a considerable power outlay to achieve.

and strength of it, he can influence the other person with nothing more than a brief request or command:

- Jones thinks Smith feels obliged to him for past favors. Furthermore, Jones thinks that his request to speed up a project by two days probably falls within a zone that Smith would consider legitimate in light of his own definition of his obligation to Jones. So Jones simply calls Smith and makes his request. Smith pauses for only a second and says yes, he'll do it.

- Manager Johnson has some power based on perceived dependence over manager Baker. When Johnson tells Baker that he wants a report done in 24 hours, Baker grudgingly considers the costs of compliance, of noncompliance, and of complaining to higher authorities. He decides that doing the report is the least costly action and tells Johnson he will do it.

- Young Porter identifies strongly with Marquette, an older manager who is not his boss. Porter thinks Marquette is the epitome of a great manager and tries to model himself after him. When Marquette asks Porter to work on a special project "that could be very valuable in improving the company's ability to meet new competitive products," Porter agrees without hesitation and works 15 hours per week above and beyond his normal hours to get the project done and done well.

When used to influence others, each of the four types of power has different advantages and drawbacks. For example, power based on perceived expertise or on identification with a manager can often be used to influence attitudes as well as someone's immediate behavior and thus can have a lasting impact. It is very difficult to influence attitudes by using power based on perceived dependence, but if it can be done, it usually has the advantage of being able to influence a much broader range of behavior than the other methods do. When exercising power based on perceived expertise, for example, one can only influence attitudes and behavior within that narrow zone defined by the "expertise."

The drawbacks associated with the use of power based on perceived dependence are particularly important to recognize. A person who feels dependent on a manager for rewards (or lack of punishments) might quickly agree to a request from the manager but then not follow through—especially if the manager cannot easily find out if the person has obeyed or not. Repeated influence attempts based on perceived dependence also seem to encourage the other person to try to gain some power to balance the manager's. And perhaps most important; using power based on perceived dependence in a coercive way is very risky. Coercion invites retaliation.

For instance, in the example in which Tim Babcock took such extreme steps to save the division he was assigned to "turn around," his development and use of power based on perceived dependence could have led to mass resignation and the collapse of the division. Babcock fully recognized this risk, however, and behaved as he did because he felt there was simply *no other way* that he could gain the very large amount of quick cooperation needed to save the division.

Effective managers will often draw on more than one form of power to influence someone, or they will combine power with persuasion. In general, they do so because a combination can be more potent and less risky than any single method, as the following description shows:

One of the best managers we have in the company has lots of power based on one thing or another over most people. But he seldom if ever just tells or asks someone to do something. He almost always takes a few minutes to try to persuade them. The power he has over people generally induces them to listen carefully and certainly disposes them to be influenced. That, of course, makes the persuasion process go quickly and easily. And he never risks getting the other person mad or upset by making what that person thinks is an unfair request or command.

It is also common for managers not to coercively exercise power based on perceived dependence by itself, but to combine it with other methods to reduce the risk of retaliation. In this way, managers are able to have a large impact without leaving the bitter aftertaste of punishment alone.

Indirect Influence Methods

Effective managers also rely on two types of less direct methods to influence those on whom they are dependent. In the first way, they use any or all of the face-to-face methods to influence other people, who in turn have some specific impact on a desired person.

Product manager Stein needed plant manager Billings to "sign off" on a new product idea (Product X) which Billings thought was terrible. Stein decided that there was no way he could logically persuade Billings because Billings just would not listen to him. With time, Stein felt, he could have broken through that barrier. But he did not have that time. Stein also realized that Billings would never, just because of some deal or favor, sign off on a product he did not believe in. Stein also felt it not worth the risk of trying to force Billings to sign off, so here is what he did:

• On Monday, Stein got Reynolds, a person Billings respected, to send Billings two market research studies that were very favorable to Product X, with a note attached saying, "Have you seen this? I found them rather surprising. I am not sure if I entirely believe them, but still. . . ."

• On Tuesday, Stein got a representative of one of the company's biggest customers to mention casually to Billings on the phone that he had heard a rumor about Product X being introduced soon and was "glad to see you guys are on your toes as usual."

• On Wednesday, Stein had two industrial engineers stand about three feet away from Billings as they were waiting for a meeting to begin and talk about the favorable test results on Product X.

• On Thursday, Stein set up a meeting to talk about Product X with Billings and invited only people whom Billings liked or respected and who also felt favorably about Product X.

• On Friday, Stein went to see Billings and asked him if he was willing to sign off on Product X. He was.

This type of manipulation of the environments of others can influence both behavior and attitudes and can often succeed when other influence methods fail. But it has a number of serious drawbacks. It takes considerable time and energy, and it is quite risky. Many people think it is wrong to try to influence others in this way, even people who, without consciously recognizing it, use this technique themselves. If they think someone is trying, or has tried, to manipulate them, they may retaliate. Furthermore, people who gain the reputation of being manipulators seriously undermine their own capacities for developing power and for influencing others. Almost no one, for example, will want to identify with a manipulator. And virtually no one accepts, at face value, a manipulator's sincere attempts at persuasion. In extreme cases, a reputation as a manipulator can completely ruin a manager's career.

A second way in which managers indirectly influence others is by making permanent changes in an individual's or a group's environment. They change job descriptions, the formal systems that measure performance, the extrinsic incentives available, the tools, people, and other resources that the people or groups work with, the architecture, the norms or values of work groups, and so on. If the manager is successful in making the changes, and the changes have the desired effect on the individual or group, that effect will be sustained over time.

Effective managers recognize that changes in the forces that surround a person can have great impact on that person's behavior. Unlike many of the other influence methods, this one doesn't require a large expenditure of limited resources or effort on the part of the manager on an ongoing basis. Once such a change has been successfully made, it works independently of the manager.

This method of influence is used by all managers to some degree. Many, however, use it sparingly simply because they do not have the power to change the forces acting on the person they wish to influence. In many organizations, only the top managers have the power to change the formal measurement systems, the extrinsic incentives available, the architecture, and so on.

GENERATING AND USING POWER SUCCESSFULLY

Managers who are successful at acquiring considerable power and using it to manage their dependence on others tend to share a number of common characteristics:

1 They are sensitive to what others consider to be legitimate behavior in acquiring and using power. They recognize that the four types of power carry with them certain "obligations" regarding their acquisition and use. A person who gains a considerable amount of power based on his perceived expertise is generally expected to be an expert in certain areas. If it ever becomes publicly known that the person is clearly not an expert in those areas, such a person will probably be labeled a "fraud" and will not only lose his power but will suffer other reprimands too.

A person with whom a number of people identify is expected to act like an ideal leader. If he clearly lets people down, he will not only lose that power, he will also suffer the righteous anger of his ex-followers. Many managers who have created or used power based on perceived dependence in ways that their employees have felt unfair, such as in requesting overtime work, have ended up with unions.

2 They have good intuitive understanding of the various types of power and methods of influence. They are sensitive to what types of power are easiest to develop with different types of people. They recognize, for example, that professionals tend to be more influenced by perceived expertise than by other forms of power. They also have a grasp of all the various methods of influence and what each can accomplish, at what costs, and with what risks. (See Exhibit 1.) They are good at recognizing the specific conditions in any situation and then at selecting an influence method that is compatible with those conditions.

3 They tend to develop all the types of power, to some degree, and they use all the influence methods mentioned in the exhibit. Unlike managers who are not very good at influencing people, effective managers usually do not think that only some of the methods are useful or that only some of the methods are moral. They recognize that any of the methods, used under the right circumstances, can help contribute to organizational effectiveness with few dysfunctional consequences. At the same time, they generally try to avoid those methods that are more risky than others and those that may have dysfunctional consequences. For example, they manipulate the environment of others only when absolutely necessary.

4 They establish career goals and seek out managerial positions that allow them to successfully develop and use power. They look for jobs, for example, that use their backgrounds and skills to control or manage some critically important problem or environmental contingency that an organization faces. They recognize that success in that type of job makes others dependent on them and increases their own perceived expertise. They also seek jobs that do not demand a type or a volume of power that is inconsistent with their own skills.

5 They use all of their resources, formal authority, and power to develop still more power. To borrow Edward Banfield's metaphor, they actually look for ways to "invest" their power where they might secure a high positive return.[6] For example, by asking a person to do him two important favors, a manager might be able to finish his construction program one day ahead of schedule. That request may cost him most of the obligation-based power he has over that person, but in return he may significantly increase his perceived expertise as a manager of construction projects in the eyes of everyone in his organization.

Just as in investing money, there is always some risk involved in using power this way; it is possible to get a zero return for a sizable investment, even for the most powerful manager. Effective managers do not try to avoid risks. Instead, they look for prudent risks, just as they do when investing capital.

6 Effective managers engage in power-oriented behavior in ways that are tempered by maturity and self-control.[7] They seldom, if ever, develop and use power in impulsive ways or for their own aggrandizement.

7 Finally, they also recognize and accept as legitimate that, in using these methods, they clearly influence other people's behavior and lives. Unlike many less effective managers, they are reasonably comfortable in using power to influence people. They recognize, often only intuitively, what this article is all about—that their attempts to establish power and use it are an absolutely necessary part of the successful fulfillment of their difficult managerial role.

---

[6] See Edward C. Banfield, *Political Influence* (New York: Free Press, 1965), Chapter 11.
[7] See David C. McClelland and David H. Burnham, "Power Is the Great Motivator," Harvard Business Review, March-April 1976, p. 100.

HOW TO CHOOSE A LEADERSHIP PATTERN

Robert Tannenbaum
Warren Schmidt

- "I put most problems into my group's hands and leave it to them to carry the ball from there. I serve merely as a catalyst, mirroring back the people's thoughts and feelings so that they can better understand them."
- "It's foolish to make decisions oneself on matters that affect people. I always talk things over with my subordinates, but I make it clear to them that I'm the one who has to have the final say."
- "Once I have decided on a course of action, I do my best to sell my ideas to my employees."
- "I'm being paid to lead. If I let a lot of other people make the decisions I should be making, then I'm not worth my salt."
- "I believe in getting things done. I can't waste time calling meetings. Someone has to call the shots around here, and I think it should be me."

Each of these statements represents a point of view about "good leadership." Considerable experience, factual data, and theoretical principles could be cited to support each statement, even though they seem to be inconsistent when placed together. Such contradictions point up the dilemma in which the modern manager frequently finds himself.

NEW PROBLEM

The problem of how the modern manager can be "democratic" in his relations with subordinates and at the same time maintain the necessary authority and control in the organization for which he is responsible has come into focus increasingly in recent years.

Earlier in the century this problem was not so acutely felt. The successful executive was generally pictured as possessing intelligence, imagination, initiative, the capacity to make rapid (and generally wise) decisions, and the ability to inspire subordinates. People tended to think of the world as being divided into "leaders" and "followers."

New Focus

Gradually, however, from the social sciences emerged the concept of "group dynamics" with its focus on *members* of the group rather than solely on the leader. Research efforts of social scientists underscored the importance of employee involvement and participation in decision making. Evidence began to challenge the efficiency of highly directive leadership, and increasing attention was paid to problems of motivation and human relations.

Through training laboratories in group development that sprang up across the country, many of the newer notions of leadership began to exert an impact. These training laboratories were carefully designed to give people a firsthand experience in full participation and decision making. The designated "leaders" deliberately attempted to reduce their own power and to make group members as responsible as possible for setting their own goals and methods within the laboratory experience.

It was perhaps inevitable that some of the people who attended the training laboratories regarded this kind of leadership as being truly "democratic" and went home with the determination to build fully participative decision making into their own organizations. Whenever their bosses made a decision without convening a staff meeting, they tended to perceive this as authoritarian behavior. The true symbol of democratic leadership to some was the meeting—and the less directed from the top, the more democratic it was.

Some of the more enthusiastic alumni of these training laboratories began to get the habit of categorizing leader behavior as "democratic" or "authoritarian." The boss who made too many decisions himself was thought of as an authoritarian, and his directive behavior was often attributed solely to his personality.

New Need

The net result of the research findings and of the human relations training based upon them has been to call into question the stereotype of an effective leader. Consequently, the modern manager often finds himself in an uncomfortable state of mind.

Often he is not quite sure how to behave; there are times when he is torn between exerting "strong" leadership and "permissive" leadership. Sometimes new knowledge pushes him in one direction ("I should really get the group to help make this decision"), but at the same time his experience pushes him in another direction ("I really understand the problem better than the group and therefore I should make the decision"). He is not sure when a group decision is really appropriate or when holding a staff meeting serves merely as a device for avoiding his own decision-making responsibility.

The purpose of our article is to suggest a framework which managers may find useful in grappling with this dilemma. First, we shall look at the different patterns of leadership behavior that the manager can choose from in relating himself to his subordinates. Then, we shall turn to some of the questions suggested by this range of patterns. For instance, how important is it for a manager's subordinates to know what type of leadership he is using in a situation? What factors should he consider in deciding on a leadership pattern? What difference do his long-run objectives make as compared to his immediate objectives?

RANGE OF BEHAVIOR

Exhibit 1 presents the continuum or range of possible leadership behavior available to a manager. Each type of action is related to the degree of authority used by the boss and to the amount of freedom available to his subordinates in reaching decisions. The actions seen on the extreme left characterize the manager who maintains a high degree of control while those seen on the extreme right characterize the manager who releases a high degree of control. Neither extreme is absolute; authority and freedom are never without their limitations.

Now let us look more closely at each of the behavior points occurring along this continuum.

The manager makes the decision and announces it. In this case the boss identifies a problem, considers alternative solutions, chooses one of them, and then reports this decision to his subordinates for implementation. He may or may not give consideration to what he believes his subordinates will think or feel about his decision; in any case, he provides no opportunity for them to participate directly in the decision-making process. Coercion may or may not be used or implied.

EXHIBIT 1 Continuum of leadership behavior.

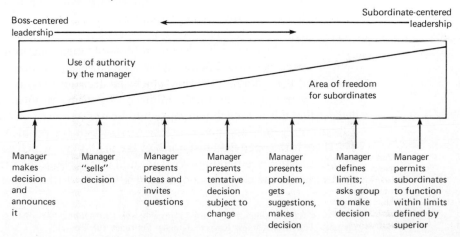

The manager "sells" his decision. Here the manager, as before, takes responsibility for identifying the problem and arriving at a decision. However, rather than simply announcing it, he takes the additional step of persuading his subordinates to accept it. In doing so, he recognizes the possibility of some resistance among those who will be faced with the decision, and seeks to reduce this resistance by indicating, for example, what the employees have to gain from his decision.

The manager presents his ideas, invites questions. Here the boss who has arrived at a decision and who seeks acceptance of his ideas provides an opportunity for his subordinates to get a fuller explanation of his thinking and his intentions. After presenting the ideas, he invites questions so that his associates can better understand what he is trying to accomplish. This "give and take" also enables the manager and the subordinates to explore more fully the implications of the decision.

The manager presents a tentative decision subject to change. This kind of behavior permits the subordinates to exert some influence on the decision. The initiative for identifying and diagnosing the problem remains with the boss. Before meeting with his staff, he has thought the problem through and arrived at a decision—but only a tentative one. Before finalizing it, he presents his proposed solution for the reaction of those who will be affected by it. He says in effect, "I'd like to hear what you have to say about this plan that I have developed. I'll appreciate your frank reactions, but will reserve for myself the final decision."

The manager presents the problem, gets suggestions, and then makes his decision. Up to this point the boss has come before the group with a solution of his own. Not so in this case. The subordinates now get the first chance to suggest solutions. The manager's initial role involves identifying the problem. He might, for example, say something of this sort: "We are faced with a number of complaints from newspapers and the general public on our service policy. What is wrong here? What ideas do you have for coming to grips with this problem?"

The function of the group becomes one of increasing the manager's repertory of possible solutions to the problem. The purpose is to capitalize on the knowledge and experience of those who are on the "firing line." From the expanded list of alternatives developed by the manager and his subordinates, the manager then selects the solution that he regards as most promising.[1]

The manager defines the limits and requests the group to make a decision. At this point the manager passes to the group (possibly including himself as a member) the right to make decisions. Before doing so, however, he defines the problem to be solved and the boundaries within which the decision must be made.

An example might be the handling of a parking problem at a plant. The boss decides that this is something that should be worked on by the people involved, so he calls them together and points up the existence of the problem. Then he tells them:

"There is the open field just north of the main plant which has been designated for additional employee parking. We can build underground or surface multilevel facilities as long as the cost does not exceed $100,000. Within these limits we are free to

---

[1] For a fuller explanation of this approach, see Leo Moore, "Too Much Management, Too Little Change," *Harvard Business Review,* January-February 1956, p. 41.

work out whatever solution makes sense to us. After we decide on a specific plan, the company will spend the available money in whatever way we indicate."

The manager permits the group to make decisions within prescribed limits. This represents an extreme degree of group freedom only occasionally encountered in formal organizations, as, for instance, in many research groups. Here the team of managers or engineers undertakes the identification and diagnosis of the problem, develops alternative procedures for solving it, and decides on one or more of these alternative solutions. The only limits directly imposed on the group by the organization are those specified by the superior of the team's boss. If the boss participates in the decision-making process, he attempts to do so with no more authority than any other member of the group. He commits himself in advance to assist in implementing whatever decision the group makes.

KEY QUESTIONS

As the continuum in Exhibit 1 demonstrates, there are a number of alternative ways in which a manager can relate himself to the group or individuals he is supervising. At the extreme left of the range, the emphasis is on the manager—on what *he* is interested in, how *he* sees things, how *he* feels about them. As we move toward the subordinate-centered end of the continuum, however, the focus is increasingly on the subordinates—on what *they* are interested in, how *they* look at things, how *they* feel about them.

When business leadership is regarded in this way, a number of questions arise. Let us take four of special importance:

Can a boss ever relinquish his responsibility by delegating it to someone else? Our view is that the manager must expect to be held responsible by his superior for the quality of the decisions made, even though operationally these decisions may have been made on a group basis. He should, therefore, be ready to accept whatever risk is involved whenever he delegates decision-making power to his subordinates. Delegation is not a way of "passing the buck." Also, it should be emphasized that the amount of freedom the boss gives to his subordinates cannot be greater than the freedom which he himself has been given by his own superior.

Should the manager participate with his subordinates once he has delegated responsibility to them? The manager should carefully think over this question and decide on his role prior to involving the subordinate group. He should ask if his presence will inhibit or facilitate the problem-solving process. There may be some instances when he should leave the group to let it solve the problem for itself. Typically, however, the boss has useful ideas to contribute, and should function as an additional member of the group. In the latter instance, it is important that he indicate clearly to the group that he sees himself in a *member* role rather than in an authority role.

How important is it for the group to recognize what kind of leadership behavior the boss is using? It makes a great deal of difference. Many relationship problems between boss and subordinate occur because the boss fails to make clear how he plans to use his authority. If, for example, he actually intends to make a certain decision himself, but the subordinate group gets the impression that he has delegated this authority, considerable confusion and resentment are likely to follow. Problems may also occur when the boss uses a "democratic" facade to conceal the fact that he has already made a decision which he hopes the group will accept as its own. The attempt to "make them think it was their idea in the first place" is a risky one. We believe that it is highly important for the manager to be honest and clear in describing what authority he is keeping and what role he is asking his subordinates to assume in solving a particular problem.

Can you tell how "democratic" a manager is by the number of decisions his subordinates make? The sheer *number* of decisions is not an accurate index of the amount of freedom that a subordinate group enjoys. More important is the *significance* of the decisions which the boss entrusts to his subordinates. Obviously a decision on how to arrange desks is of an entirely different order from a decision involving the introduction of new electronic data-processing equipment. Even though the widest possible limits are given in dealing with the first issue, the group will sense no particular degree of responsibility. For a boss to permit the group to decide equipment policy, even within rather narrow limits, would reflect a greater degree of confidence in them on his part.

DECIDING HOW TO LEAD

Now let us turn from the types of leadership which are possible in a company situation to the question of what types are *practical* and *desirable*. What factors or forces should a manager consider in deciding how to manage? Three are of particular importance:

- Forces in the manager
- Forces in the subordinates
- Forces in the situation

We should like briefly to describe these elements and indicate how they might influence a manager's action in a decision-making situation.[2] The strength of each of them will, of course, vary from instance to instance, but the manager who is sensitive to them can better assess the problems which face him and determine which mode of leadership behavior is most appropriate for him.

Forces in the Manager

The manager's behavior in any given instance will be influenced greatly by the many forces operating within his own personality. He will, of course, perceive his leadership problems in a unique way on the basis of his background, knowledge, and experience. Among the important internal forces affecting him will be the following:

[2] See also Robert Tannenbaum and Fred Massarik, "Participation by Subordinates in the Managerial Decision-Making Process," *Canadian Journal of Economics and Political Science,* August 1950, p. 413.

1 *His value system* How strongly does he feel that individuals should have a share in making the decisions which affect them? Or, how convinced is he that the official who is paid to assume responsibility should personally carry the burden of decision-making? The strength of his convictions on questions like these will tend to move the manager to one end or the other of the continuum shown in Exhibit I. His behavior will also be influenced by the relative importance that he attaches to organizational efficiency, personal growth of subordinates, and company profits.[3]

2 *His confidence in his subordinates* Managers differ greatly in the amount of trust they have in other people generally, and this carries over to the particular employees they supervise at a given time. In viewing his particular group of subordinates, the manager is likely to consider their knowledge and competence with respect to the problem. A central question he might ask himself is: "Who is best qualified to deal with this problem?" Often he may, justifiably or not, have more confidence in his own capabilities than in those of his subordinates.

3 *His own leadership inclinations* There are some managers who seem to function more comfortably and naturally as highly directive leaders. Resolving problems and issuing orders come easily to them. Other managers seem to operate more comfortably in a team role, where they are continually sharing many of their functions with their subordinates.

4 *His feelings of security in an uncertain situation* The manager who releases control over the decision-making process thereby reduces the predictability of the outcome. Some managers have a greater need than others for predictability and stability in their environment. This "tolerance for ambiguity" is being viewed increasingly by psychologists as a key variable in a person's manner of dealing with problems.

The manager brings these and other highly personal variables to each situation he faces. If he can see them as forces which, consciously or unconsciously, influence his behavior, he can better understand what makes him prefer to act in a given way. And understanding this, he can often make himself more effective.

Forces in the Subordinate

Before deciding how to lead a certain group, the manager will also want to consider a number of forces affecting his subordinates' behavior. He will want to remember that each employee, like himself, is influenced by many personality variables. In addition, each subordinate has a set of expectations about how the boss should act in relation to him (the phrase "expected behavior" is one we hear more and more often these days at discussions of leadership and teaching). The better the manager understands these factors, the more accurately he can determine what kind of behavior on his part will enable his subordinates to act most effectively.

Generally speaking, the manager can permit his subordinates greater freedom if the following essential conditions exist:

[3] See Chris Argyris, "Top Management Dilemma: Company Needs vs. Individual Development," *Personnel,* September 1955, pp. 123-134.

- If the subordinates have relatively high needs for independence. (As we all know, people differ greatly in the amount of direction that they desire.)
- If the subordinates have a readiness to assume responsibility for decision making. (Some see additional responsibility as a tribute to their ability; others see it as "passing the buck.")
- If they have a relatively high tolerance for ambiguity. (Some employees prefer to have clear-cut directives given to them; others prefer a wider area of freedom.)
- If they are interested in the problem and feel that it is important.
- If they understand and identify with the goals of the organization.
- If they have the necessary knowledge and experience to deal with the problem.
- If they have learned to expect to share in decision making. (Persons who have come to expect strong leadership and are then suddenly confronted with the request to share more fully in decision making are often upset by this new experience. On the other hand, persons who have enjoyed a considerable amount of freedom resent the boss who begins to make all the decisions himself.)

The manager will probably tend to make fuller use of his own authority if the above conditions do *not* exist; at times there may be no realistic alternative to running a "one-man show."

The restrictive effect of many of the forces will, of course, be greatly modified by the general feeling of confidence which subordinates have in the boss. Where they have learned to respect and trust him, he is free to vary his behavior. He will feel certain that he will not be perceived as an authoritarian boss on those occasions when he makes decisions by himself. Similarly, he will not be seen as using staff meetings to avoid his decision-making responsibility. In a climate of mutual confidence and respect, people tend to feel less threatened by deviations from normal practice, which in turn makes possible a higher degree of flexibility in the whole relationship.

Forces in the Situation

In addition to the forces which exist in the manager himself and in his subordinates, certain characteristics of the general situation will also affect the manager's behavior. Among the more critical environmental pressures that surround him are those which stem from the organization, the work group, the nature of the problem, and the pressures of time. Let us look briefly at each of these:

Type of Organization   Like individuals, organizations have values and traditions which inevitably influence the behavior of the people who work in them. The manager who is a newcomer to a company quickly discovers that certain kinds of behavior are approved while others are not. He also discovers that to deviate radically from what is generally accepted is likely to create problems for him.

These values and traditions are communicated in numerous ways—through job descriptions, policy pronouncements, and public statements by top executives. Some organizations, for example, hold to the notion that the desirable executive is one who is dynamic, imaginative, decisive, and persuasive. Other organizations put more emphasis upon the importance of the executive's ability to work effectively with people—his human relations skills. The fact that his superiors have a defined concept of what the good executive should be will very likely push the manager toward one end or the other of the behavioral range.

In addition to the above, the amount of employee participation is influenced by such variables as the size of the working units, their geographical distribution, and the degree of inter- and intra-organizational security required to attain company goals. For example, the wide geographical dispersion of an organization may preclude a practical system of participative decision making, even though this would otherwise be desirable. Similarly, the size of the working units or the need for keeping plans confidential may make it necessary for the boss to exercise more control than would otherwise be the case. Factors like these may limit considerably the manager's ability to function flexibly on the continuum.

Group Effectiveness   Before turning decision-making responsibility over to a subordinate group, the boss should consider how effectively its members work together as a unit.

One of the relevant factors here is the experience the group has had in working together. It can generally be expected that a group which has functioned for some time will have developed habits of cooperation and thus be able to tackle a problem more effectively than a new group. It can also be expected that a group of people with similar backgrounds and interests will work more quickly and easily than people with dissimilar backgrounds, because the communication problems are likely to be less complex.

The degree of confidence that the members have in their ability to solve problems as a group is also a key consideration. Finally, such group variables as cohesiveness, permissiveness, mutual acceptance, and commonality of purpose will exert subtle but powerful influence on the group's functioning.

The Problem Itself   The nature of the problem may determine what degree of authority should be delegated by the manager to his subordinates. Obviously he will ask himself whether they have the kind of knowledge which is needed. It is possible to do them a real disservice by assigning a problem that their experience does not equip them to handle.

Since the problems faced in large or growing industries increasingly require knowledge of specialists from many different fields, it might be inferred that the more complex a problem, the more anxious a manager will be to get some assistance in solving it. However, this is not always the case. There will be times when the very complexity of the problem calls for one person to work it out. For example, if the manager has most of the background and factual data relevant to a given issue, it may be easier for him to think it through himself than to take the time to fill in his staff on all the pertinent background information.

The key question to ask, of course, is: "Have I heard the ideas of everyone who has the necessary knowledge to make a significant contribution to the solution of this problem?"

The Pressure of Time   This is perhaps the most clearly felt pressure on the manager (in spite of the fact that it may sometimes be imagined). The more that he feels the need for an immediate decision, the more difficult it is to involve other people. In organizations which are in a constant state of "crisis" and "crash programming" one is likely to find managers personally using a high degree of authority with relatively little delegation to subordinates. When the time pressure is less intense, however, it becomes much more possible to bring subordinates in on the decision-making process.

These, then, are the principal forces that impinge on the manager in any given instance and that tend to determine his tactical behavior in relation to his subordinates. In each case his behavior ideally will be that which makes possible the most effective attainment of his immediate goal within the limits facing him.

LONG-RUN STRATEGY

As the manager works with his organization on the problems that come up day by day, his choice of a leadership pattern is usually limited. He must take account of the forces just described and, within the restrictions they impose on him, do the best that he can. But as he looks ahead months or even years, he can shift his thinking from tactics to large-scale strategy. No longer need he be fettered by all of the forces mentioned, for he can view many of them as variables over which he has some control. He can, for example, gain new insights or skills for himself, supply training for individual subordinates, and provide participative experiences for his employee group.

In trying to bring about a change in these variables, however, he is faced with a challenging question: At which point along the continuum *should* he act?

Attaining Objectives

The answer depends largely on what he wants to accomplish. Let us suppose that he is interested in the same objectives that most modern managers seek to attain when they can shift their attention from the pressure of immediate assignments:

1 To raise the level of employee motivation
2 To increase the readiness of subordinates to accept change
3 To improve the quality of all managerial decisions
4 To develop teamwork and morale
5 To further the individual development of employees

In recent years the manager has been deluged with a flow of advice on how best to achieve these longer-run objectives. It is little wonder that he is often both bewildered and annoyed. However, there are some guidelines which he can usefully follow in making a decision.

Most research and much of the experience of recent years give a strong factual basis to the theory that a fairly high degree of subordinate-centered behavior is associated with the accomplishment of the five purposes mentioned.[4] This does not mean that a manager should always leave all decisions to his assistants. To provide the individual or the group with greater freedom than they are ready for at any given time may very well tend to generate anxieties and therefore inhibit rather than facilitate the attainment of desired objectives. But this should not keep the manager from making a continuing effort to confront his subordinates with the challenge of freedom.

CONCLUSION

In summary, there are two implications in the basic thesis that we have been developing. The first is that the successful leader is one who is keenly aware of those forces which are most relevant to his behavior at any given time. He accurately understands himself, the individuals and group he is dealing with, and the company and broader social environment in which he operates. And certainly he is able to assess the present readiness for growth of his subordinates.

But this sensitivity or understanding is not enough, which brings us to the second implication. The successful leader is one who is able to behave appropriately in the light of these perceptions. If direction is in order, he is able to direct; if considerable participative freedom is called for, he is able to provide such freedom.

Thus, the successful manager of men can be primarily characterized neither as a strong leader nor as a permissive one. Rather, he is one who maintains a high batting average in accurately assessing the forces that determine what his most appropriate behavior at any given time should be and in actually being able to behave accordingly. Being both insightful and flexible, he is less likely to see the problems of leadership as a dilemma.

[4] For example, see Warren H. Schmidt and Paul C. Buchanan, *Techniques that Produce Teamwork* (New London: Arthur C. Croft Publications, 1954); and Morris S. Viteles, *Motivation and Morale in Industry* (New York: W.W. Norton & Company, Inc., 1953).

RETROSPECTIVE COMMENTARY

Since this article was first published in 1958, there have been many changes in organizations and in the world that have affected leadership pattern. While the article's continued popularity attests to its essential validity, we believe it can be reconsidered and updated to reflect subsequent societal changes and new management concepts.

The reasons for the article's continued relevance can be summarized briefly:

• The article contains insights and perspectives which mesh well with, and help clarify, the experiences of managers, other leaders, and students of leadership.

Thus it is useful to individuals in a wide variety of organizations—industrial, governmental, educational, religious, and community.

• The concept of leadership the article defines is reflected in a continuum of leadership behavior (see Exhibit 1 in original article). Rather than offering a choice between two styles of leadership, democratic or authoritarian, it sanctions a range of behavior.

• The concept does not dictate to managers but helps them to analyze their own behavior. The continuum permits them to review their behavior within a context of other alternatives, without any style being labeled right or wrong.

(We have sometimes wondered if we have, perhaps, made it too easy for anyone to justify his or her style of leadership. It may be a small step between being non-judgmental and giving the impression that all behavior is equally valid and useful. The latter was not our intention. Indeed, the thrust of our endorsement was for the manager who is insightful in assessing relevant forces within himself, others, and the situation, and who can be flexible in responding to these forces.)

In recognizing that our article can be updated, we are acknowledging that organizations do not exist in a vacuum but are affected by changes that occur in society. Consider, for example, the implications for organizations of these recent social developments:

• The youth revolution that expresses distrust and even contempt for organizations identified with the establishment.

• The civil rights movement that demands all minority groups be given a greater opportunity for participation and influence in the organizational processes.

• The ecology and consumer movements that challenge the right of managers to make decisions without considering the interest of people outside the organization.

• The increasing national concern with the quality of working life and its relationship to worker productivity, participation, and satisfaction.

These and other societal changes make effective leadership in this decade a more challenging task, requiring even greater sensitivity and flexibility than was needed in the 1950's. Today's manager is more likely to deal with employees who resent being treated as subordinates, who may be highly critical of any organizational system, who expect to be consulted and to exert influence, and who often stand on the edge of alienation from the institution that needs their loyalty and commitment. In addition, he is frequently confronted by a highly turbulent, unpredictable environment.

In response to these social pressures, new concepts of management have engaged in organizations. Open-system theory, with its emphasis on subsystems' interdependency *and* on the interaction of an organization with its environment, has made a powerful impact on managers' approach to problems. Organization development has emerged as a new behavioral science approach to the improvement of individual, group, organizational, and interorganizational performance. New research has

added to our understanding of motivation in the work situation. More and more executives have become concerned with social responsibility and have explored the feasibility of social audits. And a growing number of organizations, in Europe and in the United States, have conducted experiments in industrial democracy.

In light of these developments, we submit the following thoughts on how we would rewrite certain points in our original article.

The article described forces in the manager, subordinates, and the situation as givens, with the leadership pattern a resultant of these forces. We would now give more attention to the *interdependency* of these forces. For example, such interdependency occurs in: (a) the interplay between the manager's confidence in his subordinates, their readiness to assume responsibility, and the level of group effectiveness; and (b) the impact of the behavior of the manager on that of his subordinates, and vice versa.

In discussing the forces in the situation, we primarily identified organizational phenomena. We would now include forces lying outside the organization, and would explore the relevant interdependencies between the organization and its environment.

In the original article, we presented the size of the rectangle in Exhibit 1 as a given, with its boundaries already determined by external forces—in effect, a closed system. We would now recognize the possibility of the manager and/or his subordinates taking the initiative to change those boundaries through interaction with relevant external forces—both within their own organization and in the larger society.

The article portrayed the manager as the principal and almost unilateral actor. He initiated and determined group functions, assumed responsibility, and exercised control. Subordinates made inputs and assumed power only at the will of the manager. Although the manager might have taken into account forces outside himself, it was *he* who decided where to operate on the continuum—that is, whether to announce a decision instead of trying to sell his idea to his subordinates, whether to invite questions, to let subordinates decide an issue, and so on. While the manager has retained this clear prerogative in many organizations, it has been challenged in others. Even in situations where he has retained it, however, the balance in the relationship between manager and subordinates at any given time is arrived at by interaction—direct or indirect—between the two parties.

Although power and its use by the manager played a role in our article, we now realize that our concern with cooperation and collaboration, common goals, commitment, trust, and mutual caring limited our vision with respect to the realities of power. We did not attempt to deal with unions, other forms of joint worker action, or with individual workers' expressions of resistance. Today, we would recognize much more clearly the power available to *all* parties, and the factors that underlie the interrelated decisions on whether to use it.

In the original article, we used the terms "manager" and "subordinate." We are now uncomfortable with "subordinate" because of its demeaning, dependency-laden connotations and prefer "nonmanager." The titles "manager" and "nonmanager" make the terminological difference functional rather than hierarchical.

We assumed fairly traditional organizational structures in our original article. Now we would alter our formulation to reflect newer organizational modes which are slowly emerging, such as industrial democracy, intentional communities, and "phenomenarchy."* These

* For a description of phenomenarchy, see Will McWhinney, "Phenomenarchy: A Suggestion for Social Redesign," *Journal of Applied Behavioral Science,* May 1973.

new modes are based on observations such as the following:

- Both manager and nonmanagers may be governing forces in their group's environment, contributing to the definition of the total area of freedom.
- A group can function without a manager, with managerial functions being shared by group members.
- A group, as a unit, can be delegated authority and can assume responsibility within a larger organizational context.

Our thoughts on the question of leadership have prompted us to design a new behavior continuum (see Exhibit 2) in which the total area of freedom shared by manager and nonmanagers is constantly redefined by interactions between them and the forces in the environment.

The arrows in the exhibit indicate the continual flow of interdependent influence among systems and people. The points on the continuum designate the types of manager and nonmanager behavior that become possible with any given amount of freedom available to each. The new continuum is both more complex and more dynamic than the 1958 version, reflecting the organizational and societal realities of today.

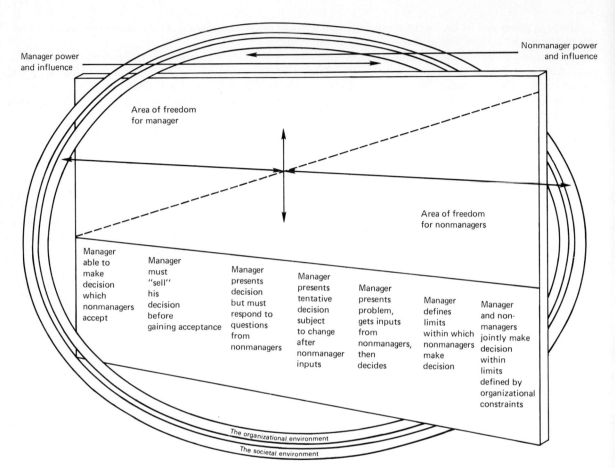

EXHIBIT 2 Continuum of manager-nonmanager behavior.

PART FOUR

GETTING THE JOB DONE: ACTION PLANNING AND IMPLEMENTATION

Part 4 assumes a thorough understanding of the concepts presented in Parts 1–3. To these concepts we now add specific principles of action planning and implementation. Our focus is on learning to develop good action plans and to anticipate contingencies. This requires knowledge of oneself and others to develop plans that will produce desired behaviors (culture), leading to required outcomes. The applied managerial focus of this book makes Part 4 the natural culmination of Parts 1–3. However, the importance of being able to act effectively requires a thorough understanding of the situation. The cases in this part are especially challenging in this regard, since they cannot be easily described in terms of one or a few concepts presented thus far.

The text—on preliminary considerations for action planning and implementation—briefly describes the key criteria used to assess the viability of an action plan. Since action planning is more of an art than a science, these criteria only serve as general guidelines. The text reviews the criteria as a series of questions:

1 Is the plan consistent with the analysis?
2 Is the plan time-sequenced in a logical order?
3 What is the probability of success at each step of the plan?
4 Does the plan take into account possible contingencies?
5 Does the plan anticipate secondary consequences?
6 Is the plan realistic given the amount of influence the actor has in the organization?
7 Does the actor have the necessary competence to implement the specific steps?
8 Does the plan consider how it impinges on other relevant actors?

Case 1 involves making changes in a sales force. Maureen Frye, a young MBA, is an assistant product manager and one of the few women managers in a conservative organization. She was given a mandate to develop a plan for changing the call patterns of 60 salespeople responsible for selling extruded titanium alloy products, which have annual sales of over $100 million. Frye obtained support from her boss, Hugh Salk (the product manager of Titanium Alloys), to shift call patterns toward larger accounts based upon the results of a computer simulation study. She first attempted to effect this change about a year ago with little success. Since then Frye has obtained the support of Salk's boss, the vice president of marketing, and the vice president of sales to develop an action plan within the next 3 months for changing the call patterns of sales representatives. A successful plan will require an understanding of why her initial plan failed.

Case 2 also concerns a young MBA, John Mitchell, who is recruited by Richard Hicks, a vice president of the National Chemical Company, to work as the assistant to the president of the recently acquired TEXCORP. Mitchell is put into a highly visible position in an organization rife with internal politics but possessing considerable opportunity. Mitchell begins highly enthusiastic, but by the end of the case is seriously considering resigning from the company. Before making this decision, he must determine if there is an effective plan he can develop that will justify staying with the company. He has failed in previous efforts to improve both organizational performance and his own situation and must take this into account in developing an action plan.

Cases 3 and 4 also concern a young MBA, but one in a different situation from Frye and Mitchell. Directly after graduation from business school, Peter Olafson was hired as general manager of Cable King Television Company of Saint Paul, a part of Universal Communication Systems, Inc., which is run by the entrepreneurial William Jurgens. Olafson, who had no previous experience in this industry or as a general manager, considered himself fortunate to get this job. After 7 months, Olafson has experienced a number of frustrating personnel and operating problems. Conflict exists within his management group and he has had to twice revise the planned startup of the Saint Paul system. He has 2 weeks to prepare for a meeting with his new boss's superior, Chet Knowles. One week before this meeting he finds out that William Jurgens and Scoop Harwood, the new vice president of operations and Knowles' boss, will also be visiting. Despite 60–80 hours of work each week, Olafson has been unsuccessful in understanding and resolving his many problems. He is faced with a situation in which he must prepare a number of different plans.

The two readings supplement the text and offer some practical guidelines on developing effective action plans and styles of managerial action. Reading 1 provides a framework for developing an action plan that builds directly on the text. It is also based on concepts introduced in earlier parts of the book. The basic steps presented are to (1) describe present conditions, (2) assess or evaluate present conditions, (3) define goals, (4) formulate the problem, (5) develop a solution-finding strategy, (6) generate solution alternatives, (7) evaluate alternatives and make a choice, (8) implement, and (9) monitor changes. The framework is general enough to be applied to any action planning situation.

Reading 2 focuses on the question of what management style is effective in taking action. This reading reviews common patterns of low achievers, who despite their raw abilities, are relatively ineffective. These patterns—including the tendency to "wing it;" inappropriate attention to detail; lack of a handle on priorities; inability to move quickly enough; lack of boldness, nerve, and self-confidence; tolerance of ineffective subordinates; failure to seek advice or help; and personal blind spots— share the general problems of being inappropriate attempts for consistency. In contrast, high performers appear versatile to the point of inconsistency, but show a different type of inconsistency. While they use a variety of techniques and change their style to fit the situation, they have in common the ability to perform careful analysis and develop general operating strategies, and they are aware of classical dilemmas that confront managers and from which they can learn. High achievers also provide excellent motivation to subordinates, effectively manage their bosses and themselves, and focus on one task of prime importance at a time.

SOME PRELIMINARY THOUGHTS ON ACTION PLANNING AND IMPLEMENTATION

John J. Gabarro
Leonard A. Schlesinger

This brief note describes some useful criteria for assessing the viability of an action plan. Skillful implementation of an action plan is very much an art, and this is one reason why relatively little has been written on the topic. Many concepts are available for diagnosing organizational problems and implementing large-scale change, but relatively few "models" are available for action planning and implementation. Action planning is largely a matter of conceiving how best to attain desired goals given the resources and time available. Doing this effectively requires thinking of processes that can be set in motion, as well as anticipating likely outcomes and contingencies. This note briefly describes some questions you can ask yourself as you assess and develop action plans and foresee possible problems in implementing them.

Before covering these questions, however, let us spell out four assumptions about action planning and implementation in the "real world" as compared to the classroom.

1 In the actual implementation of an action plan, you will encounter some contingencies that you will not have anticipated beforehand, regardless of how carefully you have thought through your action plan.

2 However, there will be fewer unanticipated problems if you have carefully thought through the a priori action plan.

3 The most critical contingencies can be identified beforehand—if you have a good grasp of the problem, the context, and the actors involved.

4 In real situations (as compared to case problems where the data are largely historical in nature), implementation of an action plan is an iterative and interactive *process* through which you and others can generate new data.

Furthermore, we are assuming here that an action plan is based on a thorough analysis and diagnosis of the problem(s), as well as a consideration of alternatives.

Given these assumptions, the following eight questions are useful in criticizing an action plan.

1 Is your action plan consistent with your analysis?   If your action plan is not consistent with your previous analysis it is a sign that something is wrong with your analysis, your action plan, or both. Often it means that you're following "gut feelings" in your action plan (which may or may not be better than your rational analysis). Whatever the case, the implication is that you need to recheck both your analysis and action plan to search for conflicting assumptions or inconsistencies.

Assuming that your action plan does follow your diagnosis, then the practicality of your action plan is a test of the relevance of the conclusions you drew from your analysis. If you discover that you can implement your action plan only at great economic or human cost, it suggests that your diagnosis is inadequate and you should reconsider other alternatives.

2 Is your action plan time-sequenced in a logical order?   Consider these questions: Is your action plan sequenced so that the proposed steps are time-phased in a realistic way? That is, are immediate issues dealt with before longer-term issues, but are related to overall goals? Does your plan deal with urgent problems in a timely manner? Are your implementation steps sequenced in a logical order? That is, if what happens in step A has a bearing on what you can do at step B, is step A undertaken before step B? Do your early action steps unnecessarily preclude future options prematurely?

3 What is the probability of success at each step of your implementation plan?   If the likelihood of success of a given action step is slight, you obviously need to reconsider it. If the probability of a given action step is highly uncertain, you need to develop other alternatives or secure better information.

4 Does your plan consider possible contingencies?   To be realistic, your action plan needs to consider "what if" possibilities. This is especially important for the critical elements of your plan.

5 Does your action plan anticipate secondary consequences?   Any action plan that is based on a particular set of actions directed at specific individuals or groups must also consider the effect of this action on all potentially impacted individuals or groups.

6 Is your action plan realistic given your influence (formal or informal) within the organization?   Actions are to a large extent contingent on roles. For example, a vice president of sales can change or alter a sales commission system; a district sales manager cannot. The degree of formal authority and informal influence you possess (and over whom and what) are important determinants of what you can and cannot do.

7 Do you have the personal competence necessary to implement your action steps?
Put more directly, do you have the personal, interpersonal, group, or leadership skills required to pull off your action plan? If your action plan is going to surface conflict, do you have the necessary conflict resolution skills to implement it? This question is especially relevant to actual situations in which you must be able to implement actions with reasonable skill. In simplest terms, your action plan must fit your capabilities as a person.

8 Have you considered how your action plan impinges on other relevant actors? This question is really a restatement of questions 4 and 5, but is more sharply focused.

All of these questions have one element in common: mentally rehearsing the possible outcomes of the proposed actions in your plan. To a large extent, this is what we attempt to do in our discussions and critiques of action plans in class. It is terribly important not only to plan the "devil's advocate" in your analysis (in terms of critical assumptions and conclusions), but also to be critical of your action plan as well. In real managerial situations, it is often useful to do this with someone else or with a group of people whose judgment and intentions you trust.

The one aspect of action planning that these questions have tended to *underemphasize* is that implementation is a process. Implementation is evolutionary and not quite as predictable as these questions might imply. However, the better job you do in your action planning, the fewer unanticipated problems you are likely to encounter when you actually implement your decisions.

QUAKER STEEL AND ALLOY CORPORATION

John J. Gabarro

In December 1978, Maureen Frye was given a mandate to develop a plan for changing the call patterns of salespeople responsible for selling extruded titanium alloy products. As assistant product manager (APM) of Titanium Alloys, Frye was responsible for all of Quaker's extruded titanium alloy products, which amounted to more than $100 million in 1978. Frye was asked to have the plan completed by March 30, 1979 so that it could be implemented the following calendar year.

The decision to have Frye develop such a plan was arrived at in a meeting attended by Frye, Hugh Salk (her supervisor and product manager for all Titanium Alloys), the vice president of marketing (Salk's supervisor), and vice president of sales. The meeting had been called by Salk in early December to obtain "top-side acceptance" of several ideas that Frye had developed for improving Quaker Alloys' sales and penetration in the extruded titanium alloys market.

Frye believed that a systematic reallocation of the sales force's time from small accounts to medium and large accounts could result in increases in sales of up to $12–$25 million in extruded titanium products. During 1977 she had conducted a number of computer simulations that had convinced her of the utility of the change in time allocation. Salk had been impressed by Frye's concept and her underlying analysis when she first presented it to him in 1977. Salk asked her to brief James Bethancourt, vice president of marketing, on the concept in early 1978. Bethancourt shared Salk's interest and had studied the concept in some depth. The early December meeting had been arranged by Salk to gain the acceptance of Larry Israel, vice president of sales, so that Frye could begin work on an implementation plan. Salk felt that the meeting was especially important since an earlier attempt by Frye to change call patterns had failed.

Both Salk and Bethancourt believed that the reallocation of salespeople's time could yield significant benefits not only in titanium but also in other alloys. However, both also believed that it made most sense to try the concept first with titanium extruded products before proceeding further. As Bethancourt put it, "This is the sort of thing you try out on one product type and see what happens—if it works, it will catch on."

QUAKER STEEL AND ALLOY CORPORATION

The Quaker Steel and Alloy Corporation was founded in 1890 to mine, refine, produce, and sell iron and iron ore. The firm was originally called the Holderness Iron Works because of its location in the small Quaker town of Holderness, Pa., on the banks of the Ohio River. The company prospered and changed its name in 1917 to Quaker Steel and Alloy Corporation. The company was generally referred to as Quaker Alloys or simply Quaker within the industry.

During the 1930s, the company began to specialize in the production and sales of other alloyed metals, such as tungsten and nickel, in addition to steel. By the early 1960s, Quaker had become one of the world's major manufacturers of specialized metal alloys, and its product line included alloys of steel, tungsten, titanium, nickel, magnesium, cobalt, zirconium, and vanadium. Quaker's strategy had been to specialize in high-margin, high-quality metal alloys to the virtual exclusion of most low-margin, price-sensitive products. Quaker had buttressed this strategy with heavy investments in research, new-process development, and new plant facilities. It also practiced a strong philosophy of providing customers with technical service and assistance.

Quaker's competitors consisted of small specialized producers of alloys of rare metals as well as large U.S. and Japanese steel manufacturers. The latter group of firms tended to compete primarily for larger-volume business in which a rare metal was alloyed with steel. Competition from Japanese manufacturers had become particularly keen since the early 1970s, especially for large-volume accounts. Quaker management observed that despite their geographic distance, Japanese producers and their trading affiliates were very responsive in developing and servicing large customers.

By 1978, Quaker's annual sales were nearly $1.4 billion. Quaker's margins, returns on sales, and return on investment were the highest in the steel and metal alloys industry. Its return on investment was significantly greater than that of its nearest competitor, a position it had enjoyed for nearly 20 years. Although Quaker was widely respected within the industry for both its products and technology, it was viewed by most of its competitors as being somewhat unique and different from other manufacturers of steel and alloyed metals.

Much of this difference had its roots in the company's practices and culture, which in turn could be traced to the firm's founders, both of whom were Quakers. The company's headquarters, R&D facilities, and more than one-third of its plants were located in Holderness, Pa., and the company prided itself on having a small-town feeling despite its size and diversity. Although most of the inhabitants of Holderness were no longer practicing Quakers, many of the founders' original values permeated both the community and the company. These values continued to be espoused and practiced by the firm's top management. One manager who was based in New York City described this culture in the following way: "It's hard to know where Holderness begins and where Quaker Alloys ends. If you work for Quaker you live in Holderness, even if your address is on Long Island."

Some of the company's more prevalent norms included an atmosphere of friendliness, openness in discussing differences of opinion, and a generally accepted norm of influence through persuasion and competence rather than through formal authority. As a result, considerable emphasis was put on participation in decisionmaking and leadership by example rather than by fiat. Other values that were attributed to the founders included an emphasis on equality and fairness, conservatism in dress, civic responsibility, hard work, deference to one's elders, and what management described as a "hard-nosed" approach to business decisions.

Typically, managers who joined Quaker from other steel or metal producers found the company a frustrating place in which to work. For this and other reasons, most of Quaker's managerial positions are filled from within. Turnover among blue-collar and white-collar employees was a quarter of the industry's average, regardless of location. Labor-management relations were also characterized as the best in the industry. This climate dated back to the early 1930s when Quaker's top management invited several trade and craft unions to organize its operations.

CORPORATE ORGANIZATION

Quaker was organized along fairly strict functional lines with the mining, refining, manufacturing, research and engineering, and sales and marketing divisions reporting directly to the president. (See Exhibit 1 for a corporate organization chart.) A small but highly profitable chemical products division reported to the chairperson of the board. The chemical products division had been started in the 1960s to manufacture solvents and lubricants used in the production of steel and metal alloys, but it operated independently of the other divisions. (Only 5% of its output went to Quaker's own manufacturing operations.)

As the company continued to grow and diversify into new alloys during the 1950s, management found that communication between functions had become more difficult. Top management believed that three factors had enabled Quaker to overcome these functional barriers and maintain its responsiveness to the marketplace. The first was the small-town atmosphere of friendliness and openness that management believed provided a basis for informal communication across functional boundaries. The second was a policy implemented in the early 1950s that required all managers above a certain rank (third line supervisor) to spend a year working in Holderness to become acclimated to the company's procedures, facilities, organization, and practices. This policy was felt to be especially important since most transactions across organizational lines are conducted through personal contacts and relationships. The third factor was the concept of "responsibility lines." Under this concept, many managers—and even whole divisions and departments—were responsible to other functions or departments, even though there were no formal lines of authority that linked them. These responsibility lines were shown on organization charts as heavy

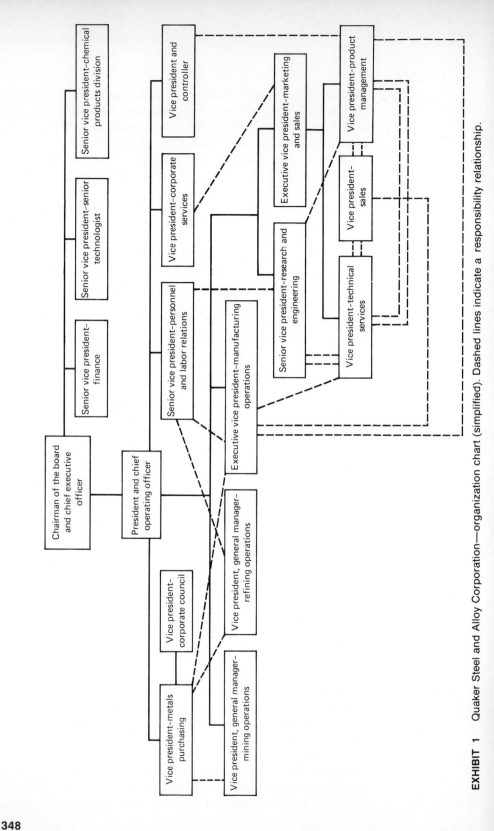

EXHIBIT 1 Quaker Steel and Alloy Corporation—organization chart (simplified). Dashed lines indicate a responsibility relationship.

dotted lines to indicate strong informal relationships. Because of this "formalized" informal procedure, it was not uncommon for a person to have two or even three persons to whom he or she was equally responsible, even when these people were in different geographic locations.

MAUREEN FRYE

Frye was 29 years old and a graduate of Harvard Business School. She had joined Quaker 3 years earlier, upon completion of an MBA. Frye had spent her first 6 months at Quaker in the sales representatives' training program and an additional 3 months as a market analyst. Both assignments were in preparation for her becoming an assistant product manager, the position for which she was originally recruited. Before attending Harvard, Frye had earned a BS degree in metallurgy and an MS degree in physical chemistry from MIT. She had no previous work experience.

Several factors had led to Frye's decision to join Quaker. The assistant product manager's position offered her an opportunity to use her technical background as well as her MBA concentrations in marketing and finance. Frye had been especially impressed by the responsibility the job offered (managing part of a product line that exceeded $100 million in sales). She was further impressed by the company itself and the opportunities it offered. These attractions were also supported by several personal factors. Her husband had received a PhD in metallurgy from MIT the year that Frye received her MBA and he, too, had been offered a job in Quaker's R&D laboratories, which he had found very attractive. Both Frye and her husband had limited their job searches to companies in cities that would allow them to continue to live together. Although both had received attractive offers in New York, Chicago, and Pittsburgh, each had independently ranked their offer from Quaker as being the most desirable. In addition, both were favorably impressed by the friendliness, cleanliness, and appearance of Holderness as a community in which to live. They were especially attracted by the many cultural and civic activities offered by the town. Ultimately, both she and her husband found the decision to join Quaker a relatively easy one.

Despite Quaker's attractiveness, Frye had felt some initial misgivings about joining a company that was in an industry in which women managers were rare. She was the only woman manager at her level in the marketing and sales division. To her knowledge, there were only a dozen other women managers in the entire corporation who were not in charge of clerical operations. These women, including herself, were still at relatively low levels of middle management. The only exception to this pattern was a historical one. In the 1950s, the R&D Division had been led by Olivia More. More had, in fact, become one of the "living legends" in Quaker's history, and both Frye and her husband had heard many stories about More's brilliance, dedication, and plain-speaking manner. An older technician had described her to Frye as follows:

> Old Livy was a giant around here. She was smart as a tack and she really knew the business. She was a real lady and even though she had all these degrees, she was as much at home in the mills as she was in the lab. She treated you like an equal and made you feel like your opinion mattered. People would do anything for her and still will—even people who never

met her. All you had to say was that "it was for Olivia More" and people would break their backs to get it done. Working for her on that project was one of the greatest honors I've had at Quaker Alloys.

More had retired as a senior vice president in 1961 and, although now in her eighties, she continued to serve as a part-time senior technologist and consultant.

Although Frye expected some difficulties in working within an all-male environment, she had found most people cooperative. If anything, she felt that having been hired to fill a management position as an outsider without previous experience with Quaker Alloys was a greater source of problems. Her boss, Hugh Salk, had discussed this potential problem with her on several occasions. His major advice had been to "Stay with it, work hard, learn the 'Quaker Alloys way of doing things,' and the problem will take care of itself." Nonetheless, even after 2 years in her current job, she continued to sense occasional resentment toward her, especially among some of the older people in product management and sales. Frye also wondered about how much of the resistance she had encountered in getting people to implement her suggestions was due to the fact that she was a woman.

MARKETING AND SALES DIVISION

Quaker's marketing and sales division was organized into three major departments, each of which was headed by a vice president. These departments were field sales, corporate marketing, and technical support services. (See Exhibit 2 for an organization chart of the marketing and sales division.) The field sales operations consisted of more than 600 sales representatives assigned to 19 district sales offices in the United States, Canada, and Europe. The district sales offices reported to one of three regional vice presidents based on geographic location. Average sales per salesperson exceeded $2 million.

The corporate marketing and the technical support services departments had been established to support the efforts of the sales force. More specifically, the technical support services department provided technical assistance on complex customer problems, and it conducted developmental work to modify or develop alloys to meet specific customer needs. It also served as a liaison with the R&D laboratories.

The marketing department consisted of eight product management groups, each of which focused on managing a particular metal-based family of alloys, as shown in Exhibit 2. Product managers and assistant product managers were responsible for developing product strategy, making market and financial projections, and providing needed product liaison with technical support services, manufacturing, R&D, and the controller's office. They were also responsible for coordinating the efforts of the sales representatives who sold their product. Product and assistant product managers were also held accountable for product profitability and volume. Larger products, such as titanium, steel, tungsten, and nickel-based alloys, had as many as three assistant product managers, each of whom focused on a type of product or a form of product application. Assistant product managers had profit and sales responsibility for their product lines.

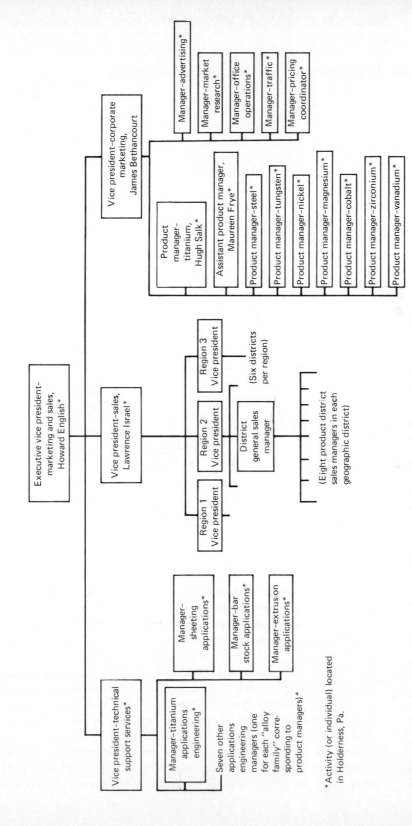

EXHIBIT 2 Quaker Steel and Alloy Corporation—organization of marketing and sales operations.

Executive vice president—marketing and sales, Howard English*

Vice president—corporate marketing, James Bethancourt

Manager—advertising*
Manager—market research*
Manager—office operations*
Manager—traffic*
Manager—pricing coordinator*

Product manager—titanium, Hugh Salk*
Assistant product manager, Maureen Frye*
Product manager—steel*
Product manager—tungsten*
Product manager—nickel*
Product manager—magnesium*
Product manager—cobalt*
Product manager—zirconium*
Product manager—vanadium*

Vice president—sales, Lawrence Israel*

Region 1 Vice president
Region 2 Vice president
Region 3 Vice president

(Six districts per region)

District general sales manager

(Eight product district sales managers in each geographic district)

Vice president—technical support services*

Manager—titanium applications engineering*

Seven other applications engineering managers (one for each "alloy family" corresponding to product managers)*

Manager—sheeting applications*
Manager—bar stock applications*
Manager—extrusion applications*

*Activity (or individual) located in Holderness, Pa.

351

RELATIONSHIP BETWEEN PRODUCT MANAGERS AND THE SALES FORCE

The relationship between the product management groups and the sales force appeared somewhat complicated to outsiders because of the number of responsibility lines that cut across the two departments. Exhibit 3 shows the relationships between the titanium products group and the Chicago district sales office, one of Quaker's largest sales districts. Each of the 19 district sales offices was headed by a general sales manager. Under each general sales manager were eight district sales managers (DSMs), each of whom was responsible for the sales of one of the eight alloys produced by Quaker. The titanium DSM essentially reported to two supervisors: to the district's general sales manager for administrative issues and coordinating sales efforts on accounts that purchased products from more than one product alloy family, and to the titanium product manager on issues dealing with titanium alloys. The titanium district sales force was typically divided into three groups: sheeting, bar stock, and extrusion sales (over which Frye had responsibility as APM).

The specialized alloys business was characterized by advanced metallurgical products and processes. Quaker sold to customers in high-technology industries or in need of highly specialized alloys. For this reason, Quaker's sales representatives had to maintain close contact with technical support services and the product management groups in Holderness. This contact was needed to gain support in servicing customer needs and problems.

While the DSMs were responsible for all titanium sales in their territories, product managers and APMs were responsible for coordinating the efforts of the salespeople selling their products. Frye explained the relationship as follows:

> I don't have direct autocratic control over the DSMs or their salespeople. I do have a high degree of influence, but there is a certain amount of persuasion that has to be used, especially with some of them who are more concerned with their prerogatives at times than in getting the job done.

SALES DEPARTMENT

Field sales personnel were recruited centrally by the personnel department in Holderness. The company sought people with undergraduate or graduate degrees in engineering and metallurgy, and it recruited primarily from schools in Pennsylvania and the Midwest. All new salespeople went through a training program in Holderness for 5–10 months that consisted of lectures, role playing, case discussions, and plant and laboratory tours. The program included a major orientation phase, a series of sales clinics, and intensive product technology training. Salespeople were paid on a straight salary basis and increases in pay were related to promotion to higher-seniority levels or job categories. This practice was consistent with Quaker's policy of "paying for the job" and moving more experienced people to more critical positions.

District sales offices were located in 19 major industrial centers. Sales representatives were assigned to territories based on volume of sales and geographical proximity within a district. The geographic division of labor was used to minimize the salesperson's traveling time. Salespeople usually spent 4 days a week on the road,

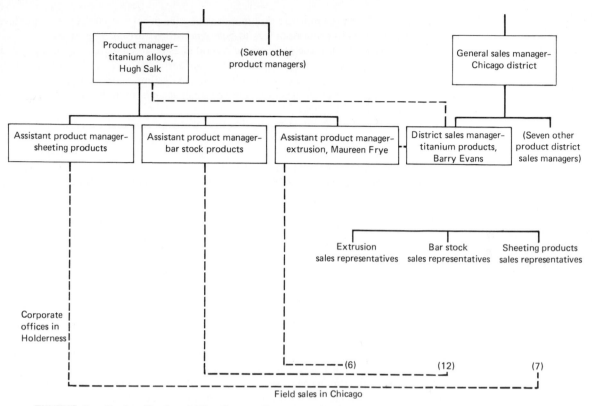

EXHIBIT 3   Quaker Steel and Alloy Corporation—organizational relationships between Chicago sales office and product manager for titanium alloys. Dashed lines indicate a responsibility relationship.

often not returning home at night. One day a week was usually spent in the office "touching base" and doing clerical work.

The Quaker philosophy of openness and friendliness extended to the sales office, and it gave the company a reputation for helpfulness and service to its customers. Larry Israel, vice president of sales, believed this was one of Quaker's distinctive advantages and one of the reasons why many customers remained loyal to Quaker on more standard alloys despite the higher margins the company charged.

District sales managers generally were loath to be autocratic with their salespeople. Instead, they preferred to provide general direction and expected the salespeople to make most decisions. As one DSM described it, "we see ourselves more as helpers than bosses." Barry Evans, the Chicago DSM for titanium sales, elaborated on the DSM's role:

> I wouldn't say that it's 100 percent either permissive or participative management, but it leans a great deal in those directions. We search for salespeople who are self-starters, who supply their own motivation. Because we are organized so loosely, the salespeople have no authority over staff functions, technical services, or the R&D groups in Holderness. Our solution to problems that require the services of various groups in Holderness depends on

the individual sales representative's skill in motivating the proper people at the proper level in other departments to bring resources to bear against his customers' problems.

It takes three sides of a triangle to make a good sales representative—knowledge of the customer, the product, and the company. The younger ones have the knowledge of the product and the technology, but they don't know the customer and they don't know the company. It is easier for them to get to know the small account than the larger one, because the small fellow needs his help.

I see a major part of my job as motivating the salespeople to handle themselves properly in their relationships with other departments so as to get maximum efforts from those departments to solve our customer's problems. This is the reason that Bethancourt and Israel insist that no one should be a DSM without extensive experience in Holderness. The DSM needs this experience to understand all the departments and services we have as resources.

Sales representatives were responsible for all accounts within their territory regardless of the size of the accounts. A young salesperson in the New York district office described work activities to the casewriter as follows:

You go where the business is, but you often get mouse-trapped into spending several hours with a very small account. Small accounts depend on us to give them help, and most of the time they are problems we can solve for them ourselves without help from Holderness. When you're in the area and you have an hour left in the day, you drop in to see a small account and before you know it you've spent a couple of hours. But it's hard for me to refuse to help an account that's been buying 10,000 pounds from me for the last 5 years.

Big accounts are much harder to crack. You need an appointment and you have to see a lot of people—the purchasing agents, product engineers, manufacturing engineers, etc. Unless you can get a fast answer from Holderness, they lose interest.

Sales representatives in the Chicago and New York offices considered their greatest motivator to be the experience of a successful sale. They then ranked the experience of actually working with customers on problems as the next highest source of motivation and satisfaction. All rated monetary rewards and incentives lower on the scale. The Chicago DSM explained to the casewriter that a modest cash bonus existed, but that he did not use it since none of his sales representatives really deserved it.

Frye and several DSMs believed that larger accounts were more difficult to develop than small- or medium-size accounts. However, they felt that the major problem in selling large accounts was not price sensitivity. Rather, the key deterrent was the long lead time needed to sell a large account. This lead time could range from 3 to 18 months. The problems posed by large accounts were also more technically complex and usually required extensive assistance from technical support services and sometimes the R&D laboratories. It was also common for such a sale to require work in technical support service's development laboratories.

EXTRUDED TITANIUM ALLOYS SALES FORCE

In total, 60 sales representatives sold extruded titanium products. Of this number, 52 were located in North America and the remainder overseas. As noted earlier, the representatives were distributed across the 19 general sales districts and reported to the DSMs for titanium alloys. See Exhibit 4 for the location and distribution of these sales personnel.

The number of full-time extruded products sales representatives assigned to a district varied considerably. Larger sales districts, such as Chicago, New York, and San Francisco, had as many as six extrusion salespeople; smaller offices, such as New Orleans and Paris, had as few as one or two. Unfortunately, Frye had not been able to spend as much time in the field as she had hoped and, therefore, she knew only a small number of salespeople well. She had spent much of her time in 1977 and early 1978 developing and refining the model and running the simulations. In addition, much of her time in early 1978 was devoted to assisting Salk in managing product allocations that were necessitated by a contraction in the availability of raw titanium ore in late 1977. Resultantly, she had spent far less time in the field than she had originally hoped.

However, Frye had had many interactions with the 19 DSMs at annual meetings, through correspondence, and over the telephone. She had come to know the DSMs of the three largest districts and the Houston district quite well. Frye believed she had established a particularly strong working relationship with Barry Evans, the titanium DSM in Chicago. In fact, she had discussed the time reallocation concept with Evans in some detail during a routine visit to Chicago in late 1977. Both he and a senior sales representative, who happened to be in the office that day, seemed quite receptive to the idea. In fact, the senior salesperson had told Frye in early October that he had altered his call pattern so that he could call on more large accounts. He

EXHIBIT 4   LOCATION AND DISTRIBUTION OF EXTRUDED TITANIUM
ALLOY PRODUCTS SALES REPRESENTATIVES

North America			
Chicago	6	Toronto	3
New York	6	Montreal	3
San Francisco	6	Holderness, Pa.	3
Los Angeles	5	Minneapolis	3
Houston	4	Boston	3
Raleigh, N.C.*	3	Kansas City*	2
Denver*	3	New Orleans*	2
International			
Munich*	2	London*	1
Zurich*	2	Paris*	1
Hong Kong	2		

* Efforts of full-time titanium extrusion salespeople were supplemented by assistance from titanium-bar or titanium-sheet sales specialists in this district.

also said that he believed this change would make a difference in his sales volume once some of the larger accounts he had been cultivating were ready to complete their sales agreements.

BACKGROUND ON THE SALES TIME REALLOCATION CONCEPT

The time reallocation concept dated back to early 1977 when Maureen Frye was faced with statistics that showed a decline in the total tonnage of titanium extruded products sold in 1976 (even though sales revenues had increased because of price increases). In analyzing the sales figures, she realized that a great deal of the sales representatives' efforts were allocated to small accounts and that only 35 percent of the field sales effort for 1977 was planned on customers who produced 85 percent of the dollar volume. Starting with the conviction that the distribution of sales effort was unbalanced, she initiated a series of computer simulations to optimize sales effort. In doing the analyses, she divided customers into six categories defined by total annual sales. The categories were:

Category	Sales class
More than $1,000,000	1
More than $500,000	2
More than $250,000	3
More than $100,000	4
More than $50,000	5
Less than $50,000	6

The simulations were completed by late fall of 1977. Her findings showed that, regardless of assumptions, the computer model could not justify investing time in accounts that sold less than $50,000 (class 6), and that from an optimization standpoint, investing time in class 5 accounts was undesirable. The simulation also showed that a reduction as slight as 20 percent in the time spent in class 6 accounts resulted in an indicated minimum return of $12–$25 million per year. Frye found that this conclusion held even under the most conservative assumptions. She concluded that time spent in class 6 accounts should be reduced by at least 30 percent and redistributed to the other classes. When she completed the analysis, she discussed it with Salk. Salk was impressed and asked her to run the simulations under a variety of additional assumptions. Again, the same pattern of results was found.

Frye explained the implications of the proposed changes in time allocation to the casewriter.

> When we say that the time should be trebled on an account, that does not necessarily mean three times as many calls. The customer contact does not necessarily increase threefold, but the time spent on behalf of the account should. It can be spent at Holderness, or on the phone to technical support services. It can be spent on visits by these people to our plants; it can be spent in libraries. It is time spent "noodling" that account. The salesperson is selling in depth to support calls on key accounts. The salesperson becomes the focal point or catalyst for the potential utilization of all types of resources within Quaker Alloys.
>
> Salespeople play this role with varying degrees of success depending on the degree of respect the groups here have for a sales representative. One person can call and get things going like that! Another person may have a much better reason, but because his or her posture may not be as healthy in Holderness, he or she may have to work twice or three times as hard to get the resource employed. Or the person may have a record of having cried "wolf" a couple of times. There is nothing better than a good track record for getting resources, and there is nothing more retarding than a poor record.

Although the simulations showed that salespeople, as a whole, should spend very little time with smaller accounts, Frye felt that the individual salespeople themselves should determine which of the small accounts to eliminate.

As a result of these conclusions, Frye sent a memo to the titanium extrusion sales representatives in late 1977, instructing them to reduce their time in class 6 accounts by 30 percent and to reallocate it to larger-size accounts. The memo included a brief description of the rationale for making the change. In response to the memo, one of the titanium DSMs called her to say that he had received several complaints from the salespeople about its arbitrary nature. The DSM suggested that she provide the DSMs with a more-detailed explanation of the desired change.

Based on this suggestion, Frye presented the computer findings to the DSMs at the yearly sales meeting in January 1978, after she had discussed the concept and simulations with the vice president of marketing. Frye commented on the meeting as follows.

> We gave them a rough outline of what we wanted done and we expected the DSMs to follow through as they saw fit. They all agreed to make these changes. However, as of November 30, 1978, the distribution of effort today differs very little from what it was in January. The recommended shifts in sales efforts did not take place. The sales representatives apparently did not accept the recommendations, and a great imbalance in sales effort still exists.

Frye discussed her disappointment over the lack of change with Salk, who concluded that they had not done a careful enough job in planning the change. Salk suggested that two steps were needed. The first step was to get acceptance of the idea from Israel and Bethancourt, which led to the early December meeting. The second step was to allow herself enough time to prepare a plan for implementing the change so that the probability of its success would be increased. Both Bethancourt and Israel agreed with Salk's analysis that a good implementation plan was needed. Bethancourt added that the concept was potentially very powerful and that Frye should take as much time as needed to implement it within the extrusion sales force. He also asked Frye to feel free to question any organizational assumptions or practices that she felt might impede its successful implementation and that they could be discussed during the March meeting. "But most of all," he added, "we need an implementation plan that will work."

TEXTILE CORPORATION OF AMERICA

Jeanne Deschamps
Louis B. Barnes
Leonard A. Schlesinger

In 1963, the Textile Corporation of America (Texcorp) was formed through the merger of three family-owned companies:

1 The Smith-Abbott Mills, located in Fitchburg, Mass., a firm known for its high-grade spun rayon and wool-blended fabrics. Smith-Abbott was headed up by William R. Abbott.

2 The North Carolina Mills, which specialized in fine cotton fabrics and staple synthetic fabrics. North Carolina Mills was owned by members of the Ford family and presided over by Robert W. Ford.

3 Carolina Cotton Company, a single, large mill located in South Carolina and owned by John S. Rand. The company produced high-quality cotton print cloth.

Since the three companies' product lines were not directly competitive with each other, the merger was looked upon as a potential bonanza by Abbott, Ford, and Rand whose combined companies became a major force in the fine textiles industry. Texcorp sales for 1963 were $45 million.

Because North Carolina Mills accounted for the largest portion ($25 million) of Texcorp's 1963 sales, Robert Ford and his management team were able to dominate the new company during its first few years. Furthermore, family loyalties and long-standing reporting practices in each of the three companies meant that Texcorp existed largely as a single company in name only. Accounting functions for all three firms were moved to a corporate office in New York City, and a few other functions were integrated, but Abbott and Rand stayed out of New York to a large extent. Abbott, for example, kept an office in the New York headquarters, attended board meetings, and oversaw the Fitchburg and other Smith-Abbott operations, but spent much of his time vacationing in Europe and playing golf. In 1967, Abbott began to spend more time in New York City, partly because his wife had contracted a crippling long-term illness.

By 1967, it was clear that the fine cotton fabric market was declining in the United States. In June 1967, Abbott suggested to the Texcorp management that they discuss the possibilities of being acquired by the National Chemical Company. National Chemical was a multinational corporation with 1967 sales of more than $2 billion. National had recently begun to actively diversify into nonchemical markets, and several Texcorp executives were personal friends of National executives. It was among these personal friends that discussions of a possible acquisition of Texcorp began.

By November 1967, these informal conversations had developed into official discussions between National's acquisition department and Texcorp management. A purchase price was agreed upon, and a presentation was made to National's board of directors late in November. They voted favorably, and Texcorp was acquired with the idea that it would be part of National's nonchemicals business group under Richard M. Hicks. With this acquisition, the nonchemicals business would account for almost one-half of National's total business. It included more than 20 new businesses and recent acquisitions. At the time of the Texcorp negotiations and acquisition, Hicks was on a prolonged business trip to Europe, where some of National's new nonchemical businesses were located. Upon his return from Europe, Hicks was asked by National's chairperson, William Scott, to become acquainted with the Texcorp management situation.

In the exchange of Texcorp stock for National Chemical stock, the owners of Texcorp became wealthy individuals. Abbott became one of the largest individual shareholders of National Chemical common stock. Ford, then more than 65 years old, agreed to step down as president of Texcorp at the initiative of Hicks. Rand indicated that he was not interested in being president of Texcorp. Consequently, Abbott became the new chief executive officer. Ford, although not entirely pleased with the new management arrangement, had considerable financial security in that his family's trust fund now owned more than $10 million of National Chemical stock.

At the same time, Hicks agreed that Abbott should probably make several other organizational changes. Andrew Thompson, who had been a star salesperson for Smith-Abbott Mills, consequently became vice president of sales for Smith-Abbott Mills. Walter Hogan, a former plant manager for Smith-Abbott, became vice president of manufacturing. Bob Cleaves was given the position of vice president for sales at Carolina Cotton Company.

Texcorp's 1967 sales were $65 million with profits of $2 million, a slight dip from 1966 profits. It was the first decline in profitability since 1963. After 4 months under National Chemical's ownership, Hicks confided to a friend that he was afraid that National Chemical had acquired a "turkey" in Texcorp. He had also requested a well-known executive recruiting firm to search for qualified top executive talent within the textile industry who might be suitable to bring into Texcorp's operations. (Exhibit 1 depicts Texcorp's organization as it existed in February 1968. Exhibit 2 outlines the background of key company personnel.)

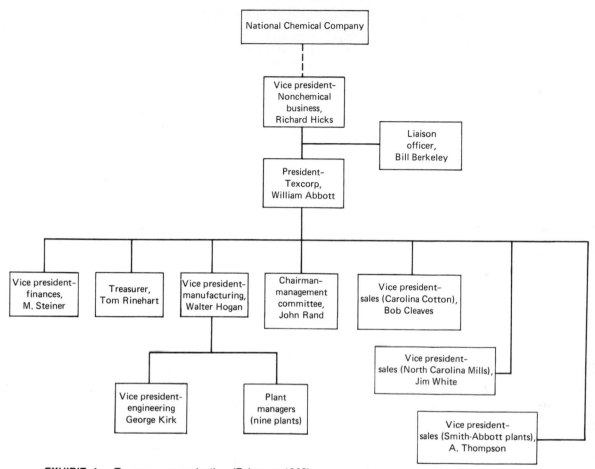

EXHIBIT 1 Texcorp—organization (February 1968).

JOHN MITCHELL, MBA

John Mitchell, 27, was married and had one child. He grew up in Darien, Conn., and graduated from Harvard College in 1963. Mitchell chose to attend Harvard because of its reputation as a politically liberal school. During his first two years of school he remained a political conservative, but during his junior and senior years he became a committed liberal. He took courses in religion and psychology and briefly considered becoming a minister. After graduation he thought about entering law or medical school, but his father wanted him to go to Harvard Business School. He then received an MBA in 1965 and joined a Peace Corps project in the Far East, where he taught industrial psychology. Mitchell's experiences overseas further strengthened his political liberalism (labeled radicalism by his mother) and his increasing unwillingness to compromise with "the establishment" perspective.

EXHIBIT 2   PERSONAL BACKGROUND OF TEXCORP PERSONNEL

Name	Age	Background
William Abbott*	55	Former president of Smith-Abbott Mills, former All-American football player from Princeton; independently wealthy
Andrew Thompson	41	Former salesperson for Smith-Abbott Mills, former professional golfer; long-time friend of Abbott
Walter Hogan*	62	Former plant manager of Smith-Abbott Mills, former football coach; long-time friend of Abbott and his father, the founder of Smith-Abbott Mills
John Rand*	66	Former president of Carolina Cotton; 1925 graduate of Harvard College; independently wealthy
Martin Steiner	42	Former chief financial officer for North Carolina Mills
George Kirk	45	Hired in 1964; chief engineer for 4 Texcorp engineers; office located in North Carolina
Sam Jarvis*	54	Plant manager of Carolina Cotton Plant; brother-in-law of John Rand
Bob Hogan	36	Plant manager of Smith-Abbott Mills; son of Walter Hogan
Jim White	55	Former sales manager of North Carolina Mills
Bob Cleaves*	42	Former president of a small textile company bought by Texcorp in 1964; independently wealthy; a bachelor
Tom Rinehart*	63	Treasurer of Texcorp; former treasurer of North Carolina Mills
Bill Davis	50	Plant manager of largest North Carolina Mills plant, appointed in 1965; son-in-law of John Rand
Bill Berkeley	29	Received MBA from University of California, Berkeley; hired by National Chemical in 1967; worked for Hicks since December 1967
Richard Hicks	50	Vice president of National Chemical; 1949 graduate of Harvard Business School; known as a "real professional" by other National Chemical executives

* Indicates that an employment contract was in effect. These contracts, which lasted through 1971, guaranteed salaries ranging from $40,000 to $70,000 per year.

During his college and graduate school years, Mitchell liked to think of himself as good at the "gamesmanship" of life. He prided himself on his ability to describe the games people played. In high school, for example, Mitchell was often called an "apple polisher" because his school work seemed to follow the particular concerns of his various teachers. He was a straight A student. At college, he rarely cut classes and was on the dean's list for all 4 years. Active in athletics, he was a starting fullback for the Harvard football team. To Mitchell, even football was a "psychological game." Commenting on his football experiences, he said:

If the coach was in a mean mood, you'd growl and hit somebody. If not, you'd joke and try to have fun. Hell, the guys that were on the field to make the big plays not only *did* the right things in practice, but *thought* and *said* the right things, too. It was all a fantastically complicated game.

Mitchell earned a varsity letter each year in college.

While at Harvard Business School, Mitchell participated in many lengthy discussions about business's social responsibilities and was sometimes shocked by what he considered to be the narrow-mindedness of some classmates. He wondered if the business world could offer him the satisfaction he needed in life. Because of these doubts as well as an interest in psychology, Mitchell became involved in a research project at school that eventually resulted in the coauthorship of a book on the psychological aspects of motivation.

In 1968 Mitchell decided to return to the United States after 3 years in the Peace Corps. He did not think he had the patience to be an effective teacher, although he believed himself to have been successful as a teacher in the Peace Corps. At the same time, the U.S. business world in 1968 intrigued him because of the new emphasis being placed on business integrity and social responsibility. Mitchell hoped he could find a job that offered an outlet for his continually growing social conscience while also testing him in a "real" business organization. As he noted,

> I've always wanted to see if I could compete with my classmates from HBS. But at the same time, I loved travel and living in other cultures. For the last 3 years, however, I kept wondering, if I were back in the states, would I be such a hot shot? And could I handle business life and its lack of social conscience?

MITCHELL AND NATIONAL CHEMICAL COMPANY

Hicks, as vice president of National Chemical with responsibilities for Texcorp, heard about Mitchell through family friends. Hicks initially wrote Mitchell and asked him to visit National Chemical's offices in New York so that they might talk about the company's operations overseas. When they met, Mitchell told Hicks that the chemical industry didn't really interest him because it was dominated by large corporations; Hicks, however, was impressed with Mitchell and persisted in discussing career opportunities with him. After many meetings and several offers, Mitchell agreed to work as assistant to Texcorp president William Abbott. Mitchell would be trained for a year in the textile business and then transfer to a textile mill that National was planning to buy overseas. The job sounded ideal to Mitchell. He would be able to test himself in the world of big business and also indulge his interest in travel and living abroad. The Mitchells rented a small house in Darien, Conn.

In July 1968, Mitchell began work at Texcorp, which was located in an office building about 10 blocks from National Chemical's corporate office in New York. Hicks had told Abbott very little about his new assistant, except he was to train him for a year. Since Mitchell knew nothing about the textile business, he requested and spent his first 2 months in the mills—part of this time as a loom operator, even though this was theoretically against union regulations.

Mitchell's initial impressions of Texcorp and its management were quite favorable. Abbott had told Mitchell to see Thompson, the vice president of sales for

Smith-Abbott products and the second in command at Texcorp, if there were any "problems" with his training. Thompson was very outgoing and personable. Mitchell spent most of his training time at the large Smith-Abbott Mill in Fitchburg. While the workers believed him to be a "spy from the chemical company" at first, they soon relaxed and Mitchell was able to develop several strong friendships in a short time. Since he was living in a motel in Fitchburg without his family, he spent 12 to 14 hours a day at work and got to know the personnel on both the day and night shifts at the mill.

When he returned to New York and Texcorp headquarters in September, Mitchell found Abbott had not planned anything for him to do. While Abbott spoke to him for about 20 minutes each day to find out how he was getting along, Mitchell felt that no one was really interested in what he did. Consequently, when the opportunity arose (due to others' lack of interest), he willingly accepted responsibility for helping to collect and organize the financial figures for the first Texcorp 5-year plan for 1969–1974. (Systematic planning was one of the most well-developed management techniques at National Chemical.)

While Mitchell worked on the plan, he also learned more about personnel at Texcorp's headquarters. He observed that four offices, which he called "executive row," were large, spacious, and thickly carpeted, while the rest of the Texcorp offices were relatively modest. The four offices were occupied by Abbott; Walter Hogan, the vice president of manufacturing; John Rand, the chairperson of the management committee; and Tom Rinehart, corporate treasurer. Mitchell discovered that despite the plush offices, Rand and Rinehart were rarely involved in the regular management meetings, and Hogan was not highly respected by many of the headquarters personnel.

Although he seemed to get along well with Texcorp executives, Mitchell found that they had little in common to justify his spending much time socializing with them. As he noted to the casewriter,

> I was young and unimportant. Also, I didn't play golf and I didn't drink. I had tomato juice at lunch while they typically boozed it up.

Bill Berkeley was the National Chemical liaison officer assigned to Texcorp by Hicks shortly after the acquisition. (The executive recruiter had reported that there was literally no real executive talent available in the textile industry.) Berkeley became Mitchell's closest friend, since both were close in age and the only people at Texcorp under 40. Also, both Mitchell and Berkeley reported to Hicks. Mitchell remarked on their relationship:

> Bill Berkeley and I got along very well. . . . Berkeley spent half of every day over at Texcorp talking to Abbott or one of the financial vice presidents about liaison work. You know, fill this form in, the appropriations meeting is next month, etc.
>
> Berkeley and I were different from the rest of Texcorp management. I discovered that I was the only person who could use a slide rule at Texcorp, except for Kirk. . . . But he's an engineer. . . . I don't know. It sure seems like some of those people waste a lot of time and stuff trying to butter up Bill Abbott, and there's so little real *analysis*.

As the month of October wore on and his work on the 5-year plan came to an end, Mitchell began to feel frustrated and bored. One day he went around the Texcorp office asking executives if they had any jobs or projects he might help them with. He spent a day filing expense reports, and 3 days drawing graphs and charts showing loom utilization for the first half of 1968. He later noted:

> It was really dull. I didn't think it would be like this. I talked with Andy Thompson and he didn't know. . . . None of them really knew what to do with me. First I was a "spy," then a "bright kid with a lot of potential." You could only ask someone for work so many times, then you just had to try and "make" work.

And, in early November,

> I finally talked to Andy. I told him I was really going out of my mind. And I talked to Bob Cleaves (the vice president of sales for Carolina Cotton). Anyway, they both told me I should lay it on the line to Abbott. "Talk to him at Oscar's," they said. [Oscar's was a large bar and restaurant often frequented by Texcorp executives.] I wanted to ask him for more responsibility. Hell, I had absolutely zero then. He must know how I felt . . . but he was so damned silent. No one ever knew what was on his mind . . . except Andy, of course. Those two were like father and son.

Because Abbott seemed constantly preoccupied and was often out of the office, Mitchell had been reluctant up to this point to speak to him about his job. ("If I catch him wrong, he'll just see me as a complainer, or worse, an overly ambitious 'whiz kid,' " he explained to his wife.) As was established in the November 1967 reorganization, Abbott ran Texcorp with the help of Thompson and Hogan, two executives who had come to New York with him from Smith-Abbott Mills in Fitchburg. Thompson and Abbott were particularly close, and virtually all company decisions were made by them. While president of Texcorp, Abbott also continued to direct Smith-Abbott Mills personally, and he and Thompson spent 5 to 8 days a month in Fitchburg.

During the second week of November, Mitchell spoke to Hicks. It was their first meeting since July, and was requested by Mitchell when he had heard that National Chemical's plans to purchase an overseas textile firm had "fallen through." Hicks' dynamic personality had been a large part of Mitchell's decision to work at Texcorp, and he enjoyed the 30-minute meeting with the National Chemical vice president. However, he also learned that plans for expansion into overseas textiles had been delayed indefinitely. According to Hicks,

> I asked Mitchell to stay at Texcorp for the time being, to tell me where the talent was, where the problems were, where the opportunities were and how to get there. He had free license to go anywhere in the company, talk to anybody he wanted to talk to, and Abbott wouldn't get in his way.

Finally, in mid-December 1968, Mitchell followed Thompson's advice and asked Abbott if he could speak to him at Oscar's after work. Mitchell discovered that his boss was much easier to talk to at Oscar's. Abbott liked to drink, and Mitchell found it relatively easy to ask his boss for a line position with specific responsibilities. Abbott replied that he would like to have someone like Mitchell on his "team" and would give him a position if he would pledge to stay "with him" for 3 years. As the evening progressed, Mitchell observed that Abbott spoke more and more about "loyalty" and the value of a person who would "stick it out." Mitchell was reluctant to commit himself to any time period, but at 10:30 p.m., when the two finally left Oscar's, he did remark that he would "certainly stick it out if things went well."

TEXCORP PERFORMANCE

Throughout most of December, Mitchell continued to "make work" for himself. He also signed on as a volunteer consultant for the New York Urban Coalition for Minority Affairs, a task that required him to spend at least 2 nights a week working late in New York City. He found that the excitement and satisfaction of volunteer work made his late arrival home almost worthwhile. (Mitchell often skipped dinner and arrived home at midnight.) But in late December, the November financial statements were released and the usual good humor in the Texcorp offices became strained. Sales had dropped sharply and most of the manufacturing plants were losing money. Mitchell commented that:

> They were all waiting for some kind of ax to fall from Hicks. The figures were rotten. One of our plants was showing a 22 percent loss before taxes! I didn't know what National was going to do, but I hoped they'd do it fast.

The disappointing financial statements brought no immediate response from the parent company. A number of Texcorp managers, however, began to express their concerns to Mitchell about the situation at Texcorp. Thompson and Hogan, for example, pointed to the relatively stable performance of the Smith-Abbott plants and at management meetings they emphasized the need to upgrade plant efficiency at Carolina Cotton. Sam Jarvis, Carolina Cotton's plant manager, complained openly to Mitchell and other Texcorp executives that his product mix was unprofitable because several North Carolina Mills plants were now producing what he used to produce and that he was never given the necessary funds to buy new equipment. Berkeley spent 2 or 3 days each week at the Texcorp executive offices. Berkeley and Mitchell often spoke about Texcorp's organizational problems and the need for reform. Berkeley was often asked what, if anything, the parent company might do about Texcorp in light of the poor operating results, and his usual reply was one of assurance. "Calm down, fellas," Mitchell heard him say. "Just get out there and sell a little, and we'll do all right." Privately, Berkeley admitted to Mitchell that he knew Hicks was very concerned about the poor performance, but didn't know if major policy changes were planned.

The poor performance reflected in the late 1968 financial reports prompted a Texcorp reorganization in December. Hicks created three distinct operating divisions and attempted to formally alter the family reporting and communication channels. After close consultation with Abbott, he announced the formation of temporary committees to run the three operating divisions. Each committee would have a chairperson, and the chair would rotate every quarter. It was understood that this was a short-term and temporary arrangement, and that permanent division managers would be appointed as soon as possible. Thompson was made chairperson of the consumer products division (primarily high-grade spun rayon and wool blends); Jim White (former vice president for the South Carolina Mills) was made chairperson of the industrial products division (fine cottons and synthetic fabrics); and the chair of the specialty products division was left vacant. Exhibit 3 outlines the new organization. This chart was drawn up by Berkeley, but was never identified as "official." The presence of the "unofficial reorganization chart," however, was known and accepted by Texcorp executives.

By the end of December, it was obvious that the year-end financial statements would also show sharp declines in sales and profitability. Thompson was beginning a 2-week vacation in California and Abbott was on a week's vacation in Florida. Nevertheless, Mitchell decided to put together a marketing research study of Texcorp's two biggest plants. Rather than clear this study with the two absent executives, he approached the two plant managers involved and they responded enthusiastically to his proposal. For the next several weeks, Mitchell spent most of his time at the Fitchburg plant and the South Carolina plant.

Mitchell completed the first plant's marketing study in early January. It included an analysis of profitability by product line and by major customer, and was enthusiastically accepted by the plant managers. He sent a copy of the study to Abbott but never received any comments from him. Mitchell grew increasingly impatient about his role at Texcorp.

A REQUEST FOR PROMOTION

In his 6 months at Texcorp, Mitchell had developed a close working relationship with Mary Fagan, the president's secretary. The two often had coffee together in the cafeteria in the basement of the Texcorp office building. Mitchell found her perceptive and intelligent and he discussed a wide range of company problems with her. As he mentioned to the casewriter:

> If it hadn't been for Mary, I think I'd have gone nuts in the office. For example, one day we talked about Kirk. She agreed with me that he was a brilliant engineer, but really out of sight when it comes to company politics. He would call Mary from his engineering offices [in North Carolina] just to find out what kind of a mood Abbott was in before calling him. One day he called me and asked who was meeting in the board room. He'd heard there was this big meeting and he wondered why he hadn't been invited.

In Mitchell's opinion, reorganization of Texcorp into three divisions had not straightened out the most serious company problems. Lines of authority were still unclear. Old, informal relationships still prevailed over the new (and still unofficial) lines of communication. Abbott and Thompson continued to make most decisions. Overall marketing and sales objectives were left undefined. And Mitchell became more and more disgusted with his situation. At that time, he wrote in his journal:

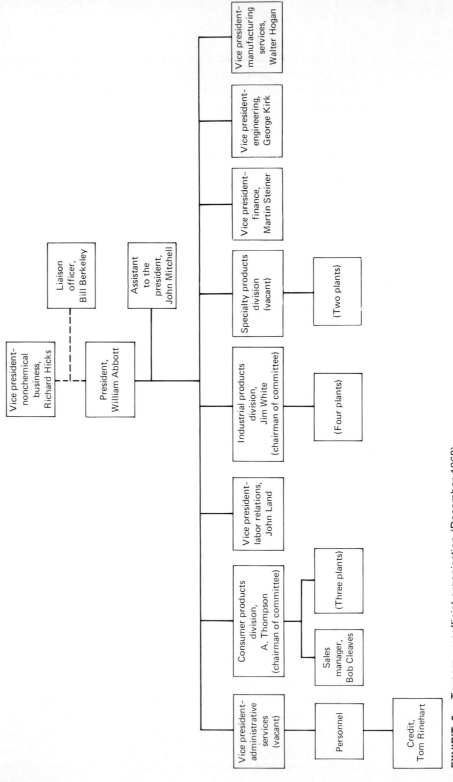

EXHIBIT 3 Texcorp—unofficial organization (December 1968).

Vice president-nonchemical business, Richard Hicks

President, William Abbott

Liaison officer, Bill Berkeley

Assistant to the president, John Mitchell

Vice president-administrative services (vacant)

Personnel

Credit, Tom Rinehart

Consumer products division, A. Thompson (chairman of committee)

Sales manager, Bob Cleaves

(Three plants)

Vice president-labor relations, John Land

Industrial products division, Jim White (chairman of committee)

(Four plants)

Specialty products division (vacant)

(Two plants)

Vice president-finance, Martin Steiner

Vice president-engineering, George Kirk

Vice president-manufacturing services, Walter Hogan

I've decided that Texcorp reminds me of a country club. Abbott and Thompson are both top golfers. They must spend $300 a month taking customers, friends, etc., golfing. And when it comes time to make a few decisions, they do it like they might select an iron. They squint down the fairway, laugh a little, say, "What the hell," and blast away. I'm convinced there are three or four of our top executives who ought to be retired . . . permanently . . . but Abbott could no more do that than he could give up his booze or his golf.

Prompted by his continued frustration and the company reorganization, Mitchell decided to write Thompson a memorandum asking for a new job. He anticipated that Thompson would show the letter to Abbott. It was delivered on January 13 and is shown in Exhibit 4.

EXHIBIT 4   MITCHELL'S MEMORANDUM TO THOMPSON

January 13, 1969

Dear Andy,

I hope this note will help you understand my, as yet unresolved, anxieties concerning my future here in Texcorp. I am putting this in writing to save you time and to facilitate any further discussions. Let me try and describe my perspective.

First, I see a lot of work to be done at all levels of the organization. Much of this work is a matter of analysis (data collection, organization, setting priorities, etc.). Systems must be set up, studies made, programs established and monitored, etc.

Second, I see a limited number of people with the background and training to accomplish all of the analytical work that has to be done.

Third, I see myself and my own selfish goals. I have spent all of my lengthy (4 years) business career doing analytical staff work. I have developed a certain facility for this kind of work. But it no longer offers the challenge I desire. I want to assume more complete responsibilities. I want to be a boss. I want to be able to look back and say, "Look, I did that . . . that's my success." When I spoke to you earlier, I hoped you might have a line position for me in your division. I have been told—and I am forced to agree—that I lack the experience to be a line manager in sales or in manufacturing. Those are the only two lines at the divisional level.

Given what I see around me, I conclude that from the organization's point of view, I should be in a position where I could move freely about; conduct market studies in the divisions, assist engineering in plant relocation studies, help establish systems and procedures, etc. (As William would say, "For Chrissake, John, we have so much to do, let's just do it!") I would need some source and position of authority that everyone saw as "legitimate" so that cooperation would be maximized. I guess my present status and title of assistant to the president seems best-suited to these organizational needs.

From a personal point of view, however, this role is less than ideal. William, I suspect, has never quite known what to do with me. I am always a little "in the way" or "under foot." My duties too often dissolve into those of a clerk–secretary–adding machine. I bear much responsibility for this, I will admit. I haven't tried to be "pushy" and I have avoided playing too many games with too many people. And I have paid a personal price: boredom. The frustration I can handle; the boredom slowly destroys me. All of this has been changing, but the deeper I get into the problems and the personalities, the less secure any "assistant-to" position becomes. I guess it comes down to the fact that I don't think being anyone's assistant will offer me the kinds of challenges I desire. (Man, this is sounding more and more presumptuous and egotistical every minute.) Anyway, from my own standpoint, I would like to be in the position of vice president of administrative services. Here I would have the challenge of line responsibility and the opportunity to test myself. (But I still wouldn't have the kind of "line" challenge and satisfaction you have when you sell a good fabric order, or a plant manager has when he reads the bottom line of his P&L statement.) In charge of administration, I would still have both the time and the authority to conduct the needed analytical studies and services. I would be available to all departments—both informally and formally. In this position I would also be able to involve myself in those kinds of administrative tasks that do not require 20 years of experience in the textile business.

Before you laugh at my conceit, let me explain why I think it's a reasonable gamble from the organization's point of view. We all agreed some time ago that the job should be created. We knew that systems were needed and that a person was needed to supervise these tasks as well as purchasing and credit (neither of which involves close or imaginative supervision). Bill Berkeley can handle the job, and I've heard his name mentioned. But he has said "No" to both of us privately, and I doubt that anyone will change his mind.

"NOW WAIT A MINUTE!! You really want me to say you can be VP of administrative services?!?!?" Yes, I'm only 27 (but, just think! I'll be 28 in June!) Yes, I just started shaving last year. Yes, only 6 months in textiles . . . only 6 months in this company. I realize William is the man to talk to in the end. It's his ball game. But with your understanding and support, my feelings, expectations, and anxieties can be more carefully presented to him. Anyway, I've got enough guts to think I can do a better job there than anyone else we've got. And I don't think it's the kind of position that a new man would be able to take over. I'd be the lowest paid VP in the city, and that'll help our budgets.

I'd like to speak with you about this note and try to cover the 100 other questions that arise from my cocky, impertinent ambition before approaching William.

If and when you show this to William, remind him he once told me to stick around because "the way we are, there are plenty of opportunities to learn." Remind him he said that, and then ask him how he learned to catch a football.

John

Meanwhile, Mitchell continued to work on the remaining plant's marketing study. It was completed in early February and focused on the declining profitability of the large Smith-Abbott mill in Fitchburg. Using it as an excuse to talk to Abbott, he tried to broach the subject of being promoted to the unfilled position of vice president of administrative services. Abbott ignored Mitchell's inquiries, and at the end of February Mitchell's letter of January 13 still remained unanswered by Thompson or Abbott. At that time, Mitchell wrote in his journal:

Well, scratch one effort. I guess they couldn't have made me vice president. Who did I think I was . . . . Oh well, it sounded good at the time. Here I am. A guy who thinks he's an expert in human relations. And I'm tied up in knots by a bunch of dumb playboys! I can't figure it out. One day I think I know why Hicks hasn't done anything. I see a little spark of hope for Abbott. And the next day I hear that Abbott has gone and wasted more money on a project that has no chance of success. You should hear the other executives talk about him. They're all losing confidence. Abbott hasn't called me into his office in almost 3 weeks now. Hell, he used to give me little odd jobs every day.

A RESIGNATION

On February 1, 1969, Berkeley announced his resignation from the National Chemical Company. On the day Berkeley left in mid-March, he and Mitchell had a long luncheon during which he talked about National Chemical and Hicks:

> John, I've worked for that man longer than any of his previous assistants, and I still don't really know him. The "in-fighting" at National is intense as hell nowadays. The president resigned last year and they still haven't filled the position. Hicks knows he's in line for the job. I'm sure the lousy 1968 Texcorp figures shook him up. Abbott keeps telling him "things will improve, things will improve," and I think he believes it! He won't listen to me. I've heard a lot of talk around the chemical company about Hicks and some of the other vice presidents. There's the "pro-Hicks" and the "anti-Hicks" factions.

Mitchell expressed his surprise at the extent of office politics at National Chemical, but admitted that he knew Hicks must be under considerable pressure. Mitchell refrained from telling Berkeley that he wished that Berkeley had prevented the communication gap between National Chemical and Texcorp by being more frank with Hicks.

TEXCORP MANAGEMENT

Mitchell began to believe that everyone in Texcorp, as well as in National Chemical, was guilty of "playing politics." Texcorp's plant managers operated with considerable independence. Martin Steiner, the vice president of finance, was the only headquarters executive who dealt with the plant personnel on a continuing basis. Yet, by January 1969, he had been unable to implement a companywide cost accounting system. The controller of Smith-Abbott Mills, for example, was very "secretive" with cost information and Steiner received only token cooperation from him. On several occasions, Steiner remarked to Mitchell that "things were sure different when old Bob Ford was running the company."

In spite of the attempts by Hicks to restructure the Texcorp organization, the old company loyalties and factions continued to exist. Abbott, Hogan, and Thompson directed the Smith-Abbott plants; White and Steiner spent most of their time dealing with the North Carolina Mills plants; and Rand and Jarvis concerned themselves with the Carolina Cotton plant. As the profitability of Carolina Cotton declined, Rand and Jarvis appeared to "mind their own business" and seemed to avoid discussions with Texcorp executives on overall policies and problems.

Management committee meetings were held monthly in the Texcorp board room. The members of this committee were Abbott, Thompson, Hogan, Rand, Steiner, Kirk, Jarvis, Cleaves, and Hicks. Mitchell was invited by Hicks to attend many of the meetings. His increasing concern over the company's viability and his interest in its management prompted Mitchell to reflect upon the patterns of communication that emerged among the Texcorp executives.

Mitchell observed that when Hicks attended the meetings, a businesslike atmosphere prevailed. The management meeting was almost formal, and the executives seemed alert. Many even took notes as the National Chemical vice president asked his pointed questions. However, Hicks was unable to attend all meetings. In his absence, Abbott would usually begin by smiling and saying, "Well, what'll we talk about today?" Mitchell felt that these meetings often degenerated into rambling discussions of the performance of the three family companies. Members of the management committee were constantly being called to the phone to "put out a fire," and little seemed to be accomplished. Mitchell soon realized that it was an "unwritten rule" that nobody paid much attention to management committee meetings or to decisions made there, for Abbott consulted later with Thompson or Hogan and decided upon the actions to be taken.

To Mitchell, the most distressing aspect of the Texcorp management and communication system was its lack of objectivity. No matter what subject was raised—from buying a new loom to expanding a product line—everyone seemed to have a known and fixed position. Texcorp executives *expected* Thompson to fight for increased expenditures for blended-wool-fabric capacity, and everyone *expected* Jarvis to say that cotton prints were the best long-term investment for the company. Mitchell observed that these expectations were never disappointed. Since the members of the management committee were already "on record" as holding certain opinions, discussions were usually routine and, thought Mitchell, uninteresting. New facts were seldom presented. The voluminous industrywide marketing statistics published by the Textile Trade Association were never cited. Texcorp executives seemed to rely on their intuition and "gut feel" for the situation. The engineering studies of Kirk were privately referred to as "worthless." Cleaves and Steiner confided "off the record" to Mitchell that on several occasions Kirk had changed facts and figures to make the studies "come out the way Abbott wanted."

Despite his feelings, Mitchell tried to remain neutral as far as office politics were concerned, but this was often difficult. He remarked:

> In a climate so politically sticky, I never covered my feelings, pulled punches, or played politics. This got me into trouble. When someone said, "How's it going?" I said, "Lousy." Still, I was everyone's friend. They [Texcorp executives] all wanted me for their assistant, but all of them lacked management expertise.

Mitchell also attempted to figure out why National Chemical (and Hicks) was so reluctant to examine the Texcorp situation. He thought one reason might be the fact that the presidency of National Chemical had been unfilled for several months and a successor had not yet been chosen.

> Hicks may be mixed up in the hassle over who gets to be president at National Chemical. He wants to sweep Texcorp under the rug because it's a bomb. They have lost at least $5 million in profits because of Texcorp, and part of this is company politics. Bill Abbott was one of the largest single stockholders in National Chemical, and he also knew Bill Scott [chairperson of the board of National Chemical]. So Abbott was formidable.

FURTHER DIFFICULTIES

In February 1969, Richard Hicks was asked by the former president of National Chemical to join him in Washington, D.C., where the ex-president had taken on a major administrative role in the Nixon administration. After conferring with the chairperson of National Chemical's board of directors, it was agreed that Hicks would spend February, March, April, and May in Washington on a special reorganization assignment for a major federal agency, working for National's ex-president. According to Hicks:

> I told National not to bother me in Washington unless they had a real problem. My single exception had to be the Texcorp situation during this period of time. Normally, I never would have gotten involved in this except that there was nobody that I could pass it on to. The textile business came out of the blue, and while Texcorp's volume was $65 million, there wasn't a soul in it who could run it.

In February, an incident occurred that Mitchell found distressing but almost humorous. Three new looms had been installed in Bill Davis' plant (North Carolina Mills), and Abbott dispatched Hogan to supervise the break-in period at the plant. Davis had not been informed and was upset when Hogan walked into his plant and began to ask questions. Davis placed calls to White and Rand, protesting Hogan's presence, and finally called Abbott. The irate plant manager said he could handle any start-up problem. Abbott explained that Hogan was just "inspecting" the new looms and said that Kirk had suggested that Hogan be present when they started operations.

Mitchell became involved in the controversy when he had lunch with Kirk the day after Hogan's arrival at North Carolina Mills. Kirk was furious. He did not respect Hogan and said he "didn't particularly care for Bill Davis" either. But he stated that he had never suggested that Hogan be sent to the plant! "Now Jim and Marty Steiner will get furious with me. They think I sicced Hogan on Davis. You should talk to them, John, and tell them what really happened." Mitchell discovered from Fagan that Kirk had, in fact, written a memo about the looms to Abbott. When questioned by Abbott, the chief engineer had evidently agreed that Hogan might "supervise the looms for a few weeks." A few days later, Mitchell mentioned the matter to Berkeley (before he had left the company). Berkeley remarked that Kirk seldom disagreed with any of Abbott's suggestions. The entire incident seemed ridiculous to Mitchell, but Berkeley pointed out that such "misunderstandings" were common at Texcorp.

In short, what really concerned Mitchell were the day-to-day politics at Texcorp:

> The number one priority here is personalities. The prime commodity people fight for is Abbott's time. I'm shocked at the amount of time spent on personalities. Eighty to 85 percent of people's time is spent warming up somebody, cooling off somebody, or on other nontask conversations.
>
> Another related commodity is information—facts about what's going on, who's talking to whom, etc. But you can't get any data from the responsible people; the secretaries are the people to talk to if you want information. Everyone relies on rumor, and people here ask the secretaries to relate casual conversations they've overheard so they can figure out which way the wind is blowing. Mary Fagan even says that Abbott has asked her to spy on me!

Many people at Texcorp seemed to use Mitchell as a confidant, and Mitchell felt he had to keep a delicate balance of discretion and candor. For instance, Steiner would complain to him that he desperately needed a new accountant, and this complaint would serve as a smokescreen if Steiner's department got behind in its work. Mitchell felt that Kirk, the head engineer, felt almost paranoid about authority. If Abbott requested that Kirk see him in his ofice, Kirk would always call Mitchell first to find out what Abbott wanted.

During March, Mitchell became increasingly aware that he was being asked more frequently to listen to the problems of various company executives. Cleaves confided in him almost daily. Cleaves' responsibilities had been reduced when Texcorp was reorganized, and he constantly spoke of retiring or quitting. Hogan also expressed personal opinions to Mitchell. His new position of manufacturing services manager was a clear demotion. Hogan was 62 years old and admitted to Mitchell that he knew "his days were numbered." Beginning in January, Steiner and White spoke to Mitchell about the financial and sales deficiencies at Texcorp. They encouraged Mitchell to "speak to someone at National Chemical" to see if Abbott could be replaced and new talent recruited. Mitchell had initially responded by speaking to Berkeley, but advised both Steiner and White that they should approach Hicks. As Mitchell observed to the casewriter:

> The atmosphere was getting thick as glue around Texcorp then. The company was going downhill. Abbott was spending more time on the links. Everyone seemed to come to me with their problems. What was I supposed to do? Except Andy. . . . He and Abbott didn't talk to me anymore. I guess they knew I thought they were both doing a lousy job. But, hell, they were in charge. All guys like Cleaves, Jarvis, and Steiner seemed to be doing was a lot of bitching.

During February and early March, Mitchell made several trips, at Hicks' request, to Washington to see Hicks about Texcorp's problems. Mitchell had become convinced beyond a doubt that Texcorp was being badly mismanaged. As Hicks recalled these visits:

> I saw Mitchell virtually every week during that period. He would fly to Washington and have dinner with me, or I would see him somehow. We made some long lists of things for him to do, because he could operate in the breach. Abbott wasn't there most of the time, and Mitchell had enough savvy to check these things out. In addition, the plant managers and the marketing people thought that Mitchell was good because he asked intelligent questions, and he was available to discuss things with. I thought that here was a superb opportunity for Mitchell to get his hands on things.

However, in early March Mitchell announced to Abbott that he was thinking about resigning from the company. He felt badly about raising the issue with Abbott because he thought that Hicks felt that Abbott should be fired, and Mitchell knew that he was partly responsible for that conclusion. Abbott reacted calmly to Mitchell's speculations about resigning and remarked that it was "too bad," but that would have to be Mitchell's decision. As Mitchell noted:

> Hell, he just sat there. The bastard. Didn't even bat an eye. I gave him the chance to try and talk me out of it. It was half a bluff anyway. Man, now I have to find another job! Wait till Hicks hears this. He's going to wonder what's been going on while he was away.

The following day, Mitchell told Cleaves what he had done. Cleaves reacted emotionally and told Mitchell he was a fool. "The future of Texcorp will rest with people like you," he exclaimed. "You're throwing away a great opportunity. You know National Chemical will have to move in soon. And when they do, you will be the one who comes out on top!" Later on that day, Abbott called Mitchell into his office and asked if he would "reconsider" his thoughts about resignation. Mitchell said he could only reconsider if "major changes" were implemented at Texcorp. Mitchell agreed to spell them out in writing. Abbott said he would read Mitchell's proposals and that they would talk about them.

Word of Mitchell's conversation with Abbott soon spread through Texcorp, and Mitchell spent the next few days answering questions about what he had said. His efforts to evade questions only seemed to add to the air of mystery and the tensions that already existed. Without exception, Texcorp managers told Mitchell that they admired his "guts" for confronting Abbott. They also hoped that Mitchell's confrontation with Abbott would help to force National Chemical into taking some action on Abbott.

During the next few weeks, Mitchell spoke several times with Hicks and planned what he would try to convey to Abbott. In early April, Texcorp's first quarter results were released. Texcorp had lost more than $1 million after taxes. Texcorp executives now spoke openly about moving to greener pastures, and the offices on executive row were generally empty. Hogan, at Abbott's suggestion, was spending all of his time at one of the large North Carolina Mills plants. Rinehart seldom came into the office, and Rand had taken a month's vacation. On one of these days, White stepped into Mitchell's office and announced that he had just spoken to Hicks to communicate to him "just how bad things are really getting at Texcorp." White smiled as he said:

> From what Hicks told me today, John, I'm sure we'll see some big changes very soon. This time, I know it will happen.

Later the same day, Mitchell received a call from Hicks who said that, in preparation for his return to the National Chemical Company from Washington on June 1, he would like Mitchell to prepare a set of recommended actions to be taken at Texcorp. While he was pleased to be thought of so highly by Hicks, Mitchell remained skeptical about the future of Texcorp and actively continued his consideration of resigning from the firm.

PETER OLAFSON (A)[1]

John J. Gabarro

Peter Olafson looked at his calendar, which read March 10, and saw that he had roughly 2 weeks to prepare for a meeting with Chet Knowles, the newly appointed director of preoperating systems for Universal Communication Systems, Inc. Knowles had just called from the company's Beverly Hills headquarters to set up a 2-day meeting with Olafson at the end of the month. The purpose of the meeting was to review several problems that Olafson's organization had been experiencing and to discuss Olafson's plans for dealing with them. It would also give Knowles a chance to meet Olafson and see the St. Paul opertions on a first-hand basis.

Olafson was general manager of Cable King Television Company of St. Paul, a cable television system serving the greater Minneapolis–St. Paul area, which had not yet begun operations. Olafson had been hired as general manager of the St. Paul system by the parent company, Universal Communication Systems, Inc. (commonly referred to within the industry as UniComm). He had joined UniComm immediately upon receiving an MBA the preceding June and had taken charge of the St. Paul operation in August after a 2-month orientation period of visiting other systems within UniComm. Olafson had felt very fortunate to have the opportunity to be a general manager this early in his career.

The St. Paul system was one of three UniComm systems that were designated preoperating systems because they had not yet commenced commercial operations. The St. Paul company had been targeted to begin service to subscribers on February 1, but was now a month behind schedule because of several major problems. The

[1] The situation described in this case is reported primarily from Olafson's point of view. Although other views of the situation have been incorporated, the case does not necessarily reflect the perceptions of all others involved. All names, places, and companies have been disguised.

newly revised "turn-on" date that Olafson had submitted to Beverly Hills was April 1, 3 weeks away, and the purpose of the meeting with Knowles was to review Olafson's plans for meeting that date.[2]

PETER OLAFSON

Olafson was 31 years old, married, and the father of two children. Before attending business school, he had been a captain in the U.S. Army Signal Corps and had held several jobs as a communications engineer. Olafson had earned a BS in electrical engineering from MIT and a master's degree in communications engineering from the University of Minnesota. Olafson had been described by classmates in business school as being a very bright, conscientious, and well-liked person who seemed to be more mature and stable than most people his age. Olafson had been raised in a small town outside of Newport, R.I., during which time his father had alternately served as captain on large privately owned yachts or merchant vessels. His father had emigrated from Norway as a young man and had risen to the master's rank in the Merchant Marine. His mother was a native of the Newport area and had lived there much of her life. Olafson had a younger brother and an older sister.

Although Olafson had never worked in cable television before joining UniComm, his interest in the area had been growing for several years. During that time, he concluded that the cable television field offered great potential for growth and opportunity. It was one of the few remaining parts of the communications business that was dominated by private entrepreneurs on both the local and national levels, and the industry still offered the promise of future expansion. Thus, Olafson decided to interview companies in the industry as part of his second-year job search. UniComm was one of these companies, and Olafson was interviewed and hired by William Jurgens, the company's founder and president.

When Jurgens made him a job offer, Olafson was told that he would be in charge of the St. Paul operation. Jurgens explained that the St. Paul system was having a number of serious start-up problems and that it was a relatively high-exposure situation for UniComm. He added that the Twin Cities area promised to be a highly attractive and profitable market; it would certainly provide Olafson with a challenge. Jurgens explained that because of the departure of UniComm's vice president of operations, Jurgens would pay very close attention to the St. Paul operation. Olafson felt very fortunate to have the opportunity to work directly for Jurgens, at least initially.

Olafson had been very impressed by both UniComm and Jurgens. Jurgens had founded UniComm and had built it from a small West Coast system to a $25-million company that currently ranked in the top 20 in the industry. He had a reputation for being one of the toughest people in the cable television industry, and was seen by many as a self-made man whose ability and aggressiveness had taken him from modest beginnings in Chicago to considerable success, wealth, and influence.

---

[2] The expression *turn on* was used in the cable television industry to refer to the date on which a system began to serve customers.

Indeed, Olafson recalled Jurgens was such a demanding individual that when the new Sacramento system failed to meet his expectations, he replaced its manager and ordered its new manager to report directly to him. (Sacramento had been one of the first major franchises won by UniComm and, therefore, was a system in which Uni-Comm's visibility and stakes were high.) Jurgens had seen Sacramento as an opportunity for UniComm to develop a "showcase" system, but instead the operation had encountered enormous cost and schedule problems. To remedy the situation, Jurgens placed a promising young manager in charge of Sacramento, and he himself actively worked with the new manager.

CABLE KING TELEVISION COMPANY

Cable King Television Company of St. Paul had been legally in existence for 4 years before Olafson's arrival. The company had been formed by UniComm, which owned 85 percent of its stock, and a St. Paul businessperson who acted as the local partner. The first 3 years of its existence were spent in securing state, federal, and local franchises and obtaining permission to operate in the St. Paul area. When Olafson arrived in August, six people were already working on the design, preparation, and initial construction of the system.

BACKGROUND ON THE CURRENT SITUATION

The past 7 months had been a difficult and, at times, frustrating period for Olafson. He regularly worked 60 to 80 hours a week and, at times, Cable King's problems seemed so incessant that he would awaken in the middle of the night thinking about them. The problems began almost immediately. Upon arrival in St. Paul, Olafson discovered that instead of reporting to Jurgens, as he had assumed, he was assigned to Jim Harvey, UniComm's director of budgets and plans. Harvey had been placed in charge of all preoperating systems as well as of other tasks during Olafson's orientation period. (See Exhibit 1 for UniComm's organization at the time Olafson took charge of the St. Paul system.) Harvey had received an MBA several years before Olafson had received his degree, but had never had system operating experience. As a result, Olafson found that Harvey was unable to offer him any initial advice or guidance that was specific or helpful. In fact, the nature of their relationship was somewhat ambiguous and awkward in the beginning, because Olafson had never been formally told by Jurgens or Harvey of the reporting relationship. It just seemed to have occurred.

Olafson also discovered that the initial construction of cable lines, which was being performed by a subcontractor, was already several weeks behind schedule and that they would never meet the turn-on target at the current rate. Efforts to get the subcontractor to improve his construction pace failed, and Olafson found that the company was receiving an increasing number of complaints from local citizens about the way the subcontractor was cutting through privately owned trees and property. Thus, Olafson's first major decision was to terminate the relationship with the subcontractor and to contract with the Land O' Lakes Construction Company, a Wis-

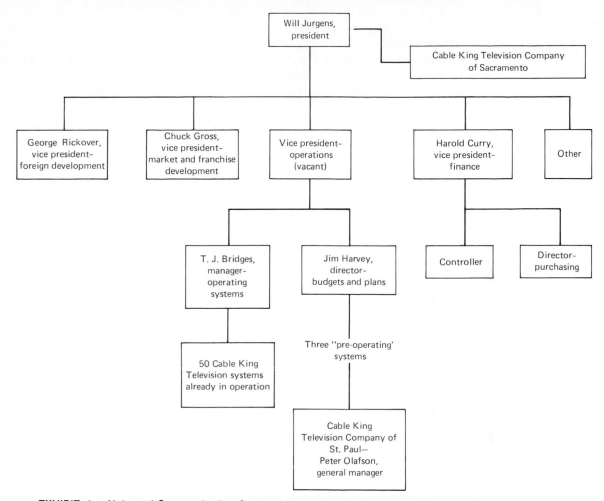

EXHIBIT 1   Universal Communication Systems, Inc.—organization prior to February 28.

consin-based firm that Olafson felt could provide better service. This decision was received somewhat reluctantly by Beverly Hills, however, because the previous subcontractor had done considerable work for UniComm in the past. Olafson felt that the former subcontractor, based in Oklahoma, was too distant to provide adequate back-up support, and he succeeded in convincing Beverly Hills that the change was necessary.

Problems with the Chief Engineer

Olafson also found that he had difficulties getting the chief engineer, Kurt Anderson, to do the planning and organizing necessary to ensure that materials arrived when needed. This planning was particularly important since four of the activities required to build the system had to be carefully coordinated if the system was to work according to specificiations and meet the targeted turn-on date. These four activities included the initial design of the system and specifications of equipment; the liaison with local utility companies so that utility pole facilities were made ready so that cable lines could be attached to them according to design specifications; the installation of the necessary power supplies, amplifiers, and taps in the system; and finally, the installation of the converting equipment in the subscriber's home and its connection to the system. (See Exhibit 2 for a more-detailed description of these activities,

EXHIBIT 2   ACTIVITIES REQUIRED TO BUILD A CABLE TELEVISION SYSTEM

The building of a cable television system took place in five interrelated phases, as outlined below.

Design and layout of the system	This first phase included the design of the total system, the decision as to where the cable was to be hung or laid, its connection to the local power company's lines, and specification of the various equipment needed to make the total system compatible. This activity was the responsibility of Cable King's chief engineer, Kurt Anderson.
Right of way	The second phase was generally referred to as gaining right of way. This involved contacting people who owned property through which the cable had to pass and obtaining from them verbal, if not written, permission to cross their property lines. This activity was performed by Cable King's right-of-way department.
Construction of the cable network	The third phase involved actually hanging or laying the cable according to the system plan. This was done by the subcontractor under the supervision of Cable King's construction department.
Installation of line equipment	The fourth phase involved the installation into the system of amplifiers and taps (into which subscribers' lines were connected), power supplies, and other equipment. Before installing this equipment (and before hanging the cable), it was necessary to go through make-ready procedures: obtaining permission from utilities to use their facilities and ensuring that the utilities made the necessary preparations so Cable King could tie into their facilities and hang cable on their poles. The installation of line equipment also involved "proofing" the system to ensure that it met the plan's requirements and specifications. Both the equipment installation and proofing functions were performed by Cable King's technical department.
Installation of subscribers' equipment	The fifth and final phase was the installation of service in subscribers' homes. This involved installing a converter on the customer's television set and connecting it into the nearest tap in the cable system. This activity was performed by Cable King's customer installation department.

These various activities were carried out by different parts of the organization, as described in Exhibit 3. The chief engineer was responsible for the overall design and specification of the system, while the construction department was responsible for supervising the subcontractor's construction of the cable network as well as for ensuring that the local power and telephone companies made their facilities ready for the cable. The technical department, which also reported to the chief engineer, was responsible for supervising the installation of the taps and amplifiers and for proofing the system. The actual installation of converters in the customer's home was performed by the installation department once the cables and line equipment were in place and the system had been "proofed."

and Exhibit 3 for a description of the St. Paul organization and the apportionment of work within it.) Since the effective functioning and overall integrity of the system depended on the compatibility of all its parts, it was crucial that the various parts of the system fit together and that the specification, delivery, and installation of these components be carefully planned and coordinated.

Olafson first became aware of Anderson's difficulties in handling planning aspects within the first few weeks at St. Paul. He discussed this problem with Harvey several times and raised it again in Beverly Hills in October, but to no avail. Anderson had originally worked as a line installer and had risen to chief engineer in the St. Louis system. He had gained a reputation within UniComm as being a first-rate technician. However, after Olafson's first 3 or 4 months, he realized that Anderson lacked the administrative ability and the knowledge needed to start a brand new operation.

EXHIBIT 3   Cable King Television Company of St. Paul—organization chart. (Numbers in parentheses represent people in each function.)

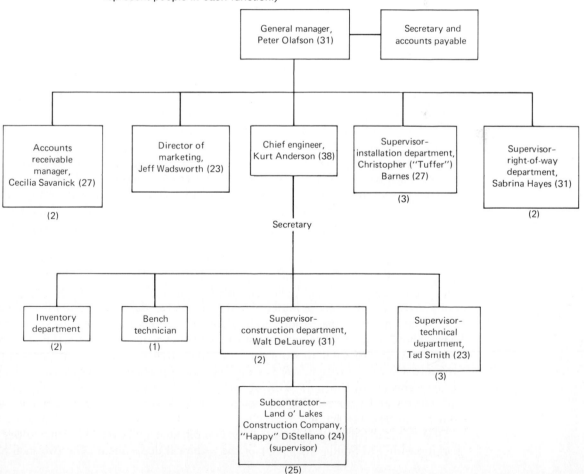

None of his previous jobs had required the detailed planning and designing needed to build a new system. Olafson felt this limitation especially keenly, because he himself had no experience in cable television and was learning about it. He needed to rely on the chief engineer's abilities and knowledge.

During his October visit to Beverly Hills, Olafson raised the possibility that Anderson be reassigned and replaced by a person with preoperating and start-up experience. However, because of the company's rapid expansion and the newness of the industry, such people were in short supply. In addition, the Beverly Hills group insisted that Anderson had the potential to handle a start-up and required only additional coaching and help from Olafson. In addition, UniComm had just relocated Anderson and his family from St. Louis to St. Paul, and Olafson suspected that the company did not wish to move him again.

Olafson took several steps to help Anderson improve the planning and coordination. One step was to have one-on-one counseling sessions with him in which Olafson tried to show Anderson how to plan better. A second step was to have Anderson call weekly construction meetings to which everyone in the organization was invited, including the new subcontractor's supervisor, "Happy" DiStellano. Olafson felt that these meetngs would also increase the sense of participation of people in the organization and would help prevent the spread of rumors by open communication. Olafson thought that these meetings were quite useful, but that Anderson did not become involved enough in them. Olafson found himself getting most of his reports directly from Anderson's two subordinates—Tad Smith, supervisor of the technical department, and Walt DeLaurey, supervisor of Cable King's construction department—despite his attempts to get Anderson more actively involved.

Olafson's third step was to establish an inventory-control reporting system. But again he found that Anderson resisted the effort. Olafson suspected that Anderson was somehow resentful because Olafson did not "trust him implicitly." Whatever the reason, Olafson continued to have difficulty in getting completed reports from Kurt on time. In fact, the inventory control problem became so great that on two occasions Cable King ran short of cable for construction. In each case, Olafson discovered the shortage during a weekly construction meeting, and it was clear that the shortage was as much of a surprise to Anderson as it was to him. The first case occurred in early December when Happy DiStellano mentioned that his crews were nearly out of cable and would have to stop construction. Fortunately, there was other work for the crews to do and Olafson handled the situation with Anderson gently, trying to explain the need for better planning. However, during this and other discussions, Olafson sensed that Anderson was angered by the implied criticism, but that he was "bottling it up." The problem of cable inventory recurred in mid-January (but some uninventoried cable was discovered in the warehouse, temporarily solving the problem). On each occasion, word of the impending problem had come from Happy during a construction meeting. During this period, Olafson discussed these problems with Harvey and again raised the possibility of Anderson's transfer, but Harvey was reluctant to take any action.

Olafson's early problems were further complicated by Anderson's difficulties in working with Tad Smith, supervisor of the technical department. The two men had several conflicts over the selection and specification of equipment. In fact, their differences over these issues occurred so frequently that Smith told Olafson several times that he was better qualified than Anderson and that he wanted Anderson's job. Despite Anderson's limitations, Olafson did not share Smith's view.

During this period, Olafson also observed that Anderson had several arguments with Cecilia Savanick, Olafson's secretary. Most of the arguments concerned errors in applications prepared by Anderson and typed by Savanick. In all of these arguments, each person attributed the errors to the other. Anderson openly described himself as a "male supremacist," and Olafson felt that this affected his ability to work with Savanick, whom Olafson found to be highly competent, precise, and mature. Although Olafson did not know for sure, he suspected that Anderson resented having his errors pointed out by a woman.

Key Personnel Assignments

During the fall, three key people joined Cable King of St. Paul. One of these was Jeff Wadsworth, a 23-year-old college graduate, who was brought in as director of marketing. Olafson saw Wadsworth as an aggressive, ambitious person who often "rubbed people the wrong way," particularly the technical personnel, in his hurry to get things done. Olafson also discovered that Wadsworth's market plans were not sufficiently detailed and that they required careful review. Unfortunately, as St. Paul's technical problems mounted, Olafson found himself with less and less time to do this. But, on the whole, he found Wadsworth competent and hard-working.

Christopher Barnes, called "Tuffer," was the second key person to join Cable King. Tuffer, a 27-year-old college graduate, had been in business for himself and had considerable "hands-on" knowledge of equipment and procedures, although he had no previous experience in cable television. Tuffer, who was hired to run the installation department, had come from a wealthy Massachusetts family, and Olafson found him very bright and knowledgeable. However, Tuffer and Anderson soon developed problems working with each other, even though Tuffer had been hired on Anderson's recommendation. Olafson believed that some of these difficulties resulted from Tuffer's many suggestions about equipment selection and procedures. Although many of Tuffer's ideas were excellent, some were impractical and his constant flow of new ideas eventually became a problem for everyone, including Olafson and Smith. It became such a problem that, by January, Olafson had to discuss it with Tuffer. During this period, the relationship between Tuffer and Anderson became quite strained. Olafson suspected that some of these difficulties may have been caused by Anderson's defensiveness over not having a college degree and his resulting annoyance at Tuffer's constant flow of criticisms and suggestions.

The third key person to join Cable King was Sabrina Hayes, a 31-year-old woman with a master's degree in social work. Hayes was hired early in the fall to run the right-of-way department. The right-of-way department had been in major trouble when Olafson first arrived, and Olafson felt that Hayes had done an excellent job in organizing the department and developing good relations with property owners and future subscribers. Hayes was referred to within Cable King as the "hippy freak" because of her style of dress, but she seemed to get along quite well with most staff and very well with the public. By late winter, Olafson had come to respect and trust her judgment a great deal. Hayes was very outspoken and had considerable ability to organize and to get to the heart of a problem.

In addition to hiring these people, Olafson also promoted Savanick to manager of accounts receivable in February. Olafson encountered difficulties with Beverly Hills over this assignment, because he had offered her the job at a salary of $9000. Olafson felt this figure was appropriate for the position given the local job market, but UniComm thought that the resulting increase over her previous salary was excessive. Eventually, Beverly Hills approved an increase to only $8300. Olafson felt that Savanick had been quite disappointed by the reversal and knew that the quality of her work had suffered as a result.

Olafson encountered another salary problem when he hired Tuffer Barnes. Olafson had offered Tuffer a salary of $12,750, which he accepted. However, before Tuffer joined the company, Smith, who was earning only $8700, found out about Tuffer's salary. Smith complained vigorously to Anderson about the difference and Anderson brought the matter up with Olafson. Olafson then talked with both Anderson and Smith about it. Olafson reminded Smith that he would be reviewed in a month and told him that he would receive an increase at that time. Still, Olafson had felt extremely uncomfortable with the apparent inequity, because Smith was a likeable, effective worker with considerable cable television experience. Olafson then also discussed this problem with Tuffer to let him know that his salary had become known within the company. As a result, Tuffer voluntarily offered to accept a salary of $11,000 to smoothe the organizational problems and facilitate his entry into the organization. Tuffer explained that one of his motivations in joining Cable King was to learn some of the more technical aspects of cable television from Smith and Anderson. Thus, Tuffer joined the firm at the lower salary with the promise of an increase in 6 months.

Despite these problems, Olafson believed he had put together a good organization with high morale. It mattered to him that people worked as a team and that organization was managed with as much participation as possible. In fact, Olafson had instituted weekly companywide meetings and invited all company employees. The purpose of these meetings was to discuss the problems of various departments and to maximize the exchange of ideas among people in the company. Many employees had remarked to Olafson that they had found the weekly meetings very effective and that morale and understanding of the company's problems had increased substantially as a result of the greater interchange. The basic organization that had emerged by January is shown in Exhibit 3.

Equipment Problems

Olafson's first 6 months at St. Paul had also been complicated by several equipment problems. Although it was theoretically possible—and also desirable—to perform the activities in the order described in Exhibit 2, it was seldom practical to specify and select all of the system's equipment before the construction or installation of the various phases began. This had been particularly true in St. Paul, because Beverly Hills had delayed in making several key decisions and had made several changes in the equipment originally specified. The decision on the use of a converter (which Beverly Hills promised would be made by October) had not been made by Jurgens until early February. St. Paul was to be the first system within UniComm to use converters, and Beverly Hills had wished to defer the decision as long as possible to acquire more information. As a result of this delay, UniComm's prime supplier of converters could not deliver on time and UniComm had to turn to an alternate source, whose equipment was later found defective, thereby requiring renegotiation with the first supplier. In addition, Beverly Hills changed the power-supply ratings in December, and Harvey did not inform Olafson of this until January. Thus, the equipment that St. Paul had in inventory could not be used, and additional design changes had to be made. To further complicate the situation, Beverly Hills subsequently decided in January to have all power supplies include standby batteries. This also created problems with suppliers.

A third decision made by Beverly Hills in January changed the basic concept used for laying out the system. This decision changed the concept from one that was based on grid maps of the areas to be serviced to one that was based on the location of power supplies. The reason for the change was that it would improve the inventory control of materials in new systems. Olafson could see its advantages but also felt that the change would create many problems in adapting existing maps and plans, and would further add to the work and coordination that Kurt had to deal with. However, Olafson was unsuccessful in influencing Harvey to reverse the decision as it applied to St. Paul. This created further problems with deliveries, and the new power supplies did not arrive until the end of February.

Indeed, Olafson had felt consistently hampered by his inability to obtain support or clear direction from Harvey. The only suggestion of major substance offered by Harvey (but with which Olafson did not agree) was how to develop the system's territory. Harvey urged Olafson to develop the high-density population areas and then expand to outlying towns, because this would bring a larger number of initial subscribers into the system when the turn-on occurred. However, Olafson felt that the high-density areas were the most difficult to build in and would require the most effort to develop, causing further delay of the turn-on date. To Olafson, it made more sense to develop the easier territories first. Olafson remembered these discussions as being extremely exhausting, but never coming to a real resolution. With this exception, however, Harvey's four visits to St. Paul had been characterized by what Olafson described as "nitpicking," such as the number of uniforms the installers should be issued, and had failed to resolve any of the major problems that Olafson felt he had to deal with. Olafson suspected that some of Harvey's indecisiveness was caused by Harvey's relationship with Jurgens. Olafson had sensed from the beginning that Harvey was somewhat insecure and anxious about how he stood with Jurgens. In many ways, Olafson could understand why that might be the case. Like Olafson, Harvey was hampered by minimal operating experience in cable television. In addition, many people in UniComm saw Jurgens as strong-willed, demanding, formidable, and intimidating.

CURRENT PROBLEMS

Although many of the technical problems just described had been resolved by early March, several other problems arose that threatened the April 1 turn-on target. Olafson had attempted to deal with Anderson's inability to plan by hiring a construction coordinator in January to do it for him. However, Olafson experienced difficulties finding a qualified person given the salary limitations of the position. Finally, Olafson promoted someone from the construction ranks who had a college degree, but that person left after 2 weeks for a better salary. Olafson knew it would be difficult to find a replacement quickly, and as a result he appointed Hayes construction coordinator and reorganized the St. Paul operations in early March as shown in Exhibit 4. Olafson had been very impressed by her work as head of the right-of-way department and trusted her ability to get the job done. However, he was not completely comfortable with the way Walt DeLaurey, the construction supervisor, would react to having her as a boss, so he had not yet fully explained the new reporting relationship to him. Olafson felt that once the two began working together

EXHIBIT 4   Cable King Television Company of St. Paul—revised organization chart.

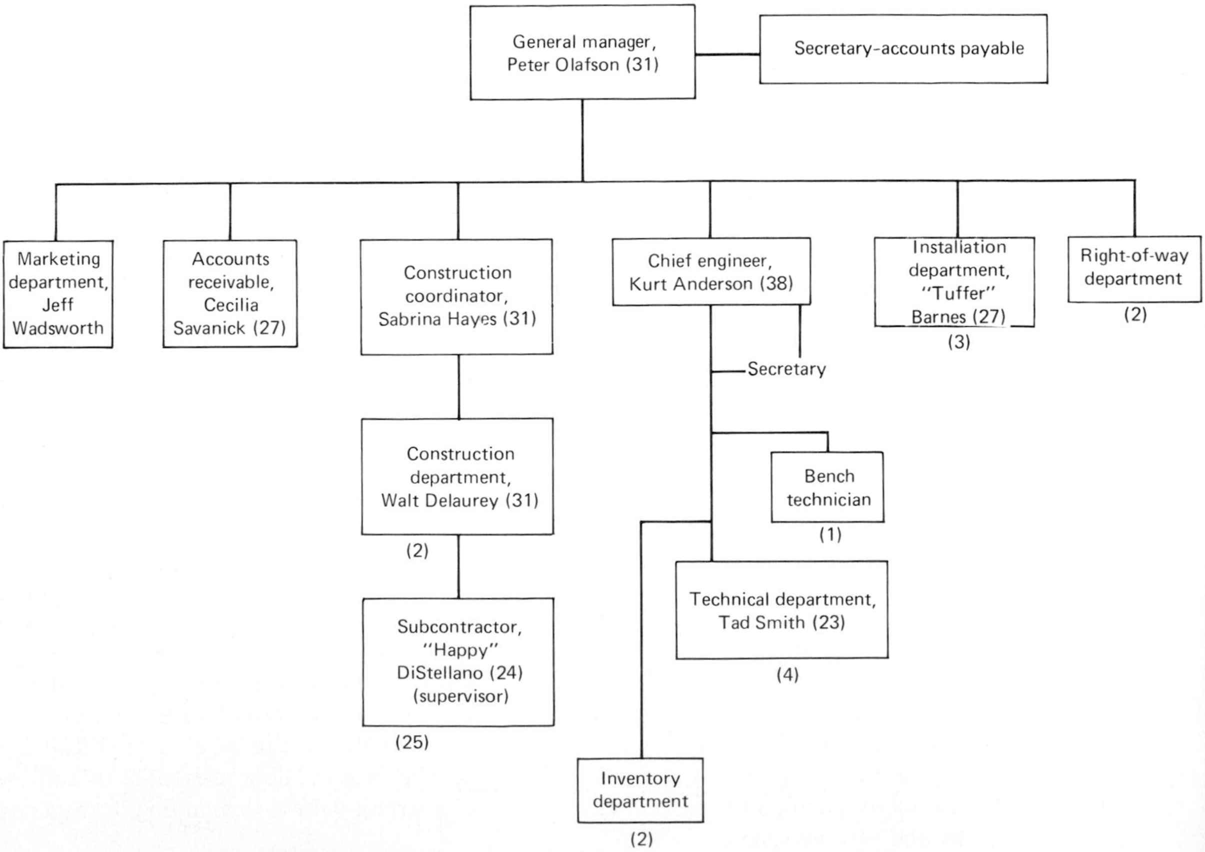

it would be easier to do so, and it would also allow Hayes time to become familiar with construction operations in greater detail. Olafson believed that involvement of Hayes in the construction effort would greatly improve the situation. Although De-Laurey was a hard-working, likeable man, he had never finished high school and had no previous experience as a supervisor; Olafson felt he had limited planning ability.

Franchise Problems

Another problem area was the current state of Cable King's franchises in four towns in the Twin Cities area. The franchises in the Twin Cities area had been awaiting approval from the Federal Communications Commission (FCC) since January 1. The delay was partly caused by an FCC suit that had not been settled until early December. Although the FCC had approved all franchises in the Twin Cities area, the state cable commission had not approved the franchises for four towns. These four towns could now choose to amend their franchises to bring them into compliance with the state commission's new rules or renegotiate the franchise on whatever terms they wished. One town wanted to renegotiate the terms of the franchise concerning the amount of community access the system would offer, that is, the number of channels and facilities that would be made available to public groups such as local school systems or libraries. A second town contended that the rates were too high. The remaining two towns were concerned with both issues but not as strongly. Olafson knew that if they wished, the towns could eventually ask for new bids and reinitiate the whole process.

Olafson also believed Beverly Hills did not fully appreciate the strength of the state commission's stand on the public access question. He had been approached numerous times by local citizens and representatives of the state cable commission concerning the amount of support Cable King was willing to give to public access in the area. As a result, Olafson had raised the issue with Harvey several times and went so far as to send Harvey a memo outlining the equipment needed to satisfy local demands. To Olafson, the funds needed were insignificant given the benefits the public and the company could derive, but everytime he raised the matter with Harvey he felt he received a "runaround." Because he failed to get a definite answer from Harvey, Olafson equivocated with the state commission on the amount of support Cable King could offer. Olafson felt that Harvey had a very unrealistic picture of the local situation and that Harvey's only concern was the effect public access had on the budget and ROI. Olafson was afraid that Cable King's equivocation might affect its reputation and relations with local citizens' groups and the state cable commission. He was particularly concerned about this because the public access question was receiving considerable publicity in the local St. Paul newspapers.

Olafson found the franchise renewals and public access question to be major problems because he did not have the time to become involved with local attorneys, town boards, and public hearings. However, Olafson did feel some relief from the immediate franchise pressures facing him because Beverly Hills had become involved in renegotiating the franchises. Beverly Hills was responsible for market and franchise development and had negotiated the original franchises. (See Exhibit 1 for UniComm's organization before February 28.) Two people from Beverly Hills— Chuck Gross, UniComm's vice president of market and franchise development, and Diana Cohen, a staff assistant—had become actively involved in the renegotiating activities. In fact, Cohen had taken it on as a project. Although Olafson felt relieved that Cohen was handling the details, he was not sure if he should ask Gross to have her report directly to him on it because of its importance. A successful resolution of the franchise problem was essential to Cable King's service, and Olafson felt uneasy about not being directly involved in its solution. On the other hand, he felt he had enough problems with the technical aspects of the system without being immersed in the franchise problem as well. Thus, he welcomed the relief of not having to supervise the franchise negotiations and hearings.

In addition, he felt somewhat uncomfortable with both Cohen and Gross because of an encounter with them during his orientation period. This encounter had left him with such negative feelings that he was eager not to tangle with them again. As part of his summer orientation, Olafson had been asked to visit the Fort Wayne system and write a report on his observations. In this report, Olafson had criticized the system's chief engineer, whom he felt was technically brilliant but ineffective as a manager, as well as the system's manager, whom he saw as not delegating enough responsibility. When he subsequently visited Beverly Hills, Gross requested his observations of the Fort Wayne operation. Olafson gave Gross a verbal summary of his impressions and, after he finished, Gross vehemently attacked him for criticizing what Gross perceived to be one of the best UniComm systems. Olafson was quite surprised by Gross's hostile and emotional reaction, and, during the ensuing exchange, Gross asked Olafson what his background was. When Olafson explained that he had just finished an MBA, Gross lectured him on how much he needed to learn about cable television. Gross, who was only 37, was recognized by many as a "wunderkind" in the industry. He had a reputation for being a sharp, smooth man with an entrepreneurial flair for being a wheeler-dealer. Like Jurgens, he, too, had been raised in the Chicago area and had worked his way up in the cable television business. Olafson resented Gross's imperious and egotistical manner and ended up feeling a distinct dislike for him.

Before meeting with Gross, Olafson had also met with Cohen. During their meeting, Olafson felt that Cohen had told him in no uncertain terms what she thought he needed to do in St. Paul. Several of her suggestions struck Olafson as being blatantly incorrect, given what he knew of the St. Paul area from his days at the University of Minnesota. When he challenged some of her statements, she became very agitated and was visibly upset when Gross arrived. As a result of these two exchanges, he had found his experience with both people to be very disturbing and was not inclined to interfere with their work in the franchise problem—particularly since he sensed that Cohen "idolized" Gross and might resent reporting to Olafson on the project.

Other Problems

Olafson had several other situations that needed to be dealt with to ensure the scheduled turn-on date. One situation was Cable King's difficulty in getting the local utility to make its facilities ready according to the promised schedule. These difficulties had becomme so great that Olafson had met with the president of the utility in mid-February. Although the meeting had gone quite well and the president had promised better service, the utility had continued to fall behind its make-ready schedule. From what Olafson could gather, he suspected that many of the problems were caused by a union steward in the utility company who was intentionally slowing down the make-ready process. Whatever the cause, the utility's make-ready speed was a severe problem. Olafson felt that since Anderson had not been successful in planning construction or dealing with the utility in the past, he would have to involve himself more deeply in these matters. If the utility did not respond, Cable King's construction would be halted in less than 3 months and the crews would have to be laid off.

Another major problem was the strained relationship between Anderson and Tuffer. As Cable King approached the turn-on date, the installation of subscriber service (Tuffer's area) became an increasingly important activity, as did the coordination between the two men. The most recent conflict between the two involved the selection of trucks to be ordered for the customer installation workers. Anderson wanted to buy open-bay pickup trucks because they would give the installer easier access to the equipment, while Tuffer wanted closed-panel trucks because of the difficult winters in St. Paul. Tuffer argued that while open-bay trucks may have been practical in San Diego, they would impose a major hardship on installers working in the St. Paul climate. Olafson finally settled the conflict by ordering open-bay trucks, except for two closed-panel trucks. These panel trucks were selected for line installers, who had to do the greatest amount of on-site preparation and therefore needed to be sheltered from the cold. This latest conflict between the two men had deepened their mutual animosity, and Olafson felt that some action needed to be taken to help them work together better.

Olafson did not expect any problems in the marketing area once the system was turned on, and felt it would simply be a question of implementing the market plan.

KNOWLES AND UNICOMM'S REORGANIZATION

Olafson was looking forward to talking with Knowles about his plans for dealing with these problems. He also felt the recently implemented reorganization at Cable King was a good first step in alleviating the coordination and planning problems. Olafson had not yet met Knowles, and this would be their first face-to-face interaction. Knowles, like several other new UniComm executives, had been brought into the company as part of a reorganization recently implemented by UniComm's newly appointed vice president of operations, "Scoop" Harwood (see Exhibit 5 for the revised UniComm organization). Harwood had previously been in charge of data communication systems for a large computer manufacturer. Before that assignment, Harwood had had a very successful career in the Signal Corps, having attained a general officer's rank at a relatively young age. Knowles, like several other executives brought in by Harwood, had previously served with a large West Coast electronics firm.

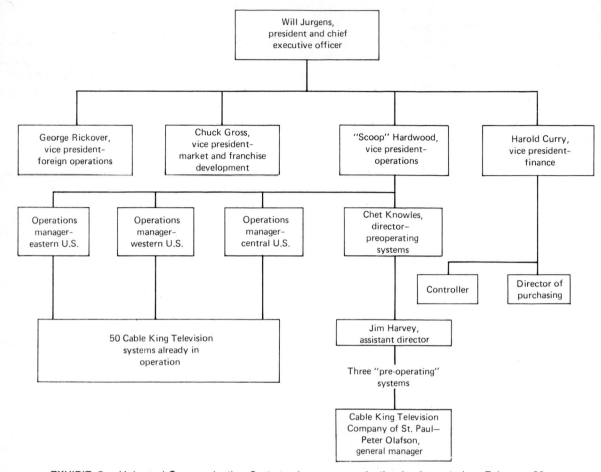

EXHIBIT 5   Universal Communication Systems, Inc.—reorganization implemented on February 20.

Olafson expected that the infusion of experienced professional managers at the top of the UniComm organization would greatly improve UniComm's effectiveness. Olafson had been very impressed by Harwood during a visit which he and Harvey had made to the St. Paul operation, as well as by the organizational changes Harwood implemented. Harwood had asked many questions during his day's visit, took voluminous notes and, in Olafson's eyes, seemed generally satisfied with the way things were going. Harvey remained relatively silent during their visit.

Although Olafson was not yet sure if he would report directly to Knowles or to Harvey (whose new title was assistant director of operating systems), he felt the situation could not help but improve. Harvey had told Olafson that he had been quite upset by his appointment to the new position, which he viewed as a demotion.

PETER OLAFSON (B)[1]

John J. Gabarro

One week after Knowles had called from Beverly Hills, Olafson received a second call from him saying that Will Jurgens, the president of UniComm, and Scoop Harwood, recently appointed vice president of operations at UniComm, would join Knowles during his visit to St. Paul. Jurgens and Harwood would arrive a day after Knowles, allowing Knowles and Olafson to use the first day to meet and discuss Olafson's plans as they had originally intended.

---

[1] The situation described in this case is reported primarily from Olafson's point of view. Although other views of the situation have been incorporated, the case does not necessarily reflect the perceptions of all others involved. All names, places, and companies have been disguised.

ACTION PLANNING AND IMPLEMENTATION: A MANAGER'S CHECKLIST

Leonard A. Schlesinger
James P. Ware

These ideas are presented as a framework for diagnosis, problem solving, and managerial action in organizational contexts. The steps listed below, and the accompanying questions, are intended as a checklist of the types of issues you should be considering, but they are by no means a complete prescription.

On the other hand, few situations require that you consider *every* element listed here. The management of change is a dynamic, ongoing process that *never* takes place as sequentially or as rationally as this list would imply. In most real-world situations, as opposed to cases, you already know a good deal about the people and prior experiences that are relevant (although a systematic review of what you know may often turn up new insights and understandings). In addition, events never turn out *exactly* as anticipated. Anticipation and contingency planning is vital, however, for it is exactly the difference between your expectations and unfolding realities that you must be sensitive to and include in new and revised plans.

With these caveats in mind, the following ideas are suggested as a basis for action planning and implementation.

Describe present conditions

- What are the actual outcomes?
  Productivity
  Satisfaction
  Growth
- What human behaviors are generating these outcomes?
  Activities
  Interactions

- How do the key people *feel* about the situation?
  Norms (external social pressures)
  Perceptions and feelings
  Underlying assumptions
  Needs
  Motives
- What are the sources (causes) of those behaviors?
  Context→Design factors↔Culture→Outcomes

Assess or evaluate present conditions

- What are the consequences?
  For the organization (costs and profits, meeting obligations, productivity)
  For the people (personal and financial rewards, careers, satisfaction, growth)
- How stable are present conditions?
- What information is lacking?
- What are the sources of available information?

Define goals

- What would be the "ideal" outcomes?
- Develop an explicit scenario of a stable future condition.

Formulate the problem (gap between what is and what ought to be)

- What type of problem is it?
  Individual
  Relationship
  Group
  Intergroup
  Leadership/motivation/power
  Total system
- What are principal, most plausible sources of the problem?
  Context
  Internal company factors   Some interaction
  Design factors   or incompatibility?
  Culture
- What are the problem parameters?
  How high are the stakes?
  What factors must change?
  What factors *can* change?
  Who controls or has influence over the key factors?
  How accurate is the available information?
  Is more information available? From whom?
  How *urgent* is the problem?
  How *important* is the problem, relative to other problems and demands?

Develop a solution-finding strategy

- What are the decisionmaker's sources of power in this situation?
  Legitimate
  Reward and punishment
  Expert
  Referent, etc.
- What are the *constraints* on a solution?
  Time
  Money

Develop a solution-finding strategy (continued)

      Organizational policies and traditions
      Expectations and previous commitments
      External realities (cultural, legal, technical)
- What are the available *resources*?
      Time
      Money
      People (insiders and outsiders)
      Existing relationships
      Power
- Should others be involved?
      In problem definition
      In data collection
      In generating alternatives
      In implementing solutions and assessing results

Generate solution alternatives

- Change design factors:
      Technology: machines, processes, product design
      Reward system: pay, promotions, benefits
      Job descriptions: work relationships, reporting relationships, task assignments, tighten or loosen room for individual initiative
      Job modification: narrowing, enlarging, enrichment
      Training and education: skills, knowledge
      Personnel changes: hiring, firing, transfers
      Selection process: new criteria, new procedures, etc.
- Attempt to directly influence culture:
      Counseling and coaching: self-insight, skill building on the job
      Third-party consultation: confrontation, control
      Task group training, team building, process consultation
      Intergroup confrontation
      Modeling more effective behaviors
- Do nothing
- Strategic questions:
      What historical relationships must be respected?
      What relationships can be exploited?
      Can current or future events become symbolic occasions for change?
      How much will compliance depend on acceptance?
- Specific possibilities and idea sources:
      Task force studies
      External consultants
      Problem-solving meetings
      Confrontation of differences
      Establishment of challenging goals
      Challenging of common assumptions
      Search for situational, rather than personal, explanations and changes
      Rewarding desired behaviors

Evaluating alternatives

- Effects
      Does the action address critical aspects of the problem?
      What are the second-order consequences? Third-order?

Evaluating alternatives (continued)

What is the probability of success?

What are the risks?

If the plan fails, what will the new situation be like?

Does the plan depend on trust, acceptance of change agent, or the responses of the affected parties?

- Costs (financial and human)
- Timing

Over what duration will actions occur?

When is the appropriate time for action?

How much time will the action require for the decision maker? For others?

- Change agent

Who is the appropriate change agent?

What skills are required?

What power and influence is required?

- Internal consistency

Are the actions consistent with underlying assumptions?

Are actions consistent with other organizational realities?

Are action elements consistent with each other?

Implement

- Unfreeze

Do the persons and/or groups who will be affected feel the need for change?

Does the plan include opportunities for developing this need?

- Change

Is the process occurring as predicted?

Are there unanticipated responses or consequences?

- Refreeze

Is the change being reinforced by other management actions?

Are the affected persons developing new patterns of stability?

What are the sources of the new stability?

Monitor changes

- Techniques

Observation

Interviews

Questionnaires

Group feedback meetings

- Generating data

Formal or informal approaches?

Frequency?

With whom?

How will feedback information be used?

- Purposes

Is the change taking place as desired?

What are the second-order consequences? Third-order?

Are further changes needed?

Was the problem defined appropriately to begin with?

Are the human and financial costs consistent with previous expectations?

Are the realized benefits comparable to the intended benefits?

MANAGERS WITH IMPACT: VERSATILE AND INCONSISTENT

C. Wickham Skinner
W. Earl Sasser

Why is it that so often after a manager has expended a lot of time and energy in discussion or planning, nothing happens? Why do so many managers who appear crisp, logical, and determined at the conference table frequently accomplish little or nothing when they return to their offices? But why do other managers work effectively both within and outside their organizations and produce a string of significant accomplishments in a short time?

Our subject in this article is the operating skills of the manager—that is, the process of getting work done and changes made rather than the process of formulating policy. We believe that at least as many management careers are damaged by weak operating skills as by a lack of competence in the realm of strategy and policy making. This belief is supported by our analysis of the activities of key managers in 31 case studies used in a course that we have both taught for several semesters. Most of these managers worked in manufacturing industries. Large and small companies and top-, middle-, and lower-level managers were almost equally represented.

While the sample is admittedly small, our analysis suggests a reasonable, but perhaps surprising, conclusion: managers who consistently accomplish a lot are notably inconsistent in their manner of attacking problems. They continually change their focus, their priorities, their behavior patterns with superiors and subordinates, and indeed, their own "executive styles." In contrast, managers who consistently accomplish little are usually predictably constant in what they concentrate on and how they go at their work. Consistency, if our findings are correct, is indeed the hobgoblin of small and inconsequential accomplishment.

We shall explore these findings in this article by analyzing the differences we noted in the operating styles of the low achievers and the high achievers.

PATTERNS OF FAILURE

For low accomplishers, consistency is the shadow of their failures. Apparently as bright, as energetic, and as mature as the high accomplishers, they sound analytical and persuasive, but their results are hollow. Meanwhile, their styles fit into one of several persistent and predictable patterns.

Tendency to "wing it": Accepting established rules of thumb without question or analysis is surprisingly frequent, even among highly trained managers. In most organizations, informal rules of thumb ease decision making with such guides as "carry two weeks' inventory," "no overtime," "promote from within," or "keep direct labor costs at 19 cents" becoming conventional wisdom.

Rules such as these may have made sense at one prior point in time but often have no current economic or strategic rationale. Unquestioning adherence to existing ways of doing things was surprisingly prevalent even among managers formally trained to analyze. The common tendency we noted was for managers to do a great deal of analysis in the first few months of a new job but after that to "wing it."

Inappropriate attention to details: On the one hand, many managers don't get involved enough with the details of their jobs. This pattern occurs more frequently among well-educated younger managers than it does among less-educated self-made managers. The cause may perhaps be the widespread acceptance of such commonly accepted notions as "a manager must stay out of detail," "a manager must learn to delegate," and "a manager must never get involved in day-to-day short-term fire fighting."

These deceptively simple notions hurt the careers of several people in our study and even, in our opinion, devastated several enterprises. In-depth knowledge at the critical level of detail provides the manager not only with the facts, but with the confidence to come to a correct decision and then to stick to it without compromise.

On the other hand, attention to details without a strategy or plan led several of our subjects into a morass where they floundered and struggled for a sense of control. When things are not going well and the pressure is on, the operating manager is often afraid to delegate much, tends to draw problems into personal control, becomes increasingly engrossed, and may be finally overwhelmed by the workload generated.

This vicious circle is a common syndrome which the reader has probably observed frequently. It is especially prevalent among older managers who have worked themselves up through the organization. Comfortable with what they know best, they stick with it and invest their energy in nearly every problem that enters their span of observation.

No handle on priorities: With the telephone constantly ringing, a never ending series of meetings and conferences, and a flurry of memos and paper-work, the operating manager can easily work day after day at a feverish pace and feel a comforting sense of accomplishment. However, quite a few managers go for months and never make much headway in the face of looming or existing problems. In some instances, the situation for which they are responsible, in fact, deteriorates.

Not moving fast enough: Determining the note of change making can also be difficult. One manager took one full year to get costs under control. Although his primary assignment to reduce costs had been spelled out, he spent most of that year asking his people to give him advice and attempting to gain their wholehearted participation and support in recommending changes. The fact was that the time available for reducing costs was short, and he simply could not afford to take a long time to get his organization to develop its own improvements or to let his ideas trickle down. His division lost the next big contract for cost reasons and had to be closed down.

Lack of boldness, nerve, and self-confidence: This theme of failure was apparent in a number of the case studies. In one situation a business school graduate assigned to a decentralized division could see after several months that the reason the division was losing money was a poor labor contract which made the company noncompetitive with foreign imports. Because the union was unwilling to renegotiate the contract, only a bold move leading to a major confrontation had any chance of straightening out the situation. The new manager recognized rightly that his boss, a middle-aged plant manager, would probably never precipitate this move. Afterward, it was learned that the young man had been placed there by the division management in the hope that with his trained analytical skills and his personality, he would bring the problem to a head. When he failed to do so because he was unwilling to make a bold and personally risky move, he was ultimately sidelined.

Tolerance of ineffective subordinates: Some managers who consider themselves excellent at developing subordinates take pride in attempting to get people to radically change their behavior. Many of these same managers are also quite reluctant about firing or replacing an individual, always hoping that his or her performance will soon improve. Some offer mild hints and suggestions for improvement; others just ignore a bad situation in the apparent hope that the individual will be able to learn on his own.

We commonly observed beliefs that "the best managers are those whose people are happy," that happiness comes from encouragement and praise, and that consistent demands for better performance are bad for morale. With this conventional wisdom often comes the simultaneous toleration of ineffective subordinates.

Not seeking advice or help: Several failures can be attributed to a kind of managerial arrogance, the inability of the manager to recognize or admit that help is needed. A director of manufacturing kept insisting to his superior vice president that he and his group could and would soon straighten out a set of problems attached to a new product that were bottlenecking all output at 50% of plan. The vice president, who was anxious to help in this situation, was held at arm's length from personal involvement. His participation not only would have been useful but probably would have defused his subsequent attack on the director of manufacturing, an attack which resulted in the latter's firing.

Similarly, some managers are unable to seek advice from knowledgeable, experienced subordinates. They seem to feel that this might admit weakness and that they must always show themselves to be equal to their own problems. The result is a waste of know-how and, perhaps worse, a negative and critical set of subordinates.

In addition, some managers feel compelled to take command, to make a showing with a decision, and to deal with situations probably better ignored or pushed "upstairs." Often no decision and delay are wiser than moving aggressively ahead.

Personal blind spots: Some managers are unaware of their own weaknesses. As they describe experiences, they do not appear to realize that they lack a certain skill or body of knowledge.

For example, a manager in a hardware manufacturing company did a fine job of improving the sales force and developing an effective sales strategy. Subsequently, he moved into marketing where he obtained good results in introducing new products, and was then promoted to executive vice president. There, he failed. His failure, we assert, was due to his blindness to the fact that he did not understand production and manufacturing operations enough to manage his subordinates. They were able to mislead him.

His approach heretofore had been to focus solely on strategy and conceptual matters, and his blind spot was not realizing that implementation, follow-up, and close attention to detail are critical in manufacturing.

OBSERVATIONS FROM PATTERNS

When the failure patterns are examined as a group, they are so numerous and so contradictory that they may seem frightening. They should be. They explain why so many managers fail at their jobs. Managers get involved in too much detail—or too little. They are too cautious or too bold. They are too critical or too accepting. They are too tough or too supportive. They delegate too much or too infrequently. They plan and analyze and procrastinate, or they blindly plunge ahead day after day without arithmetic, homework, analysis, or plan. They are excessively aware of their weaknesses and damaging compulsive tendencies, or they have blind spots.

In fact, managing is enormously difficult at any level in the organization, and no single approach works consistently. You are damned if you do and damned if you don't. The best formula seems to be "it all depends."

To get at something more useful, we took another look at these patterns. They appear at first to contradict each other as, for example, managers get into trouble by becoming too involved in details as well as not involved enough. But the key to the paradox is that no manager in the cases we examined failed because he became bogged down in details at the wrong time and then overlooked them at another time when it was equally inappropriate to do so. On the contrary, each manager who had a problem had it at one end of the scale or the other, consistently, but never at both.

In other words, low accomplishers tend to develop a set style or approach, and, when they err, it is always in the same particular direction. Consistency is their downfall, not only a general consistency of style, but also a tendency to persist in using a limited number of tools and techniques, based on a small assortment of managerial premises which they use over and over again.

In contrast, each outstanding achiever in our cases not only had a different executive style, but was inconsistent in personal style. Paradoxically, successful implementors have many styles. They are regularly inconsistent.

The paradox is revealing. The high accomplishers get into the fine detail in one situation yet stay at the strategic level in another. They delegate a lot one time or a little the next time. They are close and supportive one day and remote and demanding another. They communicate verbally with some colleagues and in writing with others. They analyze some problem in great depth for months while they move with seeming abruptness and intuition on others. They talk a great deal or are suddenly apt listeners.

It is not surprising that consistency causes managers to fail, for one cardinal imperative of life as a manager is the necessity to perceive differences—differences between one situation and another, differences between people, circumstances, motives, assumptions, and physical and technological realities. The manager analyzes in order to discern differences.

The problem is that situations change, but the ordinary executive often does not perceive it and fails to adopt a different approach. The approach that has often worked out so well will not work on what seems the same problem. Why? Because one or two critical ingredients have changed. Meanwhile, the manager is under pressure to simplify the decision-making process by extracting from experience generalizations for the next time that kind of problem is faced. Our study also indicates that the more experienced the manager, the greater the likelihood that he will have adopted one consistent approach to decision making, delegation, communication, and relationships.

While many social scientists believe that basic elements of personal behavior are rather well fixed from childhood, it is beyond the scope of this article and indeed of our competence to assay how a manager can modify his or her rather basic psychological givens—that is, motives, self-concepts, and cognitive styles. The fact is that some managers are able to modify their executive styles better than others. Our observation of successful operating managers includes men and women who seem to have always been versatile and interchangeable, and others who have apparently learned from experience to loosen their prior rigidities and adopt a more situational approach to managing.

In the balance of this article we shall offer some prescriptive concepts learned from the managers whose accomplishments were well above average and, in some cases, outstanding.

TRAITS OF SUCCESS

While the high accomplishers we studied showed much versatility and inconsistency, they were also consistent, but in a different way. They were persistent in analysis and self-discipline, which permitted them to be inconsistent in their own executive styles. Consistency was no problem for these people. They used the following approaches, concepts, and techniques.

Perform Careful Analysis

The high accomplishers were above all else analyzers. They examined each situation to get at the facts, cause-and-effect relationships, and strategic realities. The single most common cause of operating failure among the low accomplishers was their unwillingness to do this.

Careful analysis leads to an approach in operating management that is freshly tuned to the situation. While it is done in management training courses and seminars and done under pressure when the superior demands it, it is more often than not neglected. But good analysis produces power and credibility that cannot be turned aside easily. It leads to practical, realistic solutions, and, most important, develops personal confidence in the manager when he knows what is going on.

But, practically, many operating managers wing it 99% of the time. There seems to be little time to think things through. They rely on the lessons of past success. Curiously, most of the failures we observed were those of previously successful managers. What had always worked before was precisely what caused the failure. Operating skills can never be considered set; they must always be renewed, reconsidered, developed.

Develop Operating Strategy

A strategy is necessary for the manager in order to develop and hold onto a sense of direction, purpose, and objectives. But a strategy is more than a choice of objectives; it involves determining what will be difficult, making an assessment of favorable and unfavorable factors, and recognizing strengths and weaknesses.

An operating strategy can seldom be long lasting; it needs to be reanalyzed every three to six months. But it will deal with key elements of the situation such as determining the needs, wishes, and expectations of the boss and the boss's boss. It will clearly establish objectives and set priorities. It will include development of policies and plans which marshal alternatives, opportunities, and resources.

Recognize Classical Dilemmas

The high accomplishers appeared to be aware that their problems and dilemmas were not unique, that certain situations repeat themselves, and that nearly every operating manager faces at one time or another a common set of problems. These managers seemed to develop competent judgment and an element of maturity that enabled them to lift themselves beyond the bounds of their habitual responses and handle each situation appropriately.

For example, the first four to eight weeks on a new job is a critical and hazardous period. The manager must size up his subordinates at the same time that he is being sized up by them. They are especially sensitive to every signal that may indicate what it is going to be like to work for this new boss. What he does in those first few days and weeks is multiplied in its significance by those watching both "upstairs" and "downstairs."

The new boss faces a further dilemma in that whatever standards of performance he sets or does not set at the start tend to become precedents for the future. It is more difficult to criticize a poor practice after seeming to tolerate it for a month or two. But early criticism or demands for change are risky at best, for the new manager is in jeopardy of being wrong, of making a mistake, or of being unaware of perhaps valid reasons for the superficially apparent poor practice. The problem is how to avoid establishing unfortunate relations and precedents without seeming to tolerate low standards or making foolish moves.

Another set of classic issues involves information needs. The operating manager needs, but is often cut off from, information held by superiors about objectives, strategies, and priorities. The manager must know the superior's expectations for the manager's organization. The dilemma, however, is that frequently this information is not available at the lower level. It is not available because it is held upstairs purposely or, carelessly, it is not communicated downward.

Sometimes the information is not available, of course, because the executives at high levels have no plans and have not made their expectations explicit. The operating manager is often in the dark not only about what is expected but also about what should *not* be done. In these circumstances several of the managers we studied made moves that to their surprise immediately brought down upon themselves the wrath of their superiors.

Another recurring dilemma is dealing with difficult employees—those whose values or motives differ from the manager's, who have serious problems in morale, or who have negative feelings about the organization or unrealistic expectations. Dealing with upstairs may be equally difficult. The example of one manager is typical:

> How do I deal with a boss who, while brilliant and held in esteem at high levels in the industry, won't sit down long enough to plan objectives and strategy, or even read his mail. He says, 'Don't write it, tell it.' But when you talk with him, he's easily distracted. When you're discussing one problem, his mind jumps to another and he usually doesn't listen well. When you are trying to reason with him, he extends your argument to an absurd extreme, argues rhetorically, with unrealistic 'what ifs,' or makes totally unreasonable 'principles' out of points you have raised.
>
> He makes sudden, impulsive, and sometimes angry decisions based on little data and mostly on intuition. In making these hasty, long-postponed decisions, however, he often fails to consider their inevitable second-order implications. He doesn't keep me informed and seldom levels with me about what is on his mind or concerns him. We never set clear objectives or goals. He forgets from one time to the next what we've talked about or decided. Sometimes he tells me the same thing two or three times. We have few staff meetings when we can discuss our problems and plan together.
>
> When we do meet, we ramble around and reach few clear decisions unless he suddenly and sometimes angrily lays down the law. He is successful and technically competent, but as a boss he's a disaster. All I get is specific criticisms or vague praise. He has no idea really, in any depth, of what I do.

But this manager cannot be content to merely blow off steam and criticize his boss. He must learn somehow to find out what the organization and the boss need from him; he must assist the boss in the boss's own way to do some planning; he must learn to get through to him. He cannot blame things on the "disastrous boss" for he will usually be the loser if the relationship is poor and he's kept in an information vacuum. He is the one who will be criticized when things aren't letter-perfect, even if expectations are vague and never made explicit. The management of the relationship upstairs is often the responsibility of the subordinate. It's his neck; he must make the relationship work.

Other classic issues and dilemmas include the following:

How to stir up an organization that is sleepy, frozen, and stagnant.

When and how to question higher-level policies, run the system versus change the system, fight city hall.

How to handle "no-win" situations.

Whether to seek consensus, wait for it to emerge, or go ahead and make a decision.

How to identify, manage, and make use of power, clout, and pressure points in the organization.

How to overcome bureaucratic resistance, red tape, and inertia.

Use a Wide Variety of Techniques

The range of operating problems is so great that one habitual set of responses or choice of alternatives is entirely inadequate. To understand that there is a vast array of tools and techniques and that discriminating choices among them must be made is another part of the development of high accomplishers.

Our cases of operating problems indicate that the number of tools and techniques available is impressively large. Exhibit 1 is a listing of a 39-item arsenal of action-oriented techniques from which the operating manager can choose to introduce change and bring about improvements.

In spite of the existence of this powerhouse of techniques, it surprised us how many of the 31 managers felt baffled and frustrated about how little they could do in a situation. "I feel boxed in and helpless," one said. "The people and procedures and precedents are so firmly set up and frozen in place. Change is resisted by everybody around here. I can't seem to get any change accomplished whatsoever."

The reason for this myopia is reminiscent of a machinist or carpenter with a wall full of mounted tools before his eyes who scratches his head in discouragement and mutters, "I don't know how to go at this job." For instance, some managers we studied were unaware of the arsenal at hand and unfamiliar with its usage. When managers are too close to their problems, they lose perspective and, mentally locking out constructive possibilities, tend to become either conservative or unimaginative. The discouraged manager believes that nothing will work, anyway.

Sometimes the manager, in a somewhat arrogant mood, claims that the few techniques he is using or has used in the past are the proper and best ones to use again. He uses these familiar approaches whether or not analysis of the situation indicates that another approach would be better. At other times, there is either a lack of energy or the situation has begun to tailspin out of control to the point that the manager is unable to pull together the time and organization to mount a carefully planned attack on the problem. Finally, there may occur a failure of self-confidence. The manager is afraid to take the initiative and try some bold approach where visibility is high and failure will be costly.

EXHIBIT 1 SOME ACTION-ORIENTED TOOLS AND TECHNIQUES AVAILABLE TO THE OPERATING MANAGER

Structural

Formal organization
Changes in equipment and process technology methods
Physical moves, relocations
Expansion of resources, investments
Procedures, systems, routines
Job content
Job assignments
Personnel: lend, borrow, or exchange
Project, task
Long-range planning exercises
Consultants, outside advisers

Employee management and development

Reward system
Training, courses, management development, coaching
Performance evaluations
Incentives
Informal assignments
Problem-solving meetings
Short-range planning exercises
Competition: encourage and initiate
Replacement of managers
Greater participation in decision making

Communication

Short-range goals
Clear change in tone, atmosphere, system, norms, direction
Management by objectives: set objectives, get precise plan to achieve, set precise measurement
 and controls
Timing: postpone, delay, or speed up
Written announcements
Meetings
Ceremonies, speeches
Conflict resolution
Necessary commitment

Controls

Standards, norms, limits, specifications
Due dates, schedules, timing
Measurement system regarding output, individual performance, subordinates
Regular reporting sessions
Plans, reports, results

Evaluations, redesign

Evaluation of performance of unit, individuals, systems
Analysis of breakdowns
Redesign to overcome organizational weaknesses
Redesign to buttress own personal weaknesses

Change Style to Fit Situations

The dilemma of the operating managers we studied was that each person gradually adopted an executive style while different situations called for different managerial activities and tactics. Our research suggests that for each different operating situation there is a particular executive style which would be most effective.

It is a curious yet reasonable fact that nearly all managers tend to settle into a fairly rigid or limited executive style. Referring to Exhibit 2, we see that each low achiever we studied had a certain profile when his regular practices were marked on the range of the 16 attributes listed.

In contrast, the high accomplishers seemed to tune in to the fact that the demands upon a manager vary enormously from one situation and one period of time to another. The analogy of a college or university is relevant. In one period of time the institution may need a president who is strong in building a faculty. In another time, the need may be fund-raising, or strengthening relationships with the legislature and student groups, or supervising the construction of new facilities, or developing financial control. Similarly in business, the needs change from the management of growth, to new products, cost control, improved lead times, mergers, or cash management. Each focus cannot be equally important. At any given time there exists indirectly or explicitly a key *operating task,* a task which must be given top priority and which demands a particular executive style.

For example, a new production manager found himself in charge of installing a new conveyorized system for furniture finishing designed and ordered by his prede-

EXHIBIT 2   SOME ATTRIBUTES OF AN EXECUTIVE STYLE

Attributes	Range/Continuum	
Analytical patterns	Intuitive ↔	Analytical
Cognitive style	Inductive ↔	Deductive, use of generalizations
Decision-making approach	Authoritative ↔	Consultative
Decision-making speed	Fast, quick ↔	Studied, worried
Delegation	Little ↔	Much
Explicit rules of thumb	Few ↔	Many
Type of follow-up	Loose, little ↔	Much, rigorous
Communication	Informal, verbal ↔	Formal, written
Personal relationships	Supportive ↔	Demanding, challenging
Pressure, pace	Relaxed ↔	Rigorous, energetic
Availability	Easily available ↔	Remote
Boldness, audacity	Bold, risk taking ↔	Cautious, risk aversive
Focus on time dimension	Seldom ↔	Continuous
Openness to persuasion	Flexible ↔	Dogged, persistent, single-minded
Work with subordinates	One on one ↔	In a group
Work with superior	Wants support ↔	Works alone

cessor. The equipment had been approved by his boss and was scheduled to start up in ten days. A quick size-up of the equipment, however, suggested that there were going to be many start-up problems, and indeed, it was doubtful to him whether the equipment would actually work out as well as anticipated. The operating manager's industrial engineer was enthusiastic about the new equipment. However, the superintendent stated that it would never work.

If he backed off, the new manager faced a disappointed boss. If he went ahead, he would probably "be hung" with the nearly inevitable high costs and low production ahead.

He decided to do nothing and let the chips fall where they might. In fact, however, when the equipment did not work out well, his next four months were nearly disastrous. He caught hell from all sides.

What was his operating task during the first weeks? One definition could be that it was to get the organization which preceded him together and get these people to make a decision and full plans as to what to do about the new equipment.

Usually, of course, it takes months or even years to be competent at a variety of key operating tasks. In baseball, when a particular kind of pitching is called for, the manager brings in a certain relief pitcher. In business, this step is a last resort. Yet in a number of the situations we studied the manager was finally replaced when his executive style proved beyond much doubt to be inadequate for handling a certain kind of problem. In each case, the manager did not realize the need for a change in style or, if he did, was unable to make such a change. Considerable flexibility was a hallmark of the high accomplishers.

This is a big order. It says, "Be different. Don't always manage the same way." Yet only a few managers are able to accomplish this kind of self-control and discipline. Those who do act intuitively for the most part, and often by dint of experience from which they seem to learn that different behavior is called for in a new situation.

Why this step is seldom carried out is due perhaps in part to the prevailing attitudes that one must be natural and do one's thing in a natural way and that a good manager can manage anything and any situation. We believe that these notions are largely myths and that careful, honest experimentation with executive style is a tool of vast potential, seldom used.

A final concern is the widespread tendency—if our sample of 31 managers is typical—toward stagnation. The consistency that leads to an inflexible executive style and a myopic selection of operating management tools and techniques is born out of stagnation.

A high percentage of our subjects, old and young, had slipped into a kind of lethargy where one day and one experience led to another; time slid smoothly by and they became members of the gray army of low accomplishers.

A pattern of stagnation among active executives is a striking phenomenon. The very need for employing executives is to provide organizations with a mechanism for making changes as situations and circumstances change. Normal human indolence and mental lethargy on the part of those in positions of responsibility not only represent a pragmatic paradox but also raise a moral question.

At least one thing seems clear: the promise of personal reward is not enough to refuel this state of intellectual energy which we found frequently dissipated. What is needed is a state of mind which nature itself does not seem to evolve or fortify. As in the law of entropy, things run downhill.

LESSONS FROM HIGH ACHIEVERS

In summary, the high-level accomplishers share the following characteristics:

They employ the practice of analysis with great effect. They use analytical tools with such discipline and consistency that their establishment of objectives, strategies, plans, and priorities are sound and distinctly tuned to the situation. At the same time, they develop controls and information systems such that they have a flow of data which brings those details and problems requiring their attention to the surface.

From regular analysis on both the strategic and tactical levels, they decide how to allocate their time and focus their energies. They use analysis to give their work direction and so avoid the common trap of being consistent—and consistently getting into too much or too little detail.

They succeed in motivating subordinates and satisfying superiors. The words *motivating* and *satisfying* are critical. It appears that of all interactions between an executive and subordinate—leading, instructing, coaching, communicating, listening, demanding, delegating, reporting, supporting, and motivating—the key to high operating accomplishment is motivated subordinates.

Similarly, the satisfaction of the superior is vital to the manager's bottomline performance. How to be a good subordinate is a part of the operating art which is frequently neglected. Managing the relationship with those who are upstairs is as vital or more vital than managing the relationship with those who are downstairs.

They manage themselves. They understand their internal pressures and needs and their central tendencies in executive style. They discipline themselves to control anger, action, delay, or domination that could be counterproductive. They are able to modify their styles according to the needs of the situation. They are sufficiently disciplined to do the analysis necessary to provide long- and short-term directional guidance for themselves. They avoid stagnation in mental and physical diligence.

They focus on one task of prime importance at a time. Among all the tasks facing them which could be accomplished, they define and tackle the one that makes or breaks the situation in the short run. Such an explicit choice of operating task sets focus, strategy, and priorities.

Although these four characteristics form perhaps too simple a conclusion about what it takes to be successful in operating management, the fundamental message is clear from the experiences of our research subjects: analyze, motivate subordinates, mind the upstairs and downstairs relationships, understand and discipline oneself to avoid consistency, and the result could be to become one of those rare managers who always gets a great deal accomplished.

PART FIVE

MANAGING ORGANIZATIONAL EFFECTIVENESS

Part 5 marks a transition to examining the total organization. All of the concepts introduced in Parts 1–4 are needed, and a number of new ones are advanced. Part 5 focuses on taking effective managerial action to obtain desired organizational outcomes. This involves positioning an appropriate structure with the necessary supporting systems, establishing a management style to support these features, and fostering an overall culture that will lead to the desired outcomes. Conceptually, the model for managing organizational effectiveness is very similar to the text in Part 1—the framework for analyzing work groups. Of course, the task and environment facing the organization are constantly changing and thus managers must be prepared and able to change their organization as necessary to maintain the required fit of its many elements. Therefore, this part is also concerned with recognizing when change is necessary and with developing change strategies. Action planning at the organizational level is similar in many respects to action planning at the individual, interpersonal, and group levels. The relationship between these levels of action planning is especially close when one remembers that, in effect, organizational action is simply the total of the actions of its many members.

The text for part 5 provides a framework of organizational elements designed to allow assessment of organizational health, selection of improvement tools, and effective implementation of these tools. The model is composed of seven major elements: (1) key organizational processes, (2) the external environment, (3) employees and other tangible assets, (4) formal organizational arrangements, (5) the internal social system, (6) the organization's technology, and (7) the dominant coalition. These seven elements are related in complex ways and comprise a total system. In the short run the most important relationships are the cause-and-effect relationships that connect the key organizational processes with the other six elements. In the moderate run the focus is on relationships among the last six elements through the concept of alignment (or fit). In the long run the major concern is the organization's ability to adapt the relationships among these seven elements in response to both internal and external changes. The text contrasts this view of managing organizational effectiveness with some of the more commonly held beliefs about the best way to manage a total organization.

Case 1 contains many issues raised in earlier parts of the book. But a complete understanding of the situation presented in this case requires the application of the concepts developed in the text, as well as concepts from earlier models. Frank Forbus, the director of engineering at Rondell Data Corporation, has been in his job almost a year. The previous director had lasted only 10 months, and the director before him about a year. The immediate problem for Forbus is the design and production snags of the model 802, a typical experience with new-product development at Rondell. His predecessors had also faced these problems. At the same time Forbus is experiencing difficulties in managing his department and in working with other departments. As a result of his inability to understand the underlying causes of his problems, Forbus has been ineffective in resolving them.

Case 2 presents a situation in which Tom Wilson, the marketing vice president for the Bancil Corporation's toiletry division and its acting division marketing director for Europe, must exercise influence in a complex matrix structure to improve the performance of a particular product line. Wilson is located in Sunnyvale, Calif., while his key subordinate for this product line, Remy Gentile, is located in Paris; Gentile also reports to the general manager for France, Pierre Chevalier. Wilson has been unsuccessful in securing the desired cooperation from Chevalier and Gentile and must develop an action plan before visiting Gentile in Paris the next week.

Case 3 describes the highly unusual approach taken by Dee N. Hock, the iconoclastic chief executive officer of Visa International, for managing organizational effectiveness. His approach defies some general conceptions of good management and results in some unusual organizational characteristics—minimal definition of structure, rules, and procedures in an environment dedicated to ensuring constant change. The unique mission of this organization raises the question of how to measure effectiveness in the first place in order to assess the effectiveness of the organization's characteristics and Hock's management style for obtaining desired outcomes.

Case 4 provides the opportunity to assess the Japanese approach to management in the Mitsubishi Corporation. By a number of measures, this *sogo shosha* (roughly translated as *general trading firm*) is highly effective but is managed in ways very different from most American firms. These differences include guaranteed lifetime employment, slow rates of promotion, remuneration based solely upon seniority for a number of years, infrequent formal feedback, and an emphasis on shared responsibility. A thorough analysis of this case makes it possible to determine whether any organizational lessons applicable in the United States can be drawn.

Case 5 presents the challenges faced by Toshihiro Tomabechi, president of Mitsubishi International Corporation (MIC), headquartered in New York City. Tomabechi is confronted with the pressures of managing a firm having many American employees within the context of the total Mitsubishi Corporation organization. Already with annual sales of nearly $14 billion, MIC is one of the three largest foreign-controlled corporations in the United States. Since the early 1970s MIC had been involved in an Americanization program that had as a part of its effort the development of American staff. Given the nature of Mitsubishi Corporation described in the previous case, the question is raised about whether or not MIC will successfully adapt to an American environment while still functioning effectively within the total organization.

Case 6 describes the situation confronting Don Rogers, vice president and general manager of the electronic products division of Corning Glass Works. Rogers, who has been in his job about 2 years, challenges Corning's director of organization development to determine the reason for the high level of conflict present within his organization and to propose needed actions. Rogers believes that this conflict, together with external factors, accounts for low morale and poor organizational performance. He foresees increasing competition in the future and is concerned about the ability of his division to compete effectively. A number of concepts from all parts of the book must be used to understand the current situation and to develop a plan for improvement.

The three readings in this section provide further background for understanding and managing organization effectiveness. Reading 1 identifies eight characteristics of well-managed companies: (1) a bias toward action, (2) simple form and lean staff, (3) continued contact with customers, (4) productivity improvement through people, (5) operational autonomy to encourage entrepreneurship, (6) stress on one key business value, (7) emphasis on doing what they know best, and (8) simultaneous loose-tight controls.

Reading 2 discusses how to design an organization in terms of the structure, rewards, and measurement practices intended to direct members' behavior toward the organization. This approach to organization design, known as *contingency theory,* is composed of four major elements: environment, strategy, task, and the psychological characteristics of members. The concepts of differentiation and integration are used to describe how to subdivide and coordinate the tasks in an organization. The basic structures of functional, divisional, and matrix are described, along with the circumstances in which they are most appropriate. The importance of culture and leadership style are also emphasized in obtaining organizational effectiveness.

Reading 3 explores the role of management systems in organizational effectiveness. Management systems are treated as the carriers of an organization's language which, in turn, helps shape the dimensions of an organization's character. Organizational character or culture accounts for organizational outcomes. The basic components of management systems—directional signals, process phases, and management tools—are discussed.

AN INTEGRATIVE MODEL OF ORGANIZATIONAL DYNAMICS

John P. Kotter

This chapter briefly describes an integrative model of organizational dynamics that can help the assessment of organization's health, selection of improvement tools, and implementation of those choices.

MAJOR CONCEPTUAL ELEMENTS

The integrative model is made up of seven major elements: (1) key organizational processes, (2) the external environment, (3) employees and other tangible assets, (4) formal organizational arrangements, (5) the internal social system, (6) the organization's technology, and (7) the dominant coalition. These elements are included because substantial evidence exists that one must consider all seven of them to understand, assess, and predict organizational dynamics.

The first, and central, element focuses on two interdependent sets of processes, one of which involves matter and/or energy, the other information. Specifically, these key organizational processes can be defined as the major information-gathering, communication, decision-making, matter/energy transporting, and matter/energy-converting actions of the organization's employees and machines. There are many such processes in organizations, and these are usually labeled according to their purpose—such as the purchasing process, the market-planning process, the leadership process, or the production process. Taken together, these processes make up what many people would refer to as the *behavior* of a formal organization.

The second major element in this model is an organization's external environment, which is made up of two basic parts: the task environment and the wider environment. An organization's task environment can be defined as all possible suppliers (of labor, information, money, materials, etc.), markets, competitors, regulators, and associations that are relevant to the organization's current products and services. This, then, represents an organization's immediately relevant external environment. The wider environment is a residual environment that can be defined by such indicators as public attitudes, the state of technological development, the economy, the occupational system, the political system, the demographic characteristics of people and organizations, the society's social structure, current price levels, and so on.

The third element, the organization's employees and other tangible assets, can be defined as the size (or number) and internal characteristics of an organization's employees, plant and offices, equipment and tools, land, inventories, and money.

The fourth element, the formal organizational arrangements, can be defined as all formal systems that have been explicitly designed to regulate the actions of an organization's employees (and machines). These formal arrangements include structure (job design, departmentalization, reporting hierarchy, rules and plans, and teams and task forces) and operating systems (resource-allocation systems, planning systems, measurement and reward systems, and hiring and development system).

The fifth element, the organization's internal social system, is made up of two main parts: culture and social structure. Culture can be defined as those organizationally relevant norms and values shared by most employees (or subgroups of employees). Social structure is defined as the relationships that exist among employees in terms of such variables as power, affiliation, and trust.

The sixth element is the organization's technology, defined here as the major techniques (and their underlying assumptions about cause and effect) that are used by an organization's employees while engaging in organizational processes and that are programmed into its machines. This is meant to be a rather broad definition of a term that is used with several meanings. This definition would include the craft of glassblowing , methods of market research, and steel-making techniques. An important subpart of this element is called the *core technology,* which can be defined as that technology (or technologies) associated with an organization's main product or service.

The seventh and final element is an organization's dominant coalition, defined as the objectives and strategies (for the organization), the personal characteristics, and the internal relationships of that group of cooperating employees who oversee the organization as a whole and control its basic policymaking. As such a dominant coalition could be as large as 20 people (or more) or, if no one is in control, as small as zero. It could be made up of the president (or director) and his or her lieutenants as designed by the formal structure, or it could exclude some of them and/or include others.

SYSTEMS DYNAMICS FOR THE SHORT RUN

In the short run the most important relationships among the elements in this model are those of a cause-and-effect nature that connect the key organizational processes with the other elements. In a sense, the six structural elements provide the context in which the organizational processes emerge. At the same time, the processes have a continuous impact on all six other elements, which helps to maintain or change their states (see Exhibit 1).

To clarify the dynamics implicit in Exhibit 1, consider the following brief description by a manager of organizational dynamics over a 4-month period.:

In April the demand for our new product line dropped considerably. With orders down, our deliveries began to decrease and our inventories began to increase. When top management became aware of this through the weekly operating reports, they did nothing at first. They hoped that their substantial marketing efforts, which were already in effect, would bring demand back to its previous level. But when orders continued at a very low level for

EXHIBIT 1   Short-run dynamics.

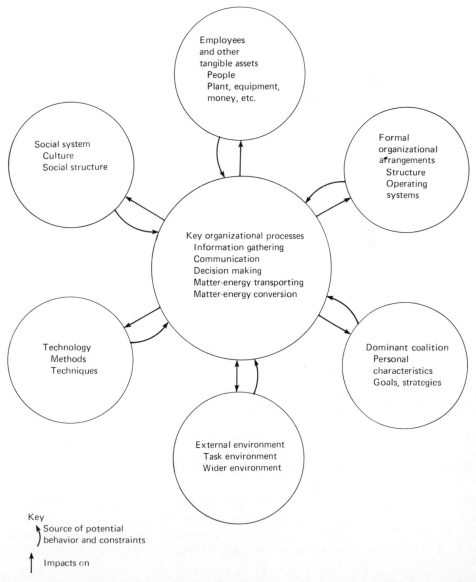

Employees
and other
tangible assets
  People
  Plant, equipment,
  money, etc.

Social system
Culture
Social structure

Formal
organizational
arrangements
  Structure
  Operating
  systems

Key organizational processes
Information gathering
Communication
Decision making
Matter-energy transporting
Matter-energy conversion

Technology
Methods
Techniques

Dominant coalition
Personal
characteristics
Goals, strategies

External environment
Task environment
Wider environment

Key
Source of potential
behavior and constraints

Impacts on

6 weeks, they decided to cut production way back and to lay off 100 people. Within 6 weeks, inventories were down to normal again and orders for the new products were back in line with production. We didn't get hurt very much financially, but I think we lost some real credibility in the eyes of our production workers. Most of them had believed we wouldn't lay off a large number of people like that.

Within the framework, shown in Exhibit 1, these events can be broken down into eight discrete cause-and-effect actions (see Exhibit 2). In some of these actions, a structural element has some clear effect on a key process: for example, the sequence of events begins with demand dropping in the external environment, which *causes* incoming orders to go down. In other actions, a key process has some effect on one or more of the structural elements: a reduced production process, for example, *causes* inventories to go down.

To understand or predict organizational dynamics in the short run, one needs to understand the two types of relationships that are present in Exhibits 1 and 2. The first of these involves the shaping of the key organizational processes by the other six structural elements. The second type involves the impact of these processes on the six structural elements.

Examples of influence relationships going from the six structural elements to the key organizational processes are shown in Exhibit 3. Such relationships have been studied by a variety of social scientists. Economists, for example, have studied how the structure of the external environment shapes organizational processes (e.g., "a monopolistic industry tends to cause inefficiency to emerge in organizational processes"). Social psychologists have studied how the social system shapes organizational processes (e.g., "anticompany norms on the part of the work force tend to cause conflict and inefficiency to emerge in organizational processes"). Administrative theorists have focused on how formal organizational arrangements shape the processes (e.g., "the installation of many rules and procedures tends to lead to more predictable and less flexible organizational processes").

Examples of possible influence relationships in the opposite direction, from the organizational processes to the structural elements, are shown in Exhibit 4. Such relationships have been studied primarily by applied social scientists and practitioners. Indeed, the various "management" disciplines are all oriented toward shaping the organizational processes (that is, gathering information, making decisions, and transporting and converting matter and energy) so as to have some impact on one of the structural elements in this model. Advertising management, for example, is concerned with gathering information and making decisions that will have a certain impact on the attitudes and behaviors of an organization's customers. Production management deals with transportation and conversion of matter and energy so as to change raw materials into a finished product (tangible assets). Research/development management focuses on gathering information and making decisions to improve the firm's core technology. Public relations management focuses on information processing and decisionmaking related to improving an organization's public image in its wider environment.

Thus, to predict an organization's behavior over a short duration, one needs (1) information on the states of the elements in the model and (2) an understanding of

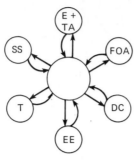

1. Demand from external environment drops, causing incoming orders to go down

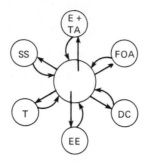

2. With the production process continuing at same rate, drop in orders causes deliveries to go down and shipments to inventory to go up.

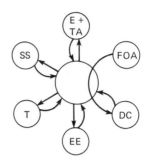

3. A formal control system maintains a process that causes top management to be alerted to these changes

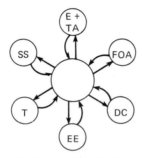

4. After watching situation for a few weeks, top management intervenes in process to slow production and reduce work force

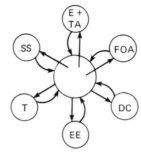

5. Their decisions are implemented— production plan is changed, people are laid off, and "no large layoff" belief is shattered

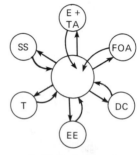

6. These changes cause production process to slow

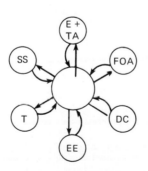

7. Shipments exceed production, causing inventories to go down

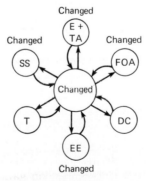

8. System restabilizes with states of five of the elements changed

EXHIBIT 2   Example of short-run cause and effect.

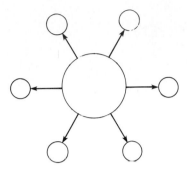

1. *External environment*—A strike in the steel industry interrupts the inflow of steel parts into the company's manufacturing processes
2. *Dominant coalition*—The president retires, and a very different type of individual is elected to succeed him, causing significant changes in the leadership processes within the company
3. *Formal arrangements*—A new compensation plan for salespeople creates a significant expansion of activity in the company's selling processes
4. *Employees and other assets*—An increase in the educational level of the corporate financial staff causes an improvement in the quality of the financial analysis process
5. *Internal social system*—An increase in the level of trust between members of production and sales units causes a significant increase in information sharing for the new product development process
6. *Technology*—The introduction of a new production-control technology completely changes the nature of the production planning and control processes

EXHIBIT 3 Examples of how each structural element might influence key processes in the short run.

EXHIBIT 4 Examples of how key processes can influence each structural element in the short run.

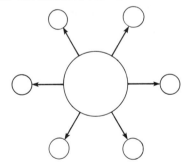

1. *External environment*—A change in the advertising process causes demand for a certain product to increase by 25 percent
2. *Dominant coalition*—A new reporting process for top management, which supplies them with more and different information about the firm's operations, causes their opinions about certain problems in the company to change considerably
3. *Formal arrangements*—A job-evaluation process causes 10 percent of middle-level jobs to be redesigned
4. *Employees and other tangible assets*—When a great deal of bitter conflict emerges in one decision-making process, it immediately causes the job satisfaction of the people involved to go down
5. *Internal social system*—A new grievance process causes the relationships between workers and management to improve
6. *Technology*—The R & D process causes the continuous expansion of the firm's core technology

the two different types of cause-and-effect relationships involved (from social science and applied social science research). The more information one has on the states of the elements and the better one understands cause-and-effect relationships, the better one can account for and predict the system's behavior over short durations.

Although cause-and-effect relationships are helpful in the short run, these are not very helpful in explaining past events or predicting future ones in a moderate to long-run time frame. To predict how an organization will evolve over a 5-year period, for example, would require estimating and tracing hundreds of cause-and-effect interactions of the type shown in Figure 2, and that is not very practical. To understand system dynamics from a moderate-run perspective, we have to move beyond cause-and-effect dynamics and examine the relationships among the six structural elements.

MODERATE-RUN DYNAMICS

The key to moderate-run dynamics lies in the relationships among the six structural elements in the model (Exhibit 5) and in the concept of alignment. As has been argued elsewhere, some of the more interesting research and theory on formal organizations completed in the past two decades has focused on the relationships among two or more of the structural elements in the model and has reached very similar conclusions. This body of research offers evidence that when an organization's formal arrangements, employees and other assets, external environment, technology, internal social system, and dominant coalition have characteristics that "fit" together, that are "consistent" and "congruent," that are "coaligned," one tends also to find efficient matter/energy processes, effective information processes, and stability within a moderate time frame. If, however, the relationships among any of the six structural elements do not fit or are nonaligned, one tends to find some inefficient matter/energy processes and ineffective decision-making processes emerging within a few months or a few years, and the situation tends to be unstable. Furthermore, the larger the nonalignment or the number of nonalignments, the greater the number of inefficient and ineffective processes that tend to emerge, and the more unstable the situation tends to be in a moderate time frame.

What constitutes aligned and nonaligned relationships among any two or more structural elements is often intuitively obvious. For example, if the goals and strategies embraced by a firm's dominant coalition are based on inaccurate assumptions about the firm's task environment, the dominant coalition and the external environment are obviously nonaligned. If the number of employees or the amount of tangible assets are not sufficient to take advantage of the economies of scale inherent in the organization's technologies, the two elements are nonaligned. If the specialization called for in the formal organizational arrangements is inconsistent with employee skills or the number of employees, again there is a nonalignment (see Exhibit 6).

Moderate-run organizational dynamics thus tend to display the following pattern. Something causes a change that creates a significant nonalignment among two (or more) of the structural elements in the model. After a period of months or years, the states of those nonaligned elements change so that their relationships are aligned

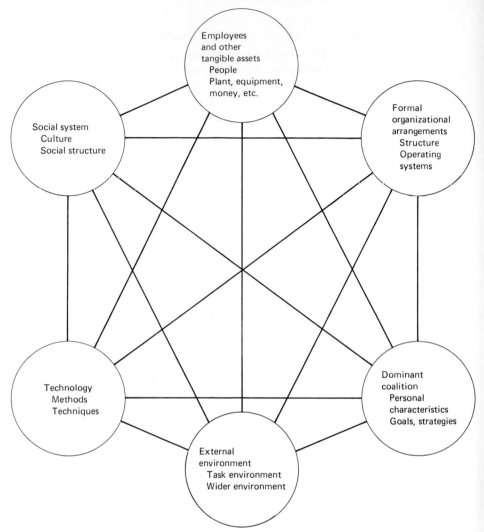

EXHIBIT 5 Relationships among these six elements play a key role in shaping moderate-run dynamics of the system.

again (or almost aligned). During that period of time problems tend to emerge and then go away, and a rather complex series of specific events (short-run cause-and-effect dynamics) occurs, which is related to the ultimate changes.

A variety of factors leads to nonalignments. Perhaps the most common is a change in an organization's external environment, which then creates a nonalignment between that element and one or more of the other structural elements. Economic recessions, new technological developments, changes in consumer tastes, competitive product developments, and new federal and state legislation quite often create nonalignments for contemporary organizations. A second common cause of nonalign-

EXHIBIT 6   EXAMPLES OF IMPORTANT RELATIONSHIPS AMONG STRUCTURAL VARIABLES

External environment—dominant coalition. If the goals and strategy that are explicitly or implicitly being followed by the dominant coalition are based on incorrect assumptions about the external environment, inefficiencies emerge and the situation is unstable in the moderate run (and thus will probably change).

Technology—employees and other tangible assets. If the number of employees or the amount of tangible assets is far too small to take advantage of the economies of scale inherent in the organization's technologies, inefficiencies emerge and the situation is unstable in the moderate run.

Dominant coalition—technology. If the dominant coalition does not have members who are skilled in understanding the organization's main technologies, inefficiencies emerge and the situation is unstable in the moderate run.

Formal organizational arrangements—employees and other tangible assets. If the specialization called for in the formal organizational arrangements is inconsistent with employee skills or the number of employees, inefficiencies emerge and the situation is unstable in the moderate run.

Formal organizational arrangements—social system. If the relationships, rules, and goals spelled out by an organization's formal arrangements are significantly different from the relationships, norms, and values in its social system, inefficiencies emerge and the situation is unstable in the moderate run.

---

ment is growth. Most modern organizations attempt to grow. They do so by expanding their task environments, developing new technologies, and adding employees and other assets. These growth-induced changes often create nonalignments with other system elements. A significant increase in employees, for example, could easily create a nonalignment with the formal organizational arrangements that were designed to fit a smaller organization. Management succession within the dominant coalition also often induces nonalignments. New leaders bring with them different skills and outlooks, a new set of relationships, and sometimes different goals for the organization. These changes can create nonalignments with any of the organization's existing structural elements. A new company president, for example, might have aspirations for growth that are not aligned with the firm's current task environment. Finally, nonalignments are also often created by actions designed to correct nonalignments. The incorporation of a new technology, for example, might eliminate a nonalignment between the organization's technology and technological developments in the external environment, yet at the same time it might create a number of new nonalignments. The new technology might require a great deal of specialization in jobs of varying complexity. The current formal arrangements might call for less specialized and more similar jobs. Current employees might not have highly specialized skills, and the current social system might stress peer relationships and little status stratification. The new technology would then create nonalignments with all three of these elements.

Once created, nonalignments tend to correct themselves by taking the path of least resistance; that is, these move toward a solution that requires a minimum use of energy. Nonalignments generally do so by realigning around that element or those elements that are most difficult and expensive to change. The speed at which this occurs can vary widely. Numerous factors can combine to correct a nonalignment in less than a month or in more than a decade. First, the more energy that is needed to correct the nonalignment, the more time it tends to take. Large and difficult changes tend to take much more time than do small and easy changes. The speed of nonalignment correction is also usually very much a function of how much energy waste an organization's dominant coalition and its external environment are willing to tolerate. Nonalignments lead to inefficiencies and waste in matter/energy processes. If a firm's dominant coalition and its external environment are willing to allow such waste and if the organization can afford this waste because of its favorable position vis-à-vis its environment, nonalignments will probably correct themselves slowly. At the extreme, it is possible under these circumstances for moderate to small nonalignments to go uncorrected for years.

To summarize, system dynamics in a moderate-run time frame are significantly shaped by the interrelationships of the six structural elements shown in Exhibit 6. An understanding of these aligned and nonaligned relationships, along with a knowledge of what tends to create nonalignments and how nonalignments tend to correct themselves, can help explain and predict organizational dynamics over a period from 6 months to 6 years.

By itself, however, knowledge of a specific nonalignment does not guarantee that one can predict an organization's specific actions over the next 7 days, for example. And an understanding of both short- and moderate-run dynamics is insufficient to predict behavior in the long run. To chart an organization's probable behavior over 10 or 20 years, one would have to do an impractical number of calculations involving (1) identification of upcoming nonalignments, (2) identification of the most probable way the organization will resolve each nonalignment, and (3) repetition of stages (1) and (2) over and over again. To understand system dynamics in the long run, one needs to consider yet another set of ideas.

LONG-RUN DYNAMICS

As most organizations grow older, the states of their seven elements tend to become increasingly complex (with more internal differentiation and more internal relationships). More diverse types of people tend to be employed. More formal arrangements usually appear. A larger and more diverse task environment is developed. A more complex internal culture emerges. Additional technologies are incorporated. The size and complexity of the dominant coalition increase. But beyond this single pattern, one can find considerable diversity in the ways organizations evolve over long periods of time.

To understand why a particular organization evolves as it does over a period of 6 to 60 years, we need to consider what elements, if any, are acting as "driving forces" and what level of adaptability is built into the system.

The degrees of impact that the six structural elements have on the seventh element of the model, the key processes, are seldom equal. It is common for some elements to be more influential than others and to remain so for significant periods of time. For example, in relatively young organizations that are run by an entrepreneur, the dominant coalition element (the entrepreneur) often tends to be much more influential than other elements. In high-technology industries, the technology element is often the most influential. In very competitive yet mature industries, the external environment element is often more influential than others. In very old, well-established, institutionlike organizations, the internal social system and the formal organizational arrangements are often the most important elements. In both professional organizations and highly capital-intensive industries, the employees and other assets are often the most important.

Because of the nature of the interdependence of the seven elements, the predominance of one or two elements can cause these to be the driving forces for the system. Regardless of the direction in which these elements move, the other elements follow to remain aligned. Thus, identification of a driving force can help predict the direction of organizational evolution in the long run. To predict the rate and ease of movement, however, one needs to consider yet another concept.

A number of organization theorists have shown clearly that the key to an organization's long-run survival and prosperity lies in its ability to adapt to inevitable external and internal changes. Within the context of our model, the logic of this observation can be expressed as follows:

1 Because some elements in the model are made up at least partially of physical and biological systems that naturally change over time and because the elements are all interdependent such that changes in one tend to affect all the others, numerous changes in the system are *inevitable* over the long run.

2 Change can easily create nonalignments.

3 Nonalignments, when not corrected quickly, drain energy from the system.

4 Therefore, unless an organization has an unlimited supply of surplus matter/energy, its ability to correct nonalignments (that is, adapt) directly affects its prosperity and survival over the long run.

Social science and managerial research suggest that an organization's ability to adapt to changes over the long run is primarily a function of the states of its structural elements. These states can range from highly constraining of organizational processes and hard to align with other structural elements to very unconstraining and easy to align (see Exhibit 7). Because the more constraining states make it difficult to adapt to changes in the short and moderate run, the organization inevitably loses some energy during slow adaptation. And, as this recurs repeatedly, or as the organization finds itself unable to make some needed changes, it can eventually drain all its surplus energy and die. Therefore, the more an organization's structural elements appear similar to the left-hand column of Exhibit 7, the more problems one would predict it would face in the long run, and the greater the chances that it will not survive. The opposite is true when its elements appear similar to those in the right-hand column.

Overall, then, to understand or predict organizational dynamics over long periods of time, one needs to identify the system's driving force (or forces) and the adaptability of its structural elements. The driving force determines the general direction of

EXHIBIT 7 EXAMPLES OF ELEMENT STATES THAT DO AND DO NOT FACILITATE SYSTEM ADAPTATION

	States that are highly constraining and hard to align with, thereby discouraging adaptation	States that are unconstraining and easy to align with, thereby facilitating adaptation
Technology	Organization possesses a single complex technology that is rapidly becoming outdated and requires large amounts of capital for equipment.	Organization possesses the most advanced technologies for its products, services, and administrative systems along with a number of alternative technologies for possible use in the future.
Social system	Key norms are not supportive of organizational flexibility and adaptability; little trust found in relationships in social structure; total power in the system is low; morale is low; little sense of shared purpose.	Key norms are supportive of organizational flexibility and adaptability; high trust found in relationships in the social structure; total power in the system is high; morale is high; high degree of shared purpose.
Employees and other tangible assets	Plant and equipment in rundown state; employees, especially middle management, are underskilled; organization has some highly specialized equipment and human skills that it doesn't need anymore.	Plant and equipment in topnotch shape; employees, especially middle management, are highly skilled; organization possesses equipment and people with skills that it doesn't need now but may need in the future.
Organizational arrangements	Formal systems are not very sophisticated but are applied in great detail, uniformly across the organization.	Different kinds of formal system exist for structuring, measuring, rewarding, selecting, and developing different types of people working on different tasks; formal systems also exist to monitor change in the organization and its environment and to change the formal systems accordingly.
Dominant coalition	A small, homogeneous, reasonably untalented group with no effective leadership; all are about the same age.	A large, reasonably heterogeneous yet cohesive group of very talented people who work together well and have plenty of effective leadership; members are of different ages.
External environment	The organization is very dependent on a large number of externalities, with little or no countervailing power.	The organization has only a limited number of strong dependencies, with a moderate amount of countervailing power over all dependencies.
	Demand for products and services is shrinking; supplies are hard to get; regulators behave with hostility and inconsistency.	Demand for products and services is growing; supplies are plentiful; regulators behave consistently and fairly.
	Public is angry at the firm; economy is in bad shape; political system isn't functioning well; overall, the environment is hostile.	Public likes the organization; economy is in good shape; political system is functioning well; overall, the environment is benevolent.

the system's evolution, and the adaptability of the structural elements helps determine its prosperity and chances of survival.

But despite their importance in determining dynamics in the long run, the system's adaptability and driving forces do not necessarily help one to understand or predict dynamics in shorter periods of time. For example, an organization that has three or four of its structural elements in states that are very unsupportive of adaption will undoubtably experience difficulties in the long run; but the organization may or may not experience problems in the moderate run depending on whether the elements are coaligned or not. To understand moderate or short-run dynamics, factors such as the alignment of elements and cause-and-effect relationships must be considered (see Exhibit 8).

SOME IMPLICATIONS FOR ORGANIZATIONAL EFFECTIVENESS

Most people, though not all, would consider an organization effective in a short-run time frame if the organization's key processes displayed a high level of matter/energy efficiency and decision-making effectiveness. In such a case, the organization would be wasting a minimum of raw materials, human energy, and machine potential. It would also be handling information in a rational way. It would not, for example, be diverting employee energy into hostile actions on or off the job, or systematically ignoring important information it needs in its decisionmaking.

Most people would probably judge an organization effective in a moderate-run time frame if they felt it was capable of maintaining its short-run effectiveness over the moderate run. That is, they would rate an organization effective if they felt it could maintain the key processes element in an efficient and effective state over a moderate time frame. In terms of our model, the structural elements are all aligned—a state of coalignment.

Most people define effectiveness in a long-run time frame as an organization's capacity to adapt quickly to the inevitable changes that occur—that is, to move quickly into a new state of coalignment when a change has caused it to go into a state of nonalignment. As we saw previously, an organization's ability to adapt is a function of the adaptability of its structural elements. Therefore, in terms of the model,

EXHIBIT 8   SYSTEMS DYNAMICS: A SUMMARY

Time frame	Key factors in shaping system dynamics
Short run (a few days to a few months)	Two types of cause-and-effect dynamics along with the current states of the seven elements
Moderate run (a few months to a few years)	The relationships—aligned or nonaligned—among the structural elements along with the short-run factors
Long run (a few years to a few decades)	The driving force and the adaptability of the structural elements along with the other moderate- and short-run factors.

an effective organization from a long-run point of view is one in which most of its structural elements are in highly adaptive states.

Overall, therefore, we would deduce that a highly effective organization, in terms of our model, is one in which the key processes are in an efficient and effective state, and the six structural elements are coaligned and are in highly adaptive states (see Exhibit 9).

This conclusion regarding organizational effectiveness may seem obvious to some readers. Nevertheless, a close examination will reveal that it is *different* from the beliefs held by many managers, researchers, and organization specialists today. Many of these people, explicitly or implicitly, think that organizational effectiveness is associated with certain "best" states—such as good leadership, a dominant market position, loyal employees, or a high level of current profitability—or with a fit among certain organizational and situational components—such as between the organizational structure and the company's strategy or between the organization and its environment. The model suggests that all these positions are partly right and partly wrong. Specifically,

1 Those who believe in contingency or fit models are correct in stating that moderate-run effectiveness is associated with a fit among system elements, not with any specific element states.

2 Those who believe in one-best-way models are correct in stating that long-run effectiveness is associated with certain best states of each element (that is, states that

EXHIBIT 9   Characteristics of a highly effective organization.

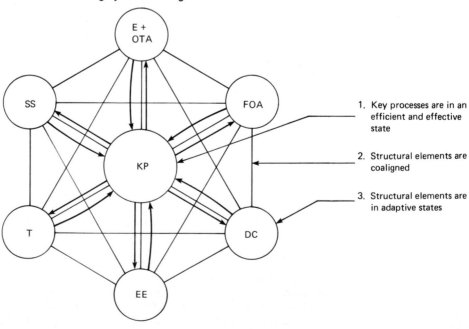

1. Key processes are in an efficient and effective state

2. Structural elements are coaligned

3. Structural elements are in adaptive states

facilitate adaptation), or in stating that short-run effectiveness is associated with a single best state in the key processes (that is, the state displaying matter/energy efficiency and effective information processing).

3 But at the same time, contingency models are wrong in asserting that fit leads to long-run effectiveness. An organization can be in a system state of coalignment and thus be performing well in the short to moderate run, and yet it may fail in the long run because most of its elements are not highly adaptive.

4 Some contingency models are also wrong in asserting that effectiveness is a function of a fit between fewer than all six of the elements in our model (for example, between just formal arrangements and the external environment or between just the social system and the technology).

5 The one-best-way models are also wrong in suggesting that an organization can achieve moderate-run effectiveness simply by getting one or more of the elements into their best states. If the overall system is significantly out of coalignment, the organization may not only perform poorly in the moderate run but may also perish as a result of the poor performance.

6 Some of the one-best-way models are also wrong in asserting that long-run effectiveness is always dependent on the adaptability of only one or two specific structural elements, such as the social system, and not on others.

7 And finally, neither the contingency models nor many of the one-best-way models are particularly sensitive to short-run dynamics and, therefore, to the problems of correcting a nonalignment or pushing an element into a more adaptive and less constraining state. Contingency or fit models often seem to imply that identification of the misfit practically solves the problem of ineffectiveness. Similarly, few one-best-way models provide realistic details about creation of their best states. In this sense, both types of model are inadequate.

In general, therefore, our model suggests that many conventional views of what is associated with organizational effectiveness are narrow and limited. These views all overlook certain correlates of effectiveness. In so doing, they can easily mislead managers and organization specialists in their efforts to improve organizational functioning.

Furthermore, one can deduce from the model that acheivement of a high level of organizational effectiveness, requires an enormous amount of good fortune or, more likely, a little good fortune combined with an ongoing series of very well made decisions, especially regarding resource allocation. Specifically, to attain a high level of effectiveness, an organization must use its limited resources successfully in three ways: (1) to ensure, in the short run, that the key organizational processes stay in an effective and efficient state, (2) to create or maintain a coalignment among the six structural elements, and (3) to push its structural elements into, or maintain them in, highly adaptive states. To do so requires that the organization be sensitive to these needs, that it monitor all three aspects of organizational effectiveness, and that it judiciously and intelligently allocate its surplus resources to these three ends.

The model does not, however, provide any simple mechanical formula for making resource allocation decisions. It only suggests that these decisions can be made more successfully if one focuses on all three aspects of effectiveness and uses the model to test the implications of alternative improvement interventions on short-, medium-, and long-run effectiveness.

Finally, a careful examination of our model also suggests that achievement of a high level of effectiveness, at least under contemporary conditions, should be very difficult. One can deduce from our model a number of reasons why organizations might develop ineffectively—reasons that relate to such factors as (1) the complexity of the system, (2) the potential for conflict between what is best for the organization and what is best for individuals, and (3) the dysfunctions caused by having excess surplus energy in the system or by not having a sufficient surplus.

USING THE MODEL

The model presented here is not meant to replace more specialized models, frameworks, and theories used by managers or organizational specialists. Nor is it meant to provide specific answers to standard questions, as does, for example, a linear programming model. Instead, it is designed to supplement existing models by raising important questions that other models might ignore, by providing a more powerful basis for understanding and predicting organizational dynamics, and by helping one to think broadly about organizational improvement issues.

More specifically, the model helps assess an organization's effectiveness level by alerting one to often-ignored aspects of effectiveness (as in Exhibit 7). It helps assess the cause of specific identified "problems" by helping to trace the dynamics leading up to them. And it provides a rational basis for identifying feasible interventions and for assessing their probable impact on the short, moderate, and long run.

RONDELL DATA
CORPORATION

John A. Seeger

"God damn it, he's done it again!" Frank Forbus threw the stack of prints and specifications on his desk in disgust. The model 802 wide-band modulator, released for production the previous Thursday, had just come back to Frank's engineering services department with a caustic note that began, "This one can't be produced, either . . ." It was the fourth time production had returned the design.

Forbus, director of engineering for the Rondell Data Corporation, was normally a quiet person. But the model 802 was stretching his patience; it was beginning to appear like other new products that had hit delays and problems in the transition from design to production during the 8 months Frank had worked for Rondell. These problems were nothing new at the sprawling, old Rondell factory; Frank's predecessor in the engineering job had run afoul of them, too, and had finallly been fired for protesting too vehemently about the other departments. But the model 802 should have been different. Frank had met 2 months earlier (on July 3, 1978) with the firm's president, Bill Hunt, and with the factory superintendent, Dave Schwab, to smooth the way for the new modulator design. He thought back to the meeting . . .

"Now, we all know there's a tight deadline on the 802," Bill Hunt said, "and Frank's done well to ask us to talk about its introduction. I'm counting on both of you to find any snags in the system, and to work together to get that first production run out by October 2. Can you do it?"

"We can do it in production if we get a clean design 2 weeks from now, as scheduled," answered Dave Schwab, the grizzled factory superintendent. "Frank and I have already talked about that, of course. I'm setting aside time in the card room and the machine shop, and we'll be ready. If the design goes over schedule, though, I'll have to fill in with other runs, and it will cost us a bundle to break in for the 802. How does it look in engineering, Frank?"

"I've just reviewed the design for the second time," Frank replied. "If Ron Porter can keep the salespeople out of our hair, and avoid any more last minute changes, we've got a shot. I've pulled the draftspersons off of three other overdue jobs to get this one out. But, Dave, that means we can't spring engineers loose to confer with your production people on manufacturing problems."

"Well, Frank, most of those problems are caused by the engineers, and we need them to resolve the difficulties. We've all agreed that production bugs come from both of us bowing to sales pressure, and putting equipment into production before the designs are really ready. That's just what we're trying to avoid on the 802. But I can't have 500 people sitting on their hands waiting for an answer from your people. We'll have to have *some* engineering support."

Bill Hunt broke in, "So long as you two can talk calmly about the problem I'm confident you can resolve it. What a relief it is, Frank, to hear the way you're approaching this. With Kilmann (the previous director of engineering), this conversation would have been a shouting match. Right, Dave?" Dave nodded and smiled.

"Now there's one other thing you should both be aware of," Hunt continued. "Doc Reeves and I talked last night about a new filtering technique, one that might improve the signal-to-noise ratio of the 802 by a factor of 2. There's a chance Doc can come up with it before the 802 reaches production, and if it's possible, I'd like to use the new filters. That would give us a real jump on the competition."

Four days after that meeting, Frank found that two of his key people on the 802 design had been called to production for an emergency consultation about a problem in final assembly: two halves of a new data transmission interface wouldn't fit together, because recent changes in the front end required a different chassis design for the rear end.

One week later, Doc Reeves proudly walked into Frank's office with the new filter design. "This won't affect the other modules of the 802 much," Doc had said. "Look, it takes three new cards, a few connectors, some changes in the wiring harness, and some new shielding, and that's all."

Frank had tried to resist the last-minute design changes, but Bill Hunt had stood firm. With considerable overtime by the engineers and draftspersons, engineering services should still be able to finish the prints in time.

Two engineers and three draftspersons went onto 12-hour days to get the 802 ready, but the prints were still 5 days late reaching Dave Schwab. Two days later, the prints came back to Frank, heavily annotated in red. Schwab had worked all day Saturday to review the job, and had found more than a dozen discrepancies in the prints—most of them caused by the new filter design and insufficient checking time before release. Correction of these design faults gave rise to a new generation of discrepancies; Schwab's cover note on the second return of the prints indicated that he had had to release the machine capacity reserved for the 802. On the third iteration, Schwab committed his photo and plating capacity to another rush job. The 802 would be at least 1 month late getting into production. Ron Porter, the vice president for sales, was furious. His customer needed 100 units *now*. Rondell was the customer's only late supplier.

"Here we go again," thought Forbus.

COMPANY HISTORY

Rondell Data Corporation traced its lineage through several generations of electronics technology. Its original founder, Bob Rondell, launched the firm in 1920 as Rondell Equipment Co. to manufacture several electrical testing devices he had invented as an engineering faculty member at a large university. The firm entered radio broadcasting equipment in 1947, and data transmission equipment in the early 1960s. A well-established corps of direct sales representatives, mostly engineers, called on industrial, scientific, and government accounts, but concentrated heavily on original equipment manufacturers. In this market, Rondell had a long-standing reputation as a source of high-quality, innovative designs. The firm's salespeople fed a continual stream of challenging problems into the engineering department, where the creative genius of Doc Reeves and several dozen other engineers "converted problems to solutions" (as the sales brochure bragged). Product design formed the spearhead of Rondell's growth.

By 1978, Rondell offered a wide range of products in its two major lines. Broadcast equipment sales had benefitted from the growth of UHF television and FM radio; it now accounted for 35 percent of company sales. Data transmission had blossomed and, in this field, an increasing number of orders called for unique specifications, ranging from specialized display panels to entirely untried designs.

The company had grown from 100 employees in 1947 to more than 800 in 1978. (Exhibits 1 and 2 show the current organization chart and the backgrounds of key employees.) Bill Hunt, who had been a student of the company's founder, had presided over most of that growth, and took great pride in preserving the family spirit of the old organization. Informal relationships between Rondell's veteran employees formed the backbone of the firm's day-to-day operations; all managers relied on personal contact, and Hunt often insisted that the absence of bureaucratic red tape was a key factor in recruiting outstanding engineering talent. The personal management approach extended throughout the factory. All exempt employees were paid a straight salary and a share of the profits. Rondell boasted an extremely loyal group of senior employees, and very low turnover in nearly all areas of the company.

The highest turnover job in the firm was director of engineering services. Forbus had joined Rondell in January 1978, replacing Jim Kilmann, who had lasted only 10 months. Kilmann, in turn, had replaced Tom MacLeod, a talented engineer who had made a promising start, but had taken to drinking after a year in the job. MacLeod's predecessor had been a genial old timer, who retired at 70, after 30 years in charge of engineering. (Doc Reeves had refused the directorship in each of the recent changes, saying, "Hell, that's no promotion for a bench man like me. I'm no administrator.")

For several years, the firm had experienced a steadily increasing number of disputes between research, engineering, sales, and production people; disputes generally centered on the problem of new-product introduction. Quarrels between departments became more numerous under MacLeod, Kilmann, and Forbus. Some managers associated these disputes with the company's recent decline in profitability—a decline that, despite higher sales and gross revenues, was beginning to bother people in 1977. Hunt commented:

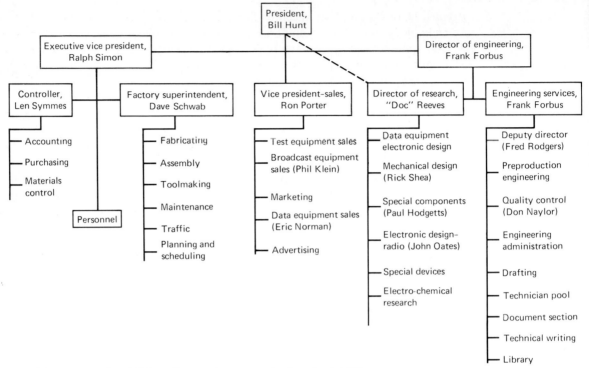

EXHIBIT 1   Rondell Data Corporation—organization chart, 1978.

Better cooperation, I'm sure, could increase our output by 5 to 10 percent. I'd hoped Kilmann could solve the problems, but pretty obviously he was too young—too arrogant. People like him—that conflict type of personality—bother me. I don't like strife, and with him it seemed I spent all my time smoothing out arguments. Kilmann tried to tell everyone else how to run their departments, without having his own house in order. That approach just wouldn't work, here at Rondell. Frank Forbus, now, seems much more in tune with our style of organization. I'm really hopeful now.

Still, we have just as many problems now as we did last year. Maybe even more. I hope Frank can get a handle on engineering services soon.

ENGINEERING DEPARTMENT: RESEARCH

According to the organization chart Forbus was in charge of both research (the product development function) and engineering services (engineering support). To Forbus, however, the relationship with research was not so clear-cut:

Doc Reeves is one of the world's unique people, and none of us would have it any other way. He's a creative genius. Sure, the chart says he works for me, but we all know Doc does his own thing. He's not the least bit interested in management routines, and I can't count on him to take any responsibility in scheduling projects, or checking budgets, or what-have-

EXHIBIT 2   BACKGROUND OF SELECTED EXECUTIVES

Executive	Position	Age	Background
Bill Hunt	President	63	Engineering graduate of an Ivy League college. Joined the company in 1946 as an engineer. Worked exclusively on development for over a year and then split his time between development and field sales work until he became assistant to the president in 1956. Became president in 1960. Together, Hunt and Simon held enough Rondell stock to command effective control of the company.
Ralph Simon	Executive vice president	65	Joined company in 1945 as a traveling representative. In 1947 became Rondell's leading salesperson for broadcast equipment. In 1954 was made treasurer, but continued to spend time selling. In 1960 was appointed executive vice president with direct responsibility for financial matters and production.
Ron Porter	Vice president of sales	50	BS in engineering. Joined the company in 1957 as a salesperson. Was influential in the establishment of the data transmission product line and did early selling himself. In 1967 was made sales manager. Extensive contacts in trade associations and industrial shows. Appointed vice president of sales in 1974.
Dave Schwab	Production manager	62	Trade school graduate; veteran of both World War II and Korean War. Joined Rondell in 1955. Promoted to production manager 7 months later after exposure of widespread irregularities in production and control departments. Reorganized production department and brought a new group of production specialists to the company.
Frank Forbus	Director of engineering	40	Master's degree in engineering. Previously division director of engineering in large industrial firm. Joined the company in 1977 as director of engineering, replacing an employee who had been dismissed because of an inability to work with sales and production personnel. As director of engineering had administrative responsibility for research personnel and complete responsibility for engineering services.
Ed Reeves	Director of research	47	Joined Rondell in 1960, working directly with Hunt to develop major innovations in data transmission equipment. Appointed director of research in 1967.
Len Symmes	Controller	43	Joined company in 1955 while attending business college. Held several jobs including production scheduling, accounting, and cost control. Named controller in 1972.

you. But as long as Doc is director of research, you can bet this company will keep on leading the field. He has more ideas per hour than most people have per year, and he keeps the whole engineering staff fired up. Everybody loves Doc—and you can count me in on that, too. In a way, he works for me, sure. But that's not what's important.

Doc Reeves—unhurried, contemplative, casual, and candid—tipped his stool back against the wall of his research cubicle and talked about what *was* important:

Development engineering. That's where the company's future rests. Either we have it there, or we don't have it.

There's no kidding ourselves that we're anything but a bunch of Rube Goldbergs here. But that's where the biggest kicks come from—from solving development problems, and dreaming up new ways of doing things. That's why I so look forward to the special contracts we get involved in. We accept them not for the revenue they represent, but because they subsidize the basic development work goes into all our basic products.

This is a fantastic place to work. I have a great crew and they can really deliver when the chips are down. Why, Bill Hunt and I (he gestured toward the neighboring cubicle, where the president's name hung over the door) are likely to find as many people here at work at 10 p.m. as at 3 p.m. The important thing here is the relationships between people; they're based on mutual respect, not on policies and procedures. Administrative red tape is a pain. It takes away from development time.

Problems? Sure, there are problems now and then. There are power interests in production, where they sometimes resist change. But I'm not a fighting man, you know. I suppose if I were, I might go in there and push my weight around a little. But I'm an engineer, and can do more for Rondell sitting right here, or working with my own people. That's what brings results.

Other members of the research department echoed these views and added additional sources of satisfaction from their work. They were proud of the personal contacts built with customers' technical staffs—contacts that increasingly involved travel to the customer's factories to serve as expert advisors in preparation of overall system design specifications. The engineers were also delighted with the department's encouragement of their personal development, continuing education, and independence on the job.

But there were problems, too. Rick Shea, of the mechanical design section, noted;

In the old days I really enjoyed the work—and the people I worked with. But now there's a lot of irritation. I don't like someone breathing down my neck. You can be hurried into jeopardizing the design.

John Oates, head of the radio electronic design section, was another designer with definite views:

Production engineering is almost nonexistent in this company. Very little is done by the preproduction section in engineering services. Frank Forbus has been trying to get preproduction into the picture, but he won't succeed because you can't start from such an ambiguous position. There have been three directors of engineering in 3 years. Frank can't hold his own against the others in the company. Kilmann was too aggressive. Perhaps no amount of tact would have succeeded.

Paul Hodgetts was head of special components in the R&D department. Like the rest of the department, he valued bench work. But he complained of engineering services.

The services don't do things we want them to do. Instead, they tell *us* what they're going to do. I should probably go to Frank, but I don't get any decisions there. I know I should go through Frank, but this holds things up, so I often go direct.

ENGINEERING SERVICES DEPARTMENT

The engineering services department (ESD) provided ancillary services to R&D, and served as liaison between engineering and the other Rondell departments. Among its main functions were drafting, management of the central technicians' pool, scheduling and expediting engineering products, documentation and publication of parts lists and engineering orders, preproduction engineering (consisting of the final integration of individual design components into mechanically compatible packages), and quality control (including inspection of incoming parts and materials, and final inspection of subassemblies and finished equipment). Top management's description of the department included the line, "ESD is responsible for maintaining cooperation with other departments, providing services to the development engineers, and freeing more valuable people in R&D from essential activities that are diversions from and beneath their main competence."

Many of the 75 ESD employees were located in other departments. Quality control people were scattered through the manufacturing and receiving areas, and technicians worked primarily in the research area or the prototype fabrication room. The remaining ESD personnel were assigned to leftover nooks and crannies near production or engineering sections. Forbus described his position:

My biggest problem is getting acceptance from the people I work with. I've moved slowly rather than risk antagonism. I saw what happened to Kilmann, and I want to avoid that. But although his precipitate action had won over a few of the younger R&D people, he certainly didn't have the department's backing. Of course, it was the resentment of other departments that eventually caused his discharge. People have been slow accepting me here. There's nothing really overt, but I get a negative reaction to my ideas.

My role in the company has never been well-defined, really. It's complicated by Doc's unique position, of course, and also by the fact that ESD sort of grew by itself over the years, as the design engineers concentrated more and more on the creative parts of product development. I wish I could be more involved in the technical side. That's been my training, and it's a lot of fun. But in our setup, the technical side is the least necessary for me to be involved in.

Schwab is hard to get along with. Before I came and after Kilmann left, there were 6 months when no one was really doing any scheduling. No work loads were figured, and unrealistic promises were made about releases. This puts us in an awkward position. We've been scheduling way beyond our capacity to manufacture or engineer.

Certain people within R&D, for instance John Oates, understand scheduling well and meet project deadlines, but this is not generally true of the rest of the R&D department, especially the mechanical engineers, who won't commit themselves. Most of the complaints come from sales and production department heads because items, such as the 802, are going to production before they are fully developed, under pressure from sales to get out the unit, and this snags the whole process. Somehow, engineering services should be able to intervene and resolve these complaints, but I haven't made much headway so far.

I should be able to go to Hunt for help, but he's too busy most of the time, and his major interest is the design side of engineering, where he got his own start. Sometimes he talks as though he's the engineering director as well as president. I have to put my foot down; there are problems here that the front office just doesn't understand.

Salespeople were often observed taking their problems directly to designers, while production frequently threw designs back at R&D, claiming they could not be produced and demanding the prompt attention of particular design engineers. The latter were frequently observed in conference with production supervisors on the assembly floor. Frank continued:

The designers seem to feel they're losing something when one of us tries to help. They feel it's a reflection on them to have someone take over what they've been doing. They seem to want to carry a project right through to the final stages, particularly the mechanical people. Consequently, engineering services people are used below their capacity to contribute, and our department is denied functions it should be performing. There's not as much use made of engineering services as there should be.

An ESD technician supervisor added his comments:

Production picks out the engineer who'll be the "bum of the month." They pick on every little detail instead of using their heads and making the minor changes that have to be made. The people with 15 to 20 years of experience shouldn't have to prove their ability any more, but they spend 4 hours defending themselves and 4 hours getting the job done. I have no one to go to when I need help. Frank Forbus is afraid. I'm trying to help him but he can't help me at this time. I'm responsible for 50 people and I've got to support them.

Fred Rodgers, who Forbus had brought with him to the company as an assistant, gave another view of the situation:

I try to get our people in preproduction to take responsibility but they're not used to it, and people in other departments don't usually see them as best qualified to solve the problem. There's a real barrier for a newcomer here. Gaining people's confidence is hard. More and more, I'm wondering whether there really is a job for me here. [Rodgers left Rondell a month later.]

Another subordinate of Forbus gave his view:

If Doc gets a new product idea, you can't argue. But he's too optimistic. He judges that others can do what he does—but there's only one Doc Reeves. We've had 900 production change orders this year—they changed 2,500 drawings. If I were in Frank's shoes, I'd put my foot down on all this new development. I'd look at the reworking we're doing and get production set up the way I wanted it. Kilmann was fired when he was doing a good job. He was getting some system in the company's operations. Of course, it hurt some people. There is no denying that Doc is the most important person in the company. What gets overlooked is that Hunt is a close second, not just politically but in terms of what he contributes technically and in customer relations.

This subordinate explained that he sometimes went out into the production department but that Schwab, the production head, resented this. Production personnel said that Kilmann had failed to show respect for oldtimers and was always meddling in other departments' business. This was the reason for his being fired, they contended. Don Taylor, in charge of quality control, commented:

> I am now much more concerned with administration and less with work. It is one of the evils you get into. There is tremendous detail in this job. I listen to everyone's opinion. Everybody is important. There shouldn't be distinctions—distinctions between people. I'm not sure whether Frank has to be a fireball like Kilmann. I think the real question is whether Frank is getting the job done. I know my job is essential. I want to supply service to the more talented people and give them information so they can do their jobs better.

SALES DEPARTMENT

Ron Porter was angry. His job was supposed to be selling, but instead it had turned into settling disputes inside the plant and making excuses to waiting customers. He jabbed a finger toward his desk:

> You see that telephone? I'm actually afraid nowadays to hear it ring. Three times out of five, it will be a customer who's hurting because we've failed to deliver on schedule. The other two calls will be from production or ESD, telling me some schedule has slipped again.
> The model 802 is typical. Absolutely typical. We padded the delivery date by 6 weeks to allow for contingencies. Within 2 months the slack had evaporated. Now it looks like we'll be lucky to ship it before Christmas. (It was now November 28.) We're *ruining* our reputation in the market. Why, just last week one of our best customers—people we've worked with for 15 years—tried to hang a penalty clause on their latest order.
> We shouldn't have to be after the engineers all the time. They should be able to see what problems they create without our telling them.

Phil Klein, head of broadcast sales under Porter, noted that many sales decisions were made by top management. He thought that sales was understaffed and had never really been able to get on top of the job.

> We have grown further and further away from engineering. The director of engineering does not pass on the information that we give him. We need better relationships there. It is very difficult for us to talk to customers about development problems without technical help. We need each other. The whole of engineering is now too isolated from the outside world. The morale of ESD is very low. They're in a bad spot—they're not well-organized.
> People don't take much to outsiders here. Much of this is because the expectation is built by top management that jobs will be filled from the bottom. So it's really tough when an outsider like Frank comes in.

Eric Norman, order and pricing coordinator for data equipment, talked about his relationships with the production department:

> Actually, I get along with them fairly well. Oh, things could be better, of course, if they were more cooperative generally. They always seem to say, "It's my bat and my ball, and we're playing by my rules." People are afraid to make production mad; there's a lot of power in there.

But you've got to understand that production has its own set of problems. And nobody in Rondell is working any harder than Dave Schwab to try to straighten things out.

PRODUCTION DEPARTMENT

Schwab had joined Rondell just after the Korean war, in which he had seen combat duty at the Yalu River and intelligence duty at Pyong Yang. Both experiences had been useful in his first year of civilian employment at Rondell: the wartime factory superintendent and several middle managers had apparently been engaging in highly questionable side deals with Rondell's suppliers. Schwab gathered the evidence, revealed the situation to Hunt, and had stood by the president in the ensuing unsavory situation. Seven months after joining the company, Schwab was named factory superintendent.

Schwab's first move had been to replace the fallen managers with a new team from outside the corporation. This group did not share the traditional Rondell emphasis on informality and friendly personal relationships, and had worked long and hard to install systematic manufacturing methods and procedures. Before the reorganization, production had controlled purchasing, stock control, and final quality control (where final assembly of products in cabinets was accomplished). Because of the wartime events, management decided on a check-and-balance system of organization and removed these three departments from production jurisdiction. The new production managers felt they had been unjustly penalized by this reorganization, particularly since they had uncovered the behavior that was detrimental to the company in the first place.

By 1978, the production department had grown to 500 employees, of whom 60 percent worked in the assembly area—an unusually pleasant environment that had been commended by *Factory* magazine for its colorful decoration, cleanliness, and low noise level. Another 30 percent of the work force, mostly skilled machinists, staffed the finishing and fabrication department. The remaining employees performed scheduling, supervisory, and maintenance duties. Production workers were not union members, were paid by the hour, and participated in both the liberal profit-sharing program and the stock purchase plan. Morale in production was traditionally high, and turnover was extremely low.

Schwab commented:

To be efficient, production has to be a self-contained department. We have to control what comes into the department and what goes out. That's why purchasing, inventory control, and quality ought to run out of this office. We'd eliminate a lot of problems with better control there. Why, even Don Naylor in QC, would rather work for me than for ESD; he's said so himself. We understand his problems better.

The other departments should be self-contained, too. That's why I always avoid the underlings, and go straight to the department heads with any questions. I always go down the line.

I have to protect my people from outside disturbances. Look what would happen if I let unfinished, half-baked designs in here—there'd be chaos. The bugs have to be found before the drawings go into the shop, and it seems I'm the one who has to find them. Look at the

802, for example. [Dave had spent most of Thanksgiving Day (it was now November 28) redpencilling the latest set of prints.] ESD should have found every one of those discrepancies. They just don't check drawings properly. They change most of the things I flag, but then they fail to trace through the impact of those changes on the rest of the design. I shouldn't have to do that.

And those engineers are tolerance crazy. They want everything to a millionth of an inch. I'm the only one in the company who's had any experience with actually machining things to a millionth of an inch. We make sure that the things that engineers say on their drawings actually have to be that way and whether they're obtainable from the kind of raw material we buy.

That shouldn't be production's responsibility, but I have to do it. Accepting bad prints wouldn't let us ship the order any quicker. We'd only make a lot of junk that had to be reworked. And that would take even longer.

This way, I get to be known as the bad guy, but I guess that's just part of the job. [Schwab paused and smiled wryly.] Of course, what really gets them is that I don't even have a degree.

Schwab had fewer bones to pick with the sales department, because he said that they trusted him.

When *we* give Ron Porter a shipping date, he knows the equipment will be shipped *then*.

You've got to recognize, though, that all of our new product problems stem from sales making absurd commitments on equipment that hasn't been fully developed. That always means trouble. Unfortunately, Hunt always backs sales up, even when they're wrong. He always favors them over us.

Ralph Simon, executive vice president of the company, had direct responsibility for Rondell's production department. He said:

There shouldn't really be a dividing of departments among top management in the company. The president should be czar over all. The production people ask me to do something for them, and I really can't do it. It creates bad feelings between engineering and production, this special attention that they [R&D] get from Bill. But then Hunt likes to dabble in design. Schwab feels that production is treated like a poor relation.

EXECUTIVE COMMITTEE

At the executive committee meeting of December 6, it was duly recorded that Schwab had accepted the prints and specifications for the model 802 modulator, and had set December 29 as the shipping date for the first 10 pieces. Hunt, as chairperson, shook his head and changed the subject quickly when Forbus tried to initiate discussion of interdepartmental coordination.

The executive committee itself was a brainchild of Rondell's controller, Len Symmes, who was well aware of the disputes that plagued the company. Symmes had convinced Hunt and Simon to meet every 2 weeks with their department heads; the meetings were formalized with Hunt, Simon, Porter, Schwab, Forbus, Reeves, Symmes, and the personnel director attending. Symmes explained his intent and the results:

Doing things collectively and informally just doesn't work as well as it used to. Things have been gradually getting worse for at least 2 years now. We had to start thinking in terms of formal organization relationships. I did the first organization chart, and the executive committee was my idea, too—but neither idea is contributing much help, I'm afraid. It takes top management to make an organization click. The rest of us can't act much differently until the top people see the need for us to change.

I had hoped the committee especially would help get the department managers into a constructive planning process. It hasn't worked out that way, because Mr. Hunt really doesn't see the need for it. He uses the meetings as a place to pass on routine information.

MERRY CHRISTMAS

"Frank, I didn't know whether to tell you now, or after the holiday." It was December 22, and Forbus was standing awkwardly in front of Hunt's desk.

"But I figured you'd work right through Christmas Day if we didn't have this talk, and that just wouldn't have been fair to you. I can't understand why we have such poor luck in the engineering director's job lately. And I don't think it's entirely your fault. But . . .

Frank only heard half of Hunt's words, and said nothing in response. He'd be paid through February 28. . . . He should use the time for searching. . . . Hunt would help all he could. . . . Jim Kilmann was supposed to be doing well at his own new job, and might need more help.

Frank cleaned out his desk, and numbly started home. The electronic carillion near his house was playing a Christmas carol. Frank thought again of Hunt's rationale: conflict still plagued Rondell—and Frank had not made it go away. Maybe somebody else could do it.

"And what did Santa Claus bring you, Frankie?" he asked himself.

"The sack. Only the empty sack."

BANCIL CORPORATION

Ram Charan
Lawrence D. Chrzanowski

Struggling to clear his mind, Remy Gentile, marketing manager in France for the toiletry division of Bancil, stumbled from bed to answer the ringing telephone.

"Allo?"

"Remy, Tom Wilson here. Sorry to bother you at this hour. Can you hear me?"

"Sacre Bleu! Do you know what time it is?"

"About 5:20 in Sunnyvale. I've been looking over the past quarter's results for our Peau Doux . . ."

"Tom, it's after 2 a.m. in Paris; hold the phone for a moment."

Remy was vexed with Tom Wilson, marketing vice president for the toiletry division and acting division marketing director for Europe, since they had already discussed the Peau Doux situation via telex no more than a month ago. When he returned to the phone, Remy spoke in a more controlled manner.

"You mentioned the Peau Doux line, Tom."

"Yes, Remy, the last quarter's results were very disappointing. Though we've increased advertising by 30 percent, sales were less than 1 percent higher. What is even more distressing, Remy, is that our competitors' sales have been growing at nearly 20 percent per year. Furthermore, our percent cost of goods sold has not decreased. Has Pierre Chevalier bought the new equipment to streamline the factory's operation?"

"No, Pierre has not yet authorized the purchase of the machines, and there is little that can be done to rationalize operations in the antiquated Peau Doux plant. Also, we have not yet succeeded in securing another distributor for the line."

"What! But that was part of the strategy with our increased advertising. I thought we agreed to . . ."

Tom Wilson hesitated for a moment. His mind was racing as he attempted to recall the specifics of the proposed toiletry division strategy for France. That strategy had guided his earlier recommendation to Gentile and Pierre Chevalier, the Bancil general manager in France, to increase advertising and to obtain a new distributor. Tom wanted to be forceful but tactful to ensure Gentile's commitment to the strategy.

"Remy, let's think about what we discussed on my last trip to Paris. Do you recall we agreed to propose to Chevalier a plan to revitalize Peau Doux's growth? If my memory serves me well, it was to increase advertising by 25 percent, groom a new national distributor, reduce manufacturing costs with new equipment, increase prices, and purchase the 'L'aube' product line to spread our marketing overhead."

"Oui, oui. We explored some ideas and I thought they needed more study."

"Remy, as you recall Peau Doux has a low margin. Cutting costs is imperative. We expected to decrease costs 5 percent by investing $45,000 in new equipment. Our test for the new strategy next year was to increase advertising this quarter and next quarter while contracting for a new distributor. The advertising was for naught. What happened?"

"I really don't know. I guess Pierre has some second thoughts."

Tom spoke faster as he grew more impatient. Gentile's asking him to repeat what he had said made him angrier. Tom realized that he must visit Paris to salvage what he could from the current test program on Peau Doux. He knew that the recent results would not support the proposed toiletry division strategy.

"Remy, I need to see what's going on and then decide how I can best assist you and Chevalier. I should visit Paris soon. How about early next week, say Monday and Tuesday?"

"Oui, that is fine."

"I'll fly in on Sunday morning. Do you think you can join me for dinner that evening at the Vietnamese restaurant we dined at last time?"

"Oui."

"Please make reservations only for two. I'm coming alone. Good night, Remy."

"Oui. Bon soir."

COMPANY BACKGROUND

Bancil Corporation of Sunnyvale, Calif., was founded in 1908 by pharmacist Dominic Bancil. During its first 50 years, its products consisted primarily of analgesics (branded pain relievers, such as aspirin), an antiseptic mouthwash, and a first-aid cream. By 1974, some of the top management positions were still held by members of the Bancil family, who typically had backgrounds as pharmacists or physicians. This tradition notwithstanding, John Stoopes, the present chief executive officer, was committed to developing a broad-based professional management team.

Bancil sales, amounting to $61 million in 1955, had grown to $380 million in 1970 and to $600 million in 1974. This sales growth had been aided by diversification and acquisition of allied businesses as well as by international expansion. Bancil's product line by 1970 included four major groups:

	Sales (in millions of dollars)	
	1970	1974
Agricultural and animal health products (weedkillers, fertilizers, feed additives)	$ 52	$141
Consumer products (Bancil original line, as well as hand creams, shampoos, and baby accessories)	205	276
Pharmaceutical products (tranquilizers, oral contraceptives, hormonal drugs)	62	107
Professional products (diagnostic reagents, automated chemical analyzers, and surgical gloves and instruments)	60	76

In 1974, Bancil's corporate organization was structured around these four product groups which, in turn, were divided into two or three divisions. Thus, in 1973 the consumer products group had been divided into the Dominic division, which handled Bancil's original product line, and the toiletry division, which was in charge of the newer product acquisitions. The objective of this separation was to direct greater attention to the toiletry products.

INTERNATIONAL OPERATIONS

International expansion had begun in the mid-1950s when Bancil exported through agents and distributors. Subsequently, marketing subsidiaries, called *national units* (NUs), were created in Europe, Africa, Latin America, and Japan. All manufacturing took place in the United States. Virtually the entire export activity consisted of Bancil's analgesic Domicil. An innovative packaging concept, large amounts of creative advertising, and considerable sales push made Domicil a common word in most of the free world, reaching even the most remote areas of Africa, Asia, and South America. A vice president of international operations exercised control at this time through letters and occasional overseas trips. By the mid-1960s, overseas marketing of pharmaceutical and professional products began, frequently through a joint venture with a local company. Increasing sales led to the construction of production facilities for many of Bancil's products in England, Kenya, Mexico, Brazil, and Japan.

Bancil's international expansion received a strong commitment from top management. John Stoopes was not only a successful business executive but also a widely read intellectual with an avid interest in South American and African cultures. This interest generated an extraordinary sense of responsibility to the developing nations and a conviction that the mature industrial societies had an obligation to help in their development. He did not want Bancil to be viewed as a firm that drained resources and money from the developing world; rather, he desired to apply Bancil's resources to worldwide health and malnutrition problems. His personal commitment as an ardent humanist was a guideline for Bancil's international operations.

While Bancil had been successful during the 1960s in its domestic diversification and international expansion, its efforts to achieve worldwide diversification had given rise to frustration. Even though the international division's specific purpose was to promote all Bancil products most advantageously throughout the world, the NUs had concentrated mainly on analgesics. As a result, the growth of the remaining products had been generally confined to the United States and thus these products were not realizing their fullest worldwide potential.

According to Bancil executives, these problems had their roots in the fact that the various product lines, though generically related, required different management strategies. For consumer products, advertising consumed 28 percent to 35 percent of sales; since production facilities did not require a large capital investment, considerable spare capacity was available to absorb impulses in demand created by advertising campaigns. For agricultural and animal health products, promotion was less than 1 percent of sales, but the capital-intensive production (a facility of minimum economic scale cost $18 million) required a marketing effort to stimulate demand consistently near full production capacity. Furthermore, the nature of the marketing activity for the professional and pharmaceutical products placed the burden on personal selling rather than on a mass promotion effort.

In response to this situation, a 1969 reorganization gave each product division worldwide responsibility for marketing its products. Regional marketing managers, reporting to the division's vice president of marketing, were given direct authority for most marketing decisions (for example, advertising, pricing, distribution channels) of their division's products in their area. The manufacturing division, with headquarters in Sunnyvale, had worldwide responsibility for production and quality control. (See Exhibit 1 for the 1969 organization chart.)

Corporate management also identified a need in key countries for a single local executive to represent Bancil's interests in local banking and political circles. There was no single criterion for selecting, from the divisions' representatives in each country, the Bancil delegate—the title given to this position. A corporate officer remarked:

> We chose whom we thought was the best business executive in each country. There was no emphasis on functional specialty or on selecting an individual from the division with the greatest volume. In one country, the major candidates were opinionated and strong-willed, and we therefore chose the individual who was the least controversial. The Bancil delegate generally had a marketing background if marketing was the primary Bancil activity in the country or a production background if Bancil had several manufacturing facilities in the country.

While international sales had grown from $99 million in 1970 to $147 million in 1972, profit performance from 1971 to 1972 had been disappointing. A consultant's report stated:

> There are excessive communications between the NUs and Sunnyvale. The marketing managers and all the agents are calling for product-line information from the divisional head-

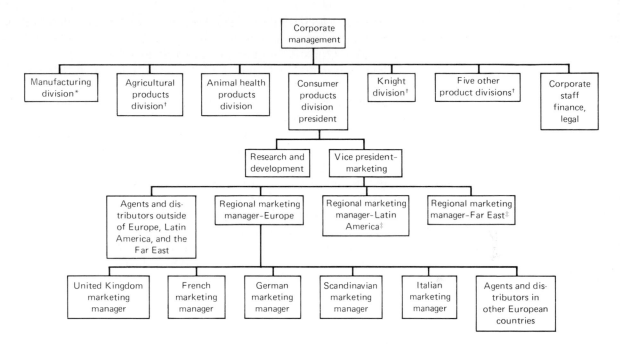

* The manufacturing division manufactured products for all the product divisions. Overseas manufacturing (not shown) reported to the manufacturing division in Sunnyvale.

† Organization similar to that of the consumer products division.

‡ Organization similar to that for Europe.

EXHIBIT 1 Bancil Corporation—1969 organization chart.

quarters. Five individuals are calling three times per week on an average, and many more are calling only slightly less often.

It appeared that a great deal of management time was spent on telex, long-distance communications, and travel. In response to these concerns, the divisions' staffs increased in each country. Overhead nearly tripled, affecting the growth rate of profits from international operations.

With the exception of financial decisions, which were dictated by corporate headquarters, most decisions on inventories, pricing, new-product offerings, and facility development were made by corporate headquarters along with the local people. However, local people felt that the key decisions were being postponed. Conflicting demands also were a problem as every division drew on the local resources for personnel, inventories, receivables, and capital investment. These demands had been manageable, however, because even though profits were below target no cash shortages had developed.

Current Organization of International Operations

To improve the performance of its international operations, Bancil instituted a reorganization in mid-1973. The new organization was a matrix of NU general managers and area vice presidents, who were responsible for total resource allocation in their geographic area, and division presidents, who were responsible for their product lines worldwide. (See Exhibit 2 for a description of the matrix in 1975.)

The general manager was the chief executive in his or her country in charge of all Bancil products. He also was Bancil's representative on the board and executive committee of local joint ventures. The Bancil delegate usually had been chosen as the general manager. The delegate was responsible for making the best use of financial, material, and personnel resources; pursuing approved strategies; searching for and identifying new business opportunities for Bancil in the NU; and developing Bancil's reputation as a responsible corporate citizen. The general manager was assisted by a financial manager, one or more plant managers, product-line marketing managers, and other functional managers as required.

The divisions were responsible for operations in the United States and Canada and for worldwide expertise on their product lines. Divisions discharged the latter responsibility through local product-line marketing managers who reported on a line basis to the NU general manager and on a functional basis to a division area market-ing director. The latter, in turn, reported to the divisional marketing vice president. Where divisions were involved in other functional activities, the organizational struc-

EXHIBIT 2 Bancil Corporation—shared responsibility matrix.

Product group vice presidents	Division presidents	France, P. Chevalier	Germany, D. Rogge	Four other national units	Argentina and Uruguay, S. Portillo	Brazil, E. Covelli	Two other national units	Four national units	General managers
Agricultural and animal health (three divisions)	Rogers division								
	Division B								
	Division C								
Consumer products (two divisions)	Dominic division								
	Toiletry division (Robert Vincent)								
Pharmaceuticals (two divisions)	Division A								
	Division B								
Professional (three divisions)	Knight division								
	Division B								
	Division C								

ture was similar to that for marketing. The flow of product-line expertise from the divisions to the NUs consisted of (1) operational inputs, such as hiring and termination policies and the structure of merit programs, and (2) technical and professional inputs to the NU marketing, production, and other staff functions on the conduct of the division's business within the NU.

Only the Dominic division was represented in every NU. Some divisions lacked representation in several NUs and, in some cases, a division did not have a marketing director in an area. For example, the Rodgers division had area marketing directors in Europe, the Far East, and Latin America, all of whom reported to the divisional vice president of marketing as did the division's U.S. marketing personnel. However, the Knight division, which had a structure similar to that of the Rodgers division, could justify area marketing directors only in Europe and Latin America.

The new matrix organization established for each country a national unit review committee (NURC) with its membership consisting of the general manager (chairperson), the financial manager, and a representative from each division with activities in the NU. Corporate executives viewed the NURC as the major mechanism for exercising shared profit responsibility. NURC met quarterly, or more frequently at the general manager's direction, to (1) review and approve divisional profit commitments generated by the general manager's staff; (2) ensure that these profit commitments, viewed as a whole, were compatible with and representative of the best use of the NU's resources; (3) monitor the NU's progress against the agreed-upon plans; and (4) review and approve salary ranges for key NU personnel. When the division's representatives acted as members of the NURC, they were expected to view themselves as responsible executives of the NU.

Strategic Planning and Control

NURC was also the framework within which general managers and division representatives established the NU's annual strategic plan and profit commitment. Strategy meetings commenced in May, at which time the general manager presented a forecast of Bancil's business in the NU for the next 5 years and the strategies to be pursued to exploit environmental opportunities. The general manager and the divisional representatives worked together between May and September to develop a mutually acceptable strategy and profit commitment. If genuine disagreement on principle arose during these deliberations, the issue could be resolved at the next level of responsibility. The profit commitment was reviewed at higher levels both within the area and within the product divisions, with the final approval coming from the corporate executive committee (CEC), which required compatible figures from the vice president of international operations and the product group executives. CEC, the major policy-making forum at Bancil, consisting of the chief executive officer, the group vice presidents, the vice president of international operations, and the corporate secretary, met monthly to resolve policy issues and to review operating performance.

For each country, results were reported separately for the various divisions represented which, in turn, were consolidated into a combined NU statement. The NU, as well as the divisions, was held accountable, though at different levels, according to its responsibilities. The division profit flow (DPF) and NU net income are shown in the following example for the Argentine national unit in 1974.

The product divisions were responsible for worldwide division profit flow (DPF), defined as net sales less all direct expenses related to divisional activity, including marketing managers' salaries, sales force, and sales office expenses. The NU was responsible for net income after charging all local divisional expenses and all NU operating expenses, such as general administration, taxes, and interest on borrowed funds. Because both the general managers and the divisions shared responsibility for profit in the international operations, the new structure was called a *shared-responsibility matrix* (SRM). The vice president of international operations and the division presidents continually monitored various performance ratios and figures (see Exhibit 3). In 1975 international operations emphasized return on resources, cash generation, and cash remittance, while the division presidents emphasized product-line return on resources, competitive market share, share of advertising, and dates of new product introductions.

The impact of the 1973 organizational shift to the SRM had been greatest for the general managers. Previously, as Bancil delegates, they had not been measured on the basis of the NU's total performance for which they were now held responsible. Also, they now determined salary adjustments, hirings, dismissals, and appointments after consultations with the divisions. In addition, general managers continued to keep abreast of important political developments in their areas, such as the appointment of a new finance minister, a general work strike, imposition of punitive taxes, and the outbreak of political strife—a not-infrequent occurrence in some countries.

Under the new organizational structure, the area marketing directors felt that their influence was waning. While they were responsible for DPF, they were not sure that they had "enough muscle" to effect appropriate allocation of resources for their products in each of the countries they served. This view was shared by Nicholas Rosati, Knight division marketing manager in Italy, who commented on his job:

	Rodgers division	Dominic division	Toiletry division	National unit
Division sales	$250,000	$800,000	$1,250,000	$2,300,000
Division expenses	160,000	650,000	970,000	1,780,000
Division profit flow (DPF)	$ 90,000	$150,000	$ 280,000	$ 520,000
NU's other expenses (general administrative, interest on loans, etc.)				350,000
NU's income before taxes				$ 170,000
Taxes				80,000
NU's net income				$ 90,000
Working capital	$100,000	$300,000	$ 700,000	

EXHIBIT 3 CONTROL FIGURES AND RATIOS*

Vice president of international operations for national unit		Division president for product line
X	Sales	X
X	Operating income: percent of sales	X
X	General manager's expense: percent of sales	
X	Selling expense: percent of sales	X
X	Nonproduction expense: percent of operating income	
X	Operating income per staff employee	
X	Percent of staff turnover	
X	Accounts receivable (days)	X
X	Inventories (days)	X
X	Fixed assets	X
X	Resources employed	X
X	Return on resources	X
X	Cash generation	
X	Cash remittances	
X	Share of market and advertising	X
X	Rate of new product introduction	X

Source: Company records.
* X indicates a figure or ratio on the organization's (NU or division) performance of interest to the vice

> The European marketing director for the Knight division keeps telling me to make more calls on hospitals and laboratories. But it is useless to make calls to solicit more orders. The general manager for Italy came from the consumer products division. He will neither allocate additional personnel to service new accounts for the Knight division nor will he purchase sufficient inventory of our products so I can promise reasonable delivery times for new accounts.

Nevertheless, divisions were anxious to increase their market penetration outside the United States and Canada, seeing such a strategy as their best avenue of growth. The recent increase in international sales and profits, which had by far exceeded that of domestic operations (see Exhibit 4), seemed to confirm the soundness of this view. Not all NU general managers shared this approach, as exemplified by the following statement from Edmundo Covelli, the general manager of Brazil:

> The divisions are continually seeking to boost their sales and increase their DPF. They are not concerned with the working capital requirements to support the sales. With the inflation rate in Brazil, my interest rate of 40 percent on short-term loans has a significant effect on my profits.

EXHIBIT 4   SALES AND PROFITS FOR BANCIL CORPORATION DOMESTIC AND INTERNATIONAL
(in millions of dollars)

Year	Domestic		International		Total	
	Sales	Profit	Sales	Profit	Sales	Profit
1955	$ 61	$ 5.5	–	–	$ 61	$ 5.5
1960	83	8.3	$ 6	$ 0.2	89	8.5
1965	121	13.5	23	1.3	144	14.8
1969	269	26.7	76	9.2	345	35.9
1970	280	27.1	99	12.3	379	39.4
1971	288	28.7	110	14.2	398	42.9
1972	313	32.5	147	15.8	460	48.3
1973	333	35.3	188	21.4	521	56.7
1974	358	36.7	242	30.9	600	67.6

Source: Company records.

THE PEAU DOUX ISSUE

The telephone conversation described at the beginning of the case involved a disagreement between Tom Wilson, who was both marketing vice president for the
toiletry division and acting division marketing director for Europe, and Pierre Chevalier, Bancil's general manager for France. It also involved Remy Gentile, who
reported on a line basis to Chevalier and on a functional basis to Wilson.

Chevalier had been the general manager of France for 18 months after having
been hired from a competitor in the consumer products business. Upon assuming the
position, he identified several organizational and operational problems in France:

> When I took this job, I had five marketing managers, a financial manager, a production
> manager, and a medical specialist reporting to me. After the consumer products division
> split, the new toiletry division wanted its own marketing manager. Nine people reporting to
> me was too many. I hired Remy for his administrative talents and had him assume respon-
> sibility for the toiletry division in addition to having the other marketing managers report
> to him. That gave me more time to work with our production people to get the cost of
> goods down.

In less than 2 years as general manager, Chevalier had reduced the cost of goods
sold by more than 3 percent by investing in new equipment and had improved the
net income for the French NU by discontinuing products that had little profit potential.

Remy Gentile had been the marketing manager for the toiletry division in France
for the past year. In addition, five other marketing managers (one for each Bancil
Corporation division operating in France) reported to him. During the previous 6
years Gentile had progressed from salesperson to sales supervisor to marketing manager within the Knight division in France. Although he had received mixed reviews

from the toiletry division, particularly on his lack of mass marketing experience, Chevalier had hired him because of his track record, his ability to learn quickly, and his outstanding judgment.

The disagreement involved the Peau Doux line of hand creams, which Bancil Corporation had purchased 5 years earlier to spread the general manager's overhead, especially in terms of marketing, over a broader product offering. Wilson's frustration resulted from Chevalier's ambivalence toward the division's strategy of increasing the marketing effort and cutting manufacturing costs on the Peau Doux line.

The total market in France for the Peau Doux product line was growing at an annual rate of 15–20 percent, according to both Wilson and Gentile. However, Peau Doux, an old, highly regarded hand cream, had been traditionally distributed through pharmacies, whereas recently introduced hand creams had been successfully sold through supermarkets. The original Peau Doux sales force was not equipped to distribute the product through other outlets. To support a second sales force for supermarket distribution, the toiletry division sought to acquire the L'aube shampoo and face cream line. When Gentile had informed Chevalier of this strategy, the latter had questioned the wisdom of the move. The current volume of the Peau Doux line was $800,000. Although less than 10 percent of Chevalier's total volume, it comprised the entire toiletry division volume in France.

Tom Wilson viewed the Peau Doux problems primarily in terms of an inadequate marketing effort. On three occasions within the past year, he or his media experts from Sunnyvale had gone to Paris to troubleshoot the Peau Doux problems. On the last trip, Robert Vincent, the toiletry division president, had joined them. On the return flight to Sunnyvale, Wilson remarked to Vincent:

> I have the suspicion that Chevalier, in disregarding our expertise, is challenging our authority. It is apparent from his indifference to our concerns and his neglect in allocating capital for new machinery that he doesn't care about the Peau Doux line. Maybe he should be told what to do directly.

Vincent responded:

> Those are very strong words, Tom. I suggest we hold tight and do a very thorough job of preparing for the budget session on our strategy in France. If Chevalier does not accept or fundamentally revises our budget, we may take appropriate measures to make corporate management aware of the existing insensitivity to the toiletry division in France. This seems to be a critical issue. If we lose now, we may never get back in the French market in the future.

After Wilson and Vincent had departed for Sunnyvale, Chevalier commented to Dufour, his area vice president:

> I have the feeling that nothing we say will alter the thinking of Wilson and Vincent. They seem to be impervious to our arguments that mass advertising and merchandising in France do not fit the Peau Doux product concept.

Andre Dufour had been a practicing pharmacist for 6 years before joining Bancil Corporation as a sales supervisor in Paris in 1962. He had progressed to sales manager and marketing manager of the consumer products division in France. After the untimely death of the existing Bancil delegate for France in 1970, he had been selected to fill that position. With the advent of SRM he had become the general manager and had been promoted to vice president for Europe a year later. Dufour had a talent for identifying market needs and for thoroughly planning and deliberately executing strategies. He was also admired for his perseverance and dedication to established objectives. Clark B. Tucker, vice president of international operations and Dufour's immediate supervisor, commented:

> When he was a pharmacist he developed an avocational interest in chess and desired to become proficient at the game. Within 5 years he successfully competed in several international tournaments and achieved the rank of International Grand Master.

In fall 1974, Dufour became the acting vice president of international operations while Tucker attended the 13-week advanced management program at the Harvard Business School. Although Dufour had considerable difficulty with the English language, he favorably impressed the corporate management at Sunnyvale with his ability to get to the heart of business problems.

The toiletry division had only limited international activities. In addition to the Peau Doux line in France, it marketed Cascada shampoos and Tempestad fragrances in Argentina. The Cascada and Tempestad lines had been acquired in 1971.

Wilson and Manual Ramirez, the toiletry division marketing director for Latin America, were ecstatic over the consumer acceptance and division performance of Cascada and Tempestad in Argentina. Revenue and DPF had quintupled since the acquisition. In his dealings with Gentile, Wilson frequently referred to the toiletry division's success in Argentina. Given this sales performance and the division's clearly stated responsibility for worldwide marketing of toiletry products, Wilson felt that his position in proposing the new strategy for France was strong.

On the other hand, Sergio Portillo, general manager of Argentina and Uruguay, and Juan Vilas, vice president for Latin American operations, had become alarmed by the cash drain from marketing the toiletry division products in Argentina. The high interest charges on funds for inventories and receivables seemed to negate the margins touted by the division executives. In describing the Cascada and Tempestad operation to Vilas, Portillo commented:

> I have roughly calculated our inventory turnover for the toiletry division products marketed in Argentina. Although my calculations are crude, the ratio based on gross sales is about 4, which is less than one-half the inventory turnover of the remainder of our products.

Neither Portillo nor Vilas shared the toiletry division's enthusiasm, and both suspected that Cascada and Tempestad were only slightly above break-even profitability. Chevalier and Dufour were aware of this concern with the toiletry products in Argentina.

As Chevalier contemplated the toiletry division strategy, he became convinced that more substantive arguments rather than just economic ones would support his position. In discussing his concerns with Dufour, Chevalier asked:

Are the toiletry division product lines really part of what John Stoopes and we want to be Bancil's business? Hand creams, shampoos, and fragrances belong to firms like Colgate-Palmolive, Procter & Gamble, and Revlon. What is Bancil contributing to the local people's welfare by producing and marketing toiletries? We have several potentially lucrative alternatives for our resources. The Rodgers division's revenues have been increasing at 18 percent. We recently completed construction of a processing plant for Rodgers and we must get sales up to our new capacity. The Knight division is introducing an electronic blood analyzer that represents a technological breakthrough. We must expand and educate our sales force to take advantage of this opportunity.

Chevalier sensed that Gentile was becoming increasingly uneasy on this issue, and the feeling was contagious. They had never faced such a situation before. Under the previous organization, NUs had been required to comply, although sometimes reluctantly, with the decisions from Sunnyvale. However, SRM was not supposed to work this way. Chevalier and Gentile stood firmly behind their position, even though they recognized the pressure on Wilson and, to a lesser degree, on Vincent. They wondered what should be the next step and who should take it. Due to the strained relationship with Wilson, they did not rule out the possibility of Wilson and Vincent's taking the Peau Doux issue to the consumer products group vice president and having it resolved within the corporate executive committee.

VISA INTERNATIONAL: THE MANAGEMENT OF CHANGE *

J. Stewart Dougherty
Robert G. Eccles

INTRODUCTION

"Is any man afraid of change? Why, what can take place without change? What, then, is more pleasing or more suitable to the universal nature? And canst thou take a bath unless the wood undergoes change? And canst thou be nourished unless the food undergoes change? And canst anything else that is useful be accomplished without change? Does thou not see, then, that for thyself also to change is just the same, and equally necessary for the universal nature?

It would be nice to claim authorship of lines which so well express the eternal dilemma of change, and current plague of bankers. However, they belong to Marcus Aurelius, Roman emperor from 161 to 180 AD.

Dee Ward Hock[1]

The roaring current of change is a current so powerful today that it overturns institutions, shifts our values and shrivels our roots. Change is the process by which the future invades our lives.

Alvin Toffler[2]

From a standing start in 1966, under the former names of BankAmericard, and then National BankAmericard, Inc. (NBI), Visa had become the largest bank card and value exchange system in the world, claiming 1980 worldwide volume of $45.7 billion. Internationally, 3.1 million merchants in 150 countries honored Visa's blue, white, and gold cards. At the end of 1980, Visa's member banks around the world maintained 94.8 million card accounts from their 100,000 offices.

---

* All oral quotations from Dee Hock are copyright © 1981 by Dee W. Hock.
[1] From the chief executive officer's speech to members of the American Bankers Association, Sept. 25, 1973.
[2] Alvin Toffler, *Future Shock,* 1970.

Visa was owned and governed by more than 14,000 financial institutions, which offered its credit cards, debit cards, travelers' checks, and merchant services. These member institutions, which were primarily commercial banks, thrift banks, savings and loans, and credit unions, were located in more than 100 countries around the globe.

Despite the sweeping size and scope of its operations, Visa International was an organization of only 500 employees, 375 of whom performed clerical operations. Its small employee population was due to the fact that Visa's member banks and member financial institutions, and *not* Visa International, issued all of Visa's products. Visa International was the overseeing administrative organization that linked the operations of the thousands of member institutions into a cohesive and efficient worldwide network.

Visa maintained two major offices in the United States: one in San Mateo, Calif., and one in McLean, Va. These offices housed Visa's sophisticated computer systems, as well as many of its key executives. The company maintained an office in Washington, D.C., for Visa's vice president for legislative affairs. Finally, various regional offices served the international membership. A London office handled Europe, the Mideast, and Africa; a Singapore office supported Asia and the Pacific; and headquarters in Miami oversaw Latin America. The offices serving these vast international territories were small, with an average of 10 employees each. Dee Hock, Visa's colorful and philosophic chief executive officer, presided over this expansive operation from a four-person office in San Francisco.

While Visa's past growth was dramatic, top management expected the future to provide an equal challenge. Total sales volume was expected to grow from the 1980 level of $45.7 billion to $180 billion by 1986. In fact, Hock felt that, in 1981, Visa's credit and debit cards had reached only 5 percent of their potential as payment devices. His view was that Visa would eventually be one or more devices that would enable individuals to exchange any asset they possessed for any good, service, or currency they desired at any time of the day or night at any location on the civilized earth. This, he explained, was the potential of electronic value exchange. "Viewed in this way," he continued, "the future is virtually without limit." To meet the special challenges of such a future, Visa had undergone a major reorganization in the early months of 1981. (See Exhibit 1 for Visa International's organization chart.)

Visa's organizational structure and employees would be strongly tested in the future months. Visa expected to experience unprecedented near-term growth, particularly outside of the United States and Canada. Further, the climate of the industry was changing rapidly. High interest rates in 1981 were resulting in massive operating losses for many U.S. Visa members. Fraud and credit writeoffs were mounting, and a major deployment of new, electronic authorization terminals would be required to halt or reverse the trend. The development of new products, systems, and services would be needed if Visa were to advance and continue to lead in this fast-changing environment.

With time, Visa's management and other observers would decide whether the company's philosophy and methods were visionary strokes of genius, destined to endure as the accepted techniques of the future, or whether they were flawed, doomed to prove undistinguished or perhaps even to fail.

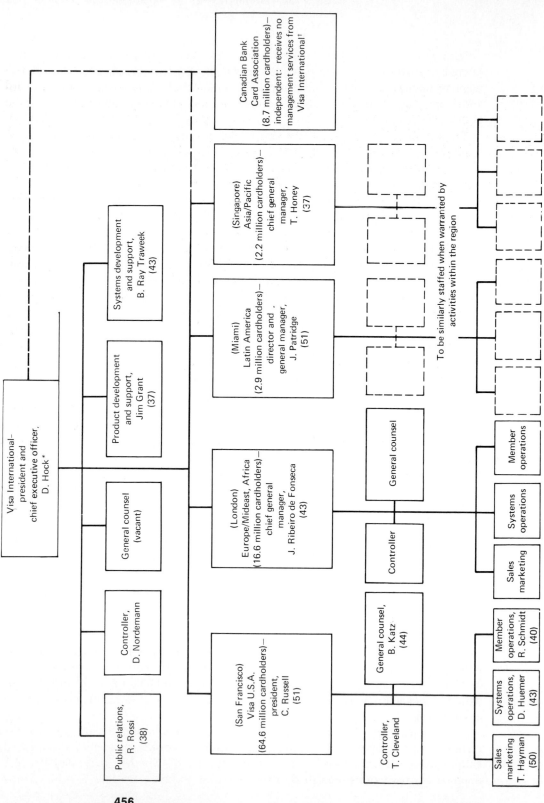

EXHIBIT 1 Visa International—organization chart.

*President and chief executive officer of Visa International also serves as chief executive officer of Visa U.S.A.

†The Canadian region is not shown because the Canadian Bank Card Association does not receive direct management services from VISA International.

COMPETITION AMONG THE CARD SYSTEMS

Competition among the various card systems was pronounced in the past, and continued to be rigorous in 1981. (See Exhibit 2 for an overview of the payment card industry.) Although MasterCharge had commenced operations after BankAmericard, it had pulled ahead of BankAmericard in the late 1960s, and rapidly increased its lead in both gross billings and the number of active accounts. When NBI was formed in July 1970, the new organization (guided by Hock's philosophy) promptly narrowed the spread between the systems. In the first quarter of 1978, Visa officially edged out MasterCharge in domestic billings, with $4.6 billion to MasterCharge's $4.5 billion. (It should be noted that MasterCharge included in its gross volume statistics the sales of other card systems with which it had interchange agreements, such as Access Card in England, Eurocard in Europe, and Diamond Credit in Japan. Therefore, it is likely that Visa surpassed MasterCharge in sales volume before the first quarter of 1978.) As of May 1981, Visa International maintained 94.8 million card accounts to the 76.7 million accounts maintained by MasterCard and its affiliates.

During the same period, American Express had become the preeminent force among the independent travel and entertainment (T&E) cards. By the end of 1980, American Express maintained 11.9 million card accounts, as compared to Diners Club's 2.9 million and Carte Blanche's 900,000 accounts. Both Diners Club and Carte Blanche had recently been acquired by Citicorp, and it was expected that they were being readied for a new competitive thrust in the marketplace.

Visa also faced stiff competition abroad. Its chief European foe was Eurocheque, the huge (35 million cards usable in 39 countries at the close of 1980) check-guarantee card that was dominated by the West German banks and championed by Deutsche Bank's Eckart van Hooven as an alternative to what he called the "US credit cards." The Eurocheque card enabled cardholders to write special personal checks (which they acquired from time to time in limited numbers from their respective banks) at locations honoring the card throughout much of the continent.

Another continental competitor for Visa was Eurocard International. Eurocard issued a T&E-type card that could be used internationally through an interchange agreement with MasterCard and other card systems in various countries.

Despite Visa's foreign competition, the company's growth outside the United States had been rapid in 1980:

Region	Growth in number of accounts, 1979–1980	Growth in sales volume, 1979–1980
Europe, the Mideast, and Africa	28%	64%
Latin America	29	93
Asia and the Pacific	31	105
Canada	10	4
United States	2	2

EXHIBIT 2

AN OVERVIEW OF THE PAYMENT CARD INDUSTRY IN 1981

In 1981 in the United States, there were four major types of payment cards: bank cards (Visa and MasterCard), travel and entertainment (T&E) cards (American Express, Carte Blanche, and Diners Club), retail store cards (for example, J.C. Penney, Sears, and Montgomery Ward), and oil and gas cards (for example, Exxon, Mobil, and Texaco).

Bank cards were issued by financial institutions, which were authorized by Visa and/or MasterCard to provide bank card services. While bank cards had initially been issued free of charge to cardholders, a majority of such cards carried an annual membership fee by 1981. Most bank cards were issued with a preapproved, revolving line of credit. Cardholders were given the option of paying their monthly bills in part or in full. Monthly interest rates were applied to all outstanding balances if the cardholder elected to pay his or her bill in installments.

Some financial institutions that issued Visa's and MasterCard's credit cards also issued a more recent product, known as the *debit card*. The debit cardholder could use his or her card in the same fashion as a credit card. The difference was that amounts charged to debit cards were directly deducted from the debit cardholder's bank account, and were not charged to a line of credit. Debit cards were thus similar to plastic, reusable checks. In some cases, credit card statements were automatically paid from deposit accounts, or debit card customers were given lines of credit in the form of overdraft, thus combining credit and debit card services.

Visa and MasterCard also produced travelers' checks that were issued by their members.

Travel and entertainment cards were issued by the three concerns listed above. Cardholders paid an annual fee for these cards. While there was no specific line of credit on T&E cards, monthly bills were payable in full upon receipt by the cardholder. Therefore, T&E cards provided no direct revolving line of credit, although by contract with banks, arrangements were made for automatic monthly payment programs for any balance the customer preferred to pay in that manner.

Structurally, the T&E and bank card industries were entirely different. The T&E firms were traditional, vertical, stockholder organizations. American Express provided a generally illustrative example. It was the sole owner of its accounts; it issued all credit to its cardholders; it owned its own computers; it set policies for its merchants; and it was the sole determiner of its corporate rate policy. As a result, Amex could provide standard quality of service, since it was singly responsible for the services it provided. On the other hand, bank card operations were conducted by the thousands of individual members of the Visa and MasterCard systems. Therefore, standard quality of service did not necessarily exist in all elements of the industry, since it depended on Visa's ability to enforce service standards on thousands of members possessing varying capabilities.

THE ISSUE OF DUALITY

Shortly after its formation, NBI altered its U.S. bylaws to prevent members of the BankAmericard system from offering MasterCharge cards as well. Hock had been committed to preserving the total separation of two systems. He had advocated this position for two primary reasons. First, he felt that confidentiality of competitive data could not be maintained if banks participated in both programs. Secondly, he saw the severe risk that competition between BankAmericard and MasterCharge would be diminished if duality (defined as the joint ownership/membership by banks of both bank card programs) were permitted to exist. Further, Hock felt that an eventual merger of the two systems could not be discounted if duality were accepted. This, he reasoned, would result in the bank card becoming, essentially, a monopoly, thereby opening the door to federal regulation of the industry. He was adamant that such an eventuality should be avoided at any cost.

MasterCard took the opposite position, making no objection to dual ownership of the competing systems and, in effect, encouraged it by condoning it.

In 1972, the Worthen Bank and Trust, located in Arkansas, sued NBI, claiming that the restriction against duality was a violation of the Sherman Antitrust Act, since it limited competition among banks by prohibiting them from embarking on aggressive, two-bank-card marketing campaigns. After nearly 5 years of legal proceedings, Visa asked the Department of Justice to indicate if it envisioned any possibility of a future attempt legally to restrain Visa from prohibiting duality.

After a lengthy investigation, the Department of Justice failed to give Visa satisfactory assurance that it would not intervene. Visa then elected to drop its restrictions on duality. It was estimated at the time that MasterCharge was offered by banks holding 50 percent of all banking assets, while Visa was offered by banks with only 25 percent of all banking assets. The remaining banks were uncommitted to either system.

Visa promptly capitalized on the new situation, and enjoyed explosive growth. Banks that had previously offered MasterCharge were welcomed as participants in Visa's program by Visa's bank sales division. Visa also wooed the uncommitted segment of the market. MasterCharge took the same approaches, but with less success. As a result, Visa signed on hundreds of new member institutions and gained millions of new cardholders. Despite Visa's success subsequent to duality, Hock remained highly skeptical of the long-term impact. He stated:

> Duality is a mistake. It should have been prevented. The effects will not fully be felt for a long time to come. It is far too early to measure the long-range impact on competition. . . . It won't be until 1981 when banks can sit back and ask, "What hath God wrought," or more properly, "What hath the Department of Justice wrought."[3]

Hock, the champion of competition and change, also feared that both systems might be ensnared by complacency, and would no longer be innovative:

> When banks were either MasterCharge *or* Visa issuers, every time one card association came up with an innovation, the members of the other would press their associations to come up with a competitive answer.

[3] *ABA Banking Journal,* July 1979.

Now, rather than press the other association for innovation, some banks just criticize whichever is the innovator. As joint owners, they can now solve competitive problems by inhibiting the innovator, rather than by spurring the laggard. I have seen a lot more of this in the past year than I have in the past and it disturbs me.[4]

VISA'S 1981 REORGANIZATION

In March 1981, Visa International underwent a major reorganization. The five worldwide regions were restructured. They had originally been established to provide an equitable means of electing members to the international board of directors and to enable the two nation-regions (Canada and the United States) to administer autonomous, national Visa corporations. The new plan enabled the remaining three regions to assume responsibility for administering the systems in their respective geographic areas and to employ staff under the direction of their own regional presidents.

Under this new plan, each of the five regions had its own board of directors, composed of senior executives who worked for member organizations in the respective regions. Each board, though different in its size and methods of electing members, embraced certain principles in common with all other boards—for example, that no single interest or area would ever be able to dominate Visa. The prime objective of the organization of Visa International was to create autonomous regional centers around the world that would be singularly capable of addressing the specific needs of their particular members. Consequently, it was planned that each region would develop its own sales, marketing, advertising, and computer systems capabilities.

Before the reorganization, no management personnel had been directly employed by Visa International. Rather, all management services had been purchased from Visa, USA. All officers of the two organizations were common, even though they reported to separate boards whose interests were not necessarily common. Conflicts of interest were governed by unique terms that were included in the management contract.

Subsequent to the reorganization, however, Visa International took direct responsibility for providing various staff services to the worldwide regions, including international legal affairs, public relations, systems development and support (computerized authorization and interchange networks; see appendixes for descriptions), and new-product development. Visa USA continued to provide advertising, accounting, payroll, research, and statistical services. Visa USA and Visa International, under a revised management contract, sold and bought services to and from one another. The entire structure continued to operate under a common staff and chief executive officer who sat on all boards, with the exception of Canada's. (Members within Canada provided their own management services.)

Under the concept of the reorganization, the regions would gradually develop the functional capabilities that were currently provided by Visa USA and the central staff of Visa International, as their respective sales volumes increased. Such increases

[4] Ibid.

would make the employment of in-house specialists economically feasible for the regions. Subsequent to the reorganization, Visa operated under the direction of small, highly decentralized management groups that were constrained by few central rules or procedures.

While most executives seemed to be generally positive about the March 1981 reorganization, some cited the potential dangers it had created. A representative sample of executive reactions to the new structure at Visa follows.

Thomas Honey, general manager of the Asia and Pacific region, remarked:

> A lot of needless duplication could take place in each region. There is a danger of regional presidents running in separate directions. If they promote Visa differently, it may be to the detriment of the worldwide image. The question is, will there come a time when someone will have to pull it all together again?

B. Ray Traweek, general manager of systems development, remarked:

> I think it has had an extremely positive effect outside of the U.S. The members in the international regions really feel that they have responsibility and authority that they never had before.

James Partridge, general manager of the Latin American region, said:

> It's a bold scheme. But if each region goes its own way, there is a risk that fragmentation could occur.

Joao Ribeiro da Fonseca, general manager of the European region, remarked:

> There's always a risk when you decentralize. The problem becomes: How do you operate under a single concept and philosophy if you have autonomous, decentralized regions?

Philip Hayman, senior vice president of sales and marketing for Visa, USA, said:

> By taking this step [reorganizing], we now have a structure that accommodates regional needs.

James Grant, general manager of product development, remarked:

> It's very positive. The regions are coming up with their own ideas, and they're committed to making them work.

VISA INTERNATIONAL'S ROLE

Visa International was an enabling organization established to serve the financial institutions that were its members and that offered its products and services. The management functions performed by Visa International for its members included international marketing; advertising and public relations services; market research; development of new products and services; operation of the vast telecommunications network for the electronic transmissions of authorizations and sales drafts among members; development of up-to-date processing and communication systems; organization of programs for cost and profit analysis and control; security and fraud control; member training and support; compilation of operating statistics; registration, protection, and control of all service marks; and other legal and legislative assistance. Additionally, Visa International established all operating rules and regulations relating to the interchange of drafts between members so that the worldwide service operated in harmony under a consistent and uniform set of mandates.

The process of defining, gaining mutual agreement among the organizing committee members, and instituting the appropriate structure for Visa International was a difficult one. Hock captured the drama surrounding the founding of Visa International in a 1977 speech:

> In 1974, the Visa International organizing committee, composed of members throughout the world, was experiencing a particularly difficult time. Differences seemed irreconcilable. Before abandoning the effort, a final meeting was held. A gift for those who had labored so hard on an apparently futile task seemed appropriate. A unique set of cuff links was designed. On one was a relief map of one-half of the world. Around it in Latin was inscribed the phrase, "Studium ad prosperandum" or "The Will to Succeed." On the other, in relief, was the other half of the world surrounded by the phrase, "Voluntas in Conveniendum" or "The Grace to Compromise." They were cast in gold and the die stored in a vault, to be broken if the effort was abandoned, or kept for the production of future sets for directors, should it succeed.
>
> At a welcoming dinner, they were presented to each member of the organizing committee with the request that they be worn throughout the meeting—on their right arm, "The Will to Succeed," and on their left, "The Grace to Compromise"—as a reminder that if the world of bank cards was to be united, it could only be through their efforts.
>
> Those cuff links are now treasured possessions. "The Will to Succeed and the Grace to Compromise" became the Visa International motto.

Hock expressed the philosophy upon which Visa International was built in this way later in 1977:

> The corporation is based upon the irrevocable principle that board and membership voting rights must be so structured as to foreclose any possibility of control, dominance, or undue influence by any institution, bank, country, or region. It is a nonstock, for-profit, membership corporation, owned and controlled by its card-issuing members worldwide. No single entity or country controls Visa International, yet no one is without representation. It has proved to be an extremely effective structure for the development of Visa as a worldwide device for the exchange of value.

On another occasion, he further elaborated upon Visa's fundamental philosophy:

> There was no pattern to which we could form the organization, since these unique needs had never before existed. We had to begin by inventing the concept, then the organization to fit it, and finally, the management that could run it. The fundamental structural idea was to make it so malleable it could be remade again and again to fit needs and people as they evolved; a structure to manage change must, itself, be infinitely changeable.

In a 1980 speech on Visa International, Hock said:

> [It is] the first truly transnational management corporation not controlled or owned by the interest of any country.

Visa International was operated under the guidance of a 21-member board of directors. These directors were elected to the international board annually by the directors of the five geographical regions that made up the international corporation.

Each region was entitled to send a minimum of two and a maximum of eight representatives to the international board, based upon the respective ratio they produced of sales volume to the worldwide total. Representation was thus automatically readjustable. As of September 1981, the regions were represented by the following numbers of directors on the international board:

Canada:	3
United States:	8
Europe/Mideast/Africa:	4
Asia/Pacific:	2
Latin America:	2

Dee Hock, as chief executive officer, sat on the board, as did a representative appointed by the Bank of America under a limited right that bank obtained as part of the consideration when its original ownership of the BankAmericard service marks was purchased by Visa International.

While the Visa International board of directors established the broad policies for the corporation, each region was designed to be an autonomous unit dedicated to fully serving its own membership. As Dee Hock said, "We do not want to do anything at the international level that the regions are capable of doing for themselves, anything at the regional level that nations are capable of doing nor anything at the national level that financial institutions are capable of doing."

MEMBER RELATIONS

The USA Turmoil Over J. C. Penney

In April 1979, at the Visa USA board of directors meeting, Dee Hock and Chuck Russell, president, informed the group that J.C. Penney, the giant retailer, had agreed to accept Visa cards in its stores. Penney was the first of the "Big Three" retailers (Penney, Sears, and Ward) to agree to accept bank cards in payment for its goods.

Under the special arrangement, Penney, which had the most advanced electronic point-of-sale network of any retailer, would link its computers directly with Visa's authorization and interchange computer network. Consequently, Penney would bypass the merchant banking step of the Visa transaction processing procedure, since it was fully capable of performing all necessary functions itself. (Under normal circumstances, a merchant would establish a contract with a Visa member to obtain authorization services and to process sales drafts that had been generated by the sales the merchant had made on Visa cards. The merchant banking step generated revenues for the Visa member providing the service to the merchant. Since J.C. Penney did not need and refused to utilize this service, no merchant banking revenues would be generated for Visa's members.) (For an understanding of the normal procedure, see Appendixes 1 and 2.)

Hock informed the board that Penney would agree to accept Visa cards only if it was permitted to link its computers directly with Visa's. Appreciating the implications of this arrangement, the board debated the issue for five hours. Finally, the plan was accepted as presented.

A storm of protest from many of Visa's members followed the public announcement of the plan. The complaining members enunciated fears that Visa would aggressively sign merchants, and thus compete with its own members. To some it appeared that Visa, rather than remaining a service organization designed to facilitate the needs of its members, was taking on a life of its own. A senior executive at Citicorp thundered that Visa was becoming a "Frankenstein monster."

Hock maintained that the Penney deal was in the best interests of Visa's members, since it opened the colossal retail chain market to bank cards. This was thought to be a critical hurdle that bank cards would have to cross if they were to become universal instruments for the exchange of value. He maintained that the Penney arrangement was unique, that Visa had no intention of changing its policies, and that member fears were groundless.

Visa, USA never again drew up a direct contract with a merchant establishment. In fact, in 1980, after most national retail chain merchants had made their bank card arrangements with various bank members, the U.S. board, at the request of Hock and Russell, eliminated Visa's authorization to deal with merchants directly.

Penney reported that 1979 sales charged to Visa accounts amounted to $100 million, or 1 percent of Penney's total sales of $11.7 billion. Volume on Penney's in-house credit card was $4.6 billion.

A Fragile Peace

> The strength of the criticism lies only in the weakness of the thing criticized.[5]

Despite Visa International's and Visa, USA's legal structures, which placed ownership and control of the corporation in the hands of directors who were elected by members, Visa's administrators had a partially contentious relationship with their members. Many members expressed concern that Visa was becoming too powerful, or that it was not adequately safeguarding their interests. Reconciling the interests of the system as a whole with those of its members who might be in opposition to any single action was an endless task. Hock described it this way:

> Since we do what we ought to do rather than what any single member wants us to do, it *rains* criticism here; this is the tropics of criticism—the monsoons are going all the time.

Subsequent to Visa's announcement of the special deal with Penney, and after the proposal outlining Visa's plan to offer a traveler's check had been publicized, Visa came under sharp attack. Visa's two largest members, Citicorp and Bank of America were, naturally, far from enthusiastic over Visa's development of a system that per-

---

[5] Dee Hock, quoting Longfellow.

mitted hundreds of Visa members to compete with the long-standing travelers' check programs of the two banks. But other, more minor operating decisions could also result in criticism being leveled at Visa. Jim Partridge made this observation:

> No matter how good relations are with our members, we are always viewed with some suspicion. It is just that we cannot harmonize all of the interests of all of the members all of the time. There is this uneasy feeling among the members that if they are not controlling us, then we will eventually control them.

Visa also faced problems in attempting to create organizational structures, business philosophies, and operating practices that would be consonant with the many disparate cultures and countries it served. Joao Ribeiro da Fonseca captured the dilemma from the European perspective when he said:

> Europe is an old lady. She can't be rushed around. She has her own pace. In the United States, everything moves at high speed. Every change is dramatic in the U.S. because of the competition and fragmentation. Europe is more conservative and tradition-oriented. People think three times before making decisions.

Whether Visa's policies and practices should be paced by the wishes of the most conservative and least innovative members or by the most aggressive and forward-looking ones was another subject that spawned contention.

Lyman Seely, chairman of Visa International, thought that the issue of the pace with which change occurred concerned U.S. members as well:

> Dee [Hock] is very impatient. He wants people to move faster. He sees very clearly how this system ought to be built. He *visualizes* the potential, and wants us to get there sooner. But many of the members think that we have moved very fast as it is.

Hock's vision actually made some members anxious that they might be outdistanced by Visa in time. Keith W. Hughes, an officer of Wells Fargo bank, once said:

> If they leapfrog into the payments system of the future, Visa could leave some of us out on an island somewhere.

VISA, USA: THE LEGAL AND ADMINISTRATIVE ENTITIES

> I submit that organizations such as NBI and Interbank could be compared to reverse holding companies in that they are owned and must be controlled by their members. They provide an equitable means of electing or removing directors who have full power to direct or remove management. The organizations are specialists in a single industry, free of the conflicts of multiple interest that are an integral part of present banking and regulatory agencies. They are uniquely structured for the job to be done, and if they are not responsive to your wishes, you must make them so.
>
> Many years ago, Burke, commenting on the nature of government, said much which is pertinent to this situation:
>
> In effect, to follow, not to force, the public inclination, to give a direction, a form, a technical dress and a specific sanction, to the general sense of the community, is the true end of legislation.

The best solution is that which is most responsive. Organizations such as NBI may give a "technical dress" or "form" but it is the general sense of the community, of you (the members), which must govern.[6]

Visa, USA (formerly NBI) was an independent corporation that administered the Visa program for the members of the system that were located in the United States. As an independent corporation, Visa, USA was regulated by its own set of bylaws, and was served by its own board of directors. (See Exhibit 3 for the organization chart of Visa, USA.)

Visa, USA's directors determined the corporation's policies and settled issues that arose in the course of its operations. However, any issue that would result in or require the amendment of the corporation's charter had to be placed before the entire membership for a vote of approval or disapproval.

[6] Dee Hock, speech of Sept. 25, 1973.

EXHIBIT 3   Visa International—Visa U.S.A. organization chart.

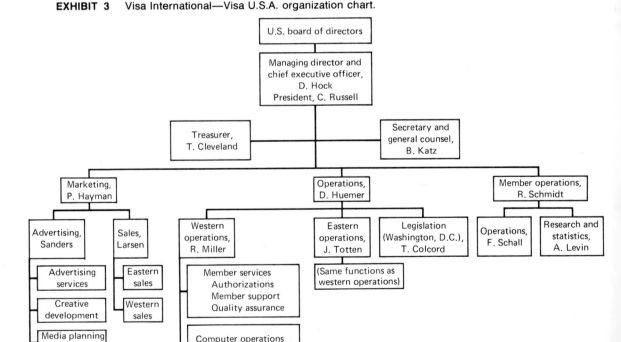

Eight of Visa, USA's 22 board members were elected by their board to serve on the Visa International board of directors and represent the interests of the members located in the United States.

To ensure that all areas of the United States would enjoy representation on Visa, USA's board, the country had been divided into 12 geographical regions. Each year, each region elected one director to serve on the Visa, USA board. Five at-large directors (with not more than one from any region) were also elected to the board by the entire membership. A sixth at-large director was elected by the smaller members only. If, for any reason, members were dissatisfied with the direction Visa was taking, a special board meeting could be called at the request of only five members, provided that they held at least 20 percent of the total votes outstanding. Such stipulations were designed to ensure that the members retained substantial power over the policies adopted by the corporation.

VISA'S CHIEF EXECUTIVE OFFICER

The opinions upon which we act in everyday affairs and those which govern the decisions of responsible business managers for the most part have little similarity with conclusions reached by exhaustive analysis and accurate measurement. The mental processes are entirely different in the two cases. In everyday life they are mostly subconscious. We know as little why we expect certain things to happen as we do the mechanism by which we recall a forgotten name. There is doubtless some analogy between the subconscious processes of "intuition" and the structure of logical deliberation, for the function of both is to anticipate the future and the possibility of prediction seems to rest upon the uniformity of nature. Hence there must be, in the one case as in the other, some sort and amount of analysis and synthesis; but the striking feature of the judging faculty is its liability to error.[7]

For prosperity doth best discover vice, and adversity doth best discover virtue.[8]

Dee Ward Hock, the 52-year-old chief executive officer of Visa International, had been raised in a small Utah town and had attended school through junior college. He had begun working part time at the age of 12, and had served in many jobs as a farm hand and factory laborer during his teens. After junior college, Hock married and then took a job as a hod carrier. In 1951, he took his first office position as a lending agent with a consumer finance company. In 1965, after 15 years with finance companies, he joined the National Bank of Commerce of Seattle (now Rainier Bank) as a consumer finance officer.

In 1966, the National Bank of Commerce became one of the first licensees of Bank of America's fledgling BankAmericard program. Hock became assistant to the head of the National Bank of Commerce's card operation. In 1968, when Bank of America was experiencing considerable difficulty in maintaining harmony among its licensees, and when the industry itself was encountering many operating difficulties, Hock

---

[7] Frank H. Knight, *Risk, Uncertainty and Profit,* 1921.
[8] Dee Hock, quoting Bacon

(then manager of Rainier's card program) suggested that a committee of licensees be formed to iron out the problems within the system. The committee was formed, and Hock was promptly elected chairman. Under Hock's leadership, the members of that committee defined a new organizational structure for the system. This led to National BankAmericard's acquisition of the U.S. card operation from Bank of America in 1970, and to the acquisition of the international program from Bank of America in 1974.

Hock and his staff ruled Visa with an iron hand in its early days. During the first year, Hock read all correspondence flowing from Visa's offices. Most executives agreed in 1981 that Hock had become more comfortable over the past few years with delegating work to his key executives. Nonetheless, he continued to probe the thoughts of his key managers with a meticulous precision that bordered on inquisition.

Hock was adamant that Visa would not become a bureaucracy. One way he helped to ensure that bureaucracy could not exist at Visa was to scorn openly the extensive use of memoranda and formal reports. Instead, he encouraged his managers to be open and to talk with one another. One recently hired executive had prepared an extensive report outlining what he intended to do with his department. He submitted this report to Hock for review. Some time later, having received no response, he asked Hock for his views on the proposal. Hock replied that he thought he had thrown the report into the wastebasket, unread. "Why should I write reports if you're not going to read them?" the employee queried. "Well," said Hock, "that's a pretty good question. What did the report say?" Fifteen minutes later, having summarized his thoughts and having received assurance that they seemed sensible, the executive was busy working to implement his ideas. Later, Hock said, "Ninety percent of all reports just reiterate the obvious. They're a waste of time. A few well-thought-out words between two people are far more productive."

An avid reader, Hock often quoted from literature. His glass-walled office on the 46th floor of the Transamerica Building, with its majestic view of San Francisco Bay, included a library stocked with the books of Yeats, Aurelius, Voltaire, Bacon, Emerson, Khayyam, Lao-tse, and others.

In the course of several interviews, Hock expressed these thoughts:

On Education

It's the classic poets, essayists, and philosophers who ought to be taught in business schools. You can learn far more about business from Bacon's and Emerson's essays, the *Meditations* of Aurelius, Gratian's maxims, and a few of Yeat's poems than you can from all the ponderous tomes ever written by professors of business administration.

Our business schools essentially teach mismanagement. They attempt to teach students that management is a science, and that's a lie. It's an art.

I would urge business school students, "Whatever you do, find time to read classic philosophy, poetry and biography. It's a good antidote to some of the junk you're being fed."

Management doesn't exist. Neither do corporations. Both are fictions. There exist instead only relationships between human beings, and the concept that brings them together.

People who graduate from management schools shouldn't assume that they know anything about management. How can you be taught something, if that something doesn't exist?

On Managing

It's feeling that moves the world. All decisions are emotional decisions. I want to know how a businessman *feels* about a situation, and why. If I know what he *thinks* about a subject, I'm not going to get anywhere, because reason and logic are not what move the world. I tell people here, "Don't send me a report; come see me or pick up the phone and tell me how you *feel* about it!"

A good manager doesn't have a single "management style!" He brings to the environment what is needed at the time, whether it's control or delegation, motivation or demand.

Most great leaders I know don't follow strict rules, but they hardly dare say so. Their stockholders and peers would be troubled if they thought these leaders were not practicing scientific management techniques, whatever they are.

Management is an art, a mystique. You can talk about it, but you can't define it. It's judgment, judgment, judgment, judgment. Judgment is developed by making sound decisions. Decisions that are based upon *all* of the *facts* are not decisions at all—they are bookkeeping entries. Making some decisions relating to matters about which little is known is the only way to develop good judgment.

The reason why things do not get done is that people get involved in what I call the "doing of the doing." You must differentiate between activity and productivity. The key to efficiency is reducing activity to the minimum and increasing productivity to the maximum. Everything but pure thought and pure action are, to some degree, infected with the doing of the doing. Reports, meetings, procedures, and all of that blather are largely the doing of the doing. Get heavily involved and you get little done. We try to avoid the "doing of the doing" at Visa, and therefore, we get a great deal done.

A manager is nearly always forced to choose between gaining the respect or affection of those he manages. If he gains affection, and not respect, he cannot manage. If he gains respect, and not affection, he can manage well, and affection frequently follows. It is ideal, but rare, to have both in the beginning.

One must never hire in one's own image. I need no one to tell me what I think and feel, or to duplicate my strengths. Rather, I am anxious to have about me people who are independent thinkers, and who have strengths which offset my weaknesses.

The best managers hire a variety of individuals, each of whom has different talents and dispositions. They then provide these individuals with an environment that encourages them to flourish in their own ways, and to achieve more than they had originally thought possible.

When you're managing properly, you reach a point where you're doing things not because they're essential, but because they're important. Most things are essential; very few are important.

Most people think that management consists of directing those over whom you have been given responsibility. That is an error. A manager has, in decreasing order of importance, four responsibilities: to manage himself; to manage his superiors; to manage his peers; and, finally, to manage his subordinates. The first responsibility is by far the most important and difficult. The second is nearly as difficult. The third is far from easy. The last is of least importance and is relatively simple if the previous three have been properly handled. Most so-called managers devote time and effort in the wrong order. They are not managers; they are administrators.

That salary which is the most exorbitant is the one not paid. If an inadequate salary results in the dissatisfaction or loss of a top employee, then the cost is enormous. The problem is that many companies look at salaries as expenses. They're not, they're investments.

On Life at Visa

Solemnity is a mystery of the body invented to conceal the defects of the mind.[8]

I persuade, prod, coerce, inspire. I do whatever I have to do to move and excite people here. Few people are indifferent at Visa. Most people either love it or dislike it here. But even if they love it, they dislike it a good portion of the time.

Many of our meetings have no agenda. If those who are numb from excess organization ever sat in on one of them, they might think it was insanity. All sorts of opinions, criticism, irreverence, and irrelevance is aired, by those in the lowest and highest positions, in an atmosphere that is often characterized by kidding and raucous laughter. It's unstructured, but fine decisions emerge swiftly even though some may be ahead of their time.

It's not complicated here—it's *simplified!* We just try to get rid of some of the theoretical crap you guys in business schools have been piling up for *years.* It's like shoveling manure out of the barn. You have to keep at it or the barn fills up and you can't get the cows in.

Visa is highly structured conceptually, philosophically, and ethically. What we do and why we do it is carefully planned. How we do it is not. We give it just enough procedural structure to make it respectable to those who are enamored of forms, job descriptions, reports, consultants' presentations, statistics, and other such impediments.

Random Reflections

There is a simple equation that should govern all relations between people. It is always in my mind. When approaching someone to whom *you* might feel inferior, it is: "I am as big to me as you are to you. Therefore, we are equals." When approached by someone who might feel inferior to you, it is: "You are as big to you as I am to me. Therefore, we are equals."

Business is not my only interest. Much of it is as dull as ditchwater. It can be stifling. It can turn you into a pompous, arrogant ass.

Any person who professes to know exactly why he does the things he does can safely be presumed to be engaged in self-delusion or prevarication.

Is this a precarious job? Does the sun come up every morning? Is is a secure environment for me personally? In one sense not at all, and in another, absolutely secure. Because at the fundamental and most important level, the job is not essential to me. There are many things which I would not do to keep it and many things which are more important.

Reflections on Dee

Is it so bad then to be misunderstood? Pythagoras was misunderstood, and Socrates, and Jesus, and Luther, and Copernicus, and Galileo, and Newton, and every pure and wise spirit that ever took flesh. To be great is to be misunderstood.[9]

[8] Dee Hock, quoting La Rochefoucauld
[9] Ralph Waldo Emerson, 1841.

The universe is change. Life is opinion.[10]

Dee Hock remarked:

Most people here care little what I think about them. But I am aware that some people are frightened of me. Their real problem is not me, but their own inability to conquer fear. I believe it was Emerson who said something to the effect that, "If we quake, it matters not at what."

Fifteen top executives at Visa reflected on Hock.

Most people at Visa are seeking Dee's attention and approval.

He's very intimidating to most people. He scares some shitless. There are some very bright people here who turn to putty when they see him—whose minds go foggy.

People are afraid of him, but no more so than they are afraid of anyone in power.

Is he fair? Absolutely. Can he be brutal? Definitely.

It's amazing that he's survived these 14 years, pushing it to the brink at all times.

He can be as unreasonable as all hell, but he's probably the finest person you'd ever want to know.

Dee manages by fear, uncertainty, and change, with fear the least important, uncertainty the most important, and change in between.

The membership is almost in awe of his ability.

I guess you'd call his the Socratic method of management. Dee will grill you when you present an idea to him, and you had best have the answers.

He's almost clairvoyant. He has an uncanny feel for what people are thinking. It's a sixth sense. I guess it would really be called "street smarts."

He's a very brilliant man. He's able to part the clouds and see the sky.

Dee is a goddamned genius, regardless of his personality.

He has an uncanny grasp of situations. He's almost always right. He's one hell of a decent human being. He gives the impression of being gruff and ruthless, but he's more of a pussycat.

He's brilliant, he's a visionary, he's a genius, but he's one of the worst administrators that we've got at Visa.

He's very demanding. He's a great thinker and a great player. He has a very difficult job. Dee is a unique man. I get along with the way his intellect plays chess.

I don't think anybody understands or totally knows Dee Hock.

[10] Marcus Aurelius.

CHANGE

> God gives us grace to accept with serenity the things that cannot be changed, courage to change the things which should be changed, and the wisdom to distinguish the one from the other.[11]

> There is nothing more difficult to take in hand, more perilous to conduct or more uncertain in its success than to take the lead in the introduction of a new order of things.[12]

> Our ability to organize and manage has created rigid structures, full of specialists resistant to change, capable of spewing out instruments of change—computers, lasers, satellites, synthetic compounds, chemical fertilizers, drugs, genetic manipulators—at a rate which has substituted a single constant which destroys all others, and that constant is change itself. What a superb dilemma: a nation of managers psychologically and structurally engineered for the management of constants whose only constant may be change itself; and as a continuing process rather than an occasional event.[13]

Visa was an organization characterized by continual job rotations, ad hoc project teams, and structural amorphousness. Managers and employees were encouraged to make decisions and to take full responsibility for their outcomes.

Project teams were regularly established to tackle new-product and new-systems developments and were also used frequently to handle normal management tasks. The travelers' check, debit card, BASE systems, check-guarantee card, and marketing programs were all developed by project teams that shepherded ideas from birth to implementation. (See Appendix 1 for an explanation of the BASE computer systems.)

In 1981, project teams worked on a variety of efforts, including the creation of a Visa money market fund, the development of a Premium card, the establishment of a worldwide network of ATMs (automated teller machines) that could be accessed by any Visa card, and the development of a system of point-of-sale terminals that would provide rapid authorizations to merchants on all purchases by using standardized magnetic-strip technology developed by Visa.

Project teams generally accomplished their tasks in a short period of time, usually fewer than 9 months. One executive said this:

> I have been on scores of project teams. It seems that as soon as you have finished with one project, you are plunged into another.

Dee Hock echoed that executive:

> There is so much change in Visa that most employees have to flail about frantically to keep their balance. They become tightrope walkers so good at anticipating change that they adjust to it before it occurs.

---

[11] Reinhold Niebuhr, 1943.
[12] Niccolo Machiavelli, *The Prince*, 1532.
[13] Dee Hock in a speech to the ABA Annual Convention, Sept. 23, 1975.

Others, too, confirmed the view that the environment was one in which change was constant. David Huemer, senior vice president of the operations division for Visa, USA, remarked:

> The one thing that is predictable is that things are going to change, so you have to keep loose, keep flexible, and not develop strong likes and prejudices, because the firm will not allow them to survive.

Fran Schall, vice president of operations support for Visa, USA, said:

> Things are never stable here. That's stimulating. You rarely have a moment to catch your breath before something else is taking off. You have to be able to juggle lots of balls at the same time. You have to be able to suddenly change your focus.

Thomas Honey remarked:

> Things are never static. You immediately begin to anticipate.

James Partridge said:

> One thing that characterizes the organization is the speed with which we can change direction.

Ron Schmidt, vice president of member operations for Visa, USA, remarked:

> The constant shifting is a matter of fact. It's not unusual. You either live with it or you leave the company.

Some executives at Visa were not sanguine about the constantly shifting and changing environment. Four individuals commented as follows:

> I think that there is a classic conflict coming up between the concept of the management of change and the concept of the management of a larger, more stable organization. I'm not saying that it will necessarily occur in the near future, but it's down the road—in perhaps 10 years or so.

> We do everything very quickly, and there's frequently not enough time to do these things the way you would really want to do them.

> In terms of getting work done, this is a well-managed company. But if you ask the staff if it is a well-managed company, they would almost universally say, "No," because Visa moves so fast that there is not the sense of order that you would find in a more stable company. There's a continuing sense of instability here.

> There is a reorganization at least once per year. That's a standing joke in the company: "This is reorganization number 812."

Most executives agreed that Hock consciously manipulated the environment to create constant change. One key employee, B. Ray Traweek, explained why he thought Hock created such an atmosphere at Visa:

> I call it the "shake the box theory of management." Dee works on some kind of sociological theory that you get more productivity if you randomly "shake the box" and move people

around. So now and then, he'll shake the hell out of things here. He'll move people around, and make them rethink what they're trying to accomplish. He wants to be sure that Visa never becomes a bureaucratic organization, so he shakes the box like crazy.

Another senior executive summed it up this way:

He loves change to keep you off balance. Just when you're comfortable, he shakes things up and you go flying. You can never get comfortable.

Hock said that he would have things no other way. To him, the future and change would be incxtricably intertwined; they would be synonymous. Consequently, he considered it vitally important that his managers were comfortable existing in an environment characterized by change. To him, those who could not adjust to change would not be able to manage it. To be so unable could prove disastrous. According to Hock,

The question that obsesses me much of the time is how to develop managers who are expert at the management of change. That is what I am trying to do at Visa. For I am convinced that a decent future for citizens of the world depends on the proper management of change.

PERFORMANCE APPRAISAL: OBJECTIVIZING FEELING

Two bonus systems were in place at Visa: one for senior management and one for other employees. The senior managers included in the special incentive plan were evaluated by their direct superiors and rated four times per year on a wholly subjective system. Performance was evaluated, and placed on a scale that ranged from satisfactory (0 percent bonus) to outstanding (45 percent bonus). Each review was thoroughly discussed with the individual, and then with management. Subsequent to these discussions, management brought the performance appraisals before the executive committee of the board for full review.

After the four quarterly reviews had been completed, an overall performance grade for the year was decided, and the appropriate bonus was determined. An outstanding annual rating would result in a bonus of 45 percent of the employee's annual salary.

An interesting aspect of the plan was that the quarterly reviews bore no necessary relationship to the final, annual performance grade. As an example, an employee who had received lesser ratings for three quarters and an excellent rating in the fourth quarter could still receive an excellent rating for the year, and hence a 30 percent bonus. Then again, the employee might receive no bonus whatsoever if he or she received a satisfactory rating for the year.

Hock described how employees were evaluated under the plan:

The single, simple criterion used to rate people in the incentive program is subjective judgment. When the system was first presented to the directors, most had reservations about grading performance on the basis of subjective judgment. Now they wouldn't do without it. It has been very successful.

Although a few slightly negative comments about the incentive system were voiced, most were highly positive. One senior executive echoed the majority of his colleagues when he said, "The bonus system is excellent."

Under the merit system for all other employees, a manager could request at any time a special cash bonus, ranging from several hundred to several thousand dollars, for any employee considered deserving. It was not uncommon for such requests to be made since, according to Bob Miller, vice president for Western operations, "We are a small organization, so our people are recognized when they do something noteworthy."

B. Ray Traweek noted the special satisfaction that he felt when he was able to award a bonus to an employee:

> It's a very rewarding part of my job. The first cash bonus I gave was as much, if not more, of a thrill for me than it was for the person receiving the bonus.

GAINING COSMIC AND ATOMIC PERSPECTIVES ON VISA

> Ah, but a man's reach should exceed his grasp,
> Or what's a heaven for?[14]

> They say that heaven is,
> Ten zillion light years away.[15]

Executives at Visa frequently described their company in words charged with notions of the future. Their expressions were often replete with allusions to the concepts of space and time. One term that was used with particular frequency was *light years.* The comments quoted below capture the essence of this theme.

In explaining Visa's progress and its current position relative to rival MasterCard, Chuck Russell said:

> Seven years ago, MasterCard was light years ahead of us. Today, I think that most people would agree that we are light years ahead of them.

Fran Schall described Hock's vision:

> He's frequently light years ahead of the industry.

Jim Grant concurred:

> It's incredible what he's done to the industry. He's been light years ahead in sensing direction.

Despite that, Hock felt that there was still a considerable distance to travel in order to reach the ultimate. When asked by *Dun's Review* in June 1978 to comment on the imminence of global, full-scale electronic value exchange, Hock replied that it was still "light years away."

[14] Robert Browning, 1855.
[15] Stevie Wonder, performing artist, 1974.

Hock saw nothing defeating in the recognition that he worked, as a mortal man with finite capabilities, toward an ideal that was light years away. Because to Hock, it was important that one keep Visa, and all human endeavor for that matter, in perspective. One had to understand the parochial relevance but universal insignificance of all things. Ironically, it was this paradox that was Hock's anchor to a focused purpose.

Hock expressed his views on the paradox of Visa in two ways. At one point, he said:

> I try to get people here to see that what we do is at the same time both ludicrous and extremely serious. It is serious because it affects thousands of people's lives, but it is ludicrous because without Visa, the world would readjust in 90 days.

Somewhat dissatisfied with that explanation, he rephrased the thought in terms with which he seemed more comfortable:

> If I take the atomic view, and look from the atom out, Visa is a vast universe. But if I take the cosmic view, looking from the universe in, Visa, all of mankind, and everything that man ever built, is an unnoticeable rash on the skin of the earth. Visa isn't a cosmic joke; it's a cosmic unnoticeable.

Hock was similarly cosmic when he expressed his views on time:

> I have little conception of time. I hardly ever know when something occurred, or what time it is, or even what day of the week it is. I'm not interested in facts and details. I'm interested in concepts and ideas.

Asked if he thought that Visa's philosophy and mission could be communicated to others through the medium of a case study, Hock replied, with a certain gleeful pessimism, "I don't think you'll come within light years of portraying what we're doing here."

MANAGING AT VISA

> A foolish consistency is the hobgoblin of little minds.[16]

Although Hock's approach to management was distinctive and highly regarded by many managers at Visa, he made no attempt to impose a single management standard upon Visa's top-level employees. In fact, he constantly encouraged his key associates to manage "not as I manage, but in whatever way works best for you." Thus, executives at Visa had developed a variety of management styles. For example, Chuck Russell took a highly personal approach to managing. Most managers perceived a major difference between Hock's and Russell's management styles. One manager commented:

> Chuck is an easygoing guy—a regular person. He's a totally different person from Dee. He isn't as driving.

[16] Ralph Waldo Emerson, 1841.

Another noted:

> Chuck Russell is one of the nicest men in the company. He's one of those guys who will just pop into your office with a cup of coffee in his hand, take a seat, and say, "How are you today." But he's not just a nice guy who occupies space—he's brilliant about this business.

Another executive expressed it this way:

> Chuck is a real delegator, and is comfortable with it. He's very pragmatic and very astute. He has good gut reactions about things.

A Visa director placed a difference between Hock and Russell in bas relief:

> When we call you [Hock], we get vision. When we call Chuck, we get answers.

Russell put it this way:

> I'm convinced that opposites attract. We [Hock and Russell] are the antithesis, which is probably why we get along. If there were two people like Dee in one organization, they couldn't peacefully coexist for 5 minutes, unless they were separated by a couple of layers of hierarchy.

David Huemer, who was in charge of 291 of Visa, USA's 387 employees, was described as being a manager who delegated responsibilities. It was mentioned that Huemer's lieutenants frequently would not know what projects the other lieutenants were working on. In the operations division, Huemer was the continual reference point. He enunciated part of his management philosophy in this way:

> I see myself as being a people manager. I don't know if it's a generally approved management technique, but I generally restructure jobs around the talents and capabilities of the individuals who are working for me. I'll restructure jobs and retrofit the organization to the people.

He continued:

> I believe in providing opportunities to people that allow them to develop their ideas, and gain the satisfaction of following a project through to completion. I feel that people deserve to gain the satisfaction that comes from succeeding at something.

Yet Huemer admitted that he was a tough boss:

> There's no question that the people under me are accountable for what they do. I want people around me who have done their homework. I don't come out of the blue, but I *do* find out if they've thought things through. I guess that makes them worry a bit.

B. Ray Traweek, head of the division that oversaw the design and development of Visa's computerized information and authorization networks, preferred a more gregarious approach to managing. He and his assistants would often meet together in his office day after day to thrash out the particulars of a plan.

> I try to get groups of people to look at problems, and then solve those problems. When we get together, we critique each other as we move toward a solution. We tend to have a quasicommittee form of management in this division.

Traweek contrasted his style with Hock's:

> I have a completely different style from Dee's. Dee feels that you have to remain somewhat aloof if you're going to have to shake up management from time to time. I tend to have more personal relationships with the people I work with.

Bob Miller, who worked under Huemer as manager of the Western operations center in San Mateo, Calif., encouraged the roughly 150 people reporting to him to make decisions and then to make them work:

> People come to see me and ask, "What am I going to do about so and so?" and I say, "Well, what are you going to do about so and so?"

Miller's comment reflected a change that was occurring at Visa—a change that nearly every manager had remarked on. As one manager put it:

> Things have changed here, in many ways. Five years ago, I would say that all decisions were made by Dee Hock. Today, he's definitely delegating more projects to a few people in order to make things happen.

It was interesting that Visa's managers, who almost universally reported that they had lacked autonomy in their careers at Visa until only recently, were generally seen to extend autonomy to their subordinates at their earliest opportunity.

BATTLING WITH AMERICAN EXPRESS

> The order is rapidly fadin'
> And the first one now will later be last
> For the times they are a-changin'.[17]

In April 1981, the solid world of banking was shaken when American Express announced that it would merge with Shearson Loeb Rhoades, the nation's second-largest brokerage firm. Until that time, American Express and the banks had peacefully occupied separate segments of the financial services market. However, since Shearson could offer its customers a money market fund investment (which banks, by law, could not), it was thought by many bankers that American Express would soon be able to compete for bank's deposits. In what appeared to be an overnight shift in strategy, American Express had become a direct competitor.

Hock had been warning bankers about the potential threat from companies such as American Express for some time. After Amex's announcement of its merger with Shearson, he went on the full offensive to rouse Visa's member bankers from any sense of complacency.

> If banks continue to be agents for American Express cards and travelers' checks, they richly deserve the loss of their business (deposits).[18]

---

[17] Bob Dylan, "The Times They Are A-Changin'," 1963.
[18] *Business Week,* May 18, 1981.

Later, he drew this analogy:

> Banking is like a walled city, which American Express has entered over the last few years with a Trojan horse. Now its sides are down and the soldiers are pouring out. It looks like war to a lot of us.[19]

Visa made two swift and strong competitive responses. First, they announced that they would issue a premium card by November 1, 1981, to compete directly with the American Express Gold Card. Secondly they announced that they would investigate the potential of offering a money market investment to Visa customers through Visa's member institutions. (Visa was already positioned in the travelers' check market, a one-time stronghold of Amex.)

Hock pledged that the Visa Premium Card would achieve a 15 percent market share in its first year, and would hold a 50 percent share within 5 years. Hock later commented on the swiftness of Visa's response to the Amex/Shearson news:

> When the news of the Amex merger was announced, we had a meeting of senior managers to decide how best to respond. In one day, we had our response. It took us very little time to figure out how we could make their move disadvantageous to them.

But at another time, he admitted that the battle with Amex was an arduous exercise:

> They [Amex] are rough, tough, smart competitors with tons of money. There is very little they will not do to achieve their objectives. The advantage at American Express is that James Robinson [chief executive officer] can say, "to the left march," and they do. I couldn't think of doing that. Each of our institutions [members] is totally independent. We leave maximum autonomy over service in individual hands. It's an enormously complex structure to run.

THE U.S. INDUSTRY'S PERFORMANCE

Record high interest rates had sharply reduced the U.S. bank card industry's profitability in 1980. It was estimated that members of the U.S. Visa system alone (which represented 54 percent of all bank card sales) posted a net loss of $336 million in 1980. At one time before the repeal of the Credit Control Act and the revision of many state usury laws, the industry was unable to charge competitive prices for its services. The industry had estimated its losses would exceed $1 billion if interest rates remained astronomical and laws remained unchanged. (See Exhibit 4 for statistics on Visa, USA, and Exhibits 5, 6, and 7 for statistics on Visa International.)

Several reasons for these losses were cited. First, an increasing number of cardholders were becoming "convenience" users, that is, they were using the card as a payment device rather than as a source of credit. Whereas only 33 percent of all volume was produced by cardholders who had been convenience users in 1978, 50 percent of all volume fell into this category in 1980. Since 65 percent of the industry's revenues were generated from interest fees charged to cardholders with extended balances, the general shift to convenience use dramatically reduced member revenues.

[19] Ibid.

EXHIBIT 4 CARD PAYMENT SERVICE FOR VISA, USA*

	1980	1979	1978	1977	1976	1975	1974	1973	1972	1971
Participating financial institutions	11,930	11,385	10,836	9,707	7,889	6,752	6,076	5,226	4,525	3,978
Merchant outlets (000)	1,866	1,936	1,972	1,661	1,321	1,204	1,050	974	913	820
Cardholders (000)	64,586	63,528	55,799	44,320	32,071	29,295	27,412	24,459	21,982	19,408
Total accounts (000)	41,669	40,986	35,999	28,407	20,697	18,897	17,675	15,780	14,182	12,521
Active accounts (000)	25,460	26,477	23,274	18,101	13,697	12,311	11,264	10,001	8,680	7,211
Gross dollar volume (millions)	28,323	27,869	22,079	15,016	11,122	8,995	7,768	6,012	4,442	3,369
Recall volume (millions)	26,054	25,270	19,814	13,494	10,077	8,175	7,015	5,425	3,996	3,011
Sales slips processed (000)	657,266	723,245	634,241	476,484	386,090	336,955	312,753	277,629	217,643	171,282
Average sale ($)	40	35	31	28	26	24	22	20	18	17
Cash advance volume ($ millions)	2,269	2,599	2,265	1,530	1,045	820	753	587	446	358
Number of cash advances (000)	14,413	17,225	16,102	12,297	9,099	7,013	6,154	4,605	3,424	2,659
Average cash advance ($)	157	151	141	124	115	117	123	128	130	135
Outstandings ($ millions)	13,208	13,127	10,347	7,217	5,238	4,391	3,852	2,993	2,305	1,787
Average outstanding balance ($)	525	502	449	399	382	356	342	299	266	248
Percent of account with outstanding balance	61.1	64.6	64.7	64.2	66.6	65.2	63.7	63.5	61.2	57.6
Percent of delinquency										
30–59 days	2.0	2.0	2.0	1.5	1.6	1.9	2.4	2.2	2.2	2.1
60–89 days	0.8	0.8	0.7	0.5	0.6	0.7	1.0	0.8	0.8	0.9
90 days and over	1.3	1.0	1.0	0.7	0.9	1.2	1.6	1.3	1.4	1.8
Total delinquency	4.1	3.8	3.7	2.7	3.1	3.8	5.0	4.3	4.4	4.8

* Figures for 1971–1975 apply to BankAmericard; thereafter, figures apply to Visa, USA.

Secondly, state usury ceilings limited the rate of interest that could be charged on outstanding balances. The average rate of interest paid by cardholders in 1979 on the total number of dollars in their possession was 14.2 percent. This figure was the average maximum rate that bank card operations were permitted to charge their cardholders under the various usury ceilings. Since the prime rate had exceeded 20 percent in 1980 and continued to hover at around this level in mid-1981, card pro-

EXHIBIT 5 VISA SYSTEM STATISTICS

Year	Worldwide number of cardholders (millions)	Worldwide sales volume ($ billions)	Worldwide number of merchant establishments honoring card (millions)
1971	25.7	$ 4.06	1.07
1972	29.1	5.48	1.29
1973	33.3	7.68	1.42
1974	38.1	10.27	1.59
1975	41.4	12.28	1.81
1976	45.2	15.22	1.95
1977	58.7	20.15	2.4
1978	66.6	24.5	2.4
1979	79.6	34.0	2.9
1980	94.8	45.7	3.1

grams were offering credit to their small, installment customers at several points below prime. Further, the Federal Reserve Board's commitment to slowing the rate of growth of the money supply argued against any likelihood of a significant decline in interest rates in the near future.

Thirdly, credit and fraud losses were escalating. Bank card industry credit and fraud losses were projected to exceed $1 billion in 1981 or 1982. In the Visa system alone, losses had increased from $290 million in 1979 to $391 million in 1980. While Visa was developing a sophisticated point-of-sale authorization system for all merchants (including small merchants, for whom such systems had not been cost-effective in the past), the project was not near completion. In addition, such remedies were costly themselves.

Hock thought that one of the major dangers posited by these developments was that only the large financial institutions would be able to remain in the system. This was ominous to Hock since it was his view that the services offered by organizations

EXHIBIT 6 VOLUME MARKET SHARES OF MAJOR ALL-PURPOSE CARDS

Card	1977	1980
Carte Blance	0.5%	0.7%
Diners Club	1.7	1.2
American Express	19.8	20.3
Interbank (MasterCard)	40.0	33.4
Visa	38.0	44.4
Total sales (for four quarters ending Sept. 30)	$48 billion	$98.6 billion

EXHIBIT 7 COUNTRIES HONORING VISA CARDS, MARCH 1981

Country	Number of merchant outlets accepting card	Countries with limited use of Visa
North America and Caribbean		
Bermuda	316	Bahamas, Barbados, British
Canada	200,638	Virgin Islands, Cayman Islands,
Commonwealth of Puerto Rico	6,782	Haiti, Jamaica, Leeward
Dominican Republic	1,000	Islands, Netherlands Antilles,
Mexico	45,296	Trinidad and Tobago, and
United States	1,866,000	Windward Islands
Virgin Islands	503	
South and Central America		
Argentina	5,500	Bolivia, British Honduras,
Brazil	66,000	Nicaragua, Paraguay, Surinam,
Chile	7,300	and Uraguay
Colombia	16,300	
Costa Rica	1,635	
Ecuador	1,645	
El Salvador	1,513	
Guatemala	1,847	
Honduras	600	
Panama	1,210	
Peru	5,136	
Venezuela	33,247	
Europe		
Andorra	570	Azores, Bulgaria,
Austria	3,310	Czechoslovakia, East Germany,
Belgium	1,227	Gibraltar, Hungary,
Cyprus	820	Lichtenstein, Madeira, Monaco,
Denmark	1,427	Poland, Romania, Russia,
Finland	4,800	Turkey, and Yugoslavia
France	121,065	
Greece	6,500	
Iceland	200	
Ireland	4,810	
Italy	56,125	
Luxembourg	567	
Malta	469	
Netherlands	1,370	
Norway	1,186	
Portugal	5,120	
Spain	99,200	
Sweden	13,500	
Switzerland	7,186	
United Kingdom	153,015	
West Germany	7,540	
Asia and the Pacific		
Australia	19,485	(See following page.)
Fiji	200	

EXHIBIT 7   (continued)

Country	Number of merchant outlets accepting card	Countries with limited use of Visa
Guam	380	Brunei, Macao, Nepal, Norfolk
Hong Kong	9,010	Islands, North Korea, Pacific
India	2,500	Islands Trust Territories,
Indonesia	245	People's Republic of China,
Japan	202,910	and South Pacific Islands
Malaysia	2,130	
New Zealand	21,160	
Philippines	7,405	
Singapore	5,985	
South Korea	415	
Taiwan	1,800	
Thailand	2,330	
Africa and the Middle East		
Israel	5,247	Botswana, Cameroon, Egypt,
Kuwait	283	Iran, Ivory Coast, Kenya,
Morocco	535	Lebanon, Lesotho, Mauritius,
Republic of South Africa	54,400	Pakistan, Saudi Arabia,
Tunisia	380	Senegal, Syria, Seychelles,
		Swaziland, and Zimbabwe

such as Visa would soon be essential to consumer banking. If the smaller institutions were unable to offer card services, they would not be able to compete effectively in the retail banking marketplace. The consequence of this would be that the large financial institutions would swallow their weak competitors, thereby lessening the degree of free competition in financial services.

Hock expressed concern that the industry's losses would serve to halt the progress being made in the area of worldwide electronic value exchange systems. In 1980 he said:

> The entire process is in jeopardy. The gains in productivity that have been achieved in the dispensing of credit and in the handling of electronic payments can easily be set back 5 years if the present situation continues.

Hock was not enunciating a totally new theme. Rather, he had warned of the potential of such a turn of events 3 years earlier. At that time, he had observed that the method of pricing bank card services was socially and economically unsound, and that it should be revised. In 1977, with bank card profits at an all-time peak, Hock had made the following comments to attendees at the American Bankcard Convention:

> I have long felt that the methods by which bank card services are priced are unsound and must be altered. . . . Let's assume that the industry is subjected to minor, adverse trends for a few years. Average merchant discounts decline one-tenth of 1 percent per year. There is a slight decline in finance charges in relation to outstandings. Chargeoffs increase one-tenth

of 1 percent each year, and money costs increase one-half of 1 percent each year. Much worse has happened before, and could easily happen again. All are fluctuations which any prudent businessman would anticipate and provide for. Applied to our industry, without a change in pricing, those minor fluctuations would soon bring our net below breakeven, with prospects of worse to come.

In a similar address in 1979, Hock repeated his comments, adding:

Well, it all happened. Those prudent businessmen did not provide for it. You are well aware what has happened to profits. Perhaps necessity will now provide the incentive for repricing [card services] which was lacking when profits were ample.

Visa's Washington lobbyist, Timothy Colcord, was working in 1981 to implement several legislative remedies, such as the federal preemption of state interest rate ceilings, and the establishment of annual card fees in those states then prohibiting them.

THE FUTURE AT VISA: DAY-TO-DAY JUDGMENTS

What is the aboriginal Self, on which a universal reliance may be grounded? What is the nature and power of that science—baffling star, without parallax, without calculable elements, which shoots a ray of beauty even into trivial and impure actions, if the least mark of independence appears? The inquiry leads us to the source, at once the essence of genius, of virtue, and of life, which we call Spontaneity or Instinct. We denote this primary wisdom as Intuition, whilst all later teachings are tuitions. In that deep force, the last fact behind which analysis cannot go, all things find their common origin. For the sense of being which in calm hours arises, we know not how, in the soul, is not diverse from things, from space, from light, from time, from man, but one with them and proceeds obviously from the same source whence their life and being also proceed.[20]

"It's very good jam," said the Queen.

"Well, I don't want any *to-day,* at any rate."

"You couldn't have it if you *did* want it," the Queen said. "The rule is, jam to-morrow and jam yesterday—but never jam *to-day.*"

"It *must* come sometimes to 'jam today'," Alice objected. "No, it can't," said the Queen. "It's jam every *other* day: to-day isn't any *other* day, you know."

"I don't understand you," said Alice. "It's dreadfully confusing."

"That's the effect of living backwards," the Queen said kindly: "It always makes one a little giddy at first—"

"Living backwards." Alice repeated in great astonishment. "I never heard of such a thing."

"—but there's one great advantage in it, that one's memory works both ways."

"I'm sure *mine* only works one way," Alice remarked. "I can't remember things before they happen."[21]

[20] Ralph Waldo Emerson, *Self-Reliance,* 1841.
[21] Lewis Carroll, *Through the Looking Glass,* 1871.

In the course of its evolution, Visa would face myriad challenges. Somewhere beyond those challenges, and fully dependent upon how, precisely, each of them had been met, lay the evolved Visa. We asked Hock to share his views on the best and worst cases for the corporation in 1990. His response was emphatic:

> I would have to be a god or a fool to answer such a question, and I am neither. I cannot make such judgments about the future.

We then asked how he determined if the course of action he chose to operate under today would be consistent with tomorrow's demands. His response implied that it was intuition that provided the guiding impulse:

> A sense of direction is infinitely more valuable than a precise plan. I have a *sense* of the direction in which Visa should be moving. I can tell you that Visa is moving in a direction that, at this time, on this day, is sound for our membership, sound for our employees, and sound for our customers. It appears to be sensible with respect to what we can deduce and what we believe about the future. We will continue to make judgments, day to day, week to week, and month to month to be certain that Visa evolves in a manner that is consistent with the principles we espouse and the needs we perceive.

In fact, Hock felt that there was a great danger inherent in the attempt to unwaveringly believe in one's vision of the future:

> People who make long-term judgments as to what the future will be tend to create rigid structures which are intended to shepherd into being a future that is identical to their own imaginings. Since they presume that they can orchestrate the future, they also presume that they can exploit it when it arrives. General Motors tried to do this, for example. The problem was that they could not predict what OPEC would do. You cannot manage change by attempting to determine, and then freeze what you will be in 10 years, or 5, or even 1.

Hock felt that Visa would succeed in its quest to be capable of the management of change because, as he said, "we are an organization that is ideally structured to deal with the unknown as it becomes known." To Hock, overemphasis on long-term planning seemed to imply an unholy conceit. This was, perhaps, why Hock said of himself, "I'm just hopelessly old-fashioned. I'm an old-fashioned futurist. I do not believe in resisting change, nor do I believe in incoherent change. It is essential to understand the past and to preserve its substance in the forms we create in the future." He was old-fashioned in the sense that, while he dared to contemplate the future, he did not presume to rule it.

Joao Ribeiro da Fonseca, in an evocative comment, expressed a similar type of humility about his stature in the face of time that reinforced the notion of "old-fashioned futurism."

> The time may come when Dee and I both feel that the job is done, the mission is accomplished, that it is time for others to take over the job. Then it is time to do something else.

He and Hock appeared to have a sweeping respect for the power of vagary, and an understanding of one's powerlessness to prevent the minutes and the hours from skimming the chapters of our personal mortalities.

CONCLUSION

An institution is the lengthened shadow of one man.[22]

It was a symphony of triumph. The notes flowed up, they spoke of rising and they were the rising itself, they were the essence and the form of upward motion, they seemed to embody every human act and thought that had ascent as its motive. It had the freedom of release and the tension of purpose. It swept space clean and left nothing but the joy of an unobstructed effort.[23]

In the field of group endeavor, you will occasionally see incredible events in which the group performs far beyond the sum of its individual talents. It happens in the symphony, in the ballet, in the theater, in sports and equally in business. It is easy to recognize and impossible to define. It is a mystique. It cannot be achieved without immense effort, training, and cooperation, but effort, training, and cooperation alone rarely create it. Some groups reach it consistently. Few can long sustain it. None can define it. We should be content to eternally strive for it and enjoy it when it occurs.

I will let greater conceits than mine determine as to whether or not Visa consistently reaches that "mystique." But I would suggest that, while a case study may reach in the right direction, it could never fully grasp the essence of Visa.[24]

Hock faced the challenge of the future with sublime optimism. He felt enduringly confident that Visa would become the premier electronic value exchange system in the world, but also that it would not achieve its full potential in his lifetime. He was also confident that, as Visa expanded around the globe, the regional structure that had been placed into being in March 1981 would permit Visa's owners and managers to respond swiftly to the vagaries of time. He remained certain that Visa's employees, baptized in the fire of flux, would understand the inevitability of change, seizing its opportunities and dismissing its bluffs. He was convinced that inherent in Visa was the pattern for future organizations that would not sacrifice individuality to what he called "the Great Gray God of Uniformity."

Then again, perhaps it was not such a cognitive thing after all. For as Hock had said, with genuine humility,

We're having an effect way out of proportion to our backgrounds. It proves the old saying that nothing is as powerful as an idea whose time has come.

APPENDIX 1: The BASE Systems

Visa International provided two computer networks to assist members and merchants in providing credit authorization information and in accomplishing the transmission of sales data between members. These two computer systems were named BASE 1 and BASE 2. BASE was an acronym for BankAmericard Authorization System, Experimental.

---

[22] Ralph Waldo Emerson, *Self-Reliance,* 1841.
[23] Ayn Rand, *Atlas Shrugged,* 1957.
[24] Dee Hock, 1981.

BASE 1

BASE 1 was an international electronic network that carried messages authorizing merchants around the world to accept Visa credit and debit cards in payment for their goods and services. It was required that any Visa transaction exceeding a specified dollar amount (the "floor limit") be authorized by the Visa member that had issued the particular card being used to make the purchase. Since many transactions requiring such authorization involved merchants and issuing banks that were distant from each other, a computerized system was the best way to provide rapid information transmission.

The BASE 1 system was a computer message-switching network consisting of a number of physical components, such as computers, terminals, communication lines, and equipment. In addition, there existed processing software for message switching and file management. The system operated 7 days per week, 24 hours per day from two locations: one near Washington, D.C., and the other near San Francisco.

The BASE 1 system was developed in 1972 at a cost of $2.5 million, and was placed in operation in April 1973. In 1974, the system processed 6 million authorizations. By 1985, the system was expected to provide 1.25 billion authorization messages. The average response time, which had been 60 seconds per message in 1973, was 2.7 seconds in 1980.

BASE 2

The BASE 2 system was an electronic data transmission (EDT) system used in cardholder billings, and in the reconciliation of accounts between members.

When a cardholder used a Visa card to make a purchase, the merchant recorded the transaction on a sales draft and gave one copy to the cardholder. The remaining copies of the draft were deposited by the merchant at the financial institution with which the merchant had established a contract for the acceptance of the merchant's drafts. The institution immediately credited the merchant with the amount of the transaction, less a discount (the merchant discount).

If the merchant's bank was the same bank that issued the card used in the purchase, the amount was simply billed by the bank directly to the cardholder's account. If the card was issued by a different Visa member, the information from the sales draft was transmitted to the issuing bank. This was done completely electronically, by means of the BASE 2 computer system. Every 24 hours, this transmission process would occur. The procedure was known as *interchange*, and was similar to the reconciliation process employed by banks to clear checks drawn on other banks. The difference between the two systems was that all Visa information was transmitted electronically through the BASE 2 system; no paperwork was returned to the card-issuing institutions.

BASE 2 became operational in the United States in November 1974, and was extended to handle international transmissions in July 1977. The BASE 2 system was developed in 1974 at a cost of under $7 million. In 1977, the system handled close to 900,000 items per day, with a total transaction volume of $22 million per day. In early 1981, the system cleared 5 million items per day, with a total daily transaction volume of $200 million.

APPENDIX 2: Fees

Visa's operations were funded by assorted fees collected from members. These funds supported Visa's international computer networks, advertising and promotional effect, staff salaries and all other expenses borne by the corporation. A cursory explanation of the fee structures is presented below.

Initial service fees. Upon election to membership in the corporation, new members paid a flat membership fee that was based upon their total assets. The 1981 fee was $6 per $1 million in assets, with a maximum initial fee of $30,000.

Quarterly service fees. Members paid a quarterly service fee amounting to .0125 percent of their total sales volume for each quarter. Visa, USA members paid .1 percent of sales, from which Visa, USA paid its international fee and other U.S. expenses.

BASE fees. Card issuers were charged an authorization fee for all authorization messages processed through the BASE 1 system and relating to their cardholders. The original fee for authorizations was $0.25 per message, but was reduced to $0.075 per message in February 1980 to reflect increased BASE operating efficiencies.

In order to encourage card issuers to provide rapid responses to requests for authorization, a new BASE 1 fee schedule took effect on October 1, 1979. Under that schedule, fees were based upon issuer response time to an authorization inquiry. The rates were:

Response time	BASE 1 authorization fee
0–3 seconds	$0.05
3.1–5 seconds	0.075
5.1–20 seconds	0.15
20.1+ seconds	0.30

Members also retained the option of having BASE central provide all authorizations for their particular accounts, at a rate of $0.06 per authorization. BASE central was staffed by Visa employees.

BASE 2 fees. Visa, USA charged issuing members $0.01 for each sales draft that was electronically transmitted back to them under the BASE 2 interchange system. The BASE 2 draft transmission rate for international transactions was $0.12 per item.

APPENDIX 3: Member Revenues

Individual members of the Visa system received revenues from one or more of the following sources. Each member had complete freedom in establishing the method and amount of charges to the merchants and cardholders it obtained.

1 Merchant discount fees
2 Issuer reimbursement fees
3 Interest charged to installment credit users
4 Cardholder annual membership fees
5 Transaction fees
6 Banking balances maintained by merchants and cardholders

These fees enabled member institutions to handle expenses related to the operation of the program, such as bookkeeping, collections, credit investigations, fraud and bad debt losses, marketing and advertising programs, and the costs of the money needed to fund the program. A description of these revenues follows.

Merchant discount fees. Merchants accepting Visa cards paid a merchant discount fee to the bank with which they deposited their sales drafts. As of 1980, the average merchant discount fee was 2.1 percent, indicating that the average merchant would receive $97.90 for each $100 of Visa draft deposits. Based upon systemwide sales of $45.7 billion in 1980, total merchant discount fees generated in that year were $959.7 million.

Issuer reimbursement fees. Merchant banks transmitting sales drafts through the BASE 2 system to card-issuing banks paid the card issuer a portion of the merchant fee they had received to help defray the issuer's costs of maintaining its Visa accounts. In April 1981, the issuer reimbursement fee was established at 1.55 percent of the amount of the sales draft, plus $0.055 per sales draft. Consequently, a merchant bank transmitting a draft in the amount of $100 to a card-issuing bank would receive $98.40 from the issuer. Since the average merchant bank had collected a merchant discount fee of $2.10 (2.1 percent) for handling the $100 sales draft, it received net revenues of $0.50 for handling the item after it had paid the issuing bank the issuer reimbursement fee.

Banks issuing cash advances to cardholders with Visa accounts established at another member bank received a cash advance fee for their services. The advancing bank was paid a cash advance fee by the issuing bank that totalled $1.75 per advance plus 0.33 percent of the amount of the advance.

Interest charges. Interest rates charged to cardholders on installment balances varied by member bank, and were often limited by state usury ceilings. Banks obtained 65% of their total bank card operation revenues from this source.

Cardholder annual membership fees. Where permitted by state law, the majority of Visa card issuers charged cardholders an annual membership fee. The fee varied, but averaged approximately $15 in 1981.

Transaction fees. Certain members charged cardholders a fee for each transaction when the cardholder used his or her Visa card to make purchases or obtain cash advances. In other cases, members charged cardholders a blanket monthy fee (approximately $1) each month that the cardholder used his or her card.

Banking balances. Merchants and cardholders tended to keep funds on deposit at the particular bank that extended Visa's services to them. Therefore banks were able to use these deposits in the course of their presumably profitable operations.

MITSUBISHI CORPORATION (A): ORGANIZATIONAL OVERVIEW

Thomas Lifson

"To the Japanese consumer, we are like the air: invisible, but pervasive, providing essential things to sustain life."

Yohei Mimura, president of Mitsubishi Corporation (MC), smiled modestly, explaining the role of the $70 billion plus organization. (See Exhibit 1 for recent financial statements.) As the largest of Japan's small number of *sogo shosha*,[1] Mitsubishi Corporation handled a range of more than 25,000 products covering a spectrum (in a popular Japanese phrase) "from noodles to space satellites." Partly because nearly all of its transactions involved other corporations, such as manufacturers or distributors, rather than the general public, MC's role and functions were poorly understood even in its native Japan. Moreover, the diversity of the functions performed by a *sogo shosha* almost paralleled the extent of its product lines, extending far beyond its core activity of trading, thereby making a clear definition of the nature of its role or strategy elusive.

Yet, for all the difficulty in understanding it, MC was clearly a very successful organization. Its corporate sales were greater than those of any other firm in Japan, equaling a third of the Japanese government's budget and ranking it among the world's five largest companies. Alone, it handled well over 10 percent of Japan's foreign trade. By 1981, the record of MC and the other giant *sogo shosha* in developing Japan's economy and trade had inspired the governments of such countries as Taiwan, South Korea, and Brazil to launch their own versions of *sogo shosha*, in the

---

[1] *Sogo shosha* is often translated as "general trading firm." Some find this translation misleadingly vague. Others have suggested using "comprehensive trading firm," or else simply using the Japanese term without translation.

EXHIBIT 1   STATEMENTS OF CONSOLIDATED INCOME AND BALANCE SHEETS, INCLUDING CONSOLIDATED SUBSIDIARIES, IN MILLIONS OF DOLLARS FOR YEARS ENDING MARCH 31, 1980 AND 1981*

	1981	1980
Total trading transactions	$70,307	$60,071
Gross trading profit	1,489	1,381
Other income		
Dividends	39	41
Lease revenues	16	22
Sundry (net)	9	25
Total	1,553	1,469
Expenses and other charges		
Selling, general, and administrative expenses	979	867
Provision for doubtful receivables	35	91
Interest	461	320
Total	1,475	1,278
Income from consolidated operations before income taxes	78	191
Income taxes	69	69
Income from consolidated operations	9	122
Equity in earnings of subsidiaries not consolidated and associated companies (net) less applicable income taxes	186	77
Net income	$ 195	$ 199
Amounts per share		
Net income	.1714	.1850
Cash dividends applicable to the year	.0332	.0345

Assets

Current assets		
Cash	$ 1,105	$ 951
Time deposits	924	981
Marketing securities	786	936
Receivables—trade		
Notes and loans	4,804	5,469
Accounts	6,488	6,816
Allowance for doubtful receivables	(324)	(346)
Unearned interest	(4)	(6)
Inventories	1,981	2,170
Advance payments to suppliers	876	745
Prepayments, etc.	278	283
Total	16,914	17,999
Investments and noncurrent receivables		
Capital stock of nonconsolidated subsidiaries and associated companies	571	466
Advances to nonconsolidated subsidiaries and associated companies	262	215
Other investments	1,018	957
Noncurrent notes, loans, and accounts receivables (trade)	3,510	2,753
Total	5,361	4,391

EXHIBIT 1   (continued)

Assets	1981	1980
Property and equipment—principally at cost less accumulated depreciation	737	647
Miscellaneous assets—deferred taxes less noncurrent and other assets	246	214
Total	$23,258	$23,251

Liabilities and shareholders' equity		
Current liabilities		
Short-term loans	$ 4,111	$ 4,745
Current maturities of long-term debt	880	864
Notes and acceptances (trade)	5,612	6,353
Accounts payable (trade)	4,130	4,158
Accrued income taxes	73	98
Other accrued expenses	207	214
Advances from customers	757	559
Deposit liabilities, etc.	252	249
Total	16,022	17,240
Long-term debt less current maturities	5,150	4,216
Liability for severance indemnities	184	178
Minority interests	24	25
Shareholders' equity		
Common stock, ¥50 par, authorized, 2.5 billion shares; issued in 1981, 1,151,950,064 shares; in 1980, 1,005,530,205 shares	273	238
Capital surplus	386	292
Retained earnings		
Appropriated for legal reserve	45	40
Unappropriated	1,175	1,023
Total	1,879	1,593
Less common stock held by consolidated subsidiaries, at cost— 1,431,629 shares	1	1
Total (net)	1,878	1,592
Total	$23,258	$23,251

Source: Company annual report.
* U.S. dollar amounts are presented solely for convenience and represent translation of yen amounts at the rate of 211:1.

hope that their own economies would benefit and grow. Other countries, including the United States, were actively investigating the possibility of creating similar institutions.

SOGO SHOSHA SECTOR

Depending on the observer, 9 to 16 firms in Japan could qualify as *sogo shosha* by virtue of their size and diversity (see Exhibit 2 for a list of the largest firms). Although some of these firms could boast of a corporate lineage of more than 350 years,

EXHIBIT 2   SIX LARGEST *SOGO SHOSHA* IN FISCAL YEAR 1980

Company	Sales*	Profits*	Assets*	Employees (thousands)
Mitsubishi Corporation	$55,183	$183	$19,647	13.0
Mitsui & Company, Ltd.	46,531	124	20,512	13.0
C. Itoh & Company, Ltd.	39,986	143	13,936	10.0
Marubeni Corporation	38,051	75	13,698	10.1
Sumitomo Corporation	33,320	119	9,028	10.0
Nissho-Iwai Company, Ltd.	26,702	37	8,600	7.9

Source: Forbes, July 6, 1981.
* Figures are on an unconsolidated basis, in millions of U.S. dollars.

the real origins of the sector lay in the last half of the nineteenth century, when Japan's 250 years of self-imposed isolation from the world's economy ended.

Critically dependent on the outside world for technologies, advanced manufacturing, and raw materials, as well as the export markets to pay for them, Japanese companies and individuals possessed almost no experience in international trade. Initially, therefore, overseas commerce had to be conducted through the services of foreign traders who flocked to the newly opened Japanese ports, finding that the ignorance and inexperience of their Japanese customers translated into rich profits for themselves. As the realization of Japan's exploitation by these foreign merchants grew, leading governmental figures as well as many private entrepreneurs came to understand that it would be essential to create Japanese-controlled trade channels, which could provide efficient and trustworthy access to the wealth of overseas opportunities.

Over time, many different kinds of firms sent representatives overseas to engage in foreign trade, experiencing varying degrees of success in coping with the risks of this entirely new type of business. Some expanded from a domestic trading base in traditional fields such as textiles, while others were established by the newly emerging Japanese industrial groups. Because of the high cost of stationing personnel overseas and the tiny number of Japanese business people capable of handling international commerce, it made economic sense for them to conduct overseas business for as wide a range of clients, performing the widest range of functions possible. Gradually, a few firms accumulated experience and achieved economies of scale sufficient to outcompete the resident foreign traders in Japan and preempt Japanese firms that might consider conducting their own transactions overseas.

From their very start, the trading firms combined international trading with active roles in Japan's domestic commerce. Then, as now, the Japanese economy featured a large number of very small firms that performed but one stage of a multiprocess production chain. These firms would buy inputs from other similarly small manufacturers, and sell outputs to another, one stage downstream in the production flow. The textile industry (in Japan, as elsewhere, historically the first truly modern manufacturing industry to develop) was particularly characterized by this pattern but so, too, were the slower developing metals, machinery, and chemical industries, among others. The early traders began to act as the coordinators of this multifirm process, identifying markets to be served, procuring raw materials, financing inventories for the manufacturers, coordinating shipments among them, and marketing the final outputs. Particularly as large-scale modern industrial facilities came to be built in Japan, often with government sponsorship for the initial plants, the traders mobilized large networks of smaller firms to perform ancillary functions necessary to channel the unprecedentedly huge volumes of raw materials and semifinished components to the new factories, and distribute the finished output at home and overseas.

As Japan's economy developed and prospered over time, so, too, did the trading firms. In essence, they operated as the eyes and ears of Japanese industry throughout the world; discovering markets, products, and processes that could be used by firms in the Japanese economy. Periodic economic fluctuations served to consolidate the positions of the largest trading firms, especially Mitsui & Co. and Mitsubishi Corporation, the trading arms of the established industrial combines.

MITSUBISHI HISTORY

In 1870, Yataro Iwasaki, a former retainer of the Tosa feudal clan,[2] established a shipping business in Osaka, the commercial capital of Japan. From this base, he began to diversify, first into shipbuilding, and then to foreign trade, metals, coal, machinery, and banking, among other fields. Iwasaki not only was extremely skillful and aggressive in his business dealings, but was also adept at understanding how to work with the Japanese government in its efforts to build up strong domestic companies in key sectors of a modern industrial economy. Problems or opportunities encountered in one field often led to the establishment of a firm in a related industry. As a result, Mitsubishi (literally, "three diamonds," named after the Iwasaki family crest), as the firm came to be called, was often the pioneer in establishing new fields of industry, especially heavy industry, in Japan.

Along with Mitsui, Sumitomo, and a few others, Mitsubishi developed into a *zaibatsu* ("financial clique") composed of several large firms in diverse industries, all under the control of a single family. Shortages of capital and professional management ability, along with the high pace of economic growth, combined to reinforce the success of these firms, which were able to establish a strong economic base early in Japan's modernization. Through World War II, the modern capital-intensive sector of the Japanese economy was dominated to an extraordinary degree by a handful of massive combines.

Iwasaki died in 1885 and was succeeded by several generations of capable Iwasaki family members. After World War I, the firm was converted from a limited partnership to a holding company. The trading department was incorporated into a key subsidiary, the predecessor of today's MC. While Mitsubishi remained smaller than

---

[2] Japan abolished its feudal system in 1868, launching the Meiji restoration.

Mitsui in trading during the entire prewar era, both firms were considerably larger and more diverse than any of the other Japanese traders. With their respective trading arms providing insight and direction for the development of new business opportunities, Mitsui and Mitsubishi *zaibatsu* developed into what were probably the two largest private firms in the world by World War II. It is estimated that each had as many as 1 million employees by the end of the war.

When the victorious Allies landed in a thoroughly vanquished Japan in 1945, they carried with them a theory of the roots of Japanese militarism that placed substantial blame on the shoulders of Japan's *zaibatsu,* and especially their trading arms. As a consequence, the *zaibatsu* holding companies were dissolved and key member firms were divided into smaller companies. In 1947, the Mitsubishi trading company was split into 139 separate trading companies.

These were difficult times. The small firms struggled to cope with uncertainties caused by their fragmentation as well as the general chaos of the Japanese economy. Present-day senior managers in MC recalled, for example, not receiving their salaries during this period, as key customers delayed paying accounts receivable. Although the 139 companies were legally separate, their members continued to interact regularly for both business and social reasons. By 1952, American theories and policies changed, and the ex-Mitsubishi trading firms quickly began merging again. By July 1954, most of the 139 companies had reconsolidated into the present corporate entity, Mitsubishi Corporation.

MITSUBISHI COMPANIES

The prewar holding company arrangement of the *zaibatsu,* however, was never revived. Nonetheless, personal ties, a sense of history, the sharing of a common name and trademark, and other factors led the former sister firms to create new linkages among the now independently owned and managed corporations. This collection of companies was known as the Mitsubishi companies.

The exact dimensions and boundaries of the Mitsubishi companies cannot be precisely defined. Although 100 or more firms could be considered of Mitsubishi parentage, the core consisted of some 20 large companies that were members of the *Kinyokai* (Friday Conference), a monthly gathering of company presidents. The firms belonging to this body had $170 billion in assets, annual sales of $114 billion, and 250,000 employees in 1979. The Friday Conference existed primarily as a means of fostering closer relationships among the firms, rather than as a policy organ. It had no authority of command over the actions of any member firm.

Members of the Friday Conference shared many types of business ties with each other. When promising new industries, such as seabed mining or urban renewal, offered opportunities, Friday Conference companies would sometimes cooperate in entering the field, thus adding to the fold of Mitsubishi companies. However, there was no guarantee of exclusivity in doing business with each other. Members could and frequently did do business with the commercial rivals of Mitsubishi companies. Nonetheless, as a broad generalization, if equally attractive products or terms were offered by a Mitsubishi company, then it would generally receive the business of other Mitsubishi companies.

Although Mitsubishi companies were fully independent of each other and business decisions were made separately, MC maintained a close relationship with members of the companies because of each company's importance in its respective industrial sector and MC's extensive commercial dealings with them. Because of this, MC was widely regarded as playing one of the leading roles among Mitsubishi companies. MC's worldwide information-gathering capacity, its range of products, and its ability to act as coordinator of other firms' activities gave it a distinct position among Mitsubishi companies; 19 percent of its total purchases and 8 percent of its sales involved them.

MITSUBISHI CORPORATION

During the fiscal year ending March 31, 1981, MC's total transactions amounted to $70.3 billion. Import and export transactions accounted for 49 percent or $34.3 billion, which was approximately 12 percent of Japan's foreign trade. During that same period, MC's total transactions by product categories were 26 percent for fuels, 18 percent for ferrous metals, 17 percent for machinery, 14 percent for foods, 9 percent for chemicals, and 8 percent for nonferrous metals; general merchandise, textiles, and project development and construction followed in that order (see Exhibit 3). As a *sogo shosha*, trade was the primary, but by no means exclusive, activity of MC.

Several examples of MC's activities were as follows:

Stable imports of crude oil were crucial to Japan as she relied nearly 100 percent on foreign sources for oil. MC handled about 700,000 barrels per day or 15 percent of Japan's total imports of crude in fiscal 1979. When the major international oil companies reduced crude supplies to nonaffiliated oil companies, the fuel division succeeded in compensating for this by increasing the volumes obtained under existing and newly negotiated direct-deal (D/D) contracts with the governments

EXHIBIT 3   BREAKDOWN OF TRADING TRANSACTIONS*

Type		Commodity	
Domestic	$28,590	Fuel	$18,382
Import	22,305	Ferrous metals	12,618
Export	11,963	Machinery	11,770
Third country	7,449	Food	9,897
	$70,307	Chemicals	6,037
		Nonferrous metals	5,321
		General merchandise	4,067
		Textiles	2,215
			$70,307

* In millions of U.S. dollars

of Middle Eastern countries, as well as similar D/D contracts from other countries.

MC's ferrous metals division handled not only ferrous metals but also raw materials for them. For instance, MC imported 22 million tons of iron ore and 19 million tons of coking coal for fiscal 1979, which was equivalent to 17 percent and 34 percent of Japan's total imports, respectively. The main supply source of coking coal handled by MC was Queensland, Australia, where MC has been engaged in coal production for many years through its subsidiary, Mitsubishi Development Pty., in a joint venture with American and Australian partners.

MC's machinery division was involved in a number of major projects in various countries around the world. For example, in September 1979, Mitsubishi Corporation received an order from the State Organization for Oil Projects of Iraq to construct an LPG production plant worth $120 million and eight gas compressor stations worth $90 million. The company signed another contract with the same organization to build a natural gas liquids plant and auxiliary facilities valued at $135 million. Before the two projects, MC had received from the same authority a $280 million contract signed in October 1979 for the construction of an oil refinery with a capacity of 150,000 barrels per day.

In another area of the world, MC's machinery division obtained an order from the Kenya Power Company, Ltd. for the supply and installation of a 15,000-kilowatt geothermal power-generating plant, the first on the African continent. On all these projects, MC worked with other companies as coordinator. These examples were only the tip of the iceberg of the $8 billion machinery-related business of MC, and such industrial plant projects on a full-turnkey basis were typical examples of MC's ability to maintain an efficient multifaceted network linking up the various functions.

MC's activities tended to be concentrated in the basic sectors of an industrialized economy: metals, fuels, food, fibers, machinery, and construction. Most of these sectors were characterized by multistage production and processing, involving many firms over the course of transformation from raw materials to finished products. MC would characteristically take on a complex role, assembling raw materials from various sources and coordinating their flow from firm to firm through the production and distribution chain. As part of its services, MC would not only buy and sell the product at various stages but would often also finance the transactions, arrange logistics, and handle the foreign exchange aspects, documentation, customs clearance, and other such details. It would use its broad expertise and global network of offices to spot emerging trends, threats, and opportunities, and mobilize its clients to counter or capitalize on these developments. The client firms could, if desired, concentrate their resources on achieving maximum efficiency in their internal operations, leaving it to the *sogo shosha* to manage the flow of inputs and outputs to and from them.

For example, as noted in the steel industry example above, MC owned equity shares in iron ore and coal mines overseas, and also entered into long-term contracts to ensure stable supplies for its Japanese steel-producing customers. But, it also set up and managed the operations of a complex logistical system involving massive transport, storage, and loading facilities, using its flexibility and economies of scale as a supplier to several firms to set up a highly efficient system to cut direct costs and minimize inventories. MC purchased basic steel and sold it to secondary and tertiary fabricators and processors. MC itself owned a network of steel service centers in Japan and overseas, and was a major marketer of the output of Japan's steel industry. In many cases, the purchasers of steel also used MC to market their products. For example, MC sold marine turbines to shipyards, and ships to shipping lines. The very ships MC used to transport coal and iron ore might well have been the end products of an earlier set of transactions arranged by MC.

In this and other industrial sectors, MC manifested what might be termed a *comprehensive commercial capacity*. Its profits were not tied to one function, product, location, or client. Instead, it managed a complex web of interfirm linkages, earning a commission or profit at each stage. Additionally, it made strategic investments at key stages of these sectors to increase its influence, its market and technical knowledge, or its security of supply or distribution, as well as to realize equity profits. More than any of the other firms involved at various stages in the production and distribution chain, MC was able to regard an industrial sector as an integrated system, and was capable of great flexibility in coping with and managing large-scale systemwide change. This allowed it to act as the organizer or rationalizer of flows of resources involving many different firms.

For instance, MC had helped introduce an entirely new technology of chicken production to Japan: the mass production of broiler chickens. MC had helped broiler growers set up large-scale environment-controlled broiler houses, providing technology, financing investments, and importing the breeding stock. MC also helped establish large-scale processing and cold storage facilities, as well as distribution and marketing channels to guarantee secure outlets for the large-scale production. One of these outlets was Kentucky Fried Chicken, which MC had successfully introduced to Japan as a joint venture. For MC, a major benefit of this activity was an expanded market for chickenfeed, since MC was also a major importer of grains into Japan, owning grain elevators and port facilities overseas, as well as feed-mixing and other grain-processing installations in Japan. MC's ability to spot opportunities and plan and coordinate change across the entire scope of this system, as well as its ability to muster financial resources, significantly reduced the uncertainty and risk for each client firm operating at a single stage.

Although historically MC concentrated its efforts on serving Japanese clients, in recent years it operated in a much more multinational mode. For example, MC entered the shoe business in the United States by procuring inexpensive shoes in Japan, which were manufactured to the specifications of a marketer and distributor. As Japanese wages rose, MC stopped exporting from Japan and began to manufacture in places such as Korea, Malaysia, Philippines, Brazil, and Eastern Europe. Moreover, MC began to design and market shoes for Western Europe and Japan as well, and became a major factor in the world shoe business, flexibly manufacturing around the world to serve a range of markets in different countries.

Unlike most of the large U.S. and European traders that specialized in commodities, metals, or petroleum, MC did *not* aim to maximize trading profits by buying low and selling high into the market. Rather, it was compensated for acting largely as a purchasing agent for a relatively fixed group of long-term clients, and received either a predetermined volume-based commission or a relatively modest trading profit established by a simultaneous purchase and sale. In March 1979, for example, MC's total uncovered purchases and sales, subject to risk from market fluctuations, were less than $850 million.

As mentioned previously, MC's profit opportunities tended to be more diffuse and long term than Western trading firms and were more closely linked to the total business volume of its clients. It was not at all uncommon for MC to take a loss on specific transactions to ultimately realize a profit on a related transaction or hoped-for stream of future business. For example, MC might lose money selling mining equipment but might gain an advantageous position for marketing its output. MC placed a high premium on providing reliable and effective service to its clients—not only supply and distribution but also information, advice, and additional special services on an as-needed basis. Although these services were often time-consuming and expensive, MC managers saw them as necessary to provide continuing incentives for clients to direct their future business to MC.

The basic cost structure of MC provided a powerful incentive to maximize transaction volume. As nearly all of its costs—personnel, office, and telecommunications—were fixed in the short run, the incremental expense of an individual transaction was usually very small. Throughout the firm there was a strong emphasis on addition of new products, clients, markets, or services. Often the service and business development efforts of one unit of the firm would result in increased business volume for another unit that dealt in a different product or geographical area.

Financing was a very important aspect of MC's service, as well as a generator of profits. In essence, MC acted as a retailer of loans, borrowing wholesale at preferential rates, and reloaning the money to finance the trade, inventories, or even capital investments of its clients. Because of its intimate contact with clients' daily business, the quality of MC's information on its clients' creditworthiness was often better than a bank could obtain, while its incremental costs for obtaining this information were quite low.

The capacity to gather and distribute information throughout all parts of its far-flung organization was an essential aspect of MC's business activity. Many regarded information as the most important commodity with which MC dealt. To support this activity, the company maintained one of the largest privately operated telex systems in the world. Each location could gain access to any or every other office of the firm through a computer-controlled system of leased lines. A telex could be addressed to an individual or to a business unit, with automatic copy-distribution capability. On an average day, more than 50,000 telexes were transmitted to and from the Tokyo office alone.

As Japan's economy reached full maturity and parity with the other advanced countries of the Western world, the scope and depth of MC's overseas activities increased. As President Mimura explained to the casewriter:

Our most fundamental role is still to bring into Japan raw materials and other resources from overseas in a steady and reliable flow, and help export the goods to pay for these. But Japan has become a major member of the global economic community, and we have a responsibility to contribute to the world's development. We're putting down roots overseas, investing in facilities to improve efficiency, giving increasingly important roles to our non-rotating overseas staff, and expanding our third-country trade.

Third-country trade referred to transactions in which Japan was neither a buyer nor a seller. Although only approximately 10 percent of MC's volume, this was the fastest-growing segment of its business. Some of the third-country trade was an outgrowth of Japan-related business. For instance, when Japanese clients moved energy- and labor-intensive operations to overseas production sites (often with MC's help), MC would usually continue to supply raw materials and market the output. But a growing portion of the third-country trade represented new business in which Mitsubishi put its global network of offices and multiservice capabilities at the disposal of foreign clients.

MC and the other *sogo shosha* did relatively little business involving brand-name consumer products requiring extensive advertising and service. Japanese manufacturers of these products generally preferred to control marketing and distribution themselves. Since the Japanese economy was developing increasingly in the direction of sophisticated consumer goods and high-technology products, the growth prospects of the basic industrial sectors in which MC was involved were poorer than they had been formerly. Moreover, although still higher than any other advanced country, the growth rate of the Japanese economy was steadily declining. Thus, MC executives saw that future growth would have to involve more and more intensive involvement of their firm in overseas-based business.

One aspect of this strategic thrust was a deepening role in overseas natural resource production. Sometimes in cooperation with leading overseas firms such as Royal Dutch Shell, or with other Mitsubishi companies, MC was undertaking the exploration and production of energy sources and mineral deposits. MC was also expanding its role in other aspects of the energy business and had become a major direct purchaser of crude oil from the oil-producing countries. MC currently imported 15 percent of Japan's total consumption.

Related to this role was a second trend: overseas project development. In the largest of these efforts, MC led a consortium of Mitsubishi companies in the development of a massive multibillion-dollar petrochemical complex at Al Jubayl in Saudi Arabia. In addition, MC had built airports in Africa and a hotel in Eastern Europe, and was exporting a complete x-ray film plant to Russia on a turnkey basis. MC's responsibilities would include identifying potential opportunities, assembling firms to supply technologies and equipment, hiring contractors, negotiating the contracts, arranging financing, supervising construction, training operators, and getting the facility in operating condition.

Thus, MC's operations and functions continued to evolve and change. Several senior executives commented that they expected this trend to continue and even accelerate. In the words of Hiromune Minagawa, managing director of the coordination division:

In a sense we provide the "software" of the Japanese economy. We can't afford to have any prejudice about where our economic future will lie. Nor can we afford to look only at short-term profits. As Japan and the world develop, and as economic eras change, we have to use our size and diversity to take risks and develop service capacities appropriate to the circumstances. Responsiveness is the key.

MITSUBISHI CORPORATION: ORGANIZATION

MC's formal organization contained product- and geography-based line units, as well as corporate staff units. Exhibit 4 presents an organization chart. Although an outside observer might well label this a *matrix organization,* the company itself referred to its organization as a *divisional system.* The most powerful and significant units were the nine product-based divisions, each headquartered in the Tokyo main office.

Following the 1954 reconsolidation of the 139 fragmented trading firms into Mitsubishi Corporation, a highly centralized organization had been purposely created to pull them into a coherently operating entity. This period of centralization successfully overcame the effects of dissolution by creating a strong corporate identity and culture and thoroughly integrating operations. However, in 1968, to achieve a better focus on the distinctive needs of the different types of industrial sectors it served, MC was divided into basic product divisions, each corresponding to a major industrial sector served by MC.

The product divisions operated as independent profit centers and were given considerable autonomy to carry out business strategies and operations for their products on a global basis. Not only purchase and sales, but also financing and such staff functions as personnel, accounting, and investments were all handled by division-level personnel, operating within general policy frameworks established by corporate units. In a sense, the product divisions were almost like separate firms.

It was rather rare for a manager to change from one product division to another. Most such transfers consisted of a temporary posting to a directly related operation, such as a transfer from the machinery division to spend a few years in the food-processing operation of the foods division. In 1980, fewer than 120 cross-divisional transfers occurred, while 1300 intradivisional transfers occurred among the more than 6300 managerial and staff employees. As entire sectors grew or declined, however, human resources could be channeled to the areas most in need. For example, the textile division was in the process of shrinking.

Both product divisions and staff divisions were subdivided into 5 to 15 departments. Departments were further subdivided into 5 to 11 sections and teams. The sections were the basic operating units of the firm, handling the buying, selling, financing, and other line functions. A section usually had 5 to 15 managerial and staff personnel, as well as several clerical support personnel to handle operations related to a specific commodity or group of products. In principle, every product MC handled was dealt with by a section.

A large number of teams (the English word was used) also existed at the same organizational level as sections. Originally, teams had been intended to be ad hoc

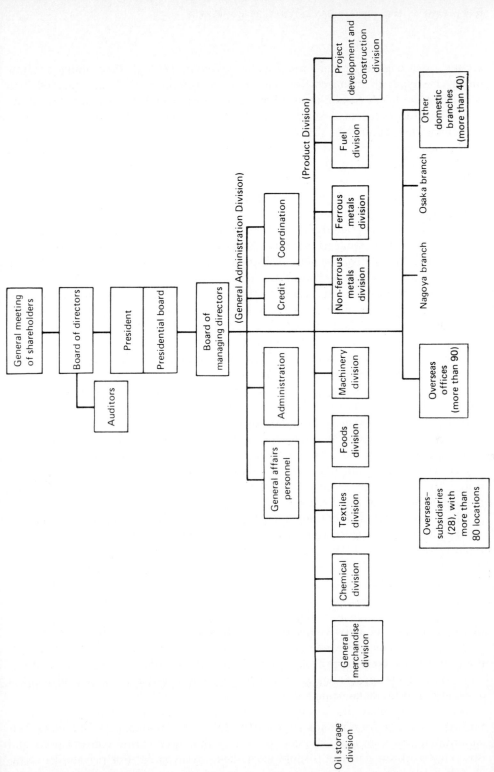

EXHIBIT 4 Mitsubishi Corporation, partial organization chart (October, 1980).

groups, often engaged in new-business development. Through their ability to draw on diverse types of managers for temporary assignments, they had succeeded in enhancing the firm's flexibility and broadening their members' perspectives. Many teams had succeeded in developing new business lines, becoming, in effect, new sections while retaining the title of team.

MC management planned to stop using the term *section* and substitute *team* as the title of its basic operating groups. While it expected no dramatic change as a result, it did hope that all managers would be encouraged to think of their work units as more flexible entities, and to regard their current work assignments as only one element of a larger career progression.

Teams and sections were headed by *team leaders* and *section managers,* whose jobs were defined as the management of the firm's business related to specific commodities. Beyond this relatively general definition of task, there were no formal job slots within the section. The leader was expected to flexibly allocate tasks and responsibilities among the members according to the need to accomplish specific operations, and also to develop the full potential of every member. As a basic philosophy, human resource development and task accomplishment were regarded as complementary aspects of leadership at this and other levels of the organization.

Departments provided supervision, guidance, and coordination for the sections reporting to them. Departments included sections trading in closely related products or markets, and had the responsibility for building and implementing coherent strategies for them. The staff of a department usually consisted of a department chief, also called a *general manager,* and one or two deputies and a few managerial assistants. General managers often took responsibility for the negotiation of larger projects and deals that would have a strategic impact on the firm's business in a product area, or else assigned this to a deputy. General managers also played a major liaison role, both horizontally, with other product departments, and vertically, with the managing director of the division.

The layout of MC's offices encouraged very intimate contact and close supervision among the members working in a department. Exhibit 5 presents the layout of a typical line department. The general manager's desk, located in a corner of the office, had a clear view of all sections. General managers were also assigned a private office, which was primarily used for confidential discussions, such as those dealing with personnel matters, or for discussions with important clients and visitors. Most general managers spent most of their time at their desks on the office floor, so as to observe the ongoing activity, and be available for consultations with their subordinates. General managers were required to review a wide range of documents, including transactions, credit approvals, plans, and other such daily and periodic matters, and indicate their approval by affixing their personal seal (the Japanese equivalent of a signature) to the documents.

Sections and teams sat together as a unit in the open-plan offices, their desks pushed together to form islands on the office floor. Section managers sat among their subordinates, in such close physical proximity that overhearing conversations and observing work on documents almost could not be avoided. For private conversa-

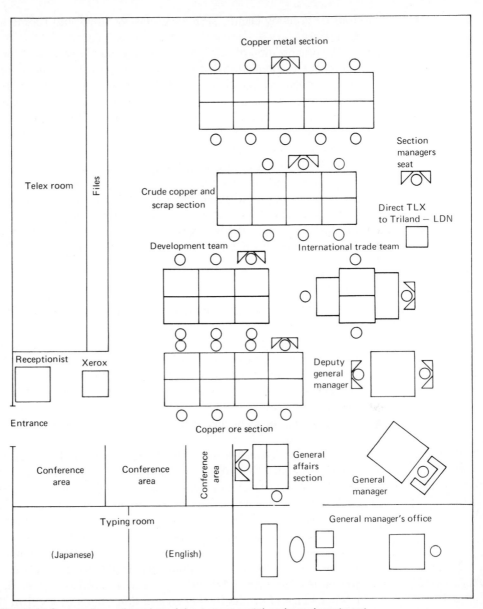

EXHIBIT 5   Mitsubishi Corporation—floorplan of the copper metal and ore department.

tions or visits by clients, several conference areas and rooms were adjacent to each department.

The organization of staff activity closely paralleled that of the line. At the top were four general administrative divisions that were at the same organizational level as the product divisions, each being headed by a managing director. The four staff divisions were labeled *coordination, general affairs and personnel, administration,* and *credit.* Each was subdivided into departments and sections, as were the line divisions. The staff divisions created policies and procedures for the line divisions to follow and also worked as a general staff for the president.

Each line division also maintained its own administrative department to implement the policies decided upon by the managing directors and corporate staff. Typically, the managers in these *line* administrative departments were drawn from the ranks of the line division itself, not from the staff divisions. This reflected MC's basic attitude that thorough familiarity with the nature of a specific business area was a prerequisite to effective administration of policies.

Domestic and Overseas Offices

About 3500 managerial and staff personnel worked in the Tokyo headquarters, assigned directly to the line and staff divisions. Additionally, more than 2800 managers and staff members, almost 1000 of them overseas, were assigned to the network of domestic and overseas offices. Almost 3400 nonrotating employees also worked in the overseas offices. Officially, the reporting lines for those working in offices went through the head of the office directly to the managing directors. But in practice, most of those stationed in an office continued to work on the same area of products or staff functions as in their home division in Tokyo, and expected to return to the same division.

The largest branches and subsidiaries, such as those in Osaka and Nagoya in Japan, or London, New York, and Sao Paulo, mirrored the structure of headquarters, with department-level units corresponding to the product divisions and section-level units handling the actual operations. Smaller offices would contain only sections to handle the various lines of business, while in the smallest representative offices, a few managers would have to cover the interests of several divisions. Many of the smallest offices had their business concentrated on one or a few commodities, such as nickel in New Caledonia or liquid natural gas in Brunei. But service in these smaller outposts was regarded as a broadening experience, bringing a manager into contact with a wider range of products, clients, and other units of the firm than would otherwise be possible in the course of a career.

Legal Status

While all domestic branches were legally part of the Mitsubishi Corporation itself, the overseas offices were divided into two groups: direct arms of the Japanese parent corporation and subsidiaries incorporated under the laws of the host country. The reasons for choosing one form over another were complex; various host countries imposed different regulations, restrictions, conditions, and taxes on direct branches as opposed to subsidiaries. Generally, however, host countries were more restrictive toward direct branches than toward local subsidiaries, even though subsidiaries often had obligations as local "citizens." Managing director Minagawa explained:

> Fundamentally, Mitsubishi Corporation is a *Japanese* company, inextricably tied to the Japanese business community. But an overseas subsidiary is a local entity, and must respond to the host country's national interests and the local community. If and when there's a conflict, we have to meet and work out an arrangement.

In only 12 overseas locations, but including such major centers as London and Singapore, were direct arms of MC considered full-status branches, permitted by local authorities to engage in a broad range of commercial activity. These 12 locales were regarded as profit centers. The other approximately 80 directly controlled arms were restricted in their activity by local authorities in important ways, and therefore were treated as cost centers, supporting the profit-making activities of other parts of the firm. These locations were assigned one of four official classifications, reflecting both the degree of commercial activity permitted and MC's expectations. Some locations were project offices, expected to be closed when a construction project or major deal was concluded, while others were limited to an information-providing and -disseminating role by local authorities; still others could negotiate, but not sign agreements.

All but 4 of the 28 overseas trading subsidiaries were wholly owned. In the other cases, local regulations made it advantageous to include local partners in the equity ownership. The subsidiaries generally enjoyed the same commercial freedoms, rights, and obligations as indigenously owned corporations, and were therefore treated as profit centers. Some subsidiaries, such as Mitsubishi International Corporation (MIC) in the United States, Mitsubishi Canada, Ltd., Mitsubishi Corporation de Brasil S.A., and Mitsubishi Australia, Ltd., maintained sizeable branch networks of their own and had sales in the billions of dollars. MIC alone had annual sales of $14 billion, and offices in 15 U.S. cities.

Officials at MC indicated a rising trend in the restrictions placed on both direct branches and subsidiaries. In many locations, the nature of a *sogo shosha* was poorly understood, and local officials were anxious to limit their activity to very specific types of functions. In countries with high unemployment, especially in Latin America, the composition of the work force was mandated by regulation. In Colombia, 90 percent of the employees had to be local citizens, while the figure was 85 percent in Chile and 75 percent in Venezuela. Salary distributions were also restricted. Peru required 80 percent of the payroll to go to Peruvians, and Brazil required 67 percent to be distributed to its citizens. Other restrictions affected the direction of trade. Some countries restricted or prohibited imports, while others insisted that trade could only be with Japan. MC officials indicated that the trend toward restrictiveness, though not fatal, was a major problem.

Other Incorporated Entities: Subsidiaries and Affiliates

In addition to the overseas subsidiaries conducting trade on the model of the parent, MC had also made investments in a wide range of other firms in both Japan and overseas. In some investments, MC owned a controlling interest; in others, its equity stake was more limited. Most of these firms performed specialized manufacturing or service operations that were part of an industrial or commercial sector in which MC had extensive dealings. Loading docks, warehouses, and manufacturing plants were all examples of the types of investments made by MC. For instance, the network of steel service centers established by MC within Japan and overseas enabled the corporation to earn profits while keeping on top of market developments and expanding its influence within the steel business in Japan.

All *sogo shosha* maintained similar networks of subsidiaries and affiliates, and these investments were a major competitive factor among them. One firm's investment in a particular operation could give it a significant advantage in capturing new business from major clients. The identities and amounts of investments could provide an important clue about the future strategy at the firms. For this reason, the exact figures regarding MC's investments were highly confidential. However, a company spokesperson commented that these subsidiaries and affiliates numbered "a few hundred," with more than half located in Japan. The equity investments were "several hundred million dollars," but this was supplemented with loans, credits, guarantees, and other financial involvements, increasing at-risk capital to several times this figure.

Most of these firms dealt with MC on virtually a daily basis, as they performed their roles in MC's overall sectoral activity. On a transaction level, the firms were well-integrated into MC's daily operations. But they also kept their own corporate identities, including their own employment practices, labor forces, and wage structures. Compared with MC, their organizations were relatively simple, performing well-defined functions in only a few locales and dealing with a more limited range of products. The total work force of these subsidiaries and affiliates consisted of about 100,000 people since, unlike MC, they often employed substantial numbers of blue-collar workers.

Each year, MC dispatched members of its own managerial staff to occupy key positions in subsidiaries and affiliates. At any one time, a few hundred MC staffers were on temporary leave, usually for a rotation of 3 to 5 years. Following this, they would normally return to their respective division in which they had previously worked. Some MC staffers, however, either stayed on in permanent managerial roles or else returned to a subsidiary following their retirement from the ranks of MC itself. In these cases, they formally left the ranks of the MC organization and were considered to be employees of the subsidiary. In one division, for example, about half of the retirees since 1970 were at work in these related companies.

Recruiting Systems

As in virtually all major Japanese companies, MC employees were recruited with the expectation that they would spend their entire careers with the firm. With few exceptions, the company hired only new graduates of universities in Japan. In recruiting, competition was very keen both among companies and students. MC was in the fortunate position of being one of the most sought-after employers in Japan. Opinion surveys of university seniors recently revealed that MC was ranked highest among the top 10 Japanese firms as a place to work. Consequently, it had instituted a careful elimination process in its recruiting procedures.

MC did not recruit for specific managerial positions, nor did students look for a position that offered a specific type of job. Generally, Japanese students were interested more in a company as a whole than a specific job, since lifetime service was their aim. Everyone entering the company did so as an employee of the firm as a whole. Only after an elaborate entrance ceremony on April 1 of each year did recruits receive an assignment to a particular position in one of the divisions. Every year divisions forecasted their own work force needs and channeled them to the managing directors' meetings. The managing directors amalgamated these needs, determined the number of recruits to be hired, and allocated slots to the various divisions. These slots were then filled with individual recruits after the hiring decisions had been made. At both the divisional and corporate levels, it was recognized that permanent employment meant that the firm could not radically increase or decrease its intake of personnel according to current business conditions. The firm had to plan to have a sufficient number of people to staff its top levels in the long run.

About 150–200 graduates were recruited each year. Each spring students graduating the following March began visiting major firms for informal discussions. Starting on October 1 of each year, at least 2000 seniors took part in recruiting interviews, which were the first step in MC's elimination process. To alleviate the problems of both students and companies caused by starting recruitment activities too early, the Ministry of Labor together with specialists from academic circles and the companies set down the following policy:

> Only students graduating next spring are able to contact companies after October 1 of the previous year and the employment contract must be made after November 1.

Therefore, in early October, the first round of interviews at MC was held. These were conducted by MC staff members who had worked in the firm for around 10 years, and who knew exactly what type of people were needed in their divisions.

Based on these preliminary interviews, about half the applicants were invited for a second round, which was conducted by specialists from the personnel department who were familiar with the general quality of the examination and who were able to compare current interviewees with those of previous years. About half of this group would be invited for the third round of interviews, which was conducted by a group generally consisting of a section manager, one or two general managers of departments, and a director. Finally, successful applicants had to be approved by all members including those of different age generations and ranks. Thus, MC's recruitment was not only the job of the personnel staff but also of all company members who would eventually guide the new recruits directly.

Because of the concept of lifetime service, the company's criterion for selection was also neither specialized knowledge nor the particular skills of the applicant. At all interviews, the qualities sought after were energy or vitality, intelligence, cooperativeness (the ability to work well with others), and the potential for developing into a capable business person. Managers also stressed that a good fit with the corporate culture was very important. In general, this stressed professionalism, cooperation, entrepreneurship, and the ability to take action. Beyond these factors, the company sought a wide variety of personality types, intending to achieve a balance among scholarly and athletic types, or physical science and humanities majors, for instance. Hiring decisions were announced in early November. Following this, a manager from corporate personnel was assigned to interview each recruit and find an appropriate initial position. Then, on April 1, the assignments would be announced after each person had formally entered the firm.

Rank and Reward

Simultaneous entry into the firm in April was important, since seniority was the major determinant of career progress and reward, at least into the latter half of a managerial career at Mitsubishi. An elaborate system of formal ranks existed (see Exhibit 6). Each new graduate entered the firm at D class. After 4 years, promotion was automatic to the C-3 class on April 1. Four years later, the C-2 class was reached. After another 3 years, C-1 class was automatically attained. After another 3 years, promotion to the B-3 class was possible, but automatic promotions ceased. In fact, only a tiny percentage were promoted to B-3 after only 3 years. Most waited at least a few more years. Some staff members reaching the mandatory retirement age of 58 did so at the rank of C-1, although most made it to the B class by retirement. Promotion beyond this level was regarded as recognition of superior management achievement and capacity.

For ranks above the B-1 level minimum ages existed, constraining the speed of promotion. For example, by the mid-forties the fastest-rising manager could potentially reach the rank of B-1. The youngest directors were in their mid-fifties. Promotion to the rank of director allowed one to retire at age 62, instead of age 58, the mandatory retirement age for lower levels. Higher ranks were allowed to retire even later. According to Toshiro Fukui of the personnel planning team, only a small percentage of managers ever achieved the rank of *sanyo,* or senior general manager, while for the rank of director the gates were even narrower. Only 2–4 people from a typical entering class of 150–200 would make it.

Individual salaries were calculated according to a formula based solely on rank and age. During the years of automatic promotion, these two criteria were directly linked. As age rose, however, the rank became more important in determining salary. Finally, at the age of 50, no further incremental salary increases were given due to age alone. The company had recently announced its intention of ending age-related salary increases in the mid-forties in several years.

Exact salary levels were confidential, but it was indicated that starting salaries were 121,000 yen (approximately $600) per month for a 22-year-old in 1980. If the

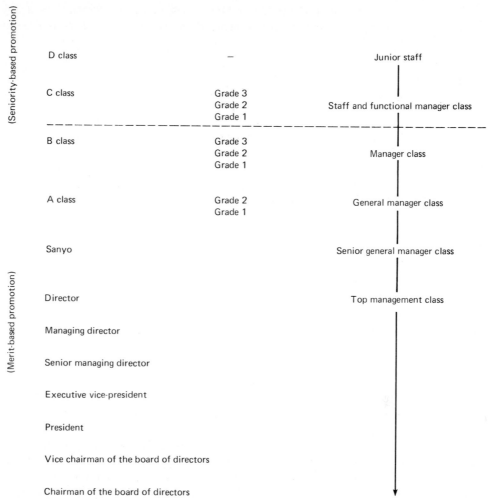

(Seniority-based promotion)			
D class	–		Junior staff
C class	Grade 3		
	Grade 2		Staff and functional manager class
	Grade 1		
B class	Grade 3		
	Grade 2		Manager class
	Grade 1		
A class	Grade 2		General manager class
	Grade 1		
Sanyo			Senior general manager class
Director			Top management class
Managing director			
Senior managing director			
Executive vice-president			
President			
Vice chairman of the board of directors			
Chairman of the board of directors			
(Merit-based promotion)			

EXHIBIT 6   Mitsubishi Corporation—rank system.

same staff member's salary a year later were taken as a baseline of 100, then a 30-year-old employee at rank C-2 would receive about 180 percent; a 38-year-old at rank B-3 would receive 250 percent, and a 49-year-old manager at A-1 would receive 350 percent. The salary differential between the lower ranking (C-1) and higher ranking (B-1) 45-year-old employee was 20 percent. In addition to the monthly salary, a bonus system existed at Mitsubishi, as in most Japanese companies.

Rank was linked to actual job titles in only a loose way. Not all managers attaining the B category were actually given the title of section manager or team leader. In fact, approximately 3000 people were in or above the B ranks, while only 2300 positions equivalent to section manager or team leader existed in the corporation. Thus, many were still acting as ordinary section or team members, despite their rank.

With the average age of MC managers and staff members at 39½ years and rising, there was considerable pressure on the upper levels of the hierarchy. According to Mr. Fukui:

> Our organization is no longer shaped like a pyramid, it's a diamond. B and above rankings now account for 46 percent of our managerial and staff members, and we fully expect it to reach 50 percent. Because we recruited very large classes of 250 or more during the 1960 era of high growth, we now have the inevitable demographic consequences to face.

The number of managers above the B rank was much smaller, since promotion to its levels was kept selective. The A class (general manager) contained only 200 persons, for instance. At the top, there were 4 executive vice presidents, about 20 managing directors, and 20 directors. All members of the board were full-time MC executives with ongoing management responsibilities. The only exception was two outside directors.

Rotation and Evaluation

The corporate personnel officials established guidelines and procedures for promotion, rotation, and evaluation of managers and staff members. But for all managers and staff members below the general managers, the actual implementation was left to the personnel officers of the line divisions. As a policy, all managers and staff members were required to rotate to a new work unit at least three times during their first 14 years in the company. Thereafter, rotations occurred as needed, but generally could be expected every several years.

Each product division created its own rotation patterns, based on the key product, functional, geographic, and client relationships in its business area. Some managers and staff members were rotated over a relatively wide range of work units related to a division's charter, becoming "generalists" whose experience, personal contacts, and perspectives bridged major interdependencies. Others were posted so as to develop in-depth expertise on particularly crucial areas of concern. These "specialists" could be grounded in technological, financial, geographic, or specific client-related expertise, for example. Obtaining the correct mix of experience, and matching these patterns to the capabilities, needs, and desires of the managers whose careers were developing was a formidable challenge to divisional management. Divisions formally planned rotations and registered the plans with corporate personnel. Actual transfers could take place at any time.

Using forms and procedures laid down by corporate personnel, the divisions also had responsibility for performance appraisal. Two different evaluations existed: one for short-term performance and one for long-term developmental potential. The key figure in carrying out these evaluations was the departmental general manager, who made a first stage appraisal, drawing on various data. Other superiors, such as a section manager, would then make more detailed appraisals. Once every 2 years, each manager and staff member was asked to write a detailed personal expectation of one's future career. This then formed the basis for an interview with the general manager, who would add comments.

Corporate personnel established a percentage for each age group that could be promoted in a given year. The promotion decisions were left to each division. Each division formed a personnel appraisal committee of from 5 to 10 managers at the general manager level. One-third of the membership in these committees was rotated each year. Rotation and promotion decisions for those at and above the general manager level were the province of the managing directors' meeting, as were overseas office general managers, and most of the deputy general manager appointments.

Training

A wide variety of educational programs existed for MC managers and staff members. After an initial corporate orientation, divisions conducted their own training courses for their assigned recruits. But on-the-job training was the fundamental philosophy of the corporation. Learning by doing while calling on colleagues for help as needed was the pattern. Each recruit was also assigned a colleague with a few years' seniority to act as counselor and overseer of development. A range of formal courses was offered by a corporate staff unit for managers and staff members at various stages of their careers. After a few years on the job, staff members were also eligible to apply for company sponsorship of overseas study. Each year MC sent several young staff members to study for MBAs and other graduate degrees at Harvard, Stanford, and other leading U.S. business schools. Higher-level managers were regularly sent overseas for advanced management training.

Planning and Control

The planning system at Mitsubishi combined both a "bottom-up" and a "top-down" approach. Formal planning made by the presidential board extended 3 years into the future, but annual revisions were made to the forecasts for each of the 3 years. The sections compiled these on a physical volume and monetary turnover basis. These were submitted to the department general managers, who held meetings with all the section managers under them. As a result of those discussions, revisions were made, and each department constructed an aggregate plan. Then, the departmental general managers submitted their plans to the managing directors of each division, and the same process was followed to produce aggregate plans of each division. Finally, the divisional plans were submitted to the president for analysis and discussion among the presidential board. Comments and revisions were made. The final decision of the board was then passed down the hierarchy, so that each unit could adjust its plans in line with the decision from top management.

The contribution of top management was intended to be strategic and macro in its thrust. One executive commented:

> We can readily determine what our expenses will be for the coming year for salaries, investments, and financial charges. Then we need to set goals that aren't too conservative and safe.

Another executive commented that top management, with its global and multidivisional perspective, was able to identify large-scale trends and opportunities, and had to guide the lower levels toward their pursuit. Both executives agreed that the actual formation and execution of plans had to be left to the operating levels. Managers at all levels stressed, however, that in addition to this formal planning exercise there was constant ongoing interchange, both horizontally and vertically. Section managers in a department, general managers in a division, and the managing directors held regular meetings for horizontal coordination, while a constant stream of formal and informal meetings between superiors and subordinates reinforced vertical coordination and control.

At the product division level, departmental results were reviewed and the immediate year's plans revised six times each year. All sections' results were reviewed by departmental general managers on a bimonthly basis, in addition to the informal daily monitoring of office floor operations.

Each product division had its own accounting staff and practices, reflecting the very different needs and practices of the business sectors they served. A corporate general accounting staff existed to maintain a common set of basic practices, and to integrate corporate financial data.

Because of the nature of its business, transactions frequently involved the efforts of more than one section, department, or product division, muddying the principle of profit-center accounting. Kenichiro Yamamoto, managing director and head of the nonferrous metals division, provided an example at the divisional level:

> For a large desalination project in the Middle East that requires a lot of copper and nickel metals as its main raw materials, we sell copper and nickel metals to a fabricator in Japan who produces cupro nickel tubes, and we supply such tubes to plant fabricators such as Mitsubishi Heavy Industries, which builds the desalination plant. Then, we sell it to the Middle East.
>
> The ability to simultaneously coordinate all of these transactions is at the heart of our commercial capability. To begin with, we give our cooperation to the machinery division by offering competitive prices for the main raw materials of copper and nickel, which enables them to become a successful contractor in the project.
>
> Then, if the machinery division sold the plant for the higher price, it would get the bigger commission. In a case like this, the heads of the two divisions would meet and try to divide fairly the whole revenue for MC following the principle of matching the contribution made to the success of the effort.

When, through the effort of one organizational unit another unit was able to add a customer, product, or market resulting in a continuing income stream, it was possible to agree to split the resulting revenue between the two units, to reward the business-generating unit. Unit A might agree to assign to unit B 30 percent of its commissions on sales to customer X, which B had developed. There were frequently such negotiations to allocate income to match contribution.

While one corporate accounting manager reported that such negotiations were often spirited, this tendency was somewhat balanced by several factors: the corporatewide stress on working for long-term common goals; the emphasis on leveraging existing business into new business involving other parts of the firm; and weight given to qualitative consensus-based evaluation of unit performance, over and above simple profit performance. One staff manager commented:

> While we look like a profit center organization on paper, in fact we're closer to an informal qualitative evaluation system in practice.

MANAGERIAL DEVELOPMENT

Several managing directors, with both line and staff responsibilities, expressed their concerns about developing future managerial resources. Yamamoto, the head of the nonferrous metals division, stated:

> Getting my people to work well is the most important job I have. Since we handle international commodities in the nonferrous metals division, we have to inculcate in them the sense to handle markets. We have to cultivate them to become internationally minded men. We have to create commodity (especially international commodity) professionals who have a deep technical knowledge and broad experience. And we have to have regional specialists who can cope with the intricacies of dealing with various countries.
>
> The person who can manage the people in addition to all these requirements is qualified to become top management. But there are only a few such slots available. (Not only in our company but in all companies over the world.) A real problem for me and for the company as a whole is how to maintain motivation in the face of this. We have to somehow infuse the spirit that they can find significance to their lives through their work. People have to take pride in the things which they accomplish on the job.

Hideo Mabuchi, managing director in charge of personnel, expressed a similar concern:

> The *sogo shosha's* biggest asset is the people who are working in it. It is not a manufacturer with production plants and facilities. We have to be able to create the ability to develop a wide range of business with the people we have. Therefore, we are constantly investing in our employees to upgrade their abilities so they can handle or create any business.
>
> One of the best ways to develop their abilities is to let them have the responsibility of running a domestic or overseas office. There, you can look across divisional boundaries and develop your general management capability. At the same time, we have to take care to develop the skills and careers of our nonrotating overseas staffs.

MANAGERIAL ROLES IN THE COPPER BUSINESS

MC's involvement in the copper business contained many elements common to most of the industrial sectors in which it operated. Several managers at various levels of the hierarchy commented on the business, their roles, and a current project with strategic importance. Yamamoto commented:

> I have to establish basic policy and manage mainly the strategic direction of our efforts. In our division, we have "old" metals, such as copper, lead, tin, and zinc, that are tied to heavy industry and whose consumption is growing slowly but steadily. Then we have "new" metals, such as aluminum, whose applications and consumption are increasing. Nickel lies somewhere between these two groups. Finally, we have silicon, titanium, and germanium, which are even newer metals, called rare metals, which will grow dramatically, finding new uses.

We have to balance our efforts among these, and we need three pillars supporting a broad business base to maintain and develop our current position of strength in the field of nonferrous metal industries. Copper is one of three major pillars of our business.

We also have to take into account the future. The future of Japanese industry—what it will manufacture, and where, for instance—is one vital element. So is the continually evolving role of the *sogo shosha*. We must also be very responsive to the aspirations of the resource-producing LDCs, who want to add value to their products before they ship them overseas.

In copper, for instance, our whole business has changed dramatically, and it continues to change. There's now only one major copper mine left in Japan, though we were once an exporter. Since Japanese smelters, whose capacities are very modern and efficient, have been almost entirely reliant on imported copper concentrates for their raw materials, they have come to operate as so-called custom smelters.

Historically, we have four stages of involvement with the copper producers; the first is outright purchase of copper concentrates for Japanese smelters. The second is long-term purchase contract of copper concentrate as a result of our loans for mine development. The third is to make equity investment in mines in order to obtain necessary raw materials. The fourth stage is to become involved in mining, smelting, refining or other value-adding activities in the resource-producing countries themselves.

We are in the midst of a change of economic eras, in the copper business. Deals such as MC's recent agreement with Kennecott Copper are part of our response to this. . . . When I look back on my career at MC, the accomplishment of this Kennecott deal will be one of my major legacies for the future.

Kennecott Deal

The Kennecott deal involved a partnership between the two firms to own, operate, expand, and modernize Kennecott's Chino mine in New Mexico. Under the terms of the agreement, MC would put up $116 million in return for a one-third interest in the partnership. Additionally, MC would pay for one-third of the modernization cost, about $80 million according to estimates, while Kennecott would put up two-thirds, or $160 million. Following modernization, output was expected to increase 70 percent, to about 110,000 tons per year. MC intended to market this output globally, mainly in the U.S. market but also exporting to Japan primarily in times of tight supply.

Seiichi Masuda, general manager of the copper metal and ore department, explained the process by which this deal evolved:

About 10 years ago we launched a study team to recommend long-term strategy for the copper business. We knew that copper supplies were limited, while demand was growing slowly but steadily, between 2 and 3 percent a year. We had to somehow be certain that we could obtain a dependable supply for Japan in times of shortage.

We also wanted to be able to deal in third-country trade in copper. The long-term loans we'd traditionally extended to copper producers usually limited us to exporting only to Japan. We felt that our best opportunities lay in expanding our business beyond Japan, whose consumption was growing slowly.

The study team issued three reports over a 10-year period. During this period, its membership changed, but because we were all rotating within the same division, there was a continuity of thinking and commitment, regardless of the specific membership. Gradually, we narrowed our focus and our list of potential countries and partners, and a consensus emerged that we should approach Kennecott. We had been dealing with them regularly since before World War II, and are currently members of a consortium engaged in deep-sea mining of manganese nodules.

After repeated approaches from us through Mitsubishi International Corporation (MIC) in New York, Kennecott proposed the Chino mine venture to us. We went to the investment administration office to get their suggestion about whom to send to Kennecott to study this specific proposal. We ended up sending two teams in February 1980, one technical and one financial and legal, with eight people representing six departments and three engineers from Mitsubishi Metal Corporation. There were lots of things brought back by these teams that had to be studied carefully to determine whether Kennecott's proposal would really be beneficial to us. For such purpose, I had to ask general managers of various departments to provide specialists from their staffs to form a study team at a working level.

After selection of the team, I went to the personnel department to let them know that a new team had been created. We also formed a special "core" team here in the copper metal and ore department to monitor it closely, and a similar team was organized within MIC. Naturally, it was necessary to do a lot of consensus building before starting the project in a formal way. When it came time to start formally, Mr. Yamamoto, the division head, and I went before the project comprehensive policy committee to explain our ideas and answer questions. There were a lot of questions on which they asked further study. The above-mentioned core team, fully assisted by the interdepartmental team, tackled these questions, spending a lot of time and effort. On the basis of this team's work, Mr. Yamamoto wrote a letter to Kennecott, setting out the terms under which we would consider participating in the Chino venture. Then, we started the negotiation, and by May, we had exchanged memoranda on the project. Following the execution of the memoranda, we proceeded to the complicated negotiation of drafting up a formal contract, and in December 1980, we signed the contract.

This wasn't just my project. It involved the division head, top management, and other departments. The help of many was necessary, so I can't really take any credit. But I do feel satisfaction in the accomplishment of the deal, and in the smooth relations which were created among members of the teams. I take real pleasure in good planning and smooth operation of a complex project. Personally, I am 100 percent sure that this is a good project, but we won't know for another 10 years.

Three Section Managers

Hidemitsu Haebara, manager of the crude copper and scrap section, described his section and role:

Even when they are buying on long-term contracts, our clients want a lot of aftercare. But our commissions are paid on a net tonnage basis, and they haven't increased much over recent years. That's why we're thinking of moving away from a commission merchant basis to more of a risk-taking (which should be manageable) position. If we don't take this initiative, we won't survive.

A *sogo shosha's* functions are always changing. We have to stay at least one step ahead of our clients. That's why we have entered the London Metal Exchange with our 60 per-cent-owned subsidiary, Triland Metals. We're also trying to establish distribution channels overseas for various copper products, to be able to operate truly globally. MC used to be an organization mainly for Japan, which lacked resources.

Haebara continued:

There are a lot of different activities which make up the typical day of my section. First, we have a meeting of all the section staff members to review pending activities and try to create new business. Then we decide on which clients to visit, and whom to send. When there are important matters, we usually send at least two, to ensure against miscommunication and to obtain better information. We keep in touch with clients' plans so that we can anticipate in advance what their requirements are. Often we have to get an overseas offer for them even before they request us for it.

A lot of the kind of information we need comes out of casual conversations with them. When we're not involved in budgeting or writing reports or urgent business, about 60 percent of our time is spent with clients. Face-to-face, you can pick up a lot, and figure out what's really on their minds. When I was stationed in the U.S., we seldom visited clients. Most business was done over the long-distance phone. Here in Tokyo, all our clients are pretty much in the same area, so we can meet them easily.

Haebara also remarked:

Young staff members don't start off by going to visit clients as a trader. They spend the first 2 or 3 years on delivery, meeting ships, handling loading and unloading. They have to learn how money flows along with the merchandise flows. They have to become familiar with invoices, letters of credit, and other documentation which are basic things in *sogo shosha*. Then, they can start visiting clients.

The managers handling trade don't actually book shipping space. That's the responsibility of the traffic department. They do the actual negotiations, since they have the market power of the entire firm. When we have a special problem, such as when the market for space is tight, we can go to them for special help. . . . They're not a profit center. Their evaluation is based on how well they cooperate with the line departments.

Tomofumi Nishimura was manager of the copper metal section:

Somehow I have to conduct discussions within my section in a way that we can agree on what direction to move. . . .I can leave most daily matters to my staff members. Therefore, my most important role as a manager—perhaps the only important one—I believe is to consider and decide which direction I should lead my section. We have to do a lot of consensus building. Many plans and proposals originate in the sections. Concrete actions are also carried out by sections. The role of those who are superior to me is more strategic and "spiritual" in nature—giving general directions, such as "Move away from commission merchant activity," or "Concentrate your activity on this."

It's my responsibility to enable section members to do good work. This means that I have to be knowledgeable about all aspects of their lives, and be close to them. I have to be aware of their physical condition, for example. Each day I look closely at their faces to see if they look tired, or if they're not in their best condition.

You have to give up your individuality somewhat in order to maintain good relations in this intense situation. The younger generation seems less willing to do this. It's not yet a major change—just a nuance. . . . We have a very powerful corporate culture here. People get more and more comfortable with our ways the longer they stay. It's really important to hire people who are flexible and who are able to immerse themselves in their work.

I think Japanese people are better at working in groups, even with people they don't necessarily like. Compared with Europe and the U.S., there's not as wide a range of variation among us. We also have a strong consciousness of MC as *my* company.

There's very broad sharing of information with all members of the section. We may go to a coffee shop during the day, or drink together after work to talk over all kinds of matters. Of course, we're all competitors for promotion in the long run, but we don't pay attention to this. People catch on quickly if you treat them as a competitor.

Nishimura also remarked:

We have a corporate policy of sending telexes overseas in English to enable our nonrotating staff members to know what's happening. But sometimes it's difficult for us to express ourselves in English, and we add Japanese at the end to make sure our meaning gets through. A fair number of Japanese language telexes also get sent out. But recently more young people are entering the company already having lived or traveled overseas. They seem to be able to use English pretty well.

Overall, communications with overseas offices is good, because we're dealing with individuals we already know very well. For instance, when I get a telex from the general manager of our nonferrous metals department in New York, I can well imagine what lies behind a simple-looking request. I worked with him for 7 or 8 years in Tokyo, and we had many long conversations together, often drinking until late at night.

Takesuke Miyoshi was manager of the copper ore section:

As far as the ore and concentrates business is concerned, our communication system has been pretty centralized. All telexes were directed to Tokyo, or at least a copy of them was sent to Tokyo, and from there they were routed to other offices, if required. This was merely because our main market for ore and concentrates was still Japanese smelters, and this fitted our needs. But since the 1970s we have been trying to broaden our markets not only in Japan but also overseas, and this trend has made communications more difficult and complicated. Apart from such commodities that would be sold by specification, there are always a lot of points and details to check and master in the ore and concentrates business. We'd like to build our capability of having overseas offices purchase and/or sell directly from and/or to third countries without going through Tokyo. But due to the nature of the business, it sometimes can be tricky, so we'd like to eliminate potential problems by centralizing communication.

Miyoshi also remarked:

I don't believe in giving direct instructions to section members, even if it causes problems. I want all members to develop their capabilities as managers by taking the initiative to figure things out. After awhile, you get to know who does what task in what way. The way of thinking in this section is to allow the greatest number of people to participate in decisionmaking in various aspects of our activities.

Two Young Section Members

Takuro Mochihara has worked 12 years at MC, including 4½ years in the Sydney, Australia office. He was currently working in the copper ore section. While growing up, he lived for 4 years in Los Angeles, where his father was posted by the Japanese government:

In Sydney, I was the only representative of nonferrous metals. For the first time, I was able to deal in commodities other than copper, and to learn about the exporting side of MC's operations. Organizationally, I was grouped with people handling coal and steel. In Japan, I'd never have an opportunity to work closely with people dealing in such relatively unrelated commodities. Because all of us shared the common experience of being expatriates together, we became quite close. Since then, I've kept up my ties with these colleagues. We go drinking or play mahjong together, all the while chatting about business, of course.

These contacts have been productive. As a result of them, for instance, I was able to introduce a manager selling tires to a mining project. Of course, in theory, I could have done that even if we hadn't worked together in Sydney. But in practice you naturally tend to pay attention to potential opportunities for the people you know. You think of them first.

Tetsuji Shibayama, who had joined MC 10 months earlier, was assigned to the copper metal section.

I wanted to join this company because I had studied international trade, concentrating on the factors affecting commodity markets. Japan must trade to survive, so I think this kind of work meets my interest and motivation.

Now, I'm living in a company-sponsored dormitory for single people. Actually, I don't eat there, or spend much time there, except sleeping, since my working hours are so long. But it has been possible for me to meet young people there from many parts of the company. Especially among those of us who joined the company last April, we can talk together easily and share our experiences.

An instructor was assigned to me when I entered this section. He explained things to me and answered my questions. At first, I was assigned a lot of clerical work with trade documents. Gradually, I've become able to assign this work to the clerical staff. When I'm asked to do something, I usually don't receive detailed instructions. It's up to me to understand the situation and ask questions or get help.

There's lots of routine work, but at least there's a wide variety of tasks. Even though our product range is quite limited, there are a lot of different functions involved in buying, selling, importing, and exporting.

MITSUBISHI CORPORATION (B): AMERICANIZATION AT MIC

Thomas Lifson

The problem with Americanization is that no one has really defined what it means. Some Japanese, as well as Americans, think that it means the taking over of the management of the company by Americans.

William Matsumoto
Director of Personnel
Mitsubishi International Corporation

Ichiro Komura leaned back in his office chair and reflected. His job as general manager of the general administration division at Mitsubishi International Corporation (MIC) in New York City usually left him precious little time for such activity. But by 8:30 p.m. on this Friday in the spring of 1981, most of his colleagues had gone home for the weekend, and the open-plan offices surrounding his desk were quiet. Instead of immediately tackling "Mount Fuji"—his subordinates' name for the daily accumulation of documents that came to his desk for review and approval—he decided to use the rare prospect of uninterrupted peace and quiet to begin the task assigned to him earlier in the day: preparation of a progress review and set of recommendations for MIC's Americanization program.

With annual sales of nearly $14 billion (see Exhibit 1 for financial statements), MIC was one of the three largest foreign-controlled corporations in the United States, and the largest Japanese operation in North America. It was a wholly owned subsidiary of Mitsubishi Corporation (MC) of Tokyo, the largest of Japan's *sogo shosha*.[1]

[1] For background, see Case 4: Mitsubishi Corporation (A).

EXHIBIT 1 STATEMENTS OF CONSOLIDATED INCOME, RETAINED EARNINGS, FINANCIAL POSITION, AND BALANCE SHEETS FOR YEARS ENDING MARCH 31, 1980 AND 1981

	1981	1980
Total trading transactions	$13,898,840,295	$11,258,165,098
Gross trading profit	$ 120,686,573	$ 112,154,511
Expenses		
Selling, general, and administrative	72,916,907	64,109,959
Interest (net)	6,463,959	19,956,829
Total	79,380,866	84,066,788
Equity in net income of affiliated companies	1,713,143	364
Income before taxes	43,018,850	28,088,087
Provision for taxes on income		
Federal and foreign	21,264,000	13,926,000
State and local	2,830,000	1,776,000
Total	24,094,000	15,702,000
Net income	18,924,850	12,386,087
Retained earnings at beginning of year	70,890,209	58,504,122
Stock dividend	(5,000,000)	
Retained earnings at end of year	$ 84,815,059	$ 70,890,209

Statements of changes in consolidated financial position

	1981	1980
Funds provided		
Net income	$ 18,924,850	$ 12,386,087
Charges (credits) to income not requiring funds— principally depreciation, amortization, equity in net income of affiliated companies, and minority interest	(2,658,947)	407,099
Total funds provided from operations	16,265,903	12,793,186
Increase in minority interest	22,786	4,920,000
Decrease in noncurrent advances, receivables, and other	8,550,253	
Increase in long-term liabilities		11,752,394
Other	108,240	
Total funds provided	24,947,182	29,465,580
Funds applied		
Increase in noncurrent advances, receivables, and other		14,926,628
Increase in investments	27,263,026	2,077,026
Increase in excess of cost over net assets acquired	39,622	1,518,982
Decrease in long-term liabilities	42,212,327	
Increase in property and equipment (net)	2,004,417	98,856
Total funds applied	71,519,392	18,621,492
Increase (decrease) in working capital	$ (46,572,210)	$ 10,844,088
Summary of changes in working capital		
Increase (decrease) in current assets		
Cash	$ (74,773,539)	$ 52,623,974
Marketable securities	(131,554,983)	94,550,929
Accounts and notes receivable	31,680,531	301,315,273
Merchandise inventory	(37,729,580)	(36,794,854)

EXHIBIT 1 **(continued)**

Statements of changes in consolidated financial position	1981	1980
Guaranty deposits and advances to suppliers	(2,645,982)	25,894,977
Prepaid expenses	(3,878,503)	(895,808)
Total	(218,902,036)	436,694,491
Increase (decrease) in current liabilities		
Loans and acceptances payable	(198,978,748)	237,652,410
Notes and accounts payable	27,657,577	187,927,040
Taxes withheld and accrued	(1,008,655)	270,953
Total	(172,329,826)	425,850,403
Increase (decrease) in working capital	$ (46,572,210)	$ 10,844,088

Assets

Current assets		
Cash (including time deposits of $26,600,000 in 1981 and $108,390,000 in 1980)	$ 39,488,251	$ 114,261,790
Marketable securities	60,220,469	191,775,452
Accounts and notes receivable		
Parent and its affiliated companies	481,984,761	423,506,304
Customers (after allowance for uncollectible accounts of $4,661,000 in 1981 and $4,085,000 in 1980)	756,959,451	777,000,975
Affiliated companies	9,599,201	16,491,203
Other	1,258,954	1,123,354
Merchandise inventory	179,901,632	217,631,212
Guaranty deposits and advances to suppliers	52,661,273	55,307,235
Prepaid expenses	3,640,104	7,518,607
Total current assets	1,585,714,096	1,804,616,132
Noncurrent advances, receivables, and other	43,464,446	54,214,699
Investments		
Investments in and advances to affiliated companies	74,182,433	45,308,113
Other investments	8,009,527	7,907,677
Total investments	82,191,960	53,215,790
Property and equipment	18,152,742	18,585,929
Excess of cost over net assets acquired	1,901,652	2,322,457
Total	$1,731,424,896	$1,932,955,007

Liabilities and stockholder's equity

Current liabilities		
Loans and acceptances payable (including commercial paper of $115,444,000 in 1981 and $157,607,000 in 1980)	$ 914,510,873	$1,113,489,621
Notes and accounts payable		
Trade creditors	480,909,134	453,180,654
Other	56,811,442	56,882,345
Taxes withheld and accrued	53,863	1,062,518
Total current liabilities	1,452,285,312	1,624,615,138

EXHIBIT 1 (continued)

Liabilities and stockholder's equity	1981	1980
Long-term liabilities	52,005,250	94,322,577
Minority interest	9,275	7,083
Stockholder's equity		
Capital stock without par value (authorized—700,000 shares; outstanding—602,500 shares in 1981 and 590,000 shares in 1980)	130,000,000	125,000,000
Retained earnings	84,815,059	70,890,209
Total stockholder's equity	214,815,059	195,890,209
Total	$1,731,424,896	$1,932,955,007

For the past several years, MIC had been struggling to adapt itself to two related imperatives: the need to generate additional business on its own, independent of the existing Japanese business base of its parent and the need to make MIC's organization more understandable and accessible to Americans while developing capable American staff to occupy important management positions in MIC. These two thrusts were together known as Americanization. During Komura's 3 years at MIC on his current rotation, he had committed himself deeply to the success of Americanization at MIC.

DEVELOPMENT OF MIC

Toshihiro Tomabechi, president of MIC, explained some of the problems and opportunities that lay behind the Americanization program:

> The basic circumstances of our business have changed in the last few years. Our exports from Japan to the United States can't really be expected to increase very much in the future. Import limitations have been imposed.
>
> In exporting from the United States, our principal business, such as grain, other farm products, coal, other raw materials, and technology exports will continue to increase. In fact, we expect major growth. But bilateral trade with Japan has its limits. So we want to export to other countries—third-country trade, as we call it—and get involved in the domestic American economy. My goal for the 1990s is to have our American-based trade, which now accounts for 15 percent of our volume, grow to a much larger share.
>
> Our Japanese staff is best at handling bilateral trade. They know Japan and Japanese markets. And they know and have extensive experience in dealing with the MC headquarters staff, whose active help is essential. But for third-country and domestic trade, we really need to have good American staff.

Yohei Mimura, the president of MC, and Tomabechi's immediate predecessor as president of MIC, shared this view and hoped that MIC could develop client relationships with U.S. firms comparable to those it enjoyed in Japan. Mimura stated:

In Japan, the integrated trading companies grew prominent by providing small, medium, and large enterprises with a sophisticated array of services. With more and more U.S. firms entering the world market, we feel that MIC, as both a *sogo shosha* and an American corporation, can play a similar role in this country.

But the achievement of this goal also raised problems. Bunichiro Tanabe, chairman of MC, cited the need to develop MIC's nonrotating staff:

> The biggest difficulty is in the area of personnel. You can't Americanize MIC's business unless you have the American staff to back that effort up. And that includes middle and top managers as well. I know it hasn't been easy until now, given the emphasis on Japan-related business and the Japanese style. It also doesn't help when people from here go out and take up an MIC assignment with the idea that they're going to a "branch office."

MIC was formed on July 1, 1954, the same date that Mitsubishi Corporation had been launched as a consolidation of more than 100 companies. Three of MC's constituent firms had by that date already established American offices, and these were combined and incorporated under U.S. laws as a subsidiary. MIC's early pioneers operated out of old and crowded offices in New York. Although these were often difficult times for Japan and MIC, several veterans of this era fondly recalled the cooperative spirit then. For instance, Mimura stated:

> Our American staff was more actively and responsibly involved in making the company go. We were smaller then and we had to depend on our American personnel to go out and obtain the crucial equipment and technology that we exported back to Japan.

As the Japanese economy recovered in the 1950s and began its intensive period of high growth in the 1960s and early 1970s, MIC also grew. Exhibit 2 lists data on MIC's current branch network. In most cities in which MIC opened branches, it was the first Japanese *sogo shosha* to do so, and it would usually be followed within a few months by the opening of offices of rival *sogo shosha*.

MIC's business growth reflected the development of the Japanese economy. As various Japanese industries, such as steel and shipbuilding, gained international competitiveness, MIC expanded its marketing capacity in the United States. The company also took an active role in licensing American technology and obtaining raw materials. But as the Japanese economy matured, wages rose, and the industrial structure shifted, an increasing portion of U.S.–Japanese trade was in products and channels handled directly by manufacturers. Mimura stated:

> This is going to reinforce our need to go beyond simple buying and selling and establish a distribution organization of our own. And this is where the efforts of our American staff are going to be so crucial. Because the age of "economic miracles" when anything and everything sold here as if by magic is well past.

Tomabechi, however, also saw new opportunities inherent in this evolutionary process:

> There's a set of basic forces which are acting to limit Japanese production in most of the basic industries: the maturing of the industries, companies, and facilities, and tight limits

EXHIBIT 2   MITSUBISHI INTERNATIONAL CORPORATION OFFICES

Office	Number of rotational staff	Number of local staff	Date established
New York headquarters	133	321	July 1954
San Francisco branch	9	37	July 1954
Los Angeles branch	28	69	May 1955
Seattle branch	9	26	May 1956
Portland branch	4	8	February 1958
Houston branch	17	32	July 1959
Chicago branch	18	84	March 1960
Detroit office	2	5	May 1970
Pittsburgh office	2	4	December 1971
Atlanta office	2	13	October 1972
Palo Alto office	0	1	July 1975
Denver office	1	2	July 1978
Philadelphia office	1	4	September 1979
St. Louis office	1	2	September 1980
Washington, D.C. representative office	3	5	March 1971

on land availability, and the high wages and costs in Japan. As a result, Japan has to go on to a new stage of integrated production on an international level.

One response of MIC to this set of changes was a program of investment in subsidiaries and affiliates in the United States. The experience, knowledge, and control over vital steps in multistage production processes obtained through these investments helped both MC and MIC play a larger role in the development of more complex international systems of production and distribution. For instance, one MIC affiliate in Oregon imported palm and coconut oils from Southeast Asia, and refined these for use in the American food-processing industry. Another potentially far more significant oil venture was MIC Petroleum, established in Houston in 1980 to participate in the petroleum industry in the United States and abroad. Along with acquisitions in refining and marketing, MIC Petroleum was undertaking oil exploration activity. Other MIC subsidiaries and affiliates did everything from finishing and warehousing steel to running export grain elevators.

The adaptation process underway required MIC to manage more complicated flows and interdependencies within itself and with other parts of the MC organization. For instance, when products exported from Japan lost their competitive edge in the United States, MIC would often turn to third-country suppliers or even domestic U.S. suppliers to fill the marketing channels it had established originally for Japanese exports. It might also help Japanese manufacturers to establish overseas procurement or production arrangements. As the business volume and reputation of MIC grew, it was able to do more things on its own, independent of MC. By 1979 MIC became the first Japanese subsidiary in America to be able to raise funds in the commercial paper market on its own, without a parent corporation guarantee. MIC enjoyed a AAA credit rating.

The keeping of trade accounts was an extremely complex matter due to multiple profit centers, foreign exchange complications, and the establishment of many special arrangements for particular clients or business lines. In principle, on deals involving other arms of MC as a buyer or seller, sharing of commissions or trading profits took place based on services and risks involved. But the increasing complexity of product and financial flows required much room for negotiation.

Because New York City was a financial center of the world and home to many multinational corporations, MIC often performed special services for other parts of MC. For example, complex, large-scale financing for overseas projects was arranged in New York City. Crude oil shipped from Saudi Arabia to MC in Japan could be paid for by MIC directly to an American oil company. Arrangements such as these in turn added layers of complexity to the interdependency of MIC and MC, and the keeping of accounts.

By 1981, MIC employed 848 persons, of whom 230 were Japanese rotational managers transferred by MC. Due to the size, importance, and scope of MIC operations, an overseas assignment in MIC had come to be regarded by some managers as highly desirable, if not essential, to a successful career path within MC. Most managers transferred to MIC came for a 5-year rotation, before returning to Japan or journeying to another overseas location. Seventy-five percent of the rotational managers came from the middle management ranks (B-1 to C-1; see Mitsubishi Corporation (A)).

THE COMING OF AMERICANIZATION

As MIC expanded into a large and successful organization, the development of a nonrotating staff was perceived by many to have received little attention. Komura explained:

> In an earlier era, with the heavy weight of our Japan-related business, the hiring of our nonrotating staffs was based on the assumption that most of the important work would be handled by the rotating staffs, and that we needed clerks and assistants to support them.

The first MIC official to openly challenge this state of affairs was Toshihiro Kido, president of MIC from 1971 to 1974. He was the first person at MIC to employ the term *Americanization*. Kido commented:

> To a considerable extent, the MIC that I came to in 1971 had its face turned to Japan. Because of this, I felt we were losing out on the vast opportunities that a country of this size and richness has to offer. I was convinced that a strong MIC, capable of moving from a more independent base in the United States and engaging in overseas transactions, would best be able to serve the interests of the parent company in Tokyo. It was then that we adopted the Americanization of MIC. The Americanization policy represented an abrupt departure from the past and it was not launched without its frictions and difficulties.

Kido aimed to increase MIC's involvement in the domestic U.S. market by establishing an extensive distribution network of its own, and by engaging in more direct investments to Americanize MIC, to make it truly self-supporting without much reliance on its parent company's business base. Kido's use of the term *Americanization* raised the hopes of many nonrotating members, while some rotating managers had difficulty understanding clearly the nature and extent of the changes contemplated.

But ultimately, the most important difficulty encountered was in the investment area. Independently of the divisional structure, MIC undertook a series of large real estate ventures in the United States. Unfortunately, in the economic downturn following the 1973 oil crisis, from which MC in Japan also suffered, many of these real estate ventures encountered difficulty. These circumstances caused Kido's successor to be primarily preoccupied with reestablishing a sound business basis for stable growth. Few immediate tangible changes in the situation of American staff members were realized. To many American staff members, this appeared to be rejection of all elements of Americanization. An American manager stated in 1981:

> Several years ago, Americanization fell flat on its face. Employees who have been here long remember this. The company has to really work to prove its sincerity this time around.

The fact that some of the investments made in the 1970s eventually turned out to be profitable reinforced the momentum of the long-term strategy of Americanization at MIC. Among those who took an interest in the formulation and implementation of a change strategy was Komura.

ICHIRO KOMURA

Komura joined MC in 1956 after graduation from one of Japan's leading universities with a major in law. His career path had included several posts relating to legal affairs. His first tour of duty in MIC began in 1962, when he spent 4½ years in New York helping to set up MIC's first legal affairs department.

Following this assignment, Komura returned to Japan to carry out duties in the personnel, labor relations, and corporate planning areas. After spending 2 years as an assistant to MC's president, he was asked in 1973 to attend a new executive education program that Harvard Business School was inaugurating in Europe. The international senior manager's program was an 8-week seminar for top-level executives in international business.

Komura then returned to Tokyo, where he was a section chief handling personnel administration and personnel development activities. During this period, he inaugurated a management education program to send several promising young MC managers each year to MBA programs at leading overseas graduate schools of business. As a result of MC's continued sponsorship of this program, the company now employed more Japanese MBA graduates than any other firm in Japan.

Komura's experiences had led him to a strong concern for the role of MC's overseas staff. He came to feel that the practice of using nonrotating staff members for support roles only was no longer viable. In his own words:

About in 1975, I began to feel that this simply couldn't go on. At my suggestion, after extensive discussions, we organized a 4-day seminar in Tokyo for local country employees, and later wrote a manual for our Japanese managers on what knowledge was needed to be able to work overseas: the dos and don'ts of being transferred overseas. I became more and more fascinated with this issue.

Then I transferred to New York. Before I arrived, I was aware that MIC President Mimura was concerned about these matters, because of internal memoranda he had sent to the personnel department in Tokyo. I had also known him very well from my first assignment in New York, when Mimura had been in charge of marine products.

When I arrived in New York in 1978, I had a series of meetings with the top executives to get their ideas and views on Americanization. Then, we set out a 3-year action plan, laying out what I thought we could accomplish. This plan considered what kind of company we want to become—a first-rate U.S. company, not just under the MC umbrella.

By spring 1981, it was time to consider where to focus future efforts, as well as to assess progress to date. Komura knew better than most that past accomplishments resulted from the efforts of many MIC members, in positions high and low. He also knew that not all employees of MIC were convinced that Americanization could succeed. But it was clear that MIC's formal organization had made some decisive changes.

MIC ORGANIZATION

Product Divisions

Similar to its parent, MIC's New York headquarters was divided into product divisions, which were profit centers formulating and implementing business strategies in their respective product areas. The volume and nature of MIC divisions varied— some were primarily import, some export, and others more than 50 percent third-country trade. (Exhibit 3 presents an organization chart for MIC.)

The heads of MIC divisions were known as *general managers,* the same title held by MC department chiefs. In general, however, the title a rotational manager held at MIC was higher than the original MC position the manager came from. This reflected MIC's smaller scope of operations. A 5-year rotation as a MIC divisional general manager offered many opportunities to demonstrate competence and vision. New York, in particular, and the United States, in general, were frequently regarded as "where the action is" in many of the globally traded commodities handled by MC divisions. For many MC divisions, the United States was a key customer, supplier, source of competition or technology, or listening post.

Network of Offices

MIC's branch network reported directly to its president, with the accounting and coordination divisions playing an intermediary role as the collector and organizer of monthly sales and profit data. There were three categories of outposts in the MIC system. The six earliest and largest branches, located in major port cities, were full-service branches, capable of buying, selling, financing, and providing a full range of

EXHIBIT 3 Mitsubishi International Corporation organization chart.

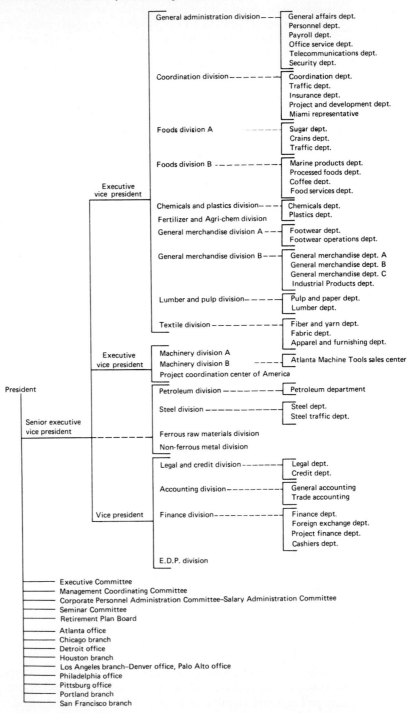

document-processing and support services. Branches contained sections corresponding to MIC New York product divisions. These branches and the sections within them operated as profit centers. The Washington, D.C. office had a special role as a listening post and source of information and advice. It did no trade and was a cost center. All other U.S. offices were considered *minibranches,* even though their official title was *office.* Some minibranches had begun as small, often single-person outposts, organizationally part of a larger branch in the same region. For example, the Detroit office was originally attached to the Chicago branch but was established independently to oversee business relationships with automotive and related industries around Detroit. In 1978, Mimura launched a program to reorganize and expand MIC's domestic network in accordance with the Americanization efforts. Existing offices had their status and role redefined as minibranches, while a series of new offices was opened. Komura explained the logic behind this program:

> The American market is wide and deep. MIC formerly was based on the waterfront: it was just oriented toward foreign trade. President Mimura wanted to enter the inland markets, to prove our reliability in daily transactions with a wide range of American companies. We want to enter into joint ventures, investments, plant construction, and many other activities not just dependent on foreign trade. We can build on the strengths of the Mitsubishi companies, Japanese industry, and our own financial ability and expertise. Partnership should be the basis of all this.

As minibranches, the offices also became profit centers, accountable for business results. On the organization chart, minibranches reported directly to the president. However, actual reporting took place through the coordination division. General managers of minibranches consulted with the coordination division from time to time about various operational matters. Rather than being assigned products and markets by headquarters' divisions, minibranches were free to develop their own business lines. Unlike full branches, minibranches were never divided into sections on the basis of MIC product divisions. Although individual traders in a minibranch could and did develop their own product specialization and expertise, their basic charter was to develop new business for MIC without the constraint of traders serving a particular divisional interest. The head of a minibranch was chosen by MIC's president from within his own organization on the basis of discussions with many others.

Minibranches did not include staff to handle the details of support work, such as accounting, invoicing, and customs clearance. For these services, a minibranch relied on New York headquarters. In return for providing these services, headquarters received a negotiated portion of the commission or trading profit earned by a minibranch on a business deal. Fee splitting and range of services provided could vary according to the particular circumstances. For example, when a minibranch began to service a client formerly developed and served by a more distant full branch, the fee split could result in 50 percent or more going to the full branch. But when minibranches developed their own clients and merely needed paperwork help, the fee could be considerably lower.

MIC top management had hoped to achieve geographic rationalization of customer service by locating minibranches closer to some existing inland customers. In practice, however, few traders were willing to assign "their" customers to someone in another office. Service to customers was a key competitive weapon, and personal relationship played a major role in providing this service. An easing of financing terms when a customer was in trouble, last-minute changes in delivery or shipping, and many other forms of service ultimately relied on judgment calls on the part of the trader as to the value of the customer, and the prospect of an ultimate return on the service investment. Traders might be willing to transfer their accounts to someone else in the *same* office, close enough for frequent consultation, information-sharing, and even joint visits when necessary. However, most strongly resisted transfer of accounts to another office, which would also, of course, take the sales and commission volume from the headquarters' accounts. As a result, in some product areas, MIC branches and minibranches had no absolute territories to call their own.

MIC top management knew that the challenge facing a new minibranch was a severe one. The low gross margin received by MIC and the impact of fee splitting required a large sales volume simply to support the overhead of a new office. In addition to the normal levels of overhead involved in running a regional outpost of a large and prestigious firm, the costs of assigning rotational Japanese mangers was higher than for locally hired personnel, due to cost-of-living adjustments and other expatriate allowances common to any multinational firm. Officials estimated that the average rotational manager in the United States cost the firm twice as much as the manager's salary in Japan. MIC top management firmly expected each minibranch to achieve profitability within just a few years and, before the 1978 launching of the minibranch program, two unprofitable offices, in Honolulu and New Orleans, were closed.

Personnel Systems

The Americanization program accelerated MIC's development of formal corporate policies and procedures. In some cases, its expatriate managers were handled in reference to MC personnel policies, while local staff were hired and managed strictly by local offices, with little effort made to coordinate practices among them, much less to contemplate the rotation of local staff among MIC offices. This had long been a source of frustration for Bill Matsumoto, MIC's personnel director since 1979. Matsumoto, a naturalized American citizen of Japanese descent, was educated primarily in the United States. He was hired by MIC in 1955 and worked in the general administration division throughout his career in MIC. When a comprehensive personnel manual was completed, Matsumoto had personally visited each MIC branch office to explain and promote it.

One significant part of this manual was a performance evaluation system. This required each employee to write his or her job description in which the main accountability factor was listed and agreed upon by the employee and his or her-supervisor and manager. Then, following a detailed format, each aspect of perform-ance was rated by the supervisor, with both sides being required to sign off. These performance evaluation procedures also required each MC general manager to add to his or her own rating, and append comments for each employee in the division. At first, intensive persuasion was necessary to get some Japanese managers to follow these procedures. Shigeru Iwashita, an MC rotational manager who, as head of MIC's personnel department, reported to Matsumoto, noted, "Some Japanese man-agers tend to avoid these discussions with Americans. It leaves them uncomfortable, and this leads to frustration and complaints by Americans." Still, although problems occurred, for many Americans it represented an opportunity to finally define their specific responsibility and authority and to obtain definitive feedback.

A related move was the installation of a formal system of job rating and reward, based on a consulting study by Hay Associates, a leading firm in the design of employment and compensation systems. MIC used the system to establish 20 job grades based on the number of Hay points, and to set salary levels for these grades. Performance ratings were reflected in a differential of up to plus or minus 20 percent, which could be given to high or low performers at a given job grade.

A small, but perhaps symbolically important step on January 1, 1979 began to change this pattern. On that date, MC and MIC activated a formal personnel ex-change agreement. According to this, all MC managers assigned to MIC were re-quired to formally resign from MC to accept a position with MIC. It was expected that they would regard their new assignment at MIC as different from being sent to overseas branch offices. Additionally, it was agreed that MIC and MC would each have the right to post their employees in each other's organization, following the principle that expatriates would receive the same employment conditions as locals, including base salary, as well as expatriate allowances to compensate for the special dislocations and expenses of service overseas.

With this agreement, the unification of MIC personnel systems could really begin to get underway. By April 1979, rotational managers were required to write their own job descriptions, so that they could be rated with Hay points. MC's support for this move was carefully cultivated. By 1981, the base salaries of rotational managers were officially being determined according to the same set of criteria as those of the American staff.

Use of the same performance appraisal forms (translated into Japanese) was also to be made mandatory on April 1, 1981. Recently, there had been discussion of the extent to which some form of management by objectives (MBO) might be applicable to MIC's situation. Some had suggested that, in place of individual goals and mea-sures, groups be given shared goals, against which all members collectively would be measured. This was being informally called *management by group objectives* (MBGO) within MIC.

In mid-1980, the first American MIC employee left for an assignment at MC headquarters. For Americans in Japan, just as for Japanese managers in the United States, need-based expatriate allowances were paid. The person chosen was an ac-counting specialist who was to work in the headquarters accounting operations.

Career Paths for Americans

To date, only a limited number of Americans occupied roles that could be considered truly managerial. Of those who did, most were located in staff, not line divisions. Komura knew that many factors lay behind this situation. One factor favoring staff promotion was the relatively fixed body of professional knowledge, often certified by a credential such as a law degree or CPA, which an American in a staff position could use as a basis of expertise. This knowledge, crucial for operating in the American business environment, was usually not fully shared by MC rotational staff. In line divisions, however, things were not so simple. Iwashita explained:

> The trading divisions will take longer to work on. Their clients may resist dealing directly with non-Japanese. As far as Japan-related business is concerned, it's hard for Americans to break in. To become a manager in a trading division requires tremendous experience, wide contacts, and the like. Also, in Japan there's no concept of the job slot. This makes it harder for Americans.

However, it was clear that Americanization of support staff functions alone would not be adequate. It was necessary to find ways to get good Americans into line positions to develop new business as well as their own careers. Iwashita described his approach:

> I've always got my antenna out listening for opportunities to create for Americans in trading. We're still in the period in which advancement opportunities have to be tailor-made. I have three lists in the back of my mind: one is the list of capable Americans who could replace Japanese traders or work effectively in Japan. Another list is of the Japanese traders who could work with and back up an American's efforts in MIC or MC. The third list consists of the specific needs and opportunities which develop out of our ever-changing business operations. I'm constantly searching for additions to this list and trying to match them to the other two lists.

The hundreds of Americans working for MIC represented a wide range of abilities, skills, experiences, and other personal characteristics. One general manager of a line division commented on MIC's nonrotating staff members:

> Roughly speaking, I think there are three generations of Americans working in MIC. The first have been here 20 years or more, from the time when New York was only a branch. Originally, they functioned as assistants. They're 45 years old or more, and have been very loyal. We must take care of them. The second group came later, and are mostly in their thirties. They have few educational credentials, but have made it to the assistant manager level. Many are quite ambitious. The third group has joined us quite recently. They are young and have good educational credentials.

Tomabechi addressed himself to the subject of recruitment:

> We're finding it easier to recruit highly qualified Americans. The American business perspective on Japan has been changing. But we also find that our name tends to be "overvalued" by Americans, since they confuse us with the entire Mitsubishi group of companies.

In the last 2 or 3 years, MIC has actively recruited a group of about 10 American MBAs from business schools, including Columbia, Wharton, and the Thunderbird

Graduate School of International Management. However, it was clear that the hiring of MBAs was not a panacea. Iwashita, who had himself received an MBA from Columbia as part of the overseas education program established by Komura, said:

> I have mixed feelings about the appropriateness of MBAs for us. For support divisions we can hire them and pay them higher salaries based on the expertise and assigned job content. But for trading divisions, so far it seems difficult. Some general managers don't want them and don't know how to use them. General managers think very carefully about how to balance their salary structure with that of other Americans. The MBAs have to start from scratch in this business, and they'll be compared with the experienced Americans. For example, both the chemicals division and the ferrous raw materials division wanted to hire an MBA. But they couldn't pay a high enough salary for fear that other non-MBA, but experienced, Americans would complain.

A related problem was the maintenance of comparability among salaries in the various MIC divisions. Several managers pointed out that MIC local staffers in divisions, such as chemicals and plastics, dealt in huge quantities, and thus interacted with relatively senior people in these well-paying industries. This tended to raise their expectations and perhaps create the possibility of their being lured from MIC by high salaries. But for MIC to meet their industry benchmark salary expectations would create severe problems of equity for comparable-level nonrotating staffers in divisions such as textiles, where outside contacts and opportunities were much more limited.

Management Education

Management education was a tool used by Komura for the Americanization program. Beginning in 1979, a week-long management development training seminar had been held two times a year. The design and teaching of the seminar was handled by a group of American business school professors who were experts on multinational corporations. Twenty-five to 30 MIC members of up to middle management level attended each session, with an approximately equal mix of rotational and nonrotational employees. The sessions were held in an isolated rural location, and the pace was kept extremely rigorous, concentrating on case studies in finance, marketing, strategy, and organizational behavior. A few cases based on MIC's own operations were included.

The response to these programs had been quite encouraging. Both nonrotational and rotational staff members found them demanding but rewarding. For case preparation, attendees were assigned to study groups that mixed nonrotational and rotational, line and staff, branch and headquarters, and experienced and new members together as a team. Although the content itself was important, Komura considered the opportunity for diverse MIC members to meet each other, share work together, and overcome difficult problems through joint effort as equally valuable. There was clear evidence that mutual understanding and respect had been augmented by these sessions.

The MIC management development seminar was the first of its kind in an overseas affiliate of MC, and had drawn attention from other affiliates as well as from Tokyo. The head of MC's management education operations had observed one entire week-long session in 1980. The session scheduled for the summer of 1981 was to be attended not only by MIC employees, but also by employees of MC affiliates in Europe, Latin America, Africa, and Australia, as well as by its Canadian organization.

MIC also launched a series of seminars for rotational managers. Komura commented:

> Most executive administration positions are still occupied by rotating personnel. They have an obligation to teach everything to the American staff. If they don't do that, nothing will happen. Therefore, we've started staff seminars to help the rotating staff understand the American environment, why we need Americanization, the U.S. law, American attitudes toward contracts, what points to be careful about, and various dos and don'ts.

Legal Considerations

One dimension of Americanization that could not be ignored was the possibility of legal or regulatory pressure on MIC. Equal Employment Opportunity laws were one factor. Thomas Tine, corporate counsel, commented:

> The personnel department takes EEO very seriously, and works hard at it. It may be a cultural problem, but the line departments seem to have little concern. I doubt it's a high priority on a day-to-day basis. If anything, they view it as part of a long-term plan.

Recently, MIC was experiencing increasing difficulty in obtaining visas for Japanese nationals to work in the United States. Matsumoto explained that the U.S. government was no longer automatically granting work visas on the basis of a company's desires. Instead, a firm was required to prove that the position in question could not be handled by an American. There was little if any recourse to these decisions. Given heightened American concerns about unemployment and trade deficits, there seemed little prospect that visa pressures would ease.

Tine explained that Japanese trading companies faced more problems than other firms:

> A Japanese manufacturing company can come over here, and the treaty (of Friendship, Commerce, and Navigation) would probably permit them the executives of their choice. Since a manufacturer doesn't need a large foreign executive staff relative to total personnel, very few problems would be presented. However, although a trading company is international, it largely serves the Japanese market. Fierce competition among them means they have to staff to best serve the Japanese manufacturers, and that means a large number of Japanese nationals in lower and middle management positions.

Comments from MIC Employees

A number of Japanse and American MIC members expressed their views on Americanization and other related concerns to the casewriter.

George Vogel had received an MBA from the Wharton School in 1979 at the age of 22 and immediately joined MIC, working in the coordination division. His interest in MIC had been sparked by his study on expanding Philadelphia's foreign trade, which had put him in contact with the recently opened MIC Philadelphia mini-branch. He commented:

As a staff member, you have to develop relationships with the Japanese line managers. They control business activities. You must demonstrate to them what you can do.

When you join this company, you have to break their stereotype of Americans. You have to show that you work just as hard and have just as much interest in the company as the rotating staff. You have to demonstrate to them that you can work at their level. You also have to show your willingness to take on responsibility. However, the rotating system means that after you get to know staff, they return to Tokyo. This can make it difficult to continually prove yourself, but it is helpful in that you get to know more people in Tokyo.

I can see a lot of changes toward Americanization—the movement is in the right direction. MIC will expand its role in the U.S., but it will take time.

Most MBAs learn specialized functions, such as finance, production, marketing, and other areas. Here, you learn to be a generalist in a Japanese system, which means you learn to do many things well. As you go higher, you get more responsibility at an earlier stage than in the American system.

There aren't many American companies where you can come up with *any* kind of project imaginable and the company will consider it. Responsibility here can be a large reward.

I want to get into a business division here, and learn the operations. Then I'd like to go to Japan and learn the operations there. It's important to work there with them on a daily basis to truly understand their situation, and for them to really know me. I'm now embarking on a career path plan.

I think the long-term financial reward here can be very good. One of my goals is to run a subsidiary. MIC would permit you to take responsibility for a subsidiary if you had the expertise and knew the MIC systems. Another goal is to run a branch office and attain a high-level position in the headquarters. The financial rewards in these cases will be competitive to U.S. companies. Someone who desires a large financial return can achieve it here if they are capable enough.

This is a frustrating and rewarding place to work. Talent is in demand. After you establish relationships and confidence, you can do a lot. Things are played by the rules—if you understand what the rules are. I'm always discovering what the rules are.

At 5:30, most of the Japanese staff stay and most of the American staff leave. I also always stay late.

Joseph Mathew joined MIC's chemicals and plastics division in 1972. His former employer, a large American chemical company, decided to relocate from New York to Houston, a move Mathew didn't wish to make. Mathew, who received a bachelor's degree in business administration in 1966, primarily marketed chemicals.

I didn't like the lack of communication, which prevailed in the early 1970s, so I started working with my boss. He suggested I approach our general manager, which I did. I told him he needed to write more memoranda explaining things to the Americans, to define job responsibilities, and to hold meetings as a division—and to include the American managers. The meetings were not successful. They would just go over the figures without reaching the substance. Then, people's schedules suddenly started having conflicts. Now, we're at the stage where we have to come up with *something*.

The American staff has started coming to me—I'm the go-between—to tell me things they couldn't say directly to a Japanese manager. Americanization has been a failure. It frightens the Japanese managers. They've been successful on the basis of the old rules. Americanization is so undefined, it's frightening to them. They have agreed to cooperate with it, but that's only superficial.

The main problem is the type of person sent over. Either they are flexible and understanding, or they are the type who don't feel any responsibility to the Americans. These types leave staff matters to personnel. I can't blame them; they're not prepared. They come here and they're just an extension of what they're doing in Japan.

Now, I've got a rotational manager working with me. He handles the Japan end of the deals I work on. My opinion was asked on whom to transfer into this position. (I had been to Japan three times, and knew quite a few people in the headquarters department.) The other Japanese agreed with my choice. But the general manager didn't. Still, we lobbied, and we got him to change his mind. He was flexible.

In my view, the type of Americans hired 15 years ago had a high school education, and could function very well in something like traffic management. They would be good at their job, but would have little potential for higher responsibility. But they stayed around, so they tended to get promoted. The Japanese managers would come over and feel superior to them, and judge all American staff by them.

It took me 5 years to make my first trip to Japan. My general manager wanted me to go sooner, but it was regarded as a reward. Now that has changed.

Japanese managers come here and live in Mamaroneck, Scarsdale, and a few other places. They work late, go out to bars together, and don't really get to know American society. They're just like Americans who work overseas.

American staff members love the freedom they have here. They can conduct their daily business any way they want. But they feel insecure. There's nobody telling them what to do. They need more structure.

I think there's hope, but we'll still lose good people because we're still learning. But there are some people in general administration, in personnel, and even in Tokyo who *understand*. I don't think we'll go back. We have EEO and the visa situation in our favor. They're committed to Americanization. They have to be.

Samuel Browning, an employee of the nonferrous metals division, joined MIC in 1957 after graduation from high school and 2 years of work in the chemical industry. He commented:

Every general manager that comes over wants to leave a mark to open up a new third-country trade, to provide service to metal clients, and to pursue and establish new ventures. There has to be an entity for younger, ambitious American managers to move up quickly into executive positions. But it will have to be non-Japan oriented. Some of us older people may sometimes feel threatened or envious. We worry about job security. Will we be pushed out? There's been an emphasis on bringing in outside people.

Shoji Yamamoto, general manager of the nonferrous metals division, was especially enthusiastic about building up MIC's own international, domestic, and third-country business base. While spending 7 years in London, Yamamoto had helped set up Triland Metals, MC's trading subsidiary, on the London Metal Exchange. In New

York, he had founded another subsidiary, Nonferrous International, which operated a domestic distribution network for fabricated copper components, and which flexibly sourced from domestic and overseas suppliers. Recently, his division had been very active in raw material procurement due to a pending joint mining venture between Kennecott Copper and MC. Yamamoto said:

> American top management comes to visit here, and we have to have good Americans who can deal with them. These people must be acceptable in the American business culture, and in the MC business culture. They can't really be successful without understanding our corporate philosophy. . . .
>
> We can't accept a higher turnover policy for Americans, even if it works in a business sense. Mitsubishi is an "establishment" company in Japan, and it just can't behave this way.
>
> You need to have complete confidence in your people in order to do business. We *could* send an American manager to work in Japan, in order to build personal credibility as a Mitsubishi person. If I can establish one case of a successful manager going to Japan, this could become a precedent. So, I'm looking for the proper situation, which I may have to create, to make a good opportunity for an American. . . . I've talked about these plans, and they have been accepted in principle by the personnel department in Japan.
>
> You need credibility and experience on a wide range of issues. For example, our Japanese clients come to us to ask us to get them a lower price when they're being hurt by market conditions. An American would tend to rely on a contract, and hold them to the price they agreed on before. The clients then wouldn't want to tell the details of the trouble to an American. A Japanese manager in the same situation would have a long background, and could make a decision on what to do on the basis of a very wide range of knowledge.
>
> One way to handle this is to spinoff the non-Japan–related business into subsidiaries, and maintain MIC for dealing with Japan-related trade. The spinoffs and MIC would need to coordinate their common resources and markets, and information and policy would have to be centralized. We'd have to be very careful to avoid conflicts. I've already made a list of issues which would require upper-level approval.

Daisuke Mizutani, general manager of the chemicals and plastics division, spoke on the training needed for MIC managers:

> We need to change the process of development of our human resources. Previously, the weight of Japanese trade in MIC's business could be covered by Japanese managers. But in the future there will be less weight to Japanese business. Our American-based business is growing, though it's still dominated by the Japan-based trade.
>
> On-the-job training is essential. In the chemical division, you need at least 8 to 10 years experience before you're ready to come to an office like New York. The range of experience offered here in New York is narrower than in Japan, so that the training you could get in Japan in 5 years would require 10 years here.
>
> In the future, I hope that we could hire and train managers for about 5 years, and then send them to Japan for further training. This could reduce the number of Japanese managers we need in New York. The big advantage of Americans is that they understand America. But they have to relate this to an understanding of Japan and the Japanese.

Eiji Kawaguchi, deputy general manager of the chemicals and plastics division, spoke on the difficulties he had experienced recently:

In the trading activity, it's very difficult for us to establish business in the United States, because American companies have no concept of the role of the *sogo shosha*. This limits our U.S. trading activity. Now, we're trying to invest in U.S. distribution facilities to establish a marketing capacity similar to that we have in Japan. The rising costs of chemical plant construction mean that even the largest companies are interested in joint ventures.

I have tried to hire a very impressive-seeming American with industry experience into this company. But in order to get people like that we have to pay much higher salaries than the other Americans here are making. The personnel department tried to cooperate to get this person, but we just couldn't obtain a consensus. Finally, we offered as much as we could, but he wouldn't accept.

We have to be able to do routine business as well as glamorous projects. Even I am sometimes responsible for very routine tasks. A highly skilled, professionally oriented American wouldn't tolerate some of the low-level tasks we need done.

Minibranch Perspectives: The View from Atlanta

The Atlanta minibranch was considered one of the most successful at developing both new business and new human resources. But its progress on these fronts had not come easily or quickly. Both MC and MIC had long enjoyed important business relationships with a few major corporations in the area, such as Coca-Cola. However, a large stream of new business volume was necessary to sustain profitable operations. The generation of trading income required the identification of new business opportunities, the careful cultivation of customers, and a thoroughgoing approach to the details of sales and service with large and small customers. Tadao Sato, manager of the Atlanta office, noted that this office had worked with import commodities as diverse as steel, reflective sheeting for highway signs, and canned goods, while developing exports such as broiler chickens, peanuts, and aluminum scrap. His progress in the aluminum scrap business represented well his type of approach.

Sato's previous assignment was in the Los Angeles branch, which was then exporting monthly two or so containers of aluminum scrap from the southeastern United States to Japan. Using his extensive network of friends in the Los Angeles branch, Sato was able to win the rights to handle these exports, even though there was some friendly joking about stealing business. Sato asked an American staff member, recruited locally in the Atlanta area, to develop sources of new supply, as well as to cultivate existing aluminum scrap dealers. A key issue in this business was agreeing on quality standards (no other metals or materials were to be mixed with the aluminum) and handling claims for damages when standards were violated. By visiting scrap dealers, maintaining regular telephone contact, and paying diligent attention to details, the nonrotating staff members were able to build up a very healthy and profitable volume. Both the Los Angeles office and the nonferrous metals division in Japan had made favorable comments on Atlanta's performance.

One feature of Atlanta's approach was delegation of tasks to others for training and development. Once the first American started in the aluminum scrap field, others were brought in to handle some of the duties as business volume grew. The small size of the office, as well as the open atmosphere encouraged by Sato, meant that people were generally aware of how a member's time or talents were utilized. The lack of any formal divisional structure meant that one person could have the freedom to take on aluminum scrap, even if peanuts were his or her primary commodity at the moment.

The experience of Veronica Washington was typical. She was one of several members of the Atlanta office who had progressed upward through a series of jobs.

> At first, I came here to work at night as a telex operator, while I studied at college during the day. Then, I moved to a job as a telephone operator and receptionist, still working in general affairs. I had a lot of spare time, so I would ask people for work to do. Then, I was able to begin buying aluminum scrap over the telephone for shipment to Japan. I'd previously worked in the traffic department at another company, so I was somewhat familiar with shipping and other things related to this work.
>
> I like the strictness, the detail orientation, and the emphasis on quality over quantity here. They're willing to actually distribute the workload according to what a person can handle. Responsibility makes me feel good. The background to all of this is the pride they have in their work.
>
> In my previous work, they would not put me in a management position, with limited college and being a woman. I don't feel any of that here. I've been given some responsibilities that frighten me. I just pinch my nose and jump in. They know their people very well here. They know when to give responsibility. They go by your abilities, whereas most companies don't. No company's ever gone by my ability. The more I accomplish, the more they give me. If you make a mistake, they will shake their finger in your face, but they don't keep it pointing at you.

Fred Guenther was another member of the Atlanta office who had been recognized as having made great career progress. He described his experiences:

> After a BA and 3 years in the Navy, I wanted something better to do, so I decided to go to grad school. I got an MBA at Georgia State, with an emphasis on international business. During the last quarter MIC was looking to hire someone. I was attracted by the idea of hands-on experience in international business, so I thought I'd take a chance. I wasn't hard-core on the money issue; the money offered wasn't great.
>
> My first assignment was to go out and develop a market for reflective sheeting—the kind used on highway signs. It was a matter of getting out and calling on governments, getting listed on bids, getting state labs to test and approve our product. It took time, but we got the business. I got the feel of putting together Japanese suppliers and American customers, and got to know how this Japanese supplier worked.
>
> One manager taught me how to write cables and telexes to Tokyo—how to get their interest and show them we're doing something for them. Each office tends to be its own fiefdom. Sometimes you have to scream and shout.
>
> We're doing a lot of exports now. We've got peanuts going from Georgia to Japan and Asia, and have worked up a poultry export business. MC is the largest poultry processor in Japan, through a subsidiary. We had to work hard to get U.S. suppliers to meet their specifications on quality and meat cutting, and to establish reliable logistics. We also had to work hard to get the Japanese guys to give us a try. We sent a couple of containers and got a lot of grumbling about packing and quality, so we tried a few other suppliers.
>
> After about 6 months of this work, I went to Japan and got to know the people there handling this business. It didn't resolve any of the problems, but the nice thing about a trading company is that everyone is looking down the road to the long-run profit. After

awhile, people wanted to do business with us. We learned how to do the job better, so things got easier.

You have to have persistence and patience, and love challenge. In this company you can't look for immediate gratification and a pat on the back. But when you do succeed, it feels awfully good.

Because markets are always changing, you're always pulling new ideas out of the file. If something wasn't moving you could always work on something else. If someone were evaluating you for profit on every item, you would feel different. But as long as you were creating something new and expanding, you got a good evaluation.

Guenther received much attention within MIC when he transferred from Atlanta to the New York headquarters. His move, which was encouraged by Sato, marked a milestone; he was the first local staff member to be assigned explicitly to a job to replace a rotating manager returning to Japan. He compared his experiences in Atlanta and New York:

The Atlanta office was free-wheeling; you do your own thing. Everybody comunicated on the same level. We had the same orientation. We looked for people with a spark in their eye to want to work on their own. People were basically similar. We worked as equals. Here [in New York], you don't get that many opportunities to interact. You're so busy during the day. Everything in the company passes through here. You don't have time to communicate well.

You have to be willing to make sacrifices to do well here. You have to subject personal feelings, or the desire to do things the American way, to the way the company does things. You have to get a handle on the way things *are* done. When I understand them, maybe I'll want to change them. But at first I accept things as they are. Japanese are picky about some small things; they like to cross the t's and dot the i's. It's made me a more careful and patient person.

The Japanese are going down the same road as U.S. and European multinationals. I feel really on the ground floor here. In 5½ years I've visited virtually every MIC office. I know who the competition is. I've got a loyalty streak in me. I've gotten offers from other companies, but I've felt, "Why take a chance when they might not be in it for the long haul?"

Mitsubishi is just in the process of getting in gear with Americanization. It will be a long road and tough. But we found in Atlanta (I hope it spreads) that if you look for motivated self-starters, they can go to explore horizons they never dreamed of.

I'm convinced that my job here in New York will give me the background and confidence in the nitty-gritty and in the risk factors. If I can get hold of these, I'd have a good chance at being general manager of Atlanta or another smaller office.

To replace Guenther in Atlanta, an arrangement new to MIC was decided upon: teaming newly hired American MBA talent with an MC rotational manager who had received an American MBA degree under MC's overseas education program. Sato explained:

When President Mimura was head of MIC, he proposed sending recent Japanese MBA graduates to U.S. offices, where they would tie together with an American MBA. The first one chosen was Makoto Asakura. We recruited an American MBA to work with him, after Fred Guenther had been transferred to New York. Makoto was told *not* to do creative business development by himself, but to transfer expertise. After an 18-month period, I'll make preliminary comments on his performance, and Mr. Komura in New York will make the final evaluation. Asakura will be required to make a report at that time, too, covering his experience, his directions, and his thoughts about Americanization.

Samuel Patrick, an MBA from Georgia State with business experience in a large American multinational manufacturer, was hired as the result of a search in the Atlanta area. Several people, including Iwashita of personnel in New York, Sato, and Asakura, were involved in interviewing candidates and making the hiring decision. Patrick commented on his reactions to working at MIC.

> The typical young American is very competitive. They want to get ahead quickly. You have to sit back and be patient. That's the hardest thing to learn. The management system is inhibiting. The tendency of the Japanese is to watch you closely. Americans would rather do than learn. I have that tendency.
>
> For Japanese, their loyalty is to the company. The company is their family. It's hard to adapt to those standards, when there's a basic philosophy of life difference. An American company wants loyalty, too. But only a degree. They expect an employee to look elsewhere when not working up to full capacity.
>
> Their profit policy is very frustrating. Japanese see a typical local business as being greedy. They work slowly and methodically on a long-term basis. Profit is not the number one priority. They want to keep their resources employed, first of all.
>
> Makoto Asakura thinks I'm fighting him, sometimes. Actually, I'm fighting the 27 years of education and growing up in the United States. . . . It's tough. . . .
>
> There's not much the company can do to make this learning process easier. Only one thing: explain their exact policies on Americanization—what they expect. At this point, there are so few people, it's experimental.

Asakura joined MC in 1968, and worked several years in the Seattle and Vancouver offices of MIC and Mitsubishi Canada, Ltd. before being sent to Stanford Business School for MBA study in 1978. He offered his views on business in Japan and the United States:

> I feel I'm able to use my MBA training better in Atlanta than I would in Tokyo. In a *sogo shosha* it's hard to sum up things by the numbers. There are so many different factors to consider. It may take 3 years to get a big order. How do you evaluate people in the meantime? We want people to work for their long-run potential—not just for immediate sales. Many aspects of work, human relations, even filing are important. You have to be an all-around player.
>
> In Japan, because of lifetime employment and the guaranteed prestige, livelihood, and social status, people at MC understand without being told where their future lies. But in the United States and Canada, people need more assurance around promotion and salaries. They always want to know, "If I do *this*, will I be given *that*?" A lot of Japanese assume Americans think the same way they do, so they don't explain or offer assurances. Americans are concerned about the details of pay and promotion. They want it to be explicit and on paper.
>
> In my own training, I made some mistakes which cost the company money. But each mistake allowed me to learn a lot. The accumulation of mistakes was the best training I got. When you make a decision and it ends up costing the company money, you feel "I shouldn't make the same mistake, and should work harder to make up the loss."

> I feel we need some compromise between the Japanese and American systems here. We are asking too much of the Americans to just adapt to our way. Our time frame is too short.

Referring to his work with Patrick, Asakura stated:

> I told him, "An MBA is just a ticket to join us. Once you join, everyone is treated equally." At first I gave him really standard business transactions, like opening letters of credit, and expanded from there to customer inquiries, sending telexes, negotiating with suppliers— price, delivery, sales contracts, shipping, etc. Sometimes it takes too long to get a response from Tokyo and he gets frustrated. I have to explain, "Look, we're waiting for another company to decide."
>
> I keep pushing him to create *new* business, to go out and meet the customers. I have to explain why some business is straightforward and other business is not. It's very hard to get him to understand that profit can come at various stages. So I explain why we want the profit to go to some other office, that we're not just evaluated on our short-term profit. In a way, we're tickling his pride, telling him that we expect him to become an overall manager, not just in charge of this profit or that profit.

Commenting on the division of labor between rotational and nonrotational staff, as well as on the course he hoped for Atlanta to follow, Sato said:

> I believe our Japanese sales staff are having a hard time to sell to local small companies, since you need to be able to talk "nitty-gritty" to them to tie to the sales.
>
> A variety of assignments will be given to American staff in both soft goods and hard goods, and their success will be examined. This kind of tryout is possible only in a small office. Our office in Atlanta now has 15 members. I fear we're beginning to get some of these large office problems. When I moved to this office almost 4 years ago, there were five people. Should we stay as a "family-style office" or should we grow in the direction of a complicated organization?

Two Views of Americans

Hiroshi Nakano, of nonferrous metals, was assigned to work in the 80-percent-owned subsidiary Nonferrous International, engaged in the distribution of copper components. He offered a sports analogy for the American and Japanese management styles:

> Communication among American managers reminds me of American football. Americans seem to need decisions or descriptions from supervisors, then they can work effectively together. It's basically a division of labor between the doers and planners.
>
> The Japanese style is more like soccer. There is a baseline of consensus about what a group should do, and the group works as a whole, with each player sensing what to do. The function of the leader is to make sure that the baseline is accepted and understood by the group.
>
> I find that having partitioned offices in NFI is very strange. You can't look in on people to keep in touch.
>
> Now, we're in the midst of trying to change things, trying to make a new style of management, neither Japanese nor American.

Hideo Murai, general manager of the coordination division, offered this view on Americans and MIC:

Americans have a sense of specialization. They want to divide their work precisely, and to understand the function of each and every person or unit precisely. This can't be done in the present MIC: Japanese-style management usually requires more generalization rather than specialization. This requirement applies even to the really good Americans who have a fast mind and considerable maturity.

I think the solution is twofold. MIC requires a marriage of functionalization and generalization. MIC operations themselves must become more functionalized to take advantage of specialized skills while still developing some generalized staff required to control and develop MIC's overall operations. These generalists will require a similar rotating career path as the Japanese staff in Japan. This rotation may even take 10 to 20 years, but must be done.

Komura's Situation

Komura had discussed Americanization with many members of MIC and MC. As a result, he knew that many different opinions existed as to its nature, importance, and timing. He was confident of the support of top management even though he realized that there might well be differences among individuals regarding specific policies or programs he might recommend as the next stage. He knew that whatever plan of action he might recommend, he would have to balance the needs, feelings, and ideas of many groups within the firm and its various external constituencies.

Komura was willing to consider a wide range of options in devising organizational tools to help MIC reach its goals. Throughout his career, he had never shied away from attempting the difficult or controversial. But he also knew that Americanization policies would require not just acceptance, but enthusiastic support if MIC were to realize its goal of creating a new type of management system: one that would combine the best energies and talents of both Americans and Japanese.

Although it was possible for a manager of his age and rank to remain in MIC longer than the normal 5-year rotation period, Komura hoped to return to Japan in another 2 years, assured that he had established an enduring framework that would provide the necessary momentum to carry Americanization through to a successful conclusion. If Americanization succeeded, MIC and MC would gain an important advantage over their Japanese rivals and would open up great possibilities of new business development in the American and international environments. But there were many risks to be considered as well. A *sogo shosha* had to live in a world of low margins, high risk, and fast change. Its major weapons for survival were flexibility and creativity, which its Japanese-style management system had fostered. If this system were jeopardized, then the very survival of MIC might even be imperiled in the future. It was important to protect and build on MIC's and MC's existing strengths, not to undermine them, in proposing any package of organizational change. Komura hoped to outline just such a package, and present it to MIC top management within a short time.

As he packed his attache case with documents to review during the weekend and put on his coat to catch a local train to Hartsdale, he thought to himself, "Everyone is watching MIC's performance on this, so we have to do it successfully. We can't fail."

CORNING GLASS WORKS (A): ELECTRONIC PRODUCTS DIVISION

Michael Beer

In July 1968 Don Rogers, vice president and general manager of the electronic products division (EPD) of Corning Glass Works, met with Corning's director of organization development at his request. He began the discussion by reflecting on the state of his organization.

> I asked you to get together with me so that I could discuss a serious problem. We have had some difficult times in my division over the past 2 years. [See Exhibit 1 for operating data on the electronic products division.] Sales have been down due to the general economy and its effects on the electronic industry. But our problems are greater than that. Our business is becoming fiercely competitive. To deal with the downturn in business, we have reduced the number of people and expenses sharply. This has been painful, but I think these actions have stemmed the tide. We are in control again. But business continues to be very competitive, morale is low, and there is a lot of conflict between groups that we can't seem to resolve. There is a lack of mutual confidence and trust. The organization is just not pulling together and the lack of coordination is affecting our ability to develop new products. Most of my key people believe that we are having conflicts because business is bad. They say that if business would only get better we will stop crabbing at each other. Frankly, I am not sure if they are right. The conflicts might be due to the pressures we are under but more likely they indicate a more fundamental problem. Can you and your group determine if the conflict between groups is serious and if so what I might do about it?

THE LARGER CORPORATION

Corning's Business

The electronic products division was one of eight line divisions in Corning Glass Works. (See Exhibit 2). Corning was recognized as a leading manufacturer of spe-

EXHIBIT 1 SALES AND OPERATING MARGIN (IN THOUSANDS OF DOLLARS), OF THE ELECTRONIC PRODUCTS DIVISION, 1961–1968

	1961	1962	1963	1964	1965	1966	1967	1968
Sales	12,723	21,745	22,836	20,036	25,320	26,553	23,852	24,034
Operating margin*	3,011	5,449	5,826	2,998	5,075	4,170	1,559	1,574

* Operating margin equals sales less manufacturing, administrative, and sales expenses.

cialty glass. Its growth and reputation were based on a strong technological capability in the invention and manufacture of glass products. This technological capability was supported by a technical staff division that conducted basic and applied, as well as product and process, research in glass and related technologies. The company had been the first to establish an industrial laboratory in the early 1900s. By 1968 its investment in R&D as a percentage of sales was quite significant compared to other companies in the industry. Company growth, which had averaged 10 percent yearly over the previous 10 years, was based on its capacity to invest new glass products that had a technological distinctiveness or capability that its competitors' products lacked. Many of these products were invented in response to a request from original equipment manufacturers (OEMs) who wanted Corning to apply its research and development strength to meet their needs. The technological edge was not limited to its product capabilities since it also had strength in manufacturing. Thus, Corning was in the unique position of growing profitably without substantial competitive pressures. Patents, technological expertise in manufacturing, and the requirement of substantial capital investment prevented other firms from posing serious threats.

Corning's R&D capability led to major businesses in the manufacture of glass envelopes[1] for incandescent lamps and television tubes. Other businesses included glass lenses for optical and ophthalmic use, laboratory glassware, refractories for glass and steel furnaces, and many other specialty glass items sold to a wide variety of industries in a wide variety of markets. A major exception to its OEM business was its position in the manufacture and sale of household consumer products for use in the kitchen. Pyrex pie plates were an early entry into this business, followed in the 1950s by the development of Corning Ware (heat-resistant cook-and-serve ovenware) and Centura (break-resistant tableware).

Corning's unique technological strengths resulted in very profitable growth for the firm from 1948 to 1967, even though this growth was uneven due to a dependence on invention in the laboratory. In 1968 Corning was in a strong financial and profit position. (See Exhibit 3 for its financial history.)

Operation of the Corporation

The trend of growth through technological breakthrough led to a number of distinct

[1] *Glass envelopes* are glass bulbs that encapsulate the electrical wiring and filaments that make up an electric light bulb or television tube.

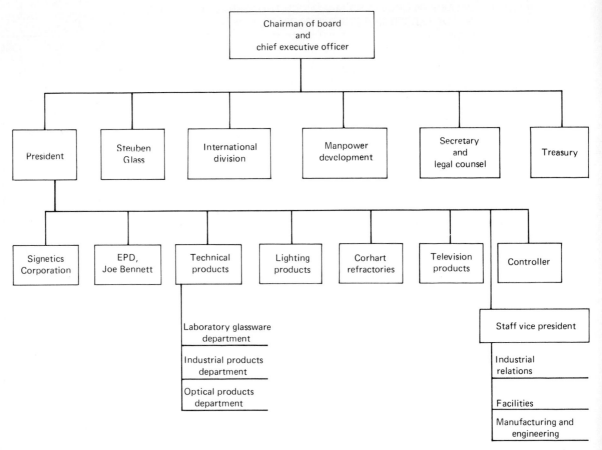

EXHIBIT 2 Corning Glass Works—organization chart

corporate characteristics. The technical staff division (R&D) was regarded as very important by top management. Its vice president reported directly to the chairperson of the board. Next to R&D, Corning's strongest functional area was manufacturing. Many of the company's top executives had been promoted from the manufacturing ranks, and it was widely regarded as the function through which one could advance to the top. To complement a strong manufacturing orientation, the company had developed a control system in which plants were viewed as profit centers. Thus, bottom-line results were measured by gross margin (plant sales less cost of manufacture) at the plant level and operating margin (total gross margin less selling and administrative expenses) at the divisional level. Financial results were reported every 28 days and were reviewed 13 times a year. These period reviews were conducted at all levels of the corporation.

The nature of Corning's business called for most divisions to maintain relatively small sales departments in which a few salespeople would service key accounts.

EXHIBIT 3 FINANCIAL HISTORY OF CORNING GLASS WORKS, 1959–1968

Consolidated statement of income*	1968	1967	1966	1965	1964	1963	1962	1961	1960	1959
Net sales	$479,089	$455,220	$444,139	$340,471	$327,612	$289,217	$262,200	$229,569	$214,871	$201,370
Dividends, interest, and other income	17,733	15,639	15,404	12,489	10,093	10,554	9,593	8,835	10,160	8,071
	496,822	470,859	459,543	352,960	337,705	299,771	271,793	238,404	225,031	209,441
Cost and expenses										
Cost of sales	335,957	310,798	291,669	237,048	229,432	199,211	184,100	160,773	158,293	138,128
Selling, general, and administrative expenses	67,251	63,253	61,172	45,612	44,525	40,012	35,088	28,972	25,538	25,380
Interest, state income taxes, and other charges	8,961	9,210	6,333	2,622	1,505	1,708	1,408	1,243	1,119	1,297
U.S. and foreign income taxes	37,886	37,779	47,195	28,989	27,221	27,264	23,100	21,490	18,026	20,300
	450,055	421,040	405,369	314,271	302,683	268,195	243,696	212,478	202,976	185,105
Net income	$ 46,767	$ 49,819	$ 54,174	$ 38,689†	$ 35,022	$ 31,576	$ 28,097	$ 25,926	$ 22,055†	$ 24,336

* All figures in thousands.
† Exclusive of nonrecurring net gain of $1,279,499 in 1965 and net loss of $2,334,024 in 1960 on contribution and sales, respectively, of investments in associated companies.

Because there were only a few key customers, virtually all the information needed by a division about its markets could be obtained by these salespeople, who maintained close relations with their customers. Thus, many divisions had limited marketing efforts. Major sales transactions between Corning and its customers were conducted at high levels of the Corning organization, since major investments were often involved for Corning. Similarly, decisions about new products were also made at a high level in the division or the corporation.

Corning Glass Works was established in Corning, N.Y. in the mid-1800s. For many years its entire operations were based in Corning. However, as the company grew, plants and sales offices were located throughout the country. In 1968 most of its 40 plants were located east of the Mississippi River. Headquarters for all but two of its divisions were located in Corning. Therefore, for most divisions, business problems could be discussed on a face-to-face basis. People from the several divisions saw each other frequently on Corning's premises, on the streets of Corning, and on social occasions. In a sense, the corporation operated like a relatively close-knit family. People at all levels and from diverse parts of the corporation interacted informally. Even top officers were addressed on a first-name basis. It would not be uncommon for top-level corporate officers to meet divisional personnel in the main office building and to informally discuss the state of their business—asking about orders, shipments, sales, and profits for the period.

HISTORY OF THE ELECTRONIC PRODUCTS DIVISION

The Business

The electronic products division (EPD) manufactured passive components[2] for several markets. More than half of EPD's sales in 1968 were OEMs who bought resistors and capacitors in large volume for use in a variety of their products. The remainder of the division's sales were to distributors, who resold the components in smaller quantities.

Much like other Corning businesses, the components business grew based upon Corning's distinct capabilities in glass, which when used as a substrate[3] gave the components desirable electrical qualities. Corning's knowledge base allowed it to develop and manufacture highly reliable components for the military market. The growth of the space program and the growing reliance in defense on missiles in the late 1950s and early 1960s demanded components that had a low probability of failure to ensure the integrity of very sophisticated and expensive systems. The government customer, however, was willing to pay premium prices for components that met its very strict specifications. In response to market demands, EPD expanded its plant operations in Bradford, Pa. and, in the early 1960s, built a new plant in Raleigh, N.C. Bradford manufactured resistors and Raleigh produced capacitors.

---

[2] A *passive component* is a device used in electrical circuitry that does not perform an electrical function by itself but acts upon or modifies an external electrical signal.

[3] A *substrate* is the material (such as carbon or glass) on which various coatings are deposited to make a resistor or capacitor of given electrical quality.

In the early 1960s the nature of EPD's business began to shift. As the military market leveled off, new commercial markets were developing and growing and EPD concentrated more of its efforts in these. For example, color television was emerging as a significant market and color sets required a larger number of components with more stringent specifications than those for black and white televisions. The growth of the data processing industry also provided a new market for EPD components. EPD, using its distinct technological capabilities in product development and manufacturing, was able to enter these new markets and quickly establish a major position in them. In 1965 EPD built a plant in Wilmington, N.C. to supply high-volume demands in the consumer electronics and data processing markets. By 1968, 60 percent of EPD's sales were to the data processing, consumer electronics (primarily television), and telecommunication (telephone) markets.

Between 1966 and 1968 the needs of commercial customers for low-cost components resulted in increased and often fierce competition among a number of firms. As companies competed for large-volume contracts from major OEMs, prices fell severely with resultant pressure on costs. It often appeared that EPD was in a commodity business.

In addition, there was continual pressure on component manufacturers for extensions of existing product lines as OEMs developed new end-use products for their growing markets. Thus, in addition to the price competition for large contracts, there was a need to respond to customers with new products that met their distinct specifications. A component manufacturer could not bid on a contract until the product had passed tests conducted in its and the customer's laboratory. Often it was also necessary to meet military specifications since commercial customers sometimes ordered against these specifications.

EPD's response to customer needs with new products was necessary because new products commanded higher prices in their early stages of development and thereby offered an opportunity for growth. As the technology of integrated circuits was introduced in the early 1960s, top management in EPD feared that the total volume of components sold would decline, making an increase in market share mandatory for survival. EPD's poor performance in 1967 and 1968 was a reflection of a major shakeout in the electronic components industry, compounded by a weakening of demand. A large number of component manufacturers were competing for what they perceived to be a declining total market in the future. Competition was on price, but quality and service were also important. Customers were giving special consideration to manufacturers that could ensure short delivery lead times (usually no more than 4 weeks) while manufacturing operations depended on long lead times. Stricter quality standards were also being demanded because poor quality often could shut down an OEM production operation.

The intense competitive pressures within a declining economy came at the time the Wilmington plant was completed in 1965. The future looked bleak indeed and some managers in EPD wondered whether the division would survive and, if so, whether it could meet Corning's high expectations for profitability and growth.

Management History

Before 1966 EPD was headed by Joe Bennett. Bennett had been in charge of the division in its infancy and nutured it into a significant business for Corning. He was an entrepreneur who was always seeking to get EPD into new businesses. Recognizing the importance of the new integrated circuit technology in the early 1960s and its threat to the passive components business, Bennett prevailed on Corning to purchase Signetics Corporation, a small company that was on the forefront of the new integrated circuits technology. Similarly, EPD had started a major effort to develop a new product and market using microcircuit technology—a technology that bridged both passive components and integrated circuits, and offered opportunities for further growth.

Scott Allen, the division's controller until 1966, described the division's strengths by pointing at Bennett.

> We always try new things. We always experiment. We set a fast pace. There is a feeling of urgency and commitment and dissatisfaction with the status quo. As an example, we are 1½ steps ahead in computer applications. This stems from Bennett and the dynamic industry we are in.

The entrepreneurial spirit, the desire to grow, and the spirit of experimentation fostered by Bennett created an air of excitement and anticipation about the future. People talked about growth and opportunity being "around the corner." These expectations were not always met. Signetics had been acquired but was operating as a separate organizational entity, resulting in relatively few promotional opportunities for EPD personnel. An even greater disappointment was the microcircuit project. It had been dropped as a failure after large sums of money were spent in its development.

Joe Bennett

Joe Bennett, who was 48 years old in 1966, was a large man with a quick and creative mind who ran the division almost single-handedly. Many key decisions were made by him, but none were made without consulting him and gaining his approval. People respected yet also feared him.

Tom Reed, product development manager for capacitors and the new microcircuit project, described Bennett and his style:

> Joe is very authoritarian with me and others. As a result, those working for Bennett who are most successful are political and manipulative.
>
> People around here do not extend themselves very much to disagree with Bennett. The way to disagree with him is in a manipulative way. If he wants something done, tell him you'll do it and carry it out immediately. Then, after a period of time go back to him and tell him that following through on his suggestion is going to cost us X number of dollars and we could make more the other way; but if he still wants to do it his way, it will be done.
>
> Bennett has a significant impact on our organization with all of us reflecting him in our managerial styles. We are all more authoritarian than before. I am less willing to let my

people make mistakes even though I think it is important that people learn from their mistakes. The pressure and unrealistic standards are transmitted down to people throughout the organization. This results in our commitments often being unrealistic.

There is little group activity and decisionmaking by the top team except where there is a specific problem. It is not a natural group. We are never together. I don't think we have been together, except at formal managers' meetings, once in the last 3 months or so. There is no cohesiveness in the group reporting to Bennett.

Bennett was a man of paradoxes. Although he was widely recognized as being extremely directive in his management style, he also had an intense interest in the behavioral sciences and their applications to management. He was widely read in the field. Mark Bell, Corning's industrial psychologist, claimed that Bennett was better read in the field than himself. In addition to reading, Bennett also attended a number of sensitivity training sessions in which participants spent a week in an unstructured group learning about themselves through the eyes of others.

Participation in the Managerial Grid Program

Bennett's interest in the behavioral sciences stimulated a number of attempts to apply behavioral sciences to management within the division. In 1965 EPD undertook a divisionwide management and organization development program called the *managerial grid*.[4] The program was to include an examination of individual management styles, group effectiveness, intergroup relations, and organizationwide problems. In all phases, action plans for improvement were to be developed.

The grid program was to have spanned a 3-year period. It was discontinued after Bennett's untimely death from cancer. Dr. Don Rogers, a director in Corning's technical staff division took over as vice president and division manager. Upon taking over the division, he asked for and received a report on the current state of the managerial grid in EPD. The report indicated that the grid had had a positive impact on the division but that phase III, which dealt with improvement of intergroup relations, was yet to come but was particularly needed.

In light of business difficulties and his relative newness in the division, Rogers decided to discontinue the program.

THE EPD IN 1968

Division Manager

The promotion of Rogers to vice president was considered unusual given his lack of line experience. However, his knowledge and background were relevant to EPD's business and he had a number of qualities that indicated his potential for a top management position.

---

[4] For more information on the managerial grid, see R. R. Blake and J. S. Mouton, *The Managerial Grid*, Gulf Publishing, Houston, 1964; and *Corporate Excellence through Grid Organization Development*, Gulf Publishing, Houston, 1968.

As director of physical research, Rogers had responsibility for all R&D work performed by the technical staffs in support of EPD's business. He was therefore knowledgeable about EPD's technology. He often sat in on many EPD meetings and had a general knowledge of their business. He had even served as a member of the board of Signetics.

Rogers also had considerable personal assets. He was very bright and a quick thinker. EPD managers were impressed with his capacity to grasp a wide variety of complex problems ranging from technical to managerial. He was always very pleasant and friendly and was able to get people to be open with him. This openness was stimulated by his readiness to share information and his own thoughts. In fact, he often surprised people with the things he was willing to reveal and discuss. He also involved people in problems and consulted them on decisions.

Despite these very positive attributes and managers' genuine liking and respect for Rogers, people did have some criticisms of him. His personality and his superior intellectual capabilities almost always assured that he was a dominant force in meetings. There were also some questions about how much confrontation Rogers did or tolerated, or how much leadership he took in difficult situations. Managers' comments about Rogers included:

He does not listen too well. His interruptions of others prevent him from sharing others' opinions and make it seem as if he really does not want criticism. What's more he has been too soft on me. He should be holding me to my goals. I have not met some of these goals and he should be climbing all over me. . . .

He is not involved enough in the problems that arise from differences in the goals of functional departments. This may be because he spends too much time away at Ion Physics and Signetics. But it doesn't change the fact that he is not involved enough. . . .

You get the same record back from him regardless of what you say. It is safe to be open with him and tell him what's on your mind, but he does not listen. . . .

Rogers is too gentlemanly, is not tough enough, has not demonstrated risk-taking, and is encumbered by Corning Glass Works philosophy and standards. I am not sure how well he fences with others in the company. . . .

Wave makers are not wanted in the division and are being pushed out. People at the top do not create and confront conflict.

EPD's Organization

In June 1968 EPD employed 1200 people, of whom 250 were salaried managerial and professional employees. It had three plants and four sales districts and with the exception of some R&D support from Corning's laboratory was a self-contained multifunctional organization. Reporting to Rogers were a controller, a manufacturing manager, a marketing manager, a sales manager, and a product development manager. (See Exhibit 4 for the organization of EPD.)

EPD's organization was representative of a typical division with two exceptions. First, the marketing and sales functions were separated by Rogers shortly after he became division manager. As he said later:

It seemed to me that marketing and sales had sufficiently different responsibilities to justify their separation. Sales, I felt, should be concerned with knocking on doors and getting the order while marketing should be concerned with strategies for pricing, new products, and the identification of new opportunities for the future. Marketing is a strategic function, as opposed to a day-to-day function.

A second difference was the existence of a product development group. Most other divisions relied totally on the technical staff division for technical product development support and only had engineering groups for manufacturing staff support. EPD's product development department was responsible for developing new products even though they also relied on the technical staff division for R&D support. In addition to product development, the product development department often became involved in manufacturing process development.

Rogers made a number of additional organizational changes shortly after his takeover.

1 EPD headquarters had been located in Raleigh. Bennett had prided himself in EPD's difference from the rest of Corning—EPD being one of only two divisions not headquartered in Corning, N.Y. At the urging of top management Rogers moved the headquarters to Corning. He believed that EPD had to learn to relate more closely to the corporation.

EXHIBIT 4 Electronic Products Division—organization chart

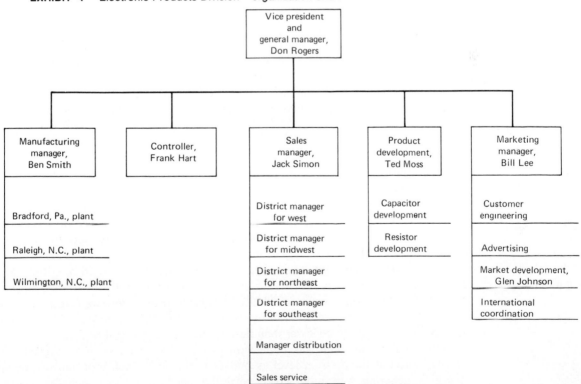

2 Before 1966 the division had been geographically decentralized. The Raleigh plant, which manufactured capacitors, not only housed the plant but also a market development group and a product development group for capacitors. Similarly, the Bradford plant had on site a market development group and a product development group for resistors. The product development managers had reported to Bennett; the market development managers to the general sales and marketing manager. In 1968 product development was consolidated under Ted Moss, who was located in Corning, even though the groups themselves remained at the plants. The market development groups were brought back to Corning.

3 Rogers also replaced all key managers with the exception of Ted Moss, the product development manager. Ben Smith, the new manufacturing manager, had held a similar job in Corning's laboratory products department. Bill Lee, the new marketing manager, had held positions in manufacturing in Corning's other divisions and had recently been in charge of corporate market planning. Frank Hart, the new controller, had worked in plants in Corning's lighting products division. Of the new division staff, only Jack Simon, the sales manager, came from within EPD. He had been a district sales manager. (See Exhibit 5 for a listing of the key managers and their backgrounds.)

4 Before 1966 a market planning function had reported to Bennett. As part of the cost-cutting efforts in 1967 and 1968, this function had been eliminated and its responsibilities given to the new marketing function.

5 One of EPD's major problems in 1966 and 1967 had been service to customers. The number of missed commitments was very high; EPD's reputation for delivery and service was slipping. Under the direction of Rogers, EPD undertook a successful program to improve service. The manufacturing manager held plant managers responsible for meeting delivery commitments and shortening delivery lead times based upon specific goals that were developed. In addition, an information system was developed by the sales service function in an effort to improve service.

EPD and the Corporation

Rogers reported to the president of Corning (see Exhibit 2) and was responsible for managing all aspects of the division's operations. He was held responsible for achieving profitability and growth goals, which were established at the end of each year (September–October) for the following year through negotiation. The division would generate its sales budget through a bottom-up process in the sales department, using price guidelines from marketing. The plants would then generate their gross margin budget based on their estimate of plant sales and costs. These would be consolidated at the top of the division and submitted to the corporate staff. Invariably, corporation staff would return to the division and, based on its corporate forecast of sales and profits, would ask the division to modify its sales and profit plans. If corporate sales were forecasted to be lower than desired, the division might be asked to increase its sales goals. The same was done with profits. This process often caused great consternation at the division level as budget proposals, which took much time and energy to generate, were modified by corporate needs.

EXHIBIT 5   BACKGROUND OF EPD EXECUTIVES

Executive	Position	Age	Background
Don Rogers	Vice president and general manager, Electronic Products Division	40	Received a PhD in chemistry from the University of Cincinnati, a master's in chemistry from St. Johns University, and a BS from Queens College in New York City. Joined Corning in 1957 as a chemist in its technical staff division. In 1961 he became manager of electronic research and in 1964 director of physical research in the same division. He was appointed as EPD's division manager in June 1966.
Bill Lee	Marketing manager	39	Received a BS in chemical engineering from Rutgers. Joined Corning in 1950 as a staff engineer, then occupied several engineering and supervisory positions in glass plants. Following an assignment in corporate market planning he gained his present position in EPD in 1967.
Ben Smith	Manufacturing manager	43	Received an engineering degree from Clarkson College. Became EPD's manufacturing manager in 1967 after numerous manufacturing positions in Corning's lighting products and technical products divisions. Started as a plant engineer and then became department foreman, production superintendent, and plant manager in several glass plants in these divisions. Just before moving to EPD, he had been manufacturing manager in the laboratory glassware department.
Ted Moss	Product development manager	45	After receiving a degree in mechanical engineering from City College in New York City, he joined Corning as a staff engineer. After 5 years in other divisions, he joined EPD in its infancy. He first served as a project engineer and then held several managerial positions in product and process development. He became manager of product development for EPD in 1968.
Frank Hart	Division controller	31	Joined Corning Glass Works in 1962 after completing a BS in industrial administration at Yale University, serving in the U.S. Army, and completing an MBA at the Harvard Business School. Before joining EPD as its division controller in 1967, he served in a variety of plant accounting positions in Cornings lighting products and television divisions.
Jack Simon	Sales manager	34	Received a degree in sociology from St. Bonaventure University. Joined Corning in 1960 as a salesperson in the Electronic Products Division. All of his experience with Corning was in EPD, where he became a district sales manager before taking over as sales manager in 1967.

EPD, along with the other divisions, was expected to grow at an average rate of 10 percent a year, the corporation's historic average growth rate. In the area of profits, EPD was expected to approach the profitability levels the corporation had come to expect of its more traditional OEM businesses. Typically, these were higher than the prevailing profitability levels among electronic component manufacturers. The ability of EPD to attain these objectives was a subject of much discussion and controversy in the division. A number of key people wondered whether both growth and profit objectives could be met. Volume could always be increased by taking low-price business, but this reduced profitability. Most people within EPD looked to new products as a major source of both new volume and profits.

FUNCTIONAL DEPARTMENTS IN 1968

Manufacturing

Resistors were manufactured in high volume at plants in Wilmington, N.C. and Bradford, Pa.; capacitors were manufactured in high volume at a plant in Raleigh, N.C. Each plant had a manager and a full complement of manufacturing functions, including production, engineering, quality control, purchasing, accounting and control, and personnel. The production superintendent had the greatest power in the plant, directing all manufacturing operations. The head of engineering was second in line of influence. The plants were held responsible for gross margin, and thus were profit centers.

The plant managers, with one exception, had grown up in EPD. Their performance was evaluated on gross margins and assorted other manufacturing variances, including delivery lead times and missed commitments to customers. Plant accounts were closed every 28 days and plant performance was reviewed in meetings in Corning 13 times each year.

The reputations of the plant managers and therefore their chance of promotion were perceived by them to be dependent on plant growth and good gross margin performance. All saw their future advancement within the manufacturing hierarchy of the company leading to the possibility of promotion to general manager of a division. Since manufacturing was the dominant function, such an expectation was not unrealistic.

Because plants were profit centers, their performance was well-known around the corporation. There were many opportunities for exchanges at plant managers' meetings, and the corporation had established an informal system for comparing plant performance. All of this heightened the individual plant manager's concerns about plant gross margin and growth.

EPD's plant managers were extremely upset with the lack of growth in the division's business. In the last 2 years their volume had shrunk and, through price cuts, their dollar volume had dropped substantially. This put enormous pressures on them for cost reduction to maintain their gross margins. While they were able to reduce some costs, gross margins still declined. With some exceptions, EPD plants had the lowest gross margins in the company. Plant managers expressed the following statements:

We're experiencing price erosion in our product lines and I don't see a large number of new products. We need something new and unique. I don't see growth potential in our existing products. . . .

We need direction on resistors. We cannot afford two plants. We need a process to allow us to make low-cost resistors. . . .

There are no operational objectives. I get the feeling that everyone is concerned but *no* clear objectives are set.

The frustration experienced by the manufacturing people was expressed most in their attitudes toward marketing and sales. They viewed the sales function as being concerned exclusively with volume and as having no concern for gross margin. They blamed sales for getting low-gross-margin business and not fighting hard enough to get better prices. Sales, in other words, was giving the store away at the plant's expense and sales wasn't penalized for it, as they saw it.

A production superintendent commented:

There is a breakdown in common agreement when it comes to pricing. Sales will sell for anything and the plant won't buy it unless 40 percent margin is involved.

Smith, the manufacturing manager, remarked:

There is a feeling of mutual distrust between sales and manufacturing because manufacturing believes sales is not putting enough of a price on the products. This is a typical problem that results when two groups have different goals.

Manufacturing's negative feelings about sales were only exceeded by their feelings about marketing. They felt that it was marketing's responsibility to provide direction to the division for profitable growth, and that such direction was not apparent. They particularly blamed Lee, the marketing manager, for lack of strong leadership. They were upset by what they called the "disappearing carrot syndrome." As manufacturing saw it, marketing would come to the plant and project a multimillion dollar market for a new resistor or capacitor (the carrot). Manufacturing, based on the projection, would run samples and make other investments in preparation for the new product only to find out 6 months or a year later that marketing was now projecting much smaller sales and profits for the product. Manufacturing's explanation of this situation was that marketing lacked the ability to forecast marketing trends accurately and was generally incompetent. They saw a need to replace the marketing manager and many others in the area.

A production superintendent remarked:

What is slowing down EPD is weak marketing, lack of marketing direction, and a very narrow product base. You can't sell what you do not have and, if you do not have it and you do not know where you are going to be in 2 years, you probably will not sell what you have.

Another production superintendent commented:

The last 5 years have left people quite cold as far as strategies are concerned. For example, marketing does not have the same strategy as we do and they give us no direction.

Smith remarked:

No one has confidence in marketing people. Plant managers don't believe them now since they have been wrong so many times.

Manufacturing was also unhappy with the product development department. They felt that product development had not always given them products that would run well on their production lines. They looked to product development to develop low-cost components and saw nothing coming. When product development requested special runs on their manufacturing lines to develop new products, they wondered what the benefits were for this sacrifice in their efficiency.

Marketing

Marketing included several functions, such as customer engineering and advertising. However, its most important function was market development, headed by Glen Johnson. It was market development's responsibility to develop sales projections for the next year, market plans for the next 3 years, analyses of market share, and plans for improving market position. One of the primary means for increasing market share was the development of new types of resistors and capacitors. It was market development's responsibility to identify these new opportunities and to ensure the development of new products in coordination with other functions. Marketing specialists reporting to Johnson had responsibility for scanning and analyzing different market segments and for developing new products in them. Measures of profitability and growth by market segment were used by them to assess their progress. Because the identification of new market opportunities was primarily marketing's responsibility (with help from sales), as was the development of the new product plan, they felt the pressure for new-product development was on them.

The marketing function had many new people, since it had been established as a separate function just a year earlier. Most of its members had transferred from the sales department, where they had been salespeople or in sales service. For example, Johnson had been a district sales manager. The marketing specialists were generally recent technical or business graduates with 1 or 2 years of sales experience.

The marketing staff felt overwhelmed with the tough job of forecasting, planning, and strategizing in a very turbulent marketplace and felt that no one appreciated their difficulties. Lee remarked:

We have not defined the resistor business. When the government business dropped, we did not face up to a need to produce at lower cost.

A marketing specialist stated:

You can't be stodgy in this business. You must be fast-moving and quick-acting. You must be decisive, adaptable, a long-range thinker and deal with a very ambiguous situation.

Some felt that Corning had such high standards for profitability on new products that it was impossible to meet them in the components business. Johnson commented:

While corporate financial people will admit that we need a different set of criteria, they informally convey to us that we are doing a lousy job, and it makes us run conservatively. The corporate environment is not a risk-taking one. We tend to want to bring a proprietary advantage to our business which we cannot do. This is slowing us down.

Glass K (a new product) took 7 years in product development. Technological development of unique characteristics is not an effective strategy in a dynamic environment. There were some original conceptions, but these quickly passed by the boards as the development process took 7 years instead of the original 3 years projected for it.

Marketing people were also critical of product development and their responsiveness to divisions needs. As marketing people saw it, product development's priorities were wrong and their projects were always late. According to Johnson:

Moss bootlegs projects. There are no ways to establish priorities in development; no criteria have even been set up. Seventy percent of his time is in process development.

Marketing felt most resentful about manufacturing's lack of cooperation and the continual criticisms that came from them. They saw the plants as conservative and unwilling to take risks. This was particularly aggravating because many of them saw themselves spending inordinate amounts of time dealing with the plants, which they felt took time away from their primary task of marketing. Johnson indicated that he would not have taken the marketing job had he known that it would involve the many frustrations of getting manufacturing and others to do things.

Sales

The products produced by the plants were sold through a direct selling force of approximately 25 salespeople organized into four sales districts. Each district was managed by a district sales manager who reported to the national sales manager. The direct sales force visited manufacturers who used passive components in their manufactured end products. Their job involved learning about manufacturers' needs by talking to purchasing agents and design engineers, and then obtaining contracts for resistors or capacitors.

In addition to direct sales, products were sold in small lot sizes through distributors. Distributor strategy and relations were the responsibility of the distributor sales manager, who reported to Jack Simon, the national sales manager. It was the distributor sales manager's job to coordinate the efforts of field salespeople in support of the objectives.

A sales service manager reported to the distribution manager. The sales service group was split geographically, with a sales service group located in each plant. The sales service group worked with the plants to expedite order processing and kept the plant informed about customer needs for delivery and service.

The sales force consisted of college graduates interested in sales or marketing careers and older and experienced salespeople who had worked in this industry for a long time. Salespeople identified strongly with their industry. Simon had risen through sales, as had all the district sales managers.

The sales task in EPD differed from that in other Corning divisions even though it also served OEM customers. It served a much larger set of customers in several markets. It had to develop a large number of relationships with purchasing agents and engineers and relied on good relationships to obtain market intelligence and an opportunity to bid on contracts. But, salespeople also had to negotiate with these same people to obtain the best possible price. They were measured on sales volume and worked hard to beat their budgeted sales target to obtain recognition from top management. They were not paid on a commission basis even though this had often been a point of some discussion and discontent.

In 1968 Simon reported mistrust, game playing, maneuvering, and office politics between sales and marketing:

> Most people [in marketing] do not believe that sales competence is high. On the other hand, we in sales do not believe that the information marketing gives us is the best.

Simon reported that major conflict developed in budget-setting sessions. This came in part because sales developed their forecast from customer canvassing, while marketing developed theirs based on analytical tools. He said:

> Conflicts are not resolved based on facts. Instead there are accusations. I don't trust them [marketing] and I don't trust that they have the capability to do their jobs.

Simon's view of manufacturing was somewhat more positive.

> Relations with manufacturing are personally good, but I have a number of concerns. I do not know and no one knows about actual cost reductions in the plant. I don't think manufacturing gets hit as hard for lack of cost reduction as sales takes it on the chin for price reductions. Another problem is Bradford's service. It's putrid! There is constant game playing in the Bradford plant.

At lower levels of the organization, relationships between sales and manufacturing were viewed as even worse. There were shouting matches over the telephone between the midwest district sales manager and the Wilmington plant manager. In one instance, sales wanted quick delivery to meet a major customer's needs. They felt that EPD's position with the customer would be hurt if it were not provided. The plant said they would not provide delivery on such short notice without upsetting plant operations. The sales service manager remarked:

> The relationship with the Bradford plant is bad. Measurement for plant managers has to change. They are not really measured on service. Things have improved somewhat, however, and they are a bit more concerned about service.

Product Development

Product development was responsible for the development of extensions to the current product line. There were generally 10–12 new-product-development projects underway and these often required significant technological development. To handle this work, the development group was divided into two parts—a development group for resistors, located in the Bradford plant (which manufactured resistors), and a development group for capacitors, located in Raleigh. No product development group was located in Wilmington. The manager of product development was located in Corning, along with the rest of the divisional staff.

The product development group was composed of technical people who had spent their careers in R&D work. While some of these people had come from the corporate R&D group, many had worked in the division for most of their careers or had held technical positions in other companies in the electronic industry. Moss, the manager of product development, described his relationships with other groups:

> In general, my department's relations with the plants are pretty good although some problems existed at Bradford. My biggest concern is with marketing. I do not feel that marketing provides detailed product specifications for new products. In addition, marketing people do not understand what is involved in specification changes. I think that writing specifications jointly with marketing would help this problem. Another problem is that marketing people have to look ahead more and predict the future better. They always need it yesterday. We need time!

Moss was also critical of Corning's technical staff division, which also did product development work for EPD.

> It is difficult to get a time schedule from them. Their direction is independent of ours since they report elsewhere. They will not wring their hands if they are behind schedule. They will more quickly try to relax requirements for the development if it is behind schedule. I need more influence on specifications when it comes to things they are working on. I often have to go upstairs to solve the problems that occur with this group.

Moss also cited problems with the sales group.

> We need comments from the sales group on our new products. I wanted to get the call reports they write and asked Simon for copies. His argument for not giving them to me is that the marketing department has the responsibility for interpretation. I finally had to go to Rogers to resolve the problem.

The Controller

It was the division controller's responsibility to maintain all accounting records for the division, to provide a financial summary every 28 days, and to report the performance of the division to the division staff and the corporate controller. It was also his responsibility to develop quarterly forecasts of business performance. Frank Hart, the division's controller, remarked:

> In most cases three-period forecasts are extremely inaccurate. It is very difficult to forecast the business this way. Our forecasts are always off. Yet it is a corporate requirement.

Not only did EPD find it difficult to forecast its business but it had difficulty explaining the reason for upturns and downturns.

New-Product-Development Process

While there were several attempts to develop completely new components or products beyond components, such as the microcircuits effort, most new-product-development effort concentrated on developing product extensions. These were resistors and capacitors with different technical characteristics than existing products and were intended to meet new market needs.

Product development was progressing far from smoothly in the division. In one case, the focus divider, a new product for the television market, was killed and resurrected four times with different parts of the organization having differing knowledge of its status at given points in time. Marketing clearly thought that this was an opportunity, and product development saw it as feasible from a technical point of view. Yet as far as sales was concerned, manufacturing's cost quotes called into question EPD's ability to compete in the marketplace. As discussions progressed on needed product modifications to reduce costs, marketing's estimate of the potential market changed and product development's estimate of technical feasibility changed. Thus, each function's management made its own estimate of the viability of this product and, at different points in time, told people in their function that the project was on or off depending on their optimism at the time. At one point, salespeople were obtaining orders for samples of the product at a time when manufacturing and marketing had decided that the product was not feasible and had killed the idea. Similar problems occurred on other projects because it was common for product development to bootleg samples for salespeople for products that did not have the commitment of manufacturing or even marketing.

In another case, severe conflict between marketing and plant personnel erupted over a new coating for resistors. Marketing had determined that a new and uniform coating was needed for competitive and efficiency reasons. They presented their views to the division's management and received what they thought was a commitment to change resistor coatings. Yet no significant progress had been made by marketing in getting plants to convert their operations. The plants questioned whether product development had proved that the new coating would work and could be manufactured to meet product specifications at no additional cost. Since they also completely distrusted marketing on the need for this change, they dragged their feet on this project. In 1968, 2 years after this project had started, there was still no project completion in sight. The marketing specialist in charge of this project would return from meetings at the plant angry and completely discouraged about his ability to influence plant people to advance the project.

The forum for the product development process was the 2-day meetings held once each accounting period (28 days) in Corning. One meeting was for new capacitor developments; the other meeting, for resistor developments. In all, approximately 20 people attended each meeting, including the division manager and immediate staff, plant managers, and a few key people in the other functions. The purpose of the meetings was to discuss, coordinate, and decide about new products. In 1968, the division was working on approximately 12 new projects.

Johnson, who chaired the meetings, typically sat at the head of the table. Rogers sat at the opposite end of the table. Johnson would publish an agenda beforehand and would direct the discussion as it moved from one project to another. For each project, progress was checked against goals as they had been agreed upon by each function at the previous review. Each function would describe in some detail what had been done in their area to support the project. For example, plant managers might describe the equipment changes made in their plant. If the goals had not been met by a function, as was often the case, new dates for the accomplishment of the goal would be extracted. While problems encountered were always described, the issue of slippage in goals and the underlying reasons for it were rarely discussed. When differences of opinion on a project did surface, there was great difficulty in resolving them. People would conclude by agreeing to disagree and moving on to the next item on the agenda. While tempers flared occasionally, there was rarely any open hostility or aggression expressed in the meetings. However, after meetings, people were often observed meeting in small groups in the hallways, over coffee, or in offices to continue the debate.

There was a continual stream of people in and out of these meetings to obtain information from subordinates in their functional area about a project's current status. It was common for a plant manager to leave the meeting to call an engineer in the plant for details about a project's status. On one occasion Ted Young, a marketing specialist, was continually mentioned as the person who knew the most about a project under discussion, yet he was not at the meeting. On other occasions, marketing specialists would be called into the meetings to provide information about a project. Plant people and product development people were sometimes brought to Corning for parts of the meeting if their input was thought to be needed.

Before 1968, product development meetings had not been attended by the division manager. In 1968 marketing asked Rogers to attend these meetings to help promote decisionmaking. Rogers became very active in the meetings. He often became involved in the discussion of a new product, particularly its technical aspects. He could be seen explaining a technical point to others who did not understand it. His viewpoints were clearly heard and felt by others, and people thought that meetings had improved since he had decided to sit in. Despite these improvements in June 1968, Johnson still dreaded the product development meetings.

> I never sleep well on the night before the meetings. I start thinking about the various projects and the problems I have in getting everyone to agree and be committed to a direction. We spend long hours in these meetings, but people just don't seem to stick to their commitments to accomplish their objectives by a given date. Projects are slipping badly and we just can't seem to get them moving. In my opinion, we also have some projects that should be killed but we can't seem to be able to do that either. Frankly, if I had it to do over again, I would not take this job. After all, how much marketing am I really doing? I seem to spend most of my time in meetings getting others to do things.

Outlook for 1969

As 1968 drew to a close, Rogers and the top management group were preparing for their second GLF (Great Leap Forward) meeting. This meeting had been instituted the previous year to discuss major problems and to develop commitment to division objectives for the coming year. Now it was time to look ahead to 1969.

In a memo to the key managers, Rogers summarized the problems that needed to be addressed in the coming year:

It is obvious that division growth is our major problem and that we need to develop new products to get growth. Achievement of budgeted operating margin is a close second. Morale has become a more acute problem and the need for communication, coordination, and the proper balance of long- and short-range efforts continue to require our attention.

As the top managers in EPD prepared for the 2-day meeting in Ithaca, N.Y., it was clear that they had survived the shakeout in the industry. But it was also clear to them that many major problems remained. They all wanted growth and saw it as their major problem, but they were not developing new products quickly enough to meet this objective nor were they in agreement about strategies, priorities, or what constituted acceptable criteria for profitability.

To complicate matters, morale was low, risk taking was down, and significant problems in communication and coordination existed. This occurred in an environment in which price-cost squeezes were continuing and competition was as fierce as ever.

As key managers prepared for their GLF meeting, the Corning organization development staff was preparing to present the results of its study of EPD to Rogers.

PUTTING EXCELLENCE INTO MANAGEMENT

Thomas J. Peters

What makes for excellence in the management of a company? Is it the use of sophisticated management techniques such as zero-based budgeting, management by objectives, matrix organization, and sector, group, or portfolio management? Is it greater use of computers to control companies that continue to grow even larger in size and more diverse in activities? Is it a battalion of specialized MBAs, well-versed in the techniques of strategic planning?

Probably not. Although most well-run companies use a fair sampling of all of these tools, they do not use them as substitutes for the basics of good management. Indeed, McKinsey & Co., a management consultant concern, has studied management practices at 37 companies that are often used as examples of well-run organizations and has found that they have eight common attributes. None of those attributes depends on "modern" management tools or gimmicks. In fact, none of them requires high technology, and none of them costs a cent to implement. All that is needed is time, energy, and a willingness on the part of management to think rather than to make use of management formulas.

The outstanding performers work hard to keep things simple. They rely on simple organizational structures, simple strategies, simple goals, and simple communications. The eight attributes that characterize their managements are:

- A bias toward action.
- Simple form and lean staff.
- Continued contact with customers.
- Productivity improvement via people.
- Operational autonomy to encourage entrepreneurship.

- Stress on one key business value.
- Emphasis on doing what they know best.
- Simultaneous loose-tight controls.

Although none of these sounds startling or new, most are conspicuously absent in many companies today. Far too many managers have lost sight of the basics—service to customers, low-cost manufacturing, productivity improvement, innovation, and risk-taking. In many cases, they have been seduced by the availability of MBAs, armed with the "latest" in strategic planning techniques. MBAs who specialize in strategy are bright, but they often cannot implement their ideas, and their companies wind up losing the capacity to act. At Standard Brands Inc., for example, Chairman F. Ross Johnson discovered this the hard way when he brought a handful of planning specialists into his consumer products company. "The guys who were bright [the strategic planners] were not the kinds of people who could implement programs," he lamented to BUSINESS WEEK. Two years later, he removed the plannners.

Another consumer products company followed a similar route, hiring a large band of young MBAs for the staffs of senior vice-presidents. The new people were assigned to build computer models for designing new products. Yet none of the products could be manufactured or brought to market. Complained one line executive: "The models incorporated 83 variables in product planning, but we were being killed by just one—cost."

Companies are being stymied not only by their own staffs but often by their structure. McKinsey studied one company where the new-product process required 223 separate committees to approve an idea before it could be put into production. Another company was restructured recently into 200 strategic business units—only to discover that it was impossible to implement 200 strategies. And even at General Electric Co., which is usually cited for its ability to structure itself according to its management needs, an executive recently complained: "Things become bureaucratic with astonishing speed. Inevitably when we wire things up, we lose vitality." Emerson Electric Co., with a much simpler structure than GE, consistently beats its huge competitor on costs—manufacturing its products in plants with fewer than 600 employees.

McKinsey's study focused on 10 well-managed companies: International Business Machines, Texas Instruments, Hewlett-Packard, 3M, Digital Equipment, Procter & Gamble, Johnson & Johnson, McDonald's, Dana, and Emerson Electric. On the surface, they have nothing in common. There is no universality of product line: Five are in high technology, one is in packaged goods, one makes medical products, one operates fast-food restaurants, and two are relatively mundane manufacturers of mechanical and electrical products. But each is a hands-on operator, not a holding company or a conglomerate. And while not every plan succeeds, in the day-to-day pursuit of their businesses these companies succeed far more often than they fail. And they succeed because of their management's almost instinctive adherence to the eight attributes.

BIAS TOWARD ACTION

In each of these companies, the key instructions are *do it, fix it, try it*. They avoid analyzing and questioning products to death, and they avoid complicated procedures for developing new ideas. Controlled experiments abound in these companies. The attitude of management is to "get some data, do it, then adjust it," rather than to wait for a perfect overall plan. The companies tend to be tinkerers rather than inventors, making small steps of progress rather than conceiving sweeping new concepts. At McDonald's Corp., for example, the objective is to do the little things regularly and well.

Ideas are solicited regularly and tested quickly. Those that work are pushed fast; those that don't are discarded just as quickly. At 3M Co., the management never kills an idea without trying it out; it just goes on the back burner.

These managements avoid long, complicated business plans for new projects. At 3M, for example, new product ideas must be proposed in less than five pages. At Procter & Gamble Co., one-page memos are the rule, but every figure in a P&G memo can be relied on unfailingly.

To ensure that they achieve results, these companies set a few well-defined goals for their managers. At Texas Instruments Inc., for one, a typical goal would be a set date for having a new plant operating or for having a designated percent of a sales force call on customers in a new market. A TI executive explained: "We've experimented a lot, but the bottom line for any senior manager is the maxim that more than two objectives is no objective."

These companies have learned to focus quickly on problems. One method is to appoint a "czar" who has responsibility for one problem across the company. At Digital Equipment Corp. and Hewlett-Packard Co., for example, there are software czars, because customer demand for programming has become the key issue for the future growth of those companies. Du Pont Co., when it discovered it was spending $800 million a year on transportation, set up a logistics czar. Other companies have productivity czars or energy czars with the power to override a manufacturing division's autonomy.

Another tool is the task force. But these companies tend to use the task force in an unusual way. Task forces are authorized to fix things, not to generate reports and paper. At Digital Equipment, TL, HP, and 3M, task forces have a short duration, seldom more than 90 days. Says a Digital Equipment executive: "When we've got a big problem here, we grab 10 senior guys and stick them in a room for a week. They come up with an answer and implement it." All members are volunteers, and they tend to be senior managers rather than junior people ordered to serve. Management espouses the busy-member theory: "We don't want people on task forces who want to become permanent task force members. We only put people on them who are so busy that their major objective is to get the problem solved and to get back to their main jobs." Every task force at TI is disbanded after its work is done, but within three months the senior operations committee formally reviews and assesses the results. TI demands that the managers who requested and ran the task force justify the time spent on it. If the task force turns out to have been useless, the manager is chided publicly, a painful penalty in TI's peer-conscious culture.

SIMPLE FORM AND LEAN STAFF

Although all ten of these companies are big—the smallest, McDonald's, has sales in excess of $1.9 billion—they are structured along "small is beautiful" lines. Emerson Electric, 3M, J&J, and HP are divided into small entrepreneurial units that—although smaller than economies of scale might suggest—manage to get things done. No HP division, for example, ever employs more than 1,200 people. TI, with 90 product customer centers, keeps each notably autonomous.

Within the units themselves, activities are kept to small, manageable groups. At Dana Corp., small teams work on productivity improvement. At the high-technology companies, small autonomous teams, headed by a product "champion," shepherd ideas through the corporate bureaucracy to ensure that they quickly receive attention from the top.

Staffs are also kept small to avoid bureaucracies. Fewer than 100 people help run Dana, a $3 billion corporation. Digital Equipment and Emerson are also noted for small staffs.

CLOSENESS TO THE CUSTOMER

The well-managed companies are customer driven—not technology driven, not product driven, not strategy driven. Constant contact with the customer provides insights that direct the company. Says one executive: "Where do you start? Not by poring over abstract market research. You start by getting out there with the customer." In a study of two fast-paced industries (scientific instruments and component manufacturing), Eric Von Hippel, associate professor at Massachusetts Institute of Technology, found that 100% of the major new product ideas—and 80% of the minor new product variations—came directly from customers.

At both IBM and Digital Equipment, top management spends at least 30 days a year conferring with top customers. No manager at IBM holds a staff job for more than three years, except in the legal, finance, and personnel departments. The reason: IBM believes that staff people are out of the mainstream because they do not meet with customers regularly.

Both companies use customer-satisfaction surveys to help determine management's compensation. Another company spends 12% of its research and development budget on sending engineers and scientists out to visit customers. One R&D chief spends two months each year with customers. At Lanier Business Products Inc., another fast growing company, the 20 most senior executives make sales calls every month.

Staying close to the customer means sales and service overkill. "Assistants to" at IBM are assigned to senior executives with the sole function of processing customer complaints within 24 hours. At Digital Equipment, J&J, IBM, and 3M, immense effort is expended to field an extraordinarily well-trained sales force. Catepillar Tractor Co., another company considered to have excellent management, spends much of its managerial talent on efforts to make a reality of its motto, "24-hour parts delivery anywhere in the world."

These companies view the customer as an integral element of their businesses. A bank officer who started his career as a J&J accountant recalls that he was required to make customer calls even though he was in a financial department. The reason: to ensure that he understood the customer's perspective and could handle a proposal with empathy.

PRODUCTIVITY IMPROVEMENTS VIA CONSENSUS

One way to get productivity increases is to install new capital equipment. But another method is often overlooked. Productivity can be improved by motivating and stimulating employees. One way to do that is to give them autonomy. At TI, shop floor teams set their own targets for production. In the years since the company has used this approach, executives say, workers have set goals that require them to stretch but that are reasonable and attainable.

The key is to motivate all of the people involved in each process. At 3M, for example, a team that includes technologists, marketers, production people, and financial types is formed early in a new product venture. It is self-sufficient and stays together from the inception to the national introduction. Although 3M is aware that this approach can lead to redundancy, it feels that the team spirit and motivation make it worthwhile.

Almost all of these companies use "corny" but effective methods to reward their workers. Badges, pins, and medals are all part of such recognition programs. Outstanding production teams at TI are invited to describe their successes to the board, as a form of recognition. Signficantly, the emphasis is never only on monetary awards.

AUTONOMY TO ENCOURAGE ENTREPRENEURSHIP

A company cannot encourage entrepreneurship if it holds its managers on so tight a leash that they cannot make decisions. Well-managed companies authorize their managers to act like entrepreneurs. Dana, for one, calls this method the "store manager" concept. Plant managers are free to make purchasing decisions and to start productivity programs on their own. As a result, these managers develop unusual programs with results that far exceed those of a division or corporate staff. And the company has a grievance rate that is a fraction of the average reported by the United Auto Workers for all the plants it represents.

The successful companies rarely will force their managers to go against their own judgment. At 3M, TI, IBM, and J&J, decisions on product promotion are not based solely on market potential. An important factor in the decision is the zeal and drive of the volunteer who champions a product. Explains one executive at TI: "In every instance of a new product failure, we had forced someone into championing it involuntarily."

The divisional management is generally responsible for replenishing its new product array. In these well-managed companies, headquarters staff may not cut off funds for divisional products arbitrarily. What is more, the divisions are allowed to reinvest most of their earnings in their own operations. Although this flies in the face of the product-portfolio concept, which dictates that a corporate chief milk mature divisions to feed those with apparently greater growth potential, these companies recognize that entrepreneurs will not be developed in corporations that give the fruits of managers' labor to someone else.

Almost all these companies strive to place new products into separate startup divisions. A manager is more likely to be recognized—and promoted—for pushing a hot new product out of his division to enable it to stand on its own than he is for simply letting his own division get overgrown.

Possibly most important at these companies, entrepreneurs are both encouraged and honored at all staff levels. TI, for one, has created a special group of "listeners"—138 senior technical people called "individual contributors"—to assess new ideas. Junior staff members are particularly encouraged to bring their ideas to one of these individuals for a one-on-one evaluation. Each "contributor" has the authority to approve substantial startup funds ($20,000 to $30,000) for product experimentation. TI's successful Speak'n'Spell device was developed this way.

IBM's Fellows Program serves a similar purpose, although it is intended to permit proven senior performers to explore their ideas rather than to open communications lines for bright comers. Such scientists have at their beck and call thousands of IBM's technical people. The Fellows tend to be highly skilled gadflies, people who can shake things up—almost invariably for the good of the company.

The operating principle at well-managed companies is to do one thing well. At IBM, the all-pervasive value is customer service. At Dana it is productivity improvement. At 3M and HP, it is new product development. At P&G it is product quality. At McDonald's it is customer service—quality, cleanliness, and value.

STRESS ON A KEY BUSINESS VALUE

At all these companies, the values are pursued with an almost religious zeal by the chief executive officers. Rene McPherson, now dean of Stanford University's Graduate School of Business but until recently Dana's CEO, incessantly preached cost reduction and productivity improvement—and the company doubled its productivity in seven years. Almost to the day when Thomas Watson Jr. retired from IBM he wrote memos to the staff on the subject of calling on customers—even stressing the proper dress for the call. TI's ex-chairman Patrick Haggerty made it a point to drop in at a development laboratory on his way home each night when he was in Dallas. And in another company, where competitive position was the prime focus, one division manager wrote 700 memos to his subordinates one year, analyzing competitors.

Such single-minded focus on a value becomes a culture for the company. Nearly every IBM employee has stories about how he or she took great pains to solve a customer's problem. New product themes even dominate 3M and HP lunchroom conversations. Every operational review at HP focuses on new products, with a minimum amount of time devoted to financial results or projections—because President John Young has made it clear that he believes that proper implementation of new-product plans automatically creates the right numbers. In fact, Young makes it a point to start new employees in the new-product process and keep them there for a few years as part of a "socialization" pattern. "I don't care if they do come from the Stanford Business School," he says. "For a few years they get their hands dirty, or we are not interested." At McDonald's the company's values are drummed into employees at Hamburger U., a training program every employee goes through.

As the employees who are steeped in the corporate culture move up the ladder, they become role models for newcomers, and the process continues. It is possibly best exemplified by contrast. American Telephone & Telegraph Co., which recently began to develop a marketing orientation, has been hamstrung in its efforts because of a lack of career telephone executives with marketing successes. When Archie J. McGill was hired from IBM to head AT&T's marketing, some long-term employees balked at his leadership because he "wasn't one of them," and so was not regarded as a model.

Another common pitfall for companies is the sending of mixed signals to line managers. One company has had real problems introducing new products despite top management's constant public stress on innovation—simply because line managers perceived the real emphasis to be on cost-cutting. They viewed top management as accountants who refused to invest or to take risks, and they consistently proposed imitative products. At another company, where the CEO insisted that his major thrust was new products, an analysis of how he spent his time over a three-month period showed that no more than 5% of his efforts were directed to new products. His stated emphasis therefore was not credible. Not surprisingly, his employees never picked up the espoused standard.

Too many messages, even when sincerely meant, can cause the same problem. One CEO complained that no matter how hard he tried to raise what he regarded as an unsatisfactory quality level he was unsuccessful. But when McKinsey questioned his subordinates, they said, "Of course he's for quality, but he's for everything else, too. We have a theme a month here." The outstanding companies, in contrast, have one theme and stick to it.

STICKING TO WHAT THEY KNOW BEST

Robert W. Johnson, the former chairman of J&J, put it this way. "Never acquire any business you don't know how to run." Edward G. Harness, CEO at P&G, says, "This company has never left its base." All of the successful companies have been able to define their strengths—marketing, customer contact, new product innovation, low-cost manufacturing—and then build on them. They have resisted the temptation to move into new businesses that look attractive but require corporate skills they do not have.

SIMULTANEOUS LOOSE-TIGHT CONTROLS

While this may sound like a contradiction, it is not. The successful companies control a few variables tightly, but allow flexibility and looseness in others. 3M uses return on sales and number of employees as yardsticks for control. Yet it gives management lots of leeway in day-to-day operations. When McPherson became president of Dana, he threw out all of the company's policy manuals and substituted a one-page philosophy statement and a control system that required divisions to report costs and revenues on a daily basis.

IBM probably has the classic story about flexible controls. After the company suffered well-published and costly problems with its System 360 computer several years ago—problems that cost hundreds of millions of dollars to fix—Watson ordered Frank T. Cary, then a vice-president to incorporate a system of checks and balances in new-product testing. The system made IBM people so cautious that they stopped taking risks. When Cary became president of IBM, one of the first things he did to reverse that attitude was to loosen some of the controls. He recognized that the new system would indeed prevent such an expensive problem from ever happening again, but its rigidity would also keep IBM from ever developing another major system.

By sticking to these eight basics, the successful companies have achieved better-than-average growth. Their managements are able not only to change but also to change quickly. They keep their sights aimed externally at their customers and competitors, and not on their own financial reports.

Excellence in management takes brute perseverance—time, repetition, and simplicity. The tools include plant visits, internal memos, and focused systems. Ignoring these rules may mean that the company slowly loses its vitality; its growth flattens, and its competitiveness is lost.

ORGANIZATION DESIGN

Jay W. Lorsch

INTRODUCTION

Managers can influence subordinates to work toward the goals of the firm in at least three primary ways. One is through their own personal contacts—by what they do and say in meetings, one-to-one sessions, speeches, plant tours, etc. The second way is by the substantive decisions they make about the allocation of resources to one activity or set of products, rather than to another. The third way is through their decisions about the definition of jobs, arrangement of organization charts, measurement and reward schemes, selection criteria for personnel, etc. The latter set of decisions concerns us here and is what is meant by organizational design.

To be more precise, *the design of the organization is composed of the structure, rewards, and measurement practices intended to direct members' behavior toward the organization's goals,* as well as the criteria used to select persons for the organization. *Structure* is the pattern of job definition, authority, and communication relationships represented in the organization charts, position descriptions, etc. *Rewards* refer to those things that an organization offers employees as its part of the psychological contract. Not only financial compensation and benefits are included, but also career opportunities, interesting work, and even meaningful personal relationships. Closely connected to this are the criteria that managers use to select new employees *Measurement* includes the control and management information system—in essence, the procedures by which plans are made and results measured and reported.

The duration of time and effort that managers devote to decisions about these design elements depends upon the size of the firm and their own level. It is a safe generalization that as managers move up in the hierarchy and/or as the size of their organization grows, they become more concerned with issues of organizational design. This is a result of the fact that with more subordinates the manager is less able to rely on personal contacts to influence subordinates. Therefore, he or she must rely more heavily on the organizational design elements of structure, rewards, measurement, and selection criteria. In this note, the focus is more on issues of structure than on the other design elements.

GOALS OF ORGANIZATION DESIGN

That organizational design decisions are intended to influence subordinates' behavior is a broad statement of the ends managers seek in making design choices. More specifically, managers are concerned with three related goals when they make design decisions:

1 To create an organizational design that provides a permanent setting in which managers can influence individuals to do their particular job

2 To achieve the pattern of collaborative effort among individual employees that is necessary for successful operations

3 To create a cost-effective organization, that is, one that not only achieves the first two goals, but does so with a minimum of duplication of effort, payroll costs, etc.

A BRIEF HISTORICAL PERSPECTIVE

Managers' concerns with these goals and the issues of organizational design are not new. Many of the earliest management writers—Fayol, Urwick, Gulick—addressed these matters. What is new, however, is our increased understanding of organizations and their operations. These writers of the early twentieth century generalized from their own experiences as practitioners in a few basic industries, such as railroads, mining, and automobiles, and concluded that the principles they learned there and then were applicable in other industries at other points in time. Furthermore, their view of the motivation of employees appears very simplistic today. Basically, they saw people as motivated solely by money: "If you paid people, they would do what you told them." We know that human needs at work are more varied and complex. Thus, the statement of the goals of organizational design also has implicit in it a recognition of the full range of rewards that motivate people to work. More recent studies have also indicated that there is no one best way to organize. As we will elaborate below, the appropriate organizational forms depend upon the human and business situation facing the firm.

While it is easy to find these flaws in the ideas of early management writers, it has not been easy for managers to discard the so-called principles that these early authors laid down: "The span of control should be between six and nine subordinates." "One boss for each person." "Authority must equal responsibility." "The line does, the staff advises." Such statements have become part of the folklore of management, at least in the United States. As a result, many managers intuitively fall back on these early ideas when they are confronted with an organizational design decision. This is not surprising, because their simplicity gives them an intuitive appeal. However, it is dangerous, since these principles ignore the infinitely varied and complex human, technological, and market conditions for which organizations must be designed. Recent managerial experience and organizational research has provided a more potent set of tools for thinking about organizational design issues. In the balance of this note, we briefly outline these ideas and describe how they shed light on the issues managers face at different organizational levels in firms of different sizes.

RECENT CONCEPTUAL DEVELOPMENT

These ideas, labeled *contingency theory,*[1] emphasize that the characteristics of an organization are contingent (depend) on the nature of the environment in which it operates, the tasks that members must perform to accomplish the firm's strategy in this environment, and the psychological characteristics of its members.

Definitions

To be more precise, four terms need to be defined. The *environment* refers to the forces and objects outside the firm with which its members must deal to achieve the organization's purposes. These may include competitors' actions, customer requirements, financial constraints, scientific and technological knowledge, etc. A common denominator is that these can be considered information that must be taken into account in making and implementing decisions inside the organization. In discussing organizational design decisions, this way of thinking about the environment is useful, and we will use it.

The organization's *strategy* is a statement of the environment(s) or business(es) relevant to the organization, the purposes of the organization within that context, and the distinctive means by which these goals will be achieved. In a sense then, the strategy defines the environment in which an organization operates. A strategy may be explicitly stated and even written down, or it may simply exist as an implicit idea based on the actions of the organization's managers over time.

The term *task* refers to the activities members must perform to achieve the organization's strategic goals in a particular environment. We will generally use this term to refer to the activities of a particular set of individuals in dealing with the environment—for example, the task of a sales unit or the task of division general managers, etc.

The *psychological characteristics of members* means the enduring personality factors that lead an individual to behave in a consistent fashion over time. It is not necessary to debate here about whether these should be labeled needs, values, interests, or all three. The important point is that individuals do have such qualities, which vary between individuals, and organizational design decisions must take these differences into account.

With these definitions in mind, there are a few central ideas that need to be understood.

---

[1] A list of the authors who have contributed to this way of thinking is included in the references.

Concept of Fit

If a three-way fit exists among an individual's psychological makeup, the nature of the task being performed, and the organizational design, the individual wil be motivated to perform that task effectively (Exhibit 1). Two examples may illustrate the point:

A production supervisor, such as a foreman, has a job in which his activities are well-defined by the technology and product specifications. In essence, his job is to ensure that his subordinates do the same thing well today they did yesterday. In this sense, the work is highly certain and predictable. Results here can be measured on a daily and even more frequent basis. This supervisor has a bachelor's degree in industrial engineering. He enjoys working with his supervisor, who provides him with clear directions for his efforts. He also finds his frequent contact with other supervisors enjoyable. The routine and predictable work also has an attraction for him. In fact, he becomes upset with too much ambiguity and confusion. For this manager and his colleagues, given their predictable task, an organizational design that emphasizes tight control and procedures is appropriate. Tighter spans of supervisory control, well-specified operating procedures, specific and frequent measurement of results—all make sense in this situation.

A group leader in a research laboratory in a consumer products company has a job in which results are not highly predictable. Her subordinates, who have PhD's, and their technical assistants are working on problems in food technology. Their progress is hard to measure, and it may take months or even years to produce meaningful results. All in all, they are involved in a highly uncertain endeavor. The group leader herself, who has a PhD in biochemistry, shares many personal characteristics with her subordinates. She prefers to work with minimum direction and maximum autonomy and does not like to be heavily involved with others, preferring often to be alone. She likes to work on complex and uncertain problems. These tasks and personal characteristics require an organizational design with a wide span of management control, with infrequent measurement in relation

EXHIBIT 1   The concept of fit

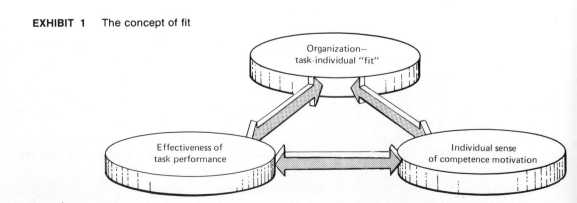

to general progress. Detailed procedures, job descriptions, and the lot are out of place here because so little work can be preprogrammed. An organizational design that has these characteristics should be motivating for this technical manager as well as for her subordinates, and thus should also lead to effective results for the laboratory.

As these two examples and Exhibit 1 are intended to illustrate, the three-way fit produces two outcomes—one is motivation for the individual and the other is performance for the organization. These results themselves are interconnected because, as the individual performs his job well and receives feedback about this, his or her need for mastery is satisfied which, in turn, encourages the individual to continue work to maintain these positive feelings. Although we will not dwell on it here, there is also a fit required between the individual and task characteristics. To be effective, the individual must have interests, skills, and needs that are consistent with his or her work. One way to ensure this fit is to use criteria for selecting personnel that recognize the need for it. Finally, we should indicate that while we have stressed mastery needs here, such a fit also enables the individual to achieve other goals as well, for example, to earn money, to gain an appropriate amount of social contact, etc.

Differentiation

The second idea that we need to introduce follows from the concept of *fit*. This is the concept of *differentiation,* which can be defined as the differences among the several units of the organization in design and members' behavior. These differences arise because a variety of tasks must be accomplished by various organizational units to cope successfully with the firm's total environment. As each unit's organization is designed to achieve a fit with its task and the characteristics of its members, it becomes differentiated from the other units with different tasks and different members. The extent of differentiation depends upon the similarity of the tasks and members in the units. To return to the preceding examples, if the factory and research laboratory were both units in the same organization, the degree of differentiation in that organization would be quite large. The factory would have a highly formalized design and members who were concerned with immediate results in terms of costs and quantity, and who believed in relatively close direction of the efforts of their subordinates. In the research laboratory, there would be a less-formalized design and members who were concerned with solving technical problems in a longer time frame, and who would want greater autonomy. If, on the other hand, the two units were factories, such as the one described above, with each operating in a separate geographic area, the degree of differentiation might be small. There might be almost no difference in members' behavior or organizational design, except for their concerns with goals pertaining to their specific location.

Differentiation is a complex commodity in that it has positive and negative consequences simultaneously. Because differentiation stems from the fact that the several units in an organization have achieved a fit with their task and human situations, and this leads to motivation and performance, an appropriate degree of differentiation is critical to the effective functioning of organizations.[2] This is its virtue. However, the negative side is that the greater the differentiation among units of an organization, the more difficult it becomes for their members to communicate across unit boundaries. For example, our factory supervisor would have great difficulty dealing with our laboratory group leaders. One thinks in the short term, the other in the long term; one is concerned with costs and productivity, the other with innovation and knowledge building; one believes in an orderly, unambiguous organization, the other relishes ambiguity and autonomy, etc. Such differences make it hard for them to understand each other's concerns and are likely to lead to conflicting ideas about how to solve mutual problems. If the laboratory leader was being asked to solve a process problem for the factory supervisor, the following dialogue might ensue:

Factory supervisor: I'd like to get this work done as quickly as possible. It's reducing our output every day.

Laboratory leader: Well, it'll take us some time to understand the factors involved, and I also have to free up a person to work on it. . . .

Factory supervisor: I understand that, but it's critical to my operation, we've got a high spoilage rate now.

Laboratory leader: (To herself—Hell, this isn't a challenging problem, none of my people will want to work on it.) I suspect we might make some progress in a month's time.

Factory supervisor: A month? You've got to be kidding! That's a month of bad product and reduced output. (To himself—my boss will eat me alive, if we don't get this solved before then.) I was hoping you could do it this week.

Laboratory leader: No way . . .

The conversation continues with no easy resolutions of these conflicting viewpoints. The fact that differentiation leads to such conflicts is connected to the third idea—the concept of integration.

Integration

Integration is simply defined as the state of collaboration among organizational units. Integration usually manifests itself in specific conversations between the representatives of units, such as the one outlined above. However, in thinking about organizational design, it is possible and necessary to generalize about the state of integration required for the organization to be effective. To do this, several dimensions are important to consider.

The first dimension is the number and patterns of units that have to collaborate to achieve the organization's purposes. Thompson has identified one useful way to think about this (Exhibit 2). Pooled integration is the simplest pattern, in which the various subsidiary units (B, C, D) have no need for integration among themselves.

---

[2] In this discussion, we have been referring to differentiation among units that stems from differences in their tasks or members and which is therefore appropriate. Of course, differentiation can result from management action that is inappropriate to the units' tasks and members. In such a case, excessive differentiation might be a liability.

They are all linked together only through their contact with the central unit A. A holding company typically has this pattern of integration among its major components. Sequential integration is where each unit must integrate its activities only with that unit preceding or following it in a process or task flow. Factories with work flow across departmental lines provide a good example of this pattern. The reciprocal pattern simply means that collaboration must be in both directions among all units. For this reason, it is the most complex pattern. The integration required among marketing, research and development, and manufacturing personnel in developing new products is often of this character. As one moves from the pooled to the sequential to the reciprocal pattern, the difficulties of achieving integration become more difficult. While this way of thinking can be useful, it is important to recognize that these pure types rarely exist in the real world.

A second dimension of integration is simply the frequency with which collaboration is necessary. For example, in a sales organization there is usually a relatively low frequency of integration required among various regional units. On infrequent occasions, the national sales manager may want to have the regional units collaborate in a national program, but usually the regions conduct their sales activity independently of each other. In contrast, in the electronic engineering and power systems departments of an aerospace firm that is trying to develop a new rocket for NASA, we see a very different picture. These engineers need frequent contact across departmental lines to make certain that the components they are each developing for the total system will work in harmony.

Closely connected to the frequency of integration required is the importance of achieving it, but these two dimensions are not necessarily identical. For example, the sales and manufacturing departments may only meet semiannually to develop an

EXHIBIT 2 Patterns of required integration

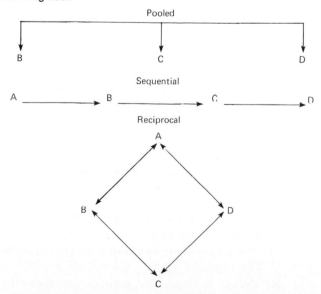

integrated production schedule, but the success of this decisionmaking may have a major impact on the firm's success.

A fourth aspect of integration to be considered in thinking about design issues is the certainty and predictability of the information. If the matters around which integration is required are highly predictable, the managers can use plans and preestablished procedures to achieve integration, and only infrequent face-to-face contact is necessary. The production scheduling example just mentioned is a case in point. If, however, the information is uncertain and complex, more face-to-face contact, as in the aerospace example, may be necessary.

As the above examples suggest, there are several ways the organizational design can be used to achieve integration. These include the management hierarchy, regular meetings, and coordination of roles, such as product or program managers, incentives that reward integrative behavior, etc. These will be fully discussed later. At this point, however, we want to emphasize that managers do have a choice about how they orient their organizational design decisions to achieving integration. To understand the appropriate choice, they need to answer the questions suggested by the factors just discussed:

How many units require integration and in what pattern?
How frequently is integration required?
How important is integration among any set of these units?
How complex and uncertain is the information being considered?

Exhibit 3 illustrates that the answers to these questions can be a rough guide to the difficulty of achieving the required integration and, therefore, to the proper mix of design elements devoted to achieving integration. For example, the greater the number of units whose efforts must be integrated and the greater their involvement in reciprocal relationships, the more the organizational design must provide mechanisms, such as teams' coordinating roles and plans, to facilitate integration. Of course, this assumes that it is important to the company's goals to achieve this integration. Whether face-to-face contact or a formal planning scheme are the best means to achieve this integration depends on the complexity and uncertainty of the information that must be handled. If the data are relatively simple and predictable, a predetermined plan might be suitable. But if the information is more uncertain and complex, the organizational design must provide mechanisms for integration that encourage greater face-to-face contact, such as teams, or a liaison role.

But this figure also includes one other issue, which affects the difficulty of achieving integration—the degree of differentiation among units. This reemphasizes the connection between differentiation and integration because, as mentioned above, the greater the differentiation among units, the more difficult it becomes to achieve integration. It is because differentiation and integration have this complex relationship that they are so important to understand as tools for thinking about organizational design. Together with the concept of fit, they give managers powerful tools for analyzing specific organizational design problems.

The suggested approach for dealing with organizational design issues basically involves three steps. First, managers must use the concepts of fit, differentiation, and

EXHIBIT 3 FACTORS AFFECTING THE DIFFICULTY OF ACHIEVING INTEGRATION.

Difficulty of achieving integration	Low	High
Degree of differentiation	Small ◄——► Large	
Number of units requiring integration	Few ◄——► Many	
Pattern of integration	Pooled ◄——► Reciprocal	
Frequency of integration required	Infrequent contact ◄——► Frequent contact—daily or more often	
Importance of integration to organization's strategy	Marginal ◄——► Critical	
Complexity and uncertainty of information	Simple and highly certain ◄——► Uncertain and highly complex	

integration to understand and assess what the environmental and human situations require of their organization. Secondly, they need to make design choices to meet those requirements. Finally, they need to consider how to implement the necessary changes. In this note, our primary emphasis is on the first two steps.

To illustrate how managers can deal with the diagnosis and design steps, we will next focus on some of the design issues managers face at three organizational levels—the functional unit, the single-business organization, and the multibusiness organization. This choice of examples is made for two reasons. First, it is a matter of common observation that most business firms build their organizations upward from functional units. This is true whether it be a small manufacturing firm with sales, manufacturing, engineering, and financial functions; a diversified multiproduct manufacturer with these same functions contained in each of several product divisions; a department store with operations, merchandising, and selling functions; or a bank with loan, trust, operations, and controller departments. Secondly, managers at each of these levels of organization are faced with different design problems and, therefore, the conceptual ideas that we have just discussed must be applied somewhat differently at each level.

ORGANIZATIONAL DESIGN IN FUNCTIONAL UNITS

Functional units are the logical place to begin this discussion not only because they are the basic building blocks upon which larger organizations are constructed, but also because they are the home of most organization members. In fact the various functions of industrial firms have become so pervasive that they have been institutionalized in the specialization in academic training in business administration and engineering schools. Undergraduates and graduate students alike can specialize in marketing, manufacturing, industrial engineering, finance, etc. They enter organizations with careers in these areas as their goals. Even the rising star on a fast career track to general management is likely to spend his or her early years in one function, and the average employee may well spend his active career in one function.

Employee Motivation

This fact points to one of the major issues facing a functional manager: to create an organizational design that provides a viable set of rewards for subordinates, including compensation and benefits, professionally stimulating work, and meaningful career opportunities. Without reviewing these issues deeply, it should be mentioned that the fit among task, individual characteristics, and organizational design is a useful way of thinking about how to create a psychological contract that is acceptable to both the members of a functional unit and to the employing organization. In essence, it is a potent tool to ensure that the measurement, rewards, and structure of a unit together accomplish the goal of motivating employees to work toward the purposes of the firm.

Division of Work

There is one aspect of achieving such a fit that is worthy of greater emphasis here: the question of job design and the division of work within the function. Job design issues certainly affect motivation. Job design decisions can also have an important bearing on a second design goal—creating a cost effective organization. For example, designing salespeople's jobs to reduce travel time creates a more cost-effective organization; similarly, addition of a second or third shift to a factory can ensure maximum machine utilization and can lower manufacturing costs. As these examples suggest, the subunits within a function can be created on the basis of occupational specialty as well as division of work by time of day or territorial responsibility. The major rationale for occupationally based units seems to be maintaining a differentiated home for specialized expertise. The major reason for creating geographic or temporal subunits within a function is often because of the opportunities for cost savings, as the previous examples also suggest.

Regardless of the basis for the division of work, there can be differences in behavior and organizational design among members of different subunits within the same function. Thus, while sales executives may refer to all controller's personnel as "shiny-bottomed bookkeepers," the controller's function in many firms is made up of a diverse set of subunits, ranging from computer programmers and systems analysts dealing with relatively complex problem-solving tasks to clerical operations with routine and repetitive tasks. Similarly, within a manufacturing function there are not only the line manufacturing supervisors but also industrial engineers, production schedulers, quality control specialists, computer programmers, etc. Although these different specialists share goals and behavior patterns that are common to their function, such as a concern with on-time delivery or low-cost operations in the case of manufacturing, they may also have differentiated approaches to these issues, and their tasks and personal characteristics may make a somewhat different organizational design appropriate. This differentiation can lead to problems of achieving integration. Thus, as functional managers consider the issues of job design and division of work, they need to think not only about achieving a fit that will lead to a motivated and efficient organization, but they also have to consider how this will affect differentiation within the function and the *potential* difficulties of achieving integration.

Achieving Integration

The word *potential* is emphasized to indicate that such difficulties can be managed if the organizational design provides a way of achieving integration among the subunits that must work together. Within most functional units, the primary device for this is the management hierarchy. The hierarchy is not only a mechanism for directing the activities of individual subunits, but it provides a means for achieving whatever integration is required within the function. For example, if the industrial engineers and mechanical engineers within a manufacturing function have difficulty agreeing upon the production methods for a new product, their common supervisor would be expected to resolve the dispute.

While the management hierarchy is usually capable of handling the information and decisionmaking required for integration within a function, occasionally other means are also necessary. Thus, we find regular meetings of the regional sales managers to coordinate sales and marketing practices, or find in a large food-processing plant that teams with representation from the various subunits (for example, scheduling, quality control, industrial engineering) are *created* to provide a vehicle for supervisors to coordinate these specialists' efforts in relation to their departments. These other means must be employed when the difficulty of achieving integration becomes too great for the hierarchy to manage. This can happen because of any combination of factors mentioned previously in Exhibit 3. Perhaps the hierarchy needs to be supplemented, because the requirement for integration within the controller's function is made more important by the impending startup of a new generation of computer. Therefore, a special project team is created. Or new pricing regulations make it necessary to create a new position of pricing coordinator on the national sales manager's staff to coordinate pricing decisions across all regions.

Applying Design Tools

The specific issues discussed so far show how the major concepts of fit, differentiation, and integration can help the functional manager think about the design problems he or she faces. They are not intended to be an all-inclusive list of design issues at this level of organization, but they are those that seem most prevalent. Before considering how these same concepts can be used at other levels of organization, two other points should be emphasized to put this discussion of functional units in perspective.

The first point is one that applies not just to this discussion, but to all that follow. The concepts that have been discussed can only be helpful as a rough map for understanding the boundaries of a particular design problem and the direction for action. There is still much room for creative invention to solve the problems once they are understood. An example of this is a factory that was having great difficulty achieving integration across its three shifts, each of which operated 7 days a week. The management of this plant had tried all the standard remedies—log books, meetings of supervisors before the shift, the factory superintendent visiting all shifts, etc. After a more careful look at the problem, it was recognized that the difficulty stemmed from the fact that the supervisors on each shift did not have time to grasp the problems on the production floor to provide reasonable direction to their workers. This led to the solution of putting the supervisors on a schedule that brought them into work and allowed them to leave 2 hours earlier than their subordinates. Thus, the supervisors were on a schedule that allowed them to grasp the problems of the previous shift before a new shift of workers started. This simple scheduling change enabled the management hierarchy to become an effective integrative tool. Such a solution may seem obvious in retrospect. But given the number of plants that have struggled with the same issue, it is obvious that creativity is also a necessary ingredient in dealing with such organizational issues.

The second point, which also applies to the rest of our discussion, is that the design elements of structure, measurement, and reward need to be considered as a package. Changes in one may also have to be accompanied by changes in others. In essence, they are all means for influencing members' behavior. If they are not designed and maintained to give consistent signals to employees about management's expectations, the results can range from confusion to chaos.

ORGANIZING THE SINGLE BUSINESS

Single-business organizations specialize in one primary business. They may be the product division of a multibusiness firm or a financially independent enterprise. In either case, the organization consists of a set of interrelated functional units whose activities are aimed at developing, producing, and marketing a common product or service to a particular set of customers.

Differentiation of Functions

Since each function needs to achieve a fit with its particular task and human situation to be effective, one design issue facing managers of single-business organizations is to maintain and/or achieve the degree of differentiation among functions appropriate to their several tasks. If functional managers handled design issues without interference, the necessary differentiation might be a natural consequence of their independent actions. However, the general managers of single businesses often feel compelled to limit such independent action on the part of their functional managers for two reasons. First, they become concerned about the issue of equity and fairness across functions. Secondly, it is easier to administrate and know what is happening in the organization if there is greater uniformity and standardization of practices. While there is no question that it is important to maintain some sense of equity in matters of compensation and benefits among various occupational groups in an organization, excessive emphasis on standardization to ease administration or because "it seems neater" can reduce differentiation and harm the organization's effectiveness.

For example, higher management often imposes the same rigid working hours on research scientists as on production personnel. Common arrival and departure times make sense when the personnel involved are operating a highly interdependent factory where schedule is critical. However, in the case of research scientists, their problem-solving and creative activity does not adhere to any schedule. Thus, the focus on regular hours is inappropriate, and the scientists become annoyed with the unnecessary rules. Their attitude is, "If they are so insistent about my being here on time, I'll damn well quit on time. No more working at night or on weekends to finish experiments." While this is a relatively trivial example, it is typical of the problems managers can encounter if they fail to understand the importance of maintaining differentiation among the functions involved in their business.

The amount of differentiation required among functions, of course, varies depending upon the nature of the organizational environment. However, in most cases, the differences across functions are much more pronounced than those discussed above within functional units. A few examples may promote an understanding of the range of such cross-functional differentiation:

As an example of minimal differentiation required across functions, consider a firm that produces corrugated containers—boxes, cartons, etc. Only two major functions are involved in this business—selling and manufacturing—and these have different goals. The sales personnel focus on prompt customer delivery, high quality, and competitive pricing. The manufacturing managers are concerned with low cost and want to avoid quality and delivery requirements, which adversely affect costs. Beyond these varying goals, there are few differences between these two functions. Both are focused on short-term results and are involved in tasks that are relatively predictable. Thus, a more formal organizational design and directive leadership makes sense to both production and sales personnel.

As an example of somewhat greater differentiation, consider a company in the cosmetics industry. There are four major functions: marketing, sales, manufacturing, and technical research. Each has a defined set of goals. Marketing personnel are concerned with effective advertising, sales promotion, and pricing policies that will lead to an expanding market share. Field sales personnel are, of course, concerned with market share, but their views on influencing it focus on maintaining shelf space in retail outlets, keeping the channels of distribution well-supplied, etc. Manufacturing personnel are concerned with an efficient operation and maintaining product quality, etc. The research personnel are involved in applied activity aimed at new products. With the marketing personnel, they share a concern with results beyond the near term. Of course, the marketing personnel also share a concern for immediate results with the manufacturing and sales function. In addition to these differences, there will be differences in management style and organizational design across these functions that will be important for each function's success, but which can impede cross-functional integration. In such a situation, management must act so that each unit develops structures, measurement schemes, and reward practices that encourage their members to focus on the appropriate set of activities and issues.

Finally, consider a business that requires an even greater amount of differentiation—a basic plastic materials business (for example, polystyrene, polyvinylchloride, etc.). Here we find the functions of sales, manufacturing, research and technical services. The manufacturing personnel, similar to those in the previous examples, are primarily concerned with near-term results in the area of cost and quality. But since they are operating a much more capital-intensive technology, they may be much less flexible than their counterparts in other businesses about interrupting product flows or process changes. The sales personnel are concerned with customer relations, competitive pricing, etc. Again, their focus is largely on the near term, but they also give some attention to the future and new products. The technical services group focuses on providing technical service to the customer in support of the sales force, and thus is concerned with immediate results. But, at the same time, it has responsibility for applied research aimed at developing new and improved products and processes and, therefore, may be also focused on the long term. Finally, the research unit is involved in more basic research—understanding the structure of the materials and using this understanding to develop entirely new products and processes as well as to improve existing ones. Their time horizon may be several years. All these units need to have widely different organizational designs and management styles, which allow each to match its highly differentiated task and members.

These examples demonstrate the range of differences that occurs in different businesses. While they are all drawn from manufacturing enterprises, similar examples can be found in service industries. Of course, these illustrations are oversimplified. For example, the financial function has been omitted even though any joint decisions involving the functions mentioned above also involves the viewpoint of the financial function—about the appropriate allocation of financial resources. In spite of such limitations, these examples do illustrate how the ideas of fit and differentiation can help us to understand what variations in behavior, management practices, and organizational design make sense among the functions in a particular business.

Using these concepts, managers need to look at each function and determine for themselves what characteristics of organizational design and behavior are necessary for that function to perform its task and to motivate the individuals who work in it. From this analysis of each function, the pattern of differences among the functions will be apparent. In such an analysis, as the examples above suggest, there are certain dimensions that previous research indicates are useful to understand:

What are the goals of each unit?

What is the time period within which each unit obtains some definitive feedback about the results of its members' efforts?

What pattern of leadership behavior is appropriate for each unit?

What pattern of structure, measurement, and rewards encourages behavior directed toward the goals, time horizon, and other aspects of the unit's task and also fits the members' personal expectations?

The dimensions suggested by these questions are really only a very crude map of the complex pattern of differences in attitudes and behavior that exist among members of different functional units. Yet if the manager concerned with how much differentiation to encourage in an organization considers these dimensions, he or she will have a useful starting point.

Grouping Functions

Understanding the issue of differentiation is important not just because of the tradeoff between differentiation and standardization in the organizational design of functional units. It also has an important bearing on another design issue concerning the manager of a single-business organization: What functions should be grouped together under a common manager? In thinking about this issue, as about other design questions, managers often tend to rely on conventional wisdom and/or emulate what other firms do.

Because most companies group marketing and the field sales force under a common manager, it seems the right thing to do. . . .

The advanced engineering design group should report to the engineering director, rather than to the research director, because its members are all engineers and not scientists. Besides that's where all the other engineering groups report. Never mind that these other mechanical and industrial engineers spend all their time in direct support of manufacturing operations.[3]

There are two essential reasons why managers consider grouping activities together. Either they want to place similar activities under a manager who understands them, or they want to place activities that require close integration under one manager to facilitate this collaboration. Therefore, the concepts of differentiation and integration can be helpful tools for such decisions. At the most basic level, simply by an awareness of these concepts, one is forced to ask if he or she is considering grouping these activities together to encourage integration or to group similar activities or both. If the answer to this question is both, clearly the decision to group activities together is a sound and easy one. On the other hand, if the answer to all parts of the question is negative, one does not want to group the units together. If in the preceding example, the advanced engineers were highly differentiated from other engineering groups and required little integration with them, there would be little logic to group them together.

The more frequently encountered and more difficult problems surround low differentiation with little requirements for integration, or a large amount of differentiation with a great need for integration. Here the organizational designer must make a tradeoff about what he or she wants to accomplish. Should the hierarchy be used to achieve integration in this instance? Or should similar activities be grouped together,

---

[3] The example of the marketing and sales force is typical of such a case. The marketing managers and field sales force may both be concerned with customers and short-run results. Therefore, the differences between them are small. Also the sales force and the marketing department are highly interdependent, since the sales force is an important element in the marketing mix.

easing the job of supervisors and perhaps facilitating their differentiation from other activities? In the latter instance, other means would have to be found to achieve integration between the units grouped together and the other parts of the organization with which they needed to be integrated.

Integration of Functions

In discussing the grouping of activities, we have necessarily sidetracked into a discussion of the integration of functions, which is another major design issue at this level of organization. As we saw in our discussion of integration within functional units, using the hierarchy is only one of several means to facilitate integration. However, even in single-business units, the hierarchy is often the fundamental mechanism for achieving integration. In fact, in businesses with low differentiation and uncomplicated integrative requirements (the corrugated container business), the hierarchy may be the only integrative device necessary. However, as the requirements for differentiation and integration become greater, other integrative devices must supplement the hierarchy. Thus, in the consumer product or pharmaceutical business described earlier, greater differentiation and a more complex requirement for integration might create a requirement for product managers, who play an integrating role, and/or a management committee made up of the heads of the several functions.

As with most organizational design issues, there are no simple rules to define the appropriate mix of integrative devices in a particular situation. However, if we accept the idea that an organization can be thought of as a system for taking in bits of information from the business environment and combining the information to reach and implement decisions, it can help us understand when certain integrative devices are appropriate. From this perspective, we can revisit the factors identified in Exhibit 3, as affecting the difficulty of achieving integration:

Number of units requiring integration
Pattern of integration (pooled, sequential, reciprocal)
Frequency of required integration
Importance of integration to organizational results
Complexity and uncertainty of information
Degree of differentiation

In theory, these factors could affect the flow of information among functional units which, in turn, affects the difficulty of achieving integration. The more that all of these factors taken together suggest difficult problems of achieving integration, the more supplements will be required for the hierarchy. Just what form these other devices should take depends importantly upon the frequency of required integration and the complexity and uncertainty of information. Both factors, which frequently are closely connected, have an important influence on whether face-to-face contact is necessary to achieve integration or whether predetermined plans, schedules, etc., once arrived at will allow units to operate in an integrated fashion without such direct contact.

For example, in a chain of variety stores, purchasing budgets may be drawn up on a quarterly basis. Once buyers and store managers agree upon the budget for a particular quarter, there may be little need for direct contact for several months. Each unit carries out its activity in a coordinated manner without any interim face-to-face contact. In this business, fashion and style do not introduce a high degree of uncertainty and change. In contrast, a group of high-priced, women's specialty stores with much more uncertainty because of fashion changes might need an integrative mechanism that encourages more direct contact between buyers and store managers.

Integrative devices that allow face-to-face contact are of basically two types—either integrating roles or cross-functional groups of managers who are constituted as a team, committee, etc., to integrate effort. Integrating roles include such positions as product managers, brand managers, program managers, project managers, and account executives. A major responsibility of such positions is to integrate the activities of peers in other functions. Such an approach makes sense when the information is sufficiently certain and simple that one person can achieve integration with his or her counterparts on a one-to-one basis.

Cross-functional groups of managers may be labeled teams, committees, task forces, etc. In specific companies, such terms have slightly different connotations. For our purposes, they are used synonymously. Such groups make sense as integrative devices when the information is so complex and uncertain that representatives from the several functions need to simultaneously understand each other's data and reach joint decisions.

Of course, individual integrating positions and cross-functional groups are not mutually exclusive. In organizations where the requirements for integration are particularly acute, both are used simultaneously. Another reason for establishing a cross-functional group in addition to an individual integrating role is that the group builds commitment to the success of integrated effort among the functional specialists assigned to it. For example, the artists, copywriters, and market information specialists assigned to an account team in an advertising agency become concerned with the overall goals of serving the account in addition to their own particular function.

In addition to these structural devices, the reward and measurement practices can also be utilized to encourage integration. The most common example is tying the compensation of functional executives not just to the results of their function, but also to business profits. This is an issue that will be discussed fully when we consider the design problems of multibusiness firms.

Single Business to Multibusiness

As a transition to issues of multibusiness organizations, we need to mention briefly a final design issue that managers of both single-business organizations and multibusiness organizations share: When does a single business become a multibusiness organization? This issue arises for the manager of a free-standing single-business enterprise when it expands and diversifies its product line. It also arises for the corporate management of a multibusiness firm and the managers of their single businesses when they consider whether to split up a product division (business) into two separate divisions or to combine a new acquisition with an existing division. In fact, within the single-business organization one of the major reasons that integrative positions and groups are needed is because the business has expanded its products and services. As it does, the quantity of cross-functional integration with which the hierarchy must deal becomes too great and other integrative devices are established. At some point in these developments, it occurs to one of those responsible for the organizational design that those in integrating positions and/or their counterparts in these groups are really running their own business and thus should be held responsible for profits.

In deciding when a single business becomes a multibusiness, the concepts of differentiation and integration again have applicability. As in any decision about division of work, the basic questions are:

1 Is the new activity sufficiently different from the existing activity to warrant treating it separately?

2 Is the new activity sufficiently free from integration with the existing activities to be managed as a separate entity?

In this instance, the differences refer to variations in customers, processes, marketing, distribution, etc., that might require personnel to adapt and develop different orientations, knowledge, and skills, and might require a different organizational design. Integration in this context refers to the extent that the proposed new business can be operated without integration with other existing activities. It is important to recognize that while the clearest case can be made for creating a new business when both great differences and little need for integration exist, there are cases when the presence of only one condition makes it desirable to create a new business. For example, when a new set of products is introduced in a consumer product company, they may be very similar to existing products, with similar customers, marketing approaches, manufacturing policies, etc. Yet because the new products can be managed independently of established products and because the managers of existing products are already overworked, the decision to establish a new business makes sense.

Although the examples that we tend to use refer to a new business as a set of new products, a new business can also refer to a decision to move into a new territory. Examples of this might be:

An East Coast department store chain expanding into the western United States

A European airline gaining the right to carry passengers from the East Coast of the United States to Caribbean resort areas

A multinational firm whose operations have been confined to the United States and Europe undertaking operations in South America.

Whether the new business is a new territory or a new set of products or services, once managers agree they are in more than one business they are faced with design issues of the structure, measurement, and reward of multibusiness organizations.

MULTIBUSINESS ORGANIZATIONS

Stratified and Simultaneous Structures

The most conventional structure for a multibusiness firm is a set of product divisions reporting to corporate executives, with staff groups also present in the corporate headquarters (Exhibit 4). Each division is self-contained, with its own manufacturing, selling, and research functions, among others. The corporate staff units are intended to provide support, services, and direction where such activity can be economically shared across the several businesses. In essence, these organizations are designed to achieve differentiation at the division level by product and within the divisions by function. Having already discussed differentiation by function earlier, it is now important to recognize that because each business faces different customers, technology, etc., it must have an organizational design and resulting behavior that fit its particular environment. This can be illustrated by returning to the example of forming a new business unit alongside existing businesses. Because of differentiation between the existing business environment and the new one, the new business management would have to make adjustments in the design of its organization and in other ways encourage its subordinates to adopt behavior that fits the new situation. It is in this sense that product or business divisions are differentiated one from the other. An important element in this is usually to develop a reward and measurement scheme that motivates key managers to work toward the profits of each business. The other integrative devices built into the design of such a divisionalized organization

EXHIBIT 4   Product divisions structure (S=sales; M=manufacturing; R=research)

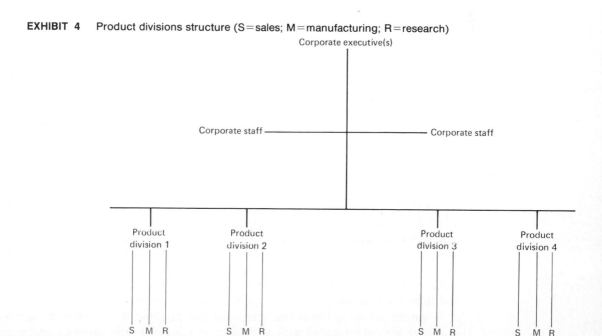

usually include the hierarchy as a major force for attaining integration within divisions and across divisions.

In summary, there are several important ways that the divisionalized structure meets the organizational design goals with which we have been concerned. First, it can create an organization that motivates the managers of each business to work toward its goals. Indeed, one of the principal arguments for this form among its advocates is the entrepreneurial zeal stimulated among divisional personnel. Secondly, it provides a structure that facilitates an appropriate flow of information; we will say more about this shortly. Finally, of course, it is an economically efficient structure. In fact, the one critical condition to make this form feasible is that it makes economic sense for each business to have its own functional resources. However, as was suggested above, it is often desirable to establish a new business even though it must share some or even all its functional resources with other businesses.

The reasons for establishing a separate business, even though sharing of functional resources is necessary, may be simply to spread the workload among several general managers and/or to improve cross-functional integration around each business. Or it may be because, while the two businesses each can support separate activities in one function, it makes economic sense to share other functional resources. A case in point is a large company in toiletries and health care. While each of its several businesses could justify its own sales force because of the variety of customers served and workload considerations, the manufacturing process serving these businesses was so technically interconnected that this resource had to be shared. A final reason that businesses might have to share functional resources is because each business has a definitive lifespan. Examples of this occur in the construction and aerospace industries, advertising, and real estate development. In such industries, it does not make sense to create new functions each time a new business venture is undertaken. Therefore, these businesses share pools of the various functional talent they require, whether these be physicists, electronics engineers, and mathematicians in aerospace companies, or artists and copywriters in advertising agencies.

The desirability of having multibusiness organizations that can share functional resources has led to a second major form for multibusiness organizations, which has been labeled *matrix, grid,* and even *multidimensional* (Exhibit 5). However, we will use the term *simultaneous* to describe such structures, because this term captures the essential differences between this structure and the product divisional structure, which is stratified. To understand why these terms seem apt, we need to return to the concepts of differentiation and integration. As was pointed out above, the product division structure (Exhibit 4) is differentiated by business at the upper level, and the hierarchy is designed to achieve integration across businesses at this level; at the next level, the hierarchy is designed to achieve integration across differentiated functions within the business. Thus, the organization is stratified in the sense that the requirements of differentiation and integration across businesses can be handled at one level and those by function at the next.

When we come to businesses that must share some or all of their functional resources, we are presented with a problem of achieving differentiation and integra-

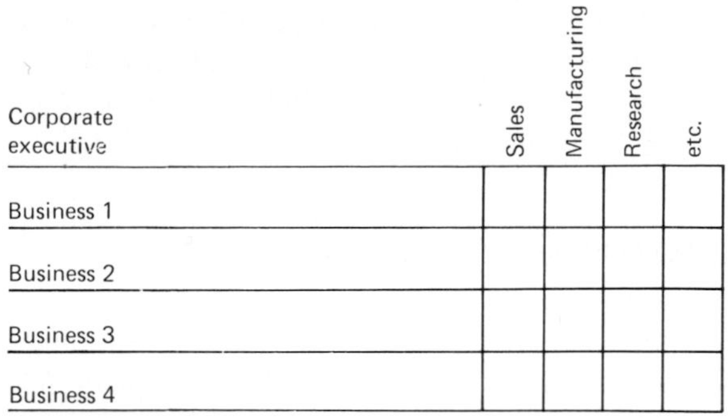

EXHIBIT 5   Simultaneous structures.

tion simultaneously along two dimensions at the same hierarchical level. Thus, the managers in charge of the functions must not only achieve integration within their functions, including allocating their resources across the various businesses, but they also need to maintain the differences between their functions and other functions. The business managers must simultaneously integrate the various functions contributing to their business and also achieve differentiated attention to the nature and goals of their business among the various functional contributors. These activities must be carried out at the same hierarchical level to ensure that the business and functional considerations are balanced. Of course, as Figure 5 illustrates, there is corporate management available to resolve any disagreements, but the complexity of the issues means that the hierarchy would quickly become overloaded as the only integrative mechanism.

For the sake of simplicity, the discussion of simultaneous organizations is limited to two dimensions—function and business. However, some multinational firms have simultaneous structure along three dimensions. For example, many U.S.-based multinational chemical companies have such a structure. Functional, product, and area dimensions cut across the organization so that all these viewpoints are represented in the complex interdependent decisions necessary for success. It also should be emphasized that while in this discussion, stratified and simultaneous structures have been considered mutually exclusive alternatives, in practice they are not. In fact, in many corporations, product divisions are created to capture the major business entities. Within these businesses, simultaneous structures are created that allow more related businesses to share functional resources. An example of this type of structure is the General Foods Corporation. It has four domestic grocery divisions, each of which focuses on a major business area, such as coffee or pet foods. Within two of these divisions, a simultaneous structure has been created with two businesses in each division sharing the functional resources of sales, manufacturing, and technical research. A simultaneous structure cannot only be utilized within a business organization, but it can also be utilized as a way of achieving differentiation and integration within a functional unit, when required. These complexities are added here not to confuse but rather to illustrate that these multiple possibilities for structuring multibusiness organizations do exist. What is required is an understanding of the requirements for differentiation and integration within and among businesses, as well as the economics of splitting or sharing functional resources. With that understanding and a good measure of creativity, a variety of structural patterns is possible.

Problems of Simultaneous Structure

Before leaving the topic of simultaneous structures, there are a few other comments about them that may be helpful. First, simultaneous structures are complex structures in which to live and work. The functional specialists working in a particular business frequently have at least two supervisors (one functional and one business). This violates the principle of unity of command, which was so sacred to early organizational writers. Also, for the organization to work at all, it is essential that any conflicts among these supervisors be resolved. This is true whether the issues be work assignments, evaluation, or compensation. A further problem within such a structure is that it often becomes difficult to hold any single person responsible for results. Instead a group of managers are the smallest accountable body that can be identified. For example, the results in business A may be affected not only by the manager of that business, but also by functional managers who work with him, but not exclusively for him in the classical line sense of the word. For these types of arrangements to work, there has to be a high level of commitment to the integrated goals of the firm as well as considerable trust among organization members. One design element that obviously can be used to develop such commitment is the reward scheme. If both compensation and career are tied to companywide results, this is one way to build such commitment. However, it would be naive to assume that this alone can achieve the desired results. It is also a matter of the top leadership and culture in the company—an issue that we will consider later.

Returning to stratified structures, there are two other design issues that warrant further consideration—the issue of grouping businesses under a company executive and the issue of achieving integration among businesses as well as with the corporate executive.

Grouping Businesses

Grouping is relatively straightforward, because it presents issues that are conceptually identical to those covered in the discussion of grouping functions within a single business. Usually, the question of grouping is raised in a company, because the span of control over the various businesses becomes too great for the existing manager(s) to handle, whether he or she be an executive vice president, chief operating officer, or president. The solution to such a problem is to create another level in the hierarchy—often labeled *group executives*. Their function is to oversee the activities of the businesses reporting to them, to integrate their activities with the corporate headquarters, and to facilitate whatever integration effort is required among these businesses. Once it is decided that the executive workload requires this addressed level, the remaining problem is to determine the businesses reporting to each executive. Here we return to the matter of the difference or similarity of the units (businesses) and how closely they must be integrated.

Ideally, units in similar businesses that require some integration should be grouped together under a common executive. If the businesses are similar, the group executive is apt to be able to understand them and provide more guidance to the business managers. If the businesses require integration (for example, because one business product is a raw material for the next, as in the paper industry), the group executive can foster the necessary cooperation. In situations where the businesses to be grouped are different but integrated, or similar but requiring no integration among them, the organizational designer is faced with the same sort of tradeoff that we found in the discussion about grouping functional units.

Cross-Divisional Integration

Thus far in this discussion, we have stressed the hierarchy and included group executives as the chief mechanism for promoting integration within the multibusiness firm. In many stratified organizations, this is adequate, because the requirements for integration are relatively simple at this level of a company's structure. By definition, the most complex requirements for integration in a stratified structure are contained within business units. As long as there is no requirement for integration among businesses, the hierarchy can manage the needed information flows and decisionmaking. These are limited in these situations to issues of resource allocation which, while important, occur at relatively infrequent intervals. For example, many so-called conglomerate firms manage highly differentiated businesses in diverse environments with the hierarchy as the only mechanism for integration. However, when company strategy requires vertical integration among businesses, as in the paper industry example above, more elaborate integrative mechanisms become necessary. The need for integration becomes more critical, the frequency of contact greater, etc.

Under such conditions, several integrative devices can supplement the hierarchy. One is, of course, a management or executive committee that meets regularly as a means of coordinating cross-business issues as well as deciding on company strategy. A second device is the compensation scheme. If business executives are tied to companywide results, as well as to the results of their own business, they are more apt to be willing to resolve cross-business conflicts. In fact, anyone experienced at this level of organization is aware, as mentioned above, that one of the major forces for differentiation among businesses is the profit-center concept. Because executives find that they are evaluated and measured on business results, they quickly identify with their business. Many articles have been devoted to the advantages and problems of profit centers and especially to the conflicts around transfer pricing (another means to facilitate cross-business integration), so we will not prolong this discussion. There is, however, one other mechanism that is sometimes used to facilitate integration—the corporate staff. For example, in vertically integrated companies, staff groups can play an integrative role by scheduling production capacity for raw-material-producing divisions to meet the needs of other divisions further downstream.

Staff Units

The corporate staff serves functions beyond promoting integration. In fact, the role of the staff groups has been a lively topic of managerial discussion for many years. For organizational architects, the critical issue seems to be the level at which staff groups should exist, the function of staff groups, and their reporting relationships. To discuss these issues, we need a working definition of the term *staff*. The term refers to any unit that is not directly involved in marketing, producing, and designing products or services. Such units include personnel, controller, planning, and legal units. What they have in common is a body of expertise that is useful to managers more directly involved in operating the businesses. What the members of these units do depends upon their specific area of expertise. In some cases they advise; in others they use their expertise to give direction; and yet in others they collect data and information about operations, which can be used as a basis to influence others. For our purposes, the central point is to recognize that staff groups can play any of these multiple roles. What the organization designer needs to do is to determine what role staff persons can usefully play in a given situation, and to make sure both members of the staff group and the units they serve are clear about their respective functions. In this process, of course, differentiated goals and time horizons will be articulated for the staff unit. For example, a controller's unit may have as its major goals the timely and accurate dispersion of financial information to operating managers. It is also important that the organization recognize that the expertise, knowledge, and information developed by staff units become a basis for influencing decisions. Even though they are not directly responsible for operating decisions, they can have an important impact on them.

The level of the organization at which a staff group should be located is a function of the differentiation of the units that use its services. For example, if the businesses of a conglomerate are highly diverse, it makes less sense to have a corporation marketing or manufacturing staff intended to serve them all. Yet even in such situations, the controller's staff and personnel staff might be highly appropriate at the corporate level to facilitate the allocation of human and financial resources among these differentiated business units. At the group level, where businesses have more in common, it might make more sense to have a small marketing or manufacturing staff to provide staff expertise to the related businesses. Similarly, in a vertically integrated firm, such as the chemical, petroleum and paper industries, where there is often more shared technology and marketing knowledge, there may be a more relevant role for a production or marketing staff at the corporate level.

Closely connected to the issue of location is one of reporting responsibility. Traditionally, most organization writers had the staff unit reporting to the general manager at the appropriate organization level. Thus, corporate staff units reported to the president, those at the group level to a group executive, and those within a business unit to the business manager. Many organizations have also followed this practice. However, because staff units usually serve specific business units no matter where they are located in the structure, the question of an individual staff member's reporting relationship has become a vexing problem. For example, a personnel manager or controller serving a division may be thought of as a member of the corporate personnel or controller's unit. Yet he or she needs to maintain a close relationship with division management. As a result of such situations, there has been an increasing tendency for organizational designers to recognize that such staff personnel are involved in dual reporting relationships similar to those in simultaneous structures. On one hand, they are responsible to their staff superior; on the other, to a line manager(s) whom they service regularly. In fact, the apparent increase in such relationships may simply result from the growing awareness by managers of the potential usefulness of simultaneous structures, and that they have adopted this form to staff units. However, another factor has also contributed to this trend. As business conditions have become more difficult in the 1980s, many members of top management have sought ways to make their organization designs more cost-effective. Consolidating staffs from several businesses and/or groups at the corporate level has been one way to accomplish this. However, the importance of retaining close ties between the staff groups and the business line managers had led to the dual reporting relationships.

CULTURE AND LEADERSHIP STYLE—THE MISSING LINK

In this discussion we have used three major concepts—fit, differentiation, and integration—to consider organizational design issues. In so doing, the focus has been on designing organizations to be consistent with the environment, strategy, and tasks of the organization and its members' characteristics. Such an emphasis is consistent with the present state of our knowledge (Exhibit 6). It is the relationship between

EXHIBIT 6   Organizational design considerations (shaded area indicates where little systematic research has been completed)

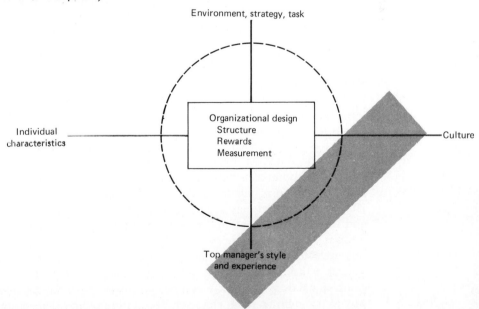

these factors and organizational design about which we have the clearest knowledge. However, as the reader is well aware, even in these areas our knowledge is still limited and there is still ample room for managerial judgment and creativity. In the shaded area of Exhibit 6, there are two other major factors about which we know much less but which also must be taken into account if the organizational design variables are to have their intended impact on members' behavior. In a broad sense, the organizational design must also be compatible with the style and experience of top management and the company's traditional culture.

The manager in charge of any organization has a persistent style of leading others with which he or she is comfortable and presumably has had some degree of success. This style is a direct outgrowth of his or her personality and is not likely to be altered easily. Therefore, although there has not been much systematic research in this direction, it seems clear that whatever design choices are made must fit not only the external conditions facing the firm and the expectations of its members, but also must be consistent with the style of the person(s) who are to lead the organization.

Similarly, beyond the leadership style of the top manager(s), the organizational design must also be compatible with their experience and talents. While we are advocating that the organizational designer start by using the ideas discussed in this paper, the resulting design may have to be altered to account for the strengths and weaknesses of available top managers. But this way of approaching the issues is preferable to the alternative, which has been often used by many organizational designers in the past, of tailoring the organization to the style and experience of top managers with little or no regard for the other factors that we have been discussing.

Culture is the shared implicit and explicit assumptions that organization members make about what is legitimate behavior in the organization. For example, in some organizations a value is placed on being self-reliant and making decisions alone. In others, more emphasis is placed on holding meetings to reach decisions. As a manager in one such company said, "Here work is attending meetings." The culture not only includes such norms about how people should behave, but also the values they are expected to hold. Furthermore, it includes general understandings about the corporate pecking order. For example, in some companies the technical research people have status and influence, while in other firms the product manager is king. Similarly, in some companies the president of a particular division is understood to be the heir apparent to the presidency of the corporation and others treat him with the deference due such status. None of these examples are written in procedure manuals or drawn on organization charts, yet it is a matter of common observation that they can have an important impact on people's behavior in a particular company. Others have labeled such sets of expectations as the *informal organization.* However, this label may suggest that somehow there is a choice between the formal and informal organization, or that they must be in opposition. In fact, the critical point is that the opposite seems to be true. In spite of limited systematic research in this area, it is clear that organizational design changes can have more immediate impact if they are consistent with the existing culture. Of course, changing the organizational design in a way that is inconsistent with the existing culture can be one way to try to bring about change in the culture of an organization, if this is a desired end, but such efforts are likely to encounter stiff resistance from organization members.

In summary, the organizational designer must create structure, rewards, and measurement that are compatible with the external environment, strategy, tasks, the members of its organization, the style of top management, and the existing culture. Accomplishing such a result may seem like an impossible task, but it really is similar to an architect planning a house. The architect starts with the character and shape of the land and the requirements of the occupants, and then considers costs, building codes, etc. To follow this analogy, the character of the plot and the occupants are similar to the environmental, strategic, task, and individual requirements facing the organizational designer. Once the ideal organization to meet these conditions is understood, the designer can then think of alternatives and tradeoffs that better fit the key planner(s). Similarly, judgments can be made about the extent to which the design is compatible with the existing culture and the extent to which changes in the design should be used as one means to shift the culture. Perhaps the architectural analogy is not a perfect one, but it does emphasize once again that the ideas described here are really just tools. Managers, like architects, must be skilled in using tools and enjoy the process of creative problem solving. Without these ingredients, the ideas described here will be of little value.

REFERENCES

Tom Burns and D. M. Stalker, *The Management of Innovation.* London: Tavistock, 1959.

Henri Fayol, *Industrial and General Administration,* Part III, Chapter I, "General Principles of Organization," Chapter II, "Elements of Administration." Paris: Dunod, 1925.

Jay Galbraith, "Organization Design: An Information Processing View." Working Paper, Massachusetts Institute of Technology, 1969.

Luther F. Gulick, "Notes on the Theory of Organizations," in *Papers on the Science of Administration,* Luther Gulick and Lyndall F. Urwick, eds. New York, Institute of Public Administration, Columbia University, 1937.

Paul Lawrence and Jay Lorsch, *Organization and Environment.* Boston, Harvard University, Graduate School of Business Administration, Division of Research, 1967.

Jay Lorsch and Stephen Allen, *Managing Diversity and Interdependence.* Boston, Harvard University, Graduate School of Business Administration, Division of Research, 1973.

Jay Lorsch and John Morse, *Organizations and Their Members: A Contingency Approach.* New York: Harper and Row, 1974.

James D. Thompson, *Organizations in Action.* New York: McGraw-Hill, 1967.

Lyndall F. Urwick, "Organization as a Technical Problem," in *Papers on the Science of Administration,* Luther Gulick and Lyndall F. Urwick, eds. New York, Institute of Public Administration, Columbia University, 1937.

Joan Woodward, *Industrial Organization: Behavior and Control,* London: Oxford University Press, 1970.

MANAGEMENT SYSTEMS: THE LANGUAGE OF ORGANIZATIONAL CHARACTER AND COMPETENCE

Thomas J. Peters

The limits of my language means the limits of my world.

Ludwig Wittgenstein

Man is an animal suspended in webs of significance he himself has spun.

Clifford Geertz

MBO, PPD, ZBB: the frustrating, gimmick-ridden, ever-changing alphabet soup of management systems. Forms, formats, forums: the mundane, boring, endless details of management systems. Senior executives might be forgiven for dismissing the whole lot as undeserving of their time and attention. But they will not be serving their companies well if they do. Consider the consequences if management systems—in all their blooming, buzzing intricacy—are ignored. At worst, conflicts between implicit values hidden among the array of systems can frustrate almost any strategic effort, no matter how carefully planned or how vital to the company's future. At best, management is in effect discarding one of its few available tools for directly shaping and controlling the climate and direction of the organization.

Most fundamentally, management systems might be conceived as the carriers of an organization's language. As such, they substantially help shape the dimensions of an organization's character. Effective top managers often use language—explicit in their words and implicit in their actions and attitudes—to reinforce or change systems, thus making the organization "speak" through them and shaping the kind of organizational character they want. Let's consider some examples.

A *Forbes* analyst summarizes Tom Clausen's monumentally successful ten-year reign at the Bank of America by noting that, "through constant questioning, he shifted the focus from loan volume to profit over time." Roy Ash of AM International says that, at core, "all businesses are the same" and that his revitalizing efforts constitute a "psychological transformation." His key is changing "not sales, not manufacturing, but . . . culture," and his chief change tool is much like Clausen's. "I see my job as one of framing the correct questions. The questioning process doesn't involve *a* question, but rather the framework of questions." Moreover, Ash asks the questions in person and during a series of field visits—not by memo and not from the head office. Both characteristics are widely noted breaks from the past.

Similarly, upon taking over at United Airlines (UAL), Ed Carlson diagnosed it as a service business that had lost sight of the customer. It had become a numbers-oriented, paper-driven bureaucracy. He introduced "MBWA," management by walking about. He and his colleagues spent 65 percent of their time in the field, working with 1,700 station managers to instill a nonbureaucratic, hands-on customer service focus. In his words, "In a service business, especially, you can't have a rigid set of rules. You can have some guidelines, but you must allow people the freedom to make a different interpretation." Similar stories are legion; for example:

• The myriad consistent, reinforcing activities by Tom Watson, Sr., to bring to life "IBM means service."
• The vast, successful array of informal activities undertaken by Chairman Ren McPherson and his colleagues at Dana Corporation to instill, over a ten-year period, a dominating sense of attention to down-the-line-induced productivity improvement (for example, featuring the semiautonomous "store manager" concept on the factory floor).

What is the point of these tales? Vignettes of superb leaders? Varieties of management style? Partly. But after systematically observing several excellent companies over the past three years, I believe I am describing a more general process of shaping and maintaining values.

In his classic study, *Leadership in Administration,* Philip Selznick reminds us:

Organizations become institutions (i.e., adaptive over the long haul) as they are infused with value. This infusion produces a distinct character and distinctive competence. When institutionalization is well advanced, distinctive outlooks, habits, and other commitments are infused, coloring all aspects of organizational life and lending it a social integration that goes well beyond formal coordination and control.

Jeffrey Pfeffer of Stanford takes the argument up a level of abstraction, from character to meaning, suggesting that:

. . . organizations can be viewed as systems of shared meanings. . . . One of the critical tasks of management involves the construction and maintenance of systems of shared meanings, shared paradigms (defined as a system of beliefs or points of view), and shared language/culture. Language, symbolism, and rituals are important elements in the process of development of shared meanings and become the focus of administrative work.

Perhaps it is possible to meld these thoughtful views into a simple definition of character: Organizational character is the embodiment of a few guiding business ideas and enduring values in mundane, daily affairs. Character deals with two extreme levels of abstraction: The highest level is ideals (for example, "IBM means service"; and at Minnesota Mining and Manufacturing, or 3M, "The 11th commandment is never kill a new product idea") and the lowest is mundane daily actions (for example, the vast arrays of informal reinforcers for the organization's guiding notions). We observe Clausen, Ash, Carlson, Watson, or McPherson imbuing a simple, basic, enduring business philosophy at every opportunity through consistent, persistent, obsessive, usually mundane reinforcements.

In my opinion these successful business leaders and scholars are describing nothing less than the *language* of organizational functioning. The Clausen and Ash tales are indeed directly about language. In Carlson's case, perhaps it is body language. What are the practical implications? Why choose to think of organizational functioning in terms so fundamental and seemingly abstract as "language"?

Quite simply. I believe that the most important—and implicit—conveyor of meaning (and hence character) in business organizations is the full set of management systems or processes. In other words, the systems are the language. And managers' days are largely taken up with management systems.

Charles Perrow addressed a related point:

> Top management directs attention: it functions as a traffic cop deciding which of the stimuli that bombard us will get through. Speeches, memos, performance reviews are obvious examples telling us to pay attention to this but not to that. Their effectiveness is limited, because their official nature may put us off guard. Once they are heard or read, their effect decays quickly. Blue-penciling words in a memo is more effective; repeated use of key words in ordinary context is more powerful still. The effect is unobtrusive, creating and changing assumptions through repetition. . . . We are only beginning to realize the extent to which natural leaders use subtle controls. . . . The leader intuits that devices that provide immediate feedback on performance are powerful correctors of behavior and potentially powerful stimulants of desired behavior.

Like Perrow, I am impressed by the power of language and character transformation embedded in everyday management systems. I believe that systems are an unparalleled tool, within the grasp of senior management, for shaping beliefs at the most fundamental levels. They are an inexorable, subtle, highly leveraged force for the patient user. Systems are the language that directs attention. And managers can learn to master the grammar of systems. There is a series of unobtrusive indicators that provide a surprisingly clear window on "how things *really* work around here."

The remainder of this paper merely serves as a nuts-and-bolts introduction to the topic. After outlining a few cases of management systems language at work, I shall propose a redefinition of management systems and suggest three ways of digging beneath their surface. Finally, I shall consider some situations in which one or more of the newly identified variables influenced the language and, over time, the character of a large organization.

READING THE LANGUAGE: BAD NEWS AND GOOD

"Read" the systems; read the problems. It's almost that simple. Here are a few examples.

Language of Time Spent

The managing director of a consumer durables company kept reiterating in speeches and private conversations that his highest priority was new products. Yet, as Exhibit 1(a) shows, his visible allocation of effort strongly suggested otherwise.

EXHIBIT 1   Reading the language of systems

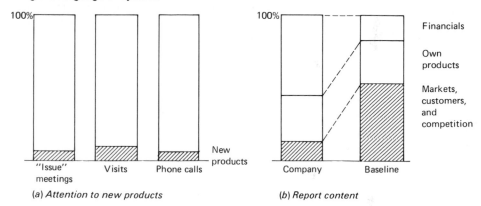

(a) *Attention to new products*

(b) *Report content*

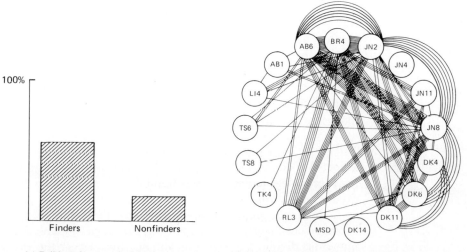

(c) *Talking about exploration: board minutes*

(d) *Committees between organizational units*

Confronted with the evidence, he responded: "The real priorities are too important to put on the formal agenda; I handle them informally." There was something in what he was saying. But down-the-line managers felt—in part because of what they saw of his visible efforts—that he wasn't serious about his stated objectives. The indicators were fair measures of what was being communicated downward. The managing director's claim that he was spending his time effectively was suspect.

Language of Reports

A large, high-technology company was being battered in the marketplace. Smaller competitors were chipping away a niche at a time. Analysis of 20 reports from the company and from similar companies with better records for rapid adaptation told part of the tale [Exhibit 1(b)]. This company was indeed preoccupied with its traditional internal concerns: financials. Its better-performing competitors had a different preoccupation: customers, competition, markets.

Language of Meetings

We used, without success, all the tricks in the analyst's book to try to discriminate between mining companies that found minerals and others that didn't. Then someone suggested looking at board meeting minutes. At least one part of the puzzle emerged [Exhibit 1(c)]: The finders talked up exploration constantly. The nonfinders didn't.

Language of Interlinks

Over a ten-year period, the number of committees required to settle "interface" issues in a $5 billion, high-technology company multiplied at a compound annual rate of 35 percent. Exhibit 1(d) depicts the 205 formal committees linking 17 organizational units that had to sign off on any new product. Inevitably, the organization's competitive reflexes became sluggish: moreover, the products that managed to clear all hurdles were "committee products." The intricate process of multiple sign-off had led to overcomplexity of product, unimaginative design, and hopelessly diffused responsibility for getting anything done.

Language of Adaptation

Sometimes action matches pronouncement and the news is good: One $2 billion, high-technology company is sustaining an annual growth rate of 30 percent. Its product line turns over approximately every five years.

A divisional annual review exemplifies the company's approach: stressing key management themes in mundane ways through systems. The company looks to its numerous divisions to spur innovation. Once a year the entire senior team devotes almost two months to conducting separate full-day reviews with each of 40 divisions. Each review day (and document) is distributed roughly as follows: 10 percent on next year's financials, 30 percent on next year's objectives, and 60 percent on new products.

The financials include only a small handful of "closely watched numbers." Short-term targets are, by the CEO's admission, "conservative, because we want managerial emphasis on product regeneration, not flogging the last dollar out of today's product slate." The objectives section focuses on a few (no more than three) concrete actions—for example, to get a new plant on line by a specific date, or to shift sales attention to a new customer segment. Typically, none of the "MBO" goals is financial.

The bulk of the review—consistent with the time-honored strategic thrust—covers new-product development. The presentations are strikingly simple. A handful of graphs vividly depict key characteristics of new products stacked up against competitors' products and customer needs.

So, then, we have five cases. Each uncovers one or more aspects of the effects of systems language on overall business character—aspects that were by no means apparent on the surface. Good news or bad, there was genuine surprise in the "reading" we unearthed.

RECONCEIVING SYSTEMS

Before setting out a new view of systems, it would be well to define what activities the term "management systems" normally encompasses. They usually include planning systems (strategic and operating), investment decision-making systems, budgeting systems, personnel systems, and the like. To this standard list, I propose to add a second major category: the committees, interface teams, and project team structures that mark any large organization.

Systems, so defined, are nothing less than the framework for almost all important managerial interaction. By thinking in terms of such a framework we can conceive of practical new avenues to follow for shaping the values, culture, character, and distinctive competence of the enterprise. Alternatively, by treating system design as a "one off" task we lose a lot of valuable leverage.

There are scores of books on would-be systems panaceas of one sort or another: MBO/R (Management by Objectives and Results), ZBB (Zero Base Budgeting), OST (Objectives, Strategies, and Tactics—a Texas Instruments invention), PPB (Program Planning and Budgeting). But there is little that describes the role of systems taken as a whole. It is useful to view systems in terms of a series of what I call *management systems components* (see Exhibit 2). These variables fall into three classes, representing three different levels of abstraction, each of which provides a distinctive vantage point for viewing the totality of the enterprise's management systems. The most general set of variables I have labeled *directional signals;* these are the systems-aided variables most directly related to value shaping. Next comes the most conventional set of components: *process phases,* such as problem solving and implementation. Finally, the lowest level of abstraction is the series of variables I call *management tools,* such as questioning routines or various aspects of management forums. I shall

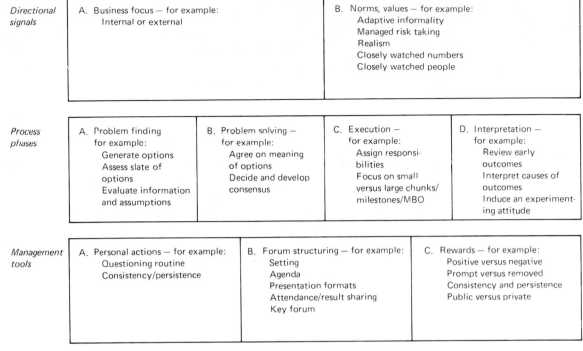

EXHIBIT 2 Management systems components

now define each of the three components more thoroughly, and then move on to illustrations.

Signals

Directional signals include business focus and norms and values. Does the set of systems, for example, focus internally or on the external environment? Does it foster creativity—by, for example, encouraging experimentation versus number-driven, buttoned-down reviews—or does it drive creativity out? In the same way, the structure of a system—and, more important, of a set of systems—can substantially affect such important norms as, say, risk taking.

Phases

Systems are machines for processing problems. The phases of the process are *problem finding, problem solving, execution,* and *interpretation.* Typically, management systems focus primarily on the problem-solving phase and only incidentally on execution and interpretation. Very few indeed focus on problem finding. Yet problem finding is the phase in which the senior manager's intuition often provides the greatest leverage for redefining what is (or ought to be) going on in the organization.

Tools

Management tools include *personal actions, forum structuring,* and *reward mechanisms.* These are the tangible activities that make up the day-to-day content of systems. Forum structuring, for example, includes presentation formats. Senior managers respond, by and large, to what they actually see. Even if the material served up is inconsistent with the proclaimed strategic direction, they will nonetheless respond to it as is. Another tool is personal actions: Questioning routines are a prime example. Again and again, we observe CEOs (such as Roy Ash) successfully revising strategic attention simply by obsessively asking the same questions. Yet many senior managers seem unaware of the power of a highly consistent questioning routine.

Those are the three sets of systems components as we now define them. Each provides a senior management team with extraordinary leverage for redirecting institutional attention. *Management gets the attention automatically through the use of systems, because systems determine what people do.* Though seldom consciously aware of the fact, senior management has wide discretion in how it uses this attention. By utilizing it purposefully and with skill, senior management can unobtrusively exert an almost irresistible leverage on the strategic direction of the organization.

DIRECTIONAL SIGNALS

Instilling values is above all a matter of consistency. If operating systems, personnel systems, strategic planning/investment systems, and daily accounting systems don't all play the same tune, then the organization's ability to maintain or shift course is impaired. Consistency, in energizing tens of thousands of people, is definitely not the hobgoblin of little minds.

Signals: Business Focus

A grocery chain executive insisted, "I don't care how good you say Procter & Gamble is, they hardly give us the time of day." Several of his colleagues jumped on his back: "Why should they? They've got their eye on the ultimate consumer." As noted earlier, UAL's Ed Carlson labored mightily to turn his bureaucrats' attention to the passenger. The million-person Bell System is now determined to achieve, in ex-Chairman John DeButts's words, "a market orientation." The biggest practical hurdle, according to many, is that it may well take a decade to get the giant enterprise's management systems focused on differentiated market concerns: for example, product, service, and segment profitability.

Over the years, a corporation frequently comes to face inward—in Roy Ash's words, "to lose sight of the purpose for which it was created and instead emphasize going through the motions." Exhibit 3 depicts the difference in focus—and some of the systems-related reasons for this difference—at two multibillion dollar companies. In Company X the systems compasses point internally, not externally. All systems—operating, strategic, and personnel—stress tight internal controls. According to outsiders, its innovative juices ceased flowing a decade ago. In Company Y, by contrast, all the systems compasses point toward productive concern with the customer. The

EXHIBIT 3 SYSTEM CONTRASTS

	Company X	Company Y
Monthly reviews	In company headquarters; three-quarters of attendees from corporate staff; almost all focus is on financial results	In the field; customer visits included; focused on new products
Annual reviews	No group-wide get-together; corporate staff "adds up the numbers" and sends down new targets that group executives virtually must buy into	A five-day session attended by up to 200 managers; focused on new products, competitive scenarios; "public" resource negotiation between line bosses
Personnel system	"Career staff" is the norm; little staff-to-line rotation, but staffs rotate every 12 to 15 months; "engineering fraternity" separate from line	Ninety percent of corporate staff jobs held by ex-line managers; typical rotation is every three to four years; those who "grew up with the product" in most key jobs
Setting	Corporate staff lives in "the tower"; central labs are 150 miles away; divisions are dispersed throughout the country, but with no local R&D support	Campus-like setting for 2,000 to 3,000 people; lots of informal but tradition-bound mechanisms force engineers, R&D, and marketing people together
General process content	All systems focus on financials; are detail- and short-term oriented; narratives are "throwaways—no one reads them"	Systems focus on "words, not numbers"; "we're interested in simple trends, not multiple regression analysis," says a senior planner (formerly a division general manager)
Top-team style	"Detail men—they'll talk about risk taking and cut you off at the knees if you risk an extra dollar"	"Evangelists," according to a division general manager, "except they are tough as nails about a promise once it's made"

consistent result has been successful adaptation to marked changes in the customer and technological environment.

An external focus rarely comes about naturally. The inherent tendency of systems, over time, is to encourage preoccupation with the internal workings of the corporation. But it is demonstrably possible to counteract the tendency, however inherent.

Signals: Norms and Values

Five sorts of interrelated norms and values are reflected in management systems: adaptive informality, managed risk taking, realism, closely watched numbers, and closely watched people.

Adaptive Informality   Consider an observation of psychologist George Miller on the Chinese social order:

From cradle to grave the Chinese are integrated into the family commune, the neighborhood commune, the larger commune. Everybody is responsible for everybody else. Somehow every farmer in the Poo Poo Valley decides at exactly the same time he is going to make war on the boo-boo fly. Now, if any one commune didn't do it at exactly the same time as the others, the effort would be wasted. So you ask them, "How did you all happen to decide at the same time?" And they say, "We talked about it." You say, "Didn't somebody from Peking tell you to wipe out the boo-boo fly?" "No," they say, "we thought it would be a good thing to do." In Russia, however, it's all decided at the top. It goes down, it's run by computers, everything is under control—and nothing works, because you can't control something that complicated. But in China, it's all kind of free. The general principles are announced from above, and how those might be implemented. And they talk about it, and suddenly millions of people decide, "That's it. You do it." And bang! They do it.

Miller's analysis raises a difficult issue about formality and informality: What is the difference between the two? By most textbook conventions, he is describing an informal process, not driven by a vast array of closely monitored rules. Conventional definitions, however, tend to equate "informal" with "loose," "unpredictable," or "unstructured." But in our observation, as in Miller's, the well-oiled informal systems tend to follow general principles more consistently than many seemingly buttoned-down formal systems.

Successful informally run organizations are almost always, like Chinese society, value driven. American examples include Dana, Digital Equipment Corporation (DEC), Hewlett Packard (HP), IBM, Koppers Corporation, 3M, Procter & Gamble (P&G), and Texas Instruments (TI).

With respect to systems, these companies are substantially similar. Most don't have vast, numbers-oriented systems. At the extreme, Dana Chairman Ren McPherson got rid of his policy manuals ten years ago and substituted a one-page statement of corporate philosophy. According to one observer, "Four hundred or so reports that used to arrive on the president's desk each month were cut back to almost nothing. Even the corporate budgets, in the conventional sense, were discontinued."

In companies where a face-to-face, informal tone permeates the daily routine, supportive aspects of systems execution crop up almost everywhere. Here are two examples:

• Dana has scores of devices that bring peers into informal contact as a substitute for formal systems. Ad hoc committees and project teams abound. Rotation among divisions and functions is regular. "Hell Week," multiday reviews that include all division and function heads in a review of results with each other, and "Dana University" are among the mechanisms used to bring managers together to swap experiences about successful productivity experiments.

• The task force often becomes but another bureaucratic encumbrance. Yet Dana, IBM, 3M, TI, and some others use the ad hoc task force with great skill. It is a key way, in all these companies, for informally calling on colleagues for short-term help. The task forces are born and die rapidly (one that lasts six months is rare at TI); attendance and membership are voluntary ("It's a free market; if you help me and do something with my advice, I'll help you"). Management fosters their use (at TI one dare not answer "no" to a query as to whether you've used the company's best talent to help you fix something or move it along). These attributes and many more stand in marked contrast to frequently observed abuses of task forces.

In a recent conversation, an executive from one of these companies readily reeled off 20 or so important systems-related vehicles—from town meetings to clubs—for ensuring that managers are in constant contact around the key business theme. Significantly, no one or two of them contributed more than fractionally to the result. It was the constant, consistent, effective reinforcement provided by the sheer number of these devices that accounted for the company's outstanding performance.

Many companies—perhaps the majority of large corporations—are much closer to the other extreme. At ITT or W.R. Grace, monthly reports are awesome in size and detail. For instance, Richard Pascale notes that, "Each month, Geneen reads all the monthly reports. They make a stack ten inches thick." In one large chemical company several group presidents insist on personally clearing *any* contact between any member of their group and a corporate staffer. Three years ago, a large transportation company held a meeting of its 40 top group managers to share results. It was the first such meeting ever, and the first time most of the participants (whose average tenure exceeded 20 years) had ever seen overall company results.

My bias toward informality (in the sense of value-driven informality) is intentional. It is my observation that "adhocracy" around a few critical business values is, in general, a good way to break the grip of bureaucracy. Moreover, as we shall see, it spurs managers toward productive risk taking. An executive summed it up recently:

> We have a few deeply held values about customers and productivity. We take every opportunity to chat about them and instill them. But, above all, we want to unleash creativity and experimentation in support of that very small handful of values. So we try our damnedest to create a physical and social environment in which the good news of successful experiments can spread rapidly on its own.

Managed Risk Taking   Systems overcontrol and excessive detail inevitably kill risk taking. Managed risk taking thrives in a physical and social environment that informally supports controlled experimentation. Supports of risk taking at 3M, for example, include:

- A new product philosophy, reiterated at every opportunity from formal town meetings to regularly scheduled informal chats.
- An integrated environment on a single campus, where engineers, marketers, and various other key actors readily get together, supported by facilities to enhance experimentation—such as a wide variety of process development units.
- Engineers and scientists in most key slots, ensuring that technical talk of new products comes naturally.
- A step-by-step approach instilled at every turn—for example, encouraging small experiments that can be done quickly.
- Evaluation systems grading the amount of venture activity spun off from mature divisions and ensuring that an idea holder can seek multiple audiences, far beyond his own group, for support.

• Systems consciously designed not to overplan, overevaluate, or kill ideas (for example, few numbers required, but a focus on first steps to test feasibility); moreover, someone who believes an idea is worthwhile is encouraged to hold on to it and work on it in a low-key way for years, until perhaps its time does come in the marketplace. Ideas are seldom killed outright or otherwise formally discouraged; if they fail to take off, they are simply allowed to fade away.

At TI a similar culture prevails. At its heart is the famed OST (Objectives, Strategies, and Tactics) system, which creates, in the words of Chairman Mark Shepard, a "fluid, project-oriented, unbounded culture." It is supported by a host of other devices such as IDEA, a program that guarantees almost anyone nonbureaucratic access to initial funds to tinker with a product notion, and armies of small "people effectiveness program" teams going after productivity opportunities ("80 percent of our people must be on a team at least once each year").

TI and 3M are alike in another crucial dimension: Action on new product ideas is taken, with rare exception, only if someone spontaneously takes on the role of product "champion" to vigorously pursue the program. "Almost every time there is a failure, it's because we pushed someone into 'championing,'" notes a senior executive.

As president of Bell & Howell, Pete Peterson consistently encouraged managed risk taking through experimentation:

> Before we let an idea get emasculated, before we let any thoroughly rational appraisal of the idea convince us that it will not work, we ask ourselves another question. Is there any way we can experiment with this idea at low cost? It is my view that the experiment is the most powerful tool for getting innovation into action. It is probably not as widely used as it should be in American industry. Quite often, if we really try, we can test the effectiveness of an idea through an experimental approach at very low cost. . . . The point I am trying to make is that if we in business can get the concept of the experiment built into our thinking and thereby get evidence on a lot of these "can'ts," "won'ts," "shouldn'ts," and so forth, more of our good ideas will be translated into action.

Unfortunately, risk taking is alarmingly easy to discourage. A company president took on a challenge much like HP's, TI's, and 3M's: to add a continually higher percentage of new products to his portfolio. He said that he was encouraging risk taking—yet in the course of his regular quarterly reviews, he came down just as hard as ever on the would-be risk takers for their inability to instantly turn ideas into profits. When he did loosen up a bit on financials, he turned to an even more subtle form of negative cue: He repeatedly asked for extensive, detailed plans as to when a certain array of future products—based on uncertain technology—would be on stream.

Even at 3M, TI, and HP, risk taking is supported by an intricate, delicate web of systems. The signals from the top must, above all, be consistent. A dissonant comment or review can kill months of painstaking work.

Realism   B. Charles Ames, president of Reliance Electric (now an Exxon subsidiary), relates the following tale:

We had planning systems of every sort—from very long term to short term. But we couldn't predict what we were going to sell next month. I virtually dismantled the five-year planning system, then the one-year planning system, then the quarterly system. We ran the company on just a 30-day system. Only then did we learn to get the numbers right. Eventually we built back up to a long-term system.

Ames was moving to instill realism into daily affairs. It is a trait that some of the top performers work hard to ensure. At GE, a manager lives or dies by the credibility of his short-term numbers. There is a complex system that allows a department manager (the lowest autonomous level) to appeal forecasts he has been asked to sign off on all the way to the top. At IBM, when there's a disagreement between staff and line and the staff estimate is approved, it's noted. There is an iron-clad historical track that records the basis of accepted projections. At Procter & Gamble, the basic communication vehicle is the famed one-page memo. It is a succinct, no-nonsense statement of essential facts.

Surprisingly, absence of realism usually coincides with overcontrol (too many systems, too many financials). It is also often closely associated with that favorite device of the hard-nosed manager, "stretch targets." Psychological research has demonstrated the efficiency of putting a 5-feet, 10-inch person in 6 feet of water. When you put him in 6 feet, 6 inches of water, however, he tends—before he drowns—to flounder about, causing untold disruption. But 6 feet, 6 inches is the depth most commonly selected: At a large energy company, forecasts were overestimated for 16 consecutive months, mainly because corporate headquarters wouldn't accept reduced estimates. Staff controllers beat the divisions into submission. It all became a joke, a game—and eventually a nightmare.

Realism is tightly linked to risk taking. When realism pervades an organization, a frequent result is willingness to take managed risks. But suspicion, mistrust, and fear tend to breed where systems are at odds with reality. Typically, more and more formal controls are imposed, starting a spiral that eventually chokes off risk taking.

Closely Watched Numbers   Dana, Emerson Electric, GE, HP, 3M, and Reliance Electric, among others, take pride in their radical decentralization into small effective units. That doesn't mean they sacrifice control. Their control is tight when it looks its loosest. Its focus, however, is not on a vast array of indicators, but on one or two closely watched numbers. For example:

• At Emerson Electric, *The New York Times* reports, "Division presidents and their top lieutenants are put under the microscope at headquarters every month by their group vice-president. The focus is more on the present than the future. Three items—inventories, profits, and sales—form a crucible for managers. They are told what they've got to do to make sure the profit is delivered each month, each quarter, and—ultimately—the full year.' "

• *Management Today* reports on Dana: "The head office does not require much in the way of written reports. The most important item is the revenue figure. In the old days it used to come up, along with much else, in an actual-against-budget tabulation by the 20th of the following month. Under the current system, the divisions transmit to head office, by phone or telex, their invoice total, and approximate profits earned, at the end of each working day."

By contrast, the companies tracking 20 or 30 variables with apparently equal intentness are legion. As a result, the signals about what's really important never get through, and the room for discretion down the line invites behavior that often borders on anarchy. "The sales incentive schemes include 83 variables," reports one executive. "Needless to say, a salesman can hide behind whichever one he chooses. Making adjustments, especially fast adjustments, is next to impossible."

A few closely watched numbers can provide a stable framework in which adaptive informality, risk taking, and realism can flourish. Only when such basic, value-driven stability exists can management move on to the next step of asking for regular, albeit controlled, risk taking.

Closely Watched People   There is at least one other obviously important piece to the value-shaping puzzle described in this section: people *per se*. The effective performers pay obsessive attention to the care and feeding of their key managers. As so often, Alfred Sloan was a pioneer. Peter Drucker reports:

> A disproportionate amount of top-committee time was taken up with decisions on people rather than policy. Moreover, Mr. Sloan left to others the chairmanship of whatever committee dealt with a specific policy area. But in any decision on people he was in the chair. Once, the committee spent hours discussing the work and assignment of a position way down the line—master mechanic in a small accessory division. I said, "Mr. Sloan, how can you afford to spend four hours on a minor job like this?" "Tell me what more important decision there is than that about the management people who do the job," he said. "If that master mechanic in Dayton is the wrong man, our decision here on the 14th floor might as well be written on water. As for taking a lot of time, that's horse apples [his strongest epithet]. How many decisions on people did we have to make last year?" Before I could answer, he had whipped out his famous "little black book" and said, "It was 143. If we didn't spend four hours on placing a man right, we'd spend 400 hours cleaning up after our mistake—and that time I wouldn't have. You think I should be a good judge of people. There's no such person. There are only people who make people decisions right, and that means slowly."

GE, Citibank, ITT, and Exxon, among others, similarly devote a seemingly disproportionate amount of time to their top few hundred managers.

The norms we have been considering are among the most significant reflections of a business's strategic tone or character. Moreover, they are closely interlinked. And none is established or maintained without the support of pervasive, multiple reinforcing mechanisms that are rooted in the full set of management systems as we have described them.

PROCESS PHASES

Systems are primary channels for major directional signals flowing through the organization. At the same time, they perform the more conventional chore of surfacing, solving, and following up on specific problems as they wend through the organization. Our concern here, however, is not with the problem-solving aspect of systems, but with their unsung role in surfacing problems, tracking implementation progress, and guiding interpretation.

Phases: Problem Finding

Problem finding is often a significant missing link in management systems. Harried managers see what is put in front of them. They seldom look for, or question, what they don't see. Henry Mintzberg and Eugene Carter reviewed 50 major investment decisions made by ten companies. In all but one, only a single option was seriously staffed out. There were plenty of "straw men"—unstaffed-out options intended for rejection by management. One good reason that multiple, well-developed options are so seldom found is that management, as a rule, just hasn't the time to study in depth a lot of different alternatives. At the very least, however, management should find a way to review the stream of decisions it sees each quarter, or year, to make sure that it is seeing (and signing off on) roughly the right things.

Consider this example. A $200 million industrial goods company was growing at 30 percent a year. The CEO was concerned that the company was becoming a bureaucracy and that its products, previously market leaders, were becoming gradually less innovative. Any *one* new product decision (the company introduces 25 to 30 new products or variations each year) seemed sensible. But he suspected that there was in general a drift toward less innovation. So he undertook an overall analysis of the previous year's new product introductions, distinguishing between marginal "me too" products and "new market definers." There were many more of the former than the latter. The exercise was conducted every four months. Repeated over the course of 18 months, the process heightened awareness of the issue and helped lead to a general shift in the desired direction.

Another neglected aspect of problem finding is somewhat easier to come to grips with: namely, identifying and evaluating key assumptions that underlie the stream of proposals that make it to the top. The four or five key judgmental parameters seldom surface in the welter of analysis; they are buried in the bowels of the organization. Very likely they were last looked at by a junior analyst weeks before the proposal hit top management's desk.

In this connection, a senior executive told me with an air of triumph that he had "found Gilbert." "Who's Gilbert?" I inquired. "He works for me, about three levels down," said my friend. "He's the guy who runs the new product-planning models. He's the one who decides that we'll jack up an elasticity from x to $x + 2$. He really makes the management calls. Do you know what this little adjustment means here?" he demanded, pushing a decision memorandum across the desk. "It means, in practical terms, that our sales force in this segment would have to more than *double* their effectiveness from 29 to 14 hours per sale. No way. No basis. Can you see why I'm glad I found Gilbert?" My friend is now undertaking a variety of steps to flush out other "Gilberts" and start unearthing the real issues.

Another company attacked the problem directly by requiring crucial assumptions to be stated early in each decision proposal. Each assumption was to be supported by a brief, one-page, one-graph summary of the factors that could change it. Additionally, the president introduced a supporting routine in meetings where the proposals were reviewed. After the "crucial assumptions" were presented, a programmed 20-minute debate ensued. Were these the right assumptions? What might an alternative set be, and how would they affect the proposal?

Harold Geneen raised reduced art to a science in his efforts to instill a common analytic discipline throughout ITT's disparate empire. "Effective immediately," he said in an early memo to his top executives, "I want every report specifically, directly, and bluntly to state at the beginning a summary of the unshakable facts. The highest art of professional management requires the ability to smell a real fact from all others—and, moreover, to have the intellectual curiosity, guts, and/or plain impoliteness if necessary to be sure what you have is indeed what we will call an unshakable fact."

Problem finding means breaking out of habitual mind sets. The systems routines we are considering exemplify the devices that can be used to accomplish this difficult task.

Phases: Problem Solving

Systems for problem-solving usually boil down to routines for making choices among options. Problem solving, however, includes two other stages that are often neglected: gaining agreement on the meaning of the options and developing consensus around the decision, once taken.

Agreement on meaning is often surprisingly difficult to achieve. It is crucially important, however, to top teams, for slight differences in interpretation at the top frequently lead to magnified distortions down the line. At a recent review, for example, the CEO of a conglomerate raised a point about inventory with a division president, who was there with his chief financial officer. The question was one of 50 or so asked that day. No discussion followed. About a week later, the financial officer launched a major project (estimated effort: four man-years) collecting data and analyzing inventory problems. He had overreacted to a casual question.

The consensus-building stage of problem solving often presents unexpected obstacles that may take months or years to surmount. Management decision systems say, in effect: "Get the options up to us, and we'll decide once and for all." But that's not what happens. Instead, the option that comes up, looking ominously large and risky, somehow doesn't feel right. So it's bounced back down, only to surface later on in a different form. Repeatedly exposing managers to small outcroppings of a key issue is usually a more efficient and effective way to build support for a major move. A precision-parts company vice-president summarized it this way:

> We knew we wanted a quality thrust. We had been looking at quality programs once a year during the planning cycle, but that was as far as it got. What really broke the log jam was creating a "quality forum." The entire top team sat down every three weeks for a half-day throughout an 8-month period to focus on various aspects of quality. As a result, a credible program slowly took shape. And we were able to monitor its successes and failures, signal our serious support, and otherwise get quality into the system as a true concern.

Phases: Execution

If it seems naïve to single out assignment of responsibilities as a systems issue, stop and consider: How often is senior management's role confined to a mere process of "advise and consent"? How many times does a presidential assignment turn out not to be an assignment at all? Simple, straightforward assignment of responsibility, duly recorded in the minutes, can become the core of an organization's real accountability systems.

Exhibit 4 illustrates an analysis of four organizations. The difference in focus was strikingly apparent from the minutes of management meetings. Companies A and B suffer from the same malady: They are laggards in responding to environmental change. Companies C and D, despite their massive size (both over $1 billion in sales), act swiftly in response to competitive moves. Since what top managers talk about this week tends to be next week's luncheon topic for their subordinates, a look at the agenda of senior management get-togethers was illuminating. In Companies C and D, the fast reactors, management spent most of its time on decisions that had due dates, follow-up protocol, and active monitoring. Managers in Companies A and B, by contrast, spent only a small fraction of their meeting time on execution-related matters. Senior management seldom got down to action-level review of "live" activities that would suggest whether or not particular programs were on target. Ed Carlson puts the point this way:

> I have a fetish about meetings where there is a lot of conversation and nothing is accomplished. If corporate policy making is going to be effective, you have to have good discussions and then decide what you want to do. We initiated the discipline very early; the minutes of those meetings were written up within 24 hours, succinctly describing the action taken and who was responsible for implementing the decision.

EXHIBIT 4 Management committee activity (shaded area represents execution-related)

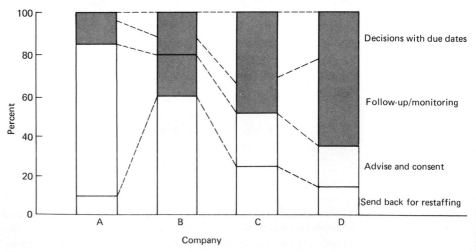

Carlson also used "follow-up squads" that, in the words of one senior executive at UAL, "would hound you to the ends of the earth to make sure that the action was taken."

And how do you shift toward execution? The most direct way is by compelling senior managers to spend their time differently, as the following example illustrates.

An engineering company had become vastly overextended and taken on projects far beyond its capability in distant outposts. Noting that senior managers spent most of their time during weekly meetings talking about the engineering issues they knew best, the chairman consciously set about shifting the focus of their agenda from engineering to the nuts and bolts of implementation. Their discussions soon took on greater relevance; more important, however, was the ripple effect that resulted as those down the line prepared their bosses for the meetings.

Another clue to effective execution is *focusing on achievable chunks of larger tasks.* Fred Brooks, the systems designer for the IBM 360, describes it in terms of milestones:

> For picking milestones there is only one relevant rule. Milestones must be concrete, specific, measurable events, defined with knife-edge sharpness. Coding, for a counter-example, is "90 percent finished" for half of the total coding time. Debugging is "99 percent complete" most of the time. "Planning complete" is an event one can proclaim almost at will. Concrete milestones, on the other hand, are 100 percent events. In fact, it is more important that milestones be sharp-edged and unambiguous than that they be easily verifiable by the boss. Rarely will a man lie about the milestone progress, if the milestone is so sharp that he can't deceive himself. But if the milestone is fuzzy, the boss often understands a different report from that which the man gives.

Milestones of the 100 percent sort are almost always to be found in superbly performing companies—but if not used with discretion, they can prove a curse in practice. Underlying this paradox is an important, if somewhat subtle, point: "Milestones thinking" entails invention of sharply defined mini-events; yet situations in which we can and should exhaustively prespecify a long future string of events are exceptional in the extreme. Moreover, the effective implementer is, above all, opportunistic; he doesn't know what the next step is until he finishes the one before.

The same caveats apply to effective management by objectives. Many executives lament the uselessness and gimmickry of MBO; it often becomes another manifestation of bureaucracy. Yet few denigrate the importance of objectives. We have observed that a certain set of attributes regularly distinguishes effective from ineffective MBO (Exhibit 5). The number of milestones may be most important. As a Texas Instruments executive noted, "More than two or three objectives is the same as no objectives."

Phases: Interpretation

An important senior-management function that is seldom handled well is interpretation of the past. We will consider three aspects here: reviewing early outcomes, interpreting cause, and inducing an experimenting attitude.

EXHIBIT 5 VARIETIES OF MBO

	Company X ("bureaucratic" MBO)	Company Y ("real" MBO)
Objectives	Many (as many as 30 for one job)	Few (no more than three)
Measures	Primarily numbers; degree of control over outcome not clear	Behaviors and control over outcomes reasonably clear
Time frame	Six to 30 months	Two to six months, occasionally 12
Coordination required	Interfaces within and outside own unit not clear	Interfaces clear, within and outside own unit
Review frequency	Reviewed once or twice a year	Discussed informally each week and formally each month or quarter
Stretch	Chosen on the basis of desirability	Chosen on the basis of achievability and need
Management process	Sent down, reviewed in private	Up and down, reviewed in public with peers as well as in private

To see the importance of reviewing early outcomes, take the case of a management that reorganizes in order to stress market segments rather than products. How does the senior executive make sure that something new is really afoot? Must he wait for a year to see whether sales results are improving? Not necessarily. In one company, the top 12 men went off-site for a full day four months after the reorganization. They checked in great detail through salesmen's call data to see if anything new was happening. They repeated the exercise twice a year for the next two years. Also, the president penciled comments all over the minutes of the new market segment boards, being particularly careful to note whether the issues under debate did or didn't seem to be in the direction of the new thrust. For any shift of direction, it should be easy to come up with a list of a dozen such early indicators of change in the patterns of practical activity.

Interpretation of causes is another neglected aspect. Few senior teams are fully alert to their opportunities to exploit management systems as learning and teaching devices. In one major chemical company, the CEO usually devotes about a third of each monthly management meeting to an exhaustive review of a seemingly tiny issue.

"How did the power costs in the old plant [one of 39] come down like that?" the CEO asked during one meeting, noting one of 20 numbers on page 26 of the monthly report. At the next meeting the division chief had the answer, an insulation project covering 80 percent of the process heating duct. "Who did it?" the CEO asked. And at the next meeting a young engineer spent 25 minutes describing the project. "Take two fellows from the central staff," the CEO proposed, "and see if you can replicate that process." Nine months later the engineer reported a $6 million savings to be realized in the first year. "Why don't you stick with it and form a little 'energy savers' unit—not on my staff, but in your division." Two years later, effective "energy savers" groups were well established in 14 to 17 operating units.

Such microscopic analyses are superb learning vehicles. They are part of a special aspect of the learning process we refer to as experimentation, or instilling a "small-win" mentality. Nobel prize-winner William Shockley (inventor of the junction transistor) summed it up at a conference on innovation in big bureaucracies:

> I distrust, by and large, any great number of sweeping principles. I lean more to being a believer in low cunning and expediency. I say to my own people, "Well, I don't know how you start a project, but maybe you can ask your boss. See if he knows someone in another company he can phone up and ask. Or step out and do an experiment." You see, there is one principle here. You don't first start on something which is going to take six man-months before you get to the answer. *You can always find something in which, in a few hours of effort, you will have made some little steps,* so there is certainly some kind of a small step before a big-scale effort. Well, that's an elementary general principle, but short of ones as elementary as that, I'm not sure I have much confidence that you can enunciate too many of them.

Most big actions are, in fact, the sum of many small steps. Taking the small seriously is a highly practical strategy for achieving an inventive, execution-oriented environment.

The process phases are the most familiar of our three major classes of management systems components. Yet even here we find a multitude of opportunities to recast management systems thinking and to use its leverage in pursuing a distinctive, effective business character.

MANAGEMENT TOOLS

Systems are the language of organization. Language shapes values and character. We have already seen much evidence of the often implicit, often pervasive effect of systems. By and large, our concern has been with major systems impacts: for example, on controlled risk taking.

In this action we shift to the lowest level of abstraction: the mundane details of system execution. Systems used effectively shift attention; their practical execution comes through meetings, the passing stream of documents, and the agglomeration of time spent on different classes of issues. These nitty-gritty "tools" include personal actions, forum structuring, and rewards.

Tools: Personal Action

The most potent way of exploiting the power of systems may well be through planned routines of personal action. *Probably the most powerful kind of personal action is a consistent, methodical questioning routine.* As we noted, Roy Ash thinks that framing the structure of questions is the CEO's key task. Geneen's search for "the unshakable facts" and Clausen's persistent profit-focused questions are analogous. Alfred Sloan was an early practitioner of this discipline, as Peter Drucker notes:

> After every meeting, no matter how many he attended, he wrote a letter of memorandum in which he identified the key question and asked: "Is this what the decision is all about?" I

asked him whether this didn't take an awful lot of time. "If a decision comes up to my level," he said, "it had better take a lot of time. If it doesn't deserve it, we'll throw it back. We make very few decisions. No one can make a great many and make them right. But we'd better know what we are deciding and what the decision is all about."

Other examples abound—though, like losing weight or permanently stopping smoking—they are easier to articulate than to execute.

Next in importance to questioning is the follow-up process. The routines of Carlson and Geneen have been discussed. All share two common properties, consistency and swiftness, whose importance would be hard to overestimate. In *Adventures of a Bystander,* Peter Drucker states the extreme case:

> The single-minded ones, the monomaniacs, are the only true achievers. The rest, the ones like me, may have more fun; but they fritter themselves away. The monomaniacs carry out a "mission"; the rest of us have "interests." Whenever anything is being accomplished, it is being done, I have learned, by a monomaniac with a mission.

While this is an extreme statement, it does not unduly exaggerate the determination and single-mindedness of Tom Watson at IBM, Theodore Vail at AT&T, or Alfred Sloan among the legendary CEOs. Among those cited in this paper, Ash, Ames, Clausen, Carlson, Geneen, Haggerty, and McPherson are of the same stripe. Persistence is not to be underrated.

Tools: Forum Structuring

Systems are implemented at particular times and places. The nitty-gritty attributes of the process can make a real difference to their success. A hotel company CEO was distressed by a downtrend in service quality despite an array of inspection systems, scoring systems tied to cash incentives, and the like. Convinced that lack of visible attention to quality was to blame, he decided to institute a "monthly execution review." Several attributes are noteworthy:

- Time commitment: two of the president's days each month and 15 to 20 top-team days per month.
- Location: at a key property chosen for a "teaching" reason (for example, maintenance effectiveness).
- Focus: specific actions taken in support of a single quality issue per trip (for example, cleanliness of public areas).
- Attention to good news, not past performance shortcomings (for example, five to ten personal awards handed out at each meeting).
- Personal follow-up after each trip (usually 30 to 40 items; action taken on these within ten working days).

After a year of these monthly execution reviews, all concerned agree that a new sense of purpose pervades the company.

The elements of forum structuring include settings, agenda, presentation formats, attendance result sharing, and key forum selection.

Settings, as we have just seen, can often be significant. One important aspect is the amount of visiting in general by top-team members. We noted the impact of the intensive, two-year field visit program by Ed Carlson. Such visits, if they are to be effective, must come to have a pattern, even if it is as subtle a pattern as the one woven in a consumer goods company. "Every time the old man comes to town," says a division head in the company, "he asks what we're proud of that we've done for a customer, large or small. He asks who our best young salesman is—and why I think so. He usually talks to the salesman, asks him what he's learned, which of our competitors he'd most like to work with—and why. It all just flows without much apparent rhyme or reason. But when he leaves after a stay of a day or two, you sure know what's on his mind. And he sure knows what's on yours. And something else: If he says, as he usually does, that he'll look into something—well, he does. Just tucks a scrap of paper in his pocket and then, bang, four or five days later you hear about some action taken."

Alistair Mant, formerly an IBM executive, describes an even more important and general attribute of setting: the myriad of systems techniques through which senior managers stay close to the product and customer—a signal readily perceived throughout the organization:

I remember, as a fairly lowly IBM employee, deploring the way the Management Review Committee—the holy of holies—concerned itself with detail out in the boondocks. Surely, I thought, they ought to stick to strategic matters. I see it better now—they were keeping their feet in the mud, and it made them better strategists. Similarly, is it just my imagination, or is it the case that the average British factory is less spick-and-span, less often painted, irrespective of its age, than its continental counterparts? Does it have pride invested in it in the same way? Is it, in its way, the spiritual temple of the enterprise, or is that the polished, paneled boardroom? My assumption is that a factory has a special character and personality when senior management understand its detailed workings in their bones, and their hands; the system as a whole has a sense of integration in a way that a split-off senior management can never achieve. A top Swedish engineering manager put it succinctly to me: "If I go down on the line, it is because I want to see if the fix on yesterday's production worked; an Englishman probably goes down because they told him in a course that the workers like it. They can tell the difference!"

Agenda are often the clearest indicator of priorities, and their importance is difficult to overemphasize. The political axiom, "He who sets the agenda controls the action," holds true for business as well—as one executive vice-president confirmed. He was bound and determined to shift the focus of senior management toward two product families that had been soundly drubbed in the marketplace because he believed them to be bellwethers of a general shortcoming in the corporation's approach to customer service and complex systems selling. There was no agreement among the top team as to the cause. So the EVP used the agenda: Over a ten-month period he scheduled 23 lengthy reviews that focused on various aspects of the issue. By brute force—that is, hours expended on the subject—the management moved gradually toward basic agreement on underlying causes and undertook some steps aimed at testing solutions.

The power of *presentation formats* is such that the CEO can often spend his time productively on their design. "Beefing up the section on competitive analysis" in investment proposals or a monthly operating review or "focusing on the bureaucratic history of a decision" can dramatically shift management's attention over time. The senior managers in one company, for example, realized that many decision issues they were seeing had been put before them time and again. So, to begin with, they announced that every decision memorandum should start with a brief historical review. When had the processing started, in response to what kinds of queries? How many times had it been up before? What had happened? Were they still trying to resolve the same issues as before? The decision-making processes got clearer fast. Part of the reason was sheer embarrassment.

Controlling attendance and the sharing of results at reviews is important on the one hand to prevent them from turning into circuses and, on the other, to ensure that they don't become private huddles, reducing people down the line to speculating about what's important to the top team now. A practical outcropping is the presence or absence of "main events." TI (with its five-day, 400-person "Strategic Planning Conference") and Dana (with its twice-a-year "Hell Week") are among companies paying obsessive attention to the main event. Alfred Sloan may have started it at GM, as Peter Drucker reports:

> There are special meetings to create common understanding, which are being held twice a year in Detroit under the chairmanship of Mr. Sloan, and at which important or acute problems are discussed. At these meetings the results of the various divisions are also shown and reasons for success and failure are discussed. Suggestions from the divisions or from central management are brought up for debate, and unplanned but effective personal contacts are established between central management and divisional personnel. About two to three hundred people attend these meetings regularly; an equal number is invited in rotation. Thus practically every senior employee—beginning perhaps at the level of plant superintendent—has an opportunity to see the business as a whole, to see his place in it and to familiarize himself with the basic policies and the program of the company.

Two recent CEO converts echo Sloan's message in describing their own new experiences:

> When my 40 division managers come together, about three times a year, we work on a critical issue. By the second meeting they're all bringing in examples of how they've done this or that. Peer pressure works.
>
> We had the first meeting ever of the top 75. They had to present three-year plans to each other. We got more real strategy thinking done in getting ready for these sessions than our formal strategic planning system had produced in the five years since its inception.

Surprising controversy swirls around the issue of sharing results. Ed Carlson broke tradition by "sharing confidential daily operating statistics previously regarded as too sensitive for the field to handle." Yet a recent *Dun's* article on productivity notes that while IBM uses several vehicles to share everyone's results with everyone else, International Harvester refuses to, because it would "just breed gamesmanship."

The nature of the information swapped is crucial. Mere comparison of abstract numerical outcomes may indeed produce stress without a compensating relief value. On the other hand, when the emphasis is on sharing tangible good- and bad-news stories about specific programs that worked (or didn't), the tone changes from scolding to learning. Northrup's successful productivity program, for instance, includes a "Quality Circles" program—a device, imported from Japan, in which ad hoc groups meet regularly to share not only results, but also ideas and success stories about tangible projects.

A regular *key forum*—the session that counts, the place where the buck stops—can be the mainstay of an effort to infuse a theme. Will it be the monthly operating review, a bi-monthly strategic progress review, a weekly meeting of the five top executives? Sometimes a management forum already in place will naturally drift into this role, but the process can also be engineered. If a chief executive wants the buck to stop around operating issues, then he can design an appropriate operating review. If a focus on new products is wanted, then part of the answer may be to create a high-visibility, monthly "new product review." Kodak recently engineered such a shift of key forums. The previous "key forum," the technical affairs committee, was disbanded and replaced in part by a strategically focused management review board. *Forbes* notes that it was a signal to insiders and outsiders alike of a major Kodak shift away from technical and toward marketing concerns.

In looking at the variables surrounding forum design and execution, we should not miss the forest for the trees. The point is simply that forums, individually and collectively, offer top management major opportunities to influence the time and attention of their senior colleagues.

Tools: Rewards

A more obvious tool that management has at its disposal is the pattern of rewards it dispenses. In the process of system execution, what forms of recognition or rebuke are handed out to staff and line executives? What kinds of actions are rewarded (or chastised) and how? Particularly effective are *frequent, public* rewards to *junior line* operators for *completed, tangible actions* in support of a major theme. Each of the italicized words in the preceding sentence designates a "reward" variable. Actually, more could have been added. We noted earlier, for instance, the sending of notes of praise to staffers for specific *small* pieces of action.

One behavioral science finding—which, remarkably, few if any psychologists dispute—is that positive reinforcement, publicly delivered immediately after a concrete action in the "right" direction, has unparalleled attention-directing power. Our view of the use of rewards in systems execution suggests the wisdom of taking advantage of this power. Sadly, few managers currently do so.

As in forum structuring, the setting in which behaviors are rewarded is vitally important—and its public/private dimension is particularly intriguing. The innovating, experimenting organizations make unparalleled use of public settings—taking advantage, we believe, of what psychologists call "social comparison." That is, the most important motivators come not from what you say to me privately in a one-to-one setting, but from what I infer my relative performance to be when you speak to me in the presence of my peers. Subtle peer pressure knows no parallel.

This set of management tools is but a small sample. Almost any of them is within the grasp of a senior executive and, if exercised consciously and persistently, can have pervasive impact. Thoughtfully managed or not—and they seldom are—all these variables and a host of others are constantly at work in every organization, shaping its basic character and competence.

CONCLUSION

Large organizations are hard to energize, hard to shift. Left to natural forces, they frequently turn sluggish, bureaucratic, and introverted. Like deposits of cholesterol, the sluggishness accrues slowly, is hard to isolate, and proves harder yet to scrape off.

The essential variable in the deterioration process is often management systems. Visibly, they grow in number and complexity. Invisibly, they perpetuate outdated value assumptions. Similarly, management systems are a critical variable in reversing a decline or spurring a new level of achievement. Even a dramatic strategic move, for instance, is likely to perturb the enterprise only briefly unless the old systems residues are attacked and remolded in parallel.

Three classes of systems success and failure provided most of the data for our review. Each has important implications for anyone trying to apply our findings. The first class emerged from our analysis of excellent, self-renewing companies. The chief implication is that a vast number and variety of interlocking, mutually supporting systems devices are required to sustain vitality; and the array is always changing, constantly being added to and subtracted from. Moreover, systems in the effectively functioning enterprise achieve a dynamic (that is, continuously redetermined) balance between two apparently opposing forces: control and encouragement of managed risk taking. In fact, the apparent opposites are not at odds. We find that the stability provided by some forms of control (for example, realism, a limited number of objectives, a very few closely watched numbers) actually enhances the propensity to innovate, experiment, and regularly take measured risks.

While the first class of success cases dealt with examples of stable, long-term, effectively functioning businesses, the second homed in on senior managements that successfully shifted their business's character (debureaucratized it, for example, or induced an innovative, external focus on the customer). The implications of these examples are in part consistent with the first class: The successful value shifters undertook a large number of systems experiments, working with most of the elements we introduced; no single program or process accounted for much of the change. The added twist was the observation that consistency and persistence over a period of years were required to bring about a significant value reorientation. Questioning routines, key forums, and other combinations of microvariables proved powerful only when they consistently and persistently reinforced new ways of doing things and altered the deeply ingrained expectations of a large number of managers. Substantial time and painstaking attention to revised patterns of agenda, closely watched numbers, and other means of controlling institutional attention are required to develop initial credibility at the top, followed by a down-the-line ripple effect of consequences.

And the third class, the failures. The most ominous implication is the myriad ways in which systems can send unintended signals or fail to achieve intended benefits. The tendency is to focus on the so-called big variables: Is the system, for example, "strategic enough"? Yet it is almost unfailingly the minor variables, such as agenda, questioning patterns, and follow-up routines that, if ignored, can torpedo otherwise positive efforts. Lack of persistence is equally fatal: It takes seemingly endless repetition to make a point. Last, there is the failure of the system to provide the settings needed to instill a desired tone. We find that effective systems invent excuses to express or parade basic values—including places and opportunities of the most mundane sort. Less powerful or effective systems fail to induce such a tone.

In summary, learning to get maximum leverage from systems, like mastering a new language, is tough going. It demands a curious blend of sensitive, meticulous care (a "good ear") and tenacity (practice). It far transcends mechanistic application of the latest best-selling technique, be it MBO, PPB, or ZBB. I earnestly believe that experimenting with bits and pieces of systems is a major, often primary, means of altering deeply held organizational values or adding major new skills. Fortunately, the raft of largely unheralded, invisible variables is almost unfailingly within senior management's grasp.

PUTTING IT ALL TOGETHER: MANAGING INDIVIDUAL AND ORGANIZATIONAL CHANGE AND DEVELOPMENT

Part 6 consists of a single case that is extremely complex and is intended to be used as an integrative exercise. This case concerns GenRad, Inc., formerly called the General Radio Company, founded in 1915. For more than 30 years it was run by its founder, Melville Eastham, who had an explicit policy of no growth. This philosophy, along with other components of his management approach, such as committee management and liberal human resource policies, became an ingrained part of the company's culture.

In 1967 the company officially declared that henceforth it would vigorously pursue growth. Over the years it had seen itself dwarfed by competitors in an industry that GenRad had founded, the test equipment industry. Under pressures from lower-level managers, Donald B. Sinclair, the incumbent president, adopted this new policy and made several acquisitions. By the end of 1972 the company was in dire financial straits and Sinclair retired.

Sinclair was replaced by William R. Thurston who substantially improved the company's performance. He made a number of changes to accomplish this. In spite of these changes a number of problems continued to persist, such as weak management information systems and poor asset management. To address these problems and to prepare the company for the future, in 1979 Thurston commissioned an internal task force, the organizational development study group, to study the company's situation and to make recommendations.

A thorough analysis of this case, recommendations for change, and a recommended implementation plan requires the integrated use of concepts from all parts of this book and provides a unique opportunity to cement the learnings we have tried to impart in these pages.

GENRAD, INC. (A)

Robert G. Eccles
J. Stewart Dougherty

INTRODUCTION

> For 35 years, until 1950, the company survived and prospered through World War I, the depression and radio boom of the 1920s, the Great Depression of the 1930s, and World War II under the continuous management of its founder. Throughout this entire period, it was the world's largest manufacturer in the electronic instrument business and, unfortunately, came to take its leadership role for granted.
>
> The founding managers and their early successors viewed growth as an undesirable phenomenon, to be discouraged because they feared that large size would force abandonment of their essential values, such as high product quality and the family atmosphere. They were afraid that in the pell mell of growth, we would all begin to go on ego trips, at the expense of what had been developed over a long period of time.

With these words, William R. Thurston, president of GenRad since 1973, reflected on the tremendous success of his company in its early years and on the reasons why the founder and early executives of the firm had come heretically to question the prudence of their firm's adoption of the free-enterprise growth ethic. For 52 years, management at GenRad steadfastly resisted the growth ethic and placidly watched its market leadership position erode and finally vaporize. During this same period, GenRad, considered by some economic historians to be the oldest electronics manufacturing firm in the world, slipped into relative obscurity as its competitors caught the world's attention and imagination with their dizzying success. Through it all GenRad had remained loyal to its early values and had refrained from changing those values while trying to adjust to a reality very different from the situation during which those beliefs had been fashioned.

By 1972, 57 years after its founding, GenRad had nearly become illiquid after recording a loss of $2.3 million on sales of $33 million. GenRad's performance after 1972 was remarkable; it resulted from the actions taken by a new management team that was installed in 1973. In many respects, GenRad's recent history has been an example of a classic management and performance turnaround.

In 1979 GenRad manufactured and marketed electronic test equipment. Fifty-five percent of the company's revenues were generated by sales of highly sophisticated test instruments referred to as *automatic test equipment* (ATE). ATE products were sold to users and manufacturers of electronic equipment, such as manufacturers of computers, peripherals, office equipment, telecommunications devices, and defense electronics. Twenty-five percent of the company's revenues were derived from sales of less sophisticated and more traditional electronic test instruments. Customers for these less exotic instruments were also participants in the electronic equipment industry. Frequently, purchasers of ATE products would be purchasers of GenRad's more standard test instruments as well. GenRad had carried many of its standard test products for years, and even for decades. Its products were designed and manufactured in the company's electronic manufacturing test (EMT) division. The remaining 20 percent of GenRad's revenues were derived from the sale of electronic testing equipment to manufacturers of mechanical equipment, such as automobiles, missiles, oil drilling platforms (onshore and offshore), engines, turbines, satellites, airframes, and bridges. The acoustics and vibration analysis (AVA) division was responsible for this portion of the company's sales. By 1979, 65 percent of the company's sales were made within the United States, 25 percent throughout Europe, and the remaining 10 percent elsewhere around the world. (A detailed description of GenRad's testing equipment is given in Appendix A.)

The ATE market was burgeoning in February 1979 when GenRad's senior officers met to conduct their annual review of the company's operations and affairs. (See Appendix B for a description of the industry environment in 1979.) At that meeting, when the participants totaled their strategic projections, it was found that GenRad's 1984 sales level was expected to exceed $400 million. This figure would represent an increase of 340 percent over GenRad's 1978 sales of $89.3 million and would reflect a 28 percent compound annual growth rate. This projection was a marked increase over the company's former 5- and 10-year compound annual growth rates of 14.2 percent and 14.4 percent, respectively. (See Exhibits 1 through 8 for detailed information on the company's financial performance.) If the projections were correct, it was safe to conclude that the GenRad of 1984 would be vastly different from the GenRad of 1979.

Given GenRad's bright prospects, one might have assumed that a sense of jubilation would have prevailed at the management meeting. There was, instead, a certain anxiety that emanated from deep within GenRad's managers—the anxiety that is born of the prospect of fundamental change. For what GenRad's managers could not deny was that, for the company to reach the 1984 that they envisioned, drastic changes would have to occur, and occur promptly.

In July 1979, a special task force was commissioned by Thurston to examine the firm's organizational and structural situation as of 1979 and to determine if the current organization was capable of carrying GenRad into the 1984 of its executives' expectations. The name of this special committee was the organizational development study group (ODSG).

HISTORY OF THE COMPANY: 1915–1972

The Eastham Years: Setting Basic Values

The General Radio Company (renamed GenRad late in 1975) was founded in 1915 by Melville Eastham, a self-taught engineer who became known for his innovative technological devices and for the strong social conscience that guided his actions as an employer and a businessman. The firm was the world's first major electronic test instrument manufacturer and essentially founded the industry. Contrary to what the firm's name implied, GenRad never manufactured radios. In 1915, the word *radio* was synonymous with the field of wireless telegraphy and thus connoted advanced technology.

Eastham's interest was in technologic excellence and innovative brilliance. From the company's earliest days, management was dedicated to manufacturing high-quality, state-of-the-art, innovative electronic test instruments. The devices were used by research and design engineers to design and test electronic products for functional reliability. GenRad's products were sold at prices that included high margins, and company profits were, therefore, flush. Products were not expected to sell in high quantities but rather to fill the specific and often solitary needs of GenRad's customers. Since engineering innovation was so highly valued at the company, creative engineers found GenRad a congenial place to work. As one executive noted, when reflecting on the relative importance of the functional personnel at the company, "The engineer was king here; nonengineers were serfs. Important serfs, true, but serfs, nonetheless."

GenRad's record in the 1920s and 1930s was impressive. For example, the company manufactured the world's first commercial vacuum tube voltmeter and wave analyzer. In the 1940s it was frequently the recipient of special military commendations for its engineering successes.

But as a result of its emphasis on technologic innovation, GenRad often fell behind in recognizing the changing dynamics of the electronic test equipment marketplace. Low-priced instruments were meeting the testing needs of a wide array of users and were gaining general market acceptance. Yet GenRad's engineers were designing exotic instruments that had fewer general applications. Therefore, the company came to cede an increasing amount of business to its more market-oriented competitors. For example, in the early 1930s, GenRad developed the first commercial oscilloscope using a cathode ray tube (CRT). Management decided that the instrument was not worth continuing to develop commercially, because "the market is too big and too willing to purchase cheaper competitive products." The company therefore abandoned the product. By 1978, the oscilloscope had annual sales of several hundred million dollars. GenRad's competitors had aggressively pursued this opportunity.

Somewhat curiously, given the company's commanding technologic lead in the field of electronic test equipment and the burgeoning demand for such equipment, Eastham committed the company to policies of slow growth and private ownership. Growth was to be fueled solely by internal earnings and limited borrowings. In 1942, the company explained its position by enunciating its philosophy on growth in an advertisement that appeared in a widely circulated technical journal. (See Exhibit 13 for the text of this advertisement.)

The company's style of management was similarly unique. In 1939, top management officially espoused a policy of management by committee. Committees were formed to look after every aspect of the business, including general management, new products, research and development, pricing, and patents. Eastham was strongly opposed to conflict (though not to "brisk, polite debate") and set the direction for the firm by merely intimating his wishes during the various committee meetings. No one in a committee was likely to dispute Eastham's opinions as to how management should proceed in conducting company affairs.

Although an emphasis was placed on management by committee, some thought that Eastham was actually in sole command. Thurston had observed:

> Even though Eastham had the various committees fully in place by the early 1940s, he continued to dominate the management of the company. People were too polite, and had too much respect for the founder to challenge him.

In the same way that the company's engineers developed products that were ahead of their time, Eastham established human resource policies that were extremely advanced for their day. Under Eastham's philosophy, job security was of paramount importance. Therefore, he disallowed plant shutdowns and layoffs. In fact, even during the Great Depression, there were no layoffs despite a steep downturn in business. Rather, production and shift schedules were revised to distribute the existing work evenly among all employees. Eastham was progressive in believing that a company's profits should be shared by stockholders, management, *and* employees; the firm pioneered in the implementation of employee benefits, profit-sharing, and bonus programs. The company maintained a liberal holiday policy and offered a relatively short work week. Another core practice at GenRad was promoting from within. Virtually all jobs in the managerial and supervisory hierarchy were filled by the advancement of understudies who had years of experience in subordinate positions.

When Eastham retired in 1948, his values were firmly established at the company. However, the sense of comprehensive direction he gave the organization departed with him. Years later, when the company faced an uncertain future, its premier engineer, Robert Fulks, remarked:

> Eastham was bright and had the entire plan for the company in his head. He created a number of rules of thumb for managers, which were consistent with his mental plan. When he left the company, he took the plan and left behind the rules of thumb. The problem was that no one knew how he had arrived at the rules, since no one really knew his plan.

The Postwar Years: Emergence of an Industry

After World War II, GenRad faced a dilemma. Many new electronics firms were growing rapidly. Military R&D money was nearly free for the asking, and success in the electronics field was becoming the rule, not the exception. As Thurston later remarked, "In the postwar years, you grew in spite of yourself."

But GenRad's top management viewed the postwar environment with concern and skepticism. They believed that a major depression was imminent and, therefore, refused to accept military R&D funds or to develop a growth strategy.

The premium GenRad paid for this policy was exorbitant. Two of the company's prime competitors, Hewlett-Packard and Tektronics (founded in 1939 and 1946, respectively), aggressively met the growing electronics industry's needs for test and measurement instrumentation by committing themselves to rapid growth and massive product development programs.

The early 1950s were troubled times for GenRad. During these years the company continued to pioneer in the development of a broad range of technically innovative products, but the percentage of new products that were successful in the marketplace declined. One reason for this lay in the fact that new-product-development engineers did not enjoy as much direct interaction with GenRad's customers as they had in earlier years. Rather, beginning in the early 1940s, the firm's sales engineers increasingly served as mediators between customers and the company's development engineers. This led to two problems. First, the company's salespeople sometimes failed to apprehend the true future needs of the market. Secondly, the company's engineers often ignored the market information communicated to them by the field salespeople, and decided to work instead on projects of their choosing. Therefore, the members of the engineering department remained removed from the customer and increasingly failed to address the real needs of the market. While GenRad was offering its customers an excellent digital voltmeter but in *only one* model, Hewlett-Packard was offering a whole *line* of digital voltmeters covering all specifications and price ranges. Further, GenRad's sales personnel were being increasingly outnumbered in the field.

Indeed, GenRad's product policy may have been outmoded altogether, given the rapid evolution of the electronics industry. Thurston described the company's product approach in this way:

> The product policy was to "skim the cream from the top," offering only one or a very few products in each instrument category, with each product the best of its type available, and priced accordingly [that is, at a substantial premium]. The concepts of product line, market segment, market share, and marketing strategy, with all their implications for industry leadership and long-term success, were simply not matters of interest.

By 1954, when Hewlett-Packard swept by GenRad in sales volume, the market had repudiated that policy. Nonetheless, GenRad's management remained confident that their policies were correct, and executives were heard to say, "We have seen them pass us on the way up, and we will see them pass us on the way down." Their prophecies proved to be unenlightened.

During the first 48 years of GenRad's history, the firm was overseen by only three presidents. Eastham was followed by Erroll H. Locke as president from 1948 to 1955. Charles C. Carey served from 1955 until his death in 1963. Both Locke and Carey had risen through the manufacturing ranks and fully espoused Eastham's management philosophies. In fact, from 1948 through 1963, Locke and Carey were presidents in name only. Out of deference to Eastham's preference for management by committee, Locke had created, in 1948, an "office of the president," which was staffed by the vice presidents of engineering, manufacturing, and marketing. Each member of the triumvirate retained an equal degree of power. The group met every Tuesday morning to negotiate the appropriate management plans for the company. One executive reflected that it was often as if three separate companies were represented at the meetings. Carey inherited and accepted without question the office of the president. GenRad's management was almost religiously dedicated to the company's founder.

Sinclair: A Time of Tentative Change

A new era was ushered in at GenRad when Dr. Donald B. Sinclair was chosen to succeed Carey as company president in 1963. After receiving his doctorate in 1936 from MIT, Sinclair joined GenRad full-time and rose through the engineering ranks. He served as chief engineer, vice president for engineering, and executive vice president and technical director before being elected president.

Upon becoming president, Sinclair immediately eliminated the triumvirate, choosing instead to take personal control and responsibility for setting the company's direction. However, he honored and even reinforced tradition in other ways. For example, he retained the process of management by committee and even expanded the committees' purview in the mid-1960s. He attempted to reinforce his predecessors' philosophy of partnership between employee and employer by preserving the cash and stock bonus plans, the profit-sharing trust, and the no-layoff policy and by introducing a stock-option plan. He adhered to the policy of promoting from within. Finally, Sinclair contined the policy of staffing the board of directors solely with company insiders.

But for all of Sinclair's attempts to preserve the harmony that had characterized GenRad's past, significant discontent with the company's traditional management philosophy and policies was being aired by 1967. Several of GenRad's junior executives expressed a consensus that the firm's preoccupation with technologic innovation (at the expense of coordinated product strategies) and its commitment to slow growth were no longer appropriate strategies given the changes taking place in the industry. Eventually, Sinclair began to agree with the dissenters, and he decided to steer the company on a new course. In 1967, he issued a manifesto entitled, "Company Policies and Objectives," which tentatively outlined his new direction for the company. He had written the manifesto with the active collaboration of Thurston. Never before had such a comprehensive statement been issued by the company's management.

1967 Statement on Policies and Objectives The document declared that for the first time in GenRad's history, management would espouse a growth policy. Simultaneously (and no less of a dramatic break with the past), the report stated that the company would adopt a focused product strategy and a narrow product line, practices that would enable the company to build upon its special strengths.

In the statement Sinclair pinpointed the weaknesses that he thought might slow the company's future progress. He noted that the company's management systems were inadequately developed and that GenRad could not grow according to plan if this condition persisted. He observed that no formal budgeting system was in place at the company and that this situation required immediate correction. He noted that planning procedures were needed and that forecasting capabilities were unsatisfactory. He indicated that inventory levels were excessive. He listed the finance-related challenges facing the company in exhaustive detail. For example, he urged increases in inventory turns, R&D effectiveness, profit margins, and growth rate. He predicted that serious problems would ensue if greater integration between manufacturing, engineering, and marketing were not achieved.

Although the statement's message often appeared to be a paradigm of focus and directness, it was simultaneously, in places, a masterpiece of ambiguity. For example, in the preface of this treatise, which outlined the radical departure that would take place from GenRad's past, the following sentences appeared:

> On the other side of the ledger, objectives should not be so developed within a comfortable consensus that further creative thinking is stultified. It is very important that objectives not become unquestioned objects of veneration and that the manner of achieving them be left as open as possible.

This 1967 announcement of the intention to pursue growth and narrow the product lines was accompanied by several determined rededications to superannuated company principles. For example, the statement reemphasized the policy of internal, private ownership of the company. Committee management was reinforced. The policy of continuous employment with no layoffs was reaffirmed: "Fluctuations in business are taken care of by adjustment of inventory and hours of work rather than by the size of the work force." The policy of promoting from within was restated. Indeed, despite the fact that the company was dramatically altering its product policy and that the competitive environment had changed drastically, the document stated that the company's traditional premium price structure would remain intact and that head-on competition on a price basis would be avoided.

Thurston characterized the response to Sinclair's statement:

> A wave of enthusiasm went through the company for the first time ever. There was a feeling of togetherness. This was the most sweeping change that had occurred at GenRad since I had joined the company, and people were excited. They were saying, "We're going to grow! Management has agreed that we're going to grow!"

Acquisitions   As these changes occurred, the company made two acquisitions in 1969, in apparent conflict with the goal to rationalize the product line. The acquired companies were Time/Data of Santa Clara, Calif., and Grason-Stadler of Concord, Mass. Time/Data manufactured testing equipment used by manufacturers of mechanical equipment (such as automobiles, oil drilling platforms, and satellites) to ensure that their products would withstand the stresses and vibrations to which they would be subjected in their end-use environments. Time/Data also manufactured sound analyzers, which were used to monitor machinery health. These instruments "listened" to operating machinery and "heard" noises that signaled impending machinery failure.

Grason-Stadler manufactured audiometers, which were used to measure and record the state of human hearing (to ensure that workers were not being affected by environmental noise levels). Management believed these instruments would be market-compatible with the company's long-established line of sound-level meters. Audiometers were used to measure noise in the industrial workplace and in outdoor areas to verify compliance with Environmental Protection Agency (EPA) noise-pollution regulations.

Management Changes

Throughout 1972, GenRad's board of directors wrestled with the issue of managerial succession at the company. After a complicated and lengthy internal selection process, they announced on December 29, 1972, that Thurston had been elected president of GenRad. Sinclair was elevated to the position of chairman and chief executive officer. Steven J. Stadler, a former partner in Grason-Stadler, was named senior vice president and chief financial officer, effective February 1973. Ivan G. Easton (formerly vice president of engineering), the chief financial officer and a 35-year veteran of the company, announced his retirement effective February 1973. Meanwhile, the enthusiasm over the new growth policy collided with the reality of the company's dramatically escalating financial problems in 1972. By January 1973, the company realized that, for the first time since the Great Depression, it had lost money. The actual loss in 1972 was a staggering $2.3 million on sales of $33 million. Over $1 million of the total loss was posted by GenRad's 1969 Time/Data acquisition. Other contributors were high R&D spending, inefficient manufacturing processes, and high inventory levels.

The news of the loss was unexpected. Given the state of the firm's financial and accounting systems, there was no sure way that management could have known the state of the company's financial condition before closing the books at year's end.

In the wake of the company's devastating 1972 financial performance, Sinclair announced in February 1973 that he would resign as chairman at the March 1974 annual meeting. Thurston was to become chief executive officer, as well as remain president of the company, at that time. In accepting the position, Thurston had agreed to shepherd the firm through a dire period in its history. Whether or not GenRad would survive as an independent company could not be foretold in 1973.

THURSTON: A VOICE FOR CHANGE

Thurston started working at GenRad in 1941 as an MIT co-op student. After receiving his BSEE in 1943, he worked full-time on classified ultra-high-frequency development projects for the U.S. Department of Defense. He received a master's degree from MIT in 1948 and that year moved to sales. One colleague had jovially noted that when Thurston left engineering and took on sales-related responsibilities, he improved the quality of both functions at the company. In 1950 he accepted the company's offer of a position in its New York sales office.

As a sales engineer in the early and mid-1950s, Thurston came to recognize that the company's products were no longer the most respected items of their kind. He warned Concord headquarters of the company's inability to compete effectively with its competitors' broad product lines and urged that the firm's product policy be developed with greater emphasis on customers' needs. In 1955, he was called back to Concord to create and staff a new market research group, which was charged with finding a means of increasing the market acceptance of the company's new products.

In 1964, during a period of slowing sales growth, Thurston was named chairperson of a group of sales and marketing executives empowered by the management committee to institute what was called the marketing planning program (MPP). Essentially, the group was to plan and coordinate the company's new-product marketing effort. This task involved examining the engineers' new-product output, selecting those products with the greatest apparent market potential, and allocating marketing resources in accordance with expected returns. It was this selection process that Thurston and his peers found problematical:

> It soon became apparent that we were generating more sound new marketing ideas than we could afford to pursue. A good case could be made for each of several individual marketing efforts. It became obvious that this approach of developing specific selling plans for each product or product line built premature enthusiasm for many marketing projects that could never be developed due to limitation of funds.

Another realization that Thurston and his associates on the MPP team reached was that the time had arrived to devise means by which to coordinate the efforts of the marketing and engineering functions relative to new and existing product-development efforts. Until 1965, there had been little coordination between the functions.

Late in 1964, Thurston was asked to attend Northeastern University's general management program. He accepted the offer to attend this program, which met one week per month for 7 months. In the meantime, the work of the MPP group continued apace. In 1966, senior management unexpectedly named him vice president for planning. By 1967, the directors agreed to the formation of a formal, permanent marketing planning committee, charged with coordinating the marketing effort. Thurston chaired this committee.

The year 1967 proved to be a watershed both in GenRad's history and in Thurston's career. Until that time, the senior management of the firm had almost pathologically sought to eliminate the development of conflict within the company. For example, during the company's first 50 years of operations, votes on company policy at employee stockholder meetings were first cast by an open showing of hands and later by ballots that were marked in view of other stockholders. This procedure mitigated against the emergence of dissenting opinions. An executive recalled that during the late 1950s, a stockholder who abstained from voting for management's platform was told, subsequent to the meeting, not to abstain from voting in the future. Since management answered to management alone, such demands went unchallenged.

As a result of top management's historic resistance to challenges to their views, Thurston felt forced at first to make all suggestions relating to what he considered to be necessary revisions in company policies with the maximum degree of tact and diplomacy. But he soon realized that the necessary changes would be long delayed if he persisted in merely hinting at his plans and ideas in the interests of avoiding a showdown. Therefore, he revised his tactics and became more assertive.

By 1967, Thurston and several other "young turks" had persuaded old-line management with the force of their arguments. By continuously challenging management's reasons for adhering to certain inbred policies, he had led them to recognize for themselves that the past approaches were no longer appropriate. When Thurston's arguments—that the company should follow growth and narrow product-line strategies—prevailed, his colleagues could not have failed to notice his success in establishing a new set of values at GenRad. When asked why he continued to flout convention by inflicting his opposing views on management, he replied, "Because I was as stubborn as they were [in attacking the old approaches that they had been defending]." In fact, he noted that many of his debates with Sinclair in committee meetings had become "shouting matches," but that they had survived those contests "with genuine mutual respect, and warm feelings." While Thurston was experimenting with open conflict, he noted that covert politics was vigorous.

In 1968 a major part of Sinclair's 1967 statement of mission became reality when the new-products committee announced that the product portfolio would be decreased from 20 product-line areas (containing over 2000 discrete products) to 3 areas. The number of products would likewise be reduced drastically. This announcement marked the company's first actual commitment to fundamental change and served to open the floodgates of transition. This "concentration policy" was to be accomplished by allocating all new-product-development resources to the three selected product areas, while milking the 17 remaining product lines.

From 1968 to 1972, Thurston pursued his duties as vice president for marketing. When he assumed the presidency of GenRad in 1973, he was faced with the challenge of steering the firm away from disaster. (See Appendix C for additional comments on Thurston and his management philosophy.)

1973: Turning Around an Ailing Company

Immediate Actions Thurston's first action as president of GenRad was to disband all committees and to thereby place key responsibilities in the hands of individual managers. In Thurston's view, the committees were impeding decisionmaking at the company. During a 1981 interview, Thurston discussed the problems associated with the committee structure:

> The problem developed when Eastham left, because the committees lost the strength and guidance that he had provided. Senior managers began to behave more like ethical trustees than aggressive entrepreneurs. What we ended up with was a company established more as a government than as a business. It was patterned after the Federalist structure to assure that a powerful minority could prevent the tyranny of the majority.

Next, Thurston took a decisive step to limit the firm's R&D expenditures, which had risen from their historical level of 10 percent of sales to 14 percent of sales in 1972. The reductions meant that entire projects were discontinued. Thurston retained the consulting firm of Arthur D. Little, Inc. (ADL), to study problems in manufacturing. Furthermore, he put the vice president of manufacturing on notice to improve efficiency in the department within 12 months or face replacement.

He also announced plans to shorten the new-product-development cycle and to improve the commercial success of future new products by continuing to upgrade the firm's marketing capabilities. He further vowed to equalize the status and influence of the engineering, manufacturing, and marketing functions, thus signaling that the engineering department would no longer be the dominant function at GenRad in terms of status and influence. Thurston expressed a strong commitment to establishing systems within the company for production inventory control, quality control, strategic planning, and project costing. Finally, he nominated three additional outside directors to the board. The first outside director in the history of the company had joined the board in 1972. After the election of these nominees, outside members had a controlling voice on the board.

As Thurston implemented his reforms, Stadler was working to right the financial side of the business. Stadler, unlike GenRad's other top managers, was not an engineer by training, although he was said by several of GenRad's executives to possess a good understanding of the firm's technology.

Manufacturing   In the wake of the manufacturing department's failure to make production and efficiency improvements, the vice president of manufacturing was replaced in March 1974 by an outsider, Walter C. Hinds, Jr. For the first time in company history, manufacturing was headed by a manager who had not risen through the ranks. Hinds noted that management had been "very reluctant to hire from the outside."

When Hinds arrived at GenRad, he found the manufacturing operation in general disarray.

> The manufacturing situation was chaos. We were operating as a large job shop, with no items being manufactured in high volume. Lot sizes ranged from 5 to 100. The average job was 26 weeks behind schedule. The production inventory control system was way out of whack. Everyone was responsible for everything. There were no clear definitions of roles or responsibilities. Quality internally was a disaster. The likelihood of an item passing final test without some sort of rework was zero. Finally, the division was working under a "one-person, one-job" concept. A manufacturing employee was assigned to manufacture 25 units of a given model from start to finish. It was incredibly inefficient.

There were other tensions as well. According to Hinds, marketing and engineering would reach decisions and then force them on manufacturing. Manufacturing was not included in a consultative role during the product-development process, and this practice led to frequent misunderstandings.

Hinds took several steps. He sent his quality engineers to work in concert with the design engineers. He hired a new purchasing manager, who awarded orders on the basis of competitive prices and not long-standing relationships, as had often been the case in the past. And he began to shift away from modular production by establishing more assembly lines at the plant, in an effort to increase quality and meet schedules. Hinds later noted that these changes had not been easy.

> I was reducing the breadth of people's jobs, and they didn't like that. Many of them were confused, upset, and irritated. By the same token, people saw that the new leadership was trying to bail the company out of a real mess.

Engineering and Marketing   In most respects, the GenRad's several engineering operations were functioning smoothly during the turnaround period. The engineering function had long been viewed as the critical determinant to the firm's success and had therefore received additional management attention in the past. This support of engineering had yielded striking engineering capabilities at the company.

However, conflicts existed between engineering and the other functions. These other functions were often viewed by those in the engineering area as poor relations. Consequently, relations between engineering and marketing personnel were awkward and unstructured. Furthermore, engineers and the company's sales personnel suffered from a poor communication network. However, given the general success of the engineering function, it was not spotlighted for emergency attention during 1973 and 1974.

As with engineering, there was a general level of satisfaction with the performance turned in by GenRad's marketing personnel. However, the problem of poor communication between marketing, manufacturing, and engineering had been noted. Thurston and Hinds sought to correct this situation by forming interfunctional project teams to handle certain aspects of the business. However, marketing was not singled out for attention during this period.

Personnel   In December 1973, Thurston took the unusual step of recruiting Richard Cambria, an outsider, to head a new personnel department. Before joining GenRad, Cambria had worked in various capacities within the personnel department at Exxon. Thurston had said that by hiring outsiders he planned to obtain the services of "those who had done it [performed the respective function] before, at large companies. We didn't want to reinvent the wheel."

Cambria characterized the company, as he saw it in late 1973, in this way:

> When I walked in the door, there was no sense of urgency. It was like a slow-motion movie here. There were no strategic plans, no sense of direction.

Cambria took action promptly. He immediately instituted the company's first formal performance appraisal system (borrowed from Exxon's system). As he studied the company, he and other senior managers concluded that the work force was too large, given the company's business level, and that benefits, in general, were far too liberal. Consequently, the company announced a work-force reduction that affected 100 employees, most of whom were located in the Massachusetts facilities. Cambria said that this, the second layoff in the company's entire history, "immediately increased the level of urgency in the company." (The company's first layoff, affecting

100 persons, had occurred in 1971 after a major cut in defense spending. Many electronics firms were affected by the spending cuts, and layoffs were widespread. The paradox of taxi drivers with doctorates was much publicized during the high-technology industry's 1971 travails.)

During 1975, more work-force reductions occurred, particularly in the nonexempt ranks. Next, Cambria trimmed employee vacations and increased the standard work week from 37½ to 40 hours. Bonuses were discontinued, and salary ranges were created for all positions, pegging GenRad salaries at the median of overall industry levels. (The company had ordered in April 1973 that employee-held stock no longer be repurchased upon retirement, to avoid the significant cash drain that this practice created. This meant that long-term employees no longer had a market for the shares they had gathered over the course of their careers with the company.)

Despite these disruptions, Cambria felt that the employees were pleased with what was happening at the company: "Most of the production people said, 'It's about time. We've been moribund.'"

When asked how long a time he thought that the employees believed GenRad had been moribund, Cambria replied, "It's bizarre, but I would say that they thought GenRad had been moribund for most of its life."

FULKS: A STUDY IN THE POWER OF INNOVATIVE BRILLIANCE

In March 1973, Robert Fulks, vice president of engineering, left the company to pursue an entrepreneurial opportunity. This was a painful loss. To replace Fulks, Thurston promoted Harold (Hal) McAleer. Fulks had led the group designing the functional board tester in 1969, and its successor designs had become the company's major product in 1979, generating 50 percent of the company's total sales. The board tester had made the company's commitment to the ATE market feasible and profitable. GenRad's entry into the ATE market was a move that would have enduringly positive consequences for the company.

In the early 1970s, after the successful introduction of the functional board tester, Fulks began to work in earnest on the development of a minicomputer to be used in GenRad's computer-driven automatic testers. (The company was then purchasing minicomputers from Digital Equipment Corporation [DEC].) Fulks saw a bright future for GenRad in the component, in-circuit, and functional ATE markets, and he wanted to be at the forefront of the industry with testing hardware (including a minicomputer) and software as well. From all accounts, Fulks' minicomputer development effort was proceeding in a phenomenally successful manner. One engineer at the company later said:

> From what I could see, Bob's minicomputer was more sophisticated than the PDP8 (DEC's minicomputer). I don't know how he did it.

While he was developing the minicomputer, Fulks had also, on his own initiative, performed a return on investment (ROI) analysis of several of the company's new products. He found that very few of these products were profitable. He submitted his findings to top management, but management's reaction was cool. "Essentially, they were not too happy with the report," he said. "I was pointing out the fact in *hard* numbers, that many products, even the popular products with good reputations, weren't making money in the late 1960s. Thurston was the only person who was interested, because he knew that costs were out of control and that profits were in trouble. But the directors and oldtimers weren't happy, because they didn't savor the prospect of changing everything around."

After the 1972 loss, however, costs had to be cut drastically. Thurston felt that the minicomputer project was one the company could no longer afford, and the project was discontinued.

Subsequently, Fulks left the company. In the late 1970, he founded Omnicomp, Inc., the pioneer manufacturer of field service testers. In May 1978, GenRad had announced that it would distribute Omnicomp's testers.

TOWARD RECOVERY: 1975–1978

By 1975 the company's sales and profits were increasing, and the strategic wisdom of the decision to push forward in the ATE field was becoming evident. Thurston issued a document in 1975 titled, "GenRad—Corporate Objectives and Strategy." It was similar in many ways to Sinclair's 1967 statement.

In this 1975 statement, Thurston reaffirmed his commitment to long-range thinking and strategic planning. He rededicated himself to the concept of maintaining a narrow product line. He observed that the company's high inventory levels would have to be reduced. He announced a decision to implement zero-based budgeting and management by objectives (MBO) systems within the company. An office for corporate planning was created. A commitment was made to adopt formal personnel and management training procedures. Furthermore, Thurston remained dedicated to the growth policy that had first been enunciated in Sinclair's 1967 statement.

Further actions were taken in 1975. In recognition of the company's continuing weakness in the areas of financial control and management information systems, a new vice president of finance was hired. The new executive reported directly to Stadler. An improved, formal performance-appraisal system was instituted, covering all employees and extending beyond the ad hoc system that was implemented to facilitate the 1974 layoffs. The capital structure was simplified by replacing the company's several unique classes of stock with a single class of conventional common stock. A more favorable debt-financing package was established with two commercial banks. Finally, the company's name was officially changed at the end of 1975 from General Radio Company to GenRad, Inc., to prevent the confusion that might arise from the word *radio* when the company was to go public in the future.

In 1976 a major recession hit the test instrument industry. GenRad's sales stalled at the 1975 level, while profits declined precipitously. However, the downturn in demand was short-lived, and in 1977 sales and earnings again improved markedly. This upturn had a strong impact on company morale and improved the prospects of GenRad's becoming a public corporation.

The company became publicly owned in June 1978. The pressure placed on management by the holders of GenRad's old stock, which was illiquid from 1973 through

1978, was relieved. But more, the move helped to change the company's image from that of a slow-moving equipment manufacturer to an advanced electronics technology firm committed to growth.

Many stock analysts were enthusiastic about GenRad's bright prospects. In fact, Thurston had later reflected:

> It wasn't until 1978, when the stock analysts told us what they saw, that we really began to believe, ourselves, that we were doing things right.

But others saw things differently. For example, Charles Hill, then an analyst with Bache Halsey Stuart Shields Inc., observed that he was not convinced that GenRad was geared for high growth as of 1978.

> The judgment is based on intangibles, but it comes from attending presentations year after year where the company talks about quality products, happy employees, and satisfaction with performance vis à vis other instrument companies. With more aggressive companies, you'd be hearing things like market value, tougher pricing policies, and paying top dollar to snare up salespeople. GenRad's simply not geared to beat the next guy.

Despite such reservations, the company's financial performance was improving dramatically. The market was growing at a rapid rate, and GenRad's technology continued to meet the market's needs. Sales in 1978 increased 23 percent over the 1977 figure to $89.4 million. Profits increased 77 percent to $6.4 million. Return on equity stood at an impressive 22.8 percent. Combined, the figures gave testimony to an impressive recovery from the company's highly unstable 1972 situation and from the 1976 recession.

STRUCTURAL CHANGE

From 1970 to 1979, GenRad's management had restructured the company on numerous occasions. After Thurston had reflected on the myriad corporate restructurings during the period, he concluded that, "Once we started the process of reorganizing, reorganizing became a fluid thing." The protean nature of GenRad's structure came to reflect its attempt to define its corporate objectives and to come to terms with its environment.

GenRad's first major reorganization occurred in 1970, when senior management at the firm suddenly announced the adoption of a matrix organizational form. The decision to reorganize under a matrix structure was conveyed to the employees by memorandum. (See Exhibit 9 for excerpts from the memorandum announcing the matrix.) The reorganization decision was made in response to the rapid change the firm was experiencing at the time. The functional organization that was replaced by the matrix was said by management to be cumbersome, since all decisions were routed through senior management. The matrix was perceived as a means of encouraging lower-level decisionmaking. Furthermore, when asked why the company had adopted the matrix form of organization in 1970, Thurston recalled:

> We had read about the matrix approach and we were intrigued. It was new and we liked to innovate.

Under the plan, the firm comprised three business areas—acoustics and signal analysis (A/SA), component and network test (C/NT), and high-frequency equipment (S/I/M)—and three functional areas—engineering, manufacturing, and marketing. Time/Data and Grason-Stadler were independently operating subsidiaries.

In retrospect, some managers claimed that the 1972 loss was partly created by the company's matrix structure. It was said that difficult decisions were either not made or were seriously delayed, since managers could not reach the compromise positions that were required under the matrix form of organization. Rather than face up to the open conflict that was inherent in the matrix decision-making process, GenRad's managers often retreated from the issues altogether and therefore compromised the effectiveness of the organization by neglecting certain essential management tasks.

The matrix organization was maintained through 1974, although a few minor revisions had been made in the matrix form up to then. Most significantly, the position of business area manager was created. Reporting to this position were an engineering manager, a marketing manager and, on a dotted-line basis, a manufacturing engineer. Unlike the engineering and marketing managers, the manufacturing engineer was not formally part of the matrix and had a straight-line reporting relationship only to the manufacturing manager. In 1974, there were four business areas. These business areas composed what was called GenRad Massachusetts (GRMass). Time/Data and Grason-Stadler remained independent subsidiaries. The business areas were responsible for generating sales forecasts for their products. These forecasts were then funneled into the marketing department. The business areas were also responsible for generating new-product designs and for developing product-marketing strategies.

Three functional operating groups were in place in 1974: engineering, manufacturing, and marketing. Central engineering, a part of engineering, was primarily a supporting resource group and provided assistance to the business areas in implementing product-development plans. Development engineering was subdivided according to business areas and had straight-line reporting relationships to the business area and to the head of engineering.

The four business areas' products were manufactured at the Concord and Bolton plants. Since the company manufactured the majority of the components needed for each product, and since components were typically manufactured at both plants, a complex set of interrelationships existed between the Concord and Bolton facilities. In effect, the two plants operated as one. There were no plant managers at either the Concord or Bolton facility. Rather, both plants were under the direct supervision of Hinds, the vice president of manufacturing.

Marketing personnel had responsibility for the consolidation of the various business area forecasts. Similar to the development engineers, they were subdivided by business area and were formally part of the matrix. Marketing generated the company's combined business forecast. Furthermore, the centralized marketing group oversaw the sales and service efforts.

During 1975, in a series of steps, another restructuring occurred. The company continued to move away from the matrix organization toward a product-line divisional organization. The business areas were termed *product-line divisions*. By the end of 1975, after several incremental changes, the firm comprised three business areas. Time/Data remained an independent operating division. Grason-Stadler, on the other hand, had been included within a business area. Sales and services remained centralized corporate functions. The matrix form was discontinued by eliminating the straight-line functional reporting relationships of development engineering and marketing. All functional engineering services were combined with the manufacturing department to form a new operations department at GRMass. Hinds was named vice president of operations. Manufacturing was not included within the business areas. The former vice president of engineering was named to head one of the business areas. Since all manufacturing and process engineers were moved to operations, and since all product-development engineers were included in the business areas, GenRad no longer had a central supporting engineering function staffed by engineers with talents and abilities covering the spectrum.

Therefore, according to the 1975 reorganization, all business areas were responsible for the administration, product-engineering, and marketing functions. Manufacturing, production engineering, production inventory control, quality assurance, purchasing, advanced engineering (a specialized R&D group that was working on the design of advanced testing equipment), sales, field service, personnel, accounting, and financial services were all provided by centralized corporate units.

During 1977, the company massaged the structure that had been established in 1975. The 1977 structure remained virtually unchanged through June 1979. The business areas were officially renamed product-line divisions. The major 1977 structural modifications related to the grouping of products within product-line divisions. For example, Grason-Stadler was once again made an independently operating subsidiary, whereas Time/Data was coupled with the acoustics and signal analysis (A/SA) business area to form the acoustic and vibration analysis (AVA) product-line division. By the close of 1977, Grason-Stadler was divested because its line of audiometers had not turned out to be as synergistic with GenRad's acoustic instruments as had originally been anticipated. (It was repurchased by Rufus Grason, one of its founders.) However, one manager had a different view relative to the divestiture:

> The company was never able to integrate entrepreneurial operations, such as Grason-Stadler. Grason-Stadler was not divested because it could not generate profits or manufacture salable products, but rather because Grason-Stadler's and GenRad's styles were in fundamental conflict.

To achieve the 1977 structural changes, several management reassignments were made. McAleer was moved from the company's electronic manufacturing test products group to the mechanical test products group. These were wholly different business segments. Upon the resignation of P. J. Macalka, vice president of marketing and international, R. G. Rogers was transferred from the test systems business area to marketing to fill the gap. Hinds' responsibilities were increased to encompass all operations functions and the general management of the company's EMT division. Thus, Hinds was also responsible for the new-product-development process for the division comprising 80 percent of the company's sales.

The EMT division's product-line managers reported to Hinds, as did the operations manager and general manager for the Futuredata subsiduary. (Futuredata is discussed in a subsequent section.)

Thurston later reflected on the intent behind the many alterations in the company's structural design:

> We were constantly attempting to design a structure that would be consonant with the strengths and weaknesses of our people. But we were simulaneously looking for a structure that could carry the company forward in a positive direction.

GENRAD'S STRUCTURE IN 1979

Overview

In July 1979, there were two product-line divisions at GenRad: the electronic manufacturing test (EMT) division and the acoustic and vibration analysis (AVA) division. The company's many disparate product lines were housed in these divisions. Manufacturing at GenRad was essentially centralized, even though certain products were manufactured in West Coast plants. All East Coast manufacturing was centralized. Sales and service was centralized, with one exception: products manufactured by Time/Data were sold by a discrete sales staff. These products were entirely different from the majority of the company's products, and the customer base for Time/Data's instruments was, likewise, different. An advanced development group was engaged in pure and applied research of a sophisticated nature. The finance, personnel, and employee-training staff functions were centralized. A copy of GenRad's 1979 organization chart is shown in Exhibit 12. (See Exhibit 15 for background information on GenRad's top management personnel.) A more detailed description of the company's 1979 structure follows.

General Organization

The EMT division was responsible for developing, manufacturing and marketing the company's ATE. Additionally, the company's industrial instrument products (older, more traditional test instruments, which were the core product line at GenRad before the firm's entry into the ATE market) were handled through EMT. Furthermore, Futuredata, Inc., a recently acquired (February 1979) microprocessor development system manufacturer, reported through the EMT division, despite the fact that it was an independent product line. Finally, the acoustics test products for AVA/East were manufactured by EMT. Eighty percent of GenRad's sales and 100 percent of its profits were generated by the EMT division in 1978, and these percentages were expected to hold steady in 1979.

The AVA division directed the marketing and engineering efforts for the company's vibration, shake-test, and machinery health analyzer products (all manufactured on the West Coast by AVA/West, formerly, Time/Data) and its acoustics test products (all manufactured for AVA/East by the manufacturing arm of the EMT division). AVA headquarters were located in Santa Clara, Calif. AVA division sales constituted 20 percent of total corporate sales in 1978.

Product-Line Management

The following is a description of the management tasks and the points of connection between personnel in the test systems product (TSP) line. The structure of the TSP line was similar to the structures of GenRad's other product-line groups in both the EMT and AVA product-line divisions.

The product line was managed by a product-line manager, a product-engineering manager, and a product-marketing manager. The product-marketing manager was responsible for generating product forecasts, developing product-marketing programs, maintaining strong communication between the field sales and service forces and the relevant product-line personnel, and coordinating new-product-development and market introduction efforts with the engineering group. Consequently, the product-marketing manager had to be aware both of the customer's needs and of existing technology to sense which new products were worth pursuing most.

The product-engineering manager was responsible for new-product-development engineering. He or she coordinated the efforts of product-engineering personnel in applying new and existing product technologies, and in developing new products and applications. These engineers specialized by product line. Three types of new-product engineers were employed by the company: hardware, software, and mechanical. These engineers worked in concert on all new products. The product-engineering manager could initiate new-product-development efforts and had access to large amounts of development capital. It was vital that product-engineering managers were intimately familiar with test equipment technologies and that they had a versatile understanding of the markets. The product-engineering manager and his or her subordinates were all reviewed on a subjective basis, as were product-marketing personnel.

Thurston had observed that the relationship between the product-engineering and product-marketing managers was the most crucial one in the company:

> The thought processes of the product-engineering and product-marketing managers must mesh very well if the product-development and marketing efforts are to succeed. There is no way to find the combined engineering and marketing talents that we need in the mind of one person. Therefore, we must rely upon the exceptionally close partnership of these two individuals. Thankfully, we have heretofore been successful in finding people who have been able to create harmonious relationships between themselves and therefore between the functions. The continued success of the interface is critical to our success.

Product-engineering managers were typically promoted from within the engineering ranks, whereas product-marketing managers were generally promoted from the regional sales manager position.

Product-line managers were responsible for facilitating the linkage of engineering and marketing personnel wherever possible. Furthermore, the product-line manager was ultimately responsible for overseeing the progress of all new-product projects and administered all funds related to new-product development. Finally, the product-line manager performed the critical task of ensuring that all product-line strategic plans, both intradivisionally and interdivisionally, were coordinated.

Manufacturing

As of July 1979, GenRad's products were manufactured in four plants. Three of the plants, controlled by the EMT division were located in Concord, Mass., Bolton Mass., and Los Angeles.

Management at GenRad had long been committed to manufacturing the majority of the components for its finished products, as opposed to finding and purchasing components externally. Therefore, GenRad's manufacturing capabilities were extremely broad. Thurston had commented that manufacturing at GenRad was

> . . . a comprehensive, vertically integrated manufacturing operation capable of producing a wide variety of products, ranging from binding posts and potentiometers selling for dimes to a few dollars, to small and large instruments priced between a few hundred to a few thousand dollars, to complex computer-controlled systems priced at hundreds of thousands of dollars apiece. It also includes a new pilot production facility for new products, material and capital-planning and production-control groups, and the company's central purchasing function.

The Concord plant had been built by the firm in 1952 and had originally offered 72,000 square feet of manufacturing space. The plant had been expanded to 350,000 square feet by 1979. The Bolton plant had been built by the firm in 1963 and had been expanded from its original size of 80,000 square feet to a 1979 size of 150,000 square feet.

The Bolton and Concord plants were used to manufacture component testers, in-circuit testers and functional testers. Additionally, the company's acoustic meters and industrial instrument test products were manufactured at both Concord and Bolton. Although the facilities were 14 miles apart, they were essentially operated as one plant.

The Bolton plant contained the following manufacturing units: sheet-metal fabrication (for test product cabinetry and the like), microelectronic circuitry fabrication, cable manufacturing, substrate manufacturing, and the final assembly of acoustics products. Additionally, it housed the company's tooling and machine shops. The facility also included offices for AVA/East engineering and marketing personnel, the New England sales and services regional office, and the software programming services unit.

The Concord plant was responsible for printed circuit board assembly, printed circuit board test, final assembly of the industrial instrument product line, final assembly of component testers, and final assembly of test systems (functional and in-circuit test equipment). The engineering and marketing functions for the component, test systems, and industrial instrument product lines were housed in the Concord facility. Other operations at Concord, such as printed circuit board manufacture, were routine and accomplished by less-skilled personnel. Printed circuit board assembly was performed under a batch process, with some boards being shunted to as many as 30 work stations before reaching completion. Final assembly operations were more project-oriented. Frequently, the final assembly function might be responsible for the manufacture of as few as two units of a given product.

All administrative functions were handled from offices at the Concord plant. Component and hardware purchases were made from the Concord offices. All shipments were received at Concord, and inventory and warehousing were centered there as well. Incoming component inspection was performed at this facility. The company's financial and manufacturing management information systems (MIS) were located in Concord. Accounting was performed in Concord, as was inventory control. Furthermore, the plant housed offices for GenRad's management staff and sales and service functions. Neither plant had a manager. Rather, Hinds and his operations team dealt with the product-line managers to coordinate the manufacturing schedule.

While each product-line division contained discrete engineering and marketing functions, manufacturing provided several resources to all product lines. Manufacturing was responsible for production-engineering and process-engineering services. The process engineers were steering manufacturing toward process automation and away from the old "one-person, one-lot" production technique. Drafting, modeling, test-engineering, and quality-engineering services were all provided by manufacturing as well. All assemblers and technicians operated from within the manufacturing division. The connection between manufacturing personnel and product-line marketing and engineering personnel was achieved by the inclusion of manufacturing personnel in the new-product-development process.

Approximately 325 people were employed within EMT manufacturing in July 1979. The employee breakdown is as follows:

Printed circuit board assembly	80
Printed circuit board test	50
Assembly operations	
Component testers	
Acoustic testers	70
Industrial instruments	
Assembly: test systems	40
Machine and sheetmetal shop	60
Microelectronic circuitry	25

The effectiveness of manufacturing personnel was measured by their ability to operate within budget and to deliver a quality product on schedule. No systems were in place at the company as of 1979 to enable management to isolate efficiency, product-mix, or volume-cost variances. A realistic rationalization of the company's product portfolio was hampered as a result of this fact. Given the changes occurring in the product mix, actual versus budgeted cost variances were often substantial.

In July 1979, a new in-circuit tester and a new component tester were being introduced. Therefore, manufacturing operations were frenzied. Demand for existing products was at an historic high, so the manufacture of new products placed considerable strain on the already taxed manufacturing function. Demands for personnel were high, but manufacturing employees were difficult to locate and hire. Some areas of the two plants were working three shifts, others two. The average work week was 48 hours. When asked to identify the key problem in manufacturing in mid-1979, Hinds stated that it lay in the inadequate material requirements planning system. He also indicated that there was a critical need for an effective manufacturing control system at the plants.

Sales and Services

The sales and services division, which sold and serviced all product lines (with the exception of Time/Data's), had nine U.S. and six European offices as well as one Canadian office. Manufacturers' representatives and distributors represented the company in other locations around the world. Ninety percent of the company's sales were made through the company's sales offices, with the remaining 10 percent handled by representatives and distributors.

There were two general sales managers within the sales and services division: one for the United States and one for Europe. In the United States, there were three regional sales offices. Each regional office had three district offices. The district offices typically included a sales manager and a service manager. The sales manager also served as district manager. Reporting to the district manager were the service manager and the sales engineers. A district office was the base for approximately 5 to 10 sales engineers. In addition to performing their management duties, district managers commonly sold products themselves.

Sales engineers held electrical engineering degrees and were generally quite experienced in test equipment sales. Sales personnel were paid on a salary and commission basis, with commissions commonly equaling 30–40 percent of their total remuneration. Salespeople were required to meet a sales quota (roughly $1 to $2 million) before being paid a commission. They were expected to give equal representation to all of the company's product lines, but most demonstrated a decided preference for a certain product or product line and developed expertise in selling it. In 1979, management faced a problem in that the great majority of the sales personnel were giving little attention to the sale of the AVA product line. This was largely due to the fact that customers for the AVA and EMT product lines were entirely different, and that the AVA products carried lower prices than the EMT products. Since sales commissions were based on total sales, salespeople were not penalized for ignoring the AVA product line. However, salary increases were based on an annual performance review, and sales personnel who were clearly focusing their sales effort on a select product group could receive lesser salary increases than those giving fair time to all of the firm's products.

Over the years, many long-standing customer relationships had been established. Therefore, much of the sales effort involved account-maintenance activities as opposed to new-account development. National accounts were serviced by national account specialists, who operated in conjunction with a district sales representative. National account specialists were intimately familiar with the entire gamut of the customer's requirements. Product specialists assisted district sales personnel in the sale of certain, generally highly sophisticated products. Product specialists were sales engineers with intimate knowledge of a particular product and expertise in selling it.

There were several potential career paths for a sales engineer. He or she was first promoted to the position of product specialist or national account specialist. From there, the career path involved a choice. The specialist could be promoted to manage a district sales office, then to lead a regional office, and finally to assume a headquarters sales and service position. Or, the employee could be promoted out of sales and service into a divisional marketing position. Promotions to marketing were usually made from the regional offices and from sales and services headquarters.

In 1979, the sales and services division was said to be functioning smoothly. Its major problems were related to personnel recruitment and the training of new and existing sales and service employees (to bring them up to date with the rapidly changing capabilities of GenRad's test equipment).

INVENTORY MANAGEMENT: A PERSISTENT PROBLEM

For most of his history, GenRad's inventory levels had been high relative to those of its competitors. In the early days of the company, these high inventories were explained by the firm's policy of maintaining steady production levels to keep employment levels constant. In periods of brisk demand, the company's policy was to quote lengthy delivery periods as a means of discouraging orders and slowing demand. The effect was to fuel the competitions' demand, since they would frequently receive the orders GenRad discouraged.

The company's excessive inventories created a significant cash drain. In fact, a large portion of GenRad's 1972 loss was attributed to high inventory-carrying costs. Therefore, Thurston proposed to reduce the inventory levels drastically and assigned Stadler the task of accomplishing the reduction. Stadler delegated the job to the vice president of finance. Neither Thurston nor Stadler set any target levels for inventories.

In 1973 and 1975, inventory levels stood at 40 percent and 37 percent of sales, respectively. By the end of 1978, levels had been reduced to 31 percent of sales. Nonetheless, the company's inventories remained substantially higher than its competitors'. The problem was made more troublesome by the fact that the rapid evolution of the test equipment industry resulted in earlier product obsolescence.

The problem was further compounded by the fact that by 1978, many managers viewed the situation as totally uncorrectable. Inventory values could not be isolated by product line, a problem that resulted in product-line managers being unable to determine if they were making progress or losing ground in their struggles to control inventory levels. Most managers redirected their attention to other areas, and a general sense of defeatism relative to controlling inventories prevailed.

SYSTEMS: A PERSISTENT WEAKNESS

Throughout GenRad's history, its management, although accurate in its assessment of the inadequacy of the company's management information systems, consistently failed to fully marshal the necessary forces to correct the problem. The irony in this was heightened by the fact that management's understanding of the flaws in the company's business systems was generally precise.

In Sinclair's 1967 policy statement, he said, relative to systems:

> As a company grows, the sheer volume of information required to describe the company's operation makes it desirable to add machines for routine processing of information. . . . We should move steadily toward the coordinated companywide system that currently goes by the name of the total system concept.

Despite the fact that Sinclair's position that the company should develop more advanced systems was sound, his plans were never adequately implemented. In fact, lack of implementation plagued many of the enlightened suggestions made by Sinclair in 1967. From 1967 until 1974, few improvements were made in the company's systems. In fact, not one of the many structural revisions implemented at the company during that time period had been accomplished by the adoption of a new set of systems. Therefore, the company's information systems remained crude or altogether absent.

Late in 1974, Thurston announced plans to implement two new systems at the company. Both represented milestones in the evolution of GenRad's financial controls. Thurston described the systems in an internal memorandum:

> A new, integrated system of financial reporting will soon be in effect to enable product and resource managers at all levels to monitor operations in comparison to the approved and budgeted product and resource plans. . . .
>
> A new project-management system has been designed and is in the process of being put into effect. This new system is designed to enable the dozens of people involved even in a single project to effectively plan and coordinate their respective contributions so as to carry out effectively the engineering, manufacturing, and marketing aspects of the new-product project while meeting time, quality, cost, product-performance, and sales volume objectives in an optimum manner.

However, implementation of the proposed systems proved difficult and troublesome. In 1975, Thurston expressed his frustration over the problem of developing and implementing needed systems and over the difficulties created by the company's inadequate systems:

> The enormous difficulty, time, and cost of developing the basic, needed information systems have, however, delayed their availability far beyond what had been expected (perhaps unrealistically) 2 years ago. Some of the most urgently needed systems are a project-cost system, product-line and business area profitability system (extending throughout GenRad), responsibility reports with transfer transactions reported and covering GenRad's worldwide operations, project-management systems, an inventory accountability system, etc.
>
> It is a corporate objective to strengthen and accelerate the development of information systems, together with their implementation and utilization, necessary to achieve effective control over the corporation's vital and essential functions at the earliest possible time.

Another systems-related problem was demonstrated by the fact that the cost accounting function at GenRad was handled by the manufacturing department until the mid-1970s. Additionally, costs by product line were not generated until 1975. Until then, there had been no means to measure these costs.

Late in 1975, in a lengthy and explicit memorandum, Thurston made an effort to clarify the roles and responsibilities of various departments and managers. For example, he wrote that responsibilities for "the completion and implementation of information systems necessary for corporate evaluation and approval, for project management, and for corporate reporting of new-product-development projects" belonged to Stadler and the finance staff. Stadler's finance-related duties were to oversee the corporation's debt structure, accounts payable policies, inventory policies, receivables policies, product-line profitability statistics, new-product profitability projections, and quarterly forecasting procedures. Furthermore, Stadler was responsible for all corporate financial relations with the banking and investment banking communities and for handling all issues related to taking the company public.

By 1977, the company's systems were still inchoate. Interestingly, after the 1977 reorganization, Thurston specifically directed his managers to concentrate on implementing the new structure and to temporarily turn their attention away from the issue of systems development. To ease management's transition to the new structure, he instructed them to "attempt to minimize the scope of any changes in accounting and information reporting until the start of the next year [1978]."

By 1979, GenRad's systems were improving but still falling far short of the needs of its operating managers. The divisions received their first balance sheets in 1979. These reports confirmed the suspicion that the divisions' asset management problems, which had been developing over time, were full blown by 1979. Individual product costs were still unavailable in 1979. After much effort, rough product-cost estimates could be provided, if needed. The industrial engineering department would attempt to extrapolate product costs based on a product's components. However, this figure would be an estimate only. One executive remarked that the industrial engineers used "fuzzy formulas" to arrive at estimated costs and that these formulas had often proved inaccurate. After the product had entered production, the industrial engineering unit would receive a detailed report from accounting outlining total manufacturing costs. However, this report was said to be extremely voluminous and cumbersome. As a practical matter, it was considered impossible for the industrial engineers to derive actual product costs based on the accounting report.

The performance appraisal system was also considered to be underdeveloped in 1979. Appraisals were primarily based on the subjective assessment of the employee's performance by his or her supervisor. When asked how an engineer might judge his performance at the company, Thurston commented, "Well, he would mostly have to have a sense about how his work was perceived by his boss." More objective performance yardsticks were generally unavailable to employees.

As a result of the weaknesses in the company's management information systems, management had come to base decisions more upon qualitative than on quantitative factors. For example, since product costs could not be generated, direct product profitability figures could not be determined. Hence, decisions relating to specific products were made on the basis of qualitative considerations (such as the importance of carrying a product to enhance the company's image as an advanced and innovative manufacturer of test products) and not on the basis of a quantitative determination (such as profitability or ROI). Over time, management had come to rely increasingly on qualitatively informed decisions. However, GenRad's explosive growth in the late 1970s had made the company's inadequacies in the area of systems more apparent and troublesome, and increased the need for new systems greatly.

Until the 1970s, the importance of the financial function had been diminished by GenRad's management. They felt that the financial personnel did not understand the company's business and that they therefore could provide little management input beyond the handling of creditor relations and the securing of necessary funds for corporate expansion.

When Thurston became GenRad's president, he began to place greater emphasis on the company's financial operations. Stadler was named second-in-command at the company. Nonetheless, the shift in values was extremely difficult to accomplish. Thurston had had little experience in the company's finance-related matters before assuming duties as president. Generally speaking, the company's line managers were uninitiated in the complexities of financial management. Therefore, the finance function was called upon to bridge a significant knowledge gap that existed at the company with respect to financial matters. This problem was compounded by the fact that the company's finance department lacked adequate systems to effectively communicate financial information. Therefore, much of the output from the finance offices appeared to the company's managers to be extraordinarily complex and opaque. Management remained hopeful that systems would improve and that the company's financial reports would become more comprehensible and useful. In the meantime, Stadler was attempting to make the major improvements that were needed in the company's historically underdeveloped financial capabilities.

NEW-PRODUCT-DEVELOPMENT PROCESS

GenRad had traditionally excelled in technological innovation and new-product development. In 1979, the company funded both pure and applied research efforts. The company's pure R&D efforts were conducted by the advanced development division. Pure R&D was the name given to research efforts designed to yield revolutionary testing methods or testing devices. The company's applied research and development programs were generally directed toward refining the testing capabilities of existing instruments or toward developing new products that were closely related to existing ones. The great majority of GenRad's research budget was devoted to applied research, which was another name for GenRad's new-product-development (NPD) process. Applied research was performed within each of GenRad's product-line divisions.

There were several stages in the new-product-development process. The process was bottom-up by nature. First, a new-product idea would be generated. This idea would often lead to what was known as "preliminary investigation," which was the formal process by which the feasibility of the product idea was explored. Approximately 10 percent of the new-product-development budget was devoted to preliminary investigations. These investigations could be instigated by the professional development engineers at the company, upon approval from the product-engineering manager. If the product idea survived preliminary investigation, a product proposal was drafted. The product proposals from all divisions were reviewed annually by senior management. Some proposals were eliminated due to budgetary constraints. Approved product proposals would then enter the project stage. Before the full-scale development of a product idea, a highly detailed project proposal would be submitted to management. The project proposal would outline production schedules, ROIs (by 1979), detailed specifications, estimated market size, projected market share, competition, and so forth, relative to the proposed product. If the project proposal were approved, the product would be passed through successive stages of design, prototype manufacturing, pilot manufacturing and, finally, full manufacturing. In 1979, this cycle took an average of 2 years to complete.

Each division received annual funding for its new-product-development effort. The new-product effort was typically budgeted at 7–12 percent of a division's projected total sales for the coming year, varying according to each division's strategic position. All project proposal negotiations were held between Thurston and the respective division general manager and division product-line managers. Division personnel would rank-order the projects, and the negotiations included gaining Thurston's approval of the major projects (his approval being granted in the context of the divisions' combined strategies) and fine-tuning the budget by weighing the strategic importance of those projects that were poised near the funding cutoff point. After the NPD budget had been established, changes in project priorities often occurred. As a given year progressed, the division general manager (in concert with the product-engineering and product-marketing managers) would normally readjust the NPD priorities to respond to such contingencies as a rapidly changing environment or an unexpected strategic shift by a competitor. Thurston had characterized the product and project approval process as being "very informal, direct and down to earth," with much open discussion between himself and the various division general managers and engineering and marketing personnel. Much of the process was said to be "intuitive" by nature.

Although many company executives lauded the project-funding process, others were critical of certain of its aspects. One executive stated that management was inordinately keen on developing technologically innovative products, and that the dangers inherent in a certain proposal, such as high financial risk or a negative expected mean value (EMV), might be overlooked if the prospect existed to develop an innovative or technologically exciting product.

In the past, the company had announced an average of six major product-development projects per year, with the average project extending over 2 years before completion and costing roughly $2 million. Management felt that the company enjoyed an above-average success ratio in developing marketable new products. New products generally took longer than planned to reach full development, but they also enjoyed longer product lives than anticipated. Development delays were explained by the fact that engineers attempted to perfect products in the development stage. Delays were increasingly costly, however, and by 1979 many executives were concerned with the skyrocketing cost of new-product development. These executives were developing techniques to measure the effectiveness of the company's applied research. However, other executives argued that the development of quantitative research-effectiveness data would not fundamentally alter the applied research funding process.

STRATEGIC PLANNING

GenRad's initial experience with formal strategic planning occurred in 1974, when the company retained Robert L. Wright (a consultant with Arthur D. Little, Inc., at the time) to help them institute such a process. Wright was concerned by the fact that GenRad's managers were examining the company's internal product strategy only, and were not looking at the corporate and product strategies being developed by their competitors. Wright felt that the firm would be highly vulnerable to competitive preemption in certain product lines if an aggressive strategic planning orientation were not adopted.

Thurston appointed a strategic planning council to coordinate the strategies and financial objectives of the business areas on a companywide basis. Under the plan, each product-line manager developed a discrete strategic plan. The product-line managers then met with their business area manager, and together developed a business area plan. The business area plan was a compilation of data on competitors' product lines, anticipated strategies, sales and growth rates, changes in product and process technologies, marketing and sales policies, and market shares. Changing environmental factors and their likely effects on the industry were also considered. Finally, based on the strategic data that had been gathered, detailed action plans were developed for each product line to maximize the effectiveness of GenRad's product-line strategies.

The various business area strategic analyses and plans would then be forwarded to the strategic planning council (which included Thurston, Stadler, and the heads of the major functional, business area, and staff units), where they would be consolidated into a master strategic plan for the company. It was thought that this bottom-up approach to strategy development would help to preserve business area autonomy and would give the business area managers a greater sense of independence.

Wright had persuaded the firm to think strategically in terms of natural businesses. A *natural business* was roughly defined as one or a group of product lines that claimed similar customers, competitors, process technologies, and functional performance capabilities. A natural business was considered to be akin to an independent business entity and could be liquidated or divested without having an adverse impact on the remainder of a company's product lines. A natural business could therefore function as an independent division. In 1974, Wright was concerned that there were many fewer natural businesses at GenRad than there were product lines—a fact which implied that the company had not yet been successful in rationalizing its product policy.

One manager made this observation about the state of the strategic process at the company in 1975:

The business areas produced massive strategic plans, but these documents detailed such issues as marketing policies, sales forecasts, and new-product-development programs. They were not, in actuality, strategic plans, since they did not include coherent sets of tactics designed to either challenge or head off the competition.

Another manager at the company felt that strategic planning at GenRad was compromised by the fact that it was essentially an annual exercise, not an ongoing process. As the executive observed, "It was a very disjointed process. The mentality here was, 'Let's get the planning out of the way so we can get back to business.'"

In 1976, corporatewide, formal strategic planning was discontinued. However, strategic planning continued at the divisional level. The discontinuation of centralized planning occurred for a number of reasons. First, Wright, who had been elected to the board of directors and had gained a reputation for asking penetrating questions about management's fundamental business assumptions, had frequently created a conflict-laden atmosphere at board of directors' and strategic planning meetings. Wright's style was said to have often been in sharp contrast to GenRad's more pacific nature. Furthermore, while the brilliance of Wright's theories on strategy was generally acknowledged, many GenRad executives did not feel that his theoretical constructs were germane to their operations. This incompatibility in management styles led to Wright's leaving the board in 1978. Secondly, business was strong from 1976 to 1978. Sophisticated strategic planning was therefore thought to be a superfluous exercise, given that the company was already operating at full capacity and that management was confident strong sales would continue. Perhaps most important, the corporatewide formal planning process did not have the full support of GenRad's managers. Many did not find the process to be valuable and believed that planning at the divisional level alone was fully satisfactory. Therefore, centralized planning expired due to lack of interest.

After 1976, the business area (and then division) general managers made annual presentations to Thurston to outline their division plans for the coming year. During these meetings, Thurston and the respective manager would arrive at a mutually acceptable division plan. Thurston, who had a clear understanding of the company's various product lines, retained sole responsibility for ensuring that the aggregated division plans melded into a coherent whole. One manager noted:

> Bill made many decisions relating to the divisions on the basis of his gut feelings as to how effective a given approach might be. Many of these were ad hoc, independent decisions. He had the overall strategy for the company in his mind, but there was no annual enunciation of that strategy.

As of mid-1979, formal, corporatewide strategic planning was still not present at GenRad.

FUTUREDATA: BROADENING PRODUCT PORTFOLIO

In February 1979, GenRad enlarged the scope of its operations by acquiring Los Angeles–based Futuredata, Inc. Futuredata was a manufacturer of microprocessor development systems (MDS). These systems were used by product designers to assist them in integrating complex microprocessors into new products. Therefore, these systems shortened the design process considerably. Microprocessor development systems were not similar to GenRad's automatic or other test instruments, since they served a laboratory design and not a manufacturing test function. Therefore, the acquisition of Futuredata meant that GenRad was entering an entirely new field.

In explaining the reasoning behind GenRad's entry into the MDS industry, Thurston stated that the microprocessor area was generally considered to hold great promise for future growth. It was thought that GenRad's involvement in the microprocessor field would give the company much-needed exposure to rapidly emerging microprocessor technology. By manufacturing and distributing development systems, GenRad's personnel would have an opportunity to interact directly with the engineers who were pioneers in microprocessor technology. Top personnel at the firm thought that this exposure to the engineers would give GenRad a clear advantage since it would gain an up-to-date understanding of developments in the field. They felt that this competitive advantage would yield future profits. Additionally, several key managers were highly optimistic over Futuredata's growth prospects.

Futhermore, Hewlett-Packard and Tektronix were thought to be making slow progress in the MDS area, and GenRad saw an opportunity to capitalize on the competition's apparent slow response in the field. However, while Hewlett-Packard and Tektronix were making slow technologic progress in the MDS market, each had devoted many times Futuredata's engineering personnel to research. Furthermore, by entering this market, GenRad was attacking Hewlett-Packard's and Tektronix's prime market territory: the engineering laboratory.

According to Dataquest, a market research firm, microprocessor system sales would grow from $74 million in 1977 to $282 million in 1982, a 31 percent compound annual growth rate. This growth rate was roughly 50 percent greater than the projected growth rate for the ATE industry. Sales in the MDS area were forecast at $90 million for 1979.

Futuredata was acquired for 240,000 shares of GenRad stock, and the company was consolidated within GenRad on a pooling-of-interests basis. Futuredata's sales for the fiscal year ending March 31, 1978, were $1 million. Sales for the fiscal year ending March 31, 1979, were forecast at $3 million. Futuredata was originally placed within the EMT division, as an independent operation.

ORGANIZATIONAL DEVELOPMENT STUDY GROUP

When members of the Organizational Development Study Group (ODSG) first convened in July 1979, they faced a paradoxical situation. GenRad was experiencing the best of times in the midst of what were, in many respects, the worst of times. In mid-1979, GenRad reflected remarkable financial strength. Orders were strong, back orders flush, and profits substantial. The company was expected to generate record sales and profits in 1979 and to set further records in 1980. The ATE industry was projected to grow at an average annual rate of 21 percent over the next 5 years. GenRad's technological lead in such areas as functional testing, testing system software, and in-circuit testing gave the company an advantageous position in this high-growth market.

But at the same time, several problems were apparent at the company. Coordination between the functions was not always smooth and this had created interpersonal strains between managers. Decisions were often delayed due to the confusion that often surrounded staff and functional overlapping. Information systems were wholly inadequate and were causing serious disruptions in day-to-day management. Managers feared that these strains would become more pronounced as the firm's sales increased.

In June 1979, Cambria hired John Ferrie to assume a new position of director of training. Thurston had been concerned for some time that GenRad's management training and career development processes were deficient. As early as 1975, he had noted that formal training programs should be adopted at the company. However, action had been postponed for budgetary reasons. By 1979, funds were made available and Cambria contacted an executive search firm to have them locate an experienced management training specialist. Ferrie was commissioned to implement training programs at all levels of the organization.

The timing of Ferrie's hiring could not have been more propitious. By July 1979, GenRad's managers were expressing with increasing fervor their dissatisfaction over work life at the firm and over the breadth and ambiguity of their responsibilities. Curiously, the managers expressed their displeasure not to Thurston but to one another and primarily to Cambria.

Cambria listened to his peers with increasing concern. He realized that someone would have to explain fully to Thurston the anxiety GenRad's managers were feeling. Cambria decided that a special task force should be commissioned to study the factors causing these problems within the firm and to generate recommendations aimed at alleviating them. He outlined the reasoning behind his decision in this way:

> We were working under a flawed matrix organization in July 1979, and the stress the matrix created was intense. Bill was high above the stress areas, so he didn't feel the pain to the extent that we were feeling it.
>
> Furthermore, we had recently reviewed the divisions' strategic plans. The plans were all highly positive and indicated a fast-paced future for the company. But many of us were concerned that the company's internal problems would prohibit us from attaining the goals outlined in the plans. So, I wrote a memo to Bill and requested that we establish a management team to take a broad look at the problems we were facing, and to concentrate on solving those that had the potential of preventing us from reaching the goals enunciated in the divisional plans.
>
> Bill agreed to the formation of the task force but didn't really share our sense of urgency. He thought it would be a long-term study. At one point he said, "Let the group work for a year or two, and at the end of that period we'll see what conclusions we can draw." Bill was taking a passive view of the task force's mission, but the other members were not, to be sure. After the first meeting, Bill fully understood that we had a problem. That's when he went into action.

The ODSG task force consisted of Thurston, Cambria, Ferrie, Hinds, Gemmell, MacKenzie, and Rogers. As one of its first actions, ODSG decided to retain the services of an outside consultant who would monitor the group's proceedings and provide a third-party voice.

Other top managers at the company gave their views on the purpose behind the formation of the ODSG. Stadler, the chief financial officer, remarked:

> We were overseeing a good number of complex businesses from Concord to California. The way the company was organized, we could not act fast. Yet we needed to act fast, given the natures of our businesses. This was a fundamental problem.
>
> Similarly, the economies of scale which accrued from the centralization of manufacturing were decreasingly important as we became more focused on the ATE market. We were not in a commodity business, didn't have mass production needs or capabilities, and therefore were not favorably influenced by such economies of scale.
>
> Finally, the traditional concept of corporate centralization was no longer appropriate to our company. Bill's span of control was extremely broad. We were simply not developing enough managers. We needed to regain the entrepreneurial touch and centralization inhibited that.

Rogers, the director of sales and service, commented:

> It was obvious that things had to change. Walt Hinds was trying to run manufacturing with a thirteenth-century manufacturing system. He was getting little help from the MIS staff, whose systems were in horrible shape. We were beginning to acquire new divisions and to enter new product lines, yet our structure did not allow us to do this effectively. The two top people at Futuredata wanted out, so there was a potential hole in our management. Omnicomp, the independent supplier of the field service testers we were marketing, was beginning to develop financial problems, and this was troublesome since field testers were becoming an important area for us. We had to consider how we would protect our place in that market. The manufacture of board testers was very complex, and we were getting bogged down, given the manufacturing situation. Finally, management in the component tester division was having trouble developing a viable long-term strategy. Our organization at the time was simply not capable of dealing with these complex problems.

McAleer, the general manager of AVA, stated:

> The company had come a long way since it had formally broken with its past [in 1967] and announced that it would pursue a growth policy. Sales were advancing rapidly, and we needed both space and people to respond to the growth that was being thrust at us. Our ability to act as managers was impeded by the organizational structure. We wanted to maintain the entrepreneurial spirit, but the organization mitigated against this. The young turks were impatient to become masters of their own destinies.

Hinds, the general manager of the EMT division, commented:

> There were many internal problems within GRMass related to the specific identification of manufacturing costs, such as overhead, product, and project costs. As a result of the continuing delays in the implementation of an effective cost-accounting system for manufacturing, we found it difficult to control the operation.
>
> Second, we were trying to manage the business with primitive systems. There was no "closed loop" between forecasting, order entry, and manufacturing.
>
> We faced problems related to recruiting, training, and retaining skilled labor, particularly technicians, machinists, and assemblers. Labor shortages were common. We were

reviewing employee grade levels and compensation packages in a crisis mode and some-times hired new personnel with lower skill levels than average for a department but at higher wage levels.

New product introductions, coupled with engineering changes on both old and new products, caused many sudden changes in the manufacturing schedule, and threw the raw-material procurement process into chaos.

Space shortages resulted in our going to second- and third-shift operations, which spread supervisory and support resources very thin. Many inexperienced personnel were used in all areas on all shifts. Personnel shifts between the Concord and Bolton plants were continuous, and this was generally disruptive.

Rob Held, European sales manager, remarked:

If you asked me to identify our major problems in 1979, I would say that they were related to our financial management systems and asset management policies.

There was a more ironic problem, as well, which is related to the fact that Bill always believes the best of people. He's not a cynic. He simply doesn't have the normal reserve of cynicism that most people have. So when things that were supposed to get done weren't done, Bill took the attitude that things would improve, and that the people would come through. But many times, they didn't.

But there's another side to the coin, too. In 1979, things were just fantastic in many respects. They almost couldn't have been better. Business was so strong that we couldn't see that we had asset management, financial management, manufacturing, and other se-lected management problems.

It was in the context of these viewpoints that ODSG members sat down to work out a plan for GenRad's future.

APPENDIX A: Overview of GenRad's Products and Product Applications

By 1979 GenRad's testing equipment, which was used to test electronic and mechanical de-vices, was specialized for use by manufacturers and other users at three stages in the manufac-turing process: (1) before manufacturing, (2) during manufacturing, and (3) after manufactur-ing.

Faults in the manufacturing of electronic and mechanical equipment are inevitable. Faults can exist in the components themselves (such as integrated circuits, including microproces-sors), the improper assembly of components onto a printed circuit board (such as poor con-nections, misplacement of components, and short circuits), and the final assembly process. Automatic test equipment and other test and measurement instruments were designed to identify actual flaws existing in a product. Automatic test equipment could be used to detect these flaws at various stages during the manufacture of a product. This computer-driven testing machinery was generally highly sophisticated. Elaborate software programs enabled the tester to perform a complex analysis of the particular product(s) being tested. Programs varied according to the particular test being conducted. Therefore, software development was an integral aspect of ATE.

Automatic test equipment was used to test electronic equipment only. There were three types of testers in the ATE category: (1) component testers, (2) in-circuit testers, and (3) functional board testers. Component testers were used to determine if individual components performed according to specifications. Relative to other ATE instruments, component testers were the least sophisticated. In-circuit testers were used to directly test each component of a printed circuit board. The device ascertained whether the components on the portion of the board being tested had the correct value, were operative, and were properly connected, as well as whether the board itself had any short or open circuits in its interconnect wiring. Functional board testers, which were highly sophisticated, tested the fully assembled circuit board to identify any defects in the board's functional performance, that is, its information-processing capabilities. A fourth device, the field service tester, then manufactured independently by Omnicomp and marketed by GenRad, was used to isolate and identify faults in electronic equipment that was in use in the field—for example, an electronic cash register installed in a retail store.

The cost effectiveness of early detection of faulty components was indicated by the following examples of product correction costs at the various manufacturing stages. In 1979, Gen-Rad estimated these typical detection and product correction costs:

$.50 to detect a faulty component at incoming inspection
$5 to detect and correct an error on a printed circuit board
$50 to detect and correct a flaw in a completed product after final assembly
$500 to detect and correct a flaw in a product in use in the field

The cost effectiveness at ATE products was enhanced by the fact that these instruments could be operated by relatively low-skilled, low-paid personnel. Further, ATE instruments performed tests exceptionally rapidly and therefore allowed a product to move through the manufacturing process more speedily than it could in a plant where ATE was not employed.

The following is a more in-depth description of ATE and mechanical test equipment.

APPENDIX B: 1979 Environment

By 1979, the wisdom of GenRad's decision in the late 1960s to focus on the ATE segment of the test and measurement industry was becoming apparent. Growth in the ATE segment of their industry was expected to outstrip growth in all other segments. According to Dataquest figures, worldwide test instrument sales had reached $2.4 billion during 1978, a 19.7 percent increase over the 1977 figure of $2 billion. However, the growth in test and measurement instrument sales was expected to slow to 17.7 percent in 1979 and to 12.4 percent in 1980. Test

ELECTRONIC MANUFACTURING TEST EQUIPMENT AND PROCESSES

Before manufacturing: component testers	During manufacturing: in-circuit and functional testers	After manufacture: field service testers
GenRad testers for incoming inspection of components were used by component manufacturers and, far more frequently, by component users (such as manufacturers of computers and other	The functional board tester was first developed by GenRad in 1969. It was this product that steered the company into the ATE industry. Computer-driven testers could determine in minutes whether a printed circuit board functioned properly. If not, the instrument guided the operator to the board's fault. (Even a trained	These compact, portable testing units were designed to return a customer's electronic products to operation after failure by allowing the service technician to diagnose faults and then replace flawed PC

ELECTRONIC MANUFACTURING TEST EQUIPMENT AND PROCESSES (continued)

Before manufacturing: component testers	During manufacturing: in-circuit and functional testers	After manufacture: field service testers
electronic equipment). Component manufacturers test their products to guarantee adherence to quality standards, while component users wish to guarantee that components will function in the application for which they are intended. Screening at the component's incoming stage has a low cost and a high payoff since it permits the elimination of flawed components before their assembly on a printed circuit board.	technician could require days to locate a fault without a tester.) Functional testers typically had a 1-year payback.	board(s) on the spot in the field. The same software used in the functional tester was used in the field tester. Programs were loaded into the field tester by portable tapes or over telephone lines. In May 1978, GenRad became a distributor for Omnicomp, Inc. Omnicomp's product was the most costly and sophisticated product in the field.
	In-circuit testers could verify both component performance and the proper assembly of a printed circuit board. These testers were generally less expensive and easier to program than functional testers and were therefore more cost effective in locating printed circuit (PC) board flaws. However, in-circuit testers could not provide the range of tests performed by the functional tester.	
The 1978 total component test market was estimated at $170 million, with GenRad's component test sales at $19 million. The price range for component testers was $1000–$500,000, with GenRad concentrating in the low end of the market by manufacturing testers in the $1000–$20,000 price category. Fairchild specialized in very sophisticated component testers ($70,000–$500,000 range) with Teradyne occupying the mid-range ($25,000–$250,000). The growth rate in this market was estimated at 15–20 percent. GenRad's customers included Beckman, Digital Equipment, Hewlett-Packard, Northern Telecom, and Pfizer Medical.	Critical features of ATE are the soft-ware programs that determine the cause of board failure by guiding the operator through a sequence of specific probes until the actual fault is located.	The 1978 market for field testers was approximately $10 million. Testers sold in the $20,000–$25,000 range. Growth was expected to be 100 percent per year for several years.
	The 1978 functional tester market was $113.3 million, with GenRad's sales (as market leader) of $42 million—triple the sales of the nearest U.S. competitor. GenRad had an installed base of 800 test systems, in use by over 250 customers in 1978. Functional testers sold in the $50,000–$500,000 price range. GenRad had a very strong position in the development of software for functional testing applications. The market was estimated to grow at 20 percent per year.	Dataquest estimated that 20 percent of the typical electronic equipment manufacturer's revenues were derived from field service. The overall market for field service, estimated at $4.6 billion in 1978, was growing at 15 percent per year. GenRad's field service tester customers included NCR, ITT Courier, Sperry Univac, the U.S. Army and Navy, and Xerox.
	The in-circuit tester market was estimated to be $36.7 million in 1978. GenRad had entered the field in 1978, and had sales of $900,000 that year. Prices for in-circuit testers ranged from $100,000 to $250,000. The market was hotly competitive. Fairchild was the market leader in 1978. GenRad, Hewlett-Packard, Computer Automation, and Teradyne all entered the market in 1978. The market was estimated to grow at 50 percent per year.	Competition in the market was becoming visible. Tektronix, already in the market (as was Hewlett-Packard), was poised to make a strong, share-protecting advance.

MECHANICAL MANUFACTURING TEST EQUIPMENT AND PROCESSES (continued)

Before manufacturing: vibration analysis systems	During manufacturing: shaker control and sound/vibration evaluation	After manufacturing: machinery health and environmental noise

GenRad's vibration analysis systems (VAS) were used during the design phase of a piece of mechanical equipment to simulate the vibration behavior of a particular design. This made it possible to optimize designs at an early stage, since a physical prototype did not have to be constructed for each design alternative under consideration. As a result, design cycle times could be reduced by months. Application included land and air transport, offshore oil rigs, and atomic energy plants.

Components and finished pieces of equipment were subjected to shake tests, which replicated the vibrations that would occur in actual operating conditions, such as road travel or rocket liftoff. The VAS used in the design phase, with slight hardware modification and completely different software, controlled the shake tests to determine components and equipment met performance specifications. GenRad held some fundamental patents in shaker control.

Sound and vibration evaluation tested for the correctness of assembly of such products as air conditioners. This testing equipment was also used to predict the reliability and operating life of pumps and compressors.

The 1978 market for VAS shaker control, sound/vibration evaluation, and machinery health testing products was estimated to be $90 million. GenRad's 1978 sales were approximately $12 million. The market was highly fragmented, although Hewlett-Packard and Spectral Dynamics were entrenched competitors, and it was expected to grow at the rate of 15–20 percent per year. Customers for these products included Carrier Corp., General Motors, Delco Remy, Fiat, BMW, AMP, Boeing, and Goodyear Atomic.

The company had entered the market through the 1969 acquisition of Time/Data. GenRad's performance in this market had been disappointing. It had been estimated by outside analysts that GenRad's mechanical equipment testing products (all products for all three stages of the

GenRad also manufactured devices that were used in the growing field of machinery health testing. With such devices, expensive and crucial machinery could be monitored to detect any changes in operating noise or vibration levels. Changes would often signal impending machinery failure. Consequently, by heeding the warnings that would be "heard" or "felt" by these testing units, the owners or operators of such equipment could take preventive measures to ensure the continued safe operation of the equipment. This reduced emergency repairs required due to unplanned breakdowns. Applications for these products included electrical and nuclear generators, oil and chemical processing equipment, and submarines.

Another form of postmanufacturing testing was the measurement of noise levels. GenRad's sound-level meters (audiometers) were used both for industrial hearing conservation (to ensure that workers were not being exposed to unsafe noise levels) and for outdoor environmental noise measurement (to ensure that EPA noise pollution regulations were adhered to by motorists, corporations, and the like).

GenRad's 1978 acoustic measurement sales of approximately $5 million gave it the largest U.S. market share of this fragmented $40 million industry. In 1979 these products were manufactued at the Bolton plant. Most of GenRad's noise level meters sold for less than $1000. The major competitor for

MECHANICAL MANUFACTURING TEST EQUIPMENT AND PROCESSES (continued)

Before manufacturing: vibration analysis systems	During manufacturing: shaker control and sound/vibration evaluation	After manufacturing: machinery health and environmental noise
	manufacturing process) had been unprofitable in 1978. GenRad lost $900,000 on its mechanical equipment testing products (all products for all three stages of manufacturing process).	this segment of the market was the Danish firm Bruel and Kjaer. Other competitors for the low-price end were Spectral Dynamiccs and Nicolet Instruments. GenRad also sold a few products aimed at the more sophisticated end of the market, where prices ranged from $12,000 to $500,000. Hewett-Packard was its main competitor for high-price market.

and measurement instrument sales were projected to reach $5 billion by 1983, for a compound annual growth rate of 15.8 percent for the period January 1979 to December 1983.

Sales in the ATE segment of the test and measurement instrument industry, however, had been $351 million in 1978 (worldwide sales of U.S. ATE manufacturers), up dramatically from the 1977 total of $240 million. Worldwide sales of American-manufactured ATE equipment was expected to jump to $900 million by 1983, for a compound annual growth rate of 21 percent from 1979 to 1983. Some segments of the ATE market were expected to grow at a far greater rate than the 21 percent rate projected for ATE overall. For example, in-circuit tester sales were projected to increase at 50 percent per year for the next few years, while portable field tester sales were projected to increase at 100 percent per year.

The burgeoning demand for ATE products could be attributed to six factors.

1 As applications for electronic technology increased, electronic devices and equipment were being integrated within a continually expanding universe of products. Consequently, the demand for instruments capable of testing these products' electronic portions was escalating.

2 Many manufacturers were backward-integrating into the manufacture of semiconductors and the assembly of printed circuit boards. Since these manufacturers needed to test the products they manufactured, the customer base for ATE was expanding.

3 Automatic test equipment reduced both the number of employees and the level of technical training needed to perform electronic product testing, thereby helping to answer the serious skill shortage problem within the electronics industry.

4 Automatic test equipment provided fast and accurate testing of what were increasingly complex semiconductor devices. There were no alternative testing methods capable of duplicating the fast, reliable results provided by automatic testers.

5 As demand for product quality increased, ATE answered the need by providing top-flight quality control for manufacturers.

6 Rapidly increasing price/performance ratios for ATE instruments decreased economic payback periods, thereby making the investment in such equipment a more attractive prospect.

Nonetheless, potential problems loomed on the horizon for ATE. In 1979, the ATE industry was changing in some important ways. First, the average product life was becoming markedly shorter. While product lives had averaged 6 to 8 years throughout the 1960s, they had dropped to 4 to 6 years in the early 1970s and to 3 to 4 years by the late 1970s. This meant that one determinant of continued success in the ATE industry was the continual ability to develop effective new products. Companies in the field could never rest on the brilliance of their past products, since obsolescence of those products was inevitable.

Second, the customer's orientation was beginning to change. Up until the early 1970s, innovative technology had been of prime importance to customers. But by 1979, even though long strides were being made in certain instrument technologies, many ATE products were increasingly standard. Therefore, direct competition was becoming more common within the ATE industry. Consequently, price and service were becoming increasingly important.

Furthermore, GenRad did battle with a broad variety of competitors, many of whom were extremely large and sophisticated and able to survive downturns in the market. New competitors were emerging in several product areas, such as in-circuit testers and field service testers. The specific competitors varied from product to product. Consequently, strategic and competitive analyses were difficult. GenRad's product lines occupied market positions ranging from high share in high-growth segments to low share in low-growth segments. Each position demanded a distinct set of tactical offensives.

Finally, forecasters were predicting a flat economy for the period from mid-1979 to mid-1980. Since changes in the state of the U.S. economy were thought to affect the test instrument market 6 to 9 months later, the forecasts indicated a business slowdown for 1980. While some forecasters thought that the ATE segment of the industry would weather the downturn well, others suggested that all segments within the test and measurement industry would see declining growth rates and possibly even negative growth. The industry slowdowns of 1971 and 1975 had led to major disruptions in GenRad's profitability, so these forecasts had potentially serious implications. Since GenRad had become a public corporation in 1978, any 1980 disruption in earnings or operations would be far more visible to customers and to prospective customers than it might have been in the past.

APPENDIX C: William R. Thurston

It was difficult to overestimate the employees' good will toward Thurston. To many of them, he was a pragmatic visionary. The fact that Thurston had brought the company through the intensely troubled period of the early 1970s, and thereby saved the careers of the firm's employees, had created a groundswell of enduring appreciation and respect for the man. Employees at GenRad saw Thurston as the type of leader who, when the efforts of all others had failed, would be the one with the ultimate solution.

Thurston himself was a subtle study in intrapersonal paradox. While he was softspoken and reflective, he had the power to sway others with the brute force of his quietly intransigent determination. While he did not cut a strikingly powerful presence, there was a transcendent staying power that seemed inherent in all of his actions, and that staying power gave his actions the edge they needed eventually to prevail.

He was an avid believer in the importance of a strong family life. Thurston vacationed each summer with his wife at two Appalachian Mountain Club camps in northern New England—one on an island in a lake and another on a lake on an island. The settings were rustic, and the camps were populated by small numbers of summer vacationers. Thurston explained that he enjoyed getting back to nature and spending time with the small bands of congenial people who traveled to the camps each year. Thurston, his wife, and one of their daughters also spent one week a year discussing thought-provoking (modern as well as classical) literature at the Great Books Summer Institute at Colby College. Approximately 250 people participated in this program each summer. His outside interests of reading classical literature, playing the piano, and landscaping (the last of which he invariably did with his wife) were further indications of his quiet traditionalism. But Thurston was also intensely interested in the notions raised in Marilyn Ferguson's futuristic book, *The Aquarian Conspiracy.* He believed that the paradigms of the future would almost certainly fail to conform with the paradigms of the past and that an age of all-encompassing change was upon man, which would be likely to improve his condition.

Although Thurston was in many ways an unyielding traditionalist, he opposed many conventional beliefs. For example, he preferred a different view from the traditional concept of the corporation. To him, the real corporation was an intangible, often unseen, entity: it was the combined efforts of the individuals working within the context of a corporation that provided the tangible reality. As a result of this conceptualization, Thurston took an extremely active interest in the welfare of GenRad's employees. He made a point of consistently monitoring the climate at the firm. As one employee had said, "Bill is unbelievably nice to people. He talks to everyone. He really cares about the people here."

EXHIBIT 1   GENRAD SALES BY GENERAL PRODUCT CATEGORIES (IN THOUSANDS OF DOLLARS)

Year*	Electronic manufacturing test		Acoustics vibration and analysis		Total
	Dollars	**Percent**	**Dollars**	**Percent**	**Total**
1978	$67,667	80%	$16,464	20%	$84,131
1977	52,527	75	17,573	25	70,100
1976	37,305	69	16,983	31	54,288
1975	35,138	66	18,070	34	53,208
1974	31,501	64	17,460	36	48,961
1973	26,362	59	18,294	41	44,656

Source: GenRad's 1978 and 1977 report on Form 10-K.

* The company did not maintain records allocating sales to product categories before 1976. Hence, amounts set forth for 1975, 1974, and 1973 are management's estimates.

EXHIBIT 2 CONSOLIDATED SUMMARY OF OPERATIONS (IN THOUSANDS OF DOLLARS)

	1969	1970	1971	1972	1973	1974	1975	1976	1977	1978
Net sales	$25,527	$26,096	$29,112	$33,105	$44,656	$48,961	$53,208	$54,288	$70,100	$84,131
Cost of goods sold	13,212	13,173	15,117	19,895	24,874	25,027	25,939	26,620	34,885	39,957
Gross profit	12,315	12,923	13,995	13,210	19,782	23,934	27,269	27,668	35,215	44,174
Research and development expense	na	3,777	4,271	na	4,195	4,899	3,955	4,422	4,992	7,145
Selling, administrative, and general	na	8,642	8,914	na	12,960	15,553	17,619	20,183	21,865	25,551
Interest expense	594	1,732	611	694	1,441	1,869	1,611	1,256	1,418	1,435
Other expense (income)		(333)	(298)	na	(71)	(613)	(363)	(18)	0	(702)
Profit before taxes	879	127	497	(2,573)	1,297	2,226	4,447	1,825	6,940	10,745
Taxes	575	81	253	(270)	662	1,179	2,100	900	3,200	4,620
Net income	304	46	244	(2,303)	635	1,047	2,347	925	3,740	6,125
Extraordinary credits	–	–	–	–	522	605	–	–	–	–
Cumulative effect of changes in accounting principle	–	–	–	–	–	1,997	–	–	–	–
Net income	304	46	244	(2,303)	1,157	3,649	2,347	925	3,740	6,125

EXHIBIT 3 SUMMARY BALANCE SHEETS (IN THOUSANDS OF DOLLARS)

Assets	1974	1975	1976	1977	1978
Cash and marketable securities	$ 925	$ 1,327	$ 506	$ 1,079	$ 5,000
Accounts receivable	13,504	12,785	14,494	18,145	17,833
Inventories	21,063	19,713	19,436	22,059	25,892
Other current assets	1,036	923	620	2,103	1,062
Subtotal	36,528	34,748	35,056	43,386	49,787
Property, plant, and equipment (net)	4,719	4,881	5,567	6,927	9,116
Good will	911	692	638	457	413
Patents and trademarks	114	73	85	53	69
Other noncurrent assets	336	432	260	269	133
Total	$42,608	$40,826	$41,606	$51,092	$59,518
Liabilities					
Notes payable	$13,152	$ 3,185	$ 4,626	$ 2,719	$ 2,669
Trade account payable	5,260	4,012	4,908	6,528	4,904
Accrued expense	3,773	3,282	3,225	5,492	6,923
Taxes payable	863	1,829	683	2,293	1,164
Subtotal	23,048	12,308	13,442	17,032	15,660
Long-term debt	2,737	9,284	7,930	10,000	10,000
Deferred taxes	1,157	924	862	927	1,263
Stockholders' equity	15,666	18,310	19,372	23,133	32,595
Total	$42,608	$40,826	$41,606	$51,092	$59,518

EXHIBIT 4   SUMMARY OF SOURCES AND USES OF FUNDS (IN THOUSANDS OF DOLLARS)

Sources	1974	1975	1976	1977	1978
Net income	$1,047	$2,347	$ 925	$3,740	$6,125
Depreciation and amortization	1,032	1,056	1,258	1,474	2,316
Deferred taxes	211	(104)	56	204	336
Total from operations	2,290	3,299	2,239	5,418	8,777
Effect of change in accounting principle	3,743				
Sale of common stock		400			3,972
Additional long-term debt		7,000		10,000	
Stock issued to employees			147	12	11
Proceeds from stock option				9	117
Total	6,033	10,699	2,386	15,439	12,877

Uses					
Additions to property, plant, and equipment	666	1,099	1,851	2,748	4,424
Cash dividends	4	5			263
Repayment of debt	487	453	1,359	7,930	
Purchase of treasury stock				10	501
Other	56	391	22	11	(83)
Total	1,613	1,948	3,232	10,699	5,105
Net increase (decrease) in working capital	4,820	8,751	(846)	4,740	7,772
Increase in cash	286	402	(821)	573	3,921
Increase in inventories	7,145	(1,350)	(277)	2,623	3,833

EXHIBIT 5 BALANCE SHEET DATA FOR SELECTED ATE MANUFACTURERS (IN MILLIONS OF DOLLARS)

Receivables (R) and payables (P)

Year	GenRad R	GenRad P	Fairchild Camera R	Fairchild Camera P	Fluke R	Fluke P	Hewlett-Packard R	Hewlett-Packard P	Tektronics R	Tektronics P	Teradyne R	Teradyne P
1978	$17.8	$ 4.9	$95.5	$30.4	$15.4	$3.4	$371.0	$71.0	$115.1	$31.0	$23.6	$ 5.7
1977	18.1	6.5	72.7	22.0	14.9	2.6	272.0	46.0	87.3	24.1	13.2	3.1
1976	14.5	4.9	82.2	23.9	12.1	3.6	234.3	31.9	70.1	17.8	11.7	2.2
1975	12.8	4.0	56.6	18.7	9.1	2.4	204.8	31.9	61.3	13.3	10.8	2.3
1974	13.5	5.3	69.0	16.7	7.7	4.9	193.7	26.5	55.2	16.7	12.0	2.7

Cash (C) and inventory (I)

Year	GenRad C	GenRad I	Fairchild Camera C	Fairchild Camera I	Fluke C	Fluke I	Hewlett-Packard C	Hewlett-Packard I	Tektronics C	Tektronics I	Teradyne C	Teradyne I
1978	$5.0	$25.9	$59.2	$90.5	$3.8	$16.7	$189.0	$356.0	$66.2	$163.5	$3.7	$20.7
1977	1.1	22.1	43.0	78.0	1.2	14.8	173.0	279.0	95.0	118.4	2.3	13.0
1976	0.5	19.4	26.9	96.6	1.6	12.1	106.8	238.0	70.5	99.1	1.8	13.1
1975	1.3	19.7	25.2	93.0	0.9	9.6	77.6	205.2	36.3	108.9	1.0	8.9
1974	0.9	21.1	33.4	73.4	0.6	7.7	13.8	195.2	18.7	95.2	2.1	11.7

Working capital (WC) and current ratio (CR)

Year	GenRad WC	GenRad CR	Fairchild Camera WC	Fairchild Camera CR	Fluke WC	Fluke CR	Hewlett-Packard WC	Hewlett-Packard CR	Tektronics WC	Tektronics CR	Teradyne WC	Teradyne CR
1978	$34.126	3.2	$123.1	1.9	$24.7	3.0	$537.0	2.3	$250.1	3.3	$25.2	2.1
1977	26.354	2.6	121.2	2.4	18.8	2.4	460.0	2.6	226.0	3.7	19.2	2.9
1976	21.968	2.7	113.9	2.1	16.4	2.7	374.1	2.7	187.8	4.1	15.6	2.3
1975	22.485	2.9	100.5	2.2	11.6	2.4	320.1	2.8	153.5	3.4	14.5	3.2
1974	13.935	1.6	93.9	2.0	8.8	2.2	237.3	2.3	107.9	2.6	13.3	2.0

Return on equity (ROE) and total debt as a percentage of total capital (LEV)

Year	GenRad ROE	GenRad LEV	Fairchild Camera ROE	Fairchild Camera LEV	Fluke ROE	Fluke LEV	Hewlett-Packard ROE	Hewlett-Packard LEV	Tektronics ROE	Tektronics LEV	Teradyne ROE	Teradyne LEV
1978	18.8%	28.0%	12.0%	31.2%	20.7%	14.6%	15.3%	8.7%	17.4%	12.7%	16.8%	36.1%
1977	16.2	35.5	6.0	30.5	17.8	12.9	14.7	6.7	16.0	14.2	15.3	3.0
1976	4.8	39.3	7.0	31.5	18.0	22.1	13.4	8.9	13.0	15.2	8.6	18.5
1975	12.8	40.5	6.3	25.3	19.6	16.8	14.9	6.4	13.0	19.4	1.7	11.4
1974	6.7	50.4	17.6	26.8	17.7	18.4	18.4	9.2	12.2	12.0	18.7	26.4

Capitalization

	GenRad		Fairchild Camera		Fluke		Hewlett-Packard		Tektronics		Teradyne	
	Dec. 31, 1978		Dec. 31, 1978		Sept. 30, 1978		Oct. 31, 1978		May 27, 1978		Dec. 31, 1978	
Short-term debt	$ 2.7	5.9%	$24.0	8.0%	$0.6	1.6%	$85.0	7.7%	$10.4	2.8%	$12.4	19.9%
Long-term debt	10.0	22.1	69.2	23.2	5.0	13.0	10.0	1.0	37.1	9.9	10.1	16.2
Preferred stock	32.6	72.0	205.9	68.8	32.8	85.4	1002.0	91.3	326.7	87.3	39.8	63.9
								100.0%		100.0%		100.0%

EXHIBIT 6   INCOME STATEMENT DATA FOR SELECTED AUTOMATIC TEST EQUIPMENT MANUFACTURERS (IN MILLIONS OF DOLLARS)

Year	GenRad		Fairchild Camera		Fluke		Hewlett-Packard		Tektronics		Teradyne	
Sales (S) and index (I)	S	I	S	I	S	I	S	I	S	I	S	I
1978	$84.1	172	$553.8	144	$79.5	238	$1751.0	195	$598.9	221	$91.7	163
1977	70.1	143	460.1	120	60.8	182	1374.0	154	455.0	168	67.8	121
1976	54.3	111	443.2	115	49.2	147	1124.0	126	366.6	135	53.7	96
1975	53.2	109	291.5	76	41.9	125	990.0	111	336.6	124	37.9	67
1974	49.0	100	384.9	100	33.4	100	893.0	100	271.4	100	56.2	100
Gross profit (GP) and margin (%)	GP	%	GP	%	GP	%	GP	%	GP	%	GP	%
1978	$44.2	52.5%	$160.7	30.1%	$47.8	60.1%	$946.0	54.0%	$332.4	55.5%	$35.1	38.3%
1977	35.2	50.2	117.5	25.5	34.4	56.6	752.0	54.7	258.9	56.9	27.1	40.0
1976	27.7	51.0	115.8	26.1	27.8	56.5	589.0	52.4	197.4	53.8	19.8	36.9
1975	27.3	51.2	82.8	28.4	22.8	54.4	527.0	53.2	173.0	51.4	12.9	34.0
1974	23.9	48.9	120.7	31.4	17.1	51.2	471.0	52.7	135.4	49.9	21.6	38.4
EBIT and margin (%)	EBIT	%	EBIT	%	EBIT	%	EBIT	%	EBIT	%	EBIT	%
1978	$12.2	14.5%	$47.9	8.6%	$13.5	17.0%	$302.0	17.2%	$100.2	16.7%	$13.6	14.8%
1977	8.4	12.0	25.5	5.5	9.1	15.0	233.0	17.0	79.8	17.5	10.6	15.6
1976	3.1	5.7	28.6	6.5	7.3	14.8	165.0	14.7	60.0	16.4	5.3	9.9
1975	6.1	11.5	21.3	7.3	6.4	15.3	151.0	15.3	51.6	15.3	1.0	2.6
1974	4.1	8.4	55.5	14.4	4.4	13.2	153.0	17.1	39.7	14.6	9.7	17.3
Pretax income (PT) and margin (%)	PT	%	PT	%	PT	%	PT	%	PT	%	PT	%
1978	$10.7	12.7%	$40.6	7.3%	$12.9	16.2%	$296.0	16.9%	$96.0	16.0%	$12.4	13.5%
1977	6.9	9.8	18.3	4.0	8.4	13.8	229.0	16.7	75.7	16.6	10.3	15.2
1976	1.8	3.3	23.1	5.2	6.9	14.0	161.0	14.3	55.2	15.1	4.9	9.1
1975	4.4	8.3	17.1	5.9	6.0	14.3	149.0	15.1	42.8	13.9	0.6	1.6
1974	2.2	4.5	51.6	13.4	4.1	12.3	144.0	16.1	38.5	14.2	8.7	15.5
Net income from continuing operations (NI) and margin (%)	NI	%	NI	%	NI	%	NI	%	NI	%	NI	%
1978	$6.1	7.3	$24.8	4.5	$6.8	8.6	$153.0	8.7	$56.8	9.5	$6.7	7.3
1977	3.7	5.3	11.2	2.4	4.5	7.4	121.0	8.8	44.0	9.7	4.9	7.2
1976	0.9	1.7	12.5	2.8	3.7	7.5	91.0	8.1	30.1	8.2	2.3	4.3
1975	2.3	4.3	10.4	3.6	3.2	7.6	84.0	8.5	26.3	7.8	0.4	1.0
1974	1.0	2.0	27.0	7.0	2.2	6.6	84.0	9.4	21.5	7.9	4.3	7.6

EXHIBIT 7 MARKET DATA FOR SELECTED AUTOMATIC TEST EQUIPMENT MANUFACTURERS

Market price

Year	GenRad High	GenRad Low	Fairchild Camera* High	Fairchild Camera* Low	Fluke High	Fluke Low	Hewlett-Packard High	Hewlett-Packard Low	Tektronix High	Tektronix Low	Teradyne High	Teradyne Low
1979	30⁵/₈	17¹/₄	65⁵/₈	28¹/₈	19³/₈	15⁷/₈	99³/₄	84	57	46⁷/₈	22¹/₂	14¹/₂
1978	24	15¹/₄	41¹/₄	22⁷/₈	17¹/₂	9	93	62	50¹/₂	32¹/₂	30¹/₂	15
1977	—	—	41¹/₈	21¹/₂	10¹/₈	6⁵/₈	87¹/₂	68¹/₂	40	28¹/₄	19⁷/₈	11¹/₄
1976	—	—	55¹/₄	36	8¹/₂	5³/₈	118	80	34³/₈	22¹/₈	21¹/₂	10¹/₂
1975	—	—	62¹/₄	17	13³/₈	4⁷/₈	121	56¹/₂	22³/₄	9	16	5³/₄
1974	—	—	64	16³/₈	11¹/₈	4⁵/₈	92¹/₂	52	23⁷/₈	9	23	5

Earnings per share (EPS) and dividends per share (DPS)

Year	GenRad EPS	GenRad DPS	Fairchild Camera* EPS	Fairchild Camera* DPS	Fluke EPS	Fluke DPS	Hewlett-Packard EPS	Hewlett-Packard DPS	Tektronix EPS	Tektronix DPS	Teradyne EPS	Teradyne DPS
Latest 12 months	$2.33	—	$4.69	—	$1.36	—	$6.12	—	$3.91	—	$1.91	—
1978	2.27	$0.5	4.12	$0.80	1.20	—	5.27	$0.50	3.19	$0.60	2.03	—
1977	1.45	—	2.01	0.80	0.81	—	4.27	0.40	2.49	0.23	1.50	—
1976	0.36	—	2.27	0.80	0.68	—	3.24	0.30	1.71	0.12	—	—
1975	0.96	—	1.94	0.80	0.60	—	3.02	0.25	1.52	0.10	0.12	—
1974	0.43	—	5.00	0.75	0.45	—	3.08	0.20	1.23	0.10	1.38	—

Price-earnings ratio

Year	GenRad 12X		Fairchild Camera* 14X		Fluke 14X		Hewlett-Packard 16X		Tektronix 13X		Teradyne 11X	
1979 to date	14X	8X	14X	6X	14X	12X	16X	14X	15X	12X	12X	8X
1978	11	7	10	6	15	8	18	12	16	10	15	7
1977	—	—	20	11	13	8	20	16	16	11	13	8
1976	—	—	24	16	13	8	36	25	20	13	30	15
1975	—	—	32	9	22	8	40	19	15	6	133	50
1974	—	—	13	3	25	10	30	17	19	7	17	4

	GenRad	Fairchild Camera*	Fluke	Hewlett-Packard	Tektronix	Teradyne
Book value per share	$11.69	$38.14	$5.68	$34.56	$18.20	$7.42
Market to book value	245.9%	171.7%	323.4%	281.4%	285.7%	283%
Total shares outstanding (thousands)	3093	5419	5782	58,020	18,102	3286
Total market value (millions)	$889.9	$355	$106.2	$5,642.4	$941.3	$69

* Merged with Schlumberger Ltd. on June 29, 1979.

EXHIBIT 8 MARKET SEGMENT DISTRIBUTION OF ORDERS, 1978*

Customer's industry	Total industry	GenRad, Inc.
Aerospace & government (including military)	19%	14%
Business equipment	8	8
Computer	9	8
Consumer	6	3
Industrial	10	18
Instruments	5	6
Medical	4	3
Peripherals	13	12
Telecommunications	21	18
Transportation and automotive	4	9
Other	1	1

SALES AND MARKET SHARE, FUNCTIONAL BOARD TESTERS, 1978*

Company	Sales (millions)	Market share (percent)
GenRad	$ 42.9	29%
Computer Automation	11.3	7
Faultfinders†	13.8	9
Fluke/Trendar	7.1	5
Hewlett-Packard	10.0	7
Instrumentation Engineering	6.5	3
Membrain†	10.5	7
Teradyne	14.3	10
Testline†	5.0	3
Zehntel	10.5	7
Others	18.1	13
Total market	$150.0	100

* Note that these figures relate to sales, market shares, and segmentations of functional board testers *only*.
† These firms acquired by Fairchild in 1979.

EXHIBIT 9 REPORT TO STOCKHOLDERS, OCT. 16, 1970

Management reorganization

A new organization, different in concept from the old, has been under study for several months. Distilled from many hours of discussion at meetings of the goals committee, the management committee, and the executive committee, there has emerged a recognition that there are two clearly distinguishable ways of looking at the structure of a company like ours. The first leads to the classical industrial organization, under which GenRad has operated since its beginning, with departments performing distinct functions, each characterized by specialized problems that require specialized knowledge to solve. The second leads to autonomous groupings, each devoted to a specific task, in all its ramifications, and each incorporating whatever functional elements are needed to accomplish that task.

The first is usually called a functional organization. The second is sometimes called a project-type organization, or a product-line organization. For the purposes of this notice, the two kinds of organization will be referred to as functional and project-type. At GenRad, the first, which is inwardly directed to what the company can do, incorporates the major functions of engineering, manufacturing, marketing, and finance. The second, which is outwardly directed to what the marketplace demands, incorporates the three concentration areas and the three manufacturing subsidiaries.

Under the new organization, these two structures will be separately recognized and administered. The first, which may be thought of as developing the corporation's resources, will be administered by Ivan G. Easton, senior vice president. The second, which may be thought of as applying the corporation's resources, will be administered by Wiliam R. Thurston who, coincident with his assumption of his new duties, will be promoted to senior vice president.

The two organizational structures obviously interact, since the project-type groups draw, to a greater or less extent, upon the functional groups. This interaction, in a small company, places managerial demands, in many cases, upon the same individual, acting in both functional and project-type capacities. Managers reporting to the president and to the two senior vice presidents may therefore, from time to time, find themselves with two masters. These relationships, which violate the classical and time-honored management rule that there must be single, clear, parallel lines of responsibility and authority, are now recognized as inherent in what has come to be known as *matrix management*. This term, which stems from the mathematical concept of a two-dimensional matrix, is clearly descriptive of the new GenRad organization when it is illustrated with functional and project-type axes running at right angles as shown in the attached exhibit.

D. B. Sinclair
President

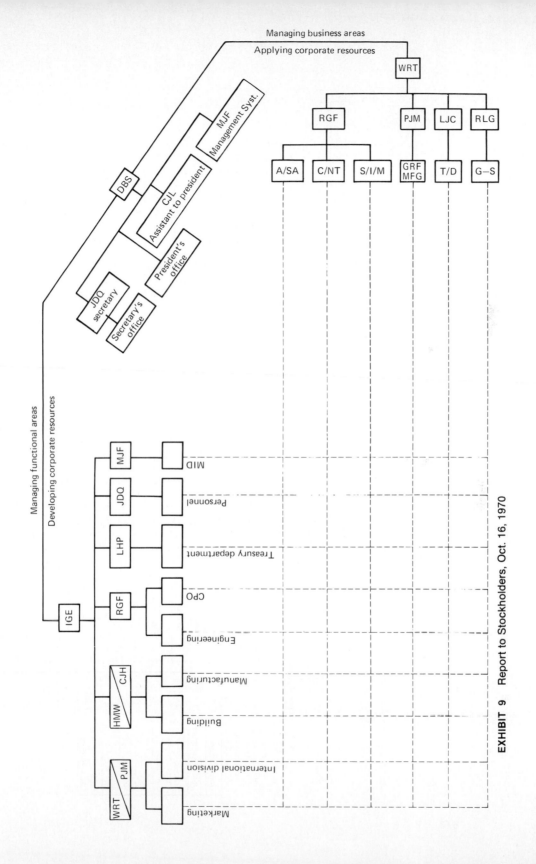

EXHIBIT 9   Report to Stockholders, Oct. 16, 1970

EXHIBIT 10 Genrad, Inc.—organization chart as of August 1975

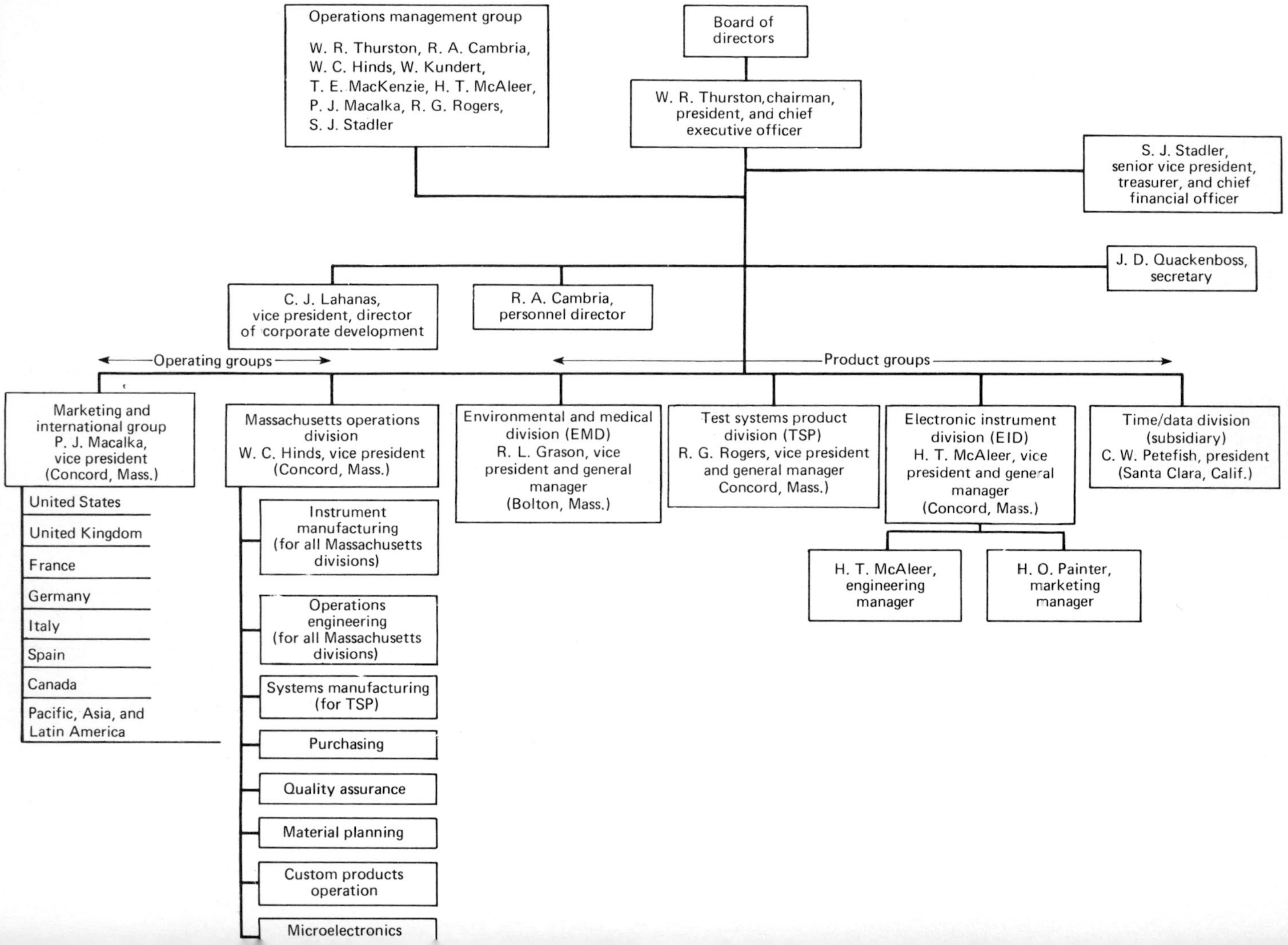

678

EXHIBIT 11 Genrad, Inc.—organization chart as of September 1977

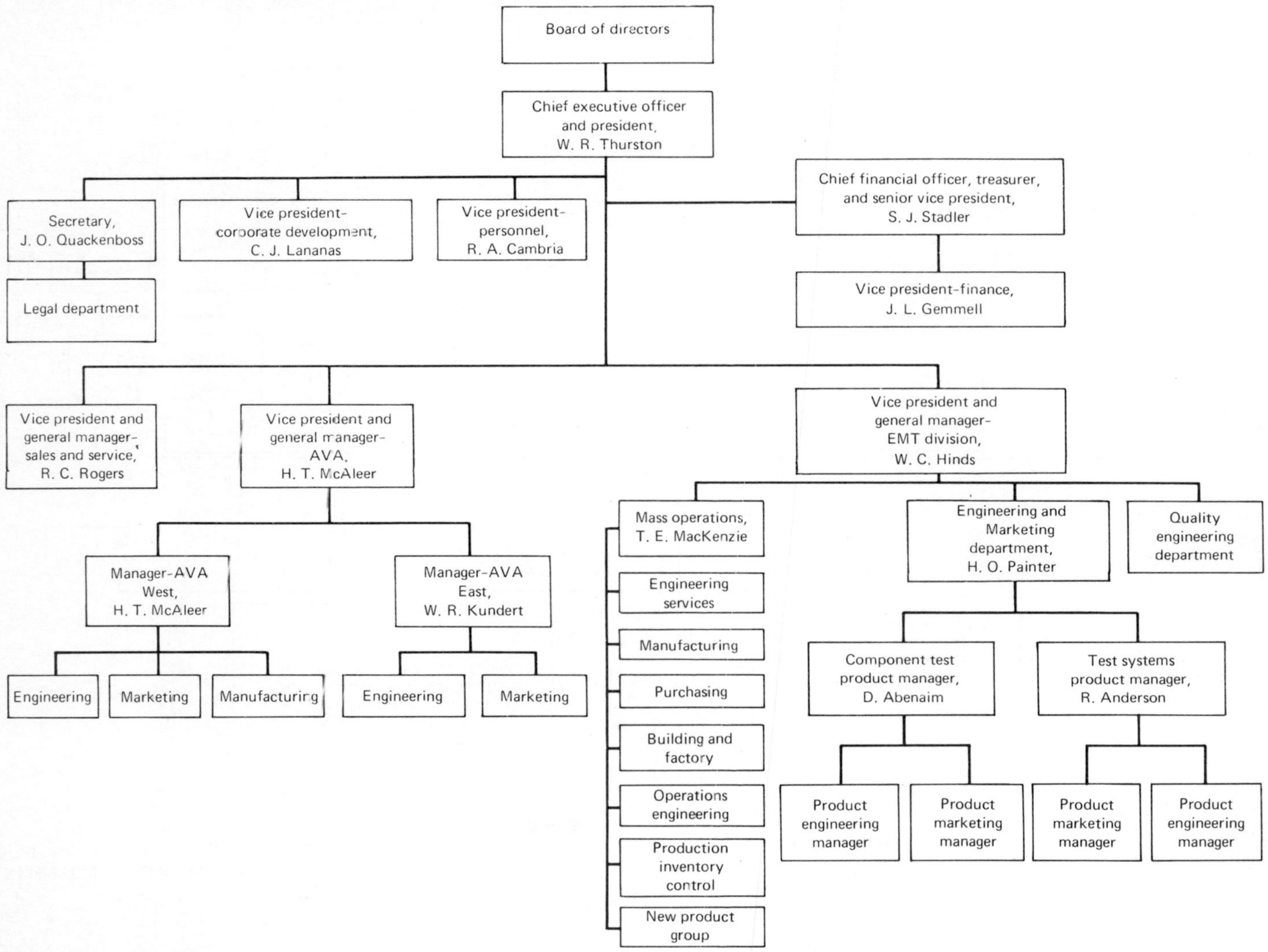

Board of directors

Chief executive officer and president, W. R. Thurston

Secretary, J. O. Quackenboss

Legal department

Vice president—corporate development, C. J. Lananas

Vice president—personnel, R. A. Cambria

Chief financial officer, treasurer, and senior vice president, S. J. Stadler

Vice president–finance, J. L. Gemmell

Vice president and general manager–sales and service, R. C. Rogers

Vice president and general manager–AVA, H. T. McAleer

Manager–AVA West, H. T. McAleer

Engineering

Marketing

Manufacturing

Manager–AVA East, W. R. Kundert

Engineering

Marketing

Vice president and general manager–EMT division, W. C. Hinds

Mass operations, T. E. MacKenzie

Engineering services

Manufacturing

Purchasing

Building and factory

Operations engineering

Production inventory control

New product group

Engineering and Marketing department, H. O. Painter

Component test product manager, D. Abenaim

Product engineering manager

Product marketing manager

Test systems product manager, R. Anderson

Product marketing manager

Product engineering manager

Quality engineering department

679

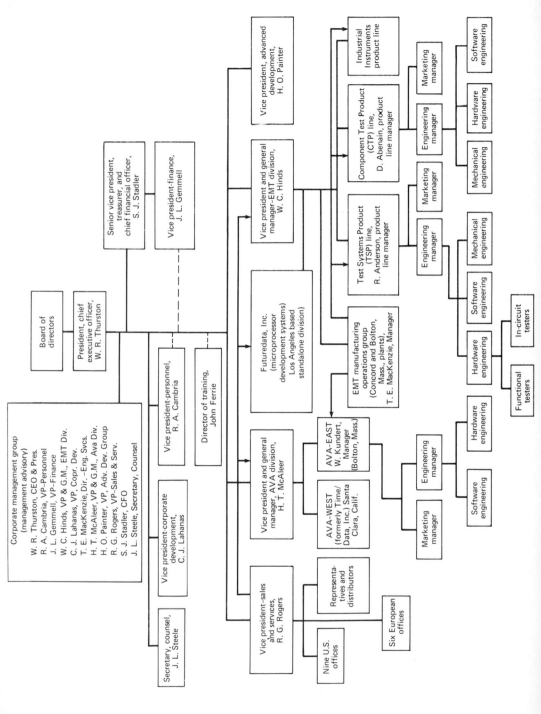

EXHIBIT 12   Genrad, Inc.—1979 organization chart

680

EXHIBIT 13 ADVERTISEMENT PLACED BY GENRAD IN FEB. 1942 ISSUE OF TECHNOLOGY REVIEW (MIT'S MONTHLY TECHNICAL JOURNAL AND ALUMNI MAGAZINE)

WE DON'T WANT TO GROW TOO LARGE!

Visitors to the laboratories and factory of General Radio are very often surprised at our size. Some think we must occupy a hole-in-the-wall, others that we are spread out over acres. Happily, we occupy a position between both of these undesirables. Our total floor space is 75,000 square feet, divided between three four-story buildings and occupying about a half a city block. Our total personnel is 287, of which 30 are engineers.

G-R does not want to grow large; only by following the basic idea upon which the company was founded in 1915 can we continue to serve our customers in the instrumentation field. That idea was to have an organization large enough to get instruments turned out, in peace time, in sufficient quantity to satisfy our customers and give us a reasonable profit; and at the same time small enough to enjoy the flexibility essential to adapting research, engineering and manufacture to the ever rapidly changing developments in the electronic art.

The type of equipment manufactured by G-R does not lend itself to production-belt methods; G-R design will never be cheapened to make mass production possible.

As soon as we grow to be a large company, we lose most of the essential direct contact between engineers and customers, and between engineers and the shop; ideas when diluted by eighteen in-betweens in an organization lose some of their sparkle and much of their originality.

Fundamentally we have only one thing to sell; engineering ideas wrapped up in cabinets with control panels. Many concerns can manufacture more economically than we; few have such a large percentage of idea-developing engineers.

If G-R grows large . . . if it grows so large that to change a machine screw from a 6-32 to an 8-32 requires a design conference, a thousand dollars in drafting time and a month's delay for tooling . . . we will cease to perform the function for which the company was established: to design and manufacture precision electrical measuring apparatus at a price consistent with both the quality of the product produced and the type of persons employed.

EXHIBIT 14 *(a)* Functional board tester

(c) Component tester

(b) In-circuit tester

EXHIBIT 15   BIOGRAPHICAL DATA ON MANAGEMENT PERSONNEL

Executive	Background
Richard A. Cambria	Joined the company in December 1973 as personnel director. Before this, he had served as manager for manpower planning and executive development at Exxon. Cambria received a BS in 1962 and a master's degree in industrial relations in 1964 from the University of Wsconsin.
John Ferrie	Joined the company in mid-1979 as director of training. From 1977 to his appointment at GenRad, Ferrie had served as director of international training at GTE Sylvania. From 1974 to 1977, he had been a training consultant. Ferrie received a BA in philosophy from All Hallows College (located in Ireland, his home country) in 1969. He received an MS in psychological counseling from Stetson University in 1971 and a PhD from the University of Massachusetts in 1975.
Robert F. Fulks	The founder and president of Omnicomp, Inc., Fulks was also founder and president of Micro Systems, Inc., a Phoenix-based subsidiary of Mirco, Inc., from 1973 to early 1975. Before that time, he was associated with General Radio Company as vice president and chief engineer. Fulks received both BS and MS degrees in electrical engineering from MIT in 1959 and joined the company that year.
J. Larry Gemmell	Joined the company in 1970 as vice president for finance, reporting to Stadler. He was responsible for the company's accounting and MIS functions. He earned a bachelor's degree in economics from Union College in 1950.
J. R. Held	Joined the company in 1974 as a controller and held positions in corporate planning from 1976 to 1978. Most recently Held served as manager of European sales and services, headquartered in the United Kingdom. He received a BS in mechanical engineering from Yale University in 1961 and an MBA from Harvard University in 1969.
Walter C. Hinds, Jr.	Appointed general manager of the electronic manufacturing test division in July 1977. From March 1974 to June 1975, he served as vice president for manufacturing; in June 1975 he assumed additional responsibilities for engineering services as vice president for operations. From 1970 until March 1974, Hinds was vice president for manufacturing at BIF, a unit of General Signal Corporation. He received a BS in engineering physics from the University of Maine in 1949 and a master's degree in industrial management from the Sloan School of MIT in 1962.
C. J. "Gus" Lahanas	After joining the company in 1951, he worked on many of the company's early marketing projects before being promoted to the position of vice president for corporate development in the mid-1970s. Lahanas received a BS in electrical engineering from MIT in 1950 and an MS degree from the same institution in 1951.
Thomas E. MacKenzie	After joining the company in 1962, he held several product-line and manufacturing management positions including, most recently, director of operations for the electronic manufacturing test division. MacKenzie earned a BS in electrical engineering in 1958 and an MS in physics in 1963 from Northeastern University.

EXHIBIT 15 BIOGRAPHICAL DATA ON MANAGEMENT PERSONNEL (continued)

Executive	Background
Harold T. McAleer	Served from April 1977 to July 1977 as general manager for the Time/Data Division. McAleer was general manager of the electronic instrument division from June 1975 to April 1977. Before that time, he held responsibility for engineering and custom products. He was named a vice president of the corporation in 1973. McAleer received an MS in electrical engineering from MIT in 1953.
Howard O. Painter	Joined the company in 1959 and remained until 1962, when he left to pursue other business interests. In 1971 he returned to GenRad. He had served in several engineering and marketing-related positions since that time. Painter earned a BS in electrical engineering from Worcester Polytechnic Institute in 1958.
Richard G. Rogers	Appointed vice president of the company and general manager with responsibility for sales and services operations in August 1977. From June 1975 to August 1977, he served as vice president of the company responsible for the test systems division. From 1973 until that time, he was general manager of the component and network testing business area. Rogers received joint BS degrees in business administration and electrical engineering from MIT in 1960 and joined the company directly thereafter.
Steven J. Stadler	Joined the company in 1969, subsequent to GenRad's purchase of Grason-Stadler, a firm in which he was a general partner. He was named chief financial officer of the firm in 1973. Stadler had served as a director since 1970. He earned a bachelor's degree in economics from Harvard University in 1948.
John L. Steele	Joined the company in 1967 and served in several capacities under the corporate secretary until he was named corporate counsel and secretary in 1979. He received a BA in geography from Dartmouth in 1963 and a degree in law from Suffolk University Law School (where he attended a night program in conjunction with holding full-time employment) in 1972.